GROWING UP

A CROSS-CULTURAL ENCYCLOPEDIA

ENCYCLOPEDIAS OF THE HUMAN EXPERIENCE

David Levinson, Series Editor

GROWING UP

A CROSS-CULTURAL ENCYCLOPEDIA

Gwen J. Broude

ABC-CLIO
Santa Barbara, California
Denver, Colorado
Oxford, England

Library of Congress Cataloging-in-Publication Data

Broude, Gwen J.
    Growing up: a cross-cultural encyclopedia/Gwen J. Broude.
        p.   cm. — (Encyclopedias of the human experience)
    Includes bibliographical references (p.   ) and index.
    1. Child development—Cross-cultural studies—Encyclopedias.
    2. Child rearing—Cross-cultural studies—Encyclopedias.   I. Title.
    3. Socialization—Cross-cultural studies—Encyclopedias.   I. Title.
    II. Series.   HQ767.84.B76   1995   305.23' 1'03—dc20   95-44079

ISBN 0-87436-767-0 (alk. paper)

02 01 00 99 98 97 96   10 9 8 7 6 5 4 3 2

ABC-CLIO, Inc.
130 Cremona Drive, P.O. Box 1911
Santa Barbara, California 93116-1911

Contents

CONTENTS

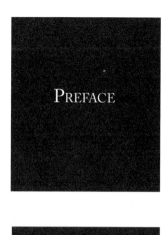

PREFACE

Any human being is the expression of a genome in an environment. The genome is the full complement of genes that the person inherits from his or her parents. The environment in which the genome is expressed can be anything from cells in the body that act as neighbors to other cells to the uterine milieu surrounding the fetus. But once a baby is born, and for the rest of the individual's life, the environment includes the culture in which the person lives. Because different cultures provide somewhat different kinds of environments, children in different cultures will be somewhat different from each other. But all infants, regardless of culture, are born with a human genome. That is, all babies begin by being very much alike in very important ways. Children in different cultures will turn out somewhat different because different environments trigger the expression of the species-typical genome in somewhat different ways. But the genome is only so plastic. It can be influenced in its expression by the environment in only limited and predictable ways. So everywhere the world over, infants, children, and adults are very much alike in very important ways. Indeed, important features of cultures are very much alike in important ways. This is because cultures are, in the final analysis, products of human beings. All human cultures, as a result, include institutions, customs, and practices that respond to the universal needs and dispositions of human babies. All human cultures provide the same kinds of environmental triggers needed by the human genome to produce a viable person.

What are examples of such environmental triggers? And what universal needs do human babies and children exhibit that require such triggers? Human infants are born relatively helpless. This means that all babies require the services of some competent caretaker. What is more, the needs of infants are the same in all cultures. A baby needs to be fed and protected from danger. Its body temperature needs to be regulated. Infants also require physical contact. A baby who is kept fed, safe, and warm but who is deprived of contact with other people cannot thrive. As youngsters mature, they also need to become competent members of their culture. They must learn practical skills and also the customs, etiquette, values, modes of social interaction, and so on of the culture in which they happen to live. And in fact, all cultures make sure that the needs of most of their infants and children are met. What is more, while mothers in all cultures get help from other people in raising children, it is usually the mother in societies the world over who takes primary responsibility for seeing to the needs of her children. Thus, mothers everywhere make sure that their babies are fed and protected from harm. Mothers toilet train their children, teach them hygiene, and instruct them in the etiquette of their culture. Mothers comfort their children, frequently by providing physical contact. And mothers make sure that their children learn the skills that they will need to become competent members of their society. Mothers everywhere, then, train, control, and nurture their children.

The environments, or cultures, in which infants and children grow up also differ in ways that affect the child's personality and behavior profile. Many cross-cultural differences in child rearing environments are themselves really practical solutions to problems posed by the ecology and economy of the culture. Thus, for example, in societies where the subsistence base depends upon both herding and farming, women typically have a relatively heavy workload. Often, they are responsible for most of the agricultural as well as household chores. Women who live in cultures of this sort usually recruit their children to help them with their tasks at an early age. Thus, as with the Gusii of Kenya, a four- or five-year-old child might be fetching wood and water, grinding grain, gardening, and harvesting. A little girl might also be required to supervise her six-month-old sibling for a number of hours every day, while her eight- or ten-year-old brother might act as shepherd. Mothers who assign chores of this sort to their children are also likely to insist that their children be responsible and obedient. And children who are recruited to do tasks tend to display a greater proportion of altruistic behaviors than do youngsters in other cultures. Thus, cross-cultural differences in child rearing environments are responses to constraints imposed by ecology and economy that then have predictable effects upon children.

Not only mother's workload, but also household structure, size of community, composition of the neighborhood, and the like will affect child rearing environments and, thus, the behavior and personality profiles of children. Thus, for example, where a number of families live under one roof, any child will have a relatively large number of siblings and cousins, and even perhaps young aunts and uncles, with whom to associate. This is in dramatic contrast with the contemporary American child who may live with a sibling or two or who may even be an only child. So the composition of the household affects the daily opportunities that a child will have to be around other youngsters. Household form also affects a mother's expectations regarding the behavior of her children. Thus, where many children live under the same roof, mothers are less tolerant of aggression in their children, perhaps because adults are concerned with maintaining harmony among household members under crowded conditions. Mothers who live in large households also tend to exhibit less affection toward their children, perhaps because they do not wish to be accused of showing favoritism toward their own youngsters and slighting their nieces and nephews. In contrast, mothers who live in nuclear family households, especially when they remain home alone with their children all day, tend to treat their youngsters as companions. The relationship between mother and child in households of this sort is friendly and relatively egalitarian in comparison with the relationship between mothers and children in other kinds of families.

While cross-cultural differences in child rearing environments lead to differences in children's behavior and personality profiles, the human developmental trajectory is also resistant to modification in important ways. Thus, even very dramatic differences in the way in which a child is raised will not create permanent differences in cognitive performance later on in the youngster's life. In rural Guatemala, an infant spends the first year of life in its cradle in a small, dark, windowless room. Other people rarely interact with the baby. Thus, the infant receives far less sensory and social stimulation than do babies in many other cultures around the world. We might expect differences in stimulation to affect a child's cognitive performance, and in fact, the scores of Guatemalan children on culture-free tests of cognitive performance are lower than those of youngsters raised in Cambridge, Massachusetts. However, by puberty, Guatemalan children have caught up, so that their scores are now equivalent to Cambridge children of their age. The Guatemalan children catch up because human children are extremely resilient. This means that, when it comes to fundamental kinds of skills and behaviors, children tend to stay on developmental course in spite of variations in what their environments deal them. Resiliency has its limits. Thus, while Guatemalan babies receive less stimulation than do babies in other cultures, they nevertheless obtain sufficient care and contact to allow them a successful developmental outcome. Children who are deprived of virtually all human contact will never catch up to the Guatemalan and Cambridge children.

Across cultures, children grow up to be the same as each other and different from one another. The profile of the child is a portrait of uniformities overlain by differences. The uniformities coincide with fundamental human needs and talents that characterize all members of our species because they have had a hand in the survival of human beings in our evolutionary past. The differences tend to be the result of differences in local circumstance, themselves dictated to some degree by practical human needs. Thus, where child rearing environments differ across cultures, and where children differ across cultures, these differences are also a reflection of the disposition of human beings everywhere to behave in ways that promote their survival.

Whiting, Beatrice B., and Carolyn Pope Edwards. (1988) *Children of Different Worlds: The Formation of Social Behavior.* Cambridge: Harvard University Press.

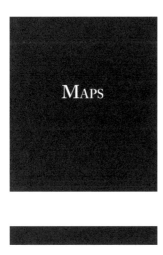

MAPS

The following maps show approximate locations
of the cultures mentioned in the text.

Africa and the Middle East

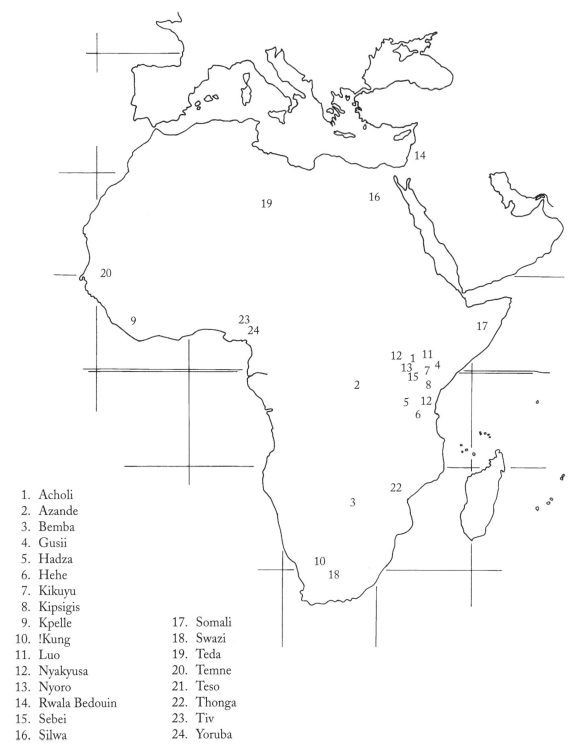

1. Acholi
2. Azande
3. Bemba
4. Gusii
5. Hadza
6. Hehe
7. Kikuyu
8. Kipsigis
9. Kpelle
10. !Kung
11. Luo
12. Nyakyusa
13. Nyoro
14. Rwala Bedouin
15. Sebei
16. Silwa
17. Somali
18. Swazi
19. Teda
20. Temne
21. Teso
22. Thonga
23. Tiv
24. Yoruba

Central and South America

1. Callinago
2. Carib
3. Chimalteco
4. Cubeo
5. Cuna
6. Haitians
7. Jamaicans
8. Jivaro
9. Maya
10. Mehinaku
11. Mixtecans
12. Shavante
13. Siriono
14. Tarahumara
15. Tepoztlán
16. Toba
17. Yahgan
18. Yanomamö

Europe and Asia

1. Ainu
2. Banoi
3. Gopalpur
4. Irish
5. Japanese
6. Koreans
7. Lakher
8. Manchu
9. Rajputs
10. Semai
11. Taitou
12. Taira

North America

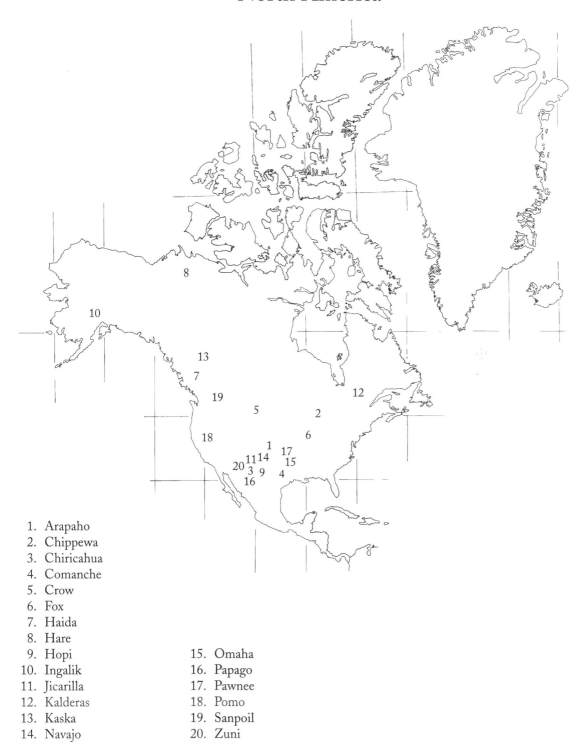

1. Arapaho
2. Chippewa
3. Chiricahua
4. Comanche
5. Crow
6. Fox
7. Haida
8. Hare
9. Hopi
10. Ingalik
11. Jicarilla
12. Kalderas
13. Kaska
14. Navajo
15. Omaha
16. Papago
17. Pawnee
18. Pomo
19. Sanpoil
20. Zuni

Oceania

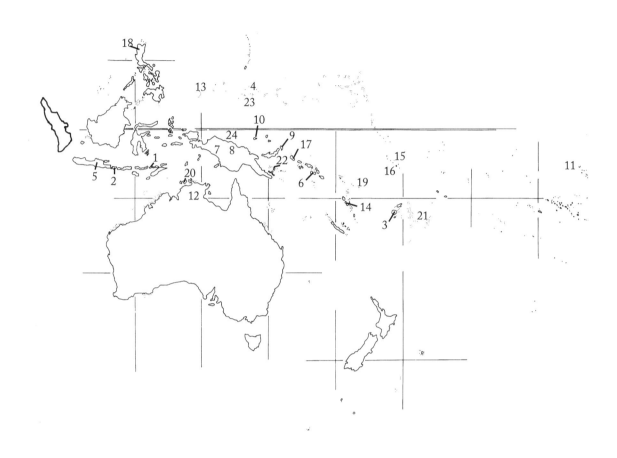

1. Alorese
2. Balinese
3. Fijians
4. Ifaluk
5. Javanese
6. Kaoka
7. Kapauku
8. Kwoma
9. Lesu
10. Manus
11. Marquesas Islanders
12. Murngin
13. Palau
14. Pentecost Islanders

15. Pukapuka
16. Samoa
17. Siuai
18. Tarong
19. Tikopia
20. Tiwi
21. Tonga
22. Trobriands
23. Truk
24. Wogeo

GROWING UP

A CROSS-CULTURAL ENCYCLOPEDIA

if the identity of the father is not known, she will have an abortion. A married Toba woman may also abort a baby if her husband has abandoned her. In the Amazon, Cubeo men claim that women do not like to have children and that they secretly have abortions when they become pregnant. Women are familiar with abortifacients, and wives who do not enjoy having sexual intercourse with their husbands do have abortions.

Abortions are condemned in a number of cultures. Sometimes this is because children are highly valued in the society. Among the Gusii of Kenya, for instance, where abortion is disapproved, women are very anxious to have as many children as possible, and the stability of a marriage is dependent upon the ability of a husband and wife to have a large family. Sometimes, abortions are disapproved because the fetus is believed to be a human being. Abortion is then understood to be a kind of murder. The association between attitudes toward abortion and beliefs about the status of the infant is also reflected in cultures that do not condemn abortion. Thus, for example, among the Toba, abortions are not regarded as immoral because newborn babies are not viewed as independent creatures. Rather, the existence of an infant depends entirely upon the parents, and especially the mother, which means that the parents have the right to decide whether it will live or die. The Javanese of Indonesia view abortions as sinful after three months of pregnancy. But before then, the fetus is "no more alive than blood," making abortion acceptable. Nevertheless, married women do not resort to abortion, and the procedure is also rare among unmarried women.

Even when abortion is officially condemned in a culture, women often know how to terminate a pregnancy. The Mexican Mixtecans do not approve of attempts to limit family size, but women do know of ways to induce abortions, including the ingestion of the juice of 12 cold lemons. Similarly, the North American

ABORTION

Sooner or later, most males and females who live to reproductive maturity become parents. In fact, the desire for children is so fundamental that sterility in a spouse constitutes grounds for divorce in many societies. On the other hand, there are sometimes better and worse times for having a baby, and women in some cultures may resort to deliberately terminating an unwanted pregnancy. The intentional termination of a pregnancy is known as abortion.

Women around the world seek abortions for a number of reasons. A woman who is unmarried may wish to terminate her pregnancy. Sometimes, this is because she cannot support a baby on her own. Sometimes, having a baby out of wedlock is too disruptive for the woman herself, for her family, for the infant, for the father, or for the community in which she lives. And in societies where premarital sex is condemned and even punished severely, an unmarried woman may seek an abortion to hide the fact that she has had sexual intercourse. In Bolivia, if a Toba woman becomes pregnant while unmarried, or

Chippewa did not approve of abortions, and the procedure was rare. But a few people said that they had heard of some women who had induced an abortion, and the practice did exist in fact. While methods for producing abortions are known and used in cultures that officially condemn the procedure, cultural attitudes do tend to affect the number of abortions that are performed. Thus, for example, while the Gusii formally condemn abortion, an unmarried girl or a new wife might obtain an abortion if she wishes to be rid of a husband who had been chosen for her by her parents. However, even most unmarried girls go on to have their babies, in spite of the fact that illegitimacy is regarded as extremely shameful.

Around the world, women use a variety of abortion methods. Abortions are not common among the Rajputs of Khalapur, India, but methods for terminating a pregnancy are known, and women may cause an abortion with a medicine that dilates the cervix when introduced into the vagina. In North America, Comanche women might have ended a pregnancy by hitting the stomach with stones. Among the Chippewa, abortions were brought on by drinking a concoction of roots or herbs, lifting heavy objects, or jumping from high places. In Micronesia, Truk women cause abortions by violent jumping or rubbing of the abdomen. A Canadian Hare woman will sometimes induce an abortion by tumbling and causing herself injury. The procedure is painful and leads to bleeding, but it results in the termination of the pregnancy. A Toba woman causes herself to abort by pressing the fetus out of her body with her thumbs.

In some cultures, abortion is not practiced, and a woman may even take measures to insure that her pregnancy is not terminated, even by accident. The North American Arapaho never resorted to abortion and indeed, they used medicines to prevent a miscarriage if a woman was fearful of losing her baby, as might happen if she did work that was too strenuous or if she was injured.

See also CHILDREN, DESIRE FOR

Geertz, Hildred. (1961) *The Javanese Family: A Study of Kinship and Socialization.*

Gladwin, Thomas, and Seymour Sarason. (1953) *Truk: Man in Paradise.*

Goldman, Irving. (1963) *The Cubeo: Indians of the Northwest Amazon.*

Hara, Hiroko Sue. (1967) *Hare Indians and Their World.*

Hilger, M. Inez. (1951) *Chippewa Child Life and Its Cultural Background.*

——— (1952) *Arapaho Child Life and Its Cultural Background.*

Hitchcock, John T., and Leigh Minturn. (1966) *The Rajputs of Khalapur, India.*

Karsten, Rafael. (1923) *The Toba Indians of the Bolivian Gran Chaco.*

LeVine, Robert A., and Barbara B. LeVine. (1966) *Nyansongo: A Gusii Community in Kenya.*

Romney, A. Kimball, and Romaine Romney. (1966) *The Mixtecans of Juxtlahuaca, Mexico.*

Wallace, Ernest, and E. Adamson Hoebel. (1952) *The Comanches: Lords of the South Plains.*

ACHIEVEMENT Individuals who strive to measure up to some standard of excellence are said to be motivated to achieve. Child training in some cultures emphasizes achievement while in others it de-emphasizes it. Attitudes toward achievement tend to be associated with other features of a society, including the economy, value system, and child rearing techniques characteristic of the culture.

In some societies, parents do not encourage children to excel. Sometimes, this is because achievement clashes with other traits that are valued in the culture. According to the New Mexican Zuni, the ideal man would never try to lead and would always avoid calling attention to himself. This emphasis on blending into the background interfered with the ability of school children to speak out in class for fear of being criticized as a "big shot." Teachers frequently allowed youngsters to work in groups and to write their answers instead of reciting them so that no child would be accused by the others of being bold or pushy. Youngsters were also permitted to recite in teams for the same reason. In cultures that de-emphasize achievement, adults are often satisfied if their children keep up with other youngsters of their age. In Mexico, Mixtecan parents do not place any emphasis on achievement. Mothers do not pressure their children to excel above other youngsters. Rather, parents set minimal standards and assume that any child will be able to achieve the desired level of performance. In the Philippines, Tarong parents also emphasize adequacy rather than excellence, and this shows up in school, where youngsters resist the teacher's attempts to reward competition and achievement. A child whose performance was inferior to that of other children would be ashamed, but a youngster who is doing well enough is perfectly happy. The reason for this sentiment is summed up by one child, who said: "We should all be the same. Then we will all be friends." Jamaican parents believe that steady attendance at school represents the road to making money quickly, and they encourage their children to go to their classes. But adults do not pressure their youngsters to do better than other children, and children may be called "thickheads" in a matter-of-fact way by parents who do not mean the term as an insult or as a provocation to motivate youngsters to do better. In Okinawa, most Tairan boys say that they would like to be the best in class, but the same boys say that they would not work harder to become best. The same youngsters do say that they would work harder if they were the worst in class. Otherwise, they would be scolded by their parents and teacher, and the other children would make fun of them. But to be average is to be good enough. Sometimes, adults who do not actively encourage youngsters to achieve will, nevertheless, appreciate superior performance in a child. The Tarong believe that children grow at their own rates and that no one can speed up the process. As a result, adults do not attempt to accelerate walking, talking, or other achievements on the part of an infant. But a child who acquires skills quickly is admired.

In some societies, success at subsistence tasks depends upon a person's desire to excel. Adults are then likely to emphasize achievement in children. The welfare of a North American Comanche family depended upon a man's skill at hunting. Boys learned this lesson early on and were encouraged early on to become excellent hunters. A boy was praised when successful at hunting, beginning with his first important kill, which was celebrated as a consequential event. Similarly, a boy's first success as a warrior was celebrated with a dance and presents, and an adolescent became determined to accompany his father or older brother on a raid. Boys wished to distinguish themselves as warriors because they might then advance to the status of war leader and even war chief. The Comanche played games of competition, such as arrow-shooting and wrestling, beginning in childhood, and those who were too old to play continued to watch the others while they played.

In some cultures, adults begin to stress achievement in school because they appreciate that a child who excels in school is likely to succeed in later life. In Thailand, all Banoi children go to school for a minimum of four years, and parents put pressure on their children to excel in school and punish failures on the part of youngsters to apply themselves. Adults want children to do well academically because success at school is tied to success in the adult world. As school performance matters more to a boy's future than to a girl's, parents place more pressure on their sons to work hard in school. In other cultures, parents are not fully committed in their support of achievement in school. Tairan mothers say that they are pleased when their children do well in school and they claim to encourage excellence and to reward children with special food for their successes. But parents do not consistently reinforce good study habits at home.

Behavioral scientists have proposed that children may have an independent motivation to be competent at the things that they do, and this shows up in the behavior of children across cultures. By the time they are adolescents, Micronesian Truk boys and girls are able to get their own food instead of having to depend upon their mothers or some other relative to be fed. Young people of this age now feel proud of their ability to take care of themselves and also to be able to provide for other members of the household. One Truk girl described her pleasure at knowing that other people heard her pounding the pestle as she prepared a meal since this meant that they would know she was strong and doing her work competently. Similarly, boys experience a good deal of pride when they are able to present members of their lineage with fish they have caught on their own. Truk adolescents also work hard to gain the approval of their parents for demonstrating that they can perform their tasks skillfully. Even when a culture disapproves of personal achievement, children may inwardly aspire to excel at something. The Arizona Hopi frowned on personal achievement, and children were taught to praise superior performance or

traits in other people but to minimize any achievements of their own. Nevertheless, while youngsters rarely talked about their own achievements, when someone else praised or paid respect to their accomplishments, they expressed pride and talked about their dreams of future personal successes.

Cultural attitudes toward achievement are associated with other features of a society. Children are more commonly encouraged to achieve in societies whose subsistence economies depend upon hunting and gathering or fishing. Perhaps this is because food is more scarce in cultures of this sort, so that the desire to achieve becomes a valuable character trait. A child's motive to achieve may also depend in part upon certain behaviors of the parents. Studies of American, Brazilian, and Turkish children have suggested that mothers of high-achieving boys are warm and encouraging, while the fathers of achieving sons are nonauthoritarian. By contrast, where fathers are authoritarian and intrusive, always telling their sons what to do, boys are not usually motivated to achieve. Finally, child rearing techniques that encourage achievement in children also tend to promote attention-seeking. Thus, the child who looks for praise from adults for good performance is at the same time being rewarded for demanding adult attention.

See also SELF-ESTEEM

Barry, Herbert, III, Irvin L. Child, and Margaret K. Bacon. (1967) "Relation of Child Training to Subsistence Economy." In *Cross-Cultural Approaches: Readings in Comparative Research,* edited by Clelland S. Ford, 246–258.

Bradburn, N. M. (1963) "Achievement and Father Dominance in Turkey." *The Journal of Abnormal and Social Psychology* 67: 464–468.

Cohen, Yehudi A. (1966) *A Study of Interpersonal Relations in a Jamaican Community.*

Gladwin, Thomas, and Seymour Sarason. (1953) *Truk: Man in Paradise.*

Leighton, Dorothea, and John Adair. (1966) *People of the Middle Place: A Study of the Zuni Indians.*

Maretzki, Thomas W., and Hatsumi Maretzki. (1966) *Taira: An Okinawan Village.*

Nydegger, William F., and Corinne Nydegger. (1966) *Tarong: An Ilocos Barrio in the Philippines.*

Piker, Steven. (1965) *An Examination of Character and Socialization in a Thai Peasant Community.*

Romney, A. Kimball, and Romaine Romney. (1966) *The Mixtecans of Juxtlahuaca, Mexico.*

Rosen, B. C. (1962) "Socialization and Achievement Motivation in Brazil." *American Sociological Review* 27: 612–624.

Rosen, B. C., and R. D'Andrade. (1959) "The Psychological Origins of Achievement Motivation." *Sociometry* 22: 185–218.

Segall, Marshall H., Pierre R. Dasen, John W. Berry, and Ype H. Poortinga. (1990) *Human Behavior in Global Perspective.*

Thompson, Laura, and Alice Joseph. (1947) *The Hopi Way.*

Wallace, Ernest, and E. Adamson Hoebel. (1952) *The Comanches: Lords of the South Plains.*

ADOLESCENCE

As a chronological stage in the life cycle, adolescence refers to the teen years. When behavioral scientists refer to adolescence, however, the focus is not so much on chronological age as it is on a psychological and sociological profile proposed to characterize teenagers distinctly, and this conception of adolescence coincides with what the man on the street also means by the term. Thus, psychologically speaking, adolescence is conventionally viewed as a time when the young person is rebellious and confused. This is the *Sturm und Drang,* or "storm and stress" account of the adolescent experience. This view of adolescence is reflected in Anna Freud's remark to the effect that any adult who behaved the way that adolescents behave would be judged as certifiably insane. In adolescence, by contrast, according to Freud, turmoil is normal and expected. Sociologically speaking, adolescence is the period during which the individual is no longer a child but has not yet attained the status of adult. While Westerners think of adolescence as an inevitable stage in the life cycle, the idea that there is a distinct era of life like adolescence first appeared in the early twentieth century. This raises the question of whether adolescence as a psychological or sociological phenomenon is inevitable.

A variety of psychological theories have claimed that the turmoil conventionally associated with adolescence is an inevitable fact of life. Those who make this claim commonly target the physical changes accompanying puberty as the source of adolescent storm and stress. As puberty is inevitable, adolescent storm and stress are regarded as inevitable. Why would puberty force this kind of psychological response in young people? Some theorists propose that the new body image and new sexual impulses demand a new self-definition by the young person. This takes its psychological toll. Other theorists propose that physical maturity implies the need for a redefinition of relationships. The newly mature young person now has to renounce ties to mother and father in favor of future commitments to a spouse. In this view, the strained relationships assumed to exist between adolescents and their parents are a result of teenagers' attempts to distance themselves emotionally from their parents.

The idea that puberty inevitably invites adolescent turmoil has been questioned by other theorists, who observe that if the onset of puberty invites adolescent turmoil because it requires a new self-definition, some cultures also provide experiences for the pubescent adolescent that might tend to minimize the problem. Thus, in a number of societies around the world, young people are required to undergo some sort of initiation rite at or around puberty. For girls, these rites are often associated with the onset of menstruation. For boys, they frequently include circumcision. Male initiation ceremonies may also include hazing and other physical and psychological challenges. In general, these rites act as public forums by which members of the young person's community recognize that the boy or girl has now attained or is about to attain physical maturity. In an important sense, then, the community is redefining the young person in light of his or her new body image and emerging sexuality. The task of redefinition, as a result, is taken out of the hands of the adolescent. In Western culture, where many people regard adolescent storm and stress as inevitable, there are no formal procedures for recognizing the fact and implications of the onset of physical maturity. Thus, adolescents are left to cope on their own.

Other theorists want to challenge the idea that puberty inevitably invites conflict between adolescents and their parents. Rather, some cultural climates unwittingly encourage collisions of this sort. The isolated nuclear family has been targeted as one source of strain between parents and teenagers. According to this view, when the primary responsibility for rearing a child is with the parents, youngsters are likely to form especially intense attachments to the mother and father. At adolescence, conflicts with parents are exaggerated because of the strength of the bond between parent and teenager. This reasoning leads to the prediction that in cultures where a number of people share the responsibility of raising a child, adolescence should not be particu-

larly stressful. In a classic study, Margaret Mead reported that in Samoa, where the entire community has a hand in the rearing of youngsters, adolescence is not particularly stressful for girls. The idea that adolescent-parent relationships need not be hostile is also supported by evidence from other cultures. For the Micronesian Truk adolescent, relationships with parents become warmer, less fraught with tension, and founded on mutual aid. Parents will continue to advise and even scold their adolescents, but physical punishment, which was common in childhood, is no longer employed unless the parent is seriously angry. The increase in good feelings between parent and child is more extreme for boys because they have typically moved out of the house of their parents by this time. There is no change in the relationship between Indonesian Javanese parents and children who have reached adolescence. Young people continue to show respect to their fathers and to have a warm relationship with their mothers. They are still dependent upon their parents for economic support and will remain so until they marry, and parents still give them advice about how to conduct their affairs. An adolescent boy may get a part-time job and spend the money that he earns as he wishes. If her mother is in business, an adolescent daughter may help her out. Otherwise, girls keep busy performing household chores. Finally, in societies where individuals are expected to remain attached to their parents for life, adolescents should not be motivated to distance themselves form their natal families. In traditional Chinese families, for example, it is assumed that a man's mother and father will always matter more to him than does his wife. In these circumstances, we would not expect the adolescent to spend any time dissociating himself from his parents. In Western society, children have traditionally been raised more or less exclusively by their parents. Further, it is assumed that the primary loyalty of an adult will be toward a spouse and not to parents. These are the conditions viewed as exaggerating adolescent storm and stress. Interestingly, however, even in American society, the relationship between most adolescents and their parents is not a stormy one. Thus, some studies indicate that most teenagers admire their parents, ask and take their advice, and look to them for emotional support.

Cultural heterogeneity has also been targeted as a cause of adolescent turmoil. Thus, where there are choices about how to make a living, whom to marry, what religion to adhere to, and so on, adolescents, who are now faced with making important decisions of this sort, find themselves confused and unsure about their futures. Choice is everywhere in Western society. The individual is theoretically free to choose a religion, political party, job, spouse, and so on. What is more, many of these choices must be made simultaneously, and in particular, sometime during adolescence.

Theorists also have suggested that where expectations about childhood behavior are dramatically different from what is expected in adulthood, adolescence becomes stressful because the rules of the game are suddenly changed on the young person. For instance, in some cultures children are not given much responsibility, yet as adults they are suddenly expected to be responsible. In some societies children are expected to be submissive, yet as adults they are supposed to be dominant. Finally, in some societies children are expected to have no interest in sex, yet as adults they are supposed to be sexually active. Where discontinuities of this sort exist, teenagers are assumed to anticipate the approach of adulthood with alarm. Where behavioral expectations for children and adults are more similar, the approach of adulthood should not be so frightening. The experience of the North American Comanche girl illustrates how continuities in what is expected of children and adults can smooth the way for the adolescent.

By the time that she arrived at adolescence, a Comanche girl had been trained in the tasks that she would be required to perform as a full-fledged adult. As a result, the transition to physical maturity did not evoke anxiety for the girl, and no puberty ceremonies existed, although some kind of ceremony or feast might be held in the case of a favorite daughter or a girl of a well-to-do family. A girl who had reached puberty was eligible to marry, and her marriage would probably have been consummated by the time she was 16. By contrast, expectations about childhood versus adult behavior tend to be discontinuous in Western societies.

The stage of life that we call adolescence can produce storm and stress for another reason. It is at this point that the young person is required to leave childhood behind and to make the shift to adult status. Where the shift to adulthood is difficult, the risk may be adolescent storm and stress. Where it is more straightforward, adolescent turmoil would not be predicted. What makes the shift to adulthood more or less problematic? Where the rules for attaining adult status are clear, the transition to adulthood is likely to be smooth. In some societies, people are assigned to age-grades. Each age-grade includes individuals of a particular age range. There are clear procedures for graduating people from one age-grade to the next. And graduation through the age-grades is guaranteed. In societies with age-grades, adolescents belong to an age-grade that includes other young people of roughly their age. Further, the graduation to adult status is clear and automatic. Finally, upon graduation, the young person is publicly recognized as an adult. This may minimize the stress associated with making the shift to adult status. Public acceptance of a young person as an adult is also associated with most initiation rites. In Kenya, the Kikuyu boy who has undergone circumcision is recognized as an adult and feels like an adult. This function of age-grading and of initiation rites reminds us of the Jewish Bar Mitzvah ceremony, at the end of which a boy can claim: "Now I am a man," although only in religious matters. In Western society, the shift to adult status is highly ambiguous and definitions of adulthood are vague. Thus, we tend to judge an individual's right to be viewed as an adult based upon economic, social, and emotional criteria, and a person can be judged as an adult on the basis of some of these criteria but not others. Nor is it clear when or how the shift to adult status is attained in Western societies.

Age-grades perform another function that may make adolescence an easier stage of life. Thus, in age-grade societies, rules regarding what responsibilities and what privileges are accorded to individuals within each age-grade are relatively clear and detailed. This means that adolescents, who are identified with a particular age-grade, know what is expected of them. They know what they can and cannot do with impunity. This contrasts with the adolescent experience in Western cultures, where the activities of young people are less constrained. There is no detailed recipe concerning what responsibilities and privileges are accorded to the adolescent. This means that people of this age are left to their own devices to a far greater degree than is true in age-grade societies. Teenagers are constructing their own adolescent experience, with the result, perhaps, that we see considerably more disruptive adolescent behavior.

Evidence from other societies suggests that cultural institutions can exaggerate or minimize adolescent storm and stress. However, it is possible that some degree of rebellion and confusion are predictable at this stage of life no matter where the adolescent lives. This prediction rests on the recognition that there may be certain facts of life about adolescents that no culture can override with entire success. Thus, for example, across cultures, the older generation sooner or later is required to cede power to the younger one, and this may mean that there are always tensions

between parents and their maturing adolescents in which the child vies for independence while the parent vies for control. As Jamaican boys and girls arrive at adolescence, they become increasingly resentful of the tendency of their parents to hold up other youngsters as models that they should try to emulate. They also become increasingly embarrassed at the floggings that Jamaican children chronically receive. Parents know this and may make a point of hitting their children in front of the children's friends, who then make fun of each other for having been flogged. An adolescent Jamaican girl usually leaves home to look for work as there are few jobs available where she has grown up. Girls are attracted to the idea of going away to work because of the freedom it affords them in contrast with the parental restrictions that bind them at home. Once an adolescent girl has left home, she is not likely to return unless she is ill or pregnant. Most Jamaicans leave school at the age of 14. Upon the completion of his education, a male begins to work full time at farming, as he will continue to do for the rest of his life. A boy is given a parcel of his father's land and may farm it as he wishes. Because parents are not responsible for the upkeep of their adolescent children, sons end up turning over one-third to one-half of what they earn to their fathers toward their expenses. Boys may spend some of their money on clothes and entertainment, but they are also expected to save some of their earnings to buy land, and parents will flog a son who spends his money in ways of which they disapprove. Boys also try to find other jobs that will allow them to earn extra money for more land and to attain economic self-sufficiency, an important motivating force for Jamaican adolescents. At this age, however, a son is still required to work on his father's land without payment and he is required to inform his father if he is working for someone else. The father can refuse to allow his son to work for a particular individual of whom he disapproves. Evolutionary theory also predicts that adolescents, who are now theoretically capable of managing on their own, will begin to find themselves at loggerheads with their parents, who wish to retain control over their children. This is because adolescents now wish to look out for their own best interests, while a parent has a stake in compelling a youngster to contribute to the parent's well-being.

Some theorists have also pointed out the adolescent is now capable of thinking in a new way. Whereas younger children think concretely, the teenager is able to suspend disbelief and think about alternate ways of doing things. This may mean that the adolescent begins to question things as they are, and this may lead to the kinds of doubts about religion, personal and parental values, social norms, and so on that we associate with adolescence. Finally, adolescents the world over may try to push the limits at least to some degree simply because they are now more competent physically and cognitively. How much adolescents collide with the older generation, how much they question the world as it is, and how much they push limits may then be influenced by the culture in which they find themselves.

See also COGNITIVE DEVELOPMENT; DEVELOPMENTAL STAGES, TRANSITIONS ACROSS; INITIATION RITES

Berk, Laura E. (1989) *Child Development.*

Blos, Peter. (1962) *On Adolescence.*

Cohen, Yehudi A. (1964) *The Transition from Childhood to Adolescence: Cross-Cultural Studies of Initiation Ceremonies, Legal Systems, and Incest Taboos.*

———. (1966) *A Study of Interpersonal Relations in a Jamaican Community.*

Erikson, Erik. (1950) *Childhood and Society.*

Freud, Anna. (1948) *The Ego and the Mechanisms of Defense.*

Geertz, Hildred. (1961) *The Javanese Family: A Study of Kinship and Socialization.*

Gladwin, Thomas, and Seymour Sarason. (1953) *Truk: Man in Paradise.*

Goethals, George W. (1967) "Adolescence: Variations on a Theme." Paper presented at Boston University, Boston, Mass. April.

Hara, Hiroko Sue. (1967) *Hare Indians and Their World.*

Mead, Margaret. (1928) *Coming of Age in Samoa.*

Van Gennep, Arnold. (1960) *The Rites of Passage.*

Wallace, Ernest, and E. Adamson Hoebel. (1952) *The Comanches: Lords of the South Plains.*

ADOPTION

In Western societies, adoption is understood to be a permanent legal transfer of an infant or child from the biological parents to another individual or couple. Typically, the relationship between the youngster and the biological parents is severed completely in favor of the new relationship between the child and the adoptive family. Individuals most typically adopt because they cannot have children of their own. Parents most typically give up a child for adoption because they do not have the financial or the emotional resources to raise a baby. In the case of foster care, children are temporarily placed under the supervision of adults who are not their biological parents. Foster parents may be financially compensated for taking care of the child, who may eventually be returned home. Adoptive or foster parents may be related to a child, but this is neither required nor expected, and usually this is not the case.

Adoptions also frequently occur in non-Western cultures, but the reasons for adoption as well as the kinds of adoption arrangements that we witness are more various than what is entailed in the Western case. Adoptions may occur at birth or at any time thereafter, and even adults may be adopted in some societies. Adoptions may be temporary or permanent, and in some cultures, individuals may be adopted a number of times in the course of a lifetime. Often, children know the identity of their biological parents and sometimes they continue to visit their birth families. Sometimes, adoption arrangements appear to be exploited by cultures as a way of allowing a fluid reorganization of social, political, or economic relationships. Adoptions across cultures occur because of infertility or because the baby is illegitimate. Parents may also give up a child to maintain the family line. Sometimes, an adoption proves financially profitable for the biological parents or for the adopted child. Adoptions will also occur if the biological mother has died or cannot produce enough milk or if a woman feels that she already has enough children. Sometimes, a person might ask to adopt a child from a good friend or kinsman. In this case, the biological parents may feel obliged to give up the child regardless of their personal preferences.

Infertility of the adoptive parents is a common motivation for adopting a child. Among the Polynesian Tongans, the two reported cases of permanent adoption were by women who were unable to have children of their own. Arrangements are made for the transfer of a child to its adoptive parents before or shortly after the baby is born. But the child only comes to live with its new family once it is weaned. The adopting family gives food to the biological mother while she is pregnant and to the baby as long as it remains with her. An infant who is adopted in this way will be named by its new parents. Among the Micronesian Truk, adoption is common when one sibling has no children or only one child while another has a large family. Again, the baby will remain with its own mother until it is weaned, although the adoptive mother will also have a major role in taking care of the infant.

Illegitimacy also leads to adoptions in a number of cultures. Babies born to unmarried girls are usually given out for adoption among the Canadian Hare, as are the children of a wife's adulterous affair. An illegitimate Northwest American Sanpoil baby was usually adopted by some married woman in the community. Such children had the option of returning to their biological mothers if they wished.

The mother's physical status may motivate her to give up a child. If a Truk mother cannot produce milk, or if she dies, a female relative is sought to nurse the baby. If no female relative is available, an unrelated woman will be asked, in which case she may also adopt the baby. Sometimes, a Hare baby will go to live in another household if the mother feels too weak to care for it or if she thinks that she already has enough children. The baby may eventually be adopted. If a Sanpoil woman with a young baby died, the infant would be adopted by some other woman, who would nurse the baby for around two years. The adoption, however, was only temporary. Weaned babies then went to live with their grandparents. Occasionally, it is the condition of the baby that motivates an adoption. Sometimes, Canadian Kalderas parents may arrange an adoption of a sick child. The father "sells" the youngster to some other man for a nominal fee. The idea is that the child will then be given a new life and will be cured.

Economic motives can also lead to adoptions. Among the Micronesian Palauans, adoptions are negotiated largely for financial reasons. Thus, adoptions can decrease the economic burden on the child's own parents. An adopted child may also benefit in terms of finances or increased opportunities by living with foster parents. Sometimes, the foster parents themselves may benefit concretely from an adoption. Adoptions are almost always conducted between close relatives, and most frequently a child is adopted by the father's sister. A set of parents may not wish to give up their child but may feel obligated to do so if there is a strong case to be made that a relative would benefit by adopting the youngster. Children can be adopted a number of times, and each time a new adoption is negotiated, the new parents make a payment for the child. This money may be used by the child's biological parents, but it must eventually be turned over to the youngster's maternal uncle, who therefore has a vested interest in seeing a niece or nephew adopted a number of times, although it is considered bad taste to acknowledge this.

Adoptions can also occur as a way of strengthening ties among political or kin groups. Traditionally, Tongan culture was characterized by various customs allowing individuals some kind of involvement in the lives of children who were not their own. Thus, a number of practices existed by which a child might be named or looked after by someone other than his parents. Sometimes, this involved a change in the rank or residence of the youngster. While all of these mechanisms fell short of real adoption, one custom, *ohi*, was a genuine adoption transaction involving changes in both the status and residence of the adopted child. *Ohi* was practiced as a way of unifying Tongan descent groups and occurred between high-ranking individuals belonging to different kin groups. Thus, for example, a woman might cement a relationship between chiefs from different districts by giving her child in adoption. Or adults without children might arrange an adoption to insure that the family line is carried on. Thus, for instance, in Japan, a childless Takashima couple will adopt a child in order to perpetuate the lineage and to insure that the ancestors will be properly cared for.

Children may also be given in adoption because the adopting family has something special to offer the youngster. Liberian Kpelle children can be adopted for as little as a few days or as much as a few years. Some adoptions are arranged so that a child can "learn the good ways" of the foster family. Some parents will send a youngster with behavior problems to live in another household for a while. One 12-year-old boy shuffled between his father's house and the household of his paternal uncle because he still wet his bed.

Some cultures treat adoption as an informal way of shifting themselves or their children from one family to another. Adoption was common among the North American Chippewa. Little children were adopted by relatives and nonrelatives, and older children and adults might ask to be adopted. Or some family might ask to adopt some particular person. There were no formal procedures for adoption. All of the involved parties simply had to agree to the adoption. In cases where a child was being adopted, the parents had to give their consent.

Sometimes, a child may be adopted on a temporary basis. When this occurs among the Tongans, a solitary relative may ask permission of the youngster's parents to take the child in for a while. Or a mother and father who find it difficult to feed their entire family may request that a relative care for one of their children for a short time. A child who has been temporarily adopted can go home at any time. Often, it is the grandparents who act as temporary surrogate parents. Children who are temporarily adopted by their grandparents will then inherit property from them when they die. Among the Tongans, temporary adoption is much more common than adoption in which a child finds a permanent home away from the youngster's biological family. Similarly, adopted Palauan children know who their own parents are, and a child can return to his own household with or without the foster parents' consent, although foster parents are not obliged to make payments for children who leave of their own accord. Among the Takashima, while the relationship between an adopted child and the natural parents is dissolved, adoptions can be revoked. This is often done for economic reasons, or, in the case of an adopted husband—that is, a man chosen by a couple to marry an adopted daughter—because of tension between the man and the household head. A revoked adoption can also be reinitiated.

Adoptions often transfer children from relatively large families to families with fewer or no children. In the case of the Takashima, a family will allow a child to be adopted if there are already a large number of children in the household, and parents are more willing to give up a boy than a girl, whereas a childless couple generally prefers to adopt a boy. An adopted child is usually a relative of the couple. If a girl is adopted, a husband will also be adopted for her when she grows up. The man then takes on the name of the household. There is some stigma attached to being an adopted husband. In Canada, a Kalderas woman may give a child to a relative or good friend who has no children. Adoption arrangements are made before the baby is born.

When a child is adopted, questions are inevitably raised about the role of the biological parents in the child's life. Sometimes the child maintains a connection with the original parents. Among the Hare, children may be adopted temporarily or permanently. Most adoptions are by relatives. Usually, adoptions occur when a child is about seven years old. Typically, the biological parents visit the child often and treat him or her affectionately. Sometimes, attempts on the part of the biological parents to maintain a relationship with their child cause trouble. Among the Kalderas, a child's natural parents may also try to involve themselves in the raising of the child, and this distresses the adoptive parents, who say of the biological mother: "She gave me the bone, but I put the meat on it." Children are usually told if they are adopted and both they and the community at large know the identities of the biological parents. In some cultures, overt attempts are made to sever the attachment between a child and the biological parents. Among the Truk of Micronesia, the adopted child is consciously kept away from the biological mother for some time to allow an attachment to form between the youngster and the new mother.

In some cultures, a person can be adopted at any age. The North American Arapaho adopted both children and adults. A person might be adopted who reminded the potential parents of a child whom they had lost. Or a friend of a dead child might be a candidate for adoption. Children who had no parents or whose parents could not raise them might be adopted. And occasionally the grandparents would adopt a child "just out of love for it." When a child was adopted, an announcement was made at one of the large tribal gatherings, usually by the adopting father, and valuable gifts such as blankets and horses were also given by the adoptive parents to anyone from another tribe who was there. An adopted child could remain at home, paying long visits to its adoptive parents and receiving gifts from them. Or the youngster could go to live with its new family, where it was treated like any other child. When an adult was adopted, no public announcements were made.

The treatment of adopted children may or may not differ from that of youngsters raised by their biological parents. Among the Hare, adoptive parents tend to expect an adopted child to work more and to show more obedience than their biological children. The Takashima say that the relationship between a child and the adoptive parents is not as close as is the attachment between parents and their own children. However, in practice it is hard to see any difference in the relationships of adopted versus biological Takashima children to other members of the family, and adopted children have the same rights as the parents' own offspring. Among the Tongans, adopted children treat their adopted kin as their own and will inherit status and property from their adopted families.

Barnett, H. G. (1960) *Being a Palauan.*

Beaglehole, Ernest, and Pearl Beaglehole. (1941) *Pangai: Village in Tonga.*

Erchak, Gerald M. (1977) *Full Respect: Kpelle Children in Adaptation.*

Gladwin, Thomas, and Seymour Sarason. (1953) *Truk: Man in Paradise.*

Hara, Hiroko Sue. (1967) *Hare Indians and Their World.*

Hilger, M. Inez. (1951) *Chippewa Child Life and Its Cultural Background.*

———. (1952) *Arapaho Child Life and Its Cultural Background.*

Norbeck, Edward. (1954) *Takashima: A Japanese Fishing Community.*

Ray, Verne. (1933) *The Sanpoil and the Nespelem: Salishan Peoples of Northeastern Washington.*

Salo, Matt, and Sheila Salo. (1977) *The Kalderas in Eastern Canada.*

Urbanowicz, Charles F. (1973) "Tongan Adoption before the Constitution of 1875." *Ethnohistory* 20: 109–123.

ADULT ROLES, TRAINING FOR

In every culture, younger generations are expected to learn the roles required of adults in their cultures. Much of the time, children pick up needed skills and knowledge from adults, although youngsters also learn from each other. Adults may explicitly teach children what they need to know. But youngsters sometimes also pick up knowledge casually. In most cultures, children begin to be recruited to do important chores at a young age, so that training for adult roles often begins early on.

Across cultures, adults frequently devote time to explicitly teaching children adult roles. Among the Mixtecans of Mexico, a girl is trained in domestic skills by her mother, who will call her older daughter away from a group of playing children in order to show her how to do some specific task with which the mother happens at the moment to be occupied. Youngsters often accompany adults who are performing some task as part of their training for adult roles. Among the Truk of Micronesia, children begin to be expected to learn adult skills as they approach adolescence, and it is at this time that a girl more regularly accompanies and assists her mother as the older woman cleans the house, does the washing, cooks, and fishes. Boys of this age should start learning to climb trees, obtain and prepare food, and fish. The intensity of training of a particular child is affected by the temperament of the parent and the number of other people in the household who are available to do the daily chores.

Adults may also depend upon verbal instruction in teaching a task. Sometimes, this takes the form of tales and legends. In India, Rajput girls sit with the other women in the evenings and listen to the stories that prepare them for the ceremonies in which they will be required to participate when they are women. The stories also impart information about what will be expected of them when they are married. Chippewa parents and grandparents lectured children on good and bad behavior. Often, children would sit in a circle to listen to an older person's advice about how to live a good life. Typically, the old men would lecture the boys, and old women the girls.

Adults will also often make miniature tools and weapons for their children. A child then uses these instruments in imitative play. Or children may actually perform some adult task with their small tools. In Ecuador, Jivaro boys begin play at blow-gun hunting when they are four years old. The father gives a small boy a miniature reed and some small darts, and the youngster shoots butterflies. A six-year-old boy is given a working miniature gun, which he uses to shoot hummingbirds as his mother works in her garden.

A herd boy looks after his charges in Transkei, South Africa.

He brings his kill to his mother, and she cooks the birds. By the time a boy is nine, he is able to bring down bigger birds, and his father begins to teach him the finer points of hunting.

In many cultures, adults depend upon observation and imitation as a major teaching strategy. Among the Tairans of Okinawa, at the harvest, adults save the best straw to make into rope, and men can be observed twisting the straw into rope on rainy days. Often older children sit by and watch the process. Very soon, the youngsters themselves are making ropes, while the four- and five-year-olds attempt to copy them. When a smaller child becomes frustrated, an older sibling will show the youngster how to twist the straw properly. No adults are directing these activities or even suggesting that the children make rope. Tairans do not explicitly tutor children in the performance of adult roles. Rather, in the view of the Tairan, children "just learn by themselves." Children are carted off to the fields and attend parties, public meetings, and rituals and therefore have ample opportunity to observe adult activities and to try to copy what they see. Little children who have accompanied their families to the fields will try to use a hoe that some adult has laid aside. Or some small children may imitate the adults who are transplanting or weeding the rice paddies. A two-year-old girl may try to cut firewood like her mother with a knife left around the house. In all likelihood, she will not be noticed by anyone, although a mother who observed her toddler brandishing such a dangerous tool would scold the child and take the knife away. But children persist in such experimentation, and a six-year-old may already be skilled at using a knife although no one has explicitly taught the child. A little girl whose mother is doing the laundry will soon start to soap up some piece of clothing on her own and then begin to clean and rinse the garment in imitation of the older woman. A Tairan mother will also encourage a toddler who copies the behavior of an older child. Imitation of baby tending is viewed as especially desirable. Mothers or older children will praise little boys or girls who are seen toting rolled up blankets or jackets on their backs in the place of real babies. The North American Seminole expected their children to learn by silent observation. A young girl would follow her mother around the camp, watching the woman as she worked, while boys studied their fathers while they hunted or carved and then secretly attempted to copy their actions. A child who imitated adult skills successfully would be rewarded, but a youngster who failed to copy a model properly would be ignored or otherwise subtly punished. A child who tried to do some chore in a novel way would be told that he was too young to think for himself. In North America, small Chippewa children imitated the activities of their parents, scaled down to size. Thus, a little girl made nets that were smaller than the standard, but according to the same technique used by her mother. Girls stayed close to their mothers and learned female skills by watching and helping them.

Children also learn adult roles simply by practicing some pursuit on their own. In Africa, Swazi boys begin to herd calves together at around six years of age and they continue to be more and more responsible for their animals as they grow older. In this way, the youngsters become competent herders and also attain consid-

erable knowledge about the terrain. Youngsters also teach each other some of the skills and knowledge that they will need in adulthood. In the Northwest Amazon, a young Cubeo boy joins an all-male group that is more or less independent of adults and spends most of his time with his peers. Each boy's group has its own leader, who helps other members of the group learn adult skills.

While adults around the world go out of their way to provide some kind of explicit training for adult roles, children typically find the prospect of doing what adults do attractive without any persuasion from the grownups. In culture after culture, we find children imitating the activities of adults on their own. Among the Philippine Tarong, children imitate adult behaviors when they play, building twig houses, stringing tobacco, cooking, and cutting cane. Youngsters will also recreate adult tools with whatever happens to be available. Thus, a can fitted with wheels, covered with banana-stalk tops, and attached to a string becomes a wagon. Or sticks and rocks become mortars and pestles. Older children also allow their younger brothers and sisters to assist in domestic tasks. As a result, little children begin to practice at sweeping the yard, preparing food for the pigs, taking care of babies, and the like. The older children laugh at the errors of the younger ones, but also help them when they make mistakes, and adults recognize that children learn valuable adult skills from their older siblings. Tairan girls who are too young to perform household chores play "house" instead, and this is a favorite activity for girls from four to ten years of age. Each girl pretends to be a mother or a child, and all of the girls meet at a play "store" to purchase household supplies. Most of their time, however, is spent in the "kitchen," where complicated meals are cooked using makeshift utensils, or real ones if the girls are lucky enough to acquire these. Everyone then sits down to eat the make-believe meal. Perhaps some boys will come along and pretend to be robbers. Or a boy may act out the role of peddler, asking one of the "mothers" if she needs anything today. Some girl may also come to "tea," with the participants acting out their proper roles as hostess and guest. Children also like to help adults with their tasks, even without an invitation. A Tairan kindergartner may watch wistfully as the adults are busy harvesting the rice until some grown-up finally gives the child some rice sheaths to take over to the threshing machine. Older children also implore adults to let them help in the fields. Children beg their parents to be allowed to help cut and haul firewood long before the adults consider them to be capable of such work.

See also CHILD NURSES; CHORES; LEARNING; PLAY

Gladwin, Thomas, and Seymour Sarason. (1953) *Truk: Man in Paradise.*

Goldman, Irving. (1963) *The Cubeo: Indians of the Northwest Amazon.*

Harner, Michael J. (1973) *The Jivaro: People of the Sacred Waterfalls.*

Hilger, M. Inez. (1951) *Chippewa Child Life and Its Cultural Background.*

Hitchcock, John T., and Leigh Minturn. (1966) *The Rajputs of Khalapur, India.*

Seminole girls learn cooking techniques from their mother.

Kuper, Hilda. (1963) *The Swazi: A South African Kingdom.*

Lefley, Harriet Phillips. (1973) *Effects of an Indian Culture Program and Familial Correlates of Self-Concept among Miccosukee and Seminole Children.* Unpublished dissertation, University of Miami, Coral Gables, Florida.

Maretzki, Thomas W., and Hatsumi Maretzki. (1966) *Taira: An Okinawan Village.*

Nydegger, William F., and Corinne Nydegger. (1966) *Tarong: An Ilocos Barrio in the Philippines.*

Romney, A. Kimball, and Romaine Romney. (1966) *The Mixtecans of Juxtlahuaca, Mexico.*

AGGRESSION

In a majority of cultures around the world, parents make some attempts to control aggression in children. In Thailand, Banoi parents disapprove of aggression directed against siblings or peers, and children are punished more for fighting with other children than for any other single kind of bad behavior. The Philippine Tarong are anxious to control aggression, and aggressive behavior toward a younger child or an adult whom the child does not know well is viewed as especially undesirable. Aggression on the part of a physically mature male is regarded as particularly grave because it can lead to serious physical consequences. Fighting is strongly disapproved unless a boy is defending himself or has been greatly provoked, and parents tell their sons to avoid any verbal insults that might result in some kind of physical confrontation. Anger directed toward other members of the family is also viewed as less acceptable on the part of a male who is approaching adulthood.

Parents across cultures often distinguish between verbal and physical aggression and treat the former as less serious than the latter. In Kenya, Gusii parents disapprove of physical aggression and harshly punish any fighting on the part of children. But as youngsters are often out of sight of their parents, they are able to engage in a considerable amount of bickering and fighting without paying the consequences. Parents do not mind if children are verbally abusive toward one another, and this indulgence of verbal aggression may explain the Gusii tendency to gossip about and blame one another when the opportunity presents itself. Tarong parents also strongly disapprove of aggressive behavior in children. In their view, a youngster who is habitually aggressive will turn into a troublemaker, lacking respect for other people. An aggressive child will be chastised and perhaps slapped, and youngsters who fight are also simply removed from the scene. But while an adult will stop any child who displays physical aggression, children are allowed to attack each other verbally.

Adults may be so anxious to prevent aggression that they restrict contact between their own children and other youngsters. Aggressive behavior is rare among the Mixtecans of Mexico. In part, this can be traced to the Mixtecan belief that aggression, anger, jealousy, and similar feelings cause a person to be ill and perhaps to die. If an individual who has yielded to angry impulses subsequently becomes sick or dies, children are warned that if they allow themselves to be angry, a similar fate will await them. Mixtecan mothers are so concerned about minimizing aggression among children that they prefer their youngsters to play alone, even though there are numerous siblings and cousins in the Mixtecan extended family household with whom to play. In fact, Mixtecan youngsters do spend much of their time in the company of close relatives of their own age, but children do not generally play with more distantly related or unrelated peers, so maternal fears about potential aggression do tend to constrain the kinds of relationships that children establish. If some other child picks a fight with her youngster, the Mixtecan mother expects her own child to come home immediately instead of retaliating, and all mothers of younger children say that they would physically punish a child who fought back instead of returning home. This is the only kind of behavior for which physical punishment of a child is approved by mothers, reflecting the special concern that parents have about aggressive behavior on the part of their youngsters. Similarly, if a fight between Micronesian Truk children becomes serious, a parent or relative of one of the youngsters will intercede. A child who has been in a major fight may subsequently be prevented from going out with the other children because he did not know how to "play nicely." In Malaysia, Semai parents do not explicitly punish aggression, but if a child displays anger, adults act shocked and the youngster is immediately taken home.

Where aggression is condemned, people often find ways of avoiding likely hostile encounters. In the South Seas, Javanese adults who are angry with each other simply stop speaking. Grown sisters, divorced couples, and debtors and creditors all deal with anger in this manner. This is also how children are encouraged to handle anger, so that playmates who are feeling hostile toward one another will avoid speaking to each other for a few days. Sometimes, children are responsible for inhibiting aggression in other youngsters. In Okinawa, Tairan youngsters eventually learn to abandon aggressive tactics to try to get what they want because such children are avoided by their peers. Thus, a child who may initially try to get his way by bullying playmates soon learns to share, ask for what he wants, and wait his turn.

Adult attitudes toward aggression in children are sometimes influenced by a parent's desire to preserve peace in the neighborhood. This is why North American Arapaho mothers would discourage fighting between their own children and those of neighboring households. When such quarrels did erupt, the parents of the children often ended up quarreling themselves as each mother stood up for her own child. Anxious to avoid these disputes, mothers told their youngsters to come away from any situation in which a fight was going on. Similar concerns motivate South Seas Javanese parents. A mother and father will punish a child who gets into a fight, no matter who was originally at fault, because they are fearful that the parents of the other child will become angry with them. North American Chippewa parents did not generally interfere when their children quarrelled. A parent whose child came and complained that some other youngster had started a fight might say: "Oh, that's all right, as long as you weren't killed." Parents who defended their own children against some other youngster would be resented by neighbors, and a parent whose child got into a fight was likely to simply cart the youngster home. Banoi parents are unhappy when their children get into fights with peers because they fear that the parents of the children will be dragged into the dispute, affecting the otherwise harmonious relationships between adults in the community. Indeed, a parent is harsher with a child who fights with a neighbor than one who fights with a sibling. Most adults say that they would prefer their own children not to retaliate when they find themselves the target of aggression from a neighbor's child.

For many parents, the question of how to deal with aggression in children is a complicated one. On the one hand, an adult may disapprove of aggressive behavior in children. But for a variety of reasons, aggression may still be tolerated, at least in some contexts. Indian Rajput mothers view aggression as a serious fault in a child, and fighting is one of the most frequently punished behaviors in youngsters. Nevertheless, Rajput children do display aggression. Small children are often allowed to express anger and even to hit a mother, aunt, or grandmother, and the adult may give in to the child in order to avoid a scene. And although they discourage aggression, adults also usually ignore quarrels between children of the same age unless physical fighting erupts or one of the youngsters cries or complains. Aggression directed toward a young sibling or cousin, however, is not tolerated by parents, largely because the physical advantage that the older child enjoys is viewed as bullying. Actual fighting between children is not common, although youngsters frequently bicker, snatch objects away from each other, call one another names, and so on. Most mothers agree that a child who has been attacked should not fight back. But fathers train their sons to defend themselves if someone starts a fight. And children do fight back when attacked. Children do not typically complain to their mothers about the aggression of some other child because they know that they will get no sympathy.

Aggression is such a problem for parents around the world in part because older children are so frequently tempted to bully younger ones. Micronesian Truk children goad, tease, and taunt one another, and this kind of meanness is especially likely to be directed by an older child against a younger one. Thus, an older child might scare a smaller one into believing that a ghost was about to attack and bite the youngster. Older children often taunt younger ones until the little victims become furious and hysterical, vainly trying to retaliate against their tormentors. The older child inevitably wins, leaving the younger one sobbing in fear and frustration. Some experts have proposed that this tendency for a bigger child to bully a younger one is a natural impulse that derives from our primate roots. Aggressive bouts figure importantly in the formation of dominance hierarchies in other primates, with older, stronger animals intimidating younger ones. In many American families, parents attempt to stop this kind of bullying on the part of an older child. But in some cultures, mothers expect older children to dominate younger ones and they do not interfere with

fights between children of different ages unless it is likely that someone will be seriously hurt. Often, an older child who is aggressive toward a younger one is really just responding to the smaller child's own attempts at domination. Interactions of this sort are especially common between four- to five-year-olds and six- to ten-year-olds. The younger children try to boss the older ones around, and the older children lose patience and retaliate. In cultures where parents do intervene in children's fights, a younger child who has been the target of an older child's aggression is likely to run to the mother for help. But in societies where mothers remain uninvolved in their children's fights, youngsters work out their differences on their own. The policy of nonintervention in children's fights is characteristic of women in some African societies, where mothers, because they keep out of their children's squabbles, are able to get on with their own work without being constantly interrupted. It is not clear how much good a woman does when she makes attempts to keep peace between feuding children. In cultures where mothers do try to mediate fights between children, youngsters often fail to obey the mother's requests to stop quarreling, with the result that the mother finds herself nagging disgruntled youngsters.

While some mothers tolerate aggression of an older sibling toward a younger one, they often expect big brothers and sisters or cousins to intervene if a younger sibling or relative is the target of some other child's aggression. Truk children below the age of ten spend most of their time playing, and in the course of a day small fights frequently break out, with one youngster taking a swipe at another. Often it is an older child who hits a younger one. If an older male relative of the victim happens to be around, he will typically retaliate against the aggressor.

Aggression is also common among siblings in societies around the world. Sometimes parents attempt to control this kind of squabbling and sometimes they adopt a laissez-faire policy.

Jamaican siblings often get into squabbles. Youngsters may chase each other around the yard, or one child may snatch something from the other. Siblings may also hit each other. Parents do not approve of this kind of play between siblings, and they are quickly punished for engaging in any activities that have the look of aggression. In North America, Chippewa parents might ignore a quarrel between siblings or they might whip the children or send them away from the house.

Parents in some societies are more tolerant of children's aggression. Tairan parents do not discourage aggressive behavior on the part of preschool children because in their view, a young child who is angry one minute is likely to forget that anything was bothering him a minute later. In fact, adults are resigned to aggression in youngsters, saying that play and fight are children's work, and hitting, pushing, biting, and rock throwing do occur among preschoolers. However, they do not approve of aggressive outbursts on the part of children, and aggression directed at a younger child by an older one is not permitted. Publicly, mothers say that they tell their children not to retaliate if another child starts a fight because fighting is bad. But parents do not like it if a child of theirs is the constant target of other children's aggression, and youngsters are in fact instructed to fight back. Children who are old enough to go to school, and whose language skills are more advanced, begin to substitute verbal for physical aggression. Similarly, in Canada, Kalderas adults will separate quarreling children. But they also minimize the importance of such fights. When adults quarrel, they say, it lasts a lifetime; children fight for one minute and forget it the next. Mormon mothers in a Texas community in the 1960s did not like it when their children fought, but some women said that youngsters should be left to "fight it out," or "settle it themselves," or "get it out of their systems." Mothers would, however,

put a stop to persistent or serious aggression against a younger child by an older one.

Aggression in children is positively approved in some societies. South American Yanomamö parents want their sons to be fierce and boys are permitted to hit their parents as well as the village girls. One father, for example, would laugh and comment on his son's ferocity when the boy, who was only four years old, beat the older man on the face and head. Children may be teased into striking adults who then cheer at the child's actions, and youngsters learn early that the appropriate way of expressing anger is to smack someone with a hand or an object. In South America, Jivaro parents encourage playful wrestling in boys, although they do not approve of fighting over possessions. When North American Comanche children got into fights, instead of separating the youngsters, adults would watch in amusement.

Over and over again, studies have suggested that boys are more aggressive than girls across cultures. We find the same sex difference in non-human primates, among whom, for instance, subadult males are much more likely to engage in what is called rough-and-tumble play than are females. Perhaps this sex difference in aggression is linked to our evolutionary heritage as hunter-gatherers. People who theorize about our evolutionary roots propose that, for 99 percent of our history as a species, men hunted and protected females and children in human groups while women gathered fruits and vegetables and took care of infants and toddlers. The division of labor is consistent with the observed sex differences in aggression that characterize children today. An association also exists between age and levels of aggression, at least in industrialized societies. In these settings, males between 14 and 30 years of age account for proportionately more violent crime than do other males or females.

Adults in many societies appear to recognize that aggression is harder to contain in males than in females. Tairan kindergarten teachers discourage aggression in both sexes, but tend to criticize a girl who is involved in some aggressive encounter regardless of whether she is responsible for the dispute. Teachers seem to believe that while girls should not and do not fight, aggression in boys is hard to restrain. Children come to understand that this is the attitude of adults, and boys gloat over their privileged position when it comes to getting away with aggression. Tairan adults expect boys to be more aggressive than girls, who are expected to be docile, well mannered, and considerate. In Thailand, Banoi adults understand that boys are more likely than girls to get into fights with other children and as a result, parents treat aggression on the part of males more severely. Girls do also display aggression. Truk girls get into fights with boys and with each other. One girl may hit another for refusing to share a coconut. Or a girl might smack a boy who had come over and beat her up for no particular reason while she was playing on the beach.

Children across cultures may sometimes be tempted to display aggression toward their parents. Parent-directed aggression is tolerated in some places but considered unacceptable in others. Once they are weaned, Banoi children find themselves displaced by the youngest baby in the household, who from then on has a monopoly on the attention of the parents. A displaced child then often attempts to attract the mother's attention by repeatedly hitting her. This aggression goes unnoticed by the mother, who continues to ignore the youngster. Sometimes, this aggressive nagging on the part of a child turns into a violent tantrum. Japanese Takashima parents expect their children to be aggressive toward them and two- and three- year-olds often hit their parents, and especially their mothers. Parents only laugh at this kind of behavior. Banoi children begin to exhibit aggression, especially toward adults, as young as a few months of age.

When infants fail to get what they want immediately, they display anger toward whomever happens to be caring for them at the time. An infant or child will repeatedly hit an adult who refuses to meet the requests of or pay attention to the youngster, and outbursts of this sort are tolerated without any punitive response on the part of the target, even if it is a parent. Parents continue to put up with attacks of this sort by their children even while they begin to show disapproval of sibling-directed aggression once a child is seven or eight years of age. Part of this restraint may be a reflection of the Banoi ethic that encourages extreme self-control in the face of another person's aggression or anger. The ideal recipe for responding to the aggression of a child, in the view of Banoi parents, is to ignore it and let it die down of its own accord or to speak sweetly to the youngster. In Jamaica, parent-directed aggression takes the form of thievery. All Jamaican children have stolen things from their parents at one time or another. These are usually valuable items, such as rings or watches. The children either discard them or give them away. Parents are careful to determine which child has stolen an item once its absence is discovered, and the guilty party is flogged. As a consequence, no youngster persists in theft of this sort for very long. In contrast with these cases, Gusii mothers punish any aggression directed toward them. Children are expected to respect authority, and it is the job of a mother to teach this lesson to her children. Aggression on the part of her child is understood by a mother to be an insult to her authority, and women will withhold food from youngsters who display aggression toward them. Across cultures, a mother is more likely to punish aggression directed toward herself if she has a heavy workload. Mothers who have many chores typically recruit their children to help them out. This places a premium on obedience on the part of the child. Thus, mothers who are forced to do many chores may punish aggression in children as part of a more general effort to create obedient, responsible children who will do what they are told when they are told to do it.

Investigations of children's aggression across cultures indicate that levels of aggressive behavior may be higher where a child lives in an extended family. Interestingly, it is in families of this type that aggression is most heavily punished. No one can be sure why this is the case. But it is possible that bickering between youngsters has the best chance of occurring in settings where there are a number of children packed together in a single household. Adults then become motivated to prevent this kind of fighting in an effort to maintain peace where many people have to coexist. Parents may also be concerned with preventing quarrels between their own children and those of their relatives for fear that such bickering will create hard feelings between the adults. Some studies of parental responses toward aggression in their children do suggest that adults are intolerant of aggression when relatives live close by and more tolerant when neighbors are unrelated to each other.

Across cultures, aggression training is also related to the presence or absence of the father in the child's daily life. Thus, where men play a salient role in the lives of their children, aggression in children is discouraged. Where fathers do not play a significant role, aggression in children is tolerated or approved. This relationship may reflect the difficulty that women have in controlling aggression in children, and especially in sons. In societies around the world, mothers complain about how hard it is to control their male children, and ill-behaved boys the world over hear the overworked warning: "Wait until your father gets home."

See also FATHERS

Broude, Gwen J. (1990) "Protest Masculinity: A Further Look at the Causes and the Concept." *Ethos* 18: 103–122.

Chagnon, Napoleon A. (1983) *Yanomamö: The Fierce People.* 3rd ed.

Cohen, Yehudi A. (1966) *A Study of Interpersonal Relations in a Jamaican Community.*

Dentan, Robert L. (1968) *The Semai: A Nonviolent People of Malaya.*

Ember, Carol R., and Melvin Ember. (1988) *Anthropology.* 5th ed.

Geertz, Hildred. (1961) *The Javanese Family: A Study of Kinship and Socialization.*

Gladwin, Thomas, and Seymour Sarason. (1953) *Truk: Man in Paradise.*

Harner, Michael J. (1973) *The Jivaro: People of the Sacred Waterfalls.*

Hilger, M. Inez. (1951) *Chippewa Child Life and Its Cultural Background.*

———. (1952) *Arapaho Child Life and Its Cultural Background.*

Hitchcock, John T., and Leigh Minturn. (1966) *The Rajputs of Khalapur, India.*

Lambert, William W. (1971) "Cross-Cultural Backgrounds to Personality Development and the Socialization of Aggression: Findings from the Six Cultures Study." In *Comparative Perspectives on Social Psychology,* edited by W. W. Lambert and R. Weisbrod, 49–61.

LeVine, Robert A., and Barbara B. LeVine. (1966) *Nyansongo: A Gusii Community in Kenya.*

Maretzki, Thomas W., and Hatsumi Maretzki. (1966) *Taira: An Okinawan Village.*

Minturn, Leigh, and William W. Lambert. (1964) *Mothers of Six Cultures: Antecedents of Child Rearing.*

Norbeck, Edward. (1954) *Takashima: A Japanese Fishing Village.*

Nydegger, William F., and Corinne Nydegger. (1966) *Tarong: An Ilocos Barrio in the Philippines.*

Piker, Steven. (1965) *An Examination of Character and Socialization in a Thai Peasant Community.*

Romney, A. Kimball, and Romaine Romney. (1966) *The Mixtecans of Juxtlahuaca, Mexico.*

Salo, Matt, and Sheila Salo. (1977) *The Kalderas in Eastern Canada.*

Segall, Marshall H., Pierre R. Dasen, and Ype H. Poortinga. (1990) *Behavior in Global Perspective: An Introduction to Cross-Cultural Psychology.*

Wallace, Ernest, and E. Adamson Hoebel. (1952) *The Comanches: Lords of the South Plains.*

Whiting, Beatrice B., and Carolyn Pope Edwards. (1988) *Children of Different Worlds: The Formation of Social Behavior.*

Whiting, Beatrice B., and John W. M. Whiting. (1975) *Children of Six Cultures: A Psycho-Cultural Analysis.*

Whiting, John W. M. (1959) "Cultural and Sociological Influences on Development." In *Growth and Development of the Child in His Setting,* 5–9.

Whiting, John W. M., Eleanor Chasdi, Helen Antonovsky, and Barbara Ayres. (1966) "The Learning of Values." In *The People of Rimrock: A Study of Values in Five Cultures,* edited by Evon Z. Vogt and Ethel M. Albert, 83–125.

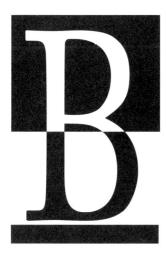

In the 1990s, an American woman who is going to have a baby can opt to have "natural" childbirth. If she does so, she will probably be required to learn breathing and relaxing techniques designed to minimize the need for anesthesia and other medical interventions during labor. Thus, "natural" childbirth is equated with intervention-free childbirth. In fact, however, cultures always intervene in childbirth, and this is so much the case that it is probably correct to say that, in the case of the human species, it is "natural" for childbirth to be dressed up with this or that cultural elaboration. Thus, for instance, societies all over the world specify who can and who cannot attend a birth. Further, certain procedures are prescribed to ease labor, hurry the delivery along, and protect the mother and infant. After the birth, specific rules are often spelled out for disposing of the placenta and the umbilical cord. The new baby is greeted and handled in culturally prescribed ways, and the behavior of the new mother and father is more or less strictly regulated. Nowhere in the world do women have babies unconstrained by cultural notions of how childbirth should be patterned.

Childbirth as Dangerous

Across cultures, childbirth is perceived as more or less dangerous. And in fact, both the woman's and the child's life are in potential jeopardy in many cultures the world over. Often, ideas about supernatural threats are superimposed upon the practical physical dangers associated with childbirth. In the Philippines, the Tarong view childbirth as a "natural thing" and, therefore, do not make a fuss over a delivery. No one expects problems, and there is no collection of people around the woman as there would be for an illness. By contrast, in Guatemala, Chimalteco women have already been told by other women that childbirth is painful and dangerous and they often cry and shout during labor, particularly at a first birth, because "there is danger of dying." In cultures where birth is feared as dangerous, the behavior of the pregnant woman and sometimes also of her husband is often regulated in an attempt to insure a safe delivery and healthy mother and baby. The Cubeo of the Northwest Amazon think of childbirth as a dangerous time for both a woman and her infant. Both are threatened by supernatural dangers, and many magical precautions are taken by the parents to protect the baby from harm while a woman is pregnant. After the baby is born, the parents observe a three-day resting period. They remain in their hammocks for most of the time and avoid engaging in any activities at all because virtually anything that a mother or father does at this time may have dire consequences for the baby. The infant's father as well as other members of his kin group are also responsible for performing a variety of rites in the service of making the baby's environment safe. The men blow tobacco smoke over all of the foods as well as the river and chant away the dangers associated with them.

Who Attends Birth

Births may be attended by the entire community. Or, the guest list may be more selective. Sometimes, women give birth alone or in the presence of just one or two helpers. Often, particular categories of people are required to be at a birth. Societies may also explicitly prevent certain people from attending a birth. Special rules regarding the participation of the expectant father at the birth of his child are also common.

Often, the husband's or wife's relatives will come to a birth. Perhaps some close friends or neighbors may also be present. The woman's female relatives or mother-in-law are sometimes singled out as mandatory attendants. Among the Gusii of Kenya, the presence of a woman's mother-in-law is required at the birth of a baby. A woman who is about to go into labor, therefore, goes to her mother-in-law's house since it is considered improper for a mother to visit the home of her son. If a woman is forced to deliver her baby elsewhere, her mother-in-law will be called to assist. When the baby has been delivered, one of the women cuts the umbilical cord, cleans out the baby's mouth, washes it with water, and feeds it juice from the leaves of a pumpkin squash plant. The mother wraps up the afterbirth in leaves and discards it on her way to bathe in the stream. She then rests with her baby in the house of her mother-in-law for a few days. A Mexican Mixtecan woman gives birth in her own house. When labor begins, the woman's mother, mother-in-law, husband, a godmother, and whoever else wishes to help at the birth are sent for. The local midwife as well as a few neighboring women and relatives, including the mother-in-law and a sister, come to help with the birth and provide moral support for a Philippine Tarong woman who is about to go into labor. People try to keep any youngsters out of the way, although everyone is too busy to bother with children unless they really get underfoot. In Jamaica, close relatives of the mother may be present at a birth, as well as the husband if he is not busy preparing water in the kitchen. The children may be sent outside to play if a woman delivers her baby in the daytime. When births occur in the evening, children are permitted to attend. People say that there is no harm in this because children do not have the sense to know what is occurring in front of their noses. No one else is allowed to be at a birth. In Okinawa, a Tairan woman who has gone into labor will go to the back room of the house, adjacent to the kitchen. A medical practitioner or midwife will be present at the birth, along with the woman's mother-in-law or other female relatives. In the cold weather, North American Chippewa women gave birth in the family wigwam unless the household contained preadolescent children. In that case, a small wigwam would be built so that the woman could be away from the children. A woman might have anyone she pleased at the birth. Usually, this included a midwife, but an expectant mother might also invite just her mother and sister, or other close female kin. All Chippewa woman knew how to help out at a birth.

Often, a crowd of people will come to the home of a woman who is in labor but will not attend the delivery itself. In Malaysia, anyone can be present at the house where a Semai woman is giving birth, and friends, relatives, and neighbors come and go continuously, bringing food and pitching in with the chores. Indeed, a husband would be insulted if fewer people showed up at his wife's labor than at that of another woman in the community. But only the midwife, husband, and female relatives enter the area where the woman is actually giving birth. No one wants to accidentally carry the odor of the birth discharge outside where the evil forces would be able to smell it and therefore be capable of causing harm to the midwife, mother, and baby. Similarly, in Thailand, when a Banoi woman is giving birth, her immediate family, including the older children, a few other relatives and a few other women whom the mother wishes to have at her side can attend. But it is generally only the midwife and perhaps another woman or two who assist at the actual delivery.

In other societies, births are more private affairs. Only the midwife and a few close relatives are informed when a Micronesian Truk woman goes into labor. The idea here is to minimize the likelihood of sorcery. In Uganda, a Sebei women may give birth on her own, although if some problem arises, the neighborhood women will come to help. In the Northwest Amazon, the Cubeo woman usually gives birth in her manioc garden. If it is her first baby, she will be assisted by her mother-in-law. Otherwise, she may deliver her baby alone, but she may ask her mother-in-law or some other women to help her if she is feeling weak. In Ecuador, a Jivaro woman gives birth assisted by her husband and mother.

In a variety of cultures, certain categories of persons are prohibited from attending a birth. Often males are required to stay away during a delivery. In Uganda, no man is permitted to attend a Sebei birth, including any male child over three years of age. Nor was a North American Comanche man, except a doctor, ever present at a delivery, although the grandfather came quickly once the baby was born to find out whether it was a boy or a girl. Among the Mixtecans, neither children nor males other than the husband are permitted to be present at a birth. Traditionally, a North American Chippewa woman did not want men at a birth and was even modest in the presence of other women, covering herself with some buckskin during labor to avoid exposure in front of onlookers.

Often, cultures explicitly indicate whether or not a husband may be present at the birth of a baby. Husbands are expected or allowed to attend births in 18 percent of 74 cultures around the world. In an additional 11 percent of these societies, a man is not often present at a birth, although there is no specific rule that prevents

him from attending. Husbands are prohibited from attending births or simply do not attend in fact in the remaining 71 percent of the 74 societies. In 11 percent of the cultures where a father cannot be present at a birth, he is still expected to perform a number of tasks associated with his wife's labor or delivery. Gusii men do not normally attend births. The husband in particular keeps away because wives simply do not want them to be present and become angry if they do show up at a delivery. In the case of a hard delivery, a husband will dig up the roots of a *chinsaga* bush. The wife will then chew and suck the roots so that their juices dissolve whatever it is in the womb that is preventing the baby from coming out. A Sebei woman will ask her husband to leave the house when labor begins because of the taboo prohibiting men from attending a birth. By contrast, in the Philippines, a Tarong husband is required to remain in the house when his wife is giving birth both to perform the chores that are required of him and to keep him from making the nonhumans angry. Among the Tairans of Okinawa, the expectant father may be present at a first birth but will remain in the front room of the house with female visitors for subsequent deliveries while his wife delivers the baby in the back room. Some Chippewa women resisted having their husbands anywhere nearby while they were in labor. Other women allowed their husbands to check on the progress of the birth. A husband might be asked to come and lift up his wife if she was too weak to get up on her own. However, men were usually not supposed to return home until the baby had been born and the mother and infant had been cleaned up.

Often, the husband is expected to perform specific duties while his wife is in labor. A Chimalteco birth is attended by the mother or mother-in-law of the woman, her husband, and a midwife, who is often a female relative. Any children in the household are packed off to stay with relatives. During labor, the husband supports his spouse. He will hold her under the arms while she squats, or she may put her arms around his waist. In Indonesia, a Javanese husband is given special herbs by the midwife. He chews these into a paste and spits them on his wife's head as added magical protection during the delivery.

First Birth

In a number of cultures, a first delivery is treated differently from subsequent births. Sometimes, this is because a first baby is accorded a special status in the society. The birth of a first son or daughter also confers a new status upon the husband and wife. They are now parents. But first births are also special because a woman does not know what to expect the first time that she has a baby, and cultural traditions sometimes take her apprehension into account. For a Gusii woman, a first birth is a major event. First-time prospective mothers are always anxious about the delivery and many are absolutely terrified. Further, there is some uncertainty about what complications may arise in the case of a first delivery. Thus, a crowd of older women is likely to attend a first birth, although only two or three women will be present for later births. A skin is put down on the floor near the bed of the mother-in-law, and this is where the expectant mother lies. If the woman is especially afraid and if labor does not progress, her own mother as well other women from the community are summoned. Sometimes, a frightened woman in labor will clamp her legs together, in which case the other women will often force them apart. They may also pinch, slap, or beat her in an attempt to hurry on her contractions. The Gusii believe that slow deliveries are caused by infidelity, so some women may also entreat her to admit her adultery. Among the Tarong, a greater crowd of people will attend a first birth, since the arrival of a first child means a change in status for the parents who can now move into a house of their own and gain some independence from their kin. A first birth is also treated as a

special occasion among the Polynesian Tongans. A first-time father throws a large feast when his wife goes into labor, and the newborn baby is placed on mats made by its grandmothers especially for the occasion.

Birth

All known cultures dictate to some degree how childbirth will be managed. There are rules concerning what a woman can and cannot ingest, what procedures should be followed to promote an easy delivery, and who should be doing what during labor. There are also conventions concerning the position in which a woman should be placed when she is giving birth. Rarely does a woman in labor lie in a horizonal position. Most frequently, women kneel or squat, allowing gravity to assist as the baby is pushed down through the birth canal.

A Mixtecan woman who is in labor eats raw eggs broken directly into her mouth by the attending women and drinks bitter tea. The idea is to promote the quick delivery of the baby. Her stomach will also be rubbed with almond oil as labor progresses. A woman gives birth kneeling on a mat. When she tires of this position, she can walk around for a while. When the baby is about to emerge, a sash is placed about the expectant mother's waist and tightened to prevent the blood and placenta from rising up through the woman's body and causing her to become ill and perhaps die. Also at this stage of delivery she is held firmly about the waist by her husband.

When a Tarong women begins to go into labor, the midwife as well as any other people who will be attending the birth are summoned. A woman who is about to have a baby will be encouraged to walk around for as long as she can. When the labor pains become stronger, someone will fetch the birth mat. Most women give birth in the kitchen, which is warm and easier to clean. When she is no longer comfortable moving around, the woman will lie down on the mat, covered by a blanket. The midwife

A midwife hangs scissors above her doorway to indicate she is on call. Later, she may use the same scissors to cut an umbilical cord.

will press her abdomen during each contraction and tie a twisted cloth around her waist to keep the blood from flowing up to her head. Her arms will also be restrained by her husband and sister. The midwife will monitor the infant's kicking movements to determine whether it is properly positioned for an easy delivery. Meanwhile, a stream of conversation is likely to be going on while everyone waits for the baby to be born. During the last stages of labor, the woman is helped to a kneeling position, supported by the midwife, whose arms are around the woman's waist. Attendants will hold her arms and legs as additional support. The midwife will try to aid the delivery by pressing down on the women's abdomen with considerable pressure during each contraction. If the delivery is a long or difficult one, various measures will also be taken to speed up the process. After the baby is delivered, the rope remains about the new mother's waist until she resumes her normal schedule, to keep the blood where it belongs. The umbilical cord is cut after the placenta is naturally expelled. After the bay is born, the mood in the kitchen becomes relaxed, with visitors joking and teasing the woman.

Chippewa women liked to kneel when giving birth, and found this preferable to lying down, as was required for hospital births. During delivery, a woman might brace herself by holding onto a tree limb slung horizontally between two poles. Some women preferred to pull on a rope fastened to a tree or part of the house frame. Once labor began, the woman was given an herb drink in an attempt to promote a quick and easy birth.

When delivery of her baby was near, a North American Sanpoil woman kneeled between two stakes hammered into the ground about 20 inches apart, leaning a knee on each stake and holding onto the stakes with her hands for further support. The old woman who assisted her rubbed the woman's stomach with downward strokes, held heated pine needles against her abdomen, and gave her hot water to drink. The assistant also told the woman what physical movements would help the progression of labor. During the delivery itself, the assistant kneeled down behind the woman and pulled down on her shoulders.

In some cultures, women like to be somewhat private when giving birth. A Jivaro woman prefers to give birth in the privacy of her garden and will feel embarrassed if the rain forces her into the house to have her baby. When the birth is imminent, two large forked sticks supporting a crossbar about two-and-one-half feet above the ground are placed in the woman's garden. During the delivery, the expectant mother squats on a clean banana leaf, her arms draped over the crossbar for support. Her husband and mother are present at the birth, one holding her arms over the crossbar and the other helping to push the baby down and out. A Tongan woman retires to a section of the house that has been separated from the rest of the dwelling area by a bark cloth partition. The two grandmothers along with an expert medicine man are present at the birth. The woman sits on her mother's lap while the older woman massages her back and applies pressure during contractions. The medicine man encourages the woman to push as hard as she can as labor progresses and catches the baby in his hands when it is finally born. A medicine man is given mats, food, bark cloth, and perhaps money as payment for assisting at a birth. In Mexico, when a Tarahumara woman goes into labor, she finds a secluded spot in which to give birth, either alone or with her husband or a female companion. She supports herself by hanging onto a branch above her head, and gives birth in a standing position, the baby falling onto a bed of grass that has been placed under her.

In Western societies, we hear about women who end up giving birth in an elevator or in the back seat of a taxicab. Women in other cultures tell of similar kinds of experiences. If a Chippewa woman began to go into labor while the family was on the move during a hunting trip, everyone would remain in one place for a few days and then the party would continue on its way. A North American Comanche woman who went into labor while on a march might simply drop back to deliver the baby and then join the other women again a few hours later.

Difficult Births

Women across cultures worry that they might have difficult deliveries, and societies have adopted strategies for trying to deal with problems during a birth. If a Tarong woman is experiencing a difficult labor, a number of remedies may be tried. Her husband may turn the house ladder upside down. Often, the woman will drink water in which the shells of naturally hatched eggs have been boiled. Sometimes, the water might contain the ashes of a bit of dried horse manure instead. The idea here is that the woman will be so disgusted at drinking the concoction that her body will want to push out the filth, expelling the baby along with it. Or some crushed ginger may be put on the woman's abdomen in the hope that the heat of the ginger will cause the baby to shift its position. Sometimes, someone will mess up the last thing that the expectant mother put in order to cause the delivery to be easier. For instance, any rice that she had recently pounded would be stirred up, or some seams of the baby clothes that she had just finished would be torn open. If a Banoi woman has a difficult time delivering her baby, the midwife will try to move things along by administering massages and rub-downs with warm water.

Among the Sanpoil, if a birth was not progressing normally, a shaman was called in. The shaman did not touch the woman, but attempted to find out what was wrong and what to do to accelerate the delivery. Among the Mixtecans, if labor does not progress rapidly enough, more extreme efforts are made to put pressure on the mother's abdomen so as to force the baby out. If

a baby is not positioned properly for delivery, the midwife will massage the mother's stomach. If the baby's hand emerges first, the appendage will be pricked with a needle in an effort to force it back up the birth canal. The woman will also be turned more or less upside down while the midwife blows on her. The goal here is to coax the baby into the right position.

In some societies, difficult births are attributed to supernatural influences. Therefore, the remedies attempt to reverse these effects. Among the Chimalteco, a hard labor is understood as a punishment from God. A diviner is summoned to find out the cause. Thus, it may be that the husband's father lies a good deal. Or the pregnant woman may have become angry with her mother-in-law or have hoarded all of the food instead of sharing it with her mother-in-law. The Cubeo blame difficult births on demonic agents. Thus, for example, if a woman dies giving birth, it may be said that the baby's father was a boa constrictor who, having come to fetch his child and having discovered a human infant instead, carried the mother away in anger. A medicine man is summoned in the case of difficult deliveries. In Micronesia, the Truk attribute a difficult birth to the effects of sorcery or, more commonly, to the actions of a ghost of some recently deceased relative of the mother who is punishing the woman's kin for their failure to meet some obligation to a member of the kin group, especially to the mother herself. If it is suspected that a ghost is causing a birth to be difficult, all of the kin of the woman come and bring her presents to show that they are not neglecting her.

Display of Pain

Cultures differ regarding their tolerance of displays of pain on the part of a woman in labor. A North American Fox woman was prohibited from crying out during labor, no matter how difficult the birth. If she made any noise, she was ridiculed by her attendants. Jamaican women attempt to control any outward signs that they are in pain for fear of being laughed at. A Samoan woman should neither squirm nor cry out in pain. By contrast, Chimalteco women often struggle, shout, and cry during labor, and a woman may hit her spouse, whose job it is to hold her while she squats in the birth position. Men joke among themselves about the violence that women direct at their husbands at delivery, and neighbors can hear the commotion coming from the house in which a birth is in progress.

Expelling the Placenta

Infection is a common cause of complications when a woman has given birth and it can be caused by the retention of pieces of placenta. Women across cultures, therefore, are concerned that the placenta be expelled cleanly and quickly after a baby has been delivered. In Japan, atten-

dants at a Takashima birth try to aid the expulsion of the placenta by gagging the woman with a wooden spoon handle. When her infant has been delivered, a Mixtecan woman promotes the expulsion of the placenta by blowing in a bottle and chewing mint seasoned with salt. This helps her to push harder. Or someone may put a feather or finger down her throat to induce nausea and to help along the expulsion of the placenta. Once the placenta is expelled, the woman can put on fresh clothing, but she will not bathe or go near water. If a Tarong woman fails to expel the placenta naturally, an attendant may press the abdomen gently while carefully pulling on the umbilical cord. If this remedy does not work, then the woman will try to blow into a bottle as hard as she can so that the effort of blowing will push out the placenta. If this strategy fails, a heated handle of a wooden ladle will be applied

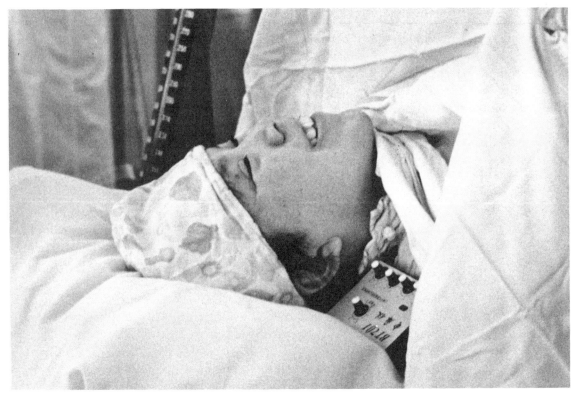

A Chinese mother smiles upon learning the daughter she has just delivered is healthy.

to the woman's abdomen. Finally, if none of these treatments succeeds, someone may sprinkle vinegar on the shorts of the new father, warm them on the stove, and place them on the woman's abdomen.

Disposal of the Placenta

In many cultures, strict rules are followed in disposing of the placenta once it has been successfully expelled. Often, proper disposal is viewed as necessary for the future welfare of the mother or baby. The Mixtecans wrap the placenta in a rag, rolled up in a straw mat, and put in a tree to insure that the baby will be able to climb trees when it grows up. Efforts are taken to see that the placenta remains very clean, as a dirty placenta is thought to lead to visual problems in the newborn baby. The Tarong put the expelled placenta into a pot with a perfect rim and cover it with half of a coconut shell. The pot is placed near the bowl in which a rope used during the birth is allowed to burn. Later that day, the new father will hang the placenta-pot in a tree. If the baby subsequently has any trouble breathing, the father will knock the pot to the ground in order to help the infant to breath better. For a first birth, the mother drinks some water into which a bit of burned and crushed placenta has been mixed. Some people say that the concoction promotes successful future births while others claim that it guards against shock to the mother's system following the birth. Among the Tairans of Okinawa, the placenta is wrapped in rice straw and disposed of in a designated spot out-of-doors behind the hearth. Meanwhile, the infant's grandmother along with other older female relatives circle the house, banging pots with pot covers, laughing, and calling out to one another. The goal of all of this activity is to insure that the new baby will become a happy and sociable child. In Uganda, the Sebei may dispose of the placenta out-of-doors, but it is more usual to bury it under the house to prevent ill-wishers from digging it up and using it for witchcraft. After a Tongan baby is born, a wide band is tied around the mother's waist for support, and pressure is applied to her abdomen until the placenta is expelled. The father then buries the placenta, wrapped in bark cloth, in a hole under a path near the house. The Banoi bury the placenta under the house to insure that the baby will not wander away from home and abandon its parents. In Mexico, the Tarahumara bury the umbilical cord so that the baby will not be stupid. The Chimalteco believe that the afterbirth remains a part of the individual for life. Thus, every person should know the location of his or her afterbirth. The afterbirth is buried under the sweathouse, which is adjacent to the family's house. If a woman gives birth away from home, the afterbirth is dried so that it can be taken back to her village to be buried as usual. In this way, when a person is sick, the soothsayer can say prayers in front of the sweathouse in which the "afterbirth lives." In adulthood, every Chimalteco is supposed to visit the sweathouse on occasion to burn a candle and say prayers, although people often forget to do this until there is some emergency.

Disposal of the Umbilical Cord

Often, cultural rules exist regarding the disposal of the umbilical cord. The cord retains importance for people in many societies because it is seen as exerting influence over the baby's future. When a Mixtecan baby's umbilical cord falls off, it is wrapped in a rag and retained so that it can be used in the treatment of various childhood eye ailments. The ailments of any child are cured by the use of an umbilical cord of a child of the opposite sex. Some Banoi parents keep the umbilical cord, waiting for it to dry and then turning it into a powder to be administered to the infant when it becomes ill, especially with stomach problems. The Comanche wrap the umbilical cord up and hang it in a hackberry tree. If the cord remains undisturbed until it rots, the baby will have a long and lucky life. The

Chippewa placed the umbilical cord in a small beaded buckskin container and attached it to the baby's cradleboard as a toy. Sometimes, a person kept the cord. Sometimes, the cord was eventually discarded in such a way as to bring good fortune to the child. For instance, a father might dispose of a boy's umbilical cord on the spot where he had killed his first animal on a hunt so that his son would become a good hunter. Or a girl's cord might be placed under some wood chips so that she would become a good wood gatherer. In Bolivia, when a Toba baby is born, the umbilical cord is cut off and guarded for some time. To discard the cord before the navel is entirely healed would be the same as throwing away the baby's life. Indeed, the baby would die soon afterwards. The Tarong appreciate that the umbilical cord was the infant's lifeline before it was born and they use a special name, *kayannak,* for a baby whose cord has not yet fallen off and who, therefore, still retains evidence of its former attachment to its mother. A cord that has fallen off is still regarded as part of the child. It is wrapped up and hung somewhere in the house, usually in a window. When the wind hits the cord, this causes the infant's chest and abdomen to become stronger so that the baby will be able to tolerate the chilly winds as it grows older and is clothed in nothing but a shirt.

Birth as Dirty

In a number of societies, the birth process is viewed as contaminating. This means that a woman who has just given birth, and perhaps also her attendants or the baby, must undergo some kind of purification before they can return to a normal life. In Canada, a Kalderas woman is considered *marime,* or unclean, after she has given birth. She remains secluded for six weeks, and any dishes or bedding that she has used during this time are thrown away. The baby is also viewed as *marime* for six weeks. In Malaysia, a Semai woman gives birth in a room that has slatted floors so that the blood and afterbirth can fall through the spaces and not contaminate the house. The odors of the blood and discharge are also believed to attract evil forces, and especially bird spirits. Assistants at a Sebei birth are considered dirty and may not milk cows until they have participated in a cleansing ceremony held two days after the delivery. At the ceremony, the women and baby wash in water in which special leaves have been boiled. The new mother must also clean her house before her husband can return. This may take a number of weeks.

Announcements of Birth

In many cultures, a new baby is more than an addition to its own family. It is a new member of the broader community. The birth of a baby, therefore, is news, and its entrance into the world soon becomes public knowledge. The Chippewa traditionally announced the birth of a baby by firing off a gun. When they heard the shot, neighbors would take off for the house where the baby had been born and play at trying to capture the child and would at the same time tell the baby to be brave and strong. The baby's relatives would throw water or a mixture of water and flour at the crowd to protect the infant from the intruders. A feast was also thrown soon after the birth. The birth of an Arapaho baby is not formally announced or celebrated. But the midwife informs a relative of the mother of the sex of the baby, and the news is passed along to everyone in the community.

Attitudes toward Hospital Births

In traditional societies that have come into contact with Western cultures, women who are accustomed to giving birth at home sometimes have the opportunity of having their babies in hospitals. The option is not always welcomed. Banoi women resist giving birth in a hospital, in part because of the expense in involved, but principally because they do not want to have their babies by themselves with no one but a strange doctor for moral support. Almost all Banoi women would rather risk the dangers of giving birth at home in the presence of their relatives. Neither did Chippewa women like to go to the hospital to give birth. They preferred squatting to lying in bed during labor. And they did not like having strange men poking at them. Truk women are very resistant to having babies in a hospital, or even away from home, and only the fear of a breech birth is likely to convince a woman to risk a hospital birth. Across cultures, then, women are happier having babies in settings with which they are familiar and surrounded by people whom they know. They tend to view hospitals as strange places populated by strangers, and even the idea of having a baby under these circumstances makes them anxious. It is, in fact, the case that expectant mothers can become anxious when in a hospital setting. Anxiety then interferes with the normal birth process, as the physiological systems responsible for promoting a smooth labor and delivery tend to shut down when a woman is anxious or stressed. The irony, then, is that the hospital, which offers a woman greater technological support in case of a difficult birth, can also lead to more difficult labors that then require technological intervention. It is because women universally prefer to have their babies in familiar settings with familiar people that hospitals have begun to relax their regulations regarding how births must proceed. Delivery rooms are now furnished like bedrooms, husbands and other acquaintances of the woman are permitted to attend births, and the expectant mother herself is allowed greater freedom to move around, eat, and so on during labor and to choose the birthing position that she prefers during delivery.

See also MOTHERS, NEW; PREGNANCY

———

Beaglehole, Ernest, and Pearl Beaglehole. (1941) *Pangai: Village in Tonga.*

Bennett, Wendell, and Robert Zingg. (1935) *The Tarahumara: An Indian Tribe of Northern Mexico.*

Broude, Gwen J., and Sarah J. Greene. (1983) "Cross-Cultural Codes on Husband-Wife Relationships." *Ethnology* 22: 263–280.

Cohen, Yehudi A. (1966) *A Study of Interpersonal Relations in a Jamaican Community.*

Denton, Robert. (1978) "Notes on Childhood in a Nonviolent Context: The Semai Case." In *Learning and Non-Aggression,* edited by Ashley Montagu, 94–143.

Geertz, Hildred. (1961) *The Javanese Family: A Study of Kinship and Socialization.*

Gladwin, Thomas, and Seymour Sarason. (1953) *Truk: Man in Paradise.*

Goldman, Irving. (1963) *The Cubeo: Indians of the Northwest Amazon.*

Goldschmidt, Walter. (1976) *The Culture and Behavior of the Sebei.*

Hara, Hiroko Sue. (1967) *Hare Indians and Their World.*

Harner, Michael J. (1973) *The Jivaro: People of the Sacred Waterfalls.*

Hilger, M. Inez. (1951) *Chippewa Child Life and Its Cultural Background.*

———. (1952) *Arapaho Child Life and Its Cultural Background.*

Hitchcock, John T., and Leigh Minturn. (1966) *The Rajputs of Khalapur, India.*

Jones, William. (1939) *Ethnography of the Fox Indians.*

Karsten, Rafael. (1923) *The Toba Indians of the Bolivian Gran Chaco.*

Kronenberg, Andreas. (1981) *The Teda of Tibesti.*

LeVine, Robert A., and Barbara B. LeVine. (1966) *Nyansongo: A Gusii Community of Kenya.*

Maretzki, Thomas W., and Hatsumi Maretzki. (1966) *Taira: An Okinawan Village.*

Mead, Margaret. (1928) *Coming of Age in Samoa.*

Norbeck, Edward. (1954) *Takashima: A Japanese Fishing Community.*

Nydegger, William F., and Corinne Nydegger. (1966) *Tarong: An Ilocos Barrio in the Philippines.*

Piker, Steven. (1965) *An Examination of Character and Socialization in a Thai Peasant Community.*

Ray, Verne. (1933) *The Sanpoil and the Nespelem: Salishan Peoples of Northeastern Washington.*

Romalis, Shelly. (1981) "An Overview." In *Childbirth: Alternatives to Medical Control,* edited by Shelly Romalis, 3–32.

Romney, A. Kimball, and Romaine Romney. (1966) *The Mixtecans of Juxtlahuaca, Mexico.*

Salo, Matt, and Sheila Salo. (1977) *The Kalderas in Eastern Canada.*

Wagley, Charles. (1949) "The Social and Religious Life of a Guatemalan Village." *American Anthropologist* 51: 3–150.

Wallace, Ernest, and E. Adamson Hoebel. (1952) *The Comanches: Lords of the South Plains.*

BIRTH ORDER

Birth order refers to the chronological position of a child relative to his or her siblings. Psychologists interested in child development have noticed that birth order is related to how a child is treated and how the child behaves. This seems to be the case both in American families and in families in cultures around the world. However, the effects of birth order turn out to be different, and sometimes even diametrically opposed, in America in comparison with other societies. Thus, in America, eldest children are typically described as seeking attention much more frequently than do younger siblings. In many other societies around the world, however, it is the youngest child who seeks help more frequently. In Kenya, Kikuyu mothers say that the youngest sibling is spoiled. People attribute this to the fact that last-born children never have to share anything with a smaller child. When a child with no younger siblings begins to demand attention, neighbors and relatives advise the mother to have another baby. Similarly, in Nigeria, the youngest Yoruba child is frequently brought up by relatives because everyone assumes that the mother will spoil the baby of the family. Among the Mixtecans of Mexico, youngest children are weaned later and are also trained in obedience, self-reliance, responsibility, and nurturance somewhat later than other children. In Thailand, the Banoi say that the last-born children are lucky because their mothers can treat them with indulgence for a longer period of time. Older siblings, by contrast, must learn to do without so much petting once younger siblings come along.

Last-born children are sometimes also a little slower than their older siblings in acquiring developmental skills. For instance, the youngest Mixtecan child tends to reach each new stage of development somewhat later than do older siblings. In part, these developmental lags may be a result of lowered expectations on the part of adults. In Kenya, a youngest Gusii child is less likely to be encouraged to walk early or to become independent of its caretakers as soon as are earlier born children. The Banoi also expect less of last-born children even when they are adolescents. A girl in particular is asked to perform fewer household tasks than other daughters if she is the youngest child.

In many societies, the birth of a firstborn baby is singled out for special attention. For instance, a first baby may be treated to more elaborate birth and naming ceremonies. Eldest children may be required to take on more responsibility but they may also be accorded more respect from and authority over younger brothers and sisters. Often, a firstborn son is treated as more special than is a firstborn daughter. A later-born infant may also receive special treatment in societies where infant mortality is a real threat. When Gusii parents have lost a number of children, they are liable to pamper a new infant more than is ordinarily the case. The same special treatment is directed toward a baby boy in a family with nothing but girls.

While firstborns often have to put up with less attention from the mother once younger siblings are born, they may get special treatment while they remain only children. For instance, a Gusii mother is more likely to take care of an older child herself instead of entrusting the youngster to a child nurse as she will do with her other children.

LeVine, Robert A., and Barbara B. LeVine. (1966) *Nyansongo: A Gusii Community in Kenya.*

Levinson, David, and Martin J. Malone. (1980) *Toward Explaining Human Culture.*

Piker, Steven. (1965) *An Examination of Character and Socialization in a Thai Peasant Community.*

Romney, A. Kimball, and Romaine Romney. (1966) *The Mixtecans of Juxtlahuaca, Mexico.*

Rosenblatt, Paul C., and Elizabeth L. Skoogberg. (1974) "Birth Order in Cross-Cultural Perspective." *Developmental Psychology* 10: 49–54.

Whiting, Beatrice B. (1971) "Folk Wisdom and Child Rearing." Paper presented at meetings of the American Association for the Advancement of Science, December.

BIRTH SPACING

In most cultures around the world, women of childbearing age have babies at regular intervals. Typically, a new baby is born once every two years. This spacing is accomplished by the fact that women's reproductive behavior represents a delicate balance between the continued production of children and activities of various sorts that interfere with reproduction. One cause of temporary infertility is simply a natural outgrowth of female physiology. Thus, ovulation is suppressed to some degree when a woman is nursing. The more a mother nurses, the more profound the suppression. As women across societies nurse infants, couples have a natural means of birth control. Typically, nursing interferes with fertility for about two years, accounting in part for the common two-year birth spacing across cultures.

Nursing is a means of birth control that demands no extra effort or planning on the part of a couple. Husbands and wives, however, may also take a more active role in spacing births. The postpartum sex taboo functions in this way. Thus, in a number of cultures, sexual intercourse between a husband and wife is prohibited for some interval of time after the birth of a child. The North American Arapaho typically avoided having other children until four or more years after a previous pregnancy. A postpartum sex taboo that lasted four years as well as the custom of nursing children for the duration of the taboo contributed to this spacing. Similarly, in Java, women typically have two babies over a three-year period. The spacing is due in part to the custom practiced by some couples of abstaining from sexual intercourse for seven months after a birth to guarantee that a baby will be able to nurse.

Abortion also serves as a conscious strategy for spacing pregnancies in a number of cultures around the world. For instance, in Bolivia, Toba couples have three or four children, spaced at two- or three-year intervals. Abortions, which are common for a variety of reasons in the society, partly account for this pattern. In some cultures, women or couples use some form of contraception. As a form of contraception, the Minnesotan Chippewa took a concoction of ingredients known only to certain individuals. In

Java, women use both drugs and spells to attempt to induce both permanent sterility, or *dikantjing* ("to be locked"), and temporary sterility, or *ngarangake* ("to make rarer").

Public opinion also acts as a kind of birth control. Chippewa married couples were advised to stay away from each other for a while after the birth of a baby, as it was regarded as shameful for people to produce children "like steps and stairs." Similarly, in Kenya, most Gusii women like to have a child every two years, and generally, wives are actively interested in having sexual intercourse when they wish to have another baby. But if a mother's children are less than two years apart, her neighbors are liable to whisper that she is oversexed.

The arrival of new babies for the duration of a woman's fertility has consequences for the makeup of families across cultures. This is illustrated by the case of the Tarong of the Philippines. Here, a woman usually has a new baby every other year as long as she is able to have children. As a result, a mother and her daughter may both be nursing a baby, and aunts and uncles will often be younger than their nieces and nephews. This rate of production is considered desirable, and one Tarong man commented that, when a child first says "mother" or "father", this is his way of asking for a new brother or sister.

While women in most nonindustrial cultures have babies every two years or so, among contemporary hunter-gatherers, for instance the Kalahari !Kung San, women give birth around once every four years. In keeping with the idea that human characteristics evolved as adaptations to our hunter-gatherer origins, we can postulate that a four-year birth spacing is the original human adaptation. The idea is supported by the fact that our ancestral cousins, the apes, also give birth once every four years. If this is correct, then it is worth our while to wonder how the shorter birth spacing characteristic of most contemporary cultures might affect development. It is possible that various developmental phenomena such as sibling rivalry, child abuse, maternal stress, and so on are the result of a spacing interval to which human infants and their parents are not ideally adapted.

See also NURSING; SEX TABOO, POSTPARTUM

Geertz, Hildred. (1961) *The Javanese Family: A Study of Kinship and Socialization.*

Hilger, M. Inez. (1951) *Chippewa Child Life and Its Cultural Background.*

———. (1952) *Arapaho Child Life and Its Cultural Background.*

Karsten, Rafael. (1923) *The Toba Indians of the Bolivian Gran Chaco.*

Konner, Melvin J. (1981) "Evolution of Human Behavior Development." In *Handbook of Cross-Cultural Human Development,* edited by Ruth H. Munroe, Robert L. Munroe, and Beatrice B. Whiting, 3–51.

Lee, Richard B. (1979) *The !Kung San: Men, Women, and Work in a Foraging Society.*

LeVine, Robert A., and Barbara B. LeVine. (1966) *Nyansongo: A Gusii Community in Kenya.*

Nydegger, William F., and Corinne Nydegger. (1966) *Tarong: An Ilocos Barrio in the Philippines.*

Piker, Steven. (1965) *An Examination of Character and Socialization in a Thai Peasant Community.*

Wagley, Charles. (1949) "The Social and Religious Life of a Guatemalan Village." *American Anthropologist* 51: 3–150.

tions in the environment will produce variations in physical and behavioral profiles. This makes good evolutionary sense. A genetic blueprint that allowed any and every environmental vicissitude to determine the nature of its expression would be in danger of constructing an organism that had less or even no chance of surviving. Natural selection, therefore, would be expected to favor genetic blueprints that tended to remain loyal to some specific tried-and-true developmental pathway in spite of environmental variation. This would increase the chances that the organism would be born with a set of characteristics that were well suited to survival.

The idea that genes remain loyal to specific developmental pathways in spite of environmental vicissitudes is called canalization. Thus, while environments are always implicated in the growth and functioning of the organism, the role of the environment is *permissive* rather than constructive. That is, environments provide the cues that permit genes to be expressed in such a way as to produce an organism by way of some relatively predictable trajectory. Environments do not construct organisms from whole cloth.

How do genetic instructions keep the developmental process on track in spite of environmental variation? First, genes may be structured in such a way that they "read" a variety of different environmental cues as if they were equivalent, allowing for the same genetic response to environmental variation. Sets of genes may also affect each other in such a way as to produce the same result in spite of environmental variation. This might occur via feedback loops. Some specific environmental cue triggers the action of one gene or subset of genes that then compensate for the environmental signal by affecting the action of some other gene or set of genes. Thus, the developmental trajectory remains on track because genes regulate each other in such a way as to produce a targeted outcome. The individual's full complement of genetic instructions may also have some built-

CANALIZATION The development of any organism, including the human organism, is dependent upon the interaction, or coaction, of the organism's genes and the environment in which the genes find themselves. This is true of prenatal development, during which the growth of the organism from a single cell to a fully formed fetus occurs because within-cell and between-cell signals allow for the expression of genetic instructions. It is the triggering of genetic instructions by cues from the gene's surroundings that accounts for the prenatal development of the individual. Genes and environment also cooperate to produce an individual's physical and behavioral profile after birth and throughout life. Thus, for example, genes that have the potential to cause cancerous cell growth may or may not express themselves depending upon whether or not they are triggered by relevant environmental cues.

While every detail of the growth and functioning of an organism is the joint product of genes and the environment in which genes find themselves, there are limits to how much varia-

in redundancy. Thus, if some set of genetic instructions is triggered by environmental cues in such a way as to pull the developmental pathway off track, some other, parallel set of instructions may be able to take over and deflect the trajectory back to a more normal course.

Some aspects of the development and functioning of an organism are in all likelihood more canalized than others. These would be the characteristics that underlie vital functions upon which survival depends. Characteristics less crucial to the organism's survival would be predicted to be more variable as a function of environmental pressure. Further, even where traits are highly canalized and, therefore, highly resistant to change, a sufficiently unusual environmental cue will be able to pull the developmental trajectory off course. Human infants and young children are surprisingly resilient in the face of food shortages, and one proposal is that the developmental trajectory of youngsters who face starvation is deflected to a parallel course that requires a less generous food supply. The youngster may be smaller than would have been the case had development followed the original pathway, but the physical appearance of the child will be typically human. However, even this parallel pathway requires some minimal input from the environment. If the child's food supply dips below some base level, the trajectory of even this highly canalized trait can be deflected from its normal course.

The idea of canalization leads us to expect that children everywhere will share a number of physical and behavioral traits in spite of variations in the way that their particular cultures pattern their experience. These shared traits are likely to be just those characteristics that are most basic to human survival and well-being. We may also expect certain cultural variations to have essentially equivalent effects on development. Other cultural variations may be expected to produce differences in the physical and behavioral profiles of children. These would be traits

less central to a person's survival and well-being. Where behaviors tailored to the details of cultural customs and institutions would best serve the welfare of the individual, we would also expect developmental pathways to be affected by environmental vicissitudes.

See also COACTION; RESILIENCY

Harper, Lawrence. (1989) *The Nurture of Human Behavior.*

Waddington, C. H. (1962) *New Patterns in Genetics and Development.*

CARETAKERS, SECONDARY

Mothers the world over are assisted in the task of rearing children. Usually, they are helped by family members, other relatives, and neighbors. In a majority of cultures, mothers recruit older siblings to help care for infants and smaller children. If no sibling is available, a cousin may be called on as a baby tender. In polygynous families, cowives may share caretaking duties. If the mother happens to live in an extended family, she has a number of kin upon whom she can depend to fill in for her. Further, in most traditional societies, other relatives live close by and can be recruited by a mother to watch her children.

In some societies where the community is small and people know each other, everyone in the neighborhood acts as a secondary caretaker. Among the Ifaluk of Micronesia, everyone in the neighborhood knows everyone else, and children can depend upon anyone who happens to be around to feed them or see to their needs. Any child can walk into any house in the village, day or night, without knocking first. In the

North American Navaho extended family, children live with perhaps 15 people or more whom they call "brother" and a number of women who are "mother." Youngsters who have been weaned come to depend as much upon their other "mothers" as the real mother to provide affection and see to their needs. Often, a woman is helped at one time or another by a variety of people with whom she has a variety of relationships. Thus, in the Philippines, a Tarong mother acts as the primary caretaker for the first month or so of her baby's life. But after this initial period, she is likely to get a significant amount of help if she happens to live in a household with appropriate surrogates with whom she gets along. No woman is ever the only caretaker of her baby. Thus, when a mother is busy, some other member of the household will see to a crying baby. If a woman is preparing a meal, the father along with the other children will take the babies and toddlers out in the yard. Once children are weaned, they spend most of their time with a secondary caretaker. Such youngsters are incorporated into the play groups made up of preschool and school-age children as they are toted about by their child nurses, and this is where the little ones may be found if they are not sleeping, eating, or away from home. Adults and siblings keep an eye on the activities of the play groups, but do not supervise any individual youngster. For Tarong preschoolers, everyone in the neighborhood is a potential caretaker. Thus, a child who is thirsty or hurt or has a broken toy can stop at a number of houses in search of help. Children may seek out whoever is closest or they may look for the person who is most likely to respond favorably to the child's request. Analogously, any adult will take on the responsibility of scolding a naughty child, and parents frequently say, "We all help to raise our children." This allows a mother to worry less if her youngster wanders from home.

The fact that a mother can count on other people to help her with caretaking means that the woman is freed up long enough to attend to subsistence and household chores. Conversely, a woman who has no such help has difficulty getting all of her work done. In Okinawa, Tairan mothers who have no one to help take care of a baby are seriously handicapped because they cannot get their work done efficiently. With a baby on her back, a woman cannot easily carry produce back from the fields and finds that her efficiency generally suffers. As a rule, Tairan babies are carried around by parents, grandparents, unmarried aunts and uncles, or older siblings while the mother is occupied with her chores. An Indian Rajput mother who has no one to assist her with caretaking and is extremely busy may administer opium to her baby to put it to sleep, although women recognize that the practice is not good for infants and should only be resorted to in an emergency.

Among the Banoi of Thailand, a woman's female relatives take on some of the responsibilities associated with child care. Female kin occasionally nurse, bathe, feed, and watch over each other's babies. Fathers also help out on occasion, but child care is viewed as women's work, and it is women who do most of the caretaking in fact. Older sisters do not tend to be recruited to care for babies. Rather, they are expected to supervise the second youngest child in the family. Boys are not expected to act as baby tenders. Among the Rajputs of India, women are confined to outdoor courtyards. Each courtyard houses a mother-in-law along with her unmarried daughters and daughters-in-law. If the women are on good terms, any of them will pick up a crying baby, and the grandmother may offer the infant a dry breast in an effort to quiet the crying. Most males, however, do not take care of infants, although old men who no longer play an important role in farming or politics will tend babies. Thus, if there is a grandfather or great uncle in a household, a mother may recruit him to watch her baby instead of asking an older child. Or sometimes, an uncle will cart an infant over to the men's platform for a while. But as soon as the baby cries, it is handed back to the women.

While women across cultures can generally rely on other people to help with child tending, the mother generally retains the role of primary caretaker. Among the Gusii of Kenya, cowives, if they are on good terms, as well as sisters-in-law, will occasionally look after and feed each other's children if the mother is out of the house all day. If she is no longer engaged in subsistence activities herself, the father's mother may also tend a grandchild when the mother is not around. An older sibling who is not formally designated as child nurse will also sometimes look after a younger brother or sister, and an initiated girl may oversee a child nurse. But the primary caretaking responsibility for young children lies with the mother and child nurse, with other people only filling in temporarily and sporadically as baby-sitters. Similarly, a Mexican Mixtecan mother will ask another female in her household to watch her child while the mother has to attend to some chore away from home, and sisters-in-law who live in the same compound may nurse each other's children if this becomes necessary. But the mother is still regarded as having primary responsibility for the care of her own child. In Canada, Hare fathers, adolescent sisters, grandmothers, or aunts will change the baby's diaper, give it a bottle, and also take care of the infant. And relatives will watch the baby when the mother is out visiting her traps or fetching spruce brush. Fathers or other male members of the household will rock the baby in its hammock and bounce it on a knee. But mothers are the primary caretakers of infants.

The situation may change as a child becomes somewhat older. This is even more likely to be the case when a new baby arrives. Often, the older child, who has monopolized the attention of its mother, is now handed over to other caretakers. In the Northwest Amazon, a Cubeo in-fant remains in its mother's care until it begins to walk and to eat solid food. From then on, the youngster is supervised by an older sibling, usually a six-year-old sister, who carries the baby around on her hip. Other people are also likely to help look after a baby of this age, including the father's mother, who feeds the infant. And once a new baby arrives in a household, care of an older infant is largely out of the hands of the mother.

Nevertheless, the mother usually retains her exclusive place in the heart of a child. A Banoi youngster receives care and attention from everyone in the household, but when a young child is upset, only the mother is an effective source of comfort. A Banoi woman whose youngster is distressed for some reason immediately nurses the child. Other caretakers come to take it for granted that they cannot successfully quiet a seriously upset youngster and they will quickly seek out the mother instead of attempting to comfort the youngster on their own. And the Banoi mother understands that she is the best source of consolation for her child.

See also CHILD NURSES; SOCIALIZATION, AGENTS OF

Goldman, Irving. (1963) *The Cubeo: Indians of the Northwest Amazon.*

Hara, Hiroko Sue. (1967) *Hare Indians and Their World.*

Hitchcock, John T., and Leigh Minturn. (1966) *The Rajputs of Khalapur, India.*

LeVine, Robert A., and Barbara B. LeVine. (1966) *Nyansongo: A Gusii Community in Kenya.*

Maretzki, Thomas W., and Hatsumi Maretzki. (1966) *Taira: An Okinawan Village.*

Nydegger, William F., and Corinne Nydegger. (1966) *Tarong: An Ilocos Barrio in the Philippines.*

Piker, Steven. (1965) *An Examination of Character and Socialization in a Thai Peasant Community.*

Romney, A. Kimball, and Romaine Romney. (1966) *The Mixtecans of Juxtlahuaca, Mexico.*

Stephens, William N. (1963) *The Family in Cross-Cultural Perspective.*

CHILD MORTALITY

In many cultures around the world, women have fewer, and sometimes dramatically fewer, surviving children than pregnancies. This means that child mortality, or child death, is a real risk in many societies. Thus, whereas women in many cultures become pregnant once every two years, the number of grown children that mothers across cultures produce is significantly less than this pregnancy rate would predict. One study of 51 cultures around the world estimates that completed families have an average of 5.8 children. This figure overestimates the number of children that will survive to maturity. The average is also inflated by societies in which women have a relatively high number of living children. Thus, for instance, the average North American Papago family has 8 living children and an average African Luo family has 10.6 surviving children. Viewed from another perspective, only one-fourth of the same 51 cultures have families with an average of 6 or more surviving children.

High infant mortality can be traced to a number of causes including complications during delivery, infantile diseases, and malnutrition. Among the Rajputs of India, child mortality is most common among children under three years of age. Children die of malaria, diarrhea, smallpox, boils, intestinal infections, and an inadequate supply of milk. The Rajputs ascribe some childhood deaths to sorcery, the evil eye, and viewing of a corpse by the youngster. The Truk of Micronesia lose a fairly large percentage of infants either from stillbirths or death shortly after birth. Some infants die as a result of prolonged labor and others because no measures are taken to induce breathing in a baby who does not begin to breathe on its own. Unsanitary birth conditions also result in the death of some babies. During a single year, over one-fifth of the babies died before their first birthdays and over one-third in the first three years of life, not counting stillbirths or births in which the mother also died. About one-half of the babies born to a Mexican Mixtecan woman survive beyond childhood. Some die at birth, but the period following weaning is also risky for a youngster. Among the Semai of Malaysia, about one-third of infant deaths may result from complications at birth. In some east Semai communities, children have less than a 50 percent chance of surviving for a year after birth. In the west, the mortality rate is half of this. Rates of infant death are related to people's attempts to protect newborn babies by way of ritual, so that people who live in the east have a greater number of food restrictions to protect infants, are more careful to observe the rules, apply the restrictions to a greater number of people, and respect the restrictions longer. On average, half of children born to Kenyan Gusii women survive to adulthood. Some individual women have few or no children despite repeated pregnancies. Women who become sterile or lose an excessive number of infants are likely to accuse a cowife of witchcraft or to blame another woman who has had similar misfortune, assuming that she has practiced witchcraft on them out of jealousy. From 1883 to the 1960s, the infant mortality rate for the Canadian Hare ranged from 21 to 88 percent for boys and from 31 to 88 percent for girls. Estimates of child mortality among some African pastoralist and agricultural societies range from 25 to over 50 percent of live births.

In some cultures, child mortality rates are different for males and females. Rajput girls die at twice the rate of boys, reflecting the preference for males in Rajput culture. The differential death rate is in part attributable to the fact that girls are less likely to receive prolonged medical care when they are ill. Differential infanticide rates for female as opposed to male babies also contribute to the higher death rate for babies. For instance, in the Northwest Amazon, Cubeo women who resort to infanticide when they do not want another baby are nevertheless likely to keep the infant if it is a boy, but not if it is a girl.

High child mortality rates affect the behavior of parents. Rajputs react to the high death rate among children by taking measures to ward off illness. Infants wear charms believed to prevent disease, and when parents refer to children who are especially frail, they will add the phrase "if he lives." A mother who had already lost two children was hesitant about purchasing good clothing for a living daughter. She was also afraid to become too attached to the little girl in case she also died. Similarly, the high mortality rate among the Micronesian Truk is reflected in their habit of waiting to name infants until it is clear that they are strong and healthy, and there is a sense that, until that happens, a child is not entirely a member of the family or community. There is no formal ceremony or mourning for a baby who dies soon after birth.

See also CHILDREN, DESIRE FOR; PARENTS' PREFERENCE FOR BOY OR GIRL

Dentan, Robert. (1978) "Notes on Childhood in a Nonviolent Context: The Semai Case." In *Learning and Non-Aggression,* edited by Ashley Montagu, 94–143.

Gladwin, Thomas, and Seymour Sarason. (1953) *Truk: Man in Paradise.*

Goldman, Irving. (1963) *The Cubeo: Indians of the Northwest Amazon.*

Goldschmidt, Walter. (1976) *The Culture and Behavior of the Sebei.*

Hara, Hiroko Sue. (1967) *Hare Indians and Their World.*

Hitchcock, John T., and Leigh Minturn. (1966) *The Rajputs of Khalapur, India.*

LeVine, Robert A., and Barbara B. LeVine. (1966) *Nyansongo: A Gusii Community in Kenya.*

Palfrey House. (n.d.) "Cross-Cultural Ratings." Unpublished codes, Harvard University, Cambridge.

Romney, A. Kimball, and Romaine Romney. (1966) *The Mixtecans of Juxtlahuaca, Mexico.*

Williamson, Laila. (1978) "Infanticide: An Anthropological Analysis." In *Infanticide and the Value of Life,* edited by Marvin Kohl, 61–75.

CHILD NURSES

While most women around the world are understood to have primary responsibility for their own children, most women also have help in tending youngsters. Further, most mothers recruit older children to take care of younger ones. Usually, the child nurse is a sibling, but if no sisters or brothers are available, a cousin will often serve as a substitute. In Mexico, a number of Mixtecan nuclear families live in one compound, so when there is no older sibling to watch a younger one, a cousin is likely to be available as a nurse, and in fact, more small children are cared for by cousins than by brothers or sisters. Across cultures, then, infants and toddlers are supervised for some part of each day by other, somewhat older children. Child nurses may feed, bathe, and generally look after their charges. In cultures where youngsters are recruited as nurses, groups of older children may be seen gathered together in play groups with infants on their backs and toddlers tagging along behind them. In the Philippines, the six-year-old Tarong youngster begins to be given additional child care responsibilities. The older child comes home from school, changes clothes, and then slings a younger sibling on the hip before going out to play with the other youngsters. A play group can consist of some 30 or more children, most of whom are younger than ten and many of whom are babies under the supervision of older siblings.

Usually, a mother will choose a boy to act as child nurse only if there are no girls to do the job. In Thailand, older Banoi girls are expected to care for the second-youngest child in the family. The baby is the responsibility of the mother and her female relatives. Boys are not recruited as child nurses. But boys are as just as likely to act as child nurses as are their sisters in some societies. A Tarong boy serves as a child nurse as often as his sister, as this allows older girls to help out in the fields or with meal preparation. Even when there are enough girls to act as nurses, a family will feel obliged to train its boys to take care of their younger siblings. Among the Tairans of Okinawa, a child nurse may be a boy or a girl. Boys, however, try to strike deals with their sisters to get out of tending their younger siblings, so caretakers are more likely to be female. Boys begin to act as child nurses at a later age than do girls, and they are more likely to ignore or abandon the baby. Sometimes, a boy will simply refuse to take care of a younger brother or sister, and mothers tend not to press the issue. By contrast, a girl who objected to baby tending would earn the disapproval both of her mother and of the other girls.

Typically, a youngster begins to act as child nurse between the ages of six and ten. This happens to coincide with the age at which people in many cultures believe that children become reasonable. Mothers, therefore, typically wait until they believe that a youngster is capable of tending a small child before giving them this kind of responsibility. Psychologists have also claimed that children are better able to take on the point of view of other people at around seven years of age, an important skill for someone who is supervising a little child. Mothers across cultures seem to notice that younger children are less sensitive to the needs of other people, and only ask them to superintend their younger siblings after they begin to develop such sensitivity. For instance, in Okinawa, Tairan adults do not think of a four- or five-year-old as responsible enough to take care of a younger child. Sometimes, a youngster of this age may end up watching a baby, but if something goes wrong, the mother is blamed and not the child nurse. Children under the age of six are said to have no sense and cannot, therefore, be held accountable for their behavior in the view of adults. A five-year-old who is carrying a baby will be praised lavishly by onlookers for displaying nurturance to another child. By contrast, Tairan children from six to twelve years of age do act as child nurses for long periods of time while the adults are away at work, and a six-year-old may watch a younger sibling all afternoon. Similarly, in Kenya, Gusii mothers typically recruit older children to supervise the infants when they are working in the fields. A child nurse may be anywhere from six to ten years old and is usually the sister of the baby, although brothers, cousins, or young aunts will do. Nurses may continue to care for their charges for two years or longer. A Gusii child nurse teaches her young charge to adopt the right position for hoisting onto the back. The nurse utters the baby word *"titi"* and the infant hugs her back and spreads his legs as she kneels down with her back to him. In Uganda, a Sebei mother will carry her infant on her back when she goes off to the fields to work. But a toddler is left home under the supervision of an older child of perhaps five or six years of age. The child nurse will be an older sibling if one is available. Otherwise, a woman will recruit a niece or nephew. Sometimes, the child caretaker will be adopted by her relative's household, remaining there until she is old enough to be circumcised. She calls the baby's parents "mother" and "father" and is prohibited from marrying any of the family's sons; her real parents are presented with

In Ecuador, a Quechua girl carries her little brother on her back.

a goat to compensate them for the loss of a daughter.

While most women prefer to recruit a child who is six years old or older as child nurse, mothers in some cultures are forced to ask young children to tend babies and toddlers. This sometimes happens with Gusii mothers, who may recruit a girl who is as young as three or four to be a baby tender. The little nurse begins to supervise her infant sibling when it is two months of age and she continues to act as child nurse to the baby until it can walk steadily. The nurse feeds, bathes, and watches the baby, all without supervision by the mother.

Child nurses perform an important function. They allow the mother the freedom to attend to chores that require her to be away from home or that are more or less incompatible with baby tending. Therefore, a woman who has handed a youngster over to the care of a sibling or cousin is not herself in a position to supervise the child nurse. And in fact, women allow older child nurses a considerable degree of autonomy. A younger nurse may depend more upon the oversight of the mother, however. And even in the case of older child nurses, the mother is often likely to be available for emergencies. Thus, for instance, among the Tarong, a preschooler is recruited to supervise and play with the next youngest sibling once a new baby is born into the family. Youngsters who are acting as supervisors are expected to tell an adult if some major or minor emergency arises, although some children take considerable initiative as caretakers. Similarly, a Tairan mother will closely supervise a younger child who is toting an infant on her back. She does not oversee an older child who is taking care of a younger one. Nevertheless, while Tairan child nurses tend to their younger siblings for hours on end without adult supervision, a child knows where the mother or grandmother can be found in case some problem arises. Among the Gusii, where a child nurse may supervise an infant or toddler for hours, the

mother is likely to be close by, as the fields in which she works are near to home.

How do children react to being recruited as nurses? Sebei children would prefer not to act as nurses. But a youngster will not refuse to watch an infant for fear of being beaten. In Micronesia, Truk children are expected to take care of younger siblings for short periods, but mothers do not recruit them for long stretches of time because youngsters clearly dislike the chore and women worry that the child nurses will become careless with their charges after a while. Some South Indian Gopalpur girls like tending to infants, but others resent their charges, viewing them as millstones around the neck. Similarly, among the Tarong, different children respond differently to the challenge of watching their younger siblings. Some youngsters are extremely patient and supportive nurses, while for others the chore is a considerable inconvenience. In Guatemala, Chimalteco girls look forward to taking care of their younger siblings. A daughter is often happy when her mother becomes pregnant because this means that the girl will be put in charge of the next-youngest child in the family. Tarong child nurses generally do not mind watching their younger brothers and sisters and often succeed at amusing their little charges with games invented for the purpose. Older children also seem to enjoy their roles as disciplinarians of a little child who has misbehaved.

Child nurses are typically nurturant toward their charges, but they are not always as skilled as the mother in dealing with a young child. A Tairan child nurse is apt to be less indulgent than the mother or grandmother and to enforce safety rules more rigorously, especially because the nurse will be blamed if something happens to her charge. Child nurses also tend to be less tolerant of disobedience than do mothers. Gopalpur nurses are not always the best of caretakers, and a jealous older sibling or cousin may refuse to give a thirsty toddler a drink or food when the mother is away. Similarly, Gusii child nurses often take some of the food left for their charges, and one child nurse was observed eating her baby brother's food while he sat by crying. Further, while a Gusii baby is treated affectionately by its child nurse, young caretakers are not always gentle with infants and sometimes a baby will be frightened by the rough handling of its child nurse. What is more, when the older child is busy playing with peers, she is likely to ignore the infant whom she is tending. More generally, younger child nurses can be inconsistent with their charges, hugging and petting them one minute and pinching or striking them out of frustration the next minute.

The habit of performing chores seems to affect a child's overall style of interacting with other people. Thus, child nurses tend to be more responsible, more nurturant, and more concerned with the welfare of their families. They are also less likely to demand help and attention from others.

See also CHORES; RESPONSIBILITY TRAINING

Beals, Alan R. (1962) *Gopalpur: A South Indian Village.*

Gladwin, Thomas, and Seymour Sarason. (1953) *Truk: Man in Paradise.*

Goldschmidt, Walter. (1976) *The Culture and Behavior of the Sebei.*

LeVine, Robert A., and Barbara B. LeVine. (1966) *Nyansongo: A Gusii Community in Kenya.*

Maretzki, Thomas W., and Hatsumi Maretzki. (1966) *Taira: An Okinawan Village.*

Nydegger, William F., and Corinne Nydegger. (1966) *Tarong: An Ilocos Barrio in the Philippines.*

Piker, Steven. (1965) *An Examination of Character and Socialization in a Thai Peasant Community.*

Romney, A. Kimball, and Romaine Romney. (1966) *The Mixtecans of Juxtlahuaca, Mexico.*

Wagley, Charles. (1949) "The Social and Religious Life of a Guatemalan Village." *American Anthropologist* 51: 3–150.

Whiting, Beatrice B. (1972) "Work and the Family: Cross-Cultural Perspectives." Paper prepared for Women: Resources for a Changing World: An International Conference. Radcliffe Institute, Radcliffe College, April.

Whiting, Beatrice B., and Carolyn Pope Edwards. (1988) *Children of Different Worlds: The Formation of Social Behavior.*

CHILDHOOD TRAITS, VALUED

In cultures around the world, adults view specific traits as the most desirable to inculcate in their children. In some degree, these traits overlap from one place to the next, reflecting perhaps the shared values of human beings as a species. Thus, parents in many cultures value honesty, generosity, and kindness in children and teach their youngsters not to lie or steal. To some degree, however, the traits a particular culture values in its children tend to reflect the characteristics that are most suitable to people living under the constraints imposed by that culture's particular physical and social settings.

A North American Chippewa parent who wished to determine a child's potential for success as an adult would send the youngster to bed without dinner. The next morning the child would be given a choice of food or charcoal. A youngster who chose the charcoal and refrained from nibbling on it would in all likelihood become something. The child who chose the food would be average. It was also assumed that children who did not sit still for the evening lectures given by adults would come to no good.

Kindness was also valued in Chippewa children, who were taught to lead a blind man, feed a hungry man, and help an old man. Sharing, too, was strongly inculcated, and a mother would have a child bring food to a neighbor so that the youngster would learn to give. Families that had an abundant supply of meat because of a good hunt would share it with other camp members so that children also saw the people around them exhibiting kindness. Chippewa parents also taught their children to value the property of other people, and if a youngster brought home some object belonging to another person, it was promptly returned. An older child who had stolen something would also be whipped. Lying in a child was taken as a sign that the youngster would not amount to anything in later life, and children who lied were disliked. So were children who boasted about things that were untrue.

Among the North American Arapaho, a child who was mean and bullied other youngsters was "crazy," and no one wanted to play with him. "Crazy" children also made other children cry and did not listen to their parents. Boys were also instructed by their fathers to be very patient, to show endurance, and to respect old people. Generosity was an especially valued trait. A father would tell his children to watch for strangers arriving at the village and to be the first to give them food. A visitor should be given a new pair of moccasins, and if there were none, then children should give away the shoes right off their own feet. A hungry dog should be fed, even with the food from the child's own mouth. Old people should be treated with special consideration, as should orphans, and God granted good luck to the person who was kind to orphaned children. A child who did not feel pity for others had "no heart." An Arapaho father told his children: "If someone wants to hit you, let him hit you." The other person would be hurt more by hitting than would the child by being hit.

Arapaho parents did not approve of boasting in children, and children who bragged were forced to prove that their claims were justified. Children were exhorted to learn to do things before they boasted of them. A little boy who bragged about catching a rabbit when in fact he had not might be taken on a hunting trip by his father to show him how hard it was to trap an animal. Arapaho youngsters tended to avoid other children who boasted. Arapaho parents also taught their children not to steal from other members of the tribe, and people known to have stolen were held up as examples of how not to behave. A younger child was forced to give back the stolen article, while an older child was punished. But stealing from a member of an enemy tribe was thought to be honorable, and adolescent boys might participate in a raiding expedition to steal horses from a hostile group.

Among the Truk of Micronesia, stealing is tolerated in young children because adults assume that they do not understand what they are doing. But an older child is expected to respect the property of others, and stealing is punished more and more severely the older the child. Truk adults do not pay much attention to lying on the part of children, in part because it is so hard to determine whether or not the youngster is telling the truth. As a result, both children and adolescents frequently tell big and little lies, usually to avoid getting into trouble for something that they have done.

Among the North American Sanpoil, the good child is the child who does not lie or steal and who is kind and refuses to speak ill of others. The good child does not waste food and always keeps clean, never allowing a day to pass without bathing in the river. Good children listen to the advice and remain true to the traditions of their tribe.

For the Gusii of Kenya, the ideal child shows unquestioning obedience to his or her parents. Obedient children are also responsible children who can do all their chores more or less on their own. Parents do not value enterprise or smartness in a youngster, and indeed, intelligence in a child is demonstrated less by brightness than by respect toward parents and other adults.

The ideal Jamaican child is undemanding, docile, and invisible, and the mother's favorite child tends to be the most subservient and submissive. By contrast, children who show independence or initiative are accused of "rudeness," a label attached to any of a child's behaviors not directly ordered by the mother. Children should also never lie or steal, and a youngster who does so is severely punished.

For a Liberian Kpelle parent, the most valued trait in a child is "full respect," and the least desirable thing that can happen is to have a child who has *lii kete,* or disrespect. A child who lacks respect will ultimately fail to show proper deference for Kpelle tradition. To have respect and to conform are the core traits of a good Kpelle child, but many youngsters seem to have *lii kete.*

The Guadalcanal Kaoka view generosity and respect for property as virtues, and children as young as two years of age are pressured to exhibit these traits even before they can actually understand what is being asked of them. In Guatemala, Chimalteco parents begin to teach their children not to lie or steal even before the youngsters have begun to talk. Otherwise, the parents warn, they will be put in jail and God will punish them.

The traits that adults value in children tend to be those that conform to the demands of the culture in which the youngster must function. In some cases, valued childhood traits coincide with demands that will be made on the youngster during the childhood years. Thus, the Gusii mother who insists upon responsibility and obedience in a child is preparing the youngster to take on the serious economic and household chores that Gusii children are asked to perform. Sometimes, adults value characteristics in children that will prepare them for success in adulthood. Thus, for instance, the traditional American emphasis on achievement and competition anticipates the dynamics of American

society, where the individual's status depends in no small part upon the person's own efforts.

The fact that parents value particular traits in children does not mean that a child will conform to the profile of the ideal child in fact. Thus, for example, Kikuyu mothers focus on generosity, obedience, and respect for elders as the most desirable traits in their children. These are the characteristics that are most compatible with Kikuyu living arrangements, which require a number of families to live together in a single household. In fact, however, Kikuyu children do not appear to be any more obedient or deferential to their elders than do American children. Similarly, American mothers value independence in their children. The American mother, who often is forced to tend to her chores and also supervise her children on her own, is likely to be grateful for a child who can manage on his or her own for a period of time. But again, American children do not seem to be any more independent than children in other cultures. Rather, they tend to seek more attention and make more demands upon their mothers than do youngsters in societies where children do not remain at home with the mother but, rather, spend their time in children's groups.

Cohen, Yehudi A. (1966) *A Study of Interpersonal Relations in a Jamaican Community.*

Erchak, Gerald M. (1977) *Full Respect: Kpelle Children in Adaptation.*

Gladwin, Thomas, and Seymour Sarason. (1953) *Truk: Man in Paradise.*

Hilger, M. Inez. (1951) *Chippewa Child Life and Its Cultural Background.*

———. (1952) *Arapaho Child Life and Its Cultural Background.*

Hogbin, Ian. (1964) *A Guadalcanal Society: The Kaoka Speakers.*

LeVine, Robert A., and Barbara B. LeVine. (1966) *Nyansongo: A Gusii Community in Kenya.*

Ray, Verne. (1933) *The Sanpoil and the Nespelem: Salishan Peoples of Northeastern Washington.*

Wagley, Charles.(1949) "The Social and Religious Life of a Guatemalan Village." *American Anthropologist* 51: 3–150.

Whiting, Beatrice B. (1978) "The Dependency Hang-Up and Experiments in Alternative Life Styles." In *Major Social Issues: A Multidisciplinary View,* edited by S. Cutler and M. Winger, 217–226.

CHILDLESSNESS

In every human culture, the expectation is that a married couple will have children, and a husband and wife without children may find themselves severely handicapped as well as heartbroken. This is because children play many valuable roles in the lives of adults. In many societies, children make critical contributions to the subsistence economy of the family. Often, people depend upon their children to take care of them in old age. Family lines are perpetuated through a person's children, and the survival of the family lineage is enormously important in many cultures. Children may also insure that a person will be remembered after death.

Children are sufficiently important in most cultures that childlessness is often sufficient grounds for divorce. Sometimes, an infertile husband or wife will permit the spouse to produce a baby with some other person. In Kenya, it is assumed that a Gusii wife will divorce a husband who is sterile or impotent because women are required to be faithful to their husbands but are also considered justified in wanting children. An older husband who can longer father children may, therefore, secretly agree to his wife's having sexual relations with another man, although this is considered to be shameful and may be resisted by the woman's grown children. Similarly, in Okinawa, if a Tairan wife fails to produce children within a year or two of her marriage, her husband or his family may force an annulment of the marriage. Or if the husband prefers to remain married to the woman, he may import another wife who can have children into his household. In Guatemala, if a Chimalteco couple fails to have children, the man assumes that his wife is to blame and he may abandon or divorce her or else bring another woman into the household.

Infertility is explained in a variety of ways across cultures. People may look for physiological causes of infertility. Among the Tarong of the Philippines, infertility is sometimes attributed to the woman, especially by men, but women often say that it is the man who is to blame, perhaps because he has only one testicle. Infertility is often attributed to supernatural influences. The Gusii believe that childlessness is a supernatural punishment. It can be caused by the curse of a father on a disobedient son, by the ancestor spirits who wish to punish a man for some transgression, or by lineage elders for ethical breaches. Even when a Gusii couple has had children, any failure to conceive promptly is a cause for worry, and the husband will visit a diviner and make costly sacrifices in order to try to reverse the curse. If nothing works, he will begin to suspect witchcraft. In polygynous Gusii families, if one wife has a miscarriage or stillbirth or fails to conceive, she is likely to accuse a cowife of witchcraft. Sometimes, infertility is attributed to a person's prior sexual behavior. In Micronesia, a Truk woman who does not conceive is suspected of having led a promiscuous sex life. This assumption may be related to the fact that barrenness is often a result of venereal disease, which becomes more likely with an increased number of sexual partners. Among the

Chimalteco, barrenness in a woman is attributed to adultery.

Men and women in many cultures also attempt to find ways of reversing infertility. The North American Arapaho sought out certain specialists in order to promote both fertility and sterility in women and fertility in men. In one treatment, a medicine man made a vapor of herbs and spread it over much of the body of the client, who then inhaled a bit of the vapor and allowed some of the herb to be placed on the tongue. The treatment was supposed to produce fertility in both men and women. The specialist was paid with the gift of a horse as well as food. In order to determine which spouse was the cause of a couple's childlessness, the specialist would cohabit with the wife of the stricken couple. If she became pregnant, then the husband was assumed to be the cause of the problem. A Tarong woman who is having trouble conceiving may drink a concoction made of boiled roots, bark, and leaves. The treatment is supposed to wash out internal impurities, as a woman must be clean in order to bear a child. In Liberia, Kpelle wives frequently pray for a child to the spirit living in the town cottonwood tree. Sometimes, a woman will visit a new baby and touch it in the hope of becoming pregnant herself as a result. The North American Chippewa used medicinal plants to treat sterility and claimed that they were effective. In some tribes, a concoction was given exclusively to women, while in others, both partners took the treatment. Among the North American Sanpoil, shamans were sometimes sought out by childless women during one of the winter dances. The shaman was able to tell the woman why she had not had any children and whether she would do so in the future. A number of remedies are available to an Indonesian Javanese couple who have no children. The wife can drink a decoction of herbs in water over which a spell has been said. Or she can have her abdomen massaged so as to "put the organs in proper position." Sometimes, a childless woman will have a long talk with a "therapist" to make her calm and happy in her heart. Then she will be able to have a baby. In Mexico, Mixtecan women employ a number of compounds that are believed to cause pregnancy. For instance, a woman who wishes to have a baby might drink a concoction of fresh pine resin boiled with roots from corn plants.

In India, a Rajput who dies without having had children becomes a ghost in an effort to remain with the living until the crucial life cycle experience of becoming a parent has been realized. A woman who cannot have children can steal the hair of a baby and present it to a sorcerer. The sorcerer will bury the hair, causing the baby to die and the barren woman to become pregnant. Or a woman may make offerings at a shrine in an effort to have a baby. Sometimes, a woman who has a child will pray at some shrine on behalf of a childless friend.

An infertile couple may also try to adopt a child. The rate of childlessness is high among the Takashima of Japan, with about 18 percent of couples in one community remaining without children. Childless couples often adopt a child so that the lineage will be perpetuated and the ancestors cared for properly. A desperate husband or wife may take extreme measures in order to procure a child. The Kpelle say that a woman old enough to have a child should be either nursing or pregnant, and a husband and wife who are having trouble producing a baby will try anything to have a child. One childless Kpelle woman would attempt to steal a child for herself when she went to market every week.

Attitudes toward childless couples vary across societies. In North America, a childless Arapaho husband and wife thought that they must have done something wrong in God's eyes. Otherwise, they would not have been deprived of a family. Other people would say that the couple was stingy and probably no good. The Javanese say: "When you are old, your children will care for you." This is not just a matter of providing for a parent's material wants. Children also provide the kind of care that money cannot buy. Thus, a woman who has a large family is regarded with envy, while one who cannot have children is to be pitied. In Uganda, a Sebei wife is anxious to have children because a childless woman is scorned by her neighbors and treated badly by her spouse, and many women say that one of the best things that can happen to a wife is to have a child. And many Sebei also say that childlessness is the very worst thing that can befall a person. The Chippewa took pride in being able to produce children, and a sterile individual was not highly esteemed. On occasion, a childless wife might be suspected of having had sexual intercourse before puberty. If she subsequently became pregnant by a new husband, everyone then knew that her former spouse had been sterile. Other people feel sorry for a Mixtecan couple who do not have many children, and the birth of a healthy child is marked by a joyful fiesta. The Tarong also view a childless couple with great sympathy, and a husband and wife with no baby of their own may be given a young relative to raise.

See also ADOPTION; CHILDREN, DESIRE FOR

Erchak, Gerald M. (1977) *Full Respect: Kpelle Children in Adaptation.*

Geertz, Hildred. (1961) *The Javanese Family: A Study of Kinship and Socialization.*

Gladwin, Thomas, and Seymour Sarason. (1953) *Truk: Man in Paradise.*

Goldschmidt, Walter. (1976) *The Culture and Behavior of the Sebei.*

Hilger, M. Inez. (1951) *Chippewa Child Life and Its Cultural Background.*

———. (1952) *Arapaho Child Life and Its Cultural Background.*

Hitchcock, John T., and Leigh Minturn. (1966) *The Rajputs of Khalapur, India.*

LeVine, Robert A., and Barbara B. LeVine. (1966) *Nyansongo: A Gusii Community in Kenya.*

Maretzki, Thomas W., and Hatsumi Maretzki. (1966) *Taira: An Okinawan Village.*

Norbeck, Edward. (1954) *Takashima: A Japanese Fishing Community.*

Nydegger, William F., and Corinne Nydegger. (1966) *Tarong: An Ilocos Barrio in the Philippines.*

Ray, Verne. (1933) *The Sanpoil and the Nespelem: Salishan Peoples of Northeastern Washington.*

Romney, A. Kimball, and Romaine Romney. (1966) *The Mixtecans of Juxtlahuaca, Mexico.*

Wagley, Charles. (1949) "The Social and Religious Life of a Guatemalan Village." *American Anthropologist* 51: 3–150.

CHILDREN, DESIRE FOR

Most men and women the world over want to have children. And from the standpoint of evolution, this is to be expected. Thus, individuals who were not motivated to reproduce would not be passing on the very traits that made reproduction a low priority for them. By contrast, those individuals who were motivated in the past to have children would be passing on those traits that made reproduction a high priority to future generations. But what makes men and women interested in having children? In part, human beings typically look forward to the emotional satisfaction that results from having a family. But people across cultures are also anxious to have children because of the many practical benefits that are conferred upon parents by a child. In recognition of this, childlessness is often grounds for divorce across cultures, and the production of children is often considered a prerequisite for a happy marriage. Thus, for example, among the Gusii of Kenya, children are necessary for a successful marriage, and a married couple generally wants as many children as possible. Some of the older Gusii bachelors are men who were unable to produce children as young husbands. Children are so important to the Mexican Mixtecans that a man and woman are not really thought of as married until they have produced a baby. A childless marriage is thought of as unnatural, and people disapprove of any woman who attempts to limit the size of her family. It is expected that a married Mixtecan couple will have children, and this is indeed the desirable outcome of marriage.

People wish to have children for a variety of pragmatic reasons. In a number of cultures, parenthood affects, and indeed improves, a person's status. A Mixtecan man wants to have children in part because fatherhood raises him from the status of youth to that of adulthood. Along with the change in status comes greater independence from his own parents. Similarly, a Japanese woman only achieves security in her husband's household if she has a child, as a childless woman can be thrown out of the house. A woman also wants a son so that she can eventually become a mother-in-law and dominate her daughter-in-law in the same way that her husband's mother has dominated her.

Often, children also improve the economic condition of a family. Children are valuable to Mixtecan adults in part because they are able to make important economic contributions to the household. Many economic projects in Mixtecan society are communal, and families with many children are better able to do the quota of work that is expected of them. Parents with fewer children, by contrast, may be forced to recruit relatives to help them fulfill their communal responsibilities. Or they may be compelled to hire unrelated people to take up the slack. Youngsters are also recruited to help their parents with the daily domestic chores. Once he is 12 years old, a boy helps his father with the herding. And older girls take care of infant siblings or cousins and supervise older children while the mother is busy with other household work. Similarly, in Mexico, a Tarahumara woman who has no children adds the herding of the sheep and goats to her other responsibilities. A mother who has a child old enough to act as a shepherd may send him off to the pasture with the animals for as long as a week at a time.

In many cultures, children are also an asset to parents in their old age. Mixtecan children are expected to support their aging parents. In Micronesia, Truk mothers and fathers both say they want to have children to help them with routine chores while the parents are still capable of working and then to take care of them in their old age.

Children are often also necessary to the maintenance of the family line. In Okinawa, children are essential to a Tairan marriage so that the father's lineage can be perpetuated, and a marriage may be annulled by a husband or his parents if a woman does not become pregnant soon after she becomes a wife. Or the husband may bring a second wife into the household. Because the production of children is so important, the Tairans favor trial marriages so that a man can be certain that his future wife is fertile.

Children may also be the guardians of a dead parent's memory. The Sebei of Uganda say that a man who has no children is not remembered once he dies. His name is thrown away and his spirit turns into an *oynatet*, causing harm to those who are still living. By contrast, a man who has many children will not be forgotten and may even become the founder of a new lineage. A Japanese man wants a son to do homage to him each day after his death, as well as to perpetuate the family line. The fate of an individual after death may also be in the hands of the person's children. The Tarahumara say that a man with no children will have a difficult time getting to heaven.

In spite of the fact that children are wanted and needed by most men and women across cultures, people may anticipate parenthood with some ambivalence. In Thailand, many Banoi women are apprehensive about childbirth itself, in part because they are afraid of a painful labor and even of dying and in part because they worry about the well-being of the baby. Some men and women are uneasy about having a family because children are a lot of trouble. Women know that motherhood means the loss of freedom and mobility as well as an increased workload. For a man, fatherhood means increased financial obligations. Many women also worry about the economic costs of having a family, and a small number of women say they do not want to have children. Both men and women are concerned that they will not be able to provide their children with the kind of superior education that would best equip them for success in later life. Parents also complain that they have so many children that they cannot provide each one with sufficient land, and virtually all say that they have more children than they want. A majority of women, however, say that they would be unhappy or ashamed if they could not have any children. For some women, childlessness implies a lonely old age. In Ecuador, a Jivaro man likes to have one of his wives accompany him when he goes hunting. A wife can manage the dogs and carry tools and provisions. As it is difficult for a woman with children to go hunting with her husband, pregnancies are not consistently welcomed by married couples, and husbands avoid frequent sexual intercourse with their wives as a means of birth control. Attitudes about having children may also be influenced by Westernization. Thus, for instance, Westernized Sebei women exhibit an interest in birth control, and men recognize that large families are expensive, especially when the children's school fees must be paid.

In a number of cultures, women feel pressured into having more children than they want.

While a Tairan woman is generally pleased when she finds that she is pregnant, women also appreciate the fact that it is hard to provide for a large family. Older family members pressure women of childbearing age to continue to have children until three sons have been produced, and some women resent these attempts on the part of their relatives. Nevertheless, even if she is no longer interested in having more children, a woman will continue to produce babies if this is the wish of her husband. Mixtecan women wish to have a number of children of both sexes, although wives tend to want a somewhat smaller family than do their husbands. Thus, women generally hope for four children, while men are happier with six. In the Northwest Amazon, Cubeo men claim that women do not want to have children because a new baby means observing a sex taboo during the lengthy period of nursing. A husband may leave a wife who fails to become pregnant because of the suspicion common to Cubeo men that a woman who has no children is secretly having abortions. What children are born, as a result, are wanted by their parents. Sometimes, prospective parents may feel positive about the theoretical benefits of having children without considering the practical drawbacks of starting a family. For Sebei adults, parenthood is important for a number of reasons, but men and women are more enthusiastic about the idea of having children than they are about having them in fact.

See also CHILDLESSNESS; CHILDREN, NUMBER OF

Benedict, Ruth. (1946) *The Chrysanthemum and the Sword.*

Bennett, Wendell, and Robert Zingg. (1935) *The Tarahumara: An Indian Tribe of Northern Mexico.*

Erchak, Gerald M. (1977) *Full Respect: Kpelle Children in Adaptation.*

Gladwin, Thomas, and Seymour Sarason. (1953) *Truk: Man in Paradise.*

Goldman, Irving. (1963) *The Cubeo: Indians of the Northwest Amazon.*

Goldschmidt, Walter. (1976) *The Culture and Behavior of the Sebei.*

Hitchcock, John T., and Leigh Minturn. (1966) *The Rajputs of Khalapur, India.*

LeVine, Robert A., and Barbara B. LeVine. (1966) *Nyansongo: A Gusii Community in Kenya.*

Maretzki, Thomas W., and Hatsumi Maretzki. (1966) *Taira: An Okinawan Village.*

Nydegger, William F., and Corinne Nydegger. (1966) *Tarong: An Ilocos Barrio in the Philippines.*

Piker, Steven. (1965) *An Examination of Character and Socialization in a Thai Peasant Community.*

Romney, A. Kimball, and Romaine Romney. (1966) *The Mixtecans of Juxtlahuaca, Mexico.*

CHILDREN, NUMBER OF

The average number of children in a completed family differs considerably from one society to the next. In one study of 51 cultures around the world, completed families had an average of 5.8 children. Women typically have more pregnancies than children across cultures, but infants and children frequently fail to survive. Thus, for example, in Mexico, Mixtecan families generally consist of no more than four to six children as a result of the high level of infant mortality. Similarly, in India, a Rajput woman typically bears from seven to nine babies. But as many as a third of these infants die, so that a family consists of an average of four or five living children. The Tarahumara of Mexico say that each person is given twelve children by God, and no more. In fact, however, a typical Tarahumara family has only two or three children because a large proportion of children do not live to maturity. In Uganda, Sebei women have an average of 7.24 births, and 4.6 living children.

The number of children in a family is also limited by the death of the mother at delivery. North American Comanche women normally bore only two children, and a mother rarely had more than three or four babies, in part because women frequently died in childbirth and in part because pregnancies were widely spaced. Spacing of babies, which is accomplished by a variety of methods, is also responsible for birthrates. These include abortion and infanticide as well as sex taboos that prohibit sexual intercourse for some period of time after a woman has had a baby. Lactation also has the effect of inhibiting ovulation, so that nursing becomes a kind of built-in contraceptive for nursing mothers. In Bolivia, Toba parents typically have three or four children spaced at two- or three-year intervals. Both abortion and infanticide contribute to the number and spacing of babies in this culture.

In some cultures, parents have fewer children than they would wish. The Chimalteco of Guatemala say that the ideal family consists of four boys and four girls, but most couples have fewer children. In other societies, parents would prefer to have relatively fewer children. Jamaican families are large, and parents bitterly complain about having so many children. The size of most families in Jamaica is inflated by the illegitimate children that are then raised by the mother's family. In Thailand, Banoi parents typically have from six to eight children, although almost all adults say that they would prefer a smaller family, perhaps just one boy and one girl. Parents with a small number of children may earn the envy of other people. In North America, some Arapaho couples had as many as ten children, but the typical family consisted of four or five. A couple who had only one child was admired for showing restraint, and men were eager to marry the daughter of such a family.

The number of siblings in a family influences the mother's treatment of her children in a number of ways. Mothers with many children typically show less warmth toward their youngsters. Other evidence suggests that it is, in fact, the number of children in the household and not only the personality of the mother that produces this effect. Thus, only children are treated warmly in comparison with children who have siblings, and oldest children receive comparatively little warmth. The youngest child in the family also enjoys a relatively high display of warmth from the mother. Thus, the same woman shows more or less warmth across time, and also directs relatively more or less warmth to the same child, depending upon the number of children with whom she has to deal. The number of siblings in a household also affects the mother's response to aggression. Thus, women with a large number of children are less tolerant of fighting among the children.

While families across cultures have an average of around six children, there is also considerable variation in family size from one culture to the next. For instance, in Kenya, the Luo have an average of 10.6 children in a completed family. By contrast, the average family among the Pomo of California consists of 1.8 children. Of 51 cultures, 11 percent have two or fewer children in a completed family. An additional 16 percent have an average of three children, while another 12 percent have four children. A completed family consists of five children in another 29 percent of the 51 societies and of six children in 10 percent. Seven children is average in 4 percent of the 51 cultures and eight is average in an additional 10 percent. Finally, 8 percent of these societies have an average of nine or more children in a completed family.

See also ABORTION; CHILD MORTALITY; INFANTICIDE; PARENTS' PREFERENCE FOR BOY OR GIRL

Bennett, Wendell, and Robert Zingg. (1935) *The Tarahumara: An Indian Tribe of Northern Mexico.*

Cohen, Yehudi A. (1966) *A Study of Interpersonal Relations in a Jamaican Community.*

Goldschmidt, Walter. (1976) *The Culture and Behavior of the Sebei.*

Hilger, M. Inez. (1952) *Arapaho Child Life and Its Cultural Background.*

Hitchcock, John T., and Leigh Minturn. (1966) *The Rajputs of Khalapur, India.*

Karsten, Rafael. (1923) *The Toba Indians of the Bolivian Gran Chaco.*

Palfrey House. (n.d.) "Cross-Cultural Ratings." Unpublished codes, Harvard University, Cambridge.

Piker, Steven. (1965) *An Examination of Character and Socialization in a Thai Peasant Community.*

Romney, A. Kimball, and Romaine Romney. (1966) *The Mixtecans of Juxtlahuaca, Mexico.*

Wagley, Charles. (1949) "The Social and Religious Life of a Guatemalan Village." *American Anthropologist* 51: 3–150.

Wallace, Ernest, and E. Adamson Hoebel. (1952) *The Comanches: Lords of the South Plains.*

CHILDREN'S ACTIVITIES

There are dramatic differences across cultures in how children spend their time each day. In some societies, children are more or less allowed to do as they please. In other cultures, youngsters are incorporated into the family work force at an early age and spend much of their time each day doing serious chores. In some societies with formal education, the major job of the child is to go to school. Or school children may be expected to do their chores every day once classes are over. Children with time on their hands often hang out in peer groups. The play activities of smaller children in these groups tend to be disorganized. Older children, by contrast, are more likely to play orderly games. Everywhere in the world, children's play includes imitation of adult activities. Children who are not otherwise occupied may also tag along after the adults, watching them do their tasks and perhaps helping them out.

In India, Rajput children are not expected to perform many tasks, and young children have no serious chores to do. Smaller children spend their time playing on the empty men's platform, in the street, or in the fields outside the village. The play of young children is not well organized. They may chase and tease each other, climb, or play seesaw on a wagon wheel. Older children may play tag or shells, or they may play at imitating some adult activity. Children are left to their own devices unless they are being especially boisterous and, therefore, attract the attention of some adult. Among the Truk of Micronesia, children spend most of their time playing until they are nine or ten years old. Small children simply hang around all day, while somewhat older children begin to engage in more organized games. Older Truk children also spend a good deal of their time swimming and making small sailboats with coconut leaf sails, which they then sail until the boats overturn beyond the reefs. The younger children play on the beach. Children also run races, throw stones, catch birds, and watch fighting fish. Only as they approach puberty do boys and girls begin to learn the skills that will be required of them as adults. In North America, Arapaho children spent their days playing, swimming, riding their horses, and imitating adult activities. They also listened for many hours to stories that some adult would tell to entertain them or to tales of tribal history or

stories about some personal experience that adults would tell to one another. Until they are around five years old, Jamaican children have little to do. They do not typically play in an organized way. Children have no toys and play no games. The only peers with whom they congregate are brothers and sisters, and interaction between them consists mainly of petty aggression, which mothers are quick to stop. Thus, youngsters are generally seen hanging around in the back yard, wandering about on their own, munching on a yam or ear of corn, talking to themselves, or just standing and staring at their feet.

While children in some societies have time on their hands, in other cultures parents recruit their youngsters to do tasks, sometimes at an early age. For these children, much of the day may be monopolized by work. In Kenya, a nine- to ten-year-old Gusii boy has the responsibility of herding the cattle each day. Meanwhile, a girl as young as five years of age may have begun to supervise younger siblings while the mother is away at work. Three-year-olds are helping their mother in the garden, and six-year-olds are doing most of the hoeing in the fields on their own. Children also fetch wood and water, grind grain, harvest produce, and cook meals. Similarly, in Ecuador, a Jivaro girl watches her infant sibling while her mother is in the garden. She also sweeps the floor, throws out the garbage, and when she is six years old, helps with the planting, weeding, and harvesting.

Children with a heavy workload do also get a chance to play. But often they are required to keep an eye on the younger siblings whom they are expected to watch. In the Philippines, a Tarong play group, as a result, can include a swarm of school-age children, many of whom have toted along the brother or sister for whom they are responsible. In Mexico, Mixtecan girls take care of and bathe younger siblings, fetch water, help with food preparation, go to market, tend the fire, take care of small farm animals,

In many cultures work is a regular activity for children. Here Bedouin children assist in sorting recently harvested olives.

clean the house, serve meals, and wash dishes and other items. A girl is constantly being asked to do this or that chore by her parents, and particularly by her mother. Boys gather farm produce or fodder and take it home, care for large animals, do some light farm work, gather firewood, and run errands. Mixtecan boys begin to work in the fields along with their fathers when they are 12 years of age. A younger son may take lunch to his father and stay with him in the fields for the afternoon.

In societies where children attend school, being a student is often viewed as the youngster's primary chore, so that children are not required to do much else besides attending to their schoolwork. For Japanese Takashima children, each day consists of school and play and it is only after their education has been completed, at about the age of 15, that they begin to fish, farm, and help with the household chores. Rajput boys who go to school may not be expected to do chores because school is thought to be enough work. Similarly, among the Tairans of Okinawa, children between two and six years of age attend morning kindergarten. After school, the youngsters play with their friends for the rest of the day, returning home only for meals. Children are permitted to play almost anywhere around the village that they choose. Youngsters may take cover in the village office building during a rainstorm or when it is excessively hot out-of-doors. Or a play group may congregate in the prayer house. Any public gathering place is open to Tairan children because youngsters are regarded as members of the community. Children will accompany their parents to the fields during harvesting or planting time. The youngsters amuse themselves and keep an eye on infant siblings while the adults are busy working. By contrast, in Micronesia, Palauan girls are expected to do a number of chores even though they also go to school. Schoolgirls take care of younger siblings, clean the house, wash clothes, collect wood and dried coconut-leaf sheaths for the fire, sweep the yard and care for the flowering plants that grow there, and help their mothers plant the sweet potatoes.

When children are not incorporated into the work force, they may tag after the adults or mimic the activities of older people. In Micronesia, Palauan boys are not required to help with adult tasks. Nevertheless, a boy will gather up his spear or net and follow after his father when the older man goes off to fish. Boys also go out fishing, skin diving, and canoeing on their own. Tarong children play at building twig houses, cooking, stringing tobacco, and cutting cane, all of which are activities performed by adults. Indeed, children usually imitate the very activities that adults are performing at the same time. Youngsters will also make copies of the tools used by adults in their daily activities, using whatever happens to be available. Some innertubing from a tire and a jar cover may be turned into a stethoscope. Or strips of bamboo may be tied together to make a sled. The imitation of adult work is an important part of Rajput children's play. Boys pretend to farm and girls to cook. Little girls like to make pretend bread out of mud, and the script that they follow remains very loyal to the steps that women follow when they make bread. Boys plow and sow wheat, and sometimes their play is a very detailed imitation of farming activities, with elaborate facsimiles of fields, which the boys then irrigate. In Uganda, Sebei children play house and also pretend to bargain for cattle or wives. They use stones of various colors as stand-ins for the cows that they trade and they pretend to drink beer as they barter. Boys also frequently hunt birds, rodents, and so on with

primitive but effective bows and arrows. The children cook and eat the animals on their own.

See also CHORES; PLAY

Cohen, Yehudi A. (1966) *A Study of Interpersonal Relations in a Jamaican Community.*

Gladwin, Thomas, and Seymour Sarason. (1953) *Truk: Man in Paradise.*

Hilger, M. Inez. (1952) *Arapaho Child Life and Its Cultural Background.*

Hitchcock, John T., and Leigh Minturn. (1966) *The Rajputs of Khalapur, India.*

Maretzki, Thomas W., and Hatsumi Maretzki. (1966) *Taira: An Okinawan Village.*

CHORES

In many traditional cultures around the world, children make serious and important contributions to the welfare of their family. They help with household chores, work alongside their parents at subsistence tasks, and tend babies. Real work begins to be assigned to youngsters at an early age by Western standards. Thus, across cultures, children most commonly begin to be recruited to do serious chores at five to seven years of age. In Uganda, a Sebei girl of four or five years of age may be left home alone by her mother to fetch water and firewood, collect vegetables, sweep the house, and superintend the younger children. By the time she is seven or eight years old, the girl will be digging in the garden as well as starting up the fire and cooking meals. A Sebei boy's main chore is herding, and boys may be taught to herd when they are four or five years of age. On the day that one brother is helping his father to herd, another will be locating a grassy area to which to take the animals on the following day. A boy who allows one of his father's animals to be eaten by a hyena or to stray into a neighbor's field will be severely beaten and may be forced to go without supper. Boys are also recruited to help plow the fields, hunt, weed, harvest, and build houses and fences when they are not herding. A seven-year-old Canadian Hare child is already making a real contribution to the household. Sometimes, a boy may get to go with his uncle or father to check the rabbit snares or fishnets, and he may be asked to do some small chores along the way. Children of this age already know how to use axes, knives, and scissors, and girls can sew. At nine years of age, boys and girls can saw and chop wood. Ten-year-old girls can embroider, bake, prepare a meal, and start the fire, and boys often fish in the summer. Girls help their mothers with the housework, often washing dishes and doing laundry and sometimes fetching water in buckets. By the time they are twelve years old, Hare children are participating more substantially in the subsistence activities of the family. Boys are accompanying the men on fishing and snaring expeditions and girls are helping the women pick berries and cut up dried fish. A child of this age may be asked to make the fire in the morning, to chop ice for washing and for drinking water, and to feed the dogs. Some thirteen-year-old boys may go along with the men on moose-hunting or wood-gathering trips and they may set rabbit snares or fishhooks of their own close to home. Some girls may sew and embroider moccasins and mittens.

Chore Assignment by Age

Across cultures, parents often begin by assigning small children less demanding tasks. Gradually, the child is given more responsibility. In Mexico, younger Mixtecan children are not assigned many tasks. Parents think that youngsters should play when it suits them and help out when it suits them. A little girl helps her mother and older sister fetch water, collects the

dishes for washing, gathers wood and blows on the fire, and runs simple errands. Little boys begin to learn how to take care of animals, do errands for their mothers, and perhaps accompany their fathers to the fields. When Mixtecan children reach five or six years of age, their contributions to the maintenance of the household begin to be taken more seriously. Boys and girls are assigned many more tasks, and chores are now assigned according to the sex of the child. The work of a youngster of this age is now viewed by the parents as a genuine contribution to the welfare of the family. Girls now begin to take care of and bathe younger siblings, fetch water, help with food preparation, go to market, tend the fire, take care of small farm animals, clean the house, serve meals, and wash dishes and other items. A girl of this age is constantly being asked to do this or that chore by her parents, and particularly by her mother. Boys gather farm produce or fodder and take it home, care for large animals, do some light farm work, gather firewood, and run errands. Mixtecan boys begin to work in the fields along with their fathers when they are twelve years old. A younger son may take lunch to his father and stay with him in the fields for the afternoon. By the time they are five years old, Philippine Tarong boys and girls are performing a number of household chores under the supervision of an adult. Children of this age carry small bottles of water, stoke the stove fire, care for the family goat, pick vegetables, help feed the chickens, cut the rice, and take the baby around the yard. Preschoolers also begin to have responsibility for supervising and playing with younger siblings when a new baby is born into the family. A six-year-old, who is now attending school, begins to be given more responsibility for caring for the goats and chickens, preparing food, cleaning the house, carrying water, and the like. The school-aged child is also asked to do more baby tending. In Kenya, Gusii children are recruited into the family work force at an early age and are expected to do a

A South African girl carries wood on her head.

variety of chores. Some of these tasks represent real contributions to the economic or domestic well-being of the household and require considerable responsibility on the part of the child. Parents begin to train toddlers to be obedient and responsible by asking them to do small chores. A child may carry a dish of food from one house to the other. Or a parent who wishes to smoke a cigarette or pipe may send a youngster off for a coal that can be used as a lighter. Children run about inviting neighbors and collecting pots and kettles when their parents are planning to throw a beer party. By the time that they are nine or ten years old, boys are expected to herd the cattle. Girls are tending babies without constant supervision as young as five years of age. Children may already be helping their mothers in the gardens when they are three years old, and by six or seven years of age, boys and girls have taken over much of the hoeing of the fields. At planting or harvest time, the entire family lives in a temporary house on the farmland and everyone pitches in to get the work done as quickly as possible. Small children may sometimes stay with relatives during these outings. But any child who does come along must expect to walk for perhaps an hour and a half to get to the field, although an older sister or the father may carry a toddler on the last leg of the trip if the youngster is beginning to slow the family's progress. In Ecuador, a Jivaro girl's main responsibility consists of watching a younger sibling while her mother is out working in the garden. This remains true until she is six years old. The child nurse is directed to rock the baby in its hammock and to keep it from eating dirt and being bitten by ants. Young girls are also expected to sweep the floor and throw out any garbage that might accumulate around the house. Once she is six, the girl will also be expected to help weed, plant, and harvest in her mother's garden. When a woman is making pottery, her young daughter will also make miniature objects out of clay in imitation of her mother. In North America, young Comanche girls were expected to carry water for the family. A slightly older girl was recruited to gather wood, and a group of girls might form a wood-gathering party. Girls accompanied older women when they went to gather fruit, nuts, and roots. And when a girl was twelve years old, she began to cook, dress hides, cut out moccasins, and put up tipis.

Age-Delayed Chore Assignment

In some cultures, parents wait until their children are somewhat older before assigning them chores. The assignment of tasks comes relatively late for Tairan children in Okinawa. One mother, when asked about the kinds of chores she expected her five-year-old to do, remarked that his work was to "play down at the beach." Another mother offered her five-year-old daughter one yen for helping to clean up after meals, but did not think that the little girl would hold up her end of the bargain because she was "still too young." One eight-year-old girl sometimes mopped the floor, fetched water, tended the baby, and served the rice at dinner, but her mother did not expect her to do these tasks on a regular basis. Rather, the girl helped out when her mother was busy. Similarly, an eleven-year-old boy might feed the pigs or chickens, supervise younger siblings, fetch wood and water, and clean the house when his mother has a lot of other work to do. Until they are ten years old, Guatemalan Chimalteco boys spend their days as they wish, performing only light chores such as carrying small piles of wood. Only when he is ten does the youngster become the constant companion of his father, working at his side like an adult and learning the skills that he will need to know as an adult.

Minimal Chore Assignment

Children in some societies are required to do relatively little work. In Micronesia, Palauan men do not actively pressure their sons to do economic chores and, in fact, they prefer the

A Navajo girl assists her mother in tending crops.

companionship of other men to that of boys when they go out to fish. A boy will tag along after his father with fish spear or net in hand and pick up various skills by observation. Boys also go out fishing, skin diving, and canoeing on their own and learn by doing. Japanese Takashima children are only asked to do a few simple chores, and older children perform such tasks as putting away their own bedding. Takashima adolescents as old as fifteen years are considered lacking in sufficient strength and experience to do a normal day's adult work. In New Guinea, Manus children are not required to do chores. When she arrives at adolescence, a girl will begin to fish with her mother, but even at this age boys are still excused from working. Micronesian Truk children spend virtually all of their time playing until they are around nine or ten years old. It is only when they are approach-

ing puberty that they begin to be expected to learn the skills and participate in the tasks that will be required of them as adults. Even as adolescents, they are excused from taking on a full adult workload. Boys are viewed as more or less unfit for much work because "they just think about women." The dramatic difference in children's workloads across cultures is illustrated by the following statistics: In Kenya, Kikuyu children spend an average of 50 percent of a typical day doing chores; in Kenya, Gusii children spend 41 percent; Kalahari !Kung boys and girls in Southern Africa 3 percent; and children in an American neighborhood only 2 percent.

Sometimes, parents encourage their children to contribute to the family's welfare, but they do not force youngsters to work. In the Northwest United States, young Sanpoil children were expected to help out with the workload, but were not absolutely required to do so. Boys helped to carry things during trips and looked after the dogs as well as performing other small tasks when they went hunting with the men. Little girls helped their mothers dig roots and pick berries and might even do these chores on their own.

Parental Recognition of the Child's Contributions

Parents in different cultures treat the efforts of their working children in noticeably different ways. In some societies, a child's successes are acknowledged in a positive way. Children may be given new tools or materials consistent with their growing accomplishments. Or youngsters may receive animals or land of their own. By the time she was twelve years old, a North American Arapaho girl was devoting her time to learning the skills that would be required of her as an adult. Her mother or grandmother was her teacher. When the girl had mastered some new technique, the woman who was supervising her would acknowledge this by providing the girl with the raw materials needed to do the task. Thus, if a girl had learned to make moccasins, her mother might get her a hide. Or if she had learned to sew, she would receive some new material. The girl would then make something, and her mother would say: "Now go on and take this to your brother's baby." At ten years of age, Jamaican children receive their own machetes. Girls then begin to help their mothers in the garden while boys do the same with their fathers in the fields. Once the youngsters become proficient in agricultural skills, they are given small plots of land, where they grow cabbage, carrots, turnips, and lettuce. The children tend their plots after school or on days when there are no classes. Most children also receive goats and calves to raise. The crops that the children tend and animals that they care for are technically their own to do with what they wish. The family eats a good deal of the produce, but if any remains, the child is supposed to be able to sell it and then use the money with the permission of the parent. In fact, the parents often hold the money for a child, and usually, it eventually disappears. Parents claim that they spend it on the children, buying clothes, schoolbooks, and so on. A Guadalcanal Kaoka boy begins to accompany his father to the fields when he is ten or eleven years old. Initially, sons help to clear the land, build fences, and cut up the seed yams. A man will sometimes give his son a plot of his own and treat the yams that grow there as the property of the boy. Hunting was essential to the economy of the Chippewa, and for this reason, boys were taught to use a bow and arrows when they were still quite young. A feast was thrown in honor of a boy's first successful kill and also when he caught his first fish. A boy might be only six years of age when his first feast was held.

By contrast, the work of children in other cultures is more or less taken for granted. Rajput mothers do not typically praise their children for performing tasks, and women tend to underestimate the importance of their children's work and the efforts that go into doing their chores. Rajput parents show impatience at the inefficiency of children who have not yet learned how to perform some task well and the child is more likely to be chastised for doing a poor job than to be praised for trying. Thus, for example, a girl may be sent away from the spinning wheel because she has broken the thread. Or a boy who is trying to feed himself will be hit by his mother for dropping the food. A Sebei mother is anxious for her daughter to become a skilled housekeeper so that her future husband will not beat her. Women also want to avoid being blamed for any inadequacies on the part of their daughters. As a result, a Sebei woman is stern with a daughter who fails to do a task properly. The girl will be abused by her mother, who may also wish stomach pains and dysentery upon her daughter as punishment for her incompetence. Mixtecan children are not usually rewarded for doing the work that is assigned to them. A father whose daughter takes him a cup of water will not acknowledge the favor that she has done for him. Rather, a child's efforts are taken for granted.

Chore Assignment by Sex

In a number of societies, the chores that are suitable for assignment to children are predominantly women's tasks. Sometimes, mothers do not mind assigning such chores to boys. Tairan children are expected to mop the floors, sweep the yards, clean the lamps, fetch water, take care of the pigs and chickens, and tend younger siblings. All of these tasks are performed by women in Tairan society, but they are allocated to both boys and girls. Mixtecan parents do not worry about assigning different tasks to younger children on the basis of sex, although it is little girls who begin to be trained to be competent caretakers. If a Mixtecan family has no daughters, a boy will be recruited to do some of the chores that are normally assigned to girls, but girls are not asked to do what are normally boys' chores. By contrast, in some cultures, mothers avoid assigning women's work to their sons. Among the Sebei, boys and girls do different kinds of chores, and these are viewed as preparation for adult male and female roles. Girls supervise younger children and do farming and household chores while boys look after the livestock. This segregation of chores by sex is maintained even when herding is not important to the family's economic well-being. A Banoi girl is encouraged by her mother to do whatever household chores she is capable of doing. By contrast, pre-adolescent boys are rarely asked to help with housework, nor do they do any serious agricultural work until they are well into their teen years. Jamaican mothers begin to recruit girls to wash and sweep the floor, do the dishes, and cook meals. Many women say that they would like their sons to help with the housework but that the boys simply refuse. In fact, girls do not like to do these chores any more than their brothers, but they are flogged for resisting and, therefore, they are more cooperative.

In some cultures, we see not only a difference in the kinds of work assigned to boys and girls but also a difference in the amount of work required of each sex. When this happens, it is often boys who have the lighter workload. Cubeo boys join an all-male play group when they are six years of age and continue as group members past adolescence. The male group is virtually independent of adults. It is the group leaders who enforce rules and punish misbehavior. The boys are welcome to help out the adults when they are at work. But the Cubeo believe that the appropriate activity for boys is play, so that a boy who does not want to work is not criticized for his choice. Girls, by contrast, who are expected to act as child nurses, remain close to home and to their mothers, spending their time with the other young girls who are also tending babies. In Liberia, a Kpelle boy has no serious chores to do until he is eleven, except that he may be asked to keep the rice birds away from the newly

planted rice crops. While Comanche girls were gradually recruited to participate in more and more household tasks, boys were not expected to do menial chores. Rather, they were indulged by adults, who treated them considerately because of the possibility that any boy might die young in war.

Chores and School

In societies where children attend school, being a student is often viewed as the youngster's primary chore, so that children are not required to do much else besides attending to their schoolwork. For Japanese Takashima children, each day consists of school and play and it is only after their education has been completed, at about the age of fifteen, that they begin to fish, farm, and help with the household chores. Rajput boys who go to school may not be expected to do chores because school is thought to be enough work. By contrast, in Micronesia, Palauan girls are expected to do a number of chores even though they also go to school. Schoolgirls take care of younger siblings, clean the house, wash clothes, collect wood and dried coconut-leaf sheaths for the fire, sweep the yard and care for the flowering plants that grow there, and help their mothers plant the sweet potatoes. When it is time for Tairans to harvest the rice, the schoolchildren are on vacation and are therefore free to help cut the rice and transport it to the threshing machines. Silkworms, which are increasingly important as income producers for Tairan families, are fed mulberry leaves by young girls. And children older than twelve occasionally help cut firewood, which is then sold for cash.

Children's Responses to Chore Assignment

How do children respond to demands on the part of adults that they perform serious chores? Youngsters the world over spend a considerable proportion of their free time imitating the activities of adults, and the idea that they make important contributions to the welfare of their families appeals to them. School-age Tarong children are pleased to be given additional work, at least until the novelty wears off, because it means that their parents view them as more grown up. Often, Mixtecan children perform chores spontaneously, imitating their older siblings and cousins rather than being explicitly asked to do some task. It is up to the Mexican Tarahumara women and children to care for the goats and sheep that form part of their livestock herds. Shepherds are often required to remain in the pastures with the animals for a week at a time, following them across the hills. Children seem to enjoy their time alone with the herds, sitting and watching the animals while wrapped in a blanket or playing games while keeping one eye on the livestock. Children who live in societies where work is expected at an early age are unlikely to believe that their daily activities are anything out of the ordinary. In Thailand, Banoi girls wash clothes, clean the house, work in the garden, fetch water, help make hats, assist with the cooking, run errands, and tend the baby beginning at eight or ten years of age. A 12-year-old girl already takes it for granted that she will regularly perform these chores and does not object when asked to do so.

Chore Assignment in Cultural Context

The amount of work that children are required to do across cultures is associated with other features of the society in which the child lives. The timing and number of chores assigned to children are related to the subsistence economy of a culture. Where parents are required to perform a large number of tasks, or where their subsistence activities are time-consuming, they are likely to recruit children into the work force at an early age and to ask them to do serious work. Gusii mothers live in a society that depends upon both agriculture and herding. In societies of this sort, special demands are made on the time of adults pursuing subsistence activities. Further, a married woman lives in a separate house with her own children, minimizing the opportunities for getting help from other women. Gusii women, as a result, are very busy by cross-cultural standards, and they require boys and girls to do numerous serious chores at an especially early age. By contrast, among the Zuni of New Mexico, members of the extended family cooperate in household chores as well as subsistence activities, with the result that there is little for children to do. And in fact, girls do not do serious household work until their teen years and boys begin to herd at roughly the same age. Task assignment is also related to cultural complexity. Children who live in moderately complex cultures work the hardest. These are societies where the population has gained significant control over the environment but where technology has not yet lightened the workload. By contrast, in very simple cultures, where control over the environment is not advanced, and in very complex cultures, where technology minimizes the work that people must do, adults ask youngsters to perform a minimum number of chores. Thus, a child is most likely to be assigned many chores in agricultural communities with dense populations.

In cultures where children are required to do serious chores, mothers are more likely to demand obedience and to punish youngsters who do not perform their tasks responsibly. In part, this is because the family's welfare and often the family's capital are being entrusted to the care of children. If a young herder is careless in his management of the herd, the family's fields may be ruined by straying animals. Or the livestock may become sick or hurt. Similarly, negligent behavior on the part of a child nurse can have disastrous results. Thus, children who are asked to take on tasks of this sort cannot afford to behave recklessly. Jamaican children, and especially girls, know that they will be flogged for refusing to do their household chores. Children are never praised for doing a task well, and even when they have done a good job, the mother is critical of the outcome. Adults say that praise makes children bad.

Chore Assignment and Behavior

Patterns of task assignment are related to the behavior profiles of children across cultures. Thus, children who are assigned numerous tasks tend to give more help and support to others than do children who do few or no tasks. Indeed, where task assignment is low, youngsters are more likely to seek help and attention. These children are also more inclined to boss others around. Certainly, the connection between task allocation and helpfulness may arise from the fact that many of the chores that children do involve contributing to the welfare of other people. The daily habit of helping others in the course of doing chores may then generalize so that children who perform many tasks become inclined to offer aid and support to other people even when this is not explicitly a part of their assigned workload. Children who perform household chores regularly are also self-assured and task-oriented in a way that youngsters who do not contribute to the welfare of the family are not.

See also CHILD NURSES; CHILDREN'S ACTIVITIES; PLAY; RESPONSIBILITY; SELF-ESTEEM

———

Barnett, H. G. (1960) *Being a Palauan.*

Bennett, Wendell, and Robert Zingg. (1935) *The Tarahumara: An Indian Tribe of Northern Mexico.*

Cohen, Yehudi A. (1966) *A Study of Interpersonal Relations in a Jamaican Community.*

Erchak, Gerald M. (1977) *Full Respect: Kpelle Children in Adaptation.*

Gladwin, Thomas, and Seymour Sarason. (1953) *Truk: Man in Paradise.*

Goldman, Irving. (1963) *The Cubeo: Indians of the Northwest Amazon.*

Goldschmidt, Walter. (1976) *The Culture and Behavior of the Sebei.*

Hara, Hiroko Sue. (1967) *Hare Indians and Their World.*

Hilger, M. Inez. (1952) *Arapaho Child Life and Its Cultural Background.*

Hitchcock, John T., and Leigh Minturn. (1966) *The Rajputs of Khalapur, India.*

Hogbin, Ian. (1964) *A Guadalcanal Society: The Kaoka Speakers.*

LeVine, Robert A., and Barbara B. LeVine. (1966) *Nyansongo: a Gusii Community in Kenya.*

Maretzki, Thomas W., and Hatsumi Maretzki. (1966) *Taira: An Okinawan Village.*

Mead, Margaret. (1931) *Growing Up in New Guinea.*

Nerlove, Sara Beth, and Ann Stanton Snipper. (1981) "Cognitive Consequences of Cultural Opportunity." In *Handbook of Cross-Cultural Human Development,* edited by Ruth H. Munroe, Robert L. Munroe, and Beatrice B. Whiting, 423–474.

Norbeck, Edward. (1954) *Takashima: A Japanese Fishing Village.*

Nydegger, William F., and Corinne Nydegger. (1966) *Tarong: An Ilocos Barrio in the Philippines.*

Piker, Steven. (1965) *An Examination of Character and Socialization in a Thai Peasant Community.*

Ray, Verne. (1933) *The Sanpoil and the Nespelem: Salishan Peoples of Northeastern Washington.*

Romney, A. Kimball. and Romaine Romney. (1966) *The Mixtecans of Juxtlahuaca, Mexico.*

Segall, Marshall H., Pierre R. Dasen, John W. Berry, and Ype H. Poortinga. (1990) *Human Behavior in Global Perspective.*

Wagley, Charles. (1949) "The Social and Religious Life of a Guatemalan Village." *American Anthropologist* 51: 3–150.

Wallace, Ernest, and E. Adamson Hoebel. (1952) *The Comanches: Lords of the South Plains.*

Whiting, Beatrice B. (1972) "Work and the Family: Cross-Cultural Perspectives." Paper prepared for Women: Resources for a Changing World: An International Conference. Radcliffe Institute, Radcliffe College, April.

Whiting, Beatrice B., and John W. M. Whiting. (1975) *Children of Six Cultures: A Psycho-Cultural Analysis.*

Whiting, John W. M., Eleanor Chasdi, Helen Antonovsky, and Barbara Ayres. (1966) "The Learning of Values." In *The People of Rimrock: A Study of Values in Five Cultures,* edited by Evon Z. Vogt and Ethel M. Albert, 83–125.

CLEANLINESS

The cleanliness of children is an important concern of mothers around the world. Often, a woman will try to make sure that a child is washed each day, even when doing so represents a considerable inconvenience for the adult. Parents tend to care more about cleanliness in babies than in older children. For babies and youngsters in some cultures, baths are fun, while in other cultures, the bath is an aversive experience for the child.

In North America, the Arapaho believed that bathing prevented illness. Therefore, every person was expected to bathe every day. A child was splashed with cool water each day from birth until it could walk. A woman took her toddler to the river with her when she went for her own bath. If the water was frozen, she would break a hole in the ice and the two would then wash.

The colder the water, the harder a woman rubbed her baby with it. Adults claimed that this made babies healthy and strong. In Micronesia, a Truk baby is usually bathed twice a day, typically by the mother. The infant is washed in some receptacle, often a wash pan filled with warmed water, and mothers are anxious that the temperature of the water be just right. If a family is lucky enough to have a bit of soap, it may be squirreled away for the baby's exclusive use. Some mothers avoid washing an infant's hair; rather, the baby's head is dressed with sweet-smelling oil just like the hair of adults. The scalps of many babies are covered with scab-like dirt because of this treatment. Once a Truk child is mobile, it is washed by its mother in the nearby spring. In Mexico, Mixtecan parents also keep their infants clean. A newborn baby is bathed and rubbed with almond oil, and infants are washed with water warmed in the sun. North American Sanpoil children are forced to get up at dawn each morning, summer or winter, and bathe in the river, ducking into the water a number of times. In Uganda, Sebei babies are washed in a basin in the house on a daily basis. A child who is old enough will be taken to the river to be bathed. A Liberian Kpelle mother bathes her baby every day unless it is cold or rainy. The mother splashes and rubs the infant with water. The baby is then dried and coated with oil or white clay as protection against illness. In some cultures, cleanliness in infants is not emphasized. In Kenya, Gusii babies are washed about once a week in cold water. Between baths, a baby's clothing and the infant itself become quite dirty.

Although adults in many cultures are concerned about bathing infants regularly, they may be less concerned about the cleanliness of older children. Some pains are taken to see to it that an Okinawan Tairan baby is kept clean, and a newborn is bathed almost every day. But an infant who is a year old or more is washed only once or twice a week. The same pattern shows up with regard to diapering. A Tairan baby's

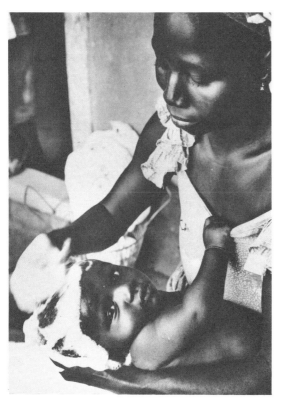

A woman washes her infant in Sierra Leone.

gartners about keeping clean and orderly. Nevertheless, a mother may scold a child for washing too often or for using too much soap, and youngsters between one and five years of age do not bathe regularly. Boys are more tolerant of being dirty than are girls, who are already concerned about how they look by three years of age.

If adults are more tolerant of dirtiness on the part of older children, a mother will often put her foot down when it comes to washing up before eating. Although Indian Rajput adults are fastidious about personal hygiene, children, who play in the dusty streets, are typically not very clean. But a mother will insist that the children wash their hands before meals. In Ecuador, Jivaro adults warn their children that if they do not wash their hands before eating, they will not grow properly. A girl is also told that if she makes beer without washing her hands, the quality of the beer will suffer.

In some cultures, babies enjoy their baths. In the Philippines, Tarong babies are bathed at least once a day. For the first few weeks, the infant is placed in a basin of warm water. Bath water is cooler after the first month or so of the Tarong infant's life, and babies at first object, although they soon become used to the change. Babies who can sit on their own are permitted to splash around in a tub of water under adult supervision, and infants enjoy these baths a good deal. A young Tairan baby is bathed in a small wash pan filled with water warmed on the kitchen hearth. Infants will bathe in the house on a cold day or outside if it is a warm day. A mother will talk to, tickle, and smile at her baby while she soaps him up and then rinses him off. Baths are less fun for the two- or three-year-old. Among the Cubeo of the Northwest Amazon, women look forward to bathing their infants. A group of mothers will often meet in the afternoon at the river to wash clothes, manioc roots and their babies together, and these group baths are fun for mothers and infants alike. An infant may also be washed at home in a ba-

diapers are changed frequently for the first two months, but after this, people are less fastidious about wet diapers, although a baby that has moved its bowels will still be quickly changed. Similarly, a Mixtecan baby is changed relatively frequently, but older babies of six to twelve months of age are changed less often.

Even when parents value cleanliness in their children, youngsters may not wash often enough to remain clean. Jamaican adults say that children should bathe each day, but in fact they do not, and children regularly walk around with coats of dirt that make the skin look dark and cause the youngsters to have a characteristic odor. Youngsters often have lice, and the children often spend time delousing each other. Tairans view cleanliness in children as extremely important. A mother will tell a dirty child to go sleep with the rats, and teachers lecture their kinder-

In Karachi, Pakistan, a woman bathes her son in the shallow lid of a cooking pot.

sin of water. In other cultures, infants dislike the experience of bathing. This may be because of the temperature of the water in which they are washed. Or it may be a result of how they are handled while being bathed. Rajput infants are given sponge baths. Mothers are rather harsh in their handling of their babies at bath time, and the infants struggle and cry while their faces and eyes are being scrubbed. In the winter, a Tairan child is sometimes dragged behind the house, screaming and kicking, to be bathed by the mother or an older sibling. A Jamaican infant gets a bath every day. The mother warms the water by letting it sit in the sun for a while "to get the chill out." Babies protest and whimper when they have to take their baths, but women say that children two or three years of age no longer object to being bathed.

In some cultures, older children are expected to wash themselves without any help from adults. In other societies, a relatively old child may still be bathed by a parent. Once Truk children can understand and use language, they are viewed as old enough to take care of themselves. This includes bathing. Sometimes, parents will take a child of this age along when they are going to bathe, but often a child who is dirty will merely be sent off by a parent or sibling to wash. The youngster will then look for some friend as company, and the two may disappear for hours, having found something interesting to do before or after their bath at the spring. By contrast, Rajput adults bathe children until they are five or six years of age.

Cohen, Yehudi A. (1966) *A Study of Interpersonal Relations in a Jamaican Community.*

Erchak, Gerald M. (1977) *Full Respect: Kpelle Children in Adaptation.*

Gladwin, Thomas, and Seymour Sarason. (1953) *Truk: Man in Paradise.*

Goldman, Irving. (1963) *The Cubeo: Indians of the Northwest Amazon.*

Goldschmidt, Walter. (1976) *The Culture and Behavior of the Sebei.*

Harner, Michael J. (1973) *The Jivaro: People of the Sacred Waterfalls.*

Hilger, M. Inez. (1952) *Arapaho Child Life and Its Cultural Background.*

Hitchcock, John T., and Leigh Minturn. (1966) *The Rajputs of Khalapur, India.*

LeVine, Robert A., and Barbara B. LeVine. (1966) *Nyansongo: A Gusii Community in Kenya.*

Maretzki, Thomas W., and Hatsumi Maretzki. (1966) *Taira: An Okinawan Village.*

Nydegger, William F., and Corinne Nydegger. (1966) *Tarong: An Ilocos Barrio in the Philippines.*

Ray, Verne. (1933) *The Sanpoil and the Nespelem: Salishan Peoples of Northeastern Washington.*

Romney, A. Kimball, and Romaine Romney. (1966) *The Mixtecans of Juxtlahuaca, Mexico.*

CLOTHING

Customs of dressing infants and children differ dramatically across cultures. Infants and babies may go naked, or they may be bundled up from head to toe. A youngster may have a small wardrobe of its own or may have to make do with a single garment. Children may be dressed so as to look like miniature versions of adults, or they may wear clothes tailored to their age. How children are clothed may depend in part upon beliefs about what is good and bad for a baby's health and what promotes growth. Customs regarding the dressing of children are also affected by climate and by attitudes toward sex and modesty. How a child is dressed may also be influenced by whether or not personal adornment is employed by a culture as a way of communicating something about a person's status.

Infants and children in some cultures wear very little clothing, even in the cold. In Kenya, Gusii infants are dressed in thin cotton cloth, which is also used to bind a baby to the back of its child nurse when it gets a bit older. Or the cloth may be used as a small blanket on which to place the infant when it is put on the ground, so that the baby ends up lying naked. This is done even on cold mornings. The mode of dress of infants is consistent with the Gusii belief that a baby's body is extremely warm and needs to become hardened by the cold. In the Philippines, a Tarong baby wears a loose shirt. Boys are covered to the navel and girls to the buttocks. Infants wear some kind of loose clothing or else nothing at all below the waist. In other cultures, children wear little or no clothes in warm weather but are provided with covering when it is cold. In North America, Chippewa infants were placed in cradleboards during the day, and their clothing at this age consisted of skins in which they were wrapped as they lay strapped in their boards. A crawling child wore nothing in the warm weather but was given a chemise made of soft deerhide when it was cold. Indian Rajput children wear only small shirts until they are toilet trained. In the winter, an untrained youngster may also wear long trousers, but the crotch will be cut out. Boys may also wear padded jackets or sleeveless sweaters and pants in the winter. A girl may wear a sari or trousers with a blouse or sleeveless sweater in cold weather, but mothers are less careful about providing their daughters with warm clothing when it is chilly. If it is especially cold, children and adults will also bundle up in quilts. Girls may also wear bangles and ankle bracelets.

In other cultures, children are more fully clothed regardless of weather. In the South Pacific, Tongan children wear some clothing beginning in infancy. A little boy wears pants and sometimes a shirt, while an older boy wears pants and a shirt or vest. Girls wear dresses. In Mexico, Tarahumara children begin to wear clothes as soon as they can walk, and children do not normally go around without clothing. A little girl wears a shirt and skirt and a boy wears a breechclout.

Children sometimes own only one garment, which they are forced to wear regardless of its condition. A Mixtecan child generally has just one serape, which is the youngster's only piece of clothing. If the garment becomes wet in the rain, it is turned inside out and put back on unless there happens to be a cooking fire over which the soaking cloak can be dried. Children who have been caught in a rainstorm must frequently sleep in their wet clothing. The serape may be a

youngster's only cover at night, even when it becomes very cold.

Dressing customs are influenced by a culture's attitudes toward sex in general and toward sex play by children in particular. In Micronesia, Truk adults pressure children into wearing clothes in order to diminish the likelihood of sex play. As the youngsters resist the pressure, parents and children become entangled in contests over dressing each day. Small children frequently wear hand-me-down undershirts that often reach down to the ground and are always dirty and ragged. Little girls also own dresses, made by their mothers and imitating the clothing of women, although shorter. Boys own short shirts that reach down to the navel and short pants with suspenders, although they often wear only the shirt or the trousers. The connection between styles of dressing and attitudes toward sex is reflected in customs for clothing maturing girls. After her first menstrual cycle, a North American Arapaho girl began to wear an apron and a blanket with the goal of covering the shape of her body. The blanket was pulled up over her head, partially covering her eyes. She wore longer dresses, and she was prohibited from showing her arms.

Cultures also frequently dress boys and girls differently. Until they were eight or nine years of age, North American Comanche boys wore no clothing, weather permitting. Girls, however, were always dressed, wearing a breechclout until adolescence and a buckskin dress thereafter. More generally, modesty is taken more seriously in the case of girls, and girls are dressed earlier and more completely than boys in many societies.

Sometimes, children's clothing is not very different from that of adults. In Guatemala, Chimalteco babies of both sexes wear a little shirt for the first six months of life. If it is warm, they go without clothing. Once an infant begins to crawl and sit by itself, a small blanket, made for the purpose, is wrapped about its waist. At one year, a girl begins to wear a little blouse and a boy to wear a small shirt like the men wear. Both still wear the blanket skirt, and some children continue to do so until they are almost five years old. By the time youngsters are five, they are dressed in small versions of adult clothing. In other societies, the clothing of children remains different from that of adults until the child approaches adolescence or adulthood. Until they are two years old, North African Teda girls wear no clothes. Their heads are also shaven, leaving a few tufts of hair. A two-year-old begins to wear a small apron adorned with cowrie shells about her waist. Her hair is now worn in many little braids. And when she is seven, a girl dresses in a cotton skirt. Her right nostril is pierced, and the hole is gradually stretched until it can accommodate a nose ring. After her first menstrual period, a girl changes her hairstyle, substituting the many small braids for three thick ones. She wears the clothing and adornment of adult women, including a cloth that covers her hair and with which she covers her mouth when being observed by a stranger.

Beaglehole, Ernest, and Pearl Beaglehole. (1941) *Pangai: Village in Tonga.*

Bennett, Wendell, and Robert Zingg. (1935) *The Tarahumara: An Indian Tribe of Northern Mexico.*

Gladwin, Thomas, and Seymour Sarason. (1953) *Truk: Man in Paradise.*

Hilger, M. Inez. (1951) *Chippewa Child Life and Its Cultural Background.*

———. (1952) *Arapaho Child Life and Its Cultural Background.*

Hitchcock, John T., and Leigh Minturn. (1966) *The Rajputs of Khalapur, India.*

Kronenberg, Andreas. (1981) *The Teda of Tibesti.*

LeVine, Robert A., and Barbara B. LeVine. (1966) *Nyansongo: A Gusii Community in Kenya.*

Nydegger, William F., and Corinne Nydegger. (1966) *Tarong: An Ilocos Barrio in the Philippines.*

Romney, A. Kimball, and Romaine Romney. (1966) *The Mixtecans of Juxtlahuaca, Mexico.*

Wagley, Charles. (1949) "The Social and Religious Life of a Guatemalan Village," *American Anthropologist* 51: 3–150.

Wallace, Ernest, and E. Adamson Hoebel. (1952) *The Comanches: Lords of the South Plains.*

COACTION

The total package of any individual's physical and behavioral characteristics is the individual's *phenotype.* Phenotypes develop as a result of the joint effect of the individual's genes and the environment in which the genes find themselves. This joint influence of genes and environment upon a phenotype is called *coaction.* The principle of coaction reminds us that any phenotype is the product of genes being expressed in an environment.

An individual is formed from a complement of genes donated from the father and mother. The complement of genes serves as a kind of blueprint or set of directions for building the individual. Genes alone, however, do not hold sufficient information for creating a person on their own. Rather, they need the cooperation of an environment. This is true from the very beginning, as the embryo and then the fetus develops from a single cell. And it continues to be true for the lifetime of the individual. For the embryo and fetus, the cooperating environment includes anything surrounding a cell, including other cells. It also includes the uterine milieu. After a baby has been born, the environment also includes the outside world.

The environment cooperates with the genes in the development of the individual by providing signals of various sorts that tell genes what to do. This means that the same set of genes can produce different phenotypes depending upon the environment in which the genes find expression. This is why pregnant women are warned that they should be quite careful about what they ingest. A woman who smokes, for instance, runs the risk of producing a small birth-weight baby who may then display particular physical and behavioral problems. The same woman will produce a different baby if she refrains from smoking. Each of these possible infants begins from the same set of genes. But a woman who smokes is providing a different uterine environment in comparison with what she would be providing if she did not smoke. The uterine environment is the milieu in which the genes find expression. Different uterine environments will provide different signals to the same set of genes, which will then build somewhat different phenotypes because the genetic instructions are being differently triggered.

We can see the joint operation of genes and environment in producing a phenotype from the earliest stages of the development of the individual. Thus for example, all individuals begin as a zygote, a single cell formed from the mother's egg and father's sperm. The zygote splits into two identical daughter cells which, in turn, continue to multiply, producing more daughter cells. The nucleus of each of these cells contains the full complement of genetic instructions. Further, the nuclei are virtually identical across cells. However, the material that surrounds the nucleus, or the cytoplasm, is not the same from one cell to the next. For the nucleus, the cytoplasm is its environment. And differences in the surrounding cytoplasm of these cells cause the genes in each cell to send out somewhat different instructions. Because each cell is now receiving different genetic instructions, each cell begins to follow a somewhat different developmental course. Furthermore, the genetic expression of each cell is also affected by the cells that are its

neighbors, partly by chemical signals sent off by neighboring cells. As each cell has a somewhat different complement of neighboring cells, the developmental trajectory of each cell is also somewhat different as a result of different neighboring cell effects. These effects of differences in cytoplasm and differences in kinds of neighboring cells cause each cell to become one of three basic tissue types: endoderm, mesoderm, or ectoderm. Similar kinds of within-cell and intercell effects then cause endodermal, mesodermal, and ectodermal cells to differentiate into more specialized kinds of body tissue; for instance, skin, heart, lungs, hair, nervous system, and so on. Eventually, an individual is produced from the continuing interaction of genes and the environments in which the genes find themselves.

We can still see genes and environments cooperating to produce phenotypes at later stages of development. For instance, a kitten's visual system is not fully mature at birth. In particular, certain connections from the eye to the cortex of the brain are not fine-tuned in newborn kittens. In order for the connections to be refined, the eyes need to be stimulated by light. This allows the genes responsible for the fine-tuning of the kitten's visual system to give the relevant cells the proper instructions for making the right connections from the kitten's eye to the kitten's brain. Thus, the cat's visual system continues to develop normally after birth because light in the outside world provides the needed environmental input for normal gene expression. We know the details of how the kitten's visual system develops because scientists can conduct research with cats that they cannot perform with human beings. However, the story of the development of the visual system in human beings follows the same general story line.

Genes and environments continue to cooperate to produce phenotypes throughout life. We see this in the behavior style that we call shyness. Very shy, or inhibited, children differ from very uninhibited children not only on a behavioral but also on a physiological level. For instance, the brain's limbic system, which is known to influence emotions, is more easily aroused in very shy children. However, shyness can be reduced if a shy child's environment is kept relatively free of stress. The absence of stress in the environment allows the genes underlying limbic system function to express themselves in such a way that there is less physiological arousal and a less intense response of shyness on the part of the child.

The idea that genes and environment may play a part in human physical and behavioral profiles is widely appreciated. However, the particular roles of genes and environments in producing phenotypes is not always well understood. Thus, for instance, we still hear about the so-called nature-nurture debate, which pits genes and environment against each other as the single cause of some physical or behavioral characteristic. For example, people argue about whether aggression or intelligence and so on are caused by a person's genes or are caused by the environment in which the individual was raised. In fact, however, no aspect of a phenotype is caused only by genes or only by environment. Every physical trait and every behavior is the result of genes being expressed in a environment. People also argue about the relative contribution of genes or the environment in producing a physical trait or behavior. Thus people may claim, for example, that while both genes and environment influence aggression, the environment is more important than are genes. The principle of coaction, however, denies that environments can be more important than genes in affecting aggression or any other aspect of an individual's phenotype. Conversely, genes can never be more important than the environment. Rather, both the complement of genes with which an individual is born and the environments in which those genes are expressed are equally important, and indeed, necessary in producing the individual's pheno-

type characteristic traits. To convince yourself that this is true, imagine what would happen if we took away an individual's genes. We would not end up with some proportion of residual phenotype for which the environment was still responsible. Similarly, if we took away the environment, we would not end up with some proportion of phenotype for which the genes were still responsible. Rather, we would end up with nothing.

Why is it attractive to believe that environments may be more important than genes in producing some traits and that genes are more important than environments in producing other traits? Perhaps this idea seems plausible because some traits have high potential variability while others are less variable. Thus, for example, we can imagine that one person might be very thin and another obese. But we have more trouble believing that a person might have 16 teeth or 32 teeth or 48 teeth. The impulse is to imagine that, where we can imagine high variability in a trait, for instance in weight, environment must have a large role to play in the ultimate outcome, while where there is little variability in a trait, for instance in number of adult teeth, genes must be playing the predominant role. The principle of coaction, however, tells us that genes and environments are equally important when it comes to growing teeth and gaining weight. When traits have low potential variability, this only means that gene expression operates within more narrow boundaries in different environments while the boundaries are wider in the case of traits with high potential variability.

The principle of coaction specifies the proper place of cultural influences in any analysis of the causes of behavior. Thus, the culture into which an individual is born provides the external environmental context in which genes are expressed. This is why a newborn baby growing up in one culture will display one physical and behavioral profile while the same baby growing up in another culture will display a somewhat different profile. It is also the case, however, that human cultures share many things in common, so that no matter where a baby is born, it will be exposed to many of the same kinds of environmental influences. And some cultural variations, while they may represent interesting differences to people interested in cross-cultural comparisons, will not make any important difference to development. It is as if the genes recognize some cultural differences as no more than variations on the same theme. Even where we do find cultural variations making a difference in physical and behavioral profiles, this is because each variation causes the individual's gene complement to be expressed in a somewhat different way. Thus, culture remains one component of the gene-environment equation.

See also CANALIZATION; RESILIENCY

Ackerman, Sandra. (1992) *Discovering the Brain.*

Harper, Lawrence. (1989) *The Nurture of Human Behavior.*

Kagan, Jerome. (1989) *Unstable Ideas: Temperament, Cognition, and Self.*

Shatz, Carla J. (1992) "The Developing Brain." *Scientific American* 267: 60–67.

Symons, Donald. (1992) "On the Use and Misuse of Darwinism in the Study of Human Behavior." In *The Adapted Mind: Evolutionary Psychology and the Generation of Culture,* edited by Jerome H. Barkow, Leda Cosmides, and John Tooby, 137–162.

COGNITIVE DEVELOPMENT

When people use the term *cognition,* they are referring to activities associated with thinking. A well-known definition of cognition focuses on the idea that cognition consists of transform-ing, reducing, and elaborating on sensory information from the environment in such a way that it can then be committed to memory and also used to produce useful behavior. Psychologists who are interested in cognitive development want to explore how thinking proceeds across the life cycle. They wish to determine whether individuals in the same developmental stage think in similar ways and whether cognitive processes change from one stage of development to the next. Underlying studies of cognitive development is the question of whether there is anything orderly and predictable about how people think. Studies indeed suggest that cognitive development is orderly at least in the sense that certain ways of thinking seem to appear earlier on in the life cycle than others. On the other hand, particular cognitive skills seem to appear at an earlier age in some cultures than in others.

Infancy

There are many descriptions of differences in cognitive performance in infants across cultures. Many of these reports suggest that African babies are more advanced than infants in a number of other societies. Thus, for example, Senegalese infants are reported to be advanced over non-African babies in language, social behavior, and adaptability. Ugandan babies are described as linguistically and socially precocious. Some reports suggest that infants of African descent raised in America still maintain an advantage over other babies born in America. There are also reports of differences in the timing of the acquisition of other cognitive skills across cultures. For instance, village Mayan youngsters acquire the idea that objects exist independent of the viewer (object permanence) some three months later than do urban American children.

If there are genuine differences in the cognitive performance of children from different cultures, to what can they be attributed? People have suggested that differences in child-rearing practices can account for these trends. Thus, for example, Jamaican babies are less sophisticated in their manipulation of drinking cups than are babies in some other cultures, but these infants have no experience with cups in their daily lives. Again, infants who are exposed to a number of caretakers are more advanced on a variety of measures of mental performance than are infants who are supervised exclusively by one caretaker. The superior performance of babies with many caretakers may be a result of the greater amount of stimulation that these youngsters are receiving. Similarly, children's performance on tests of visual skills is more advanced when the youngsters are carried around on the caretaker's shoulders and thus have unusually rich opportunities to view the world.

Arguments that emphasize the possible connections between child-rearing practices and performance on cognitive tests are trying to make a case for the influence of environmental factors on mental development. As every physical, cognitive, and behavioral trait of any individual is a joint product of genes and environment, the idea that patterns of child training affect mental performance is not contentious. We may also ask whether a society's preferred way of handling its children is in some degree influenced by dispositions of the infants themselves. For instance, in many traditional American Indian cultures, infants spent most of their time restrained in a cradleboard. And it is possible that experience as a cradleboard baby may have had physical and cognitive effects upon babies. However, we might also ask why American Indians used cradleboards whereas other American communities do not. Partly, the answer may lie in certain predispositions of American Indian versus other babies. Thus, it has been suggested that the initial physiological and temperamental profiles of American Indian infants allowed them to put up with the confinement that cradleboards require and even to welcome being packaged in this manner. By contrast, the higher activity level and restlessness of other American infants may

mean that they will not tolerate this kind of restraint. Thus, any characteristic of a child is at once the result of the youngster's makeup and the environment in which the child is operating. Similarly, any child training regime is at once a product of the requirements and beliefs of the culture and the traits that children present to those who must deal with them.

Infants across cultures also display similar trajectories in the acquisition of some cognitive skills. Thus, for instance, babies display a decline in interest in models of the human face from around four to ten months of age, after which their attention to faces increases during the second year of life. This is true of American children and also of Mayan, Ladino, and Kalahari !Kung infants. Similarly, babies from different cultures show a decrease in attention to increasingly familiar objects and a sudden increase in interest when a novel object is then presented.

Childhood

Many people who study cognition in childhood use tests of cognitive performance originally introduced by Jean Piaget, perhaps the most highly influential theorist to explore cognitive development. Piaget's tests were really small thought experiments administered by an experimenter to children of various ages. The experimenter would present the child with a problem and ask the youngster a series of questions. Piaget was interested in tapping the reasoning that lay behind the child's solution to the problems that he posed. He was looking for evidence of whether or not children of different ages could classify; organize items into an orderly series; take the perspective of another person; appreciate that objects retain their mass, volume, and so on in spite of apparent surface changes; apply rules of transitivity; and the like. Piaget claimed that children under seven years of age are not able to apply these concepts, while children roughly seven years of age are able to do so. Children who are incapable of understanding these concepts are identified as *preoperational,* while children who are capable of understanding these concepts are *concrete operational. Operations* in this context refer to the logical concepts that Piaget was testing, so that the thinking of the preoperational child proceeds in the absence of these operations, while the thinking of the concrete operational child depends upon these operations. Thus, Piaget believed in orderly cognitive development, with progressions toward more adequate thinking happening at predictable points in the life cycle. Studies of the performance of children living in Western and non-Western cultures suggest that cognitive development is indeed orderly in just the way that Piaget supposed. Thus, younger children across cultures are more rigid and less logical in their thinking, while the thinking of older children is more logical and flexible. But children in non-Western cultures take longer, and perhaps years longer, to understand and use concrete operations on Piaget's tasks. And in some studies, even adults in non-Western cultures fail tests understood to tap concrete operational thinking. Children in non-Western societies also perform less well on tests of memory. These findings have prompted people to wonder why non-Western children lag behind Western children in applying logical concepts to concrete tasks.

Even more puzzling is the claim that some adults may never become concrete operational. The idea that adults in some cultures never arrive at the concrete operational stage of cognitive development seems to many people to be improbable. This would mean, for example, that grown men and women might take tall, thin containers instead of short, fat ones when fetching water so that they would be able to bring home more water and, therefore, make fewer trips to the river. In fact, in all cultures where tests have been administered, adults remember, generalize, think abstractly, form concepts, and reason logically. Why, then, do non-

Western children, and even non-Western adults, fail on the kinds of tests that Piaget and others administer?

Cultural Effects on Cognitive Performance
Some researchers have noted that the easy verbal exchanges characteristic of cognitive testing are often alien to youngsters from non-Western cultures. Thus, for example, in Kenya, Kipsigis children are not accustomed to the kind of verbal give-and-take that characterizes conversation between adults and children in Western societies. Further, in Kipsigis culture, people are expected to remain silent in front of their elders or social superiors. These linguistic conventions may place them at a disadvantage in test-taking situations in which youngsters are required to take an active role in talking to adult interviewers. The Kpelle of Liberia believe that the knowledge that a person acquires should be kept secret from other people. When you learn some valuable bit of information, it gives you power over other people. Therefore, "you can't talk about it." A child raised in a culture with such views about the secrecy of knowledge may not be willing to provide information to strange adults on cognitive tests.

In many non-Western cultures, children are taught to show respect to their elders. They are not familiar with holding conversations with adults and would never think of questioning or contradicting an older person. Piagetian tests ask children to do just these things, and youngsters for whom this is unacceptable behavior may be at a disadvantage.

Indeed, studies suggest that children do better on cognitive tasks, including copying designs, solving puzzles, and building objects with Tinkertoys, where mothers use verbal as opposed to nonverbal styles of communication. Performance on mathematics and reading tests and on verbal memory tasks is also improved in youngsters whose mothers communicate to them verbally. It may be that a mother who talks to her

child focuses the youngster's attention on important features of objects and important relationships between features of objects, thus helping the child to make the kinds of discriminations that matter to successful cognitive performance. Indeed, children who have failed at some specific cognitive task can be helped to perform correctly if relevant aspects of the task are pointed out to them. Thus, for instance, a young child who does not appreciate that AA:BB is analogous to CC:DD but not to CC:DE, CC:DF, or CC:DG, will successfully solve equivalent analogy problems when it is pointed out that in some cases paired letters are the same while in other cases they are different.

It is also the case that Western children are used to taking tests. A child's cognitive performance also seems to be affected by the degree to which the youngster is familiar with the materials at hand. For instance, urban Mexican children who make clay pottery understand that clay is conserved even when its shape is changed before they apply the idea of conservation to weight, number, volume, and so on. It may be not only the youngster's familiarity with a particular material but also experience at manipulating the material that underwrites this kind of cognitive leap. Further, children are explicitly taught the kinds of concepts tested in Piagetian tasks in school. In many cultures, adults do not emphasize abstract skills and knowledge when teaching children. Kpelle youngsters are taught by demonstration, and what they learn is relevant to some particular concrete task. No attempts are made to generalize a lesson to other contexts. In fact, schooling is a good predictor of cognitive performance. Individuals who have been schooled perform equivalently regardless of the culture in which they live.

It is also important to remember the distinction between competence and performance. Thus, it is possible for a person to be capable of carrying out some task while not doing so in fact. As a result, if the individual is judged solely by performance, competence has the potential of being underestimated. Many people argue that non-Western children and adults are capable of applying the same logical rules in the same way as Western children and adults but that this competence does not show up on formal tests of the sort that researchers administer.

Folk Wisdom

Adults across cultures appreciate that children of different ages have predictably different cognitive capacities. Over and over, people notice that children seem to become reasonable at somewhere around the age of six or seven. The notion of reasonableness mirrors Piaget's discussion of operations. Thus, folk wisdom seems to be picking up on the same aspect of cognitive growth upon which psychological theory focuses. The Mixtecans of Mexico believe that a child slowly begins to develop awareness beginning at one year of age and is fully aware by two. A youngster starts to give evidence of reason at about six years of age, and by the time a child is eight, the ability to reason is fully developed. Both awareness and reason are assumed to emerge naturally. According to the Tarong of the Philippines, a child below the age of two or three is essentially a helpless creature without sense and without any real capacity to learn. Therefore, adults direct their efforts toward taking care of young children and protecting them from danger. A child begins to get sense starting at around the age of four and is sensible by around six years of age. This means that the youngster is now capable of learning and indeed likes to learn. The Tairans of Okinawa think of a newborn as helpless and pitiable. A child is not considered capable of knowing, learning, or understanding until the sixth birthday. Children under six have no sense. Seven-year-olds, by contrast, know what they are doing. The Jamaicans recognize that children "have sense" for different kinds of things at different ages. An eighteen-month-old has enough sense to follow an order. But even a three-year-old is not ready to urinate or defecate in the proper places on his own because "him have no sense for that." By five years of age, a child has sense enough to eliminate in an appropriate place, to control aggression, to follow correct eating etiquette, and so on. But only a seven-year-old has enough sense to be able to go to school. Children are only punished for misbehaving if adults feel that they have enough sense to know better. Therefore, a toddler will be flogged for failing to follow an order, but three-year-olds will not be punished for defecating wherever they please.

Beliefs about the cognitive abilities and limitations of a youngster affect the way in which the child is treated by other people. Among the Mixtecans, young children who hurt themselves because of their own actions are comforted by any older person who happens to be around because the Mixtecans do not think that small children are responsible for their own behavior. Adults believe that older children have now acquired the ability to reason and can, therefore, tell the difference between right and wrong. As a result, they are ridiculed for their misdeeds.

Similarly, Indian Rajput adults do not believe that it is possible to teach anything to a child who cannot yet speak. Therefore, no one tries to persuade children to behave properly until they acquire language. By contrast, youngsters who have begun to talk a little may be punished if they are told to do something but fail to do it. In Okinawa, Tairan adults say that children under six years of age "do not have sense." As a youngster without sense is not capable of learning, Tairans do not attempt to teach young children the moral virtues of their culture, nor do they seriously punish a child who steals from the gardens, throws temper tantrums, or hits another youngster because children of this age cannot be expected to know any better. Adults do work at training small children in good man-

ners. A mother will attempt to persuade her child to say "Please," "Thank you," "Good morning," "Good day," "Hello," and so on, and a baby who has not yet begun to speak may be encouraged to perform gestures that mean "Thank you," "Hello," and the like. A child who fusses or yells in response to this kind of instruction will provoke laughter on the part of onlookers, who may call the youngster a know-nothing. Seven-year-olds, by contrast, are viewed as having sense and, therefore, as knowing what they are doing. Adults now impress upon older children that their former behavior is no longer acceptable. In Thailand, Banoi parents use physical punishment to achieve compliance in older children. But they also say that there would be no point in hitting children under five or seven years of age because they would not be able to comprehend the reason for the punishment and, therefore, would not learn from the experience. The North American Chippewa assumed that young children are without reason, and therefore, if a small child stole something, the parent would simply return the object to its owner along with an explanation. Older children, who could now reason, were forced to take the stolen item back on their own. Until a Micronesian Truk baby begins to talk, it is referred to as one who "does not understand," and any behavior on the part of an infant of this age is tolerated by others. Once children have begun to understand and use language, they are considered responsible for the consequences of their behavior. They are also assumed to be able to take care of their own needs. Thus, youngsters who understand language are expected to go to bed without prodding when they are tired, to eat when they are hungry, and to go to the proper place to eliminate. Children who fail to see to their own needs will be reminded by adults to do so, but in a tone that implies that the youngster should not have needed prompting by an adult. As children grow older, it is assumed that they understand more and more, and so they are held more and more accountable for their behavior. This continues until the child reaches middle age.

See also COACTION; LEARNING; RESILIENCY; SCHOOLING

Cohen, Yehudi A. (1966) *A Study of Interpersonal Relations in a Jamaican Community.*

Erchak, Gerald M. (1977) *Full Respect: Kpelle Children in Adaptation.*

Gladwin, Thomas, and Seymour Sarason. (1953) *Truk: Man in Paradise.*

Hara, Hiroko Sue. (1967) *Hare Indians and Their World.*

Hilger, M. Inez. (1951) *Chippewa Child Life and Its Cultural Background.*

Hitchcock, John T., and Leigh Minturn. (1966) *The Rajputs of Khalapur, India.*

Kagan, Jerome, and Robert E. Klein. (1973) "Cross-Cultural Perspectives on Early Development." *American Psychologist* 28: 947–961.

Maretzki, Thomas W., and Hatsumi Maretzki. (1966) *Taira: An Okinawan Village.*

Munroe, Robert L., and Ruth H. Munroe. (1975) *Cross-Cultural Human Development.*

Nerlove, Sara Beth, and Ann Stanton Snipper. (1981) "Cognitive Consequences of Cultural Opportunity." In *Handbook of Cross-Cultural Human Development,* edited by Ruth H. Munroe, Robert L. Munroe, and Beatrice B. Whiting, 423–474.

Nydegger, William F., and Corinne Nydegger. (1966) *Tarong: An Ilocos Barrio in the Philippines.*

Piker, Steven. (1965) *An Examination of Character and Socialization in a Thai Peasant Community.*

Price-Williams, Douglas. (1981) "Concrete and Formal Operations." In *Handbook of Cross-Cultural Human Development,* edited by Ruth H. Munroe, Robert L. Munroe, and Beatrice B. Whiting, 403–422.

Romney, A. Kimball, and Romaine Romney. (1966) *The Mixtecans of Juxtlahuaca, Mexico.*

Super, Charles M. (1981) "Behavioral Development in Infancy." In *Handbook of Cross-Cultural Human Development,* edited by Ruth H. Munroe, Robert L. Munroe, and Beatrice B. Whiting, 181–270.

COMPETITION AND COOPERATION

Cultures differ noticeably in the extent to which they emphasize competition as a valuable trait to encourage in a child. Further, in a cross-cultural context, there is a kind of tension between competition and cooperation. That is, cultures that value cooperation between children do not tend to encourage competition. Conversely, some evidence indicates that children who are motivated by a competitive spirit have trouble cooperating even when cooperation is adaptive and competition is maladaptive. It looks as if cooperation and competition reflect two distinct attitudes about how individuals should pattern and evaluate their own performance in settings where other people are involved. Whether a society encourages cooperative or competitive behavior depends in part upon other features of the society.

Cooperation is highly valued in a number of societies around the world, and children in these cultures are pressured to be cooperative with other youngsters. In the Philippines, Tarong children rarely play alone. Rather, they are always incorporated into play groups made up of preschool and school-age children. The play groups engage in a variety of games such as hide-and-seek, drop the handkerchief, tag, stick tossing, and rock throwing. But no one is concerned with competing, and children will take turns "winning" with the result that the nature of the games is dramatically altered. Similarly, in Okinawa, many of the games that Tairan children play, such as racing or choosing partners, include the idea of competition, but children under the age of six do not play to win. The games of the Liberian Kpelle usually involve a number of children and emphasize cooperation. Thus, for example, in *duong,* or "water fence," a number of children hold hands to make a fence. The players sing a song and travel through town, attempting to capture other youngsters in their fence. Children's games share features with the dances of adults and also prepare youngsters for the cooperative enterprises characteristic of adult life.

Competition is valued in other cultures. North American Comanche boys played competitive games such as arrow shooting and wrestling, and those who were too old to play continued to watch the others while they played. Among the !Kung of the Kalahari Desert, camp membership is small and a child is not likely to have other youngsters of the same age with whom to play. Competition with a significantly older or younger child is not very challenging, and !Kung children do not tend to play competitive games with each other. But a youngster does compete against his or her own last best performance.

In some cultures, competition is sanctioned in children and adults, but only if the individual's activities enhance the performance of the group. Israeli children who live in kibbutzim will compete in games as members of opposing teams, but not as individuals. Similarly, a Kpelle man may strive to cut the bush faster or carry more mud than anyone else in his work group, and the man who beats his fellow worker is called a "hero." But clearly, this kind of competition ultimately benefits the work group as a whole as it gets a job done more efficiently. The same man, if he tries to outdo his peers in riding a bicycle or performing calculations, is viewed as behaving in a manner that is *kwii,* or non-Kpelle. In

North America, many of the Hopi games played by boys are competitive, but the competition is between teams instead of individuals, and give-and-take between teams is emphasized as is the difficulty of winning even in the face of talent and teamwork. Players also focus on the game itself, and not so much on winning, with the result that no one cares very much about the score when involved in a game.

There is also evidence of sex differences in cooperative and competitive behavior in children. While North American Hopi boys played games in which teams competed with one another, girls did not usually play games in which even teams competed. Rather, their play activities often mimicked the cooperative work of the women's household groups. Girls also liked pastimes such as the Pursuit Game in which a leader would chase the remaining girls along a twisted path. Any girl who stepped off the path was out of the game.

Some studies show that children who live in collectivist cultures tend to perform better in groups, while children who live in societies that emphasize individualism are more likely to do better when allowed to work on their own. Further, in cultures that emphasize competition, the older the child, the more marked the disposition to compete. For instance, when required to perform some task alone, Americans of all ages put forth more effort than they do when asked to do the same task in cooperation with other people. American ninth-graders working in pairs perform at 88 percent of the level that each child performs at the same chore alone. By contrast, Chinese ninth-graders work harder in groups, putting forth 106 percent the effort when paired up with other youngsters in comparison with what each produces alone. Cooperation is also characteristic of children raised in Israeli kibbutzim, communities operating according to an explicitly communal ethic. Thus, kibbutz youngsters are very successful at winning prizes when asked to play games that require cooperation among a group of children. By contrast, American children will opt to compete instead of cooperate when playing the same games, even when competition leads to a net loss for the youngster. The impulse to compete remains firm even when the American child knows that competition is counterproductive. Cooperation when playing games that require joint effort among a group of children is also more characteristic of youngsters raised in rural as opposed to urban settings. Thus, for example, children raised in rural Mexico or in the rural Kenyan Kipsigis culture are more willing to cooperate with each other than are children brought up in urban Mexico, urban Canada, or Los Angeles. Perhaps rural parents encourage cooperation in their children because cooperation is useful and even necessary in farming communities where people regularly help each other to plant and harvest crops, raise barns, and so on. In contrast, urban parents who encourage competition in their children may be preparing them to succeed in an environment where individual effort and achievement are important to personal success. For instance, in the Philippines, the Tarong depend heavily upon the cooperation of kin and neighbors for completing domestic and economic chores of all sorts. And it is one's neighbors and relatives who also make up a person's social world. Children, therefore, are taught the importance of neighborliness at an early age, and the practice of teasing anyone, child or adult, who is not neighborly has the effect of enforcing cooperation in youngsters as well as their elders.

See also ACHIEVEMENT

Erchak, Gerald M. (1977) *Full Respect: Kpelle Children in Adaptation.*

Gabrenya, W. K., B. Latane, and Y. E. Yang. (1983) "Social Loafing in Cross-Cultural Perspective: Chinese on Taiwan." *Journal of Cross-Cultural Psychology* 14: 368–384.

Gabrenya, W. K., Y. E. Wang, and B. Latane. (1985) "Social Loafing on an Optimizing Task: Cross-Cultural Differences among Chinese and Americans." *Journal of Cross-Cultural Psychology* 16: 223–242.

Henderson, Ronald W., and John R. Bergan. (1976) *The Cultural Context of Childhood.*

Madsen, Millard C. (1971) "Developmental and Cross-Cultural Differences in the Cooperative and Competitive Behavior of Young Children." *Journal of Cross-Cultural Psychology* 2: 365–371.

Maretzki, Thomas W., and Hatsumi Maretzki. (1966) *Taira: An Okinawan Village.*

Nydegger, William F., and Corinne Nydegger. (1966) *Tarong: An Ilocos Barrio in the Philippines.*

Segall, Marshall H., Pierre R. Dasen, John W. Berry, and Ype H. Poortinga. (1990) *Human Behavior in Global Perspective.*

Thompson, Laura, and Alice Joseph. (1947) *The Hopi Way.*

CONCEPTION, BELIEFS ABOUT

In virtually all known human cultures, people understand that conception results from sexual intercourse and that a child is the result of the joint contribution of the mother and father. The particular theories of conception articulated by societies without access to detailed information about conception and fetal development are often incorrect, however. Thus, for instance, the Cubeo of the Northwest Amazon assume that conception is caused by semen alone. The uterus grows a fetus in the same way that the earth grows vegetation when seeds are planted. According to the Truk of Micronesia, conception happens when a man's semen unites with the woman's blood. During the first three months of pregnancy, the woman's uterus is filled with nothing but blood and the pregnancy can easily be disrupted. Therefore, measures are taken to insure that the pregnant woman will take things easy and remain calm as well. Neither do people always understand when conception occurs. Among the Cubeo of the Northwest Amazon, men say that conception begins when a woman's belly begins to swell, while women believe that the cessation of the menstrual cycle marks the moment of conception. The Mexican Tarahumara think that conception occurs during or soon after menstruation. In some societies, it is assumed that each act of sexual intercourse can produce a baby even if a woman has already become pregnant. In North America, the Fox believed that a woman could conceive only if she had sexual intercourse exclusively with one man. If a woman slept with many men, a fetus would be created with each one. Soon, all of the fetuses would crush each other and be expelled from the body. The Cubeo believe that sexual intercourse during pregnancy will increase the number of children that a woman delivers, and a couple will avoid coitus once the woman begins to show.

Many societies also incorporate other ideas into their overall theories of conception that are at variance with the facts. According to rural Jamaicans, a woman becomes pregnant when sexual partners have simultaneous orgasms. The North American Chippewa believed that a child was produced by the cooperation of both parents. But specific categories of children, including twins and babies born with teeth, birthmarks, or a caul, were the result of reincarnation. Thus, it was assumed that a ghost of someone who had the characteristics of the baby had been near the mother and entered the baby's body at or around the moment of conception. The North American Arapaho believed that a woman would become pregnant if one of her relatives spoke of pregnancy or birth. People, therefore, avoided

talking about either. In Okinawa, Tairans say that it is the woman who determines the sex of a baby, and a man whose wife fails to produce sons can bring a co-wife into the household.

While most human societies understand the general role of sexual intercourse and pregnancies, the Trobriands of Melanesia did not appear to make a connection between conception and sexual intercourse. Rather, pregnancies were thought to come about because a spirit of one of the mother's dead relatives inserts a child into her uterus. As a result, the Trobriands did not recognize physiological fatherhood. Physical likenesses between fathers and children were attributed to the "molding" of the youngster that results from the close contact between the two parents.

Bennett, Wendell, and Robert Zingg. (1935) *The Tarahumara: An Indian Tribe of Northern Mexico.*

Cohen, Yehudi A. (1966) *A Study of Interpersonal Relations in a Jamaican Community.*

Gladwin, Thomas, and Seymour Sarason. (1953) *Truk: Man in Paradise.*

Goldman, Irving. (1963) *The Cubeo: Indians of the Northwest Amazon.*

Hilger, M. Inez. (1951) *Chippewa Child Life and Its Cultural Background.*

———. (1952) *Arapaho Child Life and Its Cultural Background.*

Jones, William. (1939) *Ethnography of the Fox Indians.*

Maretzki, Thomas W., and Hatsumi Maretzki. (1966) *Taira: An Okinawan Village.*

Munroe, Robert L., and Ruth H. Munroe. (1975) *Cross-Cultural Human Development.*

Romney, A. Kimball, and Romaine Romney. (1966) *The Mixtecans of Juxtlahuaca, Mexico.*

CONSISTENCY IN PARENTING

Parents differ from each other in their typical styles of interacting with their children. This is true both within and across cultures. Thus, a parent may be authoritarian, insisting that the child display unquestioning obedience. Or a parent may be firm but democratic, retaining the right to make the final decision about a child's behavior but also taking the youngster's opinions and preferences into account. Some parents adopt a laissez-faire policy of child rearing, allowing their children to do more or less what they wish. Overlaying this classification of parental styles is the attribute of consistency in parenting. While no parent can be utterly consistent in his or her management of a child, some parents are more consistent than others. Further, adults in some cultures are reported to be more inconsistent in their parenting styles than are adults in other societies. Psychologists observe that consistency in parenting is considerably more effective in producing desirable behavior in children. Inconsistency, by contrast, has a number of unintended consequences for the parent who is trying to socialize a child, all of which make it harder for the adult to obtain compliance from the youngster.

Inconsistency in parenting may be traced to a variety of causes. Some cultures, for instance, may value simultaneously personal traits that are incompatible with each other, causing parents to vacillate in the demands that they make for good behavior. Thus, for example, Indian Rajput mothers say that they value obedience in children, and the good child, in their view, is the child who obeys. Nevertheless, a mother whose youngster refuses to follow her orders is likely to get mad, calm down, and allow the child to get away without doing her bidding. This inconsistency on the mother's part follows in part from the value that is placed on dominance in Rajput culture. Dominance is equated with high status, and parents, therefore, admire willfullness in their children as an indicator that the child is a leader. As a result, parents, while they want their children to be obedient, also encourage insubordination, so that the behavior of adults tacitly teaches youngsters less about the importance of compliance than about how to deal with a temporarily angry mother when they disobey. Similarly, Rajput mothers disapprove of aggression in children, but will sometimes tolerate a temper tantrum and even hitting directed toward a mother, aunt, or grandmother on the part of a small child. Many mothers report capitulating to a child who becomes angry at them, with the result that the child is rewarded for expressing anger.

Sometimes, a parent will allow the vagaries of mood more than a consistent philosophy of child rearing to dictate how a child will be treated at any given point in time. In Thailand, Banoi parents are not very consistent in their responses to bad behavior. Thus, a parent may repeatedly ignore or only mildly rebuke some objectionable act on the part of a child but then, in a fit of pique, punish or strongly reprimand the child for the same behavior. Responses to misbehavior are influenced more by the parent's whim than the seriousness of the youngster's actions. Sometimes, parents relent after punishing a child, and this may be interpreted by the youngster as parental inconsistency. On Okinawa, a Tairan mother will scold a small child who has gotten dirty, but she is then likely to try to comfort a youngster who responds by crying, saying: "Here, here, don't cry. Mother was bad."

Frequently, a mother may prefer to exploit a style of parenting that collides with the style preferred by her husband. A Rajput man may reprimand and even beat his wife if he believes that her treatment of their daughter is too harsh. A woman, for her part, may try to shield a son from her husband if the boy has done something that is likely to be punished by his father.

Inconsistency in parenting style has a number of unintended effects upon children. First, a child whose parent is inconsistent in his or her expectations and responses from one disciplinary episode to the next may become confused about what the parent actually wants. Children of inconsistent parents may soon discover that there is no way of pleasing the parent. The same behavior may be tolerated or approved on one occasion but punished on the next. Or the parent may employ contradictory styles on different occasions in response to the same behavior. Banoi mothers often alternate between indulgent coaxing and threats or hitting in an attempt to obtain some desired behavior from a child. Incompatible behaviors may also be expected of the child at one and the same time. Thus, for example, if a Jamaican child is disobedient, the mother may administer a flogging, or she may just threaten one in the future. As mothers often make a number of conflicting demands simultaneously, children sometimes find themselves unable to avoid disobeying at least one of her orders. Children of inconsistent parents also learn that they need not pay attention to their parents' orders. Banoi parents uniformly insist that obedience is extremely important but do not in fact enforce demands for obedience in their children. Thus, Banoi children often refuse to obey their parents' commands and get away with it.

While inconsistency in parenting can be traced in part to cultural values and parental characteristics, the temperament of the child will also influence the degree to which parents are consistent or inconsistent in their management of their children. Thus, some children are temperamentally easy. Their patterns of eating and sleeping are regular, they adapt easily to changes in the environment, they have a relatively high tolerance for frustration, and they are easy to soothe when they do become upset. Parents of such children have an easier time being consistent because the children themselves are responsive to the overtures of their parents. A child whose eating and sleep schedules are irregular, who does not adapt easily to environmental change, who does not tolerate frustration, and who continues to cry and fuss while being soothed is a more difficult child to handle. Parents may first try one strategy to achieve some desired response from the child and when this does not work, they may try another. From the point of view of the observer, the parent is being inconsistent in his or her treatment of the child. Parents responding to difficult children, however, may see themselves as trying to adapt to the unresponsiveness of their children. Thus, parental consistency or inconsistency is the result of the joint influences of cultural and parental philosophies of child rearing, cultural and parental values regarding what is desirable and what is undesirable behavior on the part of a child, the parent's personal characteristics, and the personal characteristics of the child.

See also COACTION; PARENTING, STYLES OF

Berk, Laura E. (1989) *Child Development.*

Cohen, Yehudi A. (1966) *A Study of Interpersonal Relations in a Jamaican Community.*

Hitchcock, John T., and Leigh Minturn. (1966) *The Rajputs of Khalapur, India.*

Maretzki, Thomas W., and Hatsumi Maretzki. (1966) *Taira: An Okinawan Village.*

Piker, Steven. (1965) *An Examination of Character and Socialization in a Thai Peasant Community.*

CONTINUITY BETWEEN CHILDHOOD AND ADULTHOOD

Some cultures seem to emphasize the differences between children and adults while others tend to minimize them. This insight was articulated especially well by anthropologist Ruth Benedict, who observed that cultural expectations regarding the behavior of children can either be continuous or discontinuous with what will be expected of them as adults. These differences show up, for instance, in expectations about responsibility, respect, and sexuality. Thus, in some discontinuous cultures, children are not expected to be responsible members of the family and community, but are then required to behave responsibly as adults. Similarly, in some discontinuous cultures, children are required to be submissive to adults but are then expected to take on a dominant role when they are grown. Expectations regarding sexual behavior may also differ depending upon the status of the individual. By contrast, in cultures that emphasize continuity of behavior across the life cycle, responsibility may be required not only of adults but also of children, and sometimes at a quite young age. Similarly, in continuous cultures, children may not be expected to submit to adults any more than adults are expected to submit to children or each other, and sometimes sassiness in a child is positively approved. Or sometimes, children may be accorded more freedom to dominate adults than adults are accorded in dominating each other. Finally, in cultures that focus on continuity of behavior across the life cycle, expectations regarding sexual behavior may be consistent across different stages of the life cycle. Cultures also differ more generally in the degree to which they expose children to adult life. In some societies, children are more or less integrated into the daily activities of adults, while in others, children and adults lead largely separate existences. Children who understand the "ins and outs" of adult life may be more likely to experience life as continuous when they themselves become adults. By contrast, children who are shielded or excluded from participation in the adult world may be more liable to experience their lives as discontinuous as they approach adulthood.

In many societies around the world, children are recruited to do serious work at an early age. Thus for example, in Kenya, a Gusii girl begins to garden, fetch wood and water, cook meals, and tend young infants by five years of age, and boys are herding cattle on their own by nine or ten. This is in stark contrast to some industrialized societies, where the major chore for a child consists of attending school and where any chores assigned at home are viewed as building character for the future and not as important contributions to the present welfare of the family. The difference in responsibility expectations across cultures is symbolized by the fact that children in some societies are performing in earnest the same activities that children in other cultures regard as play. Thus, a child in an American home or nursery school may play at cooking and cleaning with toy pots, pans, and brooms at the same age that a child in another culture is preparing real meals and performing real household duties for the family.

Cultures also differ in the degree to which children and adults are expected to obey the same rules regarding respect, deference, dominance, and the like. In many American Indian cultures, children were not expected to be submissive to their elders any more than adults were required to be submissive to each other. A Crow father might actually show pride in a son who was disrespectful because the boy's intractability showed that "he will be a man." Adults did not understand why it would be desirable for a child to display behaviors that would be ridiculed if exhibited by an adult. By contrast, in other societies, children are expected to show unquestioning obedience to adults, while obedience in adults is not a valued trait. Among the Kpelle of Liberia, children must show "full respect" to adults, and disobedience in youngsters is among the most severely punished behaviors. Sometimes, discontinuities in behavioral expectations across the life cycle accord more freedom to the child than to the adult. Japanese adults are always meticulously unassuming in their references to themselves. A person talks of "my wretched

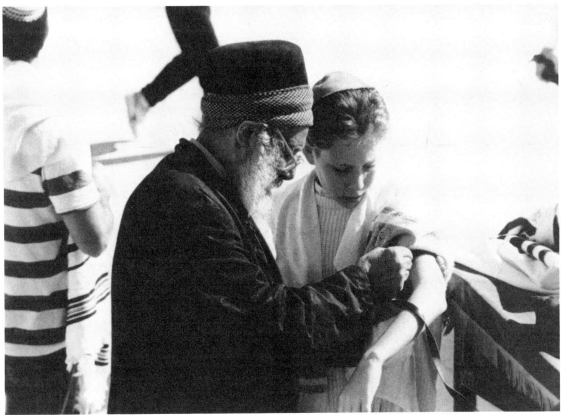

Jewish elder instructs boy in prayer ritual.

house" in comparison with "your august house," and "my miserable family" as opposed to "your honorable family." By contrast, children regularly boast about themselves and criticize each other, and it is not unusual to hear some child claiming that "my father is smarter than yours." Similarly, when children are playing together, each youngster will insist upon being the master instead of the servant. Adults agree that children are free to say what they want and know no shame but that as they grow older they will come to understand the importance of humility.

Societies also vary regarding the degree to which expectations about sexual behavior are continuous across different phases of the life cycle. The Keraki of New Guinea represent a striking example of discontinuity in a society's expectations about sexual behavior. Thus,

younger males are expected to be passive partners in homosexual relationships while somewhat older males are expected to be active homosexual partners. Mature men, by contrast, are required to make a transition to heterosexuality. By contrast, among the Lesu of New Ireland, expectations regarding the expression of sexuality remain consistent across the life cycle. Thus, Lesu children imitate the sexual behavior of adults in public, standing face to face with their genitals touching. Adults view such play as natural. Sometimes, youngsters will go off into the bush, which they know to be the preferred setting for sexual activity among their elders.

Societies also differ concerning the extent to which they incorporate children into the adult world. For instance, even as infants, Kpelle children are watching someone threshing rice, cooking, bathing, diapering a baby, weaving, scaling a fish, fixing a roof, and so on. Thus, youngsters are exposed from early on to the activities that they will be expected to perform as older children and adults. Among the Tarong of the Philippines, parents often bring young children to the fields or to parties or wakes, and youngsters are always included when something exciting is going on in the neighborhood. Relatives often take children along on trips to town, and schoolchildren help out at parties and remain as guests as long as they behave tolerably well. Children also fetch water and firewood, and can regularly be observed peeking at the activities in the kitchen, and running after each other through the yard. This is in contrast to children who live in industrialized societies, where a youngster may have no idea what adults do for a living, how they spend their leisure time, or what interests and concerns them. Children in industrialized societies are also largely ignorant of the intricacies of political life and social interactions and are often shielded from major life crises and transitions, including death and dying.

See also CHORES; DEVELOPMENTAL STAGES, TRANSITIONS ACROSS; RESPONSIBILITY

Benedict, Ruth. (1946) *The Chrysanthemum and the Sword.*

Benedict, Ruth. (1955) "Continuities and Discontinuities in Cultural Conditioning." In *Childhood in Contemporary Cultures,* edited by Margaret Mead and Martha Wolfenstein, 21–30.

Erchak, Gerald M. (1977) *Full Respect: Kpelle Children in Adaptation.*

LeVine, Robert A., and Barbara B. LeVine. (1966) *Nyansongo: A Gusii Community in Kenya.*

Nydegger, William F., and Corinne Nydegger. (1966) *Tarong: An Ilocos Barrio in the Philippines.*

Powdermaker, Hortense. (1933) *Life in Lesu: A Study of Melanesian Society in New Ireland.*

COUVADE

Couvade refers to a variety of birth customs concerning the behavior of expectant or new fathers. It is possible to distinguish between two broad kinds of couvade. First, the couvade sometimes takes the form of magical or religious practices meant to protect the man's wife and baby. Couvade customs of this sort either require men to participate in a set of activities or prohibit them from doing certain things. For example, the expectant or new father may be prohibited from hunting particular animals, eating specific foods, engaging in extramarital sex, and so on. Among the Cubeo of the Northwest Amazon, when a woman is about to go into labor, she warns her husband so that he will make sure to remain at home and to avoid engaging in any strenuous activities that might magically cause problems for the mother or baby. After the baby is born, the father and his kinsmen are required to perform numerous rites to make the infant and also the parents safe. They must blow tobacco smoke and chant over the river as well as each of the foods that are eaten by the Cubeo. For a month after the birth of the baby, the father must not tie or cut anything, or else the infant will not be able to urinate or defecate. If the father presses anything, such as sugar cane, during this period, the baby will be crushed to death. A man may not resume any of these tabooed activities until he has blown tobacco smoke and chanted over each one. The father is also prohibited from clubbing fish to death for a period of time. Otherwise, the baby's head will be injured. If a man scrapes scales from a fish, the infant navel stump will swell up. If a man drinks a certain liquid, his baby will suffer from diarrhea, and if he gets drunk, so will his infant. The Toba of Bolivia believe that if a man does strenuous work or eats certain foods after the birth of his child, the baby will be adversely affected. For instance, if he were to eat a cow's head, his son would die. Therefore, men do not exert themselves or indulge in taboo foods, especially fish, for some time after the infant is born. These practices are rooted in the idea that there is a mysterious connection between a baby and its parents for the first few days after birth. Therefore, anything that the mother or father do can have an effect on the infant. After five days have passed, or else when the navel has healed entirely, the connection between parents and baby begins to weaken and the infant begins to become an autonomous being.

By contrast, in the second form of the couvade, labeled the classical form, the expectant or new father takes to his bed and often complains of pain, exhaustion, and other similar symptoms normally identified with a woman's birth experience. The classical couvade is reported in the Philippines. Here, Tarong men experience cravings when their wives are pregnant, although they are not as strong or enduring as the cravings of the pregnant woman herself. Husbands are also lethargic and complain of feeling ill. The classical form of the couvade is quite rare. By contrast, the magico-religious form of the couvade accounts for the overwhelming majority of cultures in which the couvade occurs at all.

One explanation for the couvade suggests that it represents an expectant or new father's unconscious desire to experience vicariously pregnancy and birth. This explanation of the couvade, however, takes as its model the classical form of the couvade, which is in fact very uncommon. It is easy to see how someone might interpret pregnancy and postpartum symptoms on the part of a man as a kind of imitation of female reproductive functions. But the far more prevalent magico-religious form of the couvade

is harder to interpret in this way. Indeed, there is nothing inherently feminine about magico-religious couvade customs. Rather the only link of this form of the couvade to female reproductive functions is temporal—the two occur at the same time.

Another explanation that focuses on the magico-religious form of the couvade proposes that the couvade should not be regarded as an isolated set of customs. Indeed, in cultures where magico-religious practices are prescribed for expectant or new fathers, we also often find related kinds of customs associated with other events and activities whose outcomes are uncertain. Thus, for example, among the Kwoma of New Guinea, a new father cannot chew betel, scratch himself without using a stick, or hold a cigarette without using tweezers. All of these rules are meant to insure the new baby's well-being. But these same rules are enforced when a man plants yams, or else they will not germinate. Similarly, among the Lesu of New Ireland, new parents observe taboos on sexual activity. But the same taboos apply when their pigs are giving birth. And among the Jivaro of Ecuador, both sexual and dietary restrictions are imposed upon new fathers, but the same restrictions apply when a person is dying yarn, planting, making a signal drum, menstruating, constructing a canoe, making salt, or cooking poison, or when someone is ill. This suggests that the magico-religious form of the couvade may often represent one instance of a more general attempt on the part of people to try to affect events that are important to them but whose outcome is unpredictable. Individuals in some cultures depend upon magical or religious practices to influence all kinds of events with uncertain outcomes, and pregnancy and birth are just one set of events of this sort.

In other cultures that practice the magico-religious form of the couvade, people also mark other life cycle transitions with magico-religious practices of some kind. In these cases, the couvade appears alongside similar customs at, for instance, puberty, marriage, and death. Further, the details of the couvade in a society of this sort mimic the details of the other life transition customs. For example, in Jamaica, the Carib prohibited a new mother and father from killing or eating the flesh of certain animals. Other dietary restrictions were applied to women, and men were required to avoid activities that were physically demanding or dangerous. But the Carib were also required to follow similar kinds of dietary, sexual, and occupational taboos during other life crises and transitions, for instance, at the death of a family member. Similarly, in Northern France, a father and mother were expected to remain in bed when a new baby was born. But so did they retire to bed when a young child died. Mourners would then appear one at a time by the parents' bedside to pay their respects. Among the Lesu, the couvade customs practiced at the birth of a child are repeated at the first naming ceremony, at the appearance of a first tooth, at a feast for potential mates, at the adolescent initiation ceremony, and at weddings.

In some societies, couvade customs do not apply peculiarly to fathers. Thus, for example, among the Chiriguanoa of Paraguay, not only the father but also all of the children of a family lie in bed and fast when a new baby is born. Among the Lesu, not only the father but also the entire community participate in birth customs and also in the rituals surrounding other life transitions.

The couvade is much more common in societies where fathers also play a salient role in the lives of their children. Thus, couvade customs may represent one of the many things that fathers do for their newborn sons and daughters in societies where men are relatively active participants in the lives of their children.

See also BIRTH; INFANTS, TREATMENT OF NEWBORN

Broude, Gwen J. (1988) "Rethinking the Couvade: Cross-Cultural Evidence." *American Anthropologist* 90: 902–911.

Dawson, Warren W. (1929) *The Custom of the Couvade.*

Goldman, Irving. (1963) *The Cubeo: Indians of the Northwest Amazon.*

Harner, Michael J. (1973) *The Jivaro: People of the Sacred Waterfalls.*

Karsten, Rafael. (1923) *The Toba Indians of the Bolivian Gran Chaco.*

Karsten, Rafael. (1935) *The Headhunters of the Western Amazon.*

Nydegger, William F., and Corinne Nydegger. (1966) *Tarong: An Ilocos Barrio in the Philippines.*

Powdermaker, Hortense. (1933) *Life in Lesu: A Study of Melanesian Society in New Ireland.*

CRYING

The human infant is rightly regarded as relatively helpless. Newborn babies cannot feed or protect themselves or even regulate basic physiological functions on their own. On the other hand, babies can cry, and crying is viewed as an adaptation with which infants come equipped as compensation for their other limitations. Crying serves to summon some more competent person who can see to the baby's needs. Indeed, the sound of a baby's crying is extremely irritating to people. The impulse, therefore, for someone who hears an infant crying is to want to make it stop. This is not just because people know that a crying baby may have some acute need. Parents who are deaf do not rush to the bedside of a crying infant with the same sense of irritation as hearing adults experience. It seems as if the sound of crying is specially tailored to bother other people so that they will be inclined to pay attention to the baby.

How do adults across cultures respond to a crying infant? Overwhelmingly, crying elicits a speedy response. Thus, in 80 percent of 80 societies around the world, adults usually or always respond quickly to crying. In an additional 15 percent of these cultures, the response is prevalently speedy and nurturant. The reaction of other people to the crying of a baby is slow, perfunctory, or actually negative in only 5 percent of the 80 cultures. As a result of the predominantly quick and nurturant response of other people to the crying infant, babies in most cultures do not cry very long or very often. Thus, in 48 percent of 25 cultures around the world, babies cry infrequently and then only briefly. In 16 percent of these societies, an infant may cry occasionally, but only for short periods of time. Infrequent bouts of prolonged crying occur in 16 percent of these cultures. In only 20 percent is crying frequent, and even in these cases, babies are not typically allowed to cry for prolonged periods of time.

Virtually everywhere, the first response by caretakers to a crying baby is to feed the baby. If offering food does not work, then the caretaker will try to soothe the infant. Every Philippine Tarong mother agrees that the obvious thing to do when a baby cries is to feed it. An infant will be nursed whenever it cries and for as long as it wishes until it is weaned. If a baby does not wish to nurse, the mother will try to quiet the infant by bouncing or rocking it or, if this fails, she or some other caretaker will attempt to interest or distract the baby with odd noises or objects. As a crying baby is never ignored, a household with an especially fussy infant can be seriously disrupted. Among the Canadian Hare, a crying baby is never left to fuss for very long. The mother will try to feed the infant if she thinks that hunger is the problem. Otherwise, someone will pick the baby up and try to distract it. A crying Mexican Mixtecan baby gets the immediate attention of its mother, who attempts to quiet the baby by offering it a breast as well as other forms of comfort. Among the Javanese of Indonesia, mothers respond so quickly to the first sign of fussing in an infant that it is unusual to hear a baby crying. The infant is picked up, cleaned, and nursed. In Thailand, a Banoi mother employs a variety of techniques to try to quiet a crying child. She may feed, hold, or talk soothingly to the infant or stroke the baby's genitals or rock it in its cradle. When a more mature baby cries, the offering of food may no longer be the caretaker's first response. In Kenya, as a Gusii baby grows older and spends more of its time with substitute caretakers, nursing becomes a less common strategy for dealing with crying and distraction and playing are frequently employed instead. Banoi mothers respond to the crying of an older baby by promising a reward or giving the infant what it wants. Almost every Banoi mother says that a baby who is crying should be picked up.

In a minority of cultures, infants receive a less consistently quick and nurturant response when they cry. Sometimes this is because the mother is doing chores and cannot attend to the baby. Sometimes, the issue seems to be more one of attitude. When an Indian Rajput baby cries, the mother will respond more or less quickly if she is not occupied. If she is busy at some task that demands her attention, the baby will be required to wait. In Ecuador, a Jivaro mother goes back to work in her garden soon after a baby is born, and the infant may be left alone at home in its hammock for a number of hours at a time. Hungry babies, as a result, often cry for extended periods of time without attracting any attention. A baby whose crying wakes its mother in the middle of the night may be scolded and slapped. After the birth of her baby and before the new Banoi mother regains her strength, she spends all of her time lying next to her infant and nursing whenever the baby fusses. As she begins to regain her strength, however, a woman tends to become impatient and she now responds to her baby's crying less reliably. Thus, she may let the infant cry for a few minutes before picking it up. And she may stop nursing it after only a moment or two, leaving the baby still hungry. Mothers at this stage seem to treat nursing as an afterthought. If a baby is making enough noise, it will sooner or later be fed. If not, it is ignored while the mother attends to more interesting things. Jamaican infants are fed on a schedule. If a baby cries for food, the mother will not respond unless it is time for the infant to be nursed, and babies often cry for an hour at a time before they get a response. A baby who cries at night is also ignored, and infants can work themselves into such a rage that they become rigid and very hard to lift. When this happens, a mother may tell an older son or daughter to change the baby's diaper or move it to some other position or perhaps give it some black tea to drink. Or she may pick the baby up briefly herself, only to put it back into bed where it begins to cry again. Older siblings will not respond to a screaming infant unless specifically instructed to do so. Mothers also believe that children often cry for no good reason, so there is no point in responding to them. It makes more sense to just let the youngster "cry it out." In Japan, an Ainu baby is placed in a cradle that is hung from the ceiling. No one pays any attention when the infant cries because "babies are like talkative men and women; they must have their say."

Sometimes, caretakers will try to control crying by scaring the baby into silence. North American Sanpoil children who cried excessively were warned that they would be taken away and eaten by Owl or Bobwhite, birds who carried around baskets in which to collect crying youngsters. The Gusii will also frequently try to silence a crying baby by frightening it, for instance by pretending to call a dog to come over. Young children are likely to stop crying in response to this threat because they have already been made fearful of possible bites from animals.

In many cultures, anyone who is close enough to hear a crying baby will attempt to calm it. Indian Rajput women normally conduct their daily activities in open courtyards that are shared with the mother-in-law and sisters-in-law. If the women get along, any woman or older child will pick up a crying infant, and the baby may be passed from person to person if it refuses to quiet down. Or the grandmother might offer her breast as a pacifier. When a Javanese baby cries, all of the women within earshot stop what they are doing and direct their attention toward the infant, wondering aloud what is wrong and giving the mother advice about how to quiet the child.

Some psychologists have proposed that parents who respond to the crying of an infant will end up creating a spoiled child. Their advice has been to let a baby who is crying for no reason keep on crying. The infant will soon learn that it is futile to try to summon its caretaker with crying and the crying will then stop. Parents in other cultures, however, have different expectations about what will happen if a baby is left to cry. Tairan parents believe that if babies are allowed to cry, especially during the first four months of life, they will develop the habit of crying. Caretakers, therefore, do their utmost to keep their infants happy so that they will have no need to cry. Thus, a Tairan baby who begins to cry is immediately taken to its mother and allowed to nurse. A child nurse who allows her charge to cry is reprimanded by her playmates, and both the nurse and her friends do their best to quiet a crying child by bouncing and patting the baby or coaxing it to suck its fingers for comfort. In fact, the sound of a human infant's crying is different depending upon what the infant needs. The cry of an infant who is in pain is loud and sudden. The baby also gasps and coughs. In the case of a hungry baby, by contrast, crying builds and becomes more rhythmic. Babies do also cry when nothing seems to be wrong. The most effective way of stopping this crying is to pick the baby up. Evolutionary theorists point out that this kind of crying is probably also an adaptation. The greater the proportion of time that a helpless infant spends in proximity to some competent caretaker, the greater its chances of survival. Therefore, a baby who cries when nothing is wrong except that there is no caretaker around is increasing its likelihood of survival by summoning a caretaker who then maintains proximity with the baby in an attempt to calm it. Caretakers across cultures do respond to infant crying in such a way as to promote proximity to babies. This is what is happening when mothers who find that nursing fails to quiet the baby hold, rock, bounce, and otherwise try to comfort it. Among the Gusii, mothers appreciate that there are different kinds of infant cries that require different kinds of responses. Thus, they distinguish a hunger cry from a cry that is called *nyancha,* or "the lake." Mothers know that this cry is not caused by hunger. Some Gusii women believe that it is caused by an irritating stimulation of the genitals produced by the winds coming from Lake Victoria. What matters, however, is the mother's response to *nyancha.* Thus, the mother will put the baby on her back and walk around the house jostling the infant up and down. Child nurses who care for babies during the day will also use this strategy to calm a crying baby who will not accept food.

Responses to crying can change dramatically in the case of older children. When a Hare child over two years of age begins to cry, an adult will attempt to determine what is wrong. If the youngster continues to cry just to get attention, he or she will be ignored. A child of three or four who falls down and cries will not get a positive response from the mother, who may, instead, just say: "You are careless, you are stupid." A Mixtecan mother will comfort a child who, in her view, has a good reason for being upset, but mothers are more likely to scold or punish than to comfort a child who cries without reason. Mothers say that children who have been weaned frequently cry for not good reason. Sometimes, crying in an older child is regarded with clear disapproval by adults. In Uganda, Sebei children learn early on that crying is not approved of, and youngsters learn while quite young to inhibit any impulses to cry when they are hurt or uncomfortable. A Gusii mother has little tolerance for crying in a child who is neither hurt nor hungry, and the child who cries "for nothing" faces severe punishment. Adults repeatedly tell irritable children that they will be bitten by an animal or thrown out in the dark to be eaten by hyenas, with the result that temper tantrums are infrequent among Gusii children.

See also INFANTS, AFFECTIONATE TREATMENT OF; INFANTS, INDULGENCE OF

Barry, Herbert, III, and Leonora Paxson. (1971) "Infancy and Early Childhood: Cross-Cultural Codes 2." *Ethnology* 10: 466–508.

Batchelor, John. (1895) *The Ainu of Japan.*

Cohen, Yehudi A. (1966) *A Study of Interpersonal Relations in a Jamaican Community.*

Geertz, Hildred. (1961) *The Javanese Family: A Study of Kinship and Socialization.*

Goldman, Irving. (1963) *The Cubeo: Indians of the Northwest Amazon.*

Goldschmidt, Walter. (1976) *The Culture and Behavior of the Sebei.*

Hara, Hiroko Sue. (1967) *Hare Indians and Their World.*

Harner, Michael J. (1973) *The Jivaro: People of the Sacred Waterfalls.*

Hitchcock, John T., and Leigh Minturn. (1966) *The Rajputs of Khalapur, India.*

LeVine, Robert A., and Barbara B. LeVine. (1966) *Nyansongo: A Gusii Community in Kenya.*

Maretzki, Thomas W., and Hatsumi Maretzki. (1966) *Taira: An Okinawan Village.*

Nydegger, William F., and Corinne Nydegger. (1966) *Tarong: An Ilocos Barrio in the Philippines.*

Piker, Steven. (1965) *An Examination of Character and Socialization in a Thai Peasant Community.*

Ray, Verne. (1933) *The Sanpoil and the Nespelem: Salishan Peoples of Northeastern Washington.*

Romney, A. Kimball, and Romaine Romney. (1966) *The Mixtecans of Juxtlahuaca, Mexico.*

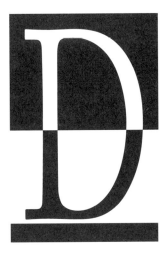

including who supervises and feeds infants and young children. They influence whether children are assigned chores. They affect if, where, and with whom children play. They influence how much time children spend with their father, mother, siblings, and other people and whether they are able to observe and even participate in adults' activities. Because the basic outline of the life of a typical family and community differs in important ways from one culture to the next, so do the daily routines of children. On the other hand, families and communities across the world are similar in many ways, with the result that we also see repeating themes in the daily routine of children across the world.

In Mexico, a Mixtecan mother gets up at around six o'clock in the morning, long before the rest of the family rises. She fetches wood from the courtyard, lights a fire, warms some coffee, and then begins to prepare the day's allotment of tortillas. When the father wakes up, he may eat some cold tortillas left over from the previous day to tide him over until breakfast is ready. He will then go off to the fields if the trip is not too long. When the children of the household get out of bed, they shake out the serapes or rebozos that they have been wearing and put them back on. The youngsters will also eat cold tortillas and may then go out into the courtyard to play. Women do not interrupt their work to tend to the children, who are thus on their own from the time that they wake up until they are called for the morning meal. One of the older girls will be asked to supervise the other youngsters while they play. Meanwhile, older boys may take the animals to the pasture or prepare more firewood in the courtyard. Breakfast is ready at around nine o'clock. The males of the household eat first while the mother serves them. The children then have breakfast while their father rests outside before going back to work in the fields. If his fields are far away from the house, a man will not return from work until the end of the day. His afternoon meal will be brought to

DAILY ROUTINE

Children do not grow up in isolation. Rather, they are raised in households that are themselves embedded in communities. Thus, the daily routine followed by the people around them affects the experience of children in profound ways. Daily routines, in turn, are affected by a variety of factors. These include the subsistence activities of parents as well as how far away from home mothers and fathers go to work and for how long. Any routine or special trips taken by parents to market or to town may influence the experience of youngsters. So will the kinds of activities in which parents engage when the workday is over. The activities of the other children in the household and the neighborhood also matter to the life of a child. Brothers, sisters, and cousins may or may not be busy with tasks. They may or may not go to school. The composition of the household as well as the size of the community in which a child lives and the nature of the relationships of people in the community also make a difference to the experience of the child. These factors and others affect who is responsible for a child's welfare,

him by his wife. Or else, a son who is not yet old enough to work all day will bring food to his father and will then remain with him in the fields until it is time to go home for the night. A woman and any daughter who has been helping to prepare breakfast will eat after everyone else has finished. If it is Friday, the mother and her children generally go to the market. On market days, youngsters are required to sit for hours at a time without making any noise. If a woman has a nursing infant, she may send someone else to market, or else she will leave the baby behind with another woman who can nurse the infant if necessary. On other days, the morning is spent preparing meals and performing other domestic chores. Girls, as well as younger boys, help to shell and grind the corn and to get the beans ready for cooking. They also clean the house and sweep the courtyard. Younger children may feed the chickens and pigs. Children are left at home under the supervision of an older girl when the mother goes to fetch water from the well, which is likely to be far from the house. When she is at home, a woman spends most of her time in the kitchen, and any youngsters who happen to be keeping her company will be recruited to help her in a variety of ways. Once a week, an older girl will also spend the day doing the wash at the river. Or the mother may do the laundry herself, in which case she takes the children along with her to play on the grass while she works. When the children are finished with their chores, they can play. Because most households are made up of a number of nuclear families sharing a single courtyard, children usually have a number of siblings and cousins as daily playmates. Younger children play in mixed-sex groups while an older girl watches them. Older children tend to break up into same-sex play groups. If the father returns home for dinner, he may play with his children for a short time, or else he may sit near them while he gossips with the other men who have also come home to eat. Males, again, eat the afternoon meal before the rest of the fam-

ily. Men who have come home for dinner are likely to spend the rest of the day conducting business with one another or attending to chores. Women may visit each other in the afternoon, taking the children along to play in the courtyard. Supper marks the end of the day. Preparations are made for the next day's meals, dishes are cleared away, and the adults sit around and chat. The children go to sleep when they are tired. By nine o'clock, everyone in the house is likely to be asleep.

Among the Tairans of Okinawa, older women wake up before the rest of the family to start up the fire, cook the sweet potatoes, and warm the soybean soup. In the winter, they are up before dawn; in summer, they rise with the sun. Children wake up next and men last. By half past six, the entire family is awake. An older child or the mother puts away blankets and mosquito nets while other youngsters fetch water from the central water tank. Once breakfast has been eaten, the women feed the pigs and everyone is ready to go off to work or school. Older people and young children stay behind in the village, which is otherwise deserted by eight o'clock. During the day, while the mother is away at work, an infant is carried about the village on the grandmother's back. If the baby begins to cry, the grandmother may offer it her breast although she has no milk. Crying babies are rushed home if the mother is nearby so that they do not have to wait very long before being fed. The adult workload is dictated by the season, but most men and women make a number of trips between their houses and the fields or forest during the course of a day so that young children see their parents a number of times even if they are being supervised by a sibling or teacher. Adults may make a trip back from the forest by ten o'clock in the morning, and mothers return home again in time to prepare lunch. People generally rest and visit after the noon meal before returning to work, and a mother will take this time to nurse and play with her baby before returning it to the

Bolivian mother and child on market day

grandmother's care. In the late afternoon, women feed the pigs again, and more water is fetched from the tank by a woman, young girl, or boy. Mothers will send their children to shop in the village store, or they may go themselves, accompanied by babies and toddlers. Young men and women use this time also to participate in joint work projects or to play games in the playground. Some adults are also gathered there supervising younger children. The evening meal is served after dark. The family eats together, and sometimes this is the only time in the course of the day that the entire household is in the same place at one time. This is the time when matters may be discussed. If it is light outside, people will go out after dinner, visiting in each other's home or hanging around the village store. Or people may attend village meetings, family gatherings, or other formal affairs. By eleven o'clock at night, beds are prepared for sleep, although the Tairans like to go to bed late, and some individuals are still likely to be awake into the early hours of the morning.

For the Rajputs of India, a typical day begins when the temple priest blows his horn before dawn. In the women's quarters, the daughter-in-law who has been assigned the job of preparing breakfast is the first member of the household to get out of bed. Other women go out to grind grain, feed the calf or churn the milk. If it is summer, the men, who sleep in the men's quarters, will also have to rise early and leave for the fields before it gets too hot to work. In the winter, they are able to stay in bed longer. The children and unmarried girls of all ages, who sleep in the women's quarters, get up later than the adults and gather around the hearth fire to wait until breakfast is ready. If it is an especially cold morning, they may build themselves a small fire in the courtyard instead. The men have breakfast after they have fed and milked the cattle. Once they are finished, the women and children eat. Families do not have meals together.

Men retire to the men's quarters or to the courtyard hearth with their food, while a woman will eat in her own room or in a corner of the courtyard facing away from everyone else. A child may eat alone or with other youngsters if a number of children are eating at the same time. After breakfast, the men go off to the fields or return to the men's house to chat and smoke. In the winter, they may be taking care of a court case, arranging a marriage, visiting, and the like. The women attend to household chores. Preschool children play out in the streets. Older boys take off for school or take the cattle to the pasture. While the animals are grazing, the young shepherds play hockey. At noon, the men come home for lunch unless it is harvesting or planting time. In this case, children bring packed lunches to the men in the fields. Schoolchildren and shepherds come home for lunch, and older men who are not in the fields may eat in the courtyard or have food brought to them by a son or daughter in the men's house. Women eat after everyone else is finished with lunch and the boys have been packed back off to school. The afternoon is quite hot, and everyone tries to stay out of the sun. Men who are at home take naps in the men's quarters or under a tree and those who are in the fields take shelter under trees. The herders pass the time chatting instead of playing more strenuous games. Little children go home or retire to some shady spot. As it cools off in midafternoon, schoolchildren return home to do their chores or to play outside. The women begin to prepare dinner, and hungry children try to extract some food from them. Before the evening meal, the men and boys feed and water the cattle. The men are served dinner in the courtyard at around eight o'clock. Women eat later on, after the men have gone. After dinner, women sit around, chatting with each other. If someone is good at telling stories, the other women and the children will gather around to hear her. Similarly, the men visit one another in

With her young children looking on, a Cherokee woman grinds meal on the Qualla Reservation in the Great Smoky Mountains, 1939.

the men's quarters. The children begin to slip off to bed, followed by the adults, the men retiring to the men's quarters and the women to their own rooms in the women's house.

A North American Sanpoil household begins to come to life before dawn as one of the older women in the family gets up to stir the fire. She then gets the children out of bed, prodding their feet with the fire tongs to hurry them up, and also wakes up the young women of the household. Babies sleep as long as they wish. When they finally wake up, they are bathed in warm water and put in their cradles. The children go off to wash in the river, the boys in their place and the girls in theirs. The older woman takes the opportunity to lecture them on some aspect of their culture while they dry off near the fire. Meanwhile, the young women go to pick berries or perform other chores before it gets too hot while the children play on the riverbank. When the men get up, they go to the sweat houses, or else they go salmon fishing. Old men bathe and then return to the house. At around ten o'clock, everyone returns home. The women cook breakfast, which includes fish that the men have caught and fresh berries that the women have gathered. If only the family is present, the children eat with the adults, with everyone seated around the mat on which the food has been placed. After breakfast, the men dress, the women helping to comb their husbands' hair. In the early afternoon, people gamble or go visiting. After the evening meal, which is similar to breakfast, the children implore the old people to tell them stories while the younger men smoke and chat outside and the young women attend to household chores. Children are in bed by dark, followed by the men and then the women. In the winter, no one eats breakfast. One meal, usually eaten in the late afternoon, is considered enough given that people are less active and that food is less abundant. Men stay at home, gossiping and smoking indoors in wintertime un-

less they have planned to go hunting. The women make baskets and do other routine chores, while the children play outside in the snow.

A Jamaican household begins to stir when the sun rises. Babies cry to be fed, the fire is lit in the kitchen, and one of the men of the family has some black tea and then goes to milk the cows. When the shops open a little after seven o'clock in the morning, children can be seen holding pails or balancing buckets on their heads on the way to sell milk. Meanwhile, the men have some black tea and roasted yams or mash and go off to the fields, where they remain until late afternoon, while the children who are old enough trudge off school. Unless it is raining, the men will bring home some yams or potatoes at the end of their workday and then head out again to find a friend or play a game of dominoes. While the men are in the fields, the women attend to household chores. They wash, mend clothing, feed the animals, work in their gardens, clean the house, and perhaps visit with a relative or neighbor. At midday, a woman prepares lunch for the schoolchildren, and food may also be sent to the men in the fields. They also take time out to discipline their preschool children, and this usually means multiple floggings every day. Usually, the family goes to bed when it is dark and after an excerpt has been read from the Bible.

Cohen, Yehudi A. (1966) *A Study of Interpersonal Relations in a Jamaican Community.*

Maretzki, Thomas W., and Hatsumi Maretzki. (1966) *Taira: an Okinawan Village.*

Minturn, Leigh, and John T. Hitchcock. (1966) *The Rajputs of Khalapur, India.*

Ray, Verne. (1933) *The Sanpoil and the Nespelem: Salish Peoples of Northeastern Washington.*

Romney, A. Kimball. and Romaine Romney. (1966) *The Mixtecans of Juxtlahuaca, Mexico.*

DEVELOPMENT, SOCIAL

Human beings belong to a species for which social relations are critical at all stages of life. Because human infants are immature, they require nurturance from responsible caretakers, and the need for caretaking continues for ten to twelve years at a minimum. Human beings also form and maintain friendships and other associations of all sorts at every stage in the life cycle, and cooperation between kin and also unrelated people is characteristic in any human endeavor that we can imagine. The profoundly social nature of human beings is reflected in panhuman social behaviors that show up in infancy and that display remarkable uniformity in infants and children across cultures. Among these are social releasers such as smiling and vocalizing, the development of attachments to caretakers, and emerging anxiety at separation from caretakers and in the presence of strangers.

Smiling

Smiling emerges and then increases at roughly the same age across a number of societies. Thus, American, Israeli, Arab Bedouin, Kalahari !Kung, and Japanese babies all display peaks in smiling between two and four months of age. The uniformity in timing of the first smile in part reflects maturation of relevant brain areas, including those that underwrite emotional responses. Areas of the brain responsible for higher mental processing also mature at this time. The appearance of the smile evokes strong feelings in parents, who often report that they feel for the first time that their baby is really responding to them when that first smile emerges. This may in part explain why there is an increase at this time in physical contact between mothers and infants in a number of cultures, including American, Israeli, and African Kipsigis communities. While the timing of smiling is uniform from society to society, frequency of smiling appears to vary from place to place. Thus, for example, Kipsigis babies smile about 20 percent of the time that they are awake. For African Zambian babies, the figure is 14 percent, for American babies, it is 10 percent, for Yugoslavian infants it is 8 percent, and for North American Navaho babies it is 5 percent.

Vocalizing

Infants across cultures also uniformly increase the rate of spontaneous vocalizations at around three or four months of age. Infants from different societies also tend to display similar absolute rates of vocalization. Thus, for instance, rural Senegal babies vocalize spontaneously at a rate of 39 percent of their waking hours. The figure is 30 percent for Japanese and Navajo babies, and 27 percent for Kenyan babies. This is in spite of the fact that a mother's vocalizations to her infant vary widely from one society to the next, with a range of 20 to 60 percent of the baby's waking time. American babies are exception to the general trend, vocalizing about 59 percent of the time that they are awake.

Attachment

An infant is considered to be attached to its caretaker when four things occur. When a baby can discriminate between its caretaker and other people, when the baby tries to maintain proximity to the caretaker, when a preference for the caretaker is indicated, and when the infant protests the caretaker's departure, we say that the baby is attached to the caretaker. This definition has its problems. In particular, it assumes that an emotional response on the part of a baby will be manifested in a specified set of behaviors, and that this will be uniformly true across infants. However, observations of how infants act vis à vis their caretakers across cultures do suggest that the relationship between an infant and its caretaker develops in a largely uniform manner around the world. Across cultures, babies show maximum distress at the absence of the mother somewhere between seven and fifteen months of age. This separation anxiety has been reported for American, !Kung, Israeli, Ugandan, Mayan, and Ladino infants among others.

Babies are maximally upset at separations from the mother just when they become mobile. This makes good evolutionary sense. Thus, separation anxiety emerges just when infants begin to be able to wander away from the mother, thus exposing themselves to danger. In an evolutionary context, danger included predators, which were common on the African savannah where our species is assumed to have evolved. Nor would an infant who became lost have much chance of surviving. The adaptation, however, remains important for human infants who, given their helplessness, can get into all sorts of trouble when they are off on their own. Human babies also display a fear of strangers at about the same age that separation anxiety emerges. Thus, an older infant who finds itself alone with an unknown person will become distressed and may begin to cry and seek the mother. Here, then, we may have another adaptation that helps the baby to avoid any risks associated with blindly trusting strangers. The appearance of separation and also stranger anxiety at the very time that infants are able to leave the mother on their own steam is underwritten by the maturation of those areas of the brain that are responsible for emotional and cognitive functioning.

Some observations also suggest that babies across cultures form a primary attachment with one caretaker, who is usually the mother. Clearly, infants also become attached to other caretakers, including the father, child nurses, relatives, and so on. If we distinguish strength of attachment to the caretaker by the degree to which an individual can comfort a baby who is upset, however, then some evidence does indicate that infants single out some particular person as the primary attachment figure. It is unclear what qualities of a person make him or her a candidate for the role of primary attachment figure. American infants who spend most of their day in day care settings nevertheless show a preference for the mother, suggesting that it is not quantity of time spent with the caretaker that makes the difference.

While separation anxiety occurs at a roughly similar age across cultures, the age of its decline is more variable from place to place. Thus, for example, few 18-month-old Mayan babies are still upset at the mother's departure. By contrast, some 60 percent of 30-month-old American infants are still upset when the mother leaves, and one-third of !Kung three-year-olds protest at the mother's departure. Israeli babies living in kibbutzim fall somewhere between these extremes, with separation anxiety becoming less common once the child reaches two years of age. Again, it is impossible to determine what accounts for these differences in the waning of separation anxiety. The number of caretakers to whom the child is exposed may make a difference. Thus, both American and !Kung children are cared for largely by the mother, while a baby living in a kibbutz has a number of caretakers. Frequency of the mother's departure may also matter as may the extent to which children are accustomed to encountering strangers.

Styles of Interacting

Across cultures, a child's age can predict how he or she relates to other people and how they respond in turn. A younger child approaches other people primarily in order to obtain help or succor. Further, a younger child is more likely to evoke nurturance from other people. Older children are more likely to be helpful to others. The major target of a one- to three-year-old Liberian Kpelle child's requests and actions is the mother. Other adults serve as the next most frequent targets, followed by older siblings. The majority of the child's interactions with the mother center around requests for help, food, comfort, and the like. A four- to six-year-old will still seek nurturance from the mother, but not nearly as often as the younger child. Further, the behavioral repertoire of older children is more varied. Thus, the four- to six-year-old is approaching people other than the mother for reasons other than the desire to get help, resources, or comfort. As children get older, they are more likely to display nurturance toward other people, and especially toward those who are younger than them. A four-year-old Kpelle child has now become part of a social group and will occasionally try to help a younger child. As Kpelle children grow older, they direct fewer of their interactions toward adults. This is especially the case with boys, who are now spending considerably more time with peers. Partly, this decrease in approaches toward adults reflects the older child's greater competence. Youngsters simply learn to do more and more on their own and so do not need to seek the assistance of grownups. But older children also approach adults less frequently than they used to because, even when they do need help, they are now willing to ask other children

Children's styles of interacting with other people also change with age. A one- to three-year-old Kpelle child who is seeking nurturance is most likely to cry or beg and plead. Younger children will also employ physical tactics, for instance pulling at the mother's clothing. By four years of age, such strategies for getting another person's attention are abandoned. Four-year-olds, however, resort to displays of affection toward an adult whose attention they wish to attract. Youngsters of this age have learned that adults usually just ignore simple requests or attempts to distract them.

By contrast, adults initiate contacts with older children at the same rate that they do with younger ones. The content of their interactions does change, so that, whereas an adult is nurturant and indulgent toward a younger child, older children are typically asked by adults to do some chore. Adults display less nurturance and indulgence toward older children and, in fact, they say that a child who receives too much attention will become spoiled.

Whereas a child who is in the presence of an adult is most likely to try to elicit nurturance, children in the presence of peers display aggression or competition as well as sociability. The same child in the presence of an infant is overwhelmingly likely to be nurturant, and even the behavior of a two-year-old in the presence of a baby will be nurturant 80 percent of the time. Thus, the social behavior of a child is highly influenced by the status of the person with whom the youngster is interacting.

Ainsworth, Mary D. (1967) *Infancy in Uganda: Infant Care and the Growth of Love.*

Bowlby, John. (1969) *Attachment and Loss. Volume 1: Attachment.*

Erchak, Gerald M. (1977) *Full Respect: Kpelle Children in Adaptation.*

Kagan, Jerome. (1976) "Emergent Themes in Human Development." *American Scientist* 64: 186–196.

Konner, Melvin. (1982) *The Tangled Wing: Biological Constraints on the Human Spirit.*

Munroe, Robert L., and Ruth H. Munroe. (1975) *Cross-Cultural Human Development.*

Super, Charles M. (1981) "Behavioral Development in Infancy." In *Handbook of Cross-Cultural Human Development,* edited by Ruth H. Munroe, Robert L. Munroe, and Beatrice B. Whiting, 181–270.

Whiting, Beatrice B., and Carolyn Pope Edwards. (1988) *Children of Different Worlds: The Formation of Social Behavior.*

DEVELOPMENT THEORIES, NATIVE

Native, or folk, theories of development appear in all known cultures around the world. Further, these theories of development try to account for the same kinds of things across cultures, and many indigenous theories echo themes found in academic accounts of human development. Thus, people the world over try to isolate the origins of children's personality and behavior profiles, sometimes emphasizing the role of biology, sometimes of environment, and sometimes the interaction of both in producing developmental outcomes. People in different cultures also express beliefs about whether or not a child's behavior and personality profile remains stable across the life cycle and whether or not development proceeds in an orderly and predictable manner. Everywhere, we also find theories about when children are most amenable to learning, how they learn, and when they become capable of reason.

Causal accounts of children's behavior and personality profiles often emphasize the role of heredity as it affects developmental outcomes. Among the Okinawan Tairans, a mother appreciates that each of her children has his or her own personality, and adults tailor their treatment of a child to the youngster's individual behavior and temperament. Adults also notice family resemblances when it comes to the personality traits of children and their parents and attribute these to the effects of heredity. A Tairan parent, therefore, is likely to be puzzled by a child who is obviously dissimilar from both of the parents. The Semai of Malaysia emphasize inborn traits as determining a child's traits. According to the Semai view, children are miniature versions of adults. As children, they are "dumb." But their physical and mental capacities will unfold naturally and without the intervention of adults. A particular child turns into a particular adult because of who the child happens to be, and parents are not responsible for the characteristics

or fate of their children. By contrast, the Philippine Tarong believe that bad behavior on the part of a child is a result of bad training. As a result, parents, while they greatly desire children, say that it is better to have no children at all than to have children who misbehave, since the parents will always be blamed for the undesirable actions of their youngsters. The Mixtecans of Mexico trace personality development to the interaction of heredity and environment, and this folk theory comes closest in spirit to current academic views of development. Thus, the Mixtecans believe that each person is unique as a result of the joint effects of inborn dispositions and learning histories. Therefore, because people inherit a set of traits through blood, and because no one ever loses his or her blood, a person's unique traits will sooner or later emerge. As a result, if someone has a bad temper, the Mixtecans will attribute this to the bad temper of the person's parents or other relative. A child inherits blood through both parents, but the mother's blood is thought to be stronger in the child and thus more likely to influence a youngster's character profile. And differences in personality or behavior tendencies among siblings are attributed to differences in the blood that has been passed down to them from parents and other relatives. Learning, however, is also assumed to have its effects upon a person's character because as a child learns, he or she is developing habits, and habits, as the Mixtecans say, are hard to unlearn. Because learning figures importantly into the Mixtecan theory of development, parents are held responsible for training their children properly. Thus, a parent whose child-rearing practices are deficient will be blamed if the youngster turns out badly. But sometimes, bad blood overrides the best efforts of a mother and father, in which case no one will criticize them for the bad behavior of their child. The idea that children come equipped to some degree with their own personality traits may be easier for people to appreciate in cultures where siblings are numerous and where, therefore, adults have the chance to observe how different the behavior patterns of children raised in the same household can be. Thus, in Kenyan communities, where anyone can see that youngsters brought up by the same mother nevertheless have different eating and sleeping habits, different responses to the same experience, different rates of growth, and so on, people believe that a mother adjusts herself to the unique needs of her baby instead of shaping the child's character by her own actions.

While adults in many cultures recognize and attempt to explain differences in the personality profiles of different children, some cultures deemphasize individual differences. The Indian Rajputs think of any individual as a member of a group rather than as a unique personality. A person is an incarnation of a soul that may have existed on earth a million times already and that may return to earth another million times. Further, any person is only a piece of the universal world-soul. The bias against viewing people as individuals is reflected in the Rajput mother's claim that all children are the same. Other cultures attribute a child's characteristics to supernatural causes. According to the Tairans, a child who is born with two cowlicks is destined to be a problem to his parents. Children, aware of this belief, will look for two cowlicks on the heads of other youngsters. A child who is successful in finding two cowlicks on the head of another child will accuse the youngster of being naughty, and a little boy who has two cowlicks will tell you without hesitation that he is naughty.

Also included in native theories of development are beliefs about the degree to which behavior and personality traits are consistent from one stage of life to the next. Some folk theories emphasize continuity, while others focus on discontinuity. For example, the Gusii of Kenya believe in the continuity of behavior across the life cycle. Thus, a bothersome child will turn out to be "bad," while an obedient, responsible, respect-

ful youngster will become a "good person." As a result, adults tend to view some children as amenable to training and others as incorrigible. The Chimalteco of Guatemala agree. Thus, a child who cries at two or three years will cry as a man when he is drinking. Similarly, a child who laughs all the time will be happy and successful as an adult. And a child who shouts and falls on the floor when his father asks him to do something will grow up to be a bad person who never does any work. A bad child cannot be changed into a good child or a good adult.

By contrast, adults in some cultures focus on the inevitable differences in children of different ages. The Semai say that a child under five or six years of age has the "heart of a macaque." Children at this age are curious and imitative. An older child has "the heart of a dog." Children have now become quarrelsome. Adults, by contrast, always remember; they have "elephant hearts." In many cultures, adults appreciate that development progresses in a stagelike manner and that the developmental program unfolds according to a blueprint of its own. The Philippine Tarong believe that development proceeds at its own pace and cannot be accelerated by experience or heredity. Therefore, no one pressures a child to walk or talk early, although people admire a child who picks up skills quickly. The North American Hopi viewed human existence as a journey along the road of life from birth to death. The person matures gradually, passing through the four stages of childhood, youth, adulthood, and old age. Each phase of development depends upon what has happened in the previous stage and prepares the individual for the next one. Graduation to each new developmental phase is marked by a "birth" or "rebirth" ceremony, thus emphasizing the idea that the stages of life are only transitory. This vision of the life cycle is represented in a Powamu ceremony sand painting. The road of life is symbolized by a yellow line marked by four crooks, one for each stage of development.

Native theories of development also include beliefs about how and when children learn and when they are capable of reason. In Mexico, the Mixtecans say that children younger than six or seven years of age are not able to learn effectively because they have not yet acquired the ability to reason. A youngster is most easily influenced by other people between the ages of 7 and 12. Once a child becomes a teenager, it becomes harder and harder to train the youngster, and by the time a person is 18 years old, the character is fixed and, therefore, not changeable by learning. Tarong parents say that it is best to teach children while they are young. "Like the old tree which is already bent, you cannot unbend." In Micronesia, Truk adults assume that little children are unteachable. As a result, they are allowed to do what they wish without interference or censure.

In many traditional cultures, adults expect children to learn by watching and doing. Repetition of an activity is also assumed to be sufficient for learning. The Rajputs believe that a child learns more efficiently by observation and imitation than by direct instruction. Among the Kpelle of Liberia, an adult will repeatedly command a child to perform some desired behavior so that it will eventually become a habit. Similarly, in Guatemala, Chimalteco boys learn ritual prayers after years of hearing them repeated over and over.

Native theories are to some degree consistent with the exigencies of the culture in which they are found. For example, mothers in different cultures have different ideas about when children are capable of performing adult tasks. These assessments, in turn, seem to be affected by when the mother is required to recruit her children as helpers. That decision, finally, depends upon how much work the mother herself does in a typical day. Thus, the lighter the mother's workload, the later she recruits her children into the work force, and the later the age at which a child is assumed to be capable of taking on serious responsibilities. Gusii mothers, who have very demanding workloads, assume that children can take on serious responsibilities quite early, and a girl of three or four may tend an infant sibling by herself for an hour or two. A six- or seven-year-old sister will feed, wash, and supervise a younger sibling on her own for hours each day. Meanwhile, a Rajput mother, whose workload is particularly light by cross-cultural standards, will still feed and bathe an eight-year-old. Certain developmental trends are also more or less universally recognized regardless of cultural context. Thus, for example, adults across societies say that children become capable of reasoning at somewhere around seven years of age. Similarly, women across cultures seem to agree that girls are generally more responsible and obedient than boys and that boys are more physically aggressive.

In most societies, ideas about how children develop are part of the folk wisdom of the culture, and when a woman becomes a mother, she has a rich body of belief about child development upon which to depend as she makes decisions about how to raise her own children. By contrast, in Western societies new parents are often unsure about what to believe when it comes to human development, and advising parents on how to raise their children has become an industry. Shelves of manuals on child development and child rearing can be found in any bookstore. Child-rearing experts host their own television programs and dole out advice to anxious mothers and fathers. Why do parents in industrial societies seek out expert advice in raising their children whereas other mothers and fathers the world over do not? Parents in Western societies may be seeking help in dealing with their children for a variety of reasons. In traditional societies, adults, and especially women, have generally had considerable experience with children by the time they are parents. In the majority of traditional societies, a mother recruits older siblings, and especially sisters, to care for younger ones while she is busy with her own chores. Child nurses tote their charges around for hours at a time, often feeding and bathing them. With this kind of prior practice under her belt, a woman from a traditional society has a good idea of what it takes to bring up a child. Parents in traditional cultures are also likely to live near their own mothers or female relatives, so when advice or support are needed, a woman does not have far to go. Where a woman leaves her natal community to live with her husband, she will often return home to give birth to her first child. And a woman who lives in her husband's community will have her mother-in-law as well as her spouse's other female relatives nearby. Traditional cultures are also stable cultures. Customs do not tend to change across generations. This means that skills learned as a child nurse remain current when a woman becomes a parent. So does the wisdom accumulated by a woman's mother and other relations and friends. Traditional societies also tend to be homogenous. Everyone shares more or less the same values and expectations. This means that parents will agree about what is the best strategy for raising a child and what is the best outcome toward which to aim. By contrast, new parents in industrial societies have frequently had no experience with babies and children. They live far from their own parents and relatives, making it hard to seek their advice. Even where parents have had prior contact with children or live close to people who can provide help and support, the rapidly changing values and demands of industrial cultures mean that skills and advice accrued in prior generations are now in some degree obsolete. Finally, because industrialized societies are often heterogenous, parents may not come from the same background and may, therefore, disagree about how to raise children and what they wish to accomplish as parents. The solution for these parents is to seek the advice of experts.

See also DEVELOPMENTAL STAGES; LEARNING

Dentan, Robert. (1978) "Notes on Childhood in a Nonviolent Context: The Semai Case." In *Learning and Non-Aggression*, edited by Ashley Montagu, 94–143.

Erchak, Gerald M. (1977) *Full Respect: Kpelle Children in Adaptation.*

Gladwin, Thomas, and Seymour Sarason. (1953) *Truk: Man in Paradise.*

Hitchcock, John T., and Leigh Minturn. (1966) *The Rajputs of Khalapur, India.*

LeVine, Robert A., and Barbara B. LeVine. (1966) *Nyansongo: A Gusii Community in Kenya.*

Maretzki, Thomas W., and Hatsumi Maretzki. (1966) *Taira: An Okinawan Village.*

Nydegger, William F., and Corinne Nydegger. (1966) *Tarong: An Ilocos Barrio in the Philippines.*

Romney, A. Kimball, and Romaine Romney. (1966) *The Mixtecans of Juxtlahuaca, Mexico.*

Thompson, Laura, and Alice Joseph. (1947) *The Hopi Way.*

Wagley, Charles. (1949) "The Social and Religious Life of a Guatemalan Village." *American Anthropologist* 51: 3–150.

Whiting, Beatrice B. (1971) "Folk Wisdom and Child Rearing." Paper presented at meetings of the American Association for the Advancement of Science, December.

DEVELOPMENTAL STAGES

Neuroscientists have observed that the development of the human being proceeds in a more or less orderly and predictable manner. Furthermore, a child's abilities during one era of life seem in some ways to be qualitatively different from those characterizing other eras. Thus, according to psychologists, the thinking, moral judgments, interpersonal relationships, and so on of children are noticeably and predictably different at different stages in the life cycle. This idea that children of different ages think, feel, and behave differently is also captured in the folk theories of development in cultures around the world. What is more, observations regarding the profiles of children in any particular stage of development overlap significantly from one culture to the next and overlap also with the formal theories of psychologists. All cultures make distinctions at a minimum between children, adults, and old people, and the folk theories of most societies also draw even finer distinctions between children of different ages. Theories of development across cultures tend to focus on the acquisition of motor skills, physical growth, the capacity to exhibit responsibility and obedience, and the emergence of reason.

The Mixtecans of Mexico think of the life cycle as being segregated into discrete stages. Each stage is associated with its own distinct profile of tendencies, capacities, and limitations. A particular stage is also identified with a specific set of roles, rights, and responsibilities. The word for infant means "in darkness." Babies are also referred to as "creatures." They have neither awareness nor the capacity to reason. As the Mixtecans assume that learning requires awareness, an infant cannot learn. A child of one or two years of age has now gained awareness, ushering in the stage of early childhood or, in the words of the Mixtecans, the era of "this child now knows." However, youngsters at this stage have not yet acquired the ability to reason. They cannot, therefore, understand the difference between good and bad and are not considered responsible when they behave badly. When, at the age of six or seven, permanent teeth begin to come in, a boy or girl enters the stage of late childhood. At this stage, a youngster has also attained reason and can be held accountable for bad behavior. Children become "youths" when

they first become aware of sex, perhaps around the age of twelve. And adulthood is marked by the attainment of economic independence. The Mixtecans recognize that different children will progress through these stages at somewhat different rates because of differences in inborn dispositions and learning histories. But all children eventually graduate naturally through these eras.

In North America, Chippewa childhood was divided into two stages, the period from birth until the child walked and the stage between walking and puberty. The third stage described the period from adolescence to the birth of the individual's first grandchild. The birth of a great-grandchild then ushered in the next stage of life and so on. The Chippewa did not reckon age in years. Rather, a young child might be described as "just old enough to remember" or as "not having any sense yet." An adult recollecting the age of an older child might describe the youngster as having been "so high," indicating the height of the child with a hand.

The Micronesian Truk recognize five broad stages of development. The baby is a person who does not understand. The child understands, but merely plays. A youth can perform productive work, but is not very responsible, while an adult is both productive and more and more responsible. Finally, the old person is no longer productive.

The African Swazi distinguish eight stages of life and mark each one ceremonially. A baby under three months of age is a "thing." Very young infants are viewed as extremely vulnerable and many, in fact, do not live. Babies of this age have not yet been named, and if they die, they are not formally mourned. An infant who is three months old enters the stage of babyhood. It is shown the moon and introduced to the world of nature. The baby is now viewed as a person and is given a name. An infant who has "teeth to chew" and "legs to run" enters the "toddler" stage, which lasts for around three years and normally ends with weaning. Whereas a baby is indulged by and rarely separated from its mother, the toddler is expected to be more independent from adults and spend a considerable amount of time with other children. The next stage of development is marked formally when a small slit is made in the lobe of each ear of the six-year-old child. Youngsters of this age are expected to take on more serious tasks and to control their emotions. The ear-slitting ceremony dramatizes this expectation. The procedure is very painful, but the children are expected to acquit themselves bravely. Puberty marks the next stage of development. Traditionally, boys were circumcised at adolescence, but the procedure is no longer practiced because so many boys died as a consequence of the operation. Marriage marks the next stage in the Swazi life cycle and is necessary for any man who wishes to be accorded the privileges of adulthood. A woman's status is increased with the birth of her first child, and reaches its height when she goes to live with her married son. At the final stage, the person who is "almost an ancestor" has earned the respect of others and oversees the education of young people and leads community rituals.

The North American Arapaho gauged a child's level of development by physical and mental milestones. Thus, the Arapaho talked about the child who still sleeps, the child who smiles, the child who has teeth, the child who walks, the child who eats alone, the child who goes to the toilet alone, the child who now knows some words, the child who is able to think, the child who is able to learn, the child who speaks the language well, and the child who has his own mind.

The name for a newborn Philippine Tarong baby is *kayannak*. The term is applied to a baby for two weeks or less, only until the umbilical cord falls off. Until then, the baby is not viewed as solidly entrenched in the world. It is not yet a separate person and its existence is in an important sense provisional. Once the cord falls off and the stump heals, the infant graduates to the

status of *tagibi*, or baby. The *tagibi* represents a successful birth and is now a full-fledged participant in this world. At adolescence, a Tarong male acquires the status of a "becoming-a-young-man." He works with his father in the fields as a member of a work group and begins to contribute to decisions made about neighborhood affairs. A Tarong boy earns recognition as an adult as a result of his own ability to act as an adult. Boys who go to school are graduated to the status of adult more slowly because a student cannot also be a man by Tarong standards. A Tarong girl who has begun to menstruate is now called by the diminutive term for young woman. She may attend wakes with the other women, serve guests at feasts, and attend parties and dances.

The first stage of life recognized by the Cubeo of the Northwest Amazon lasts from infancy until the baby learns to crawl. The crawler has arrived at stage two in the Cubeo life cycle. The child who is now walking but who still needs help is now in the third stage of life. The fourth stage takes the youngster to puberty, which then ushers in the stage of adulthood. Finally, the Cubeo recognize old age as a discrete stage of life. Different labels are employed for males and females at each stage.

The North American Comanche recognized five stages of development. The first stage was infancy. The stage of childhood included both prepubescent boys and girls, while adolescence included pubescent girls as well as unmarried warriors. The final two stages were adulthood and old age. The transitions across stages were not well defined, especially when physical signals of a change in status were lacking, as in the shift from childhood to adolescence in males or the transition to adulthood for both sexes. Thus, a male adolescent began to be considered an adult when he was capable of committing himself to the demanding life of a warrior.

For the Hare of Canada, a child remains a *be'bi*, or infant, until it can walk. A child who walks and talks is a *ts'utani*. At around 11 to 13 years of age, the young person arrives at adolescence. A boy is now called *ek'e* and a girl, *tiele*. Traditionally, adolescence ended when the person married. Nowadays, a person who becomes fully responsible for a household is an adult. The shift from adulthood to old age is not well demarcated, but a person who is 50 years or older is often called *e'si*.

The Japanese Ainu mark developmental stages by a combination of developmental advances made by the baby itself and aspects of a baby's status that are related to events external to the infant itself. A newborn baby is called *shiontek* (lump of dung) or *poishispe* (dung-covered) so that evil spirits will avoid the infant. Babies who can inflate their cheeks and make "poo-poo" or other sounds are now *ai-ai*. When another baby arrives in a household, the next youngest infant is called *ahushikore*, "it is older now." An infant becomes *yaian ibe*, "it eats food independently of its mother now," when it begins to eat an adult diet. Eventually, the youngster enters the stage of *ki yakka pirika*, "it can eat with adults now."

While some cultures draw fine distinctions among stages of development, other societies describe development in broader strokes. The North American Hopi envision the human condition as a journey along the road of life from birth to death and involving the gradual growth and development of the person. Individuals pass through the four stages of childhood, youth, adulthood, and old age. Among the Jamaicans, all children below ten years of age are "pickney," and there is no obvious transition between infancy and childhood. People say that a baby becomes a child when "him have sense" about everything. Some adults think that this happens when a child is two years old and others when the youngster is around five or seven. The difference depends upon what areas of competence the adult is emphasizing. Thus, a child gets sense about things like where to defecate, when to avoid fighting, and so on at about five years of age, but it is not until two years later that a youngster gets enough sense to go to school. The North American Cree Indians make no distinctions between children. Thus, all preadult males are "small men" and all preadult females are "small women."

See also DEVELOPMENTAL STAGES, TRANSITIONS ACROSS

Cohen, Yehudi A. (1966) *A Study of Interpersonal Relations in a Jamaican Community.*

Gladwin, Thomas, and Seymour Sarason. (1953) *Truk: Man in Paradise.*

Goldman, Irving. (1963) *The Cubeo: Indians of the Northwest Amazon.*

Hara, Hiroko Sue. (1967) *Hare Indians and Their World.*

Hilger, M. Inez. (1951) *Chippewa Child Life and Its Cultural Background.*

———. (1952) *Arapaho Child Life and Its Cultural Background.*

———. (1971) *Together with the Ainu.*

Kuper, Hilda. (1963) *The Swazi: A South African Kingdom.*

Malinowski, Bronislaw. (1929) *The Sexual Life of Savages.*

Munroe, Robert L., and Ruth H. Munroe. (1975) *Cross-Cultural Human Development.*

Nydegger, William F., and Corinne Nydegger. (1966) *Tarong: An Ilocos Barrio in the Philippines.*

Romney, A. Kimball, and Romaine Romney. (1966) *The Mixtecans of Juxtlahuaca, Mexico.*

Wallace, Ernest, and E. Adamson Hoebel. (1952) *The Comanches: Lords of the South Plains.*

Across cultures, as individuals progress through the stages of life, they must inevitably undergo changes. Some of these changes are the simple result of the fact that aging means changing physically, cognitively, emotionally, and socially. But how these inevitable changes are experienced by a child or adult is in part determined by how cultures pattern the transitions from one stage of life to the next. The cultural management of life cycle transitions influences how easy or hard these shifts turn out to be for the individual.

Age and Change

Age is exploited as the marker for determining transitions in the treatment of the child in many cultures. In Polynesia, a Tongan child receives a good deal of petting and attention for the first year and a half of life. After that, youngsters are left more or less to their own devices, coming and going wherever and whenever they wish. If a child happens to be playing around the house, the mother will expect help on some simple task and will beat a youngster who fails to obey her. For an Indonesian Javanese child, the fifth or sixth birthday marks a change in the degree of indulgence and permissiveness that can be expected from parents, and especially the father. At this point, youngsters are expected to be obedient, polite, and self-disciplined. Younger children are viewed as *durung djawa,* that is, not yet Javanese. By the age of five or six, the child is considered capable of learning more mature behavior. This includes knowing how to show respect and toward whom and knowing when it is acceptable to be familiar with another person. Among the Palauans of Micronesia, five-year-old youngsters suddenly discover that the indulgence they have come to expect from their mothers is no longer available. A little boy who clamors to be picked up will be ignored, as will

his demands to be held, cuddled, carried, fed, or amused. Children initially respond to this abrupt change in treatment with temper tantrums. At first, a mother may relent, but children are soon required to reconcile themselves to this new treatment.

A North American Zuni baby is held or carried most of the time and a mother will stop what she is doing to tend a crying baby, feeding the infant, changing its diapers, and rocking it back to sleep. The same child is ignored once it becomes a toddler, unless there is some serious problem. Adults say that a two-year-old "should know better than to be spoiled." Children are consciously trained not to hang around adults and interfere with their work, and a busy parent will simply send youngsters outside to play or place them under the supervision of older children. The change in indulgence is dramatic, and children sometimes have to be scolded as part of the process of making them self-reliant. In Liberia, Kpelle adults expect younger children to be self-centered, but four- to six-year-olds are expected to make concrete contributions to the household and they are assigned a greater range and frequency of chores than are their younger siblings. In South India, Gopalpur mothers are quick to nurse a crying child. If the baby continues to cry even after it has been fed, a sibling will rock it to sleep. But when infants become toddlers and begin to get around on their own, they can no longer expect this kind of indulgent response. Rather, a mother will now scold and grumble in response to a whining child, nursing the youngster but then shooing him or her out of the house, even while the toddler strenuously objects. This tug-of-war, in which the youngster clamors to be picked up by a rejecting mother, may go on for an entire day.

Weaning

Weaning brings with it a number of major and difficult changes for children in many societies. In the Philippines, few demands are made on a

Tarong child who has not been weaned. Youngsters have learned proper toilet habits and table manners and know how to comport themselves with modesty. Beyond this, the primary concern of the caretaker is to make the baby happy, and adults play games that are most likely to produce delighted responses on the part of the infant. Weaning, however, means a set of dramatic changes. The child is abruptly deprived of the mother's breast and also of the comfort of her lap. When youngsters resist weaning, they experience their first punishments. Crying now provokes a scolding by the mother instead of solicitous attempts on her part to relieve or distract the distressed child. And the weaned child is now supervised for a significant amount of time by some caretaker other than the mother. If there is an adequate substitute, the newly weaned youngster may not have too hard a time with this transition in caretakers. But often there is no satisfactory surrogate and the child lives through a stretch of time alternately whining and making demands for attention. Eventually, the child learns to depend upon the various relatives who reside in his household and neighborhood. Youngsters also learn at this point what they can realistically expect to obtain from other people. A child who learns these lessons leaves the world of infancy. In Mexico, Mixtecan infants experience an abrupt change when they are being weaned. A mother who has decided not to nurse her baby any longer never offers the infant the breast again. A woman will rub bitter herbs or dirt on her nipple to prevent the baby from wanting to nurse, or perhaps she will send the infant to stay with relatives for a day or two. Once the weaning process starts, a baby who cries is given coffee or perhaps milk to drink or a bit of cold tortilla or other food on which to nibble.

New Siblings

The appearance of a new sibling in the family inevitably means change for older siblings, and often the change is painful. Among the Tairans

of Okinawa, the introduction of a new baby into the household foreshadows a dramatic change in the life of the toddler who has until now lived a life filled with affection and indulgence. The youngest child in the household is carried about all day long by caretakers and nurses on demand even though solid foods have been part of the youngster's diet for a while. But when the mother discovers that she is pregnant, she begins to wean the toddler. And after the new infant is born, the older child can no longer expect to be carried around or treated with the patience and indulgence that were directed toward the former baby of the household. Youngsters respond to this double dethronement with outrage and sullenness, which eventually diminish, partly because these behaviors are ineffective in earning the child much attention. Children whose households include an older sibling or, especially, a grandmother, have a somewhat easier time. Grandmothers continue to indulge dethroned youngsters and to comfort them when they have been rebuffed or ridiculed by the mother. But all Tairan children experience the transition from youngest to second-youngest child as a difficult one.

Changes in Mother's Routine

For many children, important changes in their treatment follow the mother's return to work. At first, a Liberian Kpelle baby's needs are met immediately, and it is rare to hear an infant cry. When a woman is doing chores away from home, by contrast, a baby might have to wait before being nursed. This becomes especially likely once a baby of six months of age or older is left in the care of an older sister so that a crying infant must actually be carried off to the absent mother for feeding.

New Capabilities

In some societies, a child's demonstration of new capacities marks a formally recognized life transition. In North America, a Sanpoil boy's first successful fishing expedition is marked by a small feast thrown by the men. Similarly, the women threw a small celebration the first time that a girl gathered her first roots or fruits. The guests were mainly relatives. The food that the child had brought home was part of the feast, but the youngster was not allowed to eat any of it. All of the old people at the celebration admonished the child to work hard in order to become a success as an adult. The first deer that a boy killed was cut up by his father and a piece was distributed to every household in the village, except for that of the boy himself. The hide of the deer was made into a shirt for the young hunter.

Changes in Independence

Transitions from one stage of development to another can mean that a child now has more independence. This can signify more freedom for the child, but it can also mean that parents will be less tolerant of dependent behavior even when the youngster does not wish to be independent or responsible. Mixtecan children below the ages of five or six do whatever tasks are required of them in the presence of other people. But beginning in later childhood, youngsters will now be expected to perform important chores on their own. Girls bathe their younger siblings or cousins in the stream some distance away from home, while a boy gathers wood in the hills and works in the fields with his father. While the weaned Tarong youngster is forced to give up some of the indulgence and security experienced in infancy, children of this age also enjoy a greater degree of independence. In particular, they are no longer watched as closely by caretakers and their movements are no longer as restricted. Thus, the newly weaned child can wander about the immediate neighborhood in a way that was impossible before. This allows the youngster to join larger groups of children who may be playing in a central yard. For a Micronesian Ifaluk youngster, the introduction of a new baby in the

household means that the older child is no longer the center of attention. Now, the youngster is ignored, and a child who is no longer the baby of the house is forced to manage on his her own. On the other hand, an older brother or sister suddenly also begins to enjoy a measure of independence. Older siblings eat when they want and come and go when they want as long as they do not wander too far.

Changes in Behavioral Expectations

Parents also enforce stricter expectations regarding the behavior of children who have made a transition from one stage to the next. Tarong preschoolers are now expected to control aggressive impulses and to be responsible and obedient. Tarong preschoolers stray farther from home and begin to spend their time in play groups, and parents begin to instruct them more seriously about the rules regarding modesty, aggression, sex play, obedience, and so on. Whereas a toddler who misbehaved would simply be taken out of harm's way, the parents of an older child persuade the youngster to behave properly by administering rewards and punishments. For the Tairan child, becoming a first-grader marks an important change in status. At seven years of age, these children are now viewed as having sense, which means that they now know what they are doing. Kindergartners admire the first-grade child, who feels superior and lets the younger children know it. If a first-grader misbehaves, the teacher threatens to send the child back to kindergarten, where the students do not know anything and do not understand the teacher. Home from school, the girls enthusiastically do the household chores that signify their new status, and the eagerness of the first-graders as they practice their lessons at night contrasts sharply with the attitude of the older students. After her first menstrual cycle, a North American Arapaho girl's freedom was restricted, and she was expected to be home by dark. Girls of this age were expected not to draw attention to themselves. She should not look about carelessly and she should not giggle in the company of other people. Once they reached puberty, girls were also required to avoid their brothers and other relatives whom they called "brother." A girl was also required to learn a variety of new skills, and the woman with whom she lived began to teach her to prepare food, tan hides, and make moccasins and porcupine decorations. Kpelle parents disapprove of "friskiness," or disrespect and lack of discipline in children, but they punish friskiness mildly in a child who is not yet seven, and punishments are often softened with teasing or a smile. Once a child is seven and "has sense," the same "friskiness" is severely punished with slaps and even beatings.

Gradual Transitions

While transitions from one stage of life to the next can be dramatic and painful, they can also sometimes be rather gradual. In India, the Rajputs use the same term to designate children of all ages, and this is reflected in the slow movement and informality of shifts through the childhood years. Among the Cubeo of the Northwest Amazon, girls undergo a ten-day seclusion period at puberty. But although the girl is now marriageable, her life does not change appreciably. She is more concerned with how she looks and she now wears love charms to attract boys magically. But she continues to live with her mother and to conduct herself in her customary way. Similarly, in Thailand, as they grow older, Banoi children are expected to become more self-reliant and to follow the numerous rules of etiquette that characterize Banoi relationships. But the shift is gradual. Thus, for the five-year-old, the demands are minimal, and it is only when children are ten years of age or older that they are expected to exhibit consistently responsible and appropriate behavior. By the time Guatemalan Chimalteco children are ten years old, their activities are very similar to those of adults. They are regarded as responsible people who are

contributing to the welfare of the household, and girls may already be married by thirteen years of age. Thus, there is no abrupt transition from childhood to adulthood or any formal acknowledgement of such a transition.

Shifts in Adolescence

The transition associated with the onset of puberty can be dramatic. Or the shift can merely be background noise in the life of a young person. The Tarong make no special fuss over a girl who has begun to menstruate. The girl herself, however, is happy that she will now be referred to by the diminutive term for young woman. A girl who has begun to menstruate will now be teased about her marriage prospects. A girl who has attained sexual maturity is also allowed to participate in various adult activities. She can attend wakes along with the other women, serve food and water to guests at feasts, and go to dances and parties. There is no formal recognition among the Tarong of a boy's attainment of sexual maturity. The youngster will now go to dances and parties, and his parents will begin to think seriously about potential marriage partners for the boy. An adolescent boy is also aware of his new physiological status, and will begin to lord it over his younger siblings, bossing them about and showing off in front of them. When an Arapaho boy's voice changed, someone, usually a female relative, advised him to show respect toward other people, to avoid his sisters and any relatives called by the name of "sister," and not to pay any attention to girls. People commented that the youngster was growing into a man, but no one thought that a boy of this age was close to being mature. An Arapaho girl began to wear a wide belt decorated with beadwork or silver ornaments over her clothing when she showed signs of physical maturity. A small bag holding a section of her dried umbilical cord was strung onto the belt as were various other adornments. The skeleton of a small turtle that had been caught by the girl's mother or brother was also frequently attached to the belt. When the girl had her first menstrual period, she took off the belt. Her mother kept all of the adornments and eventually gave them to a granddaughter or niece, but the girl kept her navel-cord bag. Once she had reached puberty, a girl now wore a shawl-like garment tied around her waist and draped over her hips. For a Jamaican male, the transition to adult status is marked by subtle changes reflected in his acceptance as an equal by adult men. Thus, while a boy would never join a group of adults for any extended length of time, a male knows that he has attained adult status in the eyes of the men when he is permitted to engage in long conversations or play dominoes with them. Men will laugh at a boy who tries to be accepted by them as an adult before they think that he is ready. Adolescent boys rarely make errors of this sort, in part because they use the reactions of their parents toward them as an indication of whether they have achieved adult status in the eyes of others. If a boy's parents accord him the privileges of an adult, he can be sure that other people will too. If he is not treated as an adult by his mother and father, then neither will anyone else regard him as an adult. Males are generally recognized as adults at the age of 19. Jamaican girls can view themselves as adults when they are permitted to come and go as they please, usually when they are around 21 years old. A girl's independence, however, is not complete, as her parents continue to prevent her from behaving in ways of which they disapprove.

A somewhat more pronounced adolescent shift occurs for the Micronesian Truk male or female. The young person is no longer regarded as a child and is now an adult. This is in spite of the fact that boys and girls have already begun to do adult work before puberty and that adolescents who are now formally adults are by no means fully mature. The major change in the life of the Truk boy or girl who has now attained adult status is in the arena of sexual behavior. Adults are permitted to engage in sexual activ-

ity, whereas the preadolescent is not. But even this shift to adult is not definitive. Truk adolescents are not viewed as capable of taking on full adult responsibilities. Indeed, it is only in middle age that the individual is understood to be fully responsible. For the North American Hopi male, the adolescent shift was more dramatic. After his adolescent initiation ceremony, a Hopi male was expected to become a man abruptly, accepting both the responsibilities and privileges of manhood, avoiding fights and quarrels, and adopting the Hopi way. The transition of a Comanche girl to physical maturity was also a noteworthy occasion for both the girl and her family. But by the time that she reached adolescence, a girl was already very familiar with the tasks and roles that she would be required to perform, so that there was no anxiety associated with the transition.

Adolescent transitions can be different for the sexes. The change in status at adolescence is greater for Truk boys than for girls. All young people are regarded as adults once they have reached puberty. But boys typically move out of the house of their parents while a girl remains in her natal home until she marries. And girls, because they characteristically remain near home where other women are performing their household chores, are recruited into the work force at an earlier age than are boys. Thus, they have been gradually taking on adult responsibilities sooner than their brothers. Among the Arapaho, a girl was considered mature when she reached puberty. People did not think that a pubescent boy was mature. Thus, when a boy's voice changed, at anywhere between 14 and 17 years of age, he was no longer a child. But boys were not thought of as men until they were around 20 years of age. For a Brazilian Yanomamö girl, the transition to physical maturity is marked by her community. At her first menstruation, a girl is confined to her house for a week. Her old clothes are thrown away and she puts on new garments that have been made by her mother or older female friends. She is fed by relatives with a stick, the only way in which she is permitted to touch food during her seclusion. The girl must also scratch herself with sticks and not with her hands. Once her confinement is over, a girl is eligible to begin married life. The transition to physical maturity is not so clearly marked for Yanomamö boys. A male who is hoping to be recognized as an adult will begin to display anger when someone calls him by name, and when the adults of his village stop using his personal name, he knows that he has achieved adult male status. The transition is not abrupt.

Shifts to Old Age

The shift to old age also marks a major transition for people across cultures. In many societies, this transition is liberating for women because prohibitions upon their behavior are now lifted. For instance, before menopause, a North American Comanche woman was prevented from engaging in a variety of religious activities. As an old woman, by contrast, she was permitted to touch sacred objects, become a shaman, and obtain power from dreams. By contrast, the shift to old age was a difficult one for the Comanche man. While an adult male was ideally an aggressive, independent, energetic warrior who looked to his own interests as a sign of his status among men, an old man was expected to be wise, gentle, conciliatory, and indulgent of other people's needs. Men did not welcome the change, often preferring to die young in battle rather than suffer the indignities of being old. Sometimes, a man would try to retain the prerogatives of an adult male status by killing a younger man through bad magic. Aging Truk men and women experience a change in status that is reflected in their withdrawal from the productive activities in which they have formerly been involved. They are now dependent upon the generosity of their kin for their welfare. It is the decrease in physical stamina and mental agil-

ity that is responsible for the change in status of the elderly.

The shift to old age often means transferring power to the next generation. This may be accomplished grudgingly or with grace. In Africa, Nyoro society emphasizes the authority and power of older men over younger ones. As a result, a father can come to resent his own sons as potential usurpers of his power. The collision between older men, who wish to retain their power, and younger ones, who wish to acquire power, is recognized by the fact that the Nyoro transfer authority from father to son in a formal ceremony. After this, the heir is said to "become" his father, and his sisters' husbands now call him "father-in-law" as opposed to "brother-in-law." There is noticeable tension between members of different generations among the Guadalcanal Kaoka, in part because fathers and uncles resent the young men who will soon replace them and in part because the younger men resent the criticism and correction directed at them by males of the older generation. This mutual antagonism is communicated and also perhaps diffused by verbal duels in which younger and older men hurl obscenities at each other. A Tarong man does not view his maturing son as a potential threat to the older man's power base as long as the boy is willing to work along with his parents instead of trying to usurp authority prematurely. Similarly, a Palauan father may almost come to resent his maturing son as the younger man comes increasingly to threaten his authority. In Japan, a Takashima grandfather is the head of household and has seniority over all of the children and grandchildren who live with him. Nevertheless, a man does not typically resist turning over power to the next generation when he finds himself overtaxed by his responsibilities as the senior male of his family. Rather, he and his wife "retire," helping the next head of household and his wife to oversee the family's affairs. The old couple do whatever chores they can for the rest of their lives and are usually treated well by the younger members of the household.

Male versus Female Transitions

Shifts between stages in the life cycle can differ dramatically in content for males and females. While a Palauan mother is less indulgent of all of her older children, the withdrawal of attention is more abrupt in the case of sons. Girls, as a result, experience less emotional stress and throw fewer tantrums than their brothers at this time of life. Differences in the experience of males and females as they shift between stages also occur later in life. Thus, for example, a Truk man at 40 years of age is assumed to be at the peak of his intellectual and magical powers even though he is in physical decline. Therefore, he takes on new roles, especially those associated with magic, that require a considerable amount of responsibility. Because women are not as involved in esoteric activities, this shift toward greater responsibility is not as salient for them, and because they are never expected to do extremely heavy labor, their declining physical strength does not produce a dramatic alteration in their contribution to the welfare of the community.

See also ADOLESCENCE; CONTINUITY BETWEEN CHILDHOOD AND ADULTHOOD; PARENTS, CHILDREN'S TREATMENT OF

Barnett, H. G. (1960) *Being a Palauan.*

Beaglehole, Ernest, and Pearl Beaglehole. (1941) *Pangai: Village in Tonga.*

Beals, Alan R. (1962) *Gopalpur: A South Indian Village.*

Beattie, John. (1960) *Bunyoro: An African Kingdom.*

Chagnon, Napoleon A. (1983) *Yanomamö: The Fierce People.* 3rd ed.

Cohen, Yehudi A. (1966) *A Study of Interpersonal Relations in a Jamaican Community.*

Erchak, Gerald M. (1977) *Full Respect: Kpelle Children in Adaptation.*

Geertz, Hildred. (1961) *The Javanese Family: A Study of Kinship and Socialization.*

Gladwin, Thomas, and Seymour Sarason. (1953) *Truk: Man in Paradise.*

Goldman, Irving. (1963) *The Cubeo: Indians of the Northwest Amazon.*

Hilger, M. Inez. (1952) *Arapaho Child Life and Its Cultural Background.*

Hitchcock, John T., and Leigh Minturn. (1966) *The Rajputs of Khalapur, India.*

Hogbin, Ian. (1964) *A Guadalcanal Society: The Kaoka Speakers.*

Maretzki, Thomas W., and Hatsumi Maretzki. (1966) *Taira: An Okinawan Village.*

Norbeck, Edward. (1954) *Takashima: A Japanese Fishing Village.*

Nydegger, William F., and Corinne Nydegger. (1966) *Tarong: An Ilocos Barrio in the Philippines.*

Piker, Steven. (1965) *An Examination of Character and Socialization in a Thai Peasant Community.*

Ray, Verne. (1933) *The Sanpoil and the Nespelem: Salishan Peoples of Northeastern Washington.*

Romney, A. Kimball, and Romaine Romney. (1966) *The Mixtecans of Juxtlahuaca, Mexico.*

Stephens, William N. (1963) *The Family in Cross-Cultural Perspective.*

Thompson, Laura, and Alice Joseph. (1947) *The Hopi Way.*

Wagley, Charles. (1949) "The Social and Religious Life of a Guatemalan Village." *American Anthropologist* 51: 3–150.

Wallace, Ernest, and E. Adamson Hoebel. (1952) *The Comanches: Lords of the South Plains.*

Whiting, John W. M., Eleanor Chasdi, Helen Antonovsky, and Barbara Ayres. (1966) "The Learning of Values." In *The People of Rimrock: A Study of Values in Five Cultures,* edited by Evon Z. Vogt and Ethel M. Albert, 83–125.

DOMINANCE

Children who display dominant behavior attempt to get some other person to satisfy their needs and do so in an assertive or commanding way. Even when children do display dominance, this is not the most characteristic way in which they are likely to attempt to get other people to do things for them. Rather, youngsters most typically try to get their needs met through dependent behavior, which is a more supplicating style of interaction. Nevertheless, dominance also shows up as a behavioral style across cultures.

Dominance appears to be a natural response of older children to children who are somewhat younger and smaller. Thus, when an older child is interacting with a younger one, we see a higher than usual proportion of attempts on the part of the older child to be dominant. Adults across cultures have discovered that it is hard to train older children to resist the temptation to dominate younger ones. Indeed, in many cultures, adults expect older children to try to dominate smaller ones and they also expect children to settle disputes of this sort on their own. Parents in some cultures also expect older children to have authority over younger ones and to get a greater share of most resources over which youngsters might fight. In places where parents disapprove of dominating behavior on the part of older children, for instance in American communities where egalitarianism, fairness, taking turns, and the like may be valued, adults may attempt to interfere with dominance ploys on the part of older children, but not always successfully. Even in cultures where dominance on the part of older children is accepted, parents may expect older children to protect younger siblings from any threats from unrelated children. Younger children are not typically discouraged by the dominance ploys of older children. Across cultures, four- and five-year-olds continue to follow the older children around even though the younger children are bossed around, teased, roughhoused, and sometimes even hurt by the older ones. Younger boys seem to be particularly motivated to be with somewhat older children of their own sex. They want to do what the older children are doing.

Battles for dominance tend to occur cross-culturally between unrelated children of the same age. This is even more likely to be the case when children attend school, and especially in schools that segregate children by age. The goal appears to be to establish a rough dominance hierarchy among youngsters of more or less equal status. Detailed studies of schoolchildren in America indicate that a six- or seven-year-old boy can already accurately indicate who has power over whom in his own class. Thus, young boys are already aware of and can correctly report the dominance hierarchy that has arisen among their peers.

In cultures where a dominant style may be useful in adulthood, parents may encourage dominant behavior in their children. Among the Rajputs of India, the relative status between individuals determines patterns of dominance and submissiveness. A person obeys anyone of superior status and is dominant over anyone whose status is inferior. Parents, therefore, value dominant behavior in their children and prefer their youngsters to be bossy with their peers as this reflects leadership and intelligence on the part of the child. Dominance in children is also relatively high in some American communities. Mothers in this case may be more indulgent of dominance in their children because this style is likely to be useful to youngsters who live in a society based upon achievement and competition. Dominance by boys over girls may also be encouraged or expected in some societies. This is the case among the Gusii of Kenya, where any boy who has reached adolescence has the right to dominate a female. Similarly, in Mexico, a Mixtecan male is assumed to be dominant over all females, and a four-year-old girl may be ordered to "fetch a chair for the man" who turns out to be a three-year-old boy.

In some cultures, children direct dominance toward their mothers. This is more likely to occur in societies where mothers themselves are controlling and dominating. These are also mothers who do not work outside the home. This may mean that children in these cultures are more likely to be underfoot more often, causing mothers to make attempts to control their behavior. Further, efforts to control children increase as the noise and activity level in the house increases, especially when youngsters begin to fight. Dominance struggles are more common between mothers and sons than between mothers and daughters. Further, there is evidence that battles between mothers and sons increase when children are four or five years of age.

The consistent trend across cultures is for older children to dominate younger ones and for children, and especially boys, of the same age to engage in dominance struggles. We may be seeing here the human version of the more general tendency for animals to form dominance hierarchies. Such hierarchies appear in many species and are also characteristic of many nonhuman primates. Dominance hierarchies help to determine which animals will have access to the best mates, best territories, best food, and so on. Children may be naturally inclined to accept dominant and submissive roles when there is a clear inequality of size and competence between a pair of youngsters and to struggle for a dominant position when the status of the children is ostensibly more equal.

Hitchcock, John T., and Leigh Minturn. (1966) *The Rajputs of Khalapur, India.*

Whiting, Beatrice B., and Carolyn Pope Edwards. (1988) *Children of Different Worlds: The Formation of Social Behavior.*

Whiting, Beatrice B., and John W. M. Whiting. (1975) *Children of Six Cultures: A Psycho-Cultural Analysis.*

A primary responsibility of parents is to see that their children are adequately nourished. This is easier in some societies than in others, and in some places around the world, children sometimes go hungry. Diets are not only more adequate but also more varied some places than in others, and mealtimes are sometimes more formally defined and sometimes less so. Children are pressured to learn to eat by themselves at an early age in some societies, while in others, training to eat without help is more relaxed. Sooner or later, parents also begin to expect their children to mind their manners at meals.

Diet

In Kenya, if a Gusii mother does not have time to prepare breakfast, the children will eat leftovers such as sweet potatoes, bananas, cooked squash, dry corn, or porridge. If a child is hungry in the morning, an older sister may cook some food, or another woman may provide something to eat. But a mother who has left home in a hurry in the morning is likely to come back before lunchtime and fix the children a meal. Lunch is usually boiled sweet potatoes or dry porridge seasoned with beans, curdled milk, meat, or spinachlike leaves. Similarly, dinner consists of dry porridge with or without the same seasonings. Because the children's diet is so heavily dependent upon starch, they end up with bloated stomachs. Among the Mixtecans of Mexico, everyone who is more than a few months of age eats corn and beans every day. Meat is only eaten at fiestas, which occur about once a week, and no one has bread except on festive occasions. People eat fruits as a snack between meals. Tomatoes are added to sauces, squash is cooked and eaten as a vegetable or it may be garnished with brown sugar and eaten as a sweet. Among the Tarong of the Philippines, rice is served at every meal and is seasoned with a vegetable sauce and pickled fish, ginger, or hot peppers. Usually, a little meat or fish will be added to the sauce a few times a week at dinner. Fresh fruit is often served for dessert. A number of families may gather on a porch or under a tree to chat while eating an afternoon snack. Children may then have some cold rice or other leftovers. In a North American Fox household, the women are the first to wake up. They get the fire going and cook breakfast. The children get out of bed after the adults, and everyone eats shortly after six in the morning. Breakfast is a light meal, consisting of coffee and tea, bacon, boiled corn or potatoes, and fried or baked bread. Lunch, which is eaten sometime between eleven and two o'clock, is similar to breakfast. The most important meal is served at around seven or eight o'clock in the evening and includes the same foods that are eaten at other meals, along with some extras.

Sometimes, children begin to eat a normal adult diet as soon as they are able to chew solid food. In other cultures, however, a young child is given special food. North American Arapaho children were fed meat as soon as they could chew because meat made youngsters "strong and robust." Children who ate meat did not become sick easily. North American Sanpoil children were not allowed to eat deer bone marrow. Otherwise, they would become weak and would not be able to run uphill. Rather, they ate meat and fish from the part of the animal that had been speared. This would enable them to become strong and to survive wounds. In North America, Zuni children were allowed to eat anything that they wished, including coffee, once they were able to reach for their own food at the table. But a separate portion was prepared for a youngster if the adults were eating highly seasoned food. Even small children, however, soon began to enjoy chili and other hot food. Japanese children already begin eating bits of food during meals while still nursing. When they are weaned, they begin to eat more. A newly weaned infant is not given any special foods, and some children become finicky about food once they are weaned. Mothers occasionally try to bribe youngsters to eat by giving them sweets. Once a Jamaican baby is weaned, at about a year of age, its diet consists of sweetened black tea at breakfast, the same for lunch, porridge or mash in the afternoon, and black tea again for dinner. When a youngster can chew, roasted yam or corn cob is added. Children begin to have meat once a week beginning at three or four years of age. This is also the normal allotment of meat for adults.

In some cultures, children are hungry at least some of the time. Gusii mothers regard the feeding of their children as their first responsibility. Nevertheless, a youngster may go hungry if the mother needs to leave home in a hurry in the morning to join her work group or if the family is running out of grain foods in July and August before the new harvest. In India, Rajput children often complain that they have not had enough to eat, and mothers use food as a reward for good behavior. The Sebei of Uganda have their main meal in the late afternoon or early evening. Breakfast consists of leftovers from the previous day. Children are left to their own de-

vices during the day and are often hungry. The school tries to alleviate the problem by providing the children with porridge and sugar. Jamaican children beg for more food when a meal is over, and parents know that their youngsters are still hungry. But adults do not want their children to get used to having a "full tummy" for fear that they will then be discontented when there isn't enough food. Youngsters typically suck their fingers when a meal is over. A young child who cries for more food is ignored. An older one is flogged. Once they are five or six years of age, Jamaican children begin to hoard tidbits of food in the event of a particularly unsatisfying meal. In Indonesia, an Alorese mother returns to the field two weeks or less after the birth of her baby. The infant is fed premasticated food by a caretaker or else may on occasion be nursed by another woman. Children are weaned when they begin to walk, and from then on, they are forced to wait for the mother to return to be fed. As women stay in the fields for as long as nine hours a day, youngsters become quite hungry. No one pays much attention to their crying, and children end up begging for food during the day.

When food shortages are a fact of life for a culture, adults may ration supplies for older children and adults but still try to make sure that younger children have a more adequate diet. When food is running low, Gusii adults will limit their intake and so will children over five years of age. But younger children are fed normally, in part because they will nag their mothers otherwise and in part because they "do not understand." Sometimes, children will fight over scarce food. In Ecuador, Jivaro children often steal meat from each other. This is in part because meat is scarce in Jivaro households and also because adults do not like to give children large portions of meat on one occasion for fear that they will be upset when the portion is by necessity smaller the next time around. Children also take meat and peanuts without permission, for which they are scolded or spanked. Adults in societies where food shortages are a source of concern will try to stop children from squandering food resources. Zuni parents warned children not to waste food, and especially corn. Children were told that "corn will cry if you leave it outside," and the people believed that if food was wasted, they would be hungry.

Meals

In some cultures, more or less predictable mealtimes are observed, while in others people just eat when they are hungry. Families may have meals together. Or members of a households may eat separately. A Tarong family will eat three full meals each day if there is a child who is attending school. Otherwise, people substitute snacks for the third meal. Family members are most likely to eat together at dinner. Other meals are taken on the run if the workload is heavy or if there are special school activities to attend. Everyone eats in the kitchen, kneeling around a low table or placing the dishes on the floor. Meals are eaten with the fingers. Among the Fox of North America, if the household is small, everyone eats together. If there are many men in the family, they will eat first. Everyone sits on the ground, and the dishes of food are placed on a mat. Mealtime is very informal. People may eat from their own plates or share a plate. Sometimes, members of the family will simply eat from the serving dish. Meanwhile, conversation shifts from one topic to the next. North American Sanpoil children ate with the family unless there were strangers present. In that case, the youngsters ate later. Everyone sat around the food mat, the children usually next to their mother as it was her job to serve them. Among the Guadalcanal Kaoka, dinner is the only formal meal. Children will help themselves to the vegetables that their mother leaves in a basket before she goes off to tend to her chores. Any leftover fish that the father has brought home on the previous night will also placed in the basket, along with some roasted yams. Older girls

and boys who will be away from the house for the day take their share of food along with them and eat it cold. Supper is served a little before dark and always includes yams, taro, or sweet potatoes. Fish is also included if it is available. Otherwise, the mother cooks some greens or roasts nuts. The children sit on their beds and eat from their own dishes if enough are available. Otherwise, everyone gathers in a circle near the mother and eats from a few large bowls. The father will join his children if he is home. Or food will be set aside for him. Women generally wait to eat until after everyone else is finished.

In some societies, members of a family eat a meal or two together, but adults and children then rely on snacks at other times during the day. The North American Comanche usually had a formal meal in the morning and a main meal in the evening. During the day, both adults and children ate when they wished, if food was available. In the South Seas, Javanese families eat one large meal each day, usually at noon or sunset and supplemented by a number of snacks eaten informally and at irregular times throughout the day. Households usually have food sitting on a shelf, and members of the family take what they wish when they are hungry. It is unlikely that everyone in the family will be eating at the same time, and children are almost always snacking throughout the day. For the Rajputs, eating is a not a family affair. A man has his meals in the men's quarters or at his own hearth in the women's courtyard. A woman has her meals alone in her own room in the women's quarters, or she may eat in the corner of the courtyard facing away from the other women. Children are fed when they ask for food and may eat alone or with other youngsters, depending upon who happens to be eating when. Adults also eat when they are hungry and do not wait for specified mealtimes.

In some societies, there are no formal meals. This is true, for instance, among the Canadian Hare. Everyone eats a large meal twice a day and people snack on whatever is around when they are hungry. Children may eat candy, chewing gum, or bannock between meals. Sometimes, a child will go seven or eight hours without eating. This may happen, for instance, when children are playing at another house and have missed the meals at home and at the household that they are visiting. A mother who realizes that this has happened will give her child a large meal upon the youngster's return.

Often, young children will be fed on demand even though older children and adults eat on schedule. Thus, Gusii mothers will feed a child whenever asked unless the youngster's stomach is grossly distended. When a woman is home during the day, she will cook for the children whenever they ask for food. Rajput children often nag their mothers for food before it is ready to be served, and women try to keep bread and rice available for youngsters to munch on while they are waiting for a meal. In Micronesia, a Truk child is expected to eat when hungry, and parents do not expect their children to appear at mealtime. But youngsters who have failed to come and eat for some length of time because they have become distracted will be scolded or punished. They will also have trouble finding food for themselves if they don't come to eat when summoned, as an adult who is busy at some chore is not interested in stopping to round up food for a tardy youngster. In Guatemala, Chimalteco adults say that children under six years of age are always hungry. For this reason, they do not generally eat with the rest of the family. Rather, they have a number of meals on their own, scattered throughout the day.

Independence Training

Parents in some cultures encourage their children to learn to feed themselves at an early age.

A Japanese mother and son enjoy a meal together.

Until then, a child may eat with everyone else but be fed by an adult. By one year of age, a Japanese Takashima baby has joined the rest of the family at meals, sitting on its mother's lap to eat. Among the Tarong, little children are held and fed by an adult. Once they are one or two years old, children will be encouraged to eat by themselves. Youngsters become good at eating on their own by the time they are three years of age. Until then, mothers become irritated because their children tend to spill and thus waste rice as they attempt to get it into their mouths with their fingertips.

In other cultures, there is less pressure on children to eat on their own. Rajput children can typically feed themselves before the second birthday. But some mothers are still inclined to feed their children, perhaps because it is more convenient. The Rajputs also believe that food that is left around becomes polluted and cannot be eaten. Since the messy and inefficient eating habits of little children can cause food to become polluted, mothers may be trying to circumvent this problem by feeding young children themselves. In Indonesia, Javanese mothers are anxious to have their children eat a healthy diet, and a woman may feed her youngsters until they are five or six years old to see that they eat not only their protein soybean cake but also their rice. Children, however, are not forced to eat food that they do not want, and a youngster who is busy playing is allowed to skip a meal.

Parents are also concerned with teaching appropriate table manners. Chimalteco adults say that a good mother will teach her children to eat properly when they are about two years old. In fact, mothers wait longer than this. Eventually children learn to use three fingers when dipping their tortillas and not to drip food on the face. A youngster also learns to let an older person sit on the more desirable bench and to thank older people for the food that the child eats. A mother teaches her children good manners so that neighbors will not say that she is a bad parent. A Hare mother expects a child to eat without spilling her food by three years of age. If a little girl drops food on her clothing, her mother will say: "Look at your dress!" As soon as they are able to eat porridge, Jamaican children are given spoons and expected to eat without any adult intervention. Youngsters learn to manipulate silverware quickly, shoveling large amounts of food onto their spoons. Parents regularly chastise their children for eating like gluttons, but youngsters persist in eating this way when no one is looking. Children tend to be noisy during meals, jumping on furniture and throwing food at each other, with the result that in many families, they are required to eat separately from the adults. Kaoka parents tell their children to sit facing the center of the house when they eat so that no one will suspect them of squirreling away bits of food. Youngsters are warned not to gobble at meals or to ask for food from other people unless they are at the home of an aunt or uncle. Further, children are instructed to eat all of the food offered to them, or else to explain why they cannot finish a bit of food and then to offer it to some other person. In Okinawa, a Tairan baby is given its own spoon at about one year of age, months before weaning is likely to begin. When babies make a mess as they try to feed themselves, they may be mildly scolded, but they are also encouraged with hugs. Once they reach about two years of age, children are praised for eating neatly although sloppiness is still tolerated. Everyone at the dinner table makes a fuss over the child as he tries to eat.

Barry, Herbert, III, and Leonora Paxson. (1971) "Infancy and Childhood: Cross-Cultural Codes 2." *Ethnology* 10: 466–508.

Benedict, Ruth. (1946) *The Chrysanthemum and the Sword.*

Cohen, Yehudi A. (1966) *A Study of Interpersonal Relations in a Jamaican Community.*

Geertz, Hildred. (1961) *The Javanese Family: A Study of Kinship and Socialization.*

Gladwin, Thomas, and Seymour Sarason. (1953) *Truk: Man in Paradise.*

Goldschmidt, Walter. (1976) *The Culture and Behavior of the Sebei.*

Hara, Hiroko Sue. (1967) *Hare Indians and Their World.*

Harner, Michael J. (1973) *The Jivaro: People of the Sacred Waterfalls.*

Hilger, M. Inez. (1952) *Arapaho Child Life and Its Cultural Background.*

Hogbin, Ian. (1964) *A Guadalcanal Society: The Kaoka Speakers.*

Jones, William. (1939) *Ethnography of the Fox Indians.*

Leighton, Dorothea, and John Adair. (1966) *People of the Middle Place: A Study of the Zuni Indians.*

LeVine, Robert A., and Barbara B. LeVine. (1966) *Nyansongo: A Gusii Community in Kenya.*

Maretzki, Thomas W., and Hatsumi Maretzki. (1966) *Taira: An Okinawan Village.*

Minturn, Leigh, and John T. Hitchcock. (1966) *The Rajputs of Khalapur, India.*

Munroe, Robert L., and Ruth H. Munroe. (1975) *Cross-Cultural Human Development.*

Norbeck, Edward. (1954) *Takashima: A Japanese Fishing Community.*

Nydegger, William F., and Corinne Nydegger. (1966) *Tarong: An Ilocos Barrio in the Philippines.*

Ray, Verne. (1933) *The Sanpoil and the Nespelem: Salishan Peoples of Northeastern Washington.*

Romney, A. Kimball, and Romaine Romney. (1966) *The Mixtecans of Juxtlahuaca, Mexico.*

Wagley, Charles. (1949) "The Social and Religious Life of a Guatemalan Village." *American Anthropologist* 51: 3–150.

Wallace, Ernest, and E. Adamson Hoebel. (1952) *The Comanches: Lords of the South Plains.*

EMOTIONAL EXPRESSION

Cultures differ dramatically in their attitudes toward the expression of emotions in children. The Tarong of the Philippines believe that children should express their feelings so that "we can know what is their emotion." Youngsters are most likely to show their feelings to other members of the family. By contrast, in India, Rajput mothers attempt to train even small children to avoid open expressions of emotion. Women will try to calm children down when they become too excited or angry or when they laugh or cry too much, and a youngster may be punished for crying even when physically hurt. Cultures may also tolerate the expression of some emotions more than others. Thus, Tarong mothers do not generally approve of the overt display of aggression. Crying, on the other hand, is acceptable, and most mothers think that it is better for children to cry than to try to control themselves if something is wrong.

Fear and anger are the two emotions that are most commonly encouraged or suppressed in children. In New Mexico, Zuni children and adults alike were afraid of witches, and a Zuni woman would not display anger toward another person whom she believed to be a witch for fear of antagonizing her. Mothers taught their children never to show anger, even if they were very enraged, and even if they were in the right. In Thailand, by contrast, Banoi youngsters become accustomed to venting their anger openly early on in life. A baby who does not immediately get its way will predictably hit out at the person who is the cause of its frustration, and this open expression of hostility remains common through the childhood years. Infants and little children are not punished for displaying their anger, even when this means repeatedly hitting another child or adult. Jamaican children also regularly have fits of rage, often because they want more food than parents are willing to provide for them. Adults ignore these tantrums, saying that they cannot do anything to satisfy the child. Thus, it only makes sense to let the youngster "cry it out." Mothers also say that it is useless to respond to crying because children often just cry for no reason. They just feel like it. Infants can continue to cry without stopping for an entire hour and not attract any attention. A very young baby may be picked up and held for a few minutes, but it will then be put down again where it will continue to thrash and scream.

Sometimes, a particular emotion becomes the characteristic response across situations in a given culture, and this tendency may have its origins in child training. West Malaysian Semai adults and children alike exhibit fear toward a wide variety of events, and this tendency to be fearful is strongly reinforced beginning early in life. Thus, for example, the Semai of Malaysia believe that the violent thunderstorms that occur on an almost daily basis are caused by the supernatural in response to evil actions of human beings and especially to the ill treatment of animals. When a storm hits, the elders begin to chant to the supernatural, imploring him to save the village. As the storm draws closer, everyone becomes more terrified, and children are interrogated in case they have committed some offense to cause the storm. If a child confesses to a misdeed, a clump of his hair is cut off and burned as a compensation to the supernatural, and often, hair from all of the children is cut off in case some youngster has unknowingly committed some evil act. If the storm continues, people become more and more frantic and may begin to run into the forest. Children, as a result, see

terror in other people and experience terror themselves on a daily basis in response to these storms. Adults similarly encourage children to fear strangers. When some unknown person approaches a mother and baby, the woman will hold the infant tightly, bury its head in her chest, and cry "afraid, afraid." The child's fear of strangers is reinforced by the Semai idea of the bogeyman, a stranger said to come to collect Semai heads. Semai adults encourage children to fear many other things; for instance, fire and heights. Indeed, the goal seems to be to promote timidity as a general virtue.

Even where the open expression of emotions is not generally approved, adults may allow young children more leeway than they do older children. Among the Rajputs, who disapprove of the expression of aggression, outbursts of anger and even hitting directed toward a mother, aunt, or grandmother are sometimes tolerated in small children, and the adult may simply give in to the child in order to keep the peace. Similarly, in Micronesia, Truk children are expected to learn to control any outward signs of emotion once they reach adolescence. Crying is especially discouraged. But crying in younger children is more tolerated, and smaller children will still cry if they are seriously upset.

Attitudes toward emotional expression in children are associated with other features of culture. In a study of four East African societies, emotional expression was related to the way in which people in a culture made a living. Thus, in farming communities, the expression of emotions such as aggression, sadness, and depression is suppressed. By contrast, people who live in pastoral settings are more willing to display their emotions in the presence of others. This difference may be a result of the extent to which the expression of emotions might interfere with interpersonal relationships. Agriculturalists are sedentary. Further, people who live in farming communities often depend upon each other to cooperate in enterprises that are hard to accomplish by single households. Perhaps the unwillingness to show emotion serves the purpose of keeping the peace where people need one another and are unable to leave the scene in case of ill feelings. Pastoralists, by contrast, lead more independent lives. The pastoral life also allows an individual to pick up and move if necessary. In such a setting, ill will between people resulting from the open display of emotions is less likely to interfere with a person's way of life.

See also CRYING

Cohen, Yehudi A. (1966) *A Study of Interpersonal Relations in a Jamaican Community.*

Dentan, Robert. (1978) "Notes on Childhood in a Nonviolent Context: The Semai Case." In *Learning and Non-Aggression,* edited by Ashley Montagu, 94–143.

Edgerton, Robert B. (1971) *The Individual in Cultural Adaptation: A Study of Four East African Peoples.*

Henderson, Ronald W., and John R. Bergan. (1976) *The Cultural Context of Childhood.*

Gladwin, Thomas, and Seymour Sarason. (1953) *Truk: Man in Paradise.*

Hitchcock, John T., and Leigh Minturn. (1966) *The Rajputs of Khalapur, India.*

Leighton, Dorothea, and John Adair. (1966) *People of the Middle Place: A Study of the Zuni Indians.*

Nydegger, William F., and Corinne Nydegger. (1966) *Tarong: An Ilocos Barrio in the Philippines.*

Piker, Steven. (1965) *An Examination of Character and Socialization in a Thai Peasant Community.*

Robarchek, Clayton. (1979) "Learning To Fear: A Case Study of Emotional Conditioning." *American Ethnologist* 6: 555–567.

EVOLUTION OF HUMAN DEVELOPMENT

While child-rearing practices as well as the experiences of growing children differ widely across cultures, human infants the world over are born more or less the same. Differences in child-rearing techniques across societies are in part responses to the practical constraints that social circumstances place upon parents, including family and household form, modes of making a living, climate, size of community and the like. But characteristics of human infants as well as the human developmental trajectory evolved in a particular kind of cultural context, that of savannah hunter-gatherers, and evolutionary theory reminds us that these are the characteristics that remain with us today. So it is important to take the evolutionary baseline into account when we think about the patterning and consequences of child-rearing practices across cultures, because child-rearing techniques and environments that depart from those of our early ancestors may represent departures from the original human adaptation. In fact, American child-rearing practices display wide divergences from the hunter-gatherer baseline.

While it is impossible to be certain about the child-rearing techniques of our remote ancestors, we do have information about children's experiences in contemporary hunter-gatherer societies. The !Kung of the Kalahari are believed by some social scientists to be a model of our evolutionary past because they continue to live as hunter-gatherers in an environment similar to the one in which humans are thought to have evolved. How, then, is child rearing patterned among this hunter-gatherer group?

Among the !Kung, a woman has a baby approximately every four years. This birth spacing is large by cross-cultural standards. Spacing is partly a product of the long period of nursing, which may be four years or more and is also longer than the cross-cultural median and much longer than the American average even for women who nurse. As is typical across cultures, !Kung babies nurse many times each hour. This is characteristic of many cultures but considerably more frequent than we find among American babies, who may be nursed once every two hours at the most. The practice of frequent nursing among the !Kung is made easier by the fact that infants are carried around in a sling by their mothers during the day and sleep with them at night. Thus, an infant remains on the mother's hip, chest, or back while she is working, even when it is fast asleep. By contrast, an American infant spends most of its time in a crib, cradle, or playpen. This difference in the disposition of the baby means that American infants experience considerably less physical, sensory, and cognitive stimulation than their hunter-gatherer counterparts. They have less body contact with another individual as well as less vestibular stimulation. American infants spend most of their time lying down, whereas hunter-gatherer babies remain in a vertical position for most of the time. American infants generally find themselves looking up at the world and the people in it, while hunter-gatherer babies are at eye level with the people they meet. Further, !Kung babies, as well as infants in many other cultures, go to sleep while in physical contact with some other individual, in contrast to the experience of the typical American baby, who is put to sleep in a bed of its own. The difficulties that American parents experience as infants protest at bedtime reflect the unusual custom of expecting a baby to go to sleep without the benefit of human contact.

!Kung peer groups also differ significantly from those of American groups and also from peer groups in many other cultures. Because the !Kung live in small camps of perhaps 25 to 30 people, a particular child is unlikely to have even one other child of the same age and sex in the same camp. Thus, children aggregate in mixed-sex and mixed-age groups. This has interesting

consequences for the !Kung child. For instance, !Kung children tend not to play competitive games, as competition with a much older or much younger child is not particularly interesting. Rather, !Kung games stress improving one's own performance across time. Neither do !Kung children engage in what is called parallel play, that is, play in which children are sitting together and playing, but not with each other. Parallel play is characteristic of American toddlers and is viewed as a natural developmental phenomenon by psychologists. But a !Kung toddler usually plays in the company of older children, who can engage the child in common activities in a way that another two-year-old cannot. It is also possible that !Kung children's groups are more effective training grounds for children than are the same-age peer groups that characterize an American child's experience. Mixed groups allow older children to become accustomed to taking care of younger children, and they provide younger children with a variety of caretakers. Participation in a mixed peer group allows a youngster to integrate more easily into a social group and provides a child with models that he or she can more easily copy. Across cultures, youngsters are most attracted to and want most to attach themselves to children a little older than themselves. The mixed peer group gives them the opportunity to do so.

!Kung child rearing is also more indulgent than are the practices found in many other cultures. Thus, !Kung parents inflict less pain on their infants and exert less pressure on their children to be responsible, obedient, or self-reliant. This is in part because !Kung children are not required to do many tasks or to practice adult roles. !Kung parents are also more indulgent than parents in other cultures when it comes to toilet training, and they score very high on amount of contact between mothers and infants, as well as on response to crying.

The !Kung are a fully modern people. But they are also a hunting-gathering culture and are understood to represent the kind of setting in which our species evolved. To the extent that this assumption is justified, we can speculate that human infants have evolved to expect prolonged and very frequent nursing, relatively continuous contact with a caretaker, and an eye-level view of the world. Human children may also have evolved to function in mixed-age and mixed-sex groups that emphasize achievement over competition and that provide younger children with slightly older and more proficient role models. Children who live in a hunter-gatherer culture also interact in quite small groups of well-known people who are often relations, and a hunter-gatherer may meet no more than 500 people in a lifetime. Developmental psychologists remind us that human children are very resilient. That is, they tolerate dramatic variations in treatment while still managing to thrive. So divergences between the patterning of childhood in a hunter-gatherer world and childhood experiences in other kinds of cultures are clearly capable of producing happy, capable children and adults. However, an appreciation of the hunter-gatherer baseline can also provide clues regarding the ways in which children's environments differ from those of our ancestors and what those differences might mean for a child's developmental profile.

See also ACHIEVEMENT; BIRTH SPACING; COMPETITION AND COOPERATION; INFANTS, AFFECTIONATE TREATMENT OF; INFANTS, INDULGENCE OF; NURSING; SOCIALIZATION, AGENTS OF

Konner, Melvin J. (1981) "Evolution of Human Behavior Development." In *Handbook of Cross-Cultural Human Development*, edited by Ruth H. Munroe, Robert L. Munroe, and Beatrice B. Whiting, 3–51.

Textor, Robert B. (1967) *A Cross-Cultural Summary*.

The role of fathers in the lives of their children varies widely from one society to the next. In some cultures, a father rarely spends time with his child, while in others, fathers and children enjoy a close companionship. Fathers may routinely care for babies and children or a man may only be available for playing. Children may be expected to show considerable deference toward their fathers or the relationship between father and child may be friendly and intimate.

Minimal Role for Fathers

In a majority of societies, fathers do not play a significant role in the lives of their young children. Fathers never or only rarely interact with infants in 22 percent of 87 cultures around the world and interact with babies irregularly or only occasionally in an additional 38 percent of these societies. Thus, for example, in Kenya, it is rare to find a Gusii man paying attention to an infant. Fathers play no active role in caring for their young children, and paternal involvement is confined to such acts as occasionally telling the child nurse to get food for the baby or fetching medicine for a sick child. Fathers do not participate in any hands-on caretaking of infants. One Gusii mother observed that, if her husband were alone at home with his son and heard that a beer party was in progress, he would go off and leave his baby alone at home. Similarly, in Mexico, Mixtecan fathers do not spend much time with their younger children. During the day, they are generally in the fields. A man who does happen to be at home is usually occupied with business, so that even then his children do not receive attention from him. Indeed, fathers are not expected to contribute to the caretaking of their children. In Okinawa, Tairans view child rearing as women's work. Fathers are also away at work for most of the day, and when they come home for lunch, the children are usually off somewhere playing. As a result, a Tairan father spends minimal time with his children. A man may allow a child to accompany him to a party or to sit on his lap, but as soon as the youngster begins to become fussy, the mother or an older sibling is summoned to take over. Kindergartners will go to their fathers for help, but the youngsters are quickly sent off to look for their mothers instead. Schoolchildren are actually somewhat fearful of their fathers and a child of this age tries to remain unobtrusive when the father is at home. In Java a father is only a sporadic figure in the life of a baby. He may carry an infant on occasion when the mother is busy, but it is the mother who is the center of the baby's life.

Larger Role for Fathers

In some cultures, by contrast, men do have a considerable role in their children's lives. A father interacts frequently with his baby in 37 percent of 87 cultures around the world and enjoys a close relationship with his baby in an additional 3 percent of these cultures. When a New Ireland Lesu baby begins to walk, everyone in the family, but especially the father, is responsible for its care when the mother is away. A father is often seen in front of his house or on the beach petting and playing with his infant while his wife is busy with her chores. Men play with their babies for hours on end. In Canada, Hare fathers will change a baby's diaper, give it a bottle, rock it in its hammock, or bounce it on a knee. A father may also care for the baby in the mother's absence. The amount of caretaking expected of a Philippine Tarong father depends upon the number of other people in the household who can help the mother tend to her children. If there are a number of older girls in the house, a man will probably do little more than play with a baby and occasionally carry the youngster about. If few other caretakers are available, a father may hold the baby whenever he is not away at work and he will also feed, bathe, and change an infant. Caretaking of infants is not considered to be only women's work, and a grandfather is as likely to tend a baby as is the grandmother. One Tarong man was inseparable from his young grandson, carrying the youngster about with him whenever he was not working in the fields. The grandfather was heartbroken when the boy's mother took the child away on an extended trip until he substituted his just-weaned little niece for his grandson.

Older Children

Fathers are more likely to spend time with a child who is past infancy. Sometimes, men only begin to have extended contact with youngsters who have arrived at late childhood or adolescence. Thus, for example, among the Javanese in Indonesia, by the time a child begins walking, the father becomes a much more salient influence. Men now play, feed, bathe, and supervise their children and cuddle them until they fall asleep. A five-year-old son may go along when his father is calling on a friend. Among the Mixtecans of Mexico, sons who are twelve years of age or older accompany their fathers to the field every day and also begin to take part in the affairs of adult men more generally. An older boy, there-

fore, can expect to spend a significant amount of time each day with his father. A Jamaican father avoids having anything to do with his children until they are around ten years old. This is true even when he is at home on Sundays during the rainy season. Children who try to accompany their fathers outside of the home are severely chastised, and men explicitly state that they want nothing to do with children of this age. Children are nevertheless motivated to follow their fathers about. It is less likely, however, that a child over ten years of age will be shooed away. Among the Chimalteco of Mexico, a ten-year-old boy is now spending most of his time with his father, learning the skills that will be required of him as a man. A boy of this age is accorded the treatment of someone who is almost an adult, working for the same number of hours as an adult but being somewhat less skilled. A son now works in the fields with his father and learns also where and how to find and gather firewood. He also goes along with his father while the older man performs ritual ceremonies. Fathers are also accompanied by their sons on trips to the markets where corn is sold. Meanwhile, a Chimalteco girl is receiving the same kind of training from her mother. Fathers continue to play little or no role in the lives of young children past infancy in 11 percent of 93 cultures around the world. Men play an occasional or irregular role in the lives of their young children in 22 percent of these cultures. Men interact frequently with their young children in 57 percent of these societies and enjoy a close relationship with young children past infancy in 9 percent of these cultures.

The amount of time that a father spends with his children is predicted in part by geographic area. The salience of fathers in their children's lives is relatively high in East Asia and the insular Pacific, moderate in the Americas, and low in Africa and the circum-Mediterranean. A father is also more likely to play a relatively large role in the child's life where descent is traced either through the mother or through both parents and where marriage is monogamous or only occasionally polygynous. A father typically plays a limited role in a boy's life where sons are segregated from their families at adolescence and where circumcision is practiced at puberty.

Play

While fathers in many cultures avoid routine caretaking tasks, many more will play with their babies. In Thailand, Banoi fathers are often in or around the house when it is not working season, and a man will often play with an infant or hold it in his lap while gossiping with visitors. A fussing, crying, or restless infant, however, will quickly be handed back to its mother. In Micronesia, a Palauan father will play with his infant when he feels like it. A father may also tend to a baby when no one else is available, and men are gentle and patient with infants. But it is also understood that caretaking is not a father's role. It is the mother who is expected to feed, bathe, soothe, and love a baby. Mixtecan fathers can be playful and affectionate with their children, especially the younger ones. But fathers do not routinely take care of babies. In some societies, fathers do not even play with their children. In Uganda, Sebei fathers do not take care of or play with their children, and anyone who witnessed a man holding a baby would assume that there was some special reason for his doing so. A Gusii father does not play with his children. He does not feed his child or try to make a hurt youngster feel better. Nor do fathers show their children any physical affection.

Father as Disciplinarian

In many societies, the relationship between a man and his children is affected by his role as disciplinarian. Often, children are expected to show respect to their fathers, and this too influences the tone and content of their interactions. Gusii youngsters are afraid of their fathers, and the relationship of a man to his children sustains this fear. Children are expected to defer to their fathers so that, for example, a child will not eat from the father's bowl until given permission to do so. Gusii boys are beaten by their fathers for failing to take care of the cattle properly. A father will also demand that the mother withhold food from a child as punishment for some misdeed. Among the Chimalteco of Mexico, the father has absolute authority over the women and children of a family, and anyone who opposes his wishes will be punished by God. Fathers often threaten to whip their small sons, but they rarely do so in fact. A Mexican Tepoztlán man expects his children to fear him, and boys and girls know enough to submit to the demands of their father as long as they live at home. Children are always obedient and controlled in the presence of their father, even as adults, and a man continues to have authority over a married son who remains in his household. In many cultures, mothers depend upon their husbands to discipline the children, in part because women across cultures find it hard to control youngsters, and especially boys, on their own. Mixtecan women may ask their husbands to discipline a son on occasion. Tairan mothers can often persuade their children to behave simply by threatening that if they do not obey her they will have to "report to father." In some cultures, by contrast, fathers leave the job of disciplining children to their wives. A Rajput father is not supposed to discipline his older daughters and may even refrain from scolding his younger ones. That is the job of women.

Respect for Fathers

In many cultures, children are expected to be respectful and deferent toward their fathers. This show of deference takes many forms. Thus, fathers sometimes receive the best food or the seat of honor at meals. Sometimes, children are required to bow in the presence of their fathers or to use respectful language when addressing them.

Submissiveness of daughters is more common across societies than is submissiveness of sons. In Micronesia, a Palauan child refers to the father as "sir" or "my master." These are the same terms that are applied to the chief. Children are subordinate to their fathers, and daughters are even more submissive than sons because of their status as females. A son should never sit on a chair or stool when his father is present. Instead, he squats on the floor. A son does not use his father's belongings and he must make a token payment to the father before he smokes or shaves for the first time. While the relationship between a father and a younger child is close and affectionate among the Javanese, older children are required to remain respectfully aloof from their fathers. Older children can no longer play with their fathers or accompany them on visits, and youngsters are now restrained and formal in their interactions with their fathers. Older boys should avoid speaking to their fathers and should never eat with them at the same table. Japanese boys regularly scream at and hit their mothers when they are frustrated, but they are required to be respectful toward their fathers. Men rarely discipline their children, and when they do, a silent stare or curt admonition does the job. And fathers may make toys for their children, carry them about, or perform routine caretaking activities. But the father is the major example of an authority figure to his child, and youngsters must show their fathers respect "for training" in a culture where hierarchies matter more broadly in social relations.

In cultures where sons are expected to be submissive toward their fathers, this is sometimes because the father retains economic power over the boy. In Ireland, fathers own the land which they and their sons farm, and even when they are adults, sons take orders and work under the watchful eyes of their fathers. Neighbors refer to a man's sons as "boys," and this will remain the case even when a man is in his fifties if the father retains possession of the farm. As long as

the father is in control, his sons must defer to him in large and small matters on a daily basis. The father gets a larger piece of bread, a superior cup of tea, the tobacco for his pipe, and so on. Similarly, Gusii fathers have economic control over their grown sons, with all of the family land and cattle belonging to them. As a result, an adult man is still required to be deferential in his father's presence. The son should never embarrass, contradict, or shout at his father. In contrast, a father is free to scold his son harshly for behavior of which he disapproves. Among the Gusii, the old, wealthy, and dominating members of the community become the leaders, and this kind of social organization where rulers and followers can be easily distinguished is preferred by the people. This way of defining relationships in terms of rulers and ruled applies also to interactions between fathers and sons. A man remains head of his household, commanding deference, obedience, and loyalty even from his grown sons until he dies, and men who let themselves be controlled by their wives or sons are criticized.

In a small number of cultures, children are not required to show respect to their fathers. In rare cases, fathers are deferent toward their small children. Thus, among the Truk of Micronesia, a father cannot speak harshly or use "fight talk" toward his son. A father is supposed to obey a son who is younger than ten or eleven years and a daughter until she is seven, and no request made by the child should be refused. Similarly, among the Marquesas Islanders of Polynesia, the oldest child in a family becomes the head of the household. This means that the youngster outranks the father, and children enjoying this status can do more or less anything that they wish.

In many cultures, fathers remain remote from their children. At home, they talk only when they need to attend to business. In Mexico, a Tepoztlán father sits apart from the rest of the family when he is at home. He does not eat with other members of the household or join in on their conversation. In China, when a Taitou father works in the field with his son, neither speaks to the other. At home, they talk only when they need to attend to business. After supper, the family will gather together in the grandmother's room. The older children and younger married couples will chat about the events of the day while the grandmother plays with the infants and toddlers. Meanwhile, the grandfather usually remains apart from everyone else in order to maintain his position as head of the household. If he attempts to intrude, the conversation is likely to die down, and his wife will chase him away again so that everyone can relax.

Fathers versus Mothers

Even in those societies where fathers are most involved in the care of their children, the father's role in directly interacting with his children is trivial in comparison with that of the mother. Thus, for example, in southern Africa, !Kung fathers, who earn the highest possible rating on a cross-cultural basis when it comes to their involvement with their children, are responsible for only 10 percent of the vocal interactions directed toward a young infant in the course of a day. And only 14 percent of the contacts of a child over two years of age are with the father.

Across cultures, the relationship between a child and the father is different in tone from that between the child and the mother. Thus, interactions between a mother and her children tend to be described as warm, affectionate, loving, and informal. This is in contrast with the father-child relationship, in which men typically dominate over and command respect from their children. Mothers usually discipline their children more than do fathers because it is usually the mother who is the main caretaker, but the father is in general described as the stricter disciplinarian, tolerating less disobedience from children and doling out more severe punishment. Among the African Nyoro, a child is expected to be respect-

ful and submissive toward the father. Fathers are said to "rule" their children, and children to "fear" their fathers. This subordination of child to adult extends to a youngster's relationship to the father's brother, who is called "little" father, and even to the father's sister, or "female father." In contrast, boys and girls enjoy a friendly and intimate relationship with their mother and also with the mother's sisters. Grown men remain very fond of their mothers, and an old woman will frequently go to live with her son. In Liberia, a Kpelle boy's relationship to his father is respectful and distant, especially as the son grows older. In contrast, the mother-son relationship is quite close and affectionate, at least until his initiation. Because mothers are the primary caretakers of children, the relationship between a woman and her child also tends to be more complex than that between a man and his children. Among the Egyptian Silwa, children may quarrel with the mother in the course of the day. They may be rude and disobedient toward her and even swear at her. But a Silwan child also looks to the mother for affection, and youngsters go to their mothers when they want something, including enlisting the mother as mediator between them and their fathers. By contrast, fathers are respected and avoided. Youngsters do not bother a father who is asleep, and they make minimal noise when he is at home. As the Silwa say: "On the death of my father I eat dates; on the death of my mother I eat hot coals."

Ammar, Hammed. (1954) *Growing Up in an Egyptian Village.*

Arensberg, Conrad. (1950) *The Irish Countryman.*

Barnett, H. G. (1960) *Being a Palauan.*

Beattie, John. (1960) *Bunyoro: An African Kingdom.*

Benedict, Ruth. (1946) *The Chrysanthemum and the Sword.*

Bennett, Wendell, and Robert Zingg. (1935) *The Tarahumara: An Indian Tribe of Northern Mexico.*

Cohen, Yehudi A. (1966) *A Study of Interpersonal Relations in a Jamaican Community.*

Erchak, Gerald M. (1977) *Full Respect: Kpelle Children in Adaptation.*

Geertz, Hildred. (1961) *The Javanese Family: A Study of Kinship and Socialization.*

Goldschmidt, Walter. (1976) *The Culture and Behavior of the Sebei.*

Goodenough, Ward. (1951) "Property, Kin and Community on Truk." Yale University Publications in Anthropology 46.

Hara, Hiroko Sue. (1967) *Hare Indians and Their World.*

Hitchcock, John T., and Leigh Minturn. (1966) *The Rajputs of Khalapur, India.*

Hogbin, Ian. (1964) *A Guadalcanal Society: The Kaoka Speakers.*

Konner, Melvin J. (1981) "Evolution of Human Behavior Development." In *Handbook of Cross-Cultural Human Development,* edited by Ruth H. Munroe, Robert L. Munroe, and Beatrice B. Whiting, 3–51.

LeVine, Robert A., and Barbara B. LeVine. (1966) *Nyansongo: A Gusii Community in Kenya.*

Lewis, Oscar. (1951) *Life in a Mexican Village: Tepoztlàn Revisited.*

Maretzki, Thomas W., and Hatsumi Maretzki. (1966) *Taira: An Okinawan Village.*

Nydegger, William F., and Corinne Nydegger. (1966) *Tarong: An Ilocos Barrio in the Philippines.*

Powdermaker, Hortense. (1933) *Life in Lesu: A Study of Melanesian Society in New Ireland.*

Romney, A. Kimball, and Romaine Romney. (1966) *The Mixtecans of Juxtlahuaca, Mexico.*

Stephens, William N. (1963) *The Family in Cross-Cultural Perspective.*

Super, Charles M. (1981) "Behavioral Development in Infancy." In *Handbook of Cross-Cultural Human Development,* edited by Ruth H. Munroe, Robert L. Munroe, and Beatrice B. Whiting, 181–270.

Wagley, Charles. (1949) "The Social and Religious Life of a Guatemalan Village." *American Anthropologist* 51: 3–150.

Yang, Martin C. (1945) *A Chinese Village: Taitou, Shantung Province.*

FRIENDSHIP

In traditional societies, children and adults alike depend upon relatives for emotional and practical support as well as for social contact. But people also form special relationships that we identify as friendships. Some developmental psychologists believe that young children have a natural need to become a part of a peer group and that preadolescents have a special need for a chum or best friend. And indeed, beginning early on in life, children across cultures do begin to congregate in play groups made up of peers, while in many cultures, older children begin to adopt special friends. The peer groups of younger children may be more mixed in age and sex. But as children grow older, they tend to segregate themselves into same-sex, same-age groups and to pick out particular other children of the same sex as special friends. It is rare to hear of children older than six or seven hanging out in mixed-sex peer groups or choosing opposite-sex best friends. Sometimes, adults reinforce the tendency of children to segregate themselves by sex, but children do not seem to need this extra encouragement. Over and over, we find that boys prefer to play with boys and girls prefer to play with girls even in the absence of pressure from adults.

Even before they are three years old, Japanese children have already formed play groups. Neighborhood children of both sexes hang around the shops or the village shrine or play hopscotch or handball. Eventually, play groups become segregated by age and sex, and the "donen," or same-age group forms. Ties among children of a donen last for a lifetime and people say that the relationship of a man to his donen is more important than his relationship to his wife. In the Philippines, Tarong youngsters, who have congregated in mixed-sex, mixed-age groups of perhaps 30 or more children, begin to pair off with someone of their own age and sex in preadolescence. These friends are rarely apart, and as friends are often also cousins who live in the same neighborhood, they may even eat and sleep together, switching back and forth between households. Same-sex friends typically hold hands or express their affection by other physical gestures, although no such intimacy is ever displayed publicly between acquaintances of the opposite sex. Same-sex companions also spend much of their time talking about the opposite sex. Friends do their chores together, and this habit persists into adulthood, so that adults will also alter their work schedules in order to avoid doing their chores alone. In North America, Chippewa children began to form relationships with best friends beginning just before puberty. These friends then became lifelong chums who thought of each other almost like siblings. One friend could always count on the other for help, even after everyone had grown up and married. In Mexico, a Chimalteco boy usually has developed a special friendship with another boy by the time he is 12 or 13 years old. The two frequently get together after a day's work, spend their leisure time together, and eat dinner together, visiting the family of one of the boys on one night and the family of the other boy the next. Occasionally, the friends sleep together in the sweatbaths of one of the households, and one boy will arrange meetings with girls for the

other. Sometimes, one boy will ask his father to delay initiating a marriage for him until his friend also plans to marry so that the other boy will not be lonely without him. In North America, Kaska boys and girls form same-sex attachments beginning in late childhood, and friendships remain important until an individual marries. Adolescents are almost never seen abroad without a same-sex companion. Friends display physical affection openly. Boys may lean on each other while resting and one boy may sneak up on a friend and hug him from behind. Girls hold hands, hug, wrestle, and sit with bodies touching. Friendships among Kaska youth may be temporary, but while the relationship lasts, friends share both affection and confidences. By contrast, it is unusual to see young people of the opposite sex walking and talking together.

Friendships formed in childhood or adolescence can last for life. Sometimes, a friendship will become more important to the individual than any other relationship, including kin ties. In Melanesia, Trobriand males form same-sex friendships that are based upon mutual liking and that may last until death. These friendships provide emotional as well as concrete support to the partners. Male friends walk about with arms around each other and sleep together. Friendships are important for both sexes among the Omaha of North America, and companionships originating in childhood often last a lifetime. Among the Micronesian Truk, boys who enjoy each other's company spend progressively more time with one another and come to think of themselves as brothers, using the same word to refer to each other that is used to refer to brothers by blood. These friends come to take on some of the obligations toward each other's relatives that are owed to kin. Often the children of friends as well as the children of their children retain this same feeling of kinship toward each other. Most Truk males form a number of relationships of this sort, some of which are temporary and others permanent. "Brothers" of this sort are typically closer than real brothers, who are compelled by custom to maintain a degree of respect and aloofness with each other. Such friends have use of one another's food, clothing, possessions, and girlfriends. They may spend most of their time with each other, holding hands, lounging around, or doing their chores together. Truk girls also form similar kinds of friendships, calling each other "sister," and these relationships may be long lasting. They are not in general, however, as intimate as are the friendships of males.

Sometimes, individuals who have become good friends may formalize their relationship. Among the Kapauku of New Guinea, two people may declare themselves "best friends." Best friends are closer than brothers. They share their deepest secrets, tell each other their problems, and advise, reassure, and comfort each other. They eat, sleep, and sit together and visit one another. Each best friend helps the other during life crises. Among the North American Pawnee, formally recognized friendships bind two young men or two young women together for their entire lives, with each friend sharing the happiness and sorrow of the other. Among the Pentecost of Melanesia, ceremonial friends view one another as brothers and would never think of fighting or hurting each other. In Brazil, all Shavante boys form relationships with one or two partners while they live in the bachelors' house. These partnerships are viewed by the society as formal connections in which the participants form economic partnership and pledge reciprocal assistance. Partners sleep next to each other in the bachelors' hut and dance next to one another at ceremonies. Among the Arapaho of North America, both males and females formed very close, lifelong friendships, and these were institutionalized. When two female friends were married, their husbands might also become chums.

While friendships are important to both sexes, there is a tendency for males to have greater freedom in the choice of friends across cultures. Girls and women are likely to make friends with other female kin or with neighbors, while males exercise more choice regarding who will be their friends. Among the New Ireland Lesu, girls begin to help their mothers with chores by the time they are four or five years of age, and as a girl becomes older, more of her time is taken up with household tasks or baby tending. As a result, a little girl is usually in the company of older women, and girls do not hang around in peer groups or even with single friends. By contrast, Lesu boys, who are not assigned as many tasks as their sisters, roam about in play groups during the day. Often, boys pair off to form special friendships. Frequently, a younger boy of ten or twelve years of age develops a friendship with a boy who is a few years older. The boys keep each other company, strolling about arm in arm or holding hands. Typically, the younger boy looks up to the older friend and ends up performing various services for him.

See also PEERS; SEGREGATION OF GIRLS AND BOYS

Benedict, Ruth. (1946) *The Chrysanthemum and the Sword.*

Dorsey, George Amos, and James R. Murie. (1940) *Notes on Skidi Pawnee Society.*

Gladwin, Thomas, and Seymour Sarason. (1953) *Truk: Man in Paradise.*

Hilger, M. Inez. (1951) *Chippewa Child Life and Its Cultural Background.*

———. (1952) *Arapaho Child Life and Its Cultural Background.*

Honigmann, John J. (1949) *Culture and Ethos of Kaska Society.*

Lane, R. B. (1965) "The Melanesians of South Pentecost." In *Gods, Ghosts, and Men in Melanesia,* edited by P. Lawrence and M. J. Meggitt, 250–279.

Maybury-Lewis, David. (1967) *Akwe-Shavante Society*.

Nydegger, William F., and Corinne Nydegger. (1966) *Tarong: An Ilocos Barrio in the Philippines*.

Powdermaker, Hortense. (1933) *Life in Lesu: A Study of Melanesian Society in New Ireland*.

Wagley, Charles. (1949) "The Social and Religious Life of a Guatemalan Village." *American Anthropologist* 51: 3–150.

is no such competition for power between a boy and his grandfather as the older man has already been replaced by his own son in the power hierarchy.

Sometimes, grandparents and grandchildren have a joking relationship; that is, a relationship in which the partners are expected to exchange sexual jokes. Although Kenyan Gusii children are expected to show respect toward all adults, an exception is made in the case of grandparents. Thus, the relationship between a grandparent and grandchild is warm and friendly, and much sexual joking takes place between the pair. Nevertheless, youngsters are likely to obey the commands of a grandmother or grandfather and are not allowed to strike a grandparent. In Mexico, Tarahumara children enjoy a joking relationship with their grandparents. Thus, the flavor of the interactions between grandchildren and grandparents is humorous and often obscenely so, and this is explicitly expected by the culture.

Grandparents often act as secondary caretakers, relieving mothers to do other chores. In the Philippines, a Tarong grandmother will pack up a preschooler who is no longer nursing and cart the child along on a visit away from the immediate neighborhood. Among the Chimalteco of Guatemala, some children will spend a good part of each day at their grandparents' house, even eating meals there. In such cases, the mother comes to expect that this is where her child will be and she will not be worried when the youngster does not come home to eat. Children show this preference for grandparents because grandparents typically treat the youngsters better than do other relatives.

Grandparents may even act as a safe emotional haven for children whose parents are too busy to give them much time or attention. In Okinawa, when a new baby is born into a Tairan household, the second-youngest child finds that life has changed dramatically. The mother no longer allows the toddler to nurse, and

GRANDPARENTS In some societies around the world, the relationship between children and grandparents is formal and reserved. For instance, among the Takashima of Japan, age confers the right to respect, and grandparents are supposed to be treated with great reverence. More often, however, the relationship between grandparents and grandchildren is close and informal, sometimes in contrast to the tone of the child's relationship to other family members. In Africa, Nyoro grandparents and grandchildren have a warm and friendly relationship. A boy may joke and play with his grandfather, and the Nyoro say that grandparents spoil their children. Grandfathers are viewed as being "like brothers" to their grandsons, underscoring the intimate and egalitarian relationship between a child and a grandfather. This is in dramatic contrast to the interaction between a boy and his father. Sons are expected to be submissive and respectful toward their fathers, and the relationship between the two is said to be somewhat strained because sons eventually usurp the authority of their fathers in the group as they mature. There

Grandfather and grandson in Brazil

caretakers are no longer willing to tote the youngster around all day on their backs. This is the worst time of life for Tairan children, whose temper tantrums and sullenness are greeted by teasing or impatience by everyone except grandmothers, who indulge these youngsters and continue to reward their dependent behavior to some degree. A grandmother will help a child to dress, bathe, and eat and will comfort a youngster who is crying.

Grandparents across cultures tend to be indulgent toward grandchildren, and parents and other caretakers sometimes complain that grandparents spoil their grandchildren. A Tairan mother who is being pestered by a toddler is likely to send the child off to an older sibling or a grandmother. But when the grandmother then indulges the child, the mother may become irritated and complain that the interference of the grandmother makes it difficult for her to discipline her children. A child who is being scolded by the mother is likely to run to a grandparent for comfort, and youngsters know that, if they cannot get what they want from anyone else, they can go to a grandparent for satisfaction. Kindergarten teachers report that children who have no grandmothers are easier to manage than children who do because the latter do not cry as much and are able to do more things for themselves. Grandmothers allow their grandchildren to remain dependent for longer than parents prefer and discourage independence and responsibility on the part of their grandchildren. In North America, Comanche grandparents also spoiled their grandchildren. This was especially true in the case of the relationship between a girl and her mother's mother. Each called the other *kaku,* and the two were theoretically equal in status, and a granddaughter and grandmother were said to be closer than a girl was to her own mother. Similarly, North American Sanpoil grandparents were more indulgent of children than were parents. They defended the youngsters against the parents, rarely criticized them,

and played with them more than parents did. Often, children preferred their grandparents to their parents as a result.

The relationship between a grandfather and grandchild may be friendly and informal. In India, Rajput grandfathers are more indulgent of their grandchildren, and especially the younger ones, than are the other men with whom a youngster has contact. But sometimes, children show more respect and are more reserved toward the grandfather than toward the grandmother. This is typically because cultural norms require children to defer to men. The relationship between a Nyoro child and a grandfather is less familiar than is the relationship of a child to the grandmother, in part because youngsters have learned to show respect for elder males. A grandfather will carry a grandchild around, but children will not tease grandfathers as they do grandmothers.

Grandparents may also act as teachers to their grandchildren. A Comanche boy's father was often away at war or on a hunting trip. Thus, it fell to the grandfather to teach the child to ride, shoot, and make bows and arrows. Grandfathers passed on tribal history, tradition, religion, and legends, and the two typically enjoyed a friendly and close relationship. North American Arapaho grandparents were responsible for a major part of the instruction of their younger relatives. A grandparent might collect all of the children in the family and lecture them on proper behavior. Grandparents would tell children what to say and what not to say. They would warn children to listen to their parents, to respect people from other tribes, and not to quarrel. Grandparents as well as others took every opportunity to instruct children, and boys and girls who were nearly 20 years old continued to be the target of these diatribes.

Sometimes, parents and grandparents may end up in competition for the affection of a child. In traditional Japan, a married woman moved into her husband's household and was required to submit to the authority of her mother-in-law. This meant a child lived with both the mother and the grandmother. Frequently, a woman and her mother-in-law vied for a place in the child's life with the result that a youngster was courted by both of them. A mother was unable to object if she disapproved of the way in which her mother-in-law was treating her children, even if she thought that they were being spoiled by their grandmother. A grandmother might give a child candy even though the mother objected, and the older woman was often also able to give a child gifts that the mother could not obtain and spend time with a grandchild when a busy mother could not.

Beattie, John. (1960) *Bunyoro: An African Kingdom.*

Benedict, Ruth. (1946) *The Chrysanthemum and the Sword.*

Bennett, Wendell, and Robert Zingg. (1935) *The Tarahumara: An Indian Tribe of Northern Mexico.*

Hilger, M. Inez. (1952) *Arapaho Child Life and Its Cultural Background.*

Hitchcock, John T., and Leigh Minturn. (1966) *The Rajputs of Khalapur, India.*

LeVine, Robert A., and Barbara B. LeVine. (1966) *Nyansongo: A Gusii Community in Kenya.*

Maretzki, Thomas W., and Hatsumi Maretzki. (1966) *Taira: An Okinawan Village.*

Norbeck, Edward. (1954) *Takashima: A Japanese Fishing Community.*

Nydegger, William F., and Corinne Nydegger. (1966) *Tarong: An Ilocos Barrio in the Philippines.*

Ray, Verne. (1933) *The Sanpoil and the Nespelem: Salishan Peoples of Northeastern Washington.*

Wagley, Charles. (1949) "The Social and Religious Life of a Guatemalan Village." *American Anthropologist* 51: 3–150.

Wallace, Ernest, and E. Adamson Hoebel. (1952) *The Comanches: Lords of the South Plains.*

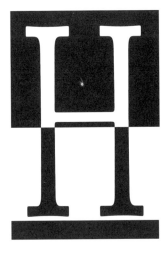

youngster. Living arrangements also affect the daily experience of a child. Family members may sleep, eat, or congregate in the same room, or different rooms or areas may be reserved for different categories of people. Sometimes, space is allocated by sex, with men conducting their daily activities outside of the purview of women and children. Sometimes, children change households at some given age.

Many children across the world live in extended families. This means that the child lives with a number aunts, uncles, and cousins as well as grandparents. The extended family may live and operate as a unit, or each nuclear family unit may function more independently. Among the Mixtecans of Mexico, the household consists of a number of related families. Each family has its own sleeping and cooking huts and eats and sleeps apart from the others, but all of the families share a courtyard. Women, children, and older people spend much of their time at home, and many of their activities take place in the courtyard, with the result that youngsters are often in the company of a number of adults and siblings and cousins of various ages. In India, the Rajputs also live in extended families. Households consist of some combination of a husband and wife along with their unmarried children and married sons with their wives and children. Anywhere between two and four generations may live in a single household. But because the Rajputs practice purdah, or the seclusion of women, there are separate houses within a family compound for males and females, and this affects the company that a child keeps. Men and male adolescents sleep and spend most of their leisure time in the men's quarters, while women, girls, and children of both sexes under three years of age are confined to the enclosed courtyard adjacent to the women's quarters most of the time. Boys who are older than three spend time with their mothers in the courtyard, but they are also free to tag along after the men. An average courtyard is inhabited by perhaps three

HOUSEHOLD COMPOSITION

For an infant and child, the household is often the focus of daily life. As a result, the composition of the household as well as living arrangements have a real and significant affect on the experience of children. Households can be small, containing only a mother and father and their unmarried children with perhaps an additional relation or two living temporarily or permanently with the family. Or households can include a number of related families. Often, a household will consist of grandmother and grandfather, along with their unmarried daughters and married sons, daughters-in-law, and grandchildren. In polygynous societies, where a man may have more than one wife at a time, each married woman may live in a house of her own along with her children. Or a man and his co-wives and their children may live together. In some American Indian cultures, as many as 30 or 40 related people may live under the same roof. These differences in household composition affect how many adults and children and how many generations live in daily contact with a

An Ovahimbo family relaxes outside their home.

women and four children, all of whom are related to each other by blood or marriage. Men's quarters house an average of five or six men and adolescent boys. The institution of purdah means that females of all ages and young children keep company almost exclusively with women, while boys over three years of age have greater access to the company of men, and male children past twelve years of age are in the presence of females only infrequently.

In some cultures, a household contains a large number of people who may live more or less independently under a single roof. In Canada, a Haida household can consist of 30 individuals, including the senior male and his wife or wives, his unmarried daughters and young sons, his married daughters and their husbands and children, a married younger brother with his wife and children, unmarried sons of his sister, a married nephew and his family, and perhaps a poor relative and a few slaves. Among the North American Pomo, a number of families lived under one roof, but each family had its own fireplace and doorway, with partitions separating the living areas of the individual family units. The traditional North American Yokut extended family lived in a longhouse. The oval dwelling was sectioned by hanging mats, with each son's family having its own hearth and, if the house was large enough, its own entrance. A longhouse is like a street, so that if you look down the middle of the house, you will be able to observe the activities of the families, each gathered around its own fire.

When a number of related nuclear families live together, a child may think of all of the members of the household as a single family unit. Among the Takashima of Japan, a household may consist of three or four generations, including the retired grandparents, the family head and his wife, and the oldest son of the head along with his wife and children. Although a household is thus composed of a number of nuclear families, no distinction is made among the members of the household on the basis of these family lines. Thus, a person does not talk about "my grandfather," but rather about "the grandfather of our household." A mother refers not to "my son" but rather to "the young person of our household."

In polygynous societies, where a man may have two or more wives at the same time, a child may live in a household along with the father's other wives as well as their children. Among the North American Crow, all of a man's wives lived in one tepee if they were sisters, and children, therefore, found themselves in a single household with their father, mother, and siblings, but also with half-siblings and their mothers. In other polygynous societies, a mother will have her own house, which she shares with her children. Among the Kipsigis of Kenya, each of a man's wives has her own homestead located on a farm. The father spends some of his time at each homestead. The two forms of polygynous household provide very different interpersonal settings for the child.

In some cultures, children change their residence as they grow older. This is more common in the case of sons than of daughters. Boys may move into a house reserved for the use of men if such an establishment exists. Once they reach adolescence, Canadian Ingalik boys live, work, and eat in the *kashim,* or men's house, chatting with each other and telling stories after dinner. Other cultures provide dormitories for older children, who remain there until they marry. These dorms may be segregated by sex. Or boys and girls may live together in the same house. Thus, for example, among the Trobrianders of Melanesia, a household includes a father and mother with their small children, but adolescents and unmarried men and women live in small bachelor's houses, each of which houses perhaps two to six individuals. In some societies, young unmarried people set up their own independent neighborhoods, villages, or the like. Among the polygynous Murngin of Australia, a husband establishes a separate household with his wives. A girl lives with her parents until she marries and moves in with her husband and co-wives if she is a junior spouse. But boys move into a different camp reserved for single men when they reach puberty. Children may also move out of the parental house and go to live with relatives. Among the Bemba of southern Africa, a child who is two or three years of age, and therefore weaned, will go to sleep in the hut of its grandparents, who may as a result have five or six youngsters underfoot. Slightly older girls may sleep in the house of a widow or of a married woman whose husband is away, while a boy will build himself a hut. Among the South African Hadza, housing accommodations are assigned on the basis of an individual's age and sex. A father and mother live in their own hut along with any children who are under five or six years old. Older boys and bachelors live in a separate hut as do older girls and unmarried women. A younger child will often go to sleep in the maternal grandmother's hut. In the Philippines, once Tarong children reach middle childhood and are able to do chores on their own, they may move in with a grandparent or perhaps an aunt who lives nearby. At first, the child may just go to eat with a relative, who fusses over the youngster and may buy the child clothes and other gifts. The child shuttles between households for a while, but if the idea of living with the relative is attractive, the transition from one household to the other is made in around six months. If the youngster does not want to move, then the relative is likely to look for a more willing one to adopt. Parents do not allow an eldest child to move in with a relative, but they are often happy to have a second child change households in this way, especially if they have two boys or two girls. Some parents, however, do not like to have their children adopted in this manner. Children do not in general mind these moves. They are not being abandoned by their parents, nor do they believe that they are, and they still have contact with their parents. Sometimes, a Tarong child will also end up living with a grandmother or aunt to whom the youngster had temporarily been sent to ease the weaning process. When this happens, the parents may find themselves eventually having to coax the child back home with gifts of food, money, and the like. The parents may even become involved in a rivalry with the relative for possession of the child.

Household composition has a number of predictable influences on child-rearing practices across cultures. Children are more likely to be treated with indulgence when the mother has other people in the household to help her with caretaking. This is especially the case where fathers and grandparents help the mother out on a daily basis. Conversely, isolation of a woman has pronounced effects upon her treatment of her children. Thus, mothers who have minimal contact with other adults are more likely than other women to reject and neglect their youngsters. This is especially true in societies with mother-child households, where the woman is the sole caretaker and where even the father has little to do with the day-to-day rearing of children.

See also SEGREGATION OF CHILDREN FROM PARENTS

Bennett, Wendell, and Robert Zingg. (1935) *The Tarahumara: An Indian Tribe of Northern Mexico.*

Gayton, Anna. (1948) *Yokuts and Western Mono Ethnography.*

Harner, Michael J. (1973) *The Jivaro: People of the Sacred Waterfalls.*

Norbeck, Edward. (1954) *Takashima: A Japanese Fishing Community.*

Nydegger, William F., and Corinne Nydegger. (1966) *Tarong: An Ilocos Barrio in the Philippines.*

Levinson, David, and Martin J. Malone. (1980) *Toward Explaining Human Culture.*

Loeb, Edwin Meyer. (1926) *Pomo Folkways.*

Maretzki, Thomas W., and Hatsumi Maretzki. (1966) *Taira: An Okinawan Village.*

Minturn, Leigh, and John T. Hitchcock. (1966) *The Rajputs of Khalapur, India.*

Niblack, Albert F. (1890) *The Coast Indians of Southern Alaska and Northern British Columbia.* Annual Reports of the Board of Regents, Smithsonian Institute.

Richards, Audrey. (1940) *Bemba Marriage and Present Economic Conditions.* Rhodes-Livingstone Papers 4.

Romney, A. Kimball, and Romaine Romney. (1966) *The Mixtecans of Juxtlahuaca, Mexico.*

Stephens, William N. (1963) *The Family in Cross-Cultural Perspective.*

Warner, W. Lloyd. (1937) *A Black Civilization: A Social Study of an Australian Tribe.*

Woodburn, J. *The Social Organization of the Hadza of North Tanzania.* Unpublished dissertation, Cambridge University.

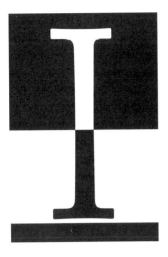

ILLEGITIMACY

In societies around the world, people make a distinction between babies born to married parents and a baby whose mother is not married. Out-of-wedlock births can disrupt the lives of the mother and father as well as the child, the parents' relatives, and the community at large. The birth of an illegitimate baby can cause problems because cultural rules regarding residence, inheritance, and legal status assume that a child's parents are married. When this is not the case, the place of the child in society can become ambiguous.

Because out-of-wedlock births are disruptive, the pregnancy of an unmarried woman can be a source of deep shame to the girl herself and to her family. Among the Gusii of Kenya, it is considered extremely shameful for an unmarried girl to become pregnant. Usually, the girl will try to persuade the father to marry her, and she may even attempt to move into his house with him. Boys, however, are hard to convince because they prefer to marry girls with whom they have not had sexual intercourse. The parents of a pregnant girl arc also anxious to scc her mar-

ried, but as a daughter is reluctant to give the name of the baby's father, the mother and father will usually try to arrange another marriage before the girl's condition becomes apparent. A pregnant girl who remains unmarried will hide herself away at home to avoid the gossip of her neighbors, who know about her disgrace. The North American Arapaho called an illegitimate child a "sweetheart child" or a "love child" because the mother and father were courting and were not married. The parents of illegitimate children lost the respect of their own relatives and the community at large, but they were not punished.

The relatives of a single pregnant girl are often anxious to see that she marries the father of the baby. If a Gusii girl has refused to identify the boy with whom she has had sexual relations, she will be forced to do so when she is in labor, as the Gusii believe that a baby cannot be delivered unless the father is known. People will then look for a resemblance between the baby and the man whom the girl has named and the girl's family will sue for damages or try to force a marriage based upon physical similarity between the baby and putative father. A Gusii girl who has had a baby out of wedlock is also frequently given as a secondary wife to an older man, who will pay a large bride price in return for the proven fertility of his young wife. Among the Chippewa of North America, girls who became pregnant while single caused a scandal but were not sent away. The parents of both the mother and father were disgraced, and everyone hoped that the two would get married. Similarly, if an unmarried Arapaho woman became pregnant, her relatives tried to persuade her and the baby's father to get married, but if they did not, then the expectant mother lived in her parents' house, where the baby was born and raised. A woman who had a baby out of wedlock had a very difficult time finding another man to marry her.

In some cultures, an illegitimate baby is not permitted to live. In India, if an unmarried

Rajput girl gives birth, everyone assumes that the baby will be killed by her relatives in order to keep the family honor intact. Among the Cuna of Panama, if a girl is pregnant and not married, her hair will be cut off. In the past, she and her baby would have been killed. Sometimes, an unmarried woman will terminate her pregnancy. Among the Kapauku of New Guinea, a girl who becomes pregnant before marriage is humiliated in front of her married peers. A girl who finds herself pregnant, therefore, attempts to induce a miscarriage if she cannot persuade the father to marry her. In some societies, illegitimate babies are adopted. In North America, an illegitimate Sanpoil child was usually adopted by a married woman in the community. The child knew the biological mother's identity, and youngsters could return to their real mothers if they wished. Among the Canadian Hare, illegitimate babies are often given up for adoption, and the mother may have already decided to arrange an adoption before the baby is born. A woman whose baby is the result of an adulterous affair may also have it adopted because her husband would resent the infant.

Out-of-wedlock births are problematic in many cultures because children often legally belong to the father's descent group. If a youngster has no legal father, then the child's status is in doubt. Further, the residence of a married mother and child is often with the father's family. Thus, the illegitimate baby has no culturally sanctioned household in which to live. The Rwala Bedouin trace descent through the father, but an illegitimate baby cannot be a member of the father's clan, as a Rwala man does not acknowledge an illegitimate child as legally his. Children of unwed mothers, as a result, have no clan identity and would have no one to depend upon for aid and protection. To the Rwala, this situation would be intolerable. As a result, when a pregnancy is detected, the relatives of the girl immediately try to induce a miscarriage. If this fails, attempts are made to persuade the father

to marry the girl. Otherwise, she is likely to commit suicide or to run away. In societies where a child belongs to the mother's kin group, premarital pregnancies do not pose insurmountable problems regarding the child's legal status. Among the Lapps, kinship is traced through both the father and mother, so an illegitimate baby still has membership in a kin group. Further, an illegitimate child can live with the mother's kin, so the youngster does not remain homeless. Similarly, among the Solomon Island Siuai, a child lives with his mother's brother and traces descent through his mother. Thus, a Siuai child whose mother is unmarried fits into society without difficulty and, indeed, such children are treated with special care by their relatives. Sometimes, a society has special rules for determining the legal status and residence of an illegitimate child. A North African Teda child who is born to an unmarried mother inherits the taboo of the mother's kin group. If a father wishes to admit paternity, he kills a goat and gives the baby a name. In this case, the child inherits the father's clan taboo and belongs to his clan. The father will then also provide the gifts at the circumcision and marriage of the child. It is the youngster who chooses whether to live with the mother or father. Some cultures extend the idea of illegitimacy to include anyone whose parents are currently unmarried. This then affects the status of the individual. Among the Toba of Bolivia, the child of a divorce is considered to be illegitimate and does not have the same rights as a person whose parents have remained married. Thus, the eldest son of a chief cannot inherit the chieftainship if his mother was divorced from his father. Rather, the eldest son of the chief's current wife becomes chief on his father's death. A father, however, does maintain contact with the sons of his divorced wife, and the son may also occasionally visit his father.

The treatment of illegitimate children may be indistinguishable from that of children born to married parents. Or an illegitimate child may be handled differently from other youngsters. An illegitimate Tairan child does not suffer any social stigma, although people do not hesitate to comment on the youngster's status in his presence. The treatment of illegitimate children is, nevertheless, identical to that of a legitimate child. By contrast, in North America, illegitimate Chippewa were stigmatized while young, but taken care of. Children without legal fathers lived with the mother's parents, and if the mother married a man who was not the child's father, the youngster remained with the maternal grandmother. More than 62 percent of Jamaican babies are illegitimate. The Church regards illegitimacy as sinful, but the average Jamaican thinks that any baby is "a blessing of God," although people also agree that it "is not the best thing" that can happen since illegitimate babies pose an economic burden for the woman's family. Women are not ashamed about having babies out of wedlock, nor are people who are illegitimate ashamed about their status. The child is supported and generally cared for by the mother's parents. This means that a woman may be forced to take care of her own younger children and the children of her unmarried daughters simultaneously. Often, a woman does not feed, clothe, and care for her daughter's children as well as she does her own. Women feel guilty about their treatment of their illegitimate grandchildren, but grandmothers are also in a difficult position as they may be in charge of as many as ten children at the same time. The dilemma faced by women because of the pregnancies of their unwed daughters leads to considerable resentment between the two. Illegitimate children generally live with their grandparents until they are grown, as a man who marries a woman who has had a baby out of wedlock generally refuses to take care of another man's children.

Premarital pregnancies do not always pose problems for a woman. Sometimes, pregnancy in an unmarried girl is viewed positively as evidence of her fertility. Among the Chimalteco of Guatemala, children are rarely born to single women, but this is because an unmarried girl who becomes pregnant is almost certain to get married, either to the father or to some other man. In fact, women commonly find a husband by becoming pregnant. If a child is born to an unmarried woman, no one thinks anything of it and when she eventually marries, the youngster will take her husband's name and may become his heir. Similarly, among the Himalayan Lepcha, a premarital pregnancy creates no problems for the girl. On the contrary, the fact that she is obviously fertile makes her more attractive as a prospective wife. In South America, a Callinago couple would marry only after the woman had demonstrated her fertility, and many women had a number of children by different men before they finally settled down in marriage.

Cohen, Yehudi A. (1966) *A Study of Interpersonal Relations in a Jamaican Community.*

Colinder, Bjorn. (1949) *The Lapps.*

Gorer, Geoffrey. (1938) *Himalayan Village: An Account of the Lepchas of Sikkim.*

Hara, Hiroko Sue. (1967) *Hare Indians and Their World.*

Hilger, M. Inez. (1951) *Chippewa Child Life and Its Cultural Background.*

———. (1952) *Arapaho Child Life and Its Cultural Background.*

Hitchcock, John T., and Leigh Minturn. (1966) *The Rajputs of Khalapur, India.*

Karsten, Rafael. (1923) *The Toba Indians of the Bolivian Gran Chaco.*

Kronenberg, Andreas. (1981) *The Teda of Tibesti.*

LeVine, Robert A., and Barbara B. LeVine. (1966) *Nyansongo: A Gusii Community In Kenya.*

Maretzki, Thomas W., and Hatsumi Maretzki. (1966) *Taira: An Okinawan Village.*

Marshall, Donald S. (1950) *Cuna Folk.* Unpublished manuscript, Harvard University.

Oliver, Douglas. (1955) *A Solomon Island Society.*

Pospisil, Leopold. (1958) *The Kapauku Papuans and Their Law.*

Raswan, Carl R. (1947) *Black Tents of Arabia.*

Ray, Verne. (1933) *The Sanpoil and the Nespelem: Salishan Peoples of Northeastern Washington.*

Wagley, Charles. (1949) "The Social and Religious Life of a Guatemalan Village." *American Anthropologist* 51: 3–150.

ILLNESS

In many cultures around the world, child mortality is a continual threat faced by parents. Among the causes of death in infants and children are childhood diseases. Diseases that are not fatal may, nevertheless, cause chronic problems for a child. Some diseases have permanent effects, such as scarring or disfigurement. Childhood diseases may also affect the developmental trajectory, causing a child to be smaller, less resilient, and so on. Traditional cultures administer treatments for the illnesses contracted by children and may also resort to preventive medicine, but often a disease that can be routinely cured by Western medical procedures is not effectively treated by indigenous methods. Diseases, therefore, can linger indefinitely. Sometimes, childhood diseases are caused by the diet on which the culture depends. In most African agricultural societies, people subsist primarily on grain and root crops, with animal protein forming a small part of their diet. As a result, a large number of African children suffer from malnutrition and diarrhea, and many die.

In Okinawa, Tairan children commonly suffer from intestinal ailments, often caused by hookworms or tapeworms. Skin disorders are also endemic, and virtually all Tairan youngsters are subject to impetigo, eczema, and other skin rashes, as well as boils. Diseases are commonly treated by bloodletting or cauteries, and babies as young as five days old may be subjected to bloodletting. The mother or grandmother will apply sake to an area of the infant's skin and then make many small cuts with a razor blade. As blood oozes from the incisions, it is mixed with sake and the mixture is then reapplied to the skin and more cuts are made. Tairan parents treat children's minor illnesses casually. A youngster who has a stomachache may be excused from going to school but then be allowed to play outside with the preschoolers.

Among the Micronesian Truk, almost all babies have intestinal parasites by the time they are a few months old, as evidenced by the swollen stomachs of virtually every Truk infant. Sometimes, the parasites are fatal. Respiratory infection, however, is the most frequent cause of death in young Truk children, especially when it turns into pneumonia. Youngsters also frequently suffer from severe diarrhea, partly as a result of the parasites. Almost all Jamaican children suffer from yaws and superficial ulcers, neither of which is treated and both of which go unhealed. Among the Rajputs of Khalapur, India, children contract typhoid, pneumonia, smallpox, chicken pox, malaria, eye and stomach infections, colds, and boils. In Malaysia, malaria is the primary cause of death in Semai babies under age one and also kills children from one to fourteen years old. A number of newborn Semai babies also die of diarrhea. Children are also susceptible to the sniffles. More severe respiratory illnesses are the second greatest cause of death in infants under age one, and over a fifth of the deaths of children between one and fourteen years old are caused by respiratory diseases. In North America, sick or fragile Chippewa babies were bathed in a decoction that might consist of catnip and cedar boughs or of other herbs, and people regularly kept dried herbs and roots hanging in their dwelling in the event of illness. A sick baby might also be given purgatives, including one made of roots and maple sugar stored as cakes and melted in water for the baby to drink. An ill infant was also held over a fire and rubbed with grease. Or sick babies might be given a second name by a person who had lived for a long time and a third name by another long-lived individual if the infant remained unwell. Among the North American Arapaho, if the mother's milk was suspected of causing illness in a nursing baby, the woman would drink an herbal decoction and then some older person would suck on her breasts to remove the bad milk. Diarrhea was treated in this manner. Sometimes, a medicine man sucked whatever part of a child's body was sick to make it better. Medicine would then be rubbed on the affected part.

Preventive medicine is practiced in a number of societies. North American Chippewa infants were bathed in water infused with certain herbs and roots so that they would be strong. Adults also allowed youngsters to eat strips of burnt cedar so that their bones would be strong and their resistance to disease great. The Arapaho believed that talking about illness caused people to be ill in fact. Therefore, they refrained from making any mention of sickness as a way of preventing it from occurring. Children were also given a decoction of peppermint plant boiled in water to prevent them from becoming ill. Or a child's face, hands, and feet might be rubbed with red paint by a medicine man while he prayed that the child would remain healthy. Tairan parents depend upon bloodletting to prevent disease, and a baby may undergo bloodletting as many as four times before the first birthday.

Many cultures attribute childhood diseases to supernatural influences. When illness is traced to supernatural causes, cures tend to be supernatural in nature. The Rajputs trace some diseases to bodily malfunctioning, but other diseases are blamed on the activities of ghosts, ancestors, or goddesses and godlings, all of whom are ca-pable of causing illness. Childhood disease is most commonly understood to be the result of supernatural intervention, especially of the evil eye or of the goddesses and godlings. The Mexican Mixtecans attribute some infant illnesses to magic of one sort or another. Magical contamination can lead to fever, vomiting, immoderate crying, or physical deformity. People with especially bright or piercing eyes are thought to be able to consciously or unconsciously cause sickness simply by looking at a victim, and babies are particularly susceptible to the evil eye. A person can also become ill as a result of evil air, and an infant can develop a swelling on the back of its head if either the baby or its mother is exposed to evil air. Mixtecans also resort to magical means to prevent illness, and infants frequently wear a shell on a cord around the neck to ward off coughs. A bag of herbs worn around the mother's waist will also protect an infant from witches' spells and from contamination by exposure to death.

The Tarong of the Philippines believe that illnesses, including tremors, tics, delirium, dizziness, and coma, are caused by the loss of the soul. Soul loss is caused by sudden frights or shocks. As a child's soul is less securely attached to the body, children are particularly vulnerable to sickness caused by soul loss. Parents will attempt to prevent the loss of a child's soul in various ways. For example, if a youngster falls down, water will be spattered at the site of the accident, and the youngster will also drink some of the water. If a child becomes ill anyway, the parents will attempt to recapture the youngster's soul by waving a piece of the child's clothing from the porch or house ladder while calling his or her name. If the child does not get better, a specialist in retrieving souls will be called in. A person may also become ill if, because of some change in routine, "something is missed." Something inside the person looks for what has been lost, causing the individual to become sick. Children are also more susceptible to this than adults.

Chills, fever, and indigestion can be caused by dead spirits visiting their earthly homes. A person who falls ill because of the actions of nonhumans may be lightly whipped with leafy twigs. The Tarong also treat sickness caused by nonhumans by attempting to trick the instigators. For instance, if two children in a row have become sick and died, the cause is assumed to be the jealousy of nonhumans. When a third child is born, therefore, the parents will pretend to abandon the infant by having it left at the side of the road. The baby will be retrieved later and taken home surreptitiously. The nonhumans, who will now believe that the child is not wanted by its parents, will not be tempted to steal it away. This kind of trickery is also used to cure deformities or other developmental abnormalities. For instance, if a child's upper teeth begin to come in below the lower teeth, the youngster is required to do some adult chore and is then renamed after an older relative. The nonhumans are thus deceived about the identity of the child. Because Tairans believe that sickness can be caused by the activities of ancestors, parents will also sometimes arrange to have a chronically ill child adopted by another family, so that the child will no longer be under the control of the parents' ancestors. Children adopted for this reason continue to live with their biological parents. However, the youngster will make occasional visits to the foster family, and gifts will be brought to the foster parents, who will then offer the presents to their ancestors in an effort to counteract the influence of the child's own ancestors. Sickness in North American Sanpoil babies was believed to occur because the parents had broken some taboo, and a shaman might be summoned to determine what prohibition had been violated if the illness was serious. Among the Semai of Malaysia, the most dreaded childhood disease is soul loss. Since souls are timid, it is almost certain that a child will lose his or her soul. A soul departs from a child as a result of some startling event such as a loud noise, so

that a bird call or the croak of a toad can precipitate soul loss. Youngsters who are suffering from soul loss display pallor, listlessness, anemia, diarrhea, or convulsions. Their speech may be irrational. The diagnosis of soul loss is made when someone has a dream indicating that the child's soul has departed. The Semai try to cure respiratory ailments in their children by making them necklaces of fragrant eaglewood bark. An expert in spells then says a spell over the necklace. The Semai say that the necklace will not always get rid of the disease but that it does make the child feel a bit better. A Semai child who has a cold will drink or take a bath in a decoction of fresh bark over which a spell has been intoned. Among the East Semai, fretful youngsters are bathed in a warm decoction of canarium leaves, while in the West, ashes of the leaves are rubbed around the infant's eyes while a spell is said. Or sometimes, the leaves of a sensitive plant may be placed under the child's pillow in the belief that the youngster will relax just as the leaves do.

Cohen, Yehudi A. (1966) *A Study of Interpersonal Relations in a Jamaican Community.*

Denton, Robert. (1978) "Notes on Childhood in a Nonviolent Context: The Semai Case." In *Learning and Non-Aggression,* edited by Ashley Montagu, 94–143.

Gladwin, Thomas, and Seymour Sarason. (1953) *Truk: Man in Paradise.*

Hilger, M. Inez. (1951) *Chippewa Child Life and Its Cultural Background.*

———. (1952) *Arapaho Child Life and Its Cultural Background.*

Hitchcock, John T., and Leigh Minturn. (1966) *The Rajputs of Khalapur, India.*

Maretzki, Thomas W., and Hatsumi Maretzki. (1966) *Taira: An Okinawan Village.*

Nydegger, William F., and Corinne Nydegger. (1966) *Tarong: An Ilocos Barrio in the Philippines.*

Ray, Verne. (1933) *The Sanpoil and the Nespelem: Salishan Peoples of Northeastern Washington.*

Romney, A. Kimball, and Romaine Romney. (1966) *The Mixtecans of Juxtlahuaca, Mexico.*

Williamson, Laila. (1978) "Infanticide: An Anthropological Analysis." In *Infanticide and the Value of Life,* edited by Marvin Kohl, 61–75.

INFANCY

In cultures around the world, infancy is singled out as a special stage of the life cycle. This is because of the special characteristics of newborn infants. Everywhere, adults understand that human babies are more or less helpless and need the more or less constant supervision of a competent caretaker if they are to survive. Beyond this, babies are regarded by adults in many societies as especially vulnerable, and the high rates of infantile disease and mortality support this view of the infant as fragile. In a number of cultures, fears about the well-being of babies are expressed in concerns about the harmful affects of supernatural influences on infants. Adults the world over also appreciate the cognitive immaturity of babies. Everywhere, infants are viewed as having no sense, and adults typically take this to mean that a baby should be treated with kindness and not be held responsible for its behavior. Thus, the shared view across cultures that babies are helpless, vulnerable, and lacking in reason leads adults to respond to infants with indulgence and concern.

For the Kenyan Gusii child, the period of greatest indulgence comes in infancy, which lasts until weaning. This is because parents are extremely worried about the survival of their infants. Adults focus on the task of meeting a baby's various needs and postpone any serious

training until a child is older. Infants are also thought to be especially susceptible to the evil eye because of their light skin. An individual who has the evil eye and looks at a child causes anything small that is near the child, such as some grain or the wool of a blanket, to adhere to the child's skin. Unless it is quickly removed, it will eventually end up in the victim's organs, causing death. Infants are also vulnerable because of their "hot blood," which makes them weak and susceptible to the cold. It is the infant's hot blood that explains its lack of strength and motor coordination. For the first week of its life, a Mexican Mixtecan baby is always near its mother, either sleeping in her arms or being rocked in the daytime. An infant may then be put in a hanging cradle during the day when it is asleep. The mother and baby remain in the house for 40 days after a birth, and during this period the woman and her baby are in constant close proximity. If the woman does leave the house, she will always take the baby along, carrying it in her rebozo. Mixtecans believe that infants are very vulnerable to the influence of witches and to the evil eye, and a number of precautions are taken to protect babies from danger. A mother and baby remain confined in the house in part to prevent the infant from being harmed by evil forces. For the same reason, a baby's head is covered with a rebozo and a pair of scissors or crossed sticks may be placed in its crib to cut any evil powers that might be lurking about. Babies also wear caps as well as nuts strung around the wrist to ward off danger. As a further precaution, only relatives can look at the baby. Among the Tarong of the Philippines, a mother and infant remain inside the house during the *dalagan* period, which may last for as much as a month. The two are confined to the bed that has been placed in the *sala*, or bed-living room, especially for this use once the baby has been born. The woman and baby are supposed to spend their time in the *sala* in quiet seclusion. In fact, however, there is a steady stream of relatives and neighbors dropping by to visit the baby. Older brothers and sisters spread themselves out on the bed and play with the infant, who gets constant attention and affection. For the first year of its life, a Jamaican infant eats and sleeps. Babies remain in the parents' bed all day, and do not usually go outside. Sometimes, an infant will be placed in a large wooden bowl and put out of doors. In Ecuador, a Jivaro baby is fed a mild hallucinogen when it is a few days old. The hope is that the infant will then achieve supernatural power, which can then help it to survive. A baby who becomes ill may receive another dose of the hallucinogen.

See also CHILD MORTALITY; CRYING; INFANTS, BELIEFS ABOUT; INFANTS, INDULGENCE OF; SUPERNATURAL INFLUENCES

Cohen, Yehudi A. (1966) *A Study of Interpersonal Relations in a Jamaican Community.*

Harner, Michael J. (1973) *The Jivaro: People of the Sacred Waterfalls.*

LeVine, Robert A., and Barbara B. LeVine. (1966) *Nyansongo: A Gusii Community of Kenya.*

Maretzki, Thomas W., and Hatsumi Maretzki. (1966) *Taira: An Okinawan Village.*

Nydegger, William F., and Corinne Nydegger. (1966) *Tarong: An Ilocos Barrio in the Philippines.*

Romney, A. Kimball, and Romaine Romney. (1966) *The Mixtecans of Juxtlahuaca, Mexico.*

INFANT-CARETAKER CLOSENESS

In the majority of societies around the world, babies are held or carried by some caretaker for most of the day. In 59 percent of 105 cultures, a young infant remains in physical contact with a caretaker for most or all of the time, and the same is true in 52 percent of 104 cultures once a baby has begun to crawl. Young babies are held and carried only rarely or occasionally in only 16 percent of 105 cultures and older babies in only 14 percent of 104 cultures. In many African societies, infants spend most of the day in body contact with the mother or other caretaker. Thus, for example, in Kenya, a Kipsigis baby spends about 70 percent of its time in body contact with its mother and only 4 percent out of her reach. For the Kikuyu of Kenya, contact between mother or caretaker and infant occurs about 68 percent of the time. For the first year of its life, a Kalahari !Kung baby is rarely far from its mother. When awake, an infant is held in a sitting or standing position in the lap of its mother or other caretaker, or it may be found in a sling on the mother's hip. When they are asleep, infants may remain in the sling. Or they may be placed on a cloth on the ground near the mother. !Kung infants remain in contact with their mothers about 79 percent of the time for the first few months of life. In most African societies, babies sleep on a special mat or rug that is placed near the caretaker. Among the Mixtecans of Mexico, infants are almost constantly in close proximity to their mothers. A baby is rocked to sleep in its mother's arms before it is put in its cradle, and often the infant will fall asleep while nursing. A baby who begins to cry will be picked up immediately by some female in the house. For the first few months of its life, a Philippine Tarong infant is rarely out of sight of its mother unless the family is poor and the woman is needed in the fields. While they are awake, babies are held by their mothers, and an infant may also sleep in her arms or between the mother and father until a younger sibling is born. Babies may be placed in a hammock to sleep, but an infant who fusses at all will be picked up again and rocked in someone's arms. A baby is never allowed to cry, and anyone who does not immediately pick up a fussing infant will be reprimanded. Thus, a mother who tries to calm a baby by singing to it instead of picking it up may be scolded by some other adult, or even by a child who has been a witness to the scene. In Indonesia, a Javanese infant is always carried about in its mother's arms when it is awake. A sleeping baby is put down on a pile of clean clothing arranged on a sleeping bench and surrounded by pillows so the infant cannot roll to the ground. As soon as a baby gives signs of crying, it is picked up and nursed. Clearly, the cross-cultural trend is in favor of regular close physical contact between infants and those who are tending them.

In a majority of societies, a baby also sleeps with its mother and perhaps also with its father, further increasing the amount of physical contact between the baby and caretaker. Among the Tairans of Okinawa, except for the first month of life, a baby is always carried about on the back of some caretaker, at least until a younger sibling is born some two or three years later. Even in its first month, someone is always close by and available to pick up a baby who shows any signs of distress. At night, an infant sleeps with its mother. Among the Sebei of Uganda, a mother carries her baby on her back more or less continuously. The infant is supported by a sling, watching its mother work from this vantage point and also napping in the sling. A child also sleeps with its mother at night for three or four years. Among the Kwoma of New Guinea, a baby is rarely put down by its mother until it is weaned. The mother of a young child asks a co-wife or other female relative to do most of her routine chores, and this allows her to spend all of her time with her baby. When she is seated on the floor of the house or outside under the porch, the baby lies on her outstretched legs. If she is walking about, the baby is cuddled in her arms or sits on her neck. In the night, the two sleep side by side.

Where babies remain in physical proximity to their mothers for most of the day, a woman may end up taking her infant along with her as she tends to her chores. Among the Cubeo of the Northwest Amazon, a baby is almost always in close proximity to its mother. The infant is carried around on its mother's hip, supported by a bark-cloth band. A sleeping baby will be placed in a tray on a hammock near its mother as she works. When the mother goes off to her garden, her baby comes along. Similarly, !Kung mothers will take any child under four years of age when they go gathering, in spite of the fact that a round-trip may be anywhere from 2 to 12 miles and even though she will be carrying anywhere from 15 to 33 pounds of vegetables on her return trip. Infants are carried in a special sling, and even older children, who may walk on their own for some part of the journey, will inevitably tire and clamor to be carried before the trip is over. A baby will remain in its sling on the mother's hip while she digs roots and gathers nuts. A Japanese baby also remains close to its mother, even when she is busy with some chore. She carries the baby with her wherever she goes and when she is working at home, she lays it on its bed nearby. Mothers talk and hum to their infants and take the baby along into the hot bath each afternoon.

An infant who is carried or held for most of the day is able to observe the activities of its caretaker from the vantage point of a hip or back. In Guatemala, a Chimalteco baby is carried about on the back of its mother, tucked in a blanket that is tied tightly about her chest. The infant remains there while the mother grinds maize, fetches wood, and washes clothes, and even while she dances for hour after hour at a fiesta. A baby may also be put in a small round hammock hung from a house beam for short intervals during the day. Here, the infant has sufficient room to move around and can easily be swung back and forth by an onlooker. Or a baby may lie or crawl around on a blanket near the door of the house while the mother works. Nevertheless, babies spend most of their time on the mother's back. Among

An Inuit mother and infant in Greenland. The child will remain close to his mother for much of the day.

the Tarahumara of Mexico, a mother places her baby on her back in a pocket fashioned from a shawl, which is then tied across the woman's chest. Infants are carted around in this manner so regularly that it seems as if the baby is part of the mother's adornment. Babies sleep inside the mother's shawl while she herds the sheep and goats and tends to her other chores.

Where an infant enjoys regular contact with a caretaker, the mother usually enlists other people to hold and carry the baby so that she can tend to other chores where the presence of a baby would be problematic. A Gusii mother nurses her infants, sleeps with her baby in her arms, and carries it on her back on long trips.

But during the day, when a mother is working in the field, an older sister or other child watches the baby, so an infant spends a good deal of its time in the company of someone other than its mother. But the fields are close to home, so even when another person is tending an infant, the mother is nearby.

An infant who is not being held or carried is often motivated to remain in the company of other people. By the time that they are one year old, Canadian Hare babies are frequently left to play on their own in the sight of some adult who is doing chores, and youngsters can be seen playing with an axe or a bit of wood, humming nonsense words to themselves. Children of this age will often try to follow an older sibling who is carrying firewood to the stove, the little one holding a stick of wood in its hand. Sometimes, a toddler whose older brother or sister is walking too fast to be followed may end up crying in frustration.

In a small number of cultures, infants are held or carried only occasionally. In Indonesia, an Alorese mother returns to the fields some ten to fourteen days after she has had a baby. The infant remains back in the village for some nine hours a day, an older sibling or other relative acting as caretaker. Where babies sleep in their own beds, proximity to a caretaker is decreased to at least some extent.

An infant may be in the presence of its caretaker continuously without, however, receiving much in the way of physical affection. A Sebei baby is regularly carried on its mother's back, and women nurse their infants on demand, but a mother does not characteristically talk to or fondle her baby or even make eye contact with the child. Among the Kpelle of Liberia, a mother may be weaving, cleaning vegetables, or chatting with another woman and paying no attention to the baby itself while she nurses her infant. The same pattern has been described for some other African mothers.

An infant who is carried about during the day and sleeps with its mother at night rarely needs to cry to make its needs known. The caretaker can usually anticipate the baby's needs before the infant has had enough time to become fussy. Similarly, a mother who is carrying an infant understands the meaning of body movements signalling that the infant is about to urinate or defecate and can hold the baby away from her body or hurry off to the proper place for eliminating. By contrast, a baby who remains in a crib, playpen, or the like has to summon a caretaker in times of need. Similarly, the caretaker discovers that the infant has urinated or defecated only after the fact, creating extra challenges when it comes to toilet training.

See also INFANTS, CARRYING DEVICES FOR

Barry, Herbert, III, and Leonora Paxson. (1971) "Infancy and Early Childhood: Cross-Cultural Codes 2." Ethnology 10: 466–508.

Benedict, Ruth. (1946) *The Chrysanthemum and the Sword.*

Bennett, Wendell, and Robert Zingg. (1935) *The Tarahumara: An Indian Tribe of Northern Mexico.*

DuBois, Cora. (1944) *The People of Alor.*

Erchak, Gerald M. (1977) *Full Respect: Kpelle Children in Adaptation.*

Geertz, Hildred. (1961) *The Javanese Family: A Study of Kinship and Socialization.*

Gladwin, Thomas, and Seymour Sarason. (1953) *Truk: Man in Paradise.*

Goldman, Irving. (1963) *The Cubeo: Indians of the Northwest Amazon.*

Goldschmidt, Walter. (1976) *The Culture and Behavior of the Sebei.*

Hara, Hiroko Sue. (1967) *Hare Indians and Their World.*

Lee, Richard B. (1979) *The !Kung San: Men, Women, and Work in a Foraging Community.*

Lee, Richard B., and Irven DeVore. (1976) *Kalahari Hunter-Gatherers: Studies of the !Kung San and Their Neighbors.*

LeVine, Robert A., and Barbara B. LeVine. (1966) *Nyansongo: A Gusii Community in Kenya.*

Maretzki, Thomas W., and Hatsumi Maretzki. (1966) *Taira: An Okinawan Village.*

Nydegger, William F., and Corinne Nydegger. (1966) *Tarong: An Ilocos Barrio in the Philippines.*

Romney, A. Kimball, and Romaine Romney. (1966) *The Mixtecans of Juxtlahuaca, Mexico.*

Whiting, John W. M. (1941) *Becoming a Kwoma.*

———. (1971) "Causes and Consequences of the Amount of Body Contact between Mother and Infant." Paper presented at the meetings of the American Anthropological Association, New York.

———. (1981) "Environmental Constraints on Infant Care Practices." In *Handbook of Cross-Cultural Human Development*, edited by Ruth H. Munroe, Robert L. Munroe, and Beatrice B. Whiting, 155–179.

INFANTICIDE

Infanticide refers to the deliberate killing of an infant. Because infanticide is usually accomplished by the mother or other close relative in private, it is often hard to establish its use in a given society. But infanticide has been practiced in societies of all kinds everywhere around the world. Thus, most cultures view infanticide as an option for doing away with unwanted infants, at least in some circumstances.

Infanticide is usually practiced on newborn babies. Suffocation is the most common form of infanticide. Thus, the infant may be buried or drowned, or it may be held to the ground, face downward, so that it cannot breathe. Abandoning the baby is another common practice. Infanticide may be frequently practiced in a given society, or it may be reserved for special cases. Infanticide is more common in societies whose subsistence base is hunting or fishing and gathering than in pastoral and agricultural cultures. This may be because children can make genuine contributions to the family's welfare when the subsistence economy is based upon farming. In agricultural societies, children are recruited to do important chores at an early age.

Infanticide is most common in the case of deformed or otherwise abnormal babies. In Mexico, the Mixtecans will take the life of an infant with a face "like an animal," but no other justifications for infanticide are recognized, and a baby with other kinds of physical deformity will be treated as normal. The Jivaro of Ecuador also practice infanticide on deformed babies. The infant is crushed under a foot. An unmarried girl may also take her baby's life if she does not believe that the infant's father will marry her. A North American Comanche infant who was deformed, diseased, or weak might be left out on the plains to die.

Infanticide may be practiced in cases where the addition of a new baby to the family represents some kind of hardship. A baby's survival may be in jeopardy because the family does not have sufficient resources to care for another person. Or the well-being of older children may be compromised if resources have to be stretched to accommodate a new infant. Infanticide was practiced in medieval society because poverty as well as famine prevented parents from being able to care properly for large families. In nomadic societies, it may be too difficult to tote a newborn baby around. Among the Kurnai of Australia, if a woman has given birth at around the time that her tribe is scheduled to move to another camp, her husband forbids her to bring the baby along. The infant is abandoned on a sheet of bark. People say that the baby has been "left behind." A baby may also be killed if it is motherless. Formerly, in Bolivia, if a Toba woman died in childbirth, her baby would be buried alive along with her as the Toba believe that parents and their baby are still a single individual. The same practice is also found in other cultures and can be traced to the fact that babies without mothers cannot easily be kept alive because there is no one available to nurse or care for them.

Multiple births commonly represent an unusual burden for parents, and infanticide is often practiced across cultures when twins are born. Overlaying the practical problems associated with multiple births is the frequently held view that such births can only be the result of malevolent supernatural influences. Among the Sebei of Uganda, it is unusual for both twins to live to maturity, and the middle triplet is said to "never survive." The babies who do not live usually die from willful neglect. If a Toba couple has twins, the first one to be born is usually put to death. Twins are viewed as unnatural because no one believes that a single man can become the father of two children at the same time. Further, no woman can adequately provide milk for two babies at once, so twins must be the result of bad luck.

In many cultures, supernatural forces are also thought to be responsible for other kinds of unusual births, and infanticide may also be practiced in these cases. Toba parents will kill a baby who is deformed or in general very sickly. Partly, the custom depends upon the assumption that the child has little chance of growing up to be a strong or useful person. But infanticide is also practiced as a result of the belief that sick children are demons, or are at least possessed by demons. As babies are thought to be mystically connected to their parents, allowing such an infant to live might mean putting the lives of the parents in jeopardy. The Australian Mining believe that colic in a baby is a result of bad magic, and colicky babies are starved to death. Siberian parents will do away with an infant who happens to be born during a storm.

In many societies, an illegitimate baby poses serious problems for the parents, their kin, the baby, and the community at large. Often, the legal status of the infant is in doubt, and cultural rules regarding who will care for the baby and where it will live are ambiguous. Premarital pregnancies may also bring deep shame upon the mother and her family. A number of cultures solve the problem of illegitimacy through the practice of abortion or infanticide. Among the Rajputs of India, a baby born out of wedlock will be killed by the relatives of the mother as

the only way of preserving the honor of the family. An unmarried Siberian woman who finds that she is pregnant will attempt to induce an abortion. If the procedure fails, she will strangle the baby after it is born.

In some cultures, infanticide is exploited as a way of influencing the sex ratio of children in a family. When this is the case, it is almost always female babies who are killed. The Rajputs, who have a preference for boys, practiced female infanticide until the beginning of the twentieth century. Girls are still less likely than boys to receive prolonged medical care, particularly if the family is poor, and the result of this is a child mortality rate that is twice as high for females than for males. In North America, Comanche parents of twins sometimes killed one or both babies, especially in the case of girls, although they might try to have the baby adopted if possible. Among some Eskimo groups, where males are more or less the only providers of food, female infanticide is also practiced. In classical Greece and Rome, parents routinely resorted to infanticide as a way of limiting the number of girls in a family.

In some societies, infanticide is also practiced in cases of rape. Among the Mossi of the Upper Volta, the baby of a woman who has been raped is always aborted or killed once it is born. Parents may also resort to infanticide when they simply do not want a baby. Among the Cubeo of the Northwest Amazon, a woman will abort or kill her child if she does not enjoy having sexual intercourse with her husband. The infant is buried alive where it was delivered. If the baby is a boy, however, she is much less likely to go through with her plans. Sometimes, a North American Sanpoil woman would deliver her baby in the woods by herself. This gave a woman who did not want her infant the chance to kill it and then take it back to camp claiming that it was born dead. If it was discovered that the woman had in fact killed the baby, she would be beaten severely.

The use of infanticide by a culture does not imply that people in the society do not love their children. The person who is elected to do away with a baby does not typically enjoy doing so. Rather, the killing of a baby is commonly viewed as a necessary evil. In cultures that do not accord full human status to a newborn baby, or where people believe that a dead infant will eventually be reborn, the task is made a bit less onerous. Sometimes, the deliberate killing of a baby is not regarded as infanticide. The Truk of Micronesia believe that infants born with some abnormality are in fact ghosts and they are killed, often by being thrown into the sea, in the same way as are spontaneously aborted fetuses. The Truk themselves do not view this as infanticide, a practice that horrifies them.

As an option for solving the problem of what to do with unwanted infants, infanticide is virtually universal. But there are cultures in which the practice is universally opposed. The Gusii of Kenya disapprove of any kind of infanticide and do not practice it in fact. Indeed, infanticide is viewed as the province of witches, who are said to force a new witch to do away with an infant of her own in order to confirm her powers. The prejudice against infanticide reflects the high value that the Gusii place on children, and the longevity of a marriage depends upon the continued ability of a husband and wife to produce offspring. Even where infanticide is tolerated, it may be disapproved if practiced excessively. Among the Sebei of Uganda, infanticide is practiced and is not punished, but a man can divorce a spouse who has killed three babies in a row.

See also ABORTION; ILLEGITIMACY; PARENTS' PREFERENCE FOR BOY OR GIRL

Czaplicka, M. A. (1914) *Aboriginal Siberia: A Study in Social Anthropology.*

Gladwin, Thomas, and Seymour Sarason. (1953) *Truk: Man in Paradise.*

Goldman, Irving. (1963) *The Cubeo: Indians of the Northwest Amazon.*

Goldschmidt, Walter. (1976) *The Culture and Behavior of the Sebei.*

Harner, Michael J. (1973) *The Jivaro: People of the Sacred Waterfalls.*

Hitchcock, John T., and Leigh Minturn. (1966) *The Rajputs of Khalapur, India.*

Howitt, A. W. (1904) *The Native Tribes of South-Eastern Australia.*

Karsten, Rafael. (1923) *The Toba Indians of the Bolivian Gran Chaco.*

LeVine, Robert A., and Barbara B. LeVine. (1966) *Nyansongo: A Gusii Community in Kenya.*

Ray, Verne. (1933) *The Sanpoil and the Nespelem: Salishan Peoples of Northeastern Washington.*

Romney, A. Kimball, and Romaine Romney. (1966) *The Mixtecans of Juxtlahuaca, Mexico.*

Skinner, E. P. (1964) *The Mossi of the Upper Volta.*

Super, Charles M. (1981) "Behavioral Development in Infancy." In *Handbook of Cross-Cultural Human Development,* edited by Ruth H. Munroe, Robert L. Munroe, and Beatrice B. Whiting, 181–270.

Wallace, Ernest, and E. Adamson Hoebel. (1952) *The Comanches: Lords of the South Plains.*

Williamson, Laila. (1978) "Infanticide: An Anthropological Analysis." In *Infanticide and the Value of Life,* edited by Marvin Kohl, 61–75.

INFANTS, AFFECTIONATE TREATMENT OF

In cultures across the world, infants tend to be treated with a considerable amount of affection by parents and other caretakers. Of a sample of 87 societies, in 79 percent caretakers are consistently affectionate to babies, and babies are usually treated with affection in an additional 13 percent of these cultures. In only 9 percent of these 87 cultures do caretakers withhold affection from infants even occasionally. In Mexico, a Mixtecan mother tends to a nursing infant whenever she is home, and the child is rewarded with many demonstrations of physical and verbal affection. In the Philippines, Tarong babies receive a considerable amount of affection from both men and women, although males are a bit less demonstrative than are females. A North American Hutterite baby is picked up, tickled, held, patted, and spoken to by anyone who happens to pass by and ends up receiving constant affectionate displays from other people.

Even when parents do not display much affection to their infants, a baby is likely to receive affectionate treatment from other people. In Kenya, Gusii mothers do not typically cuddle, kiss, or coo at their babies. But child nurses, who are responsible for a good deal of the care of a Gusii baby, often hug, kiss, and tickle their charges. Grandmothers also consistently show physical affection to their grandchildren, kissing them and gently biting a foot or hand, and aunts sometimes display the same kinds of behaviors toward young children.

The quality of affectionate handling that a baby is likely to receive depends in part upon the status of its caretaker. Thus, a baby who is treated in a generally affectionate way may nevertheless find itself buffeted around on occasion by a well-meaning baby tender. A Gusii baby is treated affectionately by its child nurse, but young caretakers are not always gentle when showing affection and will sometimes frighten a baby with their rough handling. Further, when a child nurse is busy playing with peers, she is likely to ignore the infant whom she is tending. Sometimes the generally affectionate treatment received by a baby is interrupted by less indulgent handling. In Micronesia, Truk babies are picked up, bounced, kissed, held, and talked to by men and women alike. But they are also teased. Thus, someone might offer an infant some desirable object only to take it away when the baby shows interest. Or someone might hold a cigarette near the infant's face until it becomes distressed.

While these societies are the exception, the affectionate treatment of babies is uncommon in some societies. In Uganda, Sebei women nurse their babies on demand, but nursing is not accompanied by physical affection or social interaction. Even when she is not preoccupied with other tasks or other people, a mother does not typically look at, talk to, or fondle her baby. An infant is only likely to be petted by a childless woman who is holding someone else's baby. Men are even less demonstrative toward infants and rarely care for or play with young children. Similarly, Jamaican babies are rarely fondled by their mothers and indeed, physical contact between the two is minimal. Even the occasional physical affection that they do get is cut off when a new baby comes along, and parents acknowledge that older siblings "feel neglected" when a mother's attention is turned to the youngest member of the household. Jamaican fathers are never seen to show affection for their children, and youngsters see them more or less exclusively as disciplinarians.

The degree of affectionate treatment an infant receives is associated with a number of other features of a society. For instance, a culture's mode of subsistence is a good predictor of how much affection a baby is likely to receive, and in particular, infants are treated affectionately in all hunting and gathering societies for which we have information. Cultural complexity is also able to predict the degree to which infants are shown love, warmth, and affection. The more complex the society, the less likely it is that an infant will consistently receive affectionate treatment. This relationship between complexity and display of affection may itself depend upon the fact that household structure, mode of making a

A Chinese mother and child. Parents treat their infants with affection in most world societies.

living, and so on are themselves related to the level of complexity of a society. Thus, who lives with whom, how people make a living, and other things of this sort may be the real driving forces behind variations in displays of affection toward babies. Display of affection toward babies may also reflect a more general set of attitudes about the propriety of demonstrations of affection toward other people. Thus, for instance, if Gusii mothers show less physical affection toward their babies than do women in other cultures, this may be a consequence of the more general lack of physical and even verbal demonstrativeness or intimacy between people of adjacent generations or the opposite sex. Thus, two people may not shake hands unless they are roughly the same age; a father may not enter the home of his own son; and a son, for his part, can only go as far as the foyer of his mother's dwelling.

Why is the display of affection toward infants so common across cultures? We may be seeing here the ability of babies to evoke caretaking responses from other people. Infants possess sets of attributes, including a big head, pudgy cheeks, big, round eyes, high forehead, pouty lips, and small limbs, that make them cute to most people. The effect of these characteristics is to motivate almost anyone who happens to see an infant to want to interact with and show affection to the baby. The characteristics of babies are so attractive that even toddlers are highly likely to be nurturant to infants. And human beings think that puppies, kittens, and other immature animals who share the physical profile of human babies are cute enough to take home and care for. This gut response that people have to the adorable appearance of babies is assumed to be the result of evolution. Babies in the past who had the power to evoke affection and nurturance from other people were more likely to survive, reproduce, and pass on the very traits that made other people think of them as cute and approachable. The result is that, in vir-

tually all contemporary societies, babies can count on being treated with affection.

See also CRYING; INFANTS, INDULGENCE OF

Barry, Herbert, III, and Leonora Paxson. (1971) "Infancy and Childhood: Cross-Cultural Codes 2." *Ethnology* 10: 466–508.

Cohen, Yehudi A. (1966) *A Study of Interpersonal Relations in a Jamaican Community.*

Gladwin, Thomas, and Seymour Sarason. (1953) *Truk: Man in Paradise.*

Goldschmidt, Walter. (1976) *The Culture and Behavior of the Sebei.*

LeVine, Robert A., and Barbara B. LeVine. (1966) *Nyansongo: A Gusii Community in Kenya.*

Levinson, David, and Martin J. Malone. (1980) *Toward Explaining Human Culture.*

Nydegger, William F., and Corinne Nydegger. (1966) *Tarong: An Ilocos Barrio in the Philippines.*

Rohner, Ronald P. (1975) *They Love Me, They Love Me Not: A Worldwide Study of the Effects of Parental Acceptance and Rejection.*

Romney, A. Kimball, and Romaine Romney. (1966) *The Mixtecans of Juxtlahuaca, Mexico.*

Whiting, Beatrice B., and Carolyn Pope Edwards. (1988) *Children of Different Worlds: The Formation of Social Behavior.*

 **INFANTS, BELIEFS ABOUT**

Beliefs about the nature of newborn babies are similar across many societies around the world. In part, this reflects the real profile of babies as helpless and cognitively immature. People in most cultures would agree with the assessment of the Philippine Tarong who view infants as helpless, irresponsible, and captivating. And adults the world over expend much energy in seeing to it that infants are protected and that their needs are met. Adults everywhere might also agree with the Mixtecans of Mexico who believe that infants have no awareness or reason. Indeed, the Mixtecan word for infant is "in darkness." Because the Mixtecans assume that learning depends upon awareness, infants are assumed to be unteachable. Indeed, people will sometimes use the Spanish word for "creature" when referring to infants.

Beliefs about the nature of infants are also affected by rates of mortality, which are relatively high in many societies. The result is that babies are often seen as very vulnerable. But while mortality rates can be traced to pregnancy and birth complications and to infantile diseases, adults in many cultures attribute infant fragility to supernatural causes. According to the Javanese of Indonesia, babies are extremely sensitive to sudden shocks, which include rough handling, loud noises, strong tastes, physical discomfort, and so on. A baby exposed to such influences would be *kaget,* that is, shocked, startled, and upset, allowing the evil spirits, which are forever hovering around the infant and mother, to enter the baby and cause illness or even death. Parents, therefore, are preoccupied with protecting a new infant from anything that might expose the baby to the influence of evil spirits. The Gusii of Kenya similarly believe that infants are fragile. This means that they are particularly vulnerable to evil influences that can cause fatal diseases. Parents take pains to meet all of a baby's needs in hopes of saving it from evil influences. The Mixtecans of Mexico also believe that babies under two or three months of age are very vulnerable. The evil eye, which can be directed at an infant intentionally or unintentionally, as well as the activities of witches, represent special dangers to the newborn infant, and a sleeping baby is most susceptible as it cannot protect

itself. No one except a member of the family is allowed to see an infant for fear that the baby will be harmed. An infant's face is always covered with a rebozo to protect it from the evil eye. Mothers will also place a pair of scissors or crossed sticks in a baby's crib to cut the evil powers. Or a baby may wear a nut strung around its wrist as well as a cap on its head to protect it from evil influences. The confinement of mothers and their babies inside the house for the first 40 days after a birth protects the infant to some degree from potential harm. The Tarong of the Philippines worry that infants will be harmed or killed by the jealous nonhumans, and many precautions are taken in an attempt to thwart the spiteful activities of the supernatural. The Rajputs of India believe that babies are particularly vulnerable to supernatural dangers, and many infants wear protective charms until they are around 18 months of age. A black dot worn on the forehead or foot protects babies from the evil eye, which may be directed at them by some jealous person, and mothers are supposed to avoid making a child look attractive for fear of inviting the evil eye. Ghosts can also cause a child to be ill or possessed. In Uganda, Sebei adults say that infants are susceptible to the evil eye. As it is impossible to tell who has the evil eye, an infant is shielded from visits by strangers until it gains some strength. Babies wear cowrie shells, iron neck rings, and medicinal herbs mixed with cow's milk as protection against the evil eye. Neighbors are permitted to see a baby after they have given it a small gift. Jamaicans think that vomiting in an infant is evidence that evil spirits have entered the baby's body, and parents try to protect infants by applying a gummy substance from tree bark to the child's hair. Some people keep a Bible open next to the child's head instead. Once the baby is baptized it is safe form evil influences because God will protect it.

Cultures differ regarding their attitudes about the innocence of babies. Thus, for example, the Rajputs view infants as pure. God resides in the baby, who cannot tell the difference between good and evil. A baby remains pure until it has begun to eat solid food. By contrast, Jamaicans view infants as naturally "rude," aggressive, and evil. The job of adults, therefore, is to "bend" the child through discipline and thereby to neutralize these inborn tendencies.

Cohen, Yehudi A. (1966) *A Study of Interpersonal Relations in a Jamaican Community.*

Geertz, Hildred. (1961) *The Javanese Family: A Study of Kinship and Socialization.*

Goldschmidt, Walter. (1976) *The Culture and Behavior of the Sebei.*

Hitchcock, John T., and Leigh Minturn. (1966) *The Rajputs of Khalapur, India.*

LeVine, Robert A., and Barbara B. LeVine. (1966) *Nyansongo: A Gusii Community in Kenya.*

Nydegger, William F., and Corinne Nydegger. (1966) *Tarong: An Ilocos Barrio in the Philippines.*

Romney, A. Kimball, and Romaine Romney. (1966) *The Mixtecans of Juxtlahuaca, Mexico.*

INFANTS, CARRYING DEVICES FOR

Human infants are born relatively immature and helpless compared with newborns of many other species. The immaturity of the human baby means that a mother can deliver an infant with an already large brain that has the capacity to learn much from the environment. The baby's immaturity at birth allows it to grow up to be a highly competent and widely talented adult by cross-species standards. The downside of a human baby's immaturity is that it cannot fend for itself or get around on its own.

This means that human infants have to be "packaged" in some way that keeps them safe. And unless its caretakers are willing to leave a baby in one place for the first year or so of its life, the human infant has to be carried about by some older person. Cultures across the world have invented a variety of devices for carrying infants around efficiently. Sometimes, the same device can be used to house the baby even when it is not being transported from place to place.

In a number of cultures, babies are packaged in cradleboards. This is the preferred carrying device in 16 percent of 154 cultures around the world. Cradleboards in general create a pocket into which a baby can be tucked. The back of the cradleboard is relatively stiff. Often the baby is strapped inside the device. In cultures that employ cradleboards, a baby often remains in the device for most of the day and night, being removed mainly for cleaning and changing. Once a North American Comanche woman returned to her normal work routine, her infant was placed on a "papoose board" that could be stood in a corner or carried on the mother's back when she was out gathering seeds or roots. The baby remained on the board for most of the day for the first ten months of its life. Some papoose boards were like rawhide baskets attached to a flat board, while others were made of soft buckskin attached to a board and laced up the front. Babies were bundled up in blankets in the winter before being placed in their papoose boards. Because it was hard to get infants in and out of their papoose boards, a baby, once placed in its board, remained there all day. A newborn North American Chippewa baby was too small to fit in a standard cradleboard. Therefore, an infant was first placed in a birchbark container, which was then tied to the board. As the baby grew, a larger and larger container was used until the infant could be strapped to the cradleboard itself. Cradleboards were lined with animal skins. The Chippewa used cradleboards partly for efficiency, as the boards permitted a mother to carry her baby around on her back when on the move and also keep the baby safe when put down. Cradleboards were also seen as instrumental in helping the baby's back to grow straight, and the Chippewa said that babies liked their boards and cried to be put in them. The bag containing the infant's umbilical cord was hung on its cradleboard, along with shells, feathers, or strings of beads or duck skulls or other bones strung on strips of buckskin. Sometimes, bunches of pinecones, one filled with maple sugar for the baby to suck, were suspended on the cradleboard. Images of spiderwebs were also hung from the boards to catch evil that would otherwise harm the baby. A North American Sanpoil mother did not make a cradleboard for her baby until after it was born. Until the board was ready, the baby might be wrapped up in a fur. Sanpoil babies slept in night bags for the first year of life, and sometimes an infant would also stay in the bag during the day until it was switched to the cradleboard. For the first few months of its life, a baby was only removed from the board for bathing and changing.

When cradleboards are the main carrying device, and especially when the cradleboard remains horizontal, some solution must be found for the disposal of urine and feces. In some cultures, moss is inserted into the cradleboard to act as a diaper. The moss may then be changed whenever the baby cries. Among the Chippewa, dried moss was usually used as a diaper, and babies did not typically get rashes. The moss also kept the infant smelling sweet in spite of its being confined all day on the cradleboard. Among the Sanpoil, sleeping bags were lined with fur or sweet-smelling grasses, when they could be found. If the baby was a boy, his penis was allowed to protrude from the bag. Sometimes, diapers are used. In New Mexico, Zuni babies wore diapers if the parents could afford them. Otherwise, soft rags served as a substitute. A number of American Indian societies in North America use a urine tube. The tube is placed between the baby's legs and urine then flows down the tube and out a hole in the cradleboard. Among the Comanche, a drainage tube was provided in a girl's papoose board while a boy infant's penis peeked out of an opening in the front of the board so that the baby would not get wet, but not with very good effect, so that infants were washed and powdered at the end of each day.

In cultures that use cradleboards as a carrying device, infants may be removed every so often for exercise. A Zuni baby was removed from its cradleboard a few times each day and laid on its parents' bed where it was able to kick and move about. Infants in cradleboard cultures are often permitted more time out of the board once they are old enough to become mobile on their own. Sanpoil babies continued to be put in cradleboards until they could walk. After that, the board was used for traveling or if the infant needed to sleep during the day. In North America, very young Hopi babies remained in their cradleboards virtually all of the time unless they were being bathed. The board was always held horizontally instead of being hung vertically. Once the infant reached three months of age, the cradleboard began to be abandoned except when the baby was sleeping. Babies older than six months could give up their cradleboards altogether, and one-year-olds were no longer using the boards.

In other cradleboard cultures, the baby continues to be carried about in the board even after it can move about. A ten-month-old Comanche baby began to be permitted to crawl, but when it was not playing about on the ground, the infant continued to be placed in its papoose board on its mother's back. When children got too heavy to be carried on the back, the papoose board was placed on poles and pulled along by a packhorse. Youngsters continued to be pulled about in this manner until they were old enough to ride a horse themselves. Babies were very content in the papoose board, looking around over the mother's shoulder or falling asleep as she moved about.

Westerners may wonder whether a baby can be happy strapped into a cradleboard most of the time for the first months of life. But mothers who use cradleboards say that their babies seem to do better in the board than out of it. Some modern Zuni mothers removed their month-old babies from the cradleboard. Other infants might remain strapped to the board for the first 18 months of life. Some parents claimed that babies cried much more frequently when they were not in their cradleboards. There is evidence that babies in cradleboard cultures differ physiologically from other infants. Thus, for example, Navaho babies score very low on measures of muscle tone, vigor, irritability, and reaction to pinpricks, and this profile is apparent at birth. It is possible, then, that cradleboards are used in societies where infants are physically suited to the restraint that these carrying devices enforce upon the baby. By contrast, the more active infant of European descent actively resists physical restraint, perhaps making cradleboards and similar devices impractical for these babies.

Cradleboards represent a way of packaging infants in which the package is a permanent container. Some cultures do not use permanent carrying devices. Rather, the baby is somehow tied onto the body of the caretaker. In 48 percent of 154 cultures, babies are placed in a sling or flexible pouch that is carried on the body of the caretaker. In an additional 27 percent of these cultures, the infant is simply tied to the body of the caretaker. In Mexico, a Tarahumara woman carries her baby in a shawl on her back, between her shoulders. She hoists the infant up by an arm, and the baby hangs onto the mother until she is able to adjust her shawl into a pocket housing the baby. There the baby remains for much of the time. A Guatemalan Chimalteco mother carries her baby on her back in a blanket that is tied around her chest. The infant travels with her this way wherever she goes. Thus, the infant

An Indonesian mother carries her child in a shoulder sling.

remains on the back of its mother while she grinds maize, washes clothes, and fetches firewood, and even while she dances for hours at a fiesta. In Indonesia, a Javanese infant is carried on the mother's hip, cradled in a long, narrow shawl that is tied over one shoulder to form a pocket on the opposite hip. Sometimes, the baby may be placed on the woman's back if she is traveling a long distance. Javanese children love to ride around in the mother's shawl, and youngsters under three years of age clamor to be picked up and carried. Children as old as eight years may be placed in the mother's shawl instead of being left at home in bed when they are sick. Kalahari !Kung infants are carried about in a sling that allows them maximum freedom. The

Kahn-Tineta Horn, a forceful Indian spokesperson and former beauty queen, strides through the Caughnawaga Indian Reserve in Montreal in 1971 with her daughter, Ojistoh, strapped onto a cradleboard.

baby is supported on the mother's hip, arms and legs moving about unhindered. Infants see what the mother sees and find themselves eye to eye with any child who might come along. The baby has access to the mother's breast and can nurse at will and plays with the jewelry that hangs around her neck. A Japanese baby is tied to its mother's body with sashes strung under its arms and buttocks. The sashes are wound about the mother's shoulders and tied at the waist. A woman will drape her outer jacket right over the baby in the winter. An infant learns to cling to the back of a caretaker as it is carried around, and babies are responsible for positioning themselves comfortably in their slings. Older brothers and sisters also cart infants about in the same fashion, even when they are running around or playing hopscotch.

Some societies place babies in permanent devices that cannot, however, be carted about in the way that a cradleboard can. This is the preferred method of packaging babies in 6 percent of 154 cultures. In Southern India, Gopalpur babies are housed in a cradle made of wood or fiber and hung by ropes from the ceiling of the veranda. An infant lies on its back and can watch the movement of the paper birds that hang from the mobile suspended above the cradle. A crying baby will be vigorously rocked by an older sibling until it falls asleep.

As these examples illustrate, different kinds of carrying devices are used in different geographic areas of the world. In African and South American cultures, babies are typically carried about in a sling-like contraption draped over the body of the caretaker. An African baby also generally sleeps on a mat or platform next to the mother. Often, the infant and mother are in direct skin-to-skin contact, as babies wear no clothes and women go topless in the daytime and sleep naked at night. South American babies sometimes sleep in a boxlike cradle, although a mat or hammock are most commonly used, with the infant usually sleeping with the mother. In Eurasian cultures, infants are rarely carried about in a sling. Rather, the baby spends its time in a cradle that can be carried around the house or to the fields by the mother or other caretaker. If camels, horses, or reindeer are used for transportation, the baby will be tied securely to the cradle, which will then be tied to the saddle of the animal, lashed to a sled, or carried by a rider. In these cultures, cradles are used when a baby is resting or sleeping, and in societies that use cradles, babies are held by a caretaker less than half of the day. For example, in Yugoslavia, where cradles are used, infants are in direct contact with the mother only 27 percent of the time. Even when babies are being held or carried, they are separated from the caretaker by clothing. Babies in many North American societies are swaddled and placed in cradleboards. When the mother is on the move, the board is placed on her back, the baby looking out backwards. When not being carried, the cradleboard is usually placed against some object or hung from a tree limb so that the baby will remain in an upright position. In some island societies in the Indian and Pacific Oceans, babies are carried by caretakers without the aid of a device. Among the Tikopia, a baby who cannot yet support itself is placed in a sling of bark-cloth placed on the back or side of the caretaker. But slings are not used for older infants, who hang onto the side or back of the caretaker by their own strength. Among Eskimo and northern polar region societies, babies are carried on the mother's back, under her parka and facing forward. The coat is belted at the waist and loose at the shoulders, making a roomy but secure pocket for the infant.

The association of particular carrying methods with geographic areas is accounted for in part by borrowing. One group of people copies a specific method of packaging babies from a neighbor. But choice of carrying device is also predictably associated with climate. Thus, cradleboards, swaddling, cribs, cradles, and the like are common in cold climates, while babies are more likely to be carried by the caretaker in warm climates. Apparently, adults package infants to keep them from becoming too cold where the temperature dips to relatively low levels. Where babies do not need to be bundled up for warmth, they usually travel around on the mother's back or hip, typically supported in a shawl, sling, or similar device. When babies are carried by the caretaker during the day, they also typically sleep with her at night. By contrast, an infant who is "packaged" during the day usually sleeps by itself in a crib or something of the sort.

Climate is also related to the length of time that a baby is carried about by some caretaker. Mothers who live in the tropics carry their children around for longer periods of time than do other women. This may be because the parasites that infest tropical settings represent a danger to any small child who is crawling around on the ground.

While carrying devices differ from place to place the world over, all of these packaging schemes tend to allow a baby to be rocked while it is installed in the device. Infants who are carried about in slings are rocked up and down by the action of the caretaker's body as she walks about or performs her chores. Cradles are usually either attached to some rocking device or constructed so that they can be hung from a house beam or tree limb and rocked or swung. Sometimes, and especially in Middle East cultures, a baby may be placed in a hammock. This is not surprising. Systematic studies have suggested that babies are happiest when rocked. Further, a crying baby is most effectively calmed by rocking it up and down for a total distance of three inches at 60 cycles per minute. This pattern mimics the rocking that a baby would experience on the back, hip, or chest of a mobile caretaker. This suggests that human babies are adapted to prefer a motion that coincides with what they would experience if carried about by some other person. This is a sensible adaptation for a helpless baby who is probably safest when in close proximity to a caretaker.

Barry, Herbert, III, and Leonora Paxson. (1971) "Infancy and Childhood: Cross-Cultural Codes 2." *Ethnology* 10: 466–508.

Beals, Alan R. (1962) *Gopalpur: A South Indian Village.*

Benedict, Ruth. (1946) *The Chrysanthemum and the Sword.*

Bennett, Wendell, and Robert Zingg. (1935) *The Tarahumara: An Indian Tribe of Northern Mexico.*

Freedman, Daniel G. (1974) *Human Infancy: An Evolutionary Perspective.*

Geertz, Hildred. (1961) *The Javanese Family: A Study of Kinship and Socialization.*

Hilger, M. Inez. (1951) *Chippewa Child Life and its Cultural Background.*

Leighton, Dorothea, and John Adair. (1966) *People of the Middle Place: A Study of the Zuni Indians.*

Ray, Verne. (1933) *The Sanpoil and the Nespelem: Salishan Peoples of Northeastern Washington.*

Thompson, Laura, and Alice Joseph. (1947) *The Hopi Way.*

Wagley, Charles. (1949) "The Social and Religious Life of a Guatemalan Village." *American Anthropologist* 51: 3–150.

Wallace, Ernest. and E. Adamson Hoebel. (1952) *The Comanches: Lords of the South Plains.*

Whiting, Beatrice B. (1971) "Folk Wisdom and Child Rearing." Paper presented at meetings of the American Association for the Advancement of Science, December.

Whiting, John W. M. (1971) "Causes and Consequences of the Amount of Body Contact between Mother and Infant." Paper presented at the meetings of the American Anthropological Association, New York.

Whiting, John W. M. (1981) "Environmental Constraints on Infant Care Practices." In *Handbook of Cross-Cultural Human Development,* edited by Ruth H. Munroe, Robert L. Munroe, and Beatrice B. Whiting, 155–179

INFANTS, INDULGENCE OF

An infant is treated with indulgence to the extent that its needs are met consistently and swiftly by its caretakers. If caretakers are less predictable, and even neglectful, in their responses to the infant, then caretaking is regarded as less indulgent. Indulgent caretaking is also associated with lenient treatment of an older child, while caretaking lacking in indulgence is characterized by disapproval and punishment of the child. In most of the societies around the world, infants and young children are treated indulgently. Caretakers are consistently nurturant and affectionate, meeting the demands of infants quickly and predictably, in 79 percent of 88 cultures. In an additional 12 percent of these societies, caretakers are usually affectionate but show occasional neglect toward babies. Infants experience a somewhat greater degree of deprivation in 8 percent of these cultures, and in only 1 percent are caretakers regularly harsh or neglectful toward babies. Similar patterns typify the treatment of young children. Thus, caretaking is characterized by a high degree of leniency and indulgence in 58 percent of 88 cultures around the world. Caretakers are generally permissive with children, punishing or expressing disapproval only occasionally, in an additional 25 percent of these societies. Children are treated somewhat severely in 14 percent of the 88 cultures, while persistent or severe punishment is typical of the behavior of caretakers in 3 percent of these societies.

In the Philippines, Tarong adults go out of their way to make infants comfortable. Thus, a baby is given baths to cool it off during the day, while someone will fan it at night. Many parents drape an infant's hammock with mosquito nets to keep annoying flies away. Babies are dusted with talcum powder to counteract prickly heat and offered tempting foods. According to the Tairans of Okinawa, children under six years of age are not responsible for their own behavior because they do not know any better. A baby is also a gift of God. As a result, babies require extreme indulgence, and Tairan infants receive constant attention and affection. In the Amazon, a crying Cubeo baby will be picked up and nursed or comforted immediately. Among the Banoi of Thailand, an infant can only be comforted by its mother, and women almost always respond immediately to any signs of distress on the part of their babies. A woman will always allow a crying or fussing infant to nurse and will regularly offer her infant a breast even when it is perfectly content. Mothers and other family members also hold and play with infants, talk to them soothingly, stroke their genitals, blow in their ears, and so on, even when they are not fussing. Women are indulgent with their infants in part because they genuinely enjoy the interaction and in part because they believe that the only way to reach and control a baby is through affection. In Guatemala, a Chimalteco baby is carried around everywhere in a basket on its mother's back and is nursed whenever it cries. Indeed, a woman will stop whatever she is doing to feed a fretting infant. Among the Canadian Hare, everyone, including men and women, boys and girls, likes to touch, carry, talk to, and play with a baby. If an infant is crying, someone will pick it up and try to create a distraction. In Indonesia, a crying Javanese baby is picked up by its mother and gently rocked and bounced in her arms. This is also how small babies are lulled to sleep. When it is time for an older child to go to bed, the mother, or perhaps an older sister, grandmother, or father will cuddle the youngster on his or her sleeping mat. Children are also protected from anything that might startle them, including strong tastes, loud noises, anger, frustration, and disappointment. Thus, for instance, a mother will hold her hands over a child's ears in a thunderstorm. Similarly, women try to give children whatever they want. If a baby wants some forbidden object, they will distract the infant to hide the object.

Adults and older children across cultures also like to hold and play with infants, so that indulgence of infants often extends to pleasant interactions with a baby even when it is not actually demanding attention. In Micronesia, Ifaluk infants are passed about from person to person because everyone, adults and children alike, loves to hold and play with a baby. An infant may be held by ten different people during a 30-minute conversation. A baby is never left alone until it can walk, and people insist that a baby who was isolated from other people would soon die. In New Ireland, everyone in the neighborhood plays with a Lesu baby. Whenever a group of people is collected in one place, a baby is handed around, kissed, cuddled, and jostled up and down, and men and women alike will fondle and play with an infant. Sometimes, however, caretakers only respond to infants who are actively expressing some need. Among the Rajputs of India, neither women nor the older girls who take care of babies play with infants. An old man may sometimes play with a baby whom he is watching, but primarily a caretaker ignores the infant on her hip unless it is actively fussing. Caretakers are more interested in quieting a baby than in stimulating it.

Caretakers are less indulgent in a handful of cultures. In Uganda, Sebei infants are typically carried on the mother's back during the day. But a woman may put the baby down on the floor if she is working around the house. A child is then allowed to fuss and cry until it finally falls asleep. Among the Jivaro of Ecuador, mothers leave their infants at home when they go to work in their gardens, and women typically remain away from home for hours at a time. The baby may be supervised by an older sister. A hungry infant who cries persistently may be picked up by its child nurse, who will try to quiet the baby by singing lullabies or feeding it chewed up boiled manioc. But hungry babies often cry for a considerable period of time without receiving much attention. Jamaican mothers never caress or fondle their babies during nursing, and a baby of five or six months who begins to bite when nursing is slapped. They rarely go to sleep after a meal without first crying out of hunger for a protracted period of time.

A caretaker may be in close proximity to a child without, however, displaying indulgence toward the baby. Among the Truk of Micronesia, infants receive more attention in infancy than they probably do at any other time of life. Women do not resume their workload until they are strong enough, with the result that new mothers spend all of their time lying beside, playing with, feeding, and holding their babies. But as the mother regains her strength, her response to her infant's crying is less consistent. Thus, a baby who is fussing may be ignored for a few minutes. And when the mother does respond, she may only nurse the baby for a minute or two before becoming distracted and putting it down. When the mother does begin to work again, she either remains close to home, at least until the baby can crawl, or she takes her infant with her. Nevertheless, a youngster is still unlikely to capture the mother's attention very quickly or hold it for very long. When the infant begins to crawl, a woman begins to leave the house for an hour or more with some other person who may then also wander off, leaving the baby with yet another caretaker. Similarly, if a woman happens to be preoccupied with some other activity, a youngster may not be able to capture her immediate attention even if the child has had an accident and is screaming in distress. In such cases, the mother may only look over to see whether any serious injury has occurred.

High indulgence in infancy does not guarantee the same degree of solicitude toward an older child. In Micronesia, a Palauan baby can expect to be held, carried, cuddled, and amused. Mothers are rarely far from their infants, and a woman will generally spend all of her free time pampering her baby. Toddlers, who are especially demanding, can also expect to be indulged by

their mothers, who respond to all of a youngster's demands, usually with good grace. But by five years of age, the same child will be rebuffed by the mother, who is now interested in convincing her youngster that she can no longer be counted on as a source of unconditional affection and indulgence. A child who was once carried is now forced to walk. A youngster whose cries were once answered swiftly is now ignored. Whereas the mother formerly treated her child tenderly, she is now likely to tease or shout at the youngster. Some mothers stand firm from the start in their efforts to distance their children, while others may initially relent in the face of persistent demands for attention from an insistent child. For boys, the shift is especially abrupt, and eventually, all children learn that their relationships to their mothers have changed forever. Five-year-old children are not left to fend for themselves. They continue to be supervised by an older sibling, who now takes over significant responsibility for tending the younger child. But this kind of attention does not really make up for the loss of the mother's solicitude. Similarly, an African Swazi mother carries her infant everywhere she goes in a sling on her back. A crying baby is fed immediately and is fondled not only by the mother but also by its father and other people. By contrast, a toddler remains home with the other children when the mother is off in the fields or attending to some other task, and women may be gone from home for hours. A toddler can now expect to be punished more severely, and physical punishment may now take the place of other forms of discipline.

The degree of indulgence directed toward an infant is related to the number and kind of secondary caretakers upon whom a mother can rely. Infants are most likely to be treated with indulgence in households where mothers can depend upon other people to help with caretaking. This is especially true where father and grandparents help to tend babies on a daily basis. By contrast, where a mother depends largely upon older children to help watch the baby, indulgence is not as easy to predict. Where the mother has the sole responsibility for caretaking, the baby is most likely to be neglected. Indulgence of babies also tends to be associated with other features of caretaking. Where people in a culture place a high value on the indulgence of infants, accommodations may be made to free up the mother so that she can care for her baby. Among the Truk, a new mother is supposed to refrain from doing heavy work at least until the child can crawl, and ideally for a year. The concern is not primarily for the woman's physical well-being. Rather, the goal is to allow the mother to devote herself to her baby, and this is demonstrated by cases where women who have adopted infants are also excused from routine work.

See also CRYING; INFANTS, AFFECTIONATE TREATMENT OF

Barnett, H. G. (1960) *Being a Palauan.*

Barry, Herbert, III, and Leonora Paxson. (1971) "Infancy and Early Childhood: Cross-Cultural Codes 2." *Ethnology* 10: 466–508.

Cohen, Yehudi A. (1966) *A Study of Interpersonal Relations in a Jamaican Community.*

Geertz, Hildred. (1961) *The Javanese Family: A Study of Kinship and Socialization.*

Gladwin, Thomas, and Seymour Sarason. (1953) *Truk: Man in Paradise.*

Goldman, Irving. (1963) *The Cubeo: Indians of the Northwest Amazon.*

Goldschmidt, Walter. (1976) *The Culture and Behavior of the Sebei.*

Hara, Hiroko Sue. (1967) *Hare Indians and Their World.*

Harner, Michael J. (1973) *The Jivaro: People of the Sacred Waterfalls.*

Hitchcock, John T., and Leigh Minturn. (1966) *The Rajputs of Khalapur, India.*

Kuper, Hilda. (1963) *The Swazi: A South African Kingdom.*

Levinson, David, and Martin J. Malone. (1980) *Toward Explaining Human Culture.*

Maretzki, Thomas W., and Hatsumi Maretzki. (1966) *Taira: An Okinawan Village.*

Nydegger, William F., and Corinne Nydegger. (1966) *Tarong: An Ilocos Barrio in the Philippines.*

Piker, Steven. (1965) *An Examination of Character and Socialization in a Thai Peasant Community.*

Powdermaker, Hortense. (1933) *Life in Lesu: A Study of Melanesian Society in New Ireland.*

Romney, A. Kimball, and Romaine Romney. (1966) *The Mixtecans of Juxtlahuaca, Mexico.*

Stephens, William N. (1963) *The Family in Cross-Cultural Perspective.*

Wagley, Charles. (1949) "The Social and Religious Life of a Guatemalan Village." *American Anthropologist* 51: 3–150.

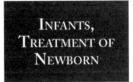

INFANTS, TREATMENT OF NEWBORN

Around the world, when an infant is born, those attending the mother and baby have similar goals in mind. The baby's physical condition is assessed and procedures may be employed to protect the baby, to help it breathe, and so on. The infant is quickly handed over to its mother. Newborn babies may be immediately allowed to nurse, or they may be required to wait until the mother begins to produce milk.

Postpartum Procedures

First, the adults who welcome the new infant into the world occupy themselves attending to its physical condition. Thus, for example, in North America, a newborn Sanpoil baby was dipped in cool water and rubbed vigorously, causing the infant to begin breathing. The baby's face was rubbed to get rid of "ugly lines" and make the features more attractive and the legs and arms were also smoothed out to make them straight. The baby was then placed in a fur wrapping and its head was bound with buckskin to eliminate the elongation that occurs at birth and make the head round. The infant was put down on some bedding and occasionally turned from side to side.

In most societies, once the baby has been cared for by some attendant it is handed over to the mother. A newborn Mexican Mixtecan baby is placed on a mat. The umbilical cord is cut, cauterized, wrapped in cloth, and greased, and grease continues to be applied to the cord stump until it falls off. Then, the baby is bathed and rubbed with almond oil. The rest of the infant's body is also rubbed with almond oil and the baby is dressed in a shirt and fed a spoonful of oil to clean out its stomach. The infant and mother are then allowed to lie down together. Similarly, in the Philippines, a newborn Tarong baby is washed in warm water and wrapped up. A small cap is then put on its head. The baby is placed on a winnowing tray treated with vinegar and gently bounced up and down to prevent it from being frightened easily. Babies are then given an oil pouch to suck. An adult will continue to offer the pouch to a baby for a number of days whenever it cries. The infant will then be put down to sleep with its mother on the slat bed that has been moved into the *sala,* or living-bedroom. The head of the bed is positioned somewhat higher than the foot so that the blood will not go to the head of anyone who is lying on it. People say that the newborn baby and its mother spend a quiet and secluded first month together in this manner, but in fact, the *sala* is the scene of much bustling activity. In Polynesia, the medicine man sucks a newborn Tongan baby's nostrils to clear its nose of mucous and then slaps the infant hard on the back to give it strength.

The baby is washed with warm water, wrapped in bark cloth, and placed in the grandmother's lap. Eventually, the infant is put down next to its mother on its own soft bed of white bark cloth. A newborn Guatemalan Chimalteco baby is put in a sweat bath along with its mother. The midwife rubs the mother and infant with a medicine bag that contains a bundle of leaves wrapped around a hot stone. The application of the medicine bag is meant to warm the baby and start the blood going, and to ease the mother's discomfort. The midwife also massages the mother and bathes the baby. It is very common across cultures for a newborn baby to be bathed, and sometimes these baths continue on a daily basis. North American Arapaho newborns were splashed with cool water as soon as the umbilical cord was cut. It was usually the grandmother, or perhaps the midwife, who administered the bath. The infant was placed face down on the woman's lap and the water was dashed on it. After its first bath, the baby was rubbed with "war paint," that is, with a red ointment. Infants continued to be splashed with water each day until the cord stump fell off, and they were bathed with cold water until they began to walk.

Protection from the Supernatural

In a number of cultures, adults assume that a baby is vulnerable to supernatural influences, and measures of some sort are taken to protect the infant from such forces. The Philippine Tarong chronically worry about the activities of the nonhumans who, because they are jealous of any good fortune on the part of human beings, are likely to try to harm or kill an infant. Therefore, new parents take many precautions against the spiteful acts of the nonhumans. As the umbilical cord is being cut, someone will light one of the ropes used during the birth. The rope, which will continue to burn until the umbilical stump falls off the baby, disguises the odor of childbirth so that the nonhumans will not be able to kill the infant. In the Northwest Amazon, a

Soon after birth, a San mother shapes her child's head.

newborn Cubeo infant is immediately bathed in warm water by its mother. She then paints the baby's face with red spots so that it will look like a jaguar child, protecting the infant against the jaguar. The rest of the baby's body is also painted red, a common practice during Cubeo ceremonies. This grants the baby human status. Sometimes, magical practices are employed that are believed to influence the baby's future behavior. Among the Banoi of Thailand, a baby is washed and placed in a cradle to which stones may be tied, the reasoning being that, as stones don't cry, the baby will not cry either. In North America, the Chippewa bathed a new baby in water in which certain plants had been boiled. The bath was thought to promote the baby's good health, and a mother might bathe her baby in treated water whenever she wished.

Nursing

In many cultures, babies are not permitted to nurse until the mother begins to produce milk. Usually, the baby is given some substitute food to eat or an object to suck to assuage its hunger until it can nurse. In Okinawa, a Tairan infant is bathed in lukewarm water, diapered, wrapped in a kimono and blankets, and laid next to the mother. The baby is given some gauze soaked in tea and sugar on which to suck until the mother begins to produce milk, and this may be the baby's only food for as long as two days if the mother is slow to lactate. A new Mixtecan mother does not immediately nurse her baby. Rather, she expels the colostrum from her breast for two days if there is some other woman who can nurse the baby and one day if there is not. The new mother has a paste made of spice rubbed on her back, hips, and breasts to encourage the production of milk. The Tarong think that colostrum is bad for the baby. Therefore, until the mother begins to produce milk, a baby is nursed by some other neighborhood woman. The Banoi believe that a new mother does not

produce milk for the first few days after birth. Newborns, therefore, are fed mush and/or milk from a bottle by the father or some female relative. A North American Chippewa mother usually nursed her baby as soon as it was born. Some old people, however, thought that a woman should wait two days before nursing because the milk was not good for the baby before then. Babies who cried before the mother's milk was ready would be fed water. In Micronesia, the Truk rub the mother's breast with coconut and then allow the baby to suck for a short while. The infant is then prevented from nursing until the mother's milk begins to flow; otherwise, the colostrum would cause it to have diarrhea. The infant is given water for the first day or so, but if the mother is still not producing milk, it will be fed coconut water or juice from sugarcane, along with other more nourishing foods such as sap from the shoots of coconut palm leaves. North American Arapaho mothers would not nurse their babies for at least two, and perhaps three or four, days after birth because they believed that the colostrum was not good for the baby. The husband, the midwife, or another woman who had attended the birth would suck on the new mother's breast until the colostrum was extracted and milk began to come in. The colostrum was spit out. Until a mother began to produce milk, the baby was nursed by another woman to whom it was carried whenever it cried. Japanese babies are not fed for the first three days of life, until the mother's milk comes in. After that, they are nursed on demand.

By contrast, in some societies, infants nurse immediately. Among the Jamaicans, colostrum is thought to be even better for a baby than milk. Therefore, a baby is allowed to nurse four hours after it is born and may continue to nurse for a number of days before the mother is producing milk. In Guatemala, Chimalteco babies are nursed as soon as they are born and from then on whenever they cry.

See also BIRTH; CRYING; INFANCY; INFANT-CARETAKER CLOSENESS; INFANTS, INDULGENCE OF; NURSING

Benedict, Ruth. (1946) *The Chrysanthemum and the Sword.*

Cohen, Yehudi A. (1966) *A Study of Interpersonal Relations in a Jamaican Community.*

Gladwin, Thomas, and Seymour Sarason. (1953) *Truk: Man in Paradise.*

Goldman, Irving. (1963) *The Cubeo: Indians of the Northwest Amazon.*

Hilger, M. Inez. (1951) *Chippewa Child Life and Its Cultural Background.*

———. (1952) *Arapaho Child Life and Its Cultural Background.*

Maretzki, Thomas W., and Hatsumi Maretzki. (1966) *Taira: An Okinawan Village.*

Nydegger, William F., and Corinne Nydegger. (1966) *Tarong: An Ilocos Barrio in the Philippines.*

Piker, Steven. (1965) *An Examination of Character and Socialization in a Thai Peasant Community.*

Ray, Verne. (1933) *The Sanpoil and the Nespelem: Salishan Peoples of Northeastern Washington.*

Romney, A. Kimball, and Romaine Romney. (1966) *The Mixtecans of Juxtlahuaca, Mexico.*

INITIATION RITES Initiation rites are ceremonies that mark the entrance of an individual into a new status. The new status may be membership into a society, as in the case of the hazing of a college student who hopes to be accepted into a fraternity. Initiation rites that mark the transition out of childhood for a boy or girl are called adolescent initiation rites. Where adolescent initiation rites are customary, the status of the initiated person is often dramatically different from that of the uninitiated child. Among the Gusii of Kenya, an uninitiated girl is called *egesagane* and a boy is called *omoisia*, meaning uncircumcised girl or boy. An adult who was called by either term would be extremely insulted, and even boys and girls who are, in fact, uncircumcised, are offended at the name since the labels imply that the person to whom they are applied is of inferior status. Often, the boy or girl who has undergone the rite is automatically graduated to adult status. Among the Jivaro of Ecuador, when a boy is about 16 years old, he will go to the forest, kill a tree sloth, and shrink its head. Two feasts are then given, and the boy's status as an adult is established. He may now wear the headpiece of an adult male and he may marry. In approximately one half of all traditional societies for which we have information, some kind of initiation rite is held at or around puberty. Initiation ceremonies are more common for girls, perhaps because the first menstrual cycle, which is such a clear indication of physical maturity for females, has no male counterpart. On the other hand, where boys do undergo initiation rites they tend to be more dramatic.

While the details of the initiation ceremony will vary greatly across cultures, puberty rites tend to share common features. Thus, ceremonies are normally overseen by community elders. Parents do not typically play a role in the rites in which their children are participating. Initiation ceremonies typically serve as an educational arena in which initiates are tutored about various community traditions and may also be taught necessary skills. Often, the initiate is forced to submit to some kind of physical ordeal. Male initiation ceremonies frequently include circumcision and female rites may include clitoridectomy. Initiates may also be expected to go without food or sleep. In cultures that hold initiation ceremonies, everyone must undergo the rite at the appropriate age. Participation is not optional. Finally, any particular ceremony typically focuses on the initiation of a single sex, and members of the opposite sex are ordinarily prohibited from witnessing the rite.

Initiation rites also tend to follow the same general blueprint across societies. The initiates are first separated in some manner from the symbols of their former lives. Typically, the young person is removed from the parents' household, with the initiates banding together to form their own group. During the transition period, the rites and all of their attendant activities are conducted. Finally, the initiates are reincorporated into the community in their new adult status.

Male adolescent rites often include a circumcision ceremony. In North Africa, a Teda boy who is ready to be circumcised picks a husband and wife as his sponsors. He calls them "my father" and "my mother" for the duration of the ceremony. His own parents do not take an active role in the ritual. The circumcision takes place in a roughly constructed hut built for the purpose. A procession of people, headed by the sponsor and other men, and followed by the candidate and then a number of uncircumcised boys, retires under a tree a short distance from the hut. It is here that the circumcision will take place. Dressed only in a sheepskin, the boy who is to be circumcised sits on a stone in front of which a hole has been dug to catch the foreskin and blood. One man sits behind the initiate and holds him around the waist. The sponsor, who performs the operation, says: "Cyeni orwu lano," that is, "Little boy look up." When the boy looks up, the foreskin is cut off, and the sponsor says: "Umri, uo lano," that is, "Man, look up." If the boy cries during the operation, the men warn him that they will slit his stomach with a knife. After the procedure has been completed, the participants and observers march back to the circumcision hut, this time with the newly circumcised boy heading the procession. The boys enter the hut, and the uncircumcised youngsters play music on a stringed instrument. The boy's father visits him immediately, congratulating him and saying: "Fortunately you are a man now." The boy remains in the hut for seven days, during which time a number of additional ceremonies are performed. At the end of the seven-day period, the initiate emerges from the hut. His female sponsor is standing in front of the hut, singing: "Garkye, garkwe," that is, "This is a man, this is a man." A number of gifts are given to the boy, after which there is a feast. The boy continues to live in the hut for another three days and is considered to be healed after another seven days have passed. Once the ceremonies are over, the circumcised boy is now a man. As such, he can kill animals and have sexual intercourse with women.

Female initiation rites typically mark the girl's first menstruation. Girls are usually secluded for some period of time. A North American Chippewa girl was secluded in a small wigwam in the woods at some distance from camp at the onset of her first menstruation. The wigwam was built by the girl herself, by her mother, or by both, perhaps with the help of a grandmother. The seclusion lasted for four to ten days. Some mothers fetched their daughters home before the ten days were up because they were afraid to leave them alone in the woods. Before entering her wigwam, the girl's cheeks and perhaps also her forehead were blackened with charcoal and her hair was tied back or else covered with buckskin or cloth. A secluded girl was not allowed to touch herself. If she had an itch, she had to scratch herself with a stick; her mother combed her hair. The girl cooked her own food, some rice which was brought out to her at sundown, and used her own dishes for eating. A secluded girl was forbidden to eat any food that was in season. If she ate berries picked by some campmate, the remaining berries would dry up; if she ate fish, subsequent fishing expeditions would be unsuccessful. The girl was more generally viewed as dangerous to the rest of the community. If she touched a plant, it would wither; a person whom she touched, or even looked at, would become paralyzed. Indeed, a girl was not allowed to touch a baby or handle the clothing of any man for a year after her first menstruation; otherwise, the affected individual would be crippled. During her seclusion, a girl was supposed to keep busy sewing inside the wigwam, chopping wood out-of-doors, and so on. The girl also received instruction from her mother about how to conduct herself in adulthood. At the end of the seclusion, the girl bathed and washed her clothes and a feast was given for her.

A New Mexican Jicarilla girl traditionally underwent a four-day-long initiation ceremony on the next full moon after her first menstruation, when she was 13 or 14 years old. Otherwise she would have bad luck and die young. The girl's mother, with the help of neighbors, began to prepare for the ceremony, gathering a large amount of food and readying the large tipi in which the initiation would take place. Meanwhile, the father looked for a singer who could perform the ceremony and a boy of the same age as his daughter to dance with her at the initiation. All boys were expected to take part in at least one girl's initiation. A man who had never done so would go bald, die early, and fail to become a leader. When the day for the initiation arrived, the boy and girl sat inside the tipi together, the girl on the south side and the boy on the north, and preparations for the initiation began. The old clothes of the boy and girl were taken away and new clothing put on them, the girl's mother dressing her daughter and some neighbor dressing the boy, starting at the feet and working their way up according to a set of prescribed rules. The eyebrows of both young people were removed, and other measures taken to prevent hair from growing at the eyebrows, under the arms or in the pubic region of the boy

and girl. Their hair was dressed and their faces painted, after which they were given "scratchers" with which to scratch themselves when necessary, as they were not permitted to use their fingers for this purpose for the next four days. They were also prohibited from allowing water to touch their lips. Therefore, drinking tubes were provided. Various other restrictions were placed upon the actions of the boy and girl. For instance, they were warned against smiling; otherwise their faces would become wrinkled before they became old. Nor were they allowed to look into water; otherwise, it would rain. The girl was given cornbread to share with the boy. This was the only food that either could eat for the remaining days of the ceremony. Then, body molding ceremonies were performed on both young people. The girl and boy were warned that their behavior during the initiation would determine what sorts of people they became later on in life. If they were obedient during the ceremony, they would be obedient adults. But a girl who lost her temper during the initiation would be short-tempered for life. The scene was now set for the initiation proper. The next phase of the ceremony began with the singing of the chanter hired by the girl's father. Then, the boy and girl were required to run in circles a number of times; this would make them fast runners. The girl and boy returned to the tipi, where they performed a variety of tasks to prepare them for their adult roles. That night, there was singing and dancing as well as a midnight feast for relatives and guests. The next three days of the ceremony proceeded in more or less the same way. On the morning of the last day, most of the guests departed, but the boy, girl, singer, and close relatives remained behind for the final rituals. The hair of the boy and girl was washed, and they were dressed in their old clothes while the singer sang. The singer then painted their faces as well as the faces of any other participants who also wished to be painted. They would then enjoy good luck. The ceremony was then over and the girl was considered marriageable. A family that could afford it might repeat the initiation within a year of the first ceremony to make sure that it would have the desired beneficial effects upon the girl's future life.

In some societies, clitoridectomies are performed as part of the initiation ceremony. Among the Kpelle of Liberia, parents say that clitoridectomies are performed to "cut the frisky" out of a girl. Friskiness, or *lii kete*, refers here to the trait of being uncontrollable, a characteristic of which the Kpelle disapprove in both sexes. A girl who is no longer frisky will be easier to control by her husband and also by Kpelle tradition more generally.

In North America, a number of cultures sent children off on vision quests. The boy or girl would spend a number of days alone in the forest, fasting and waiting for a vision. A Comanche boy who wished to attain supernatural power went on a vision quest at the time of puberty and before he had gone to war. Wearing nothing but a breechcloth and moccasins, the boy departed from camp to fast and keep vigil until he was visited in a dream by the supernatural, who revealed to the boy the particular nature of the "magic"—or power—that he would be equipped to exercise in the future. The visitation was a hallucinatory experience and was no doubt aided by the hunger and fatigue experienced on vision quests, which lasted four days or more. Chippewa children of both sexes went on fasts in the woods in order to obtain supernatural power. Youngsters might fast a number of times, beginning at four years of age. A child this young would refrain from eating for perhaps a day, whereas a child six to eight years old would fast from one to four days and a ten- to twelve-year-old from four to ten days. The idea was that the fasting child would see his or her guardian spirit in a vision. The guardian spirit gave advice and imparted knowledge and power of one sort or another to the child. Thus, a child might learn to make wind or rain, bring success

in war, predict the future, or heal disease. Thus, for instance, a child who dreamed of a thunderbird while on a fast would gain the power to stop storms, which were caused by thunderbirds. After their vision quests, individuals always carried around some symbol of their guardian spirits, such as a feather or a claw, in small bags, or "medicine bundles." The decision to go on a fast depended upon the dream that the child had the night before. Youngsters would be sent off to fast after having a dream that was considered good by their parents. Good dreams might be about thunderbirds, the sun, thunder, lightning, and other natural phenomena as well as anything pertaining to human beings or animals, except for snakes. Every boy was expected to fast, and those who did not were viewed as cowards. Almost every girl also fasted, usually for no more than four days unless the girl wished to become a medicine woman, in which case the fast lasted for ten days. Fasting was no longer effective once a child had reached puberty and began to have impure thoughts, and indeed fasting after this time was considered both disgraceful and ridiculous. Unlike the adolescent initiation rite, vision quests are not always associated with graduation to adult status. The Arapaho appreciated that when a boy's voice began to change, he was growing into manhood. But no one thought that a boy of this age was in fact a man. Arapaho males went on fasts, but only when they had "sense," and an adolescent boy did not usually have enough sense to fast.

Cohen, Yehudi A. (1964) *The Transition from Childhood to Adolescence: Cross-Cultural Studies of Initiation Ceremonies, Legal Systems, and Incest Taboos.*

Harner, Michael J. (1973) *The Jivaro: People of the Sacred Waterfalls.*

Hilger, M. Inez. (1951) *Chippewa Child Life and Its Cultural Background.*

———. (1952) *Arapaho Child Life and Its Cultural Background.*

Kronenberg, Andreas. (1981) *The Teda of Tibesti.*

LeVine, Robert A., and Barbara B. LeVine. (1966) *Nyansongo: A Gusii Community in Kenya.*

Levinson, David, and Martin J. Malone. (1980) *Toward Explaining Human Culture.*

Opler, Morris. (1942) "Adolescence Rite of the Jicarilla." *El Palacio* 49, 25–38.

van Gennep, Arnold. (1960) *The Rites of Passage.*

Wallace, Ernest, and E. Adamson Hoebel. (1952) *The Comanches: Lords of the South Plains.*

INTEGRATION INTO ADULT LIFE

In industrialized societies, the daily lives of children and adults are largely segregated. While adults are busy at their jobs, children are in school. After-school activities also typically involve other children. Neither do youngsters who live in industrial societies have much exposure to the world of adults. They do not regularly observe their parents or other adults at work. Nor do they have much of a sense of what kinds of political or social activities take up the time of adults.

Children who live in subsistence economy cultures are much better acquainted with what adult life is all about. Usually, children are already incorporated into the work force at an early age and are working alongside their parents and other adults. Even if they are not actually participating in some adult activity, they have the chance to observe what the adults are doing. Children may also be present at adult political, religious, and social events. Traditional cultures differ regarding the extent to which they integrate children into adult activities. But industrial societies are extreme in the extent to which they isolate children from adult life. In many societies, by contrast, even infants are toted along to this or that adult activity or event.

Among the Tarong of the Philippines, preschoolers may accompany their parents to the fields or to parties or wakes. Adults would not think of leaving a child at home when something exciting was going on in the neighborhood. The little children are tucked into a corner of the room to sleep when they can no longer keep their eyes open. A grandmother, aunt, or older sister who is planning a trip around town may pack up a preschooler who is no longer nursing and take the youngster along for company. Schoolchildren are allowed to help and remain at parties as long as they are not very disruptive, and youngsters can be seen fetching water and firewood, peeking at the activities in the kitchen, and running after each other through the yard. Their younger siblings, who are also present at these events, do not have this kind of freedom, and they watch the older children jealously. In Okinawa, a Tairan baby is carried on the back of a caretaker for the first two or three years of life. As a result, infants are carted through the village each day so that, by the time they are a year old, they are familiar with every corner of the village as well as everyone who lives there. A child also becomes acquainted with the various kinds of economic, social, and ceremonial activities that make up the fabric of life in his culture and participates vicariously in the business of the children and adults around him. Toddlers to six-year-olds are free to roam the village and, as members of the community, are seen as having the right to play at any public gathering place. At holiday affairs, a two-year-old may end up in the center of the dance floor, while older siblings wait around for food to be served. A small child who disrupts the activities of adults is simply given back to the mother. It is taken for granted that youngsters will be present at a holiday event, and children participate along with their parents at sporting events and dance performances. Children are sometimes asked to put on their own dance shows for the entertainment of adults. The North American Chippewa liked to visit their neighbors, meeting outside in the summertime and in a wigwam in the winter. Children, when not playing, sat and listened to the conversation of the adults during these visits. Sometimes, the conservation consisted of gossip, but often, and especially in wintertime, people recounted legends or reminisced about important past events such as wars or visits to other tribes. Adults and children alike smoked tobacco as they sat about. Often, hosts and guests simply kept one another company without talking about anything at all. In the Philippines, Tarong children have easy access to the events of adult life, and when anything interesting happens, they stop their play to watch what the grownups are doing. If a boat happens to arrive or a husband and wife get into a fight, or if some person is trying to catch a chicken for dinner, at least a few children show up to see what is going on. Children may hang around watching the activities of adults for hours at a time.

In Canada, Kalderas children are always in the vicinity of adults. When parents go off to gatherings, the youngsters are always taken along. At a large ball, a cluster of cribs and playpens may be found in the corner of the room, and children may be seen weaving in and out of a group of adults, playing a game of tag. There were a variety of adult activities in which North American Arapaho children were not allowed to participate. But they were permitted to observe what the grownups were doing. Thus, youngsters watched while the adults played games. They were taken along when their parents visited with neighbors, and sometimes the adults would tell stories specifically meant to entertain the children. Youngsters also participated along with the adults in social dances that were held at various times throughout the year.

When their parents have remained in the village, New Ireland Lesu children will follow them around. This means that youngsters are present at dance rehearsals, communal food preparations, rites, and every other activity in which adults may engage. Occasionally, a child may help out a parent by carrying some manageable item such as a taro basket to the beach. Children participate in ritual dances as soon as they can walk. Somewhat older girls are already helping their mothers with household chores and, as a result, they spend much of their time in the company of older women. Boys' play groups watch the older men fish and also help in the communal cooking. They are also allowed into the men's house and are present when the men are performing rites and holding feasts. At these occasions, the boys eat and listen to the speeches and watch the trading transactions between the older men. Among the Koreans, children are always part of the scene as adults conduct their daily affairs. Children are always attempting to help with adult tasks and to participate in adult activities. Sometimes they are shooed away and sometimes they are permitted to participate. At night, youngsters are put to bed when they have fallen asleep in the lap of some adult as they listen to the conservation going on around them.

Children may also be more nearly segregated from adult life in nonindustrialized societies. Because Indian Rajput women follow the custom of purdah, or seclusion, a Rajput baby is confined to the outdoor courtyard where its mother, grandmother, and aunts, as well as sisters, young brothers, and cousins spend their days. The infant remains in a cot when not actively fussing. A baby is so well covered by a sheet or quilt that an observer might not know that there was anyone in the cot. An infant who is awake and cranky will be carried on the hip of one of the women or older children. But as soon as it quiets down, it is placed back in the cot. Babies do not crawl about very much. The women do most of their chores on the floor of the courtyard, so a mobile baby is an inconvenience. Neither are babies encouraged to walk. Thus, a Rajput spends the first two years of his life in the company of women and children, but as a passive observer. He does not participate in any activities, nor does anyone attempt to interact with the baby except to try to stop it from crying. Youngsters who have begun to walk meander around the courtyard on their own. Or they may be treated to a short excursion out of the courtyard to visit the men's platform. Grandmothers are also more likely to take children on visits and to birth ceremonies and weddings once they have begun to walk. Or a youngster may tag along after the five- to seven-year-old children when they go off somewhere to play. But even though walkers spend more time with a greater variety of adults and older children, they do not really join in the activities of the people around them. They are still, for the most part, observers instead of participants. Similarly, Jamaican infants rarely leave the family house, nor do relatives or neighbors tend to visit each other. Therefore, babies are not exposed to the activities of the wider community for the first year of life.

Benedict, Ruth. (1946) *The Chrysanthemum and the Sword.*

Brandt, Vincent. (1971) *A Korean Village.*

Cohen, Yehudi A. (1966) *A Study of Interpersonal Relations in a Jamaican Community.*

Gladwin, Thomas, and Seymour Sarason. (1953) *Truk: Man in Paradise.*

Hilger, M. Inez. (1951) *Chippewa Child Life and Its Cultural Background.*

———. (1952) *Arapaho Child Life and Its Cultural Background.*

Hitchcock, John T., and Leigh Minturn. (1966) *The Rajputs of Khalapur, India.*

Maretzki, Thomas W., and Hatsumi Maretzki. (1966) *Taira: An Okinawan Village.*

Nydegger, William F., and Corinne Nydegger. (1966) *Tarong: An Ilocos Barrio in the Philippines.*

Powdermaker, Hortense. (1933) *Life in Lesu: A Study of Melanesian Society in New Ireland.*

Salo, Matt, and Sheila Salo. (1977) *The Kalderas in Eastern Canada.*

INTERPERSONAL ENVIRONMENT

Across cultures, children may find themselves in the company of people of different statuses. These may include other children of their own age and sex as well as children of both sexes who may be older or younger than they are. Adolescents and adults of either sex may also make up part of the interpersonal environment of a child. Further, a child may be regularly exposed to kin, to unrelated acquaintances, and to strangers. Youngsters may conduct their activities in the presence of many other people. Or they may be more segregated from people, or from certain categories of people. The network of individuals with whom a child typically interacts differs from culture to culture, and the differences affect the daily experience and also the behavior of the child. A child's interpersonal environment will be affected by a number of features of the culture in which the youngster lives. These include family form and household structure, size and composition of the community, dispersal of relatives, mode of subsistence and preferred leisure-time pursuits, identity of caretakers, nature of children's activities, and level of integration of children into adult life.

The nature and size of the household, the flow of activity within the house, and the nature of interactions between people in different households affect the patterning of a child's interpersonal relationships. Children who live in extended families including a number of mother-father-child units will be surrounded by more people of different ages than will children who live in smaller households. Where members of a household conduct their activities in common rooms, children will be embedded in interpersonal networks that are different from those of youngsters from households where specific activities or specific people are relegated to separate rooms. And where movement between households is fluid, the circle of people to whom a child is exposed will expand. The Tarong of the Philippines live in clusters of dwellings housing related families and surrounding a central yard. Houses always face the footpaths on which people travel from place to place around the village. Individuals who are not occupied with work generally spend their time sitting or doing small chores at a window or on the porch, so that a good deal of Tarong social life consists of chatting with people who happen to be passing by on a path in front of one's house. The yard is the center of activity for most of the women's daily tasks, for much of the men's nonfarm work, and for the family's leisure activities. Older people who can no longer engage in more strenuous work tend babies in the yard; animals are fed there; children play in the yard; baptisms, dances, weddings, birthdays, and funerals take place here; and an infant's first experience of the world outside its house is in the yard. Similarly, among the Tairans of Okinawa, houses can be entered easily from the street and visitors come and go freely. Houses are quite close together, so that a person in one house can carry on a conversation with someone in the neighboring house without ever leaving home.

If members of the family are segregated for some reason, the interactions of children may be more restricted, even if the family is large. Since infants and young children tend to spend most of their time with their mothers, a younger child's circle of interaction will be influenced by restraints on the mother's activities and interactions. Among the Rajputs of India, women are required to remain secluded from men. Since it is women who have the exclusive responsibility for the care of young children, a youngster of either sex under three years of age, and girls of all ages, spend their time largely in the company of females. Women are confined to large outdoor courtyards, which they share with the mother-in-law as well as sisters-in-law. Each woman also has her own indoor room. Women chat with each other all day as they work, visiting one another in their indoor rooms or remaining out of doors in the courtyard. The younger women play hide-and-seek, jacks, or dog-and-cat during the day with the children, while an older woman will tell stories or read to everyone in the evening.

In polygynous cultures, where a man may have two or more wives simultaneously, the composition of the household also influences the nature of a child's interpersonal interactions. Sometimes, as among the Gusii of Kenya, each wife has her own house, which she shares with her children. The father also has a hut of his own if he can afford it. This means that the Gusii child is isolated in some degree from other people for some part of the time. In some polygynous cultures, wives cooperate, so that the circle of people with whom the child interacts includes all of the father's wives and their children. Among the Liberian Kpelle, a child calls all of the father's co-wives "mother," and a woman may watch as well as discipline the child of her co-wife. When co-wives do not get along, this can also affect the child. Among the Gusii, any animosity that exists between co-wives infects a child's relationships with the father's other spouses as well as with their children. Thus, when a woman does not get along with her co-wife, the relationship between her children, the other woman, and the youngsters' half-siblings will be strained. When there is antagonism between Kpelle co-wives, one woman may criticize another in front of the co-wife's children, calling her lazy or the like.

In some societies, children, and especially boys, move out of the home of their parents at some point before they marry. Boys may live, or at least eat, sleep, or spend their leisure time, in houses reserved especially for males. Among the Murngin of Australia and the Nyakyusa of Africa, adolescent boys move into villages of their own. In some cultures, for instance among the Trobrianders of Melanesia, a prepubescent boy moves into the household of one of his mother's brothers. These living arrangements also affect the pattern of the child's daily social interactions.

Customs regarding who supervises infants and younger children affect a youngster's patterns of interpersonal interaction. In most societies the world over, the mother has the principle responsibility for caretaking. However, most mothers can also depend upon other people to pitch in with caretaking chores. In many cultures, an infant or younger child will be supervised by an older sibling or cousin for some part of each day. Sometimes, however, supervision of children is viewed as mainly the job of adults. Thus, infants are cared for principally by older children in 37 percent of 127 cultures around the world. Child caretakers, further, are usually female. In an additional 54 percent of these cultures, infants are primarily cared for by adult family members. Again, these are for the most part females. In the remaining 9 percent of 127 societies, infants are supervised chiefly by someone outside the family, for instance, an employed babysitter. These caretakers are overwhelmingly female. These differences in the status of secondary caretakers make a difference for a child's daily interpersonal experiences. Further, if caretakers cart their charges along as they attend to their daily chores, infants and children will find themselves in the company of a variety of kinds of people. For instance, in Okinawa, Tairan caretakers carry infants on their backs for the first few years of life, and babies and toddlers, as a result, know everyone in the village.

Mothers always play a more significant role than do fathers in the lives of their children across cultures. However, there are differences in the extent to which children interact with their fathers from place to place. Among the Lesu of New Ireland, men will take over caretaking duties when their wives are occupied with other tasks. By contrast, among the Javanese of Indonesia, baby tending is viewed as women's work, and fathers make only occasional appearances when their children are young. Older children, and particularly boys, are likely to spend more time with their fathers, especially as boys begin to be recruited into the work force. In Guatemala, an older Chimalteco boy begins to accompany his father to the fields each day. A son also goes to the market and attends ritual ceremonies with his father.

The nature of a culture's subsistence economy will affect a child's interpersonal interactions because the manner by which adults make a living influences how accessible they will be to children on a daily basis. A Mexican Mixtecan father may remain away from home for the entire day if his fields are far from home. By contrast, Tairan parents make a number of daily trips between their houses and the fields with the result that children see their parents on and off throughout the day.

The extent to which children are asked to do chores, and the kinds of chores that they do, also affect the patterning of their interpersonal associations. Across cultures, girls are recruited to help their mothers with domestic chores, including the chore of baby tending, with the result that girls spend more time with women and children than do boys. As boys begin to perform tasks, they are often thrown into the company of men. By the time he is ten years old, a

Canadian Hare boy is going on fishing and hunting trips with the men. Meanwhile, his sisters are picking berries and cutting up dried fish with the women. Sometimes, differences in task assignment for boys and girls lead to differences in the nature of social interactions that boys and girls experience. Among the Northwest Amazonian Cubeo, girls are recruited as child nurses and remain close to home, spending much of their time with their mothers and the other girls who are also supervising babies. Cubeo boys, by contrast, are playing in all-male play groups for most of the day.

In communities with central meeting places, children may have the opportunity to mix with people of different statuses. A favorite gathering place for the Tairans is the banyan tree that stands outside the village office, and dozens of children may be found playing in or under the tree at any time, where they have the opportunity of observing adults and overhearing their conversation. Similarly, village Japanese children begin to hang around in play groups before they are three years old. They weave around vehicles in the streets, play at the village shrine, and congregate in the shops to listen to the conversations of adults.

Where children are integrated into adult life, they have a greater opportunity of interacting with people occupying a variety of statuses. In the Philippines, Tarong children are taken on trips to town by older relatives. They are also allowed to attend adult parties. North American Chippewa children would sit and smoke with the adults, listening to their gossip or following along as they rehearsed stories about past events or retold legends. Sometimes, by contrast, children are confined to their own homes. In this case, their exposure to people is limited. Jamaican infants rarely leave home for the first year of life, nor do relatives or neighbors tend to visit. Thus, the infant's primary association is with its mother and, on occasion, its siblings. As the child

gets older, it has more contact with brothers and sisters.

While there are noticeable differences in children's patterns of interpersonal interaction across cultures, the majority of a young child's time is almost always spent with other children. Children are principally in the company of other youngsters in 76 percent of 131 societies. In 47 percent of these cultures, young children spend their time primarily with other youngsters of roughly their own age, while in the remaining 53 percent, they remain in the company of somewhat older, and usually female, children. Young children are supervised primarily by adults, usually of both sexes, in 24 percent of the 131 cultures. The composition of the play group affects the patterns of interpersonal interactions of the youngster, and the nature of per play groups does differ from place to place. Among the Tarong, play groups are made up of all of the neighborhood children, and a play group can include up to 40 children of various ages and both sexes. The older children often cart along the infants of whom they are in charge, with the result that a Tarong child begins to be exposed to a wide variety of other youngsters almost from birth. Some children do not have much experience playing in large groups. In Micronesia, smaller Truk children play alone close to home. Or perhaps a child may play with some neighboring children. Across cultures, play groups eventually begin to be segregated by sex at the initiative of the children themselves. This means that, by the time youngsters are perhaps six or eight, their interactions with children of the opposite sex become more limited.

The patterning of a child's social interactions influences the kinds of behaviors that the youngster will typically exhibit. Across cultures, children display altruism toward infants and toddlers, aggression toward peers, and dependence toward adults. Further, six- to ten-year-olds consistently try to dominate children who are a bit younger than they are. Thus, the behavior profiles of children are importantly affected by the company that they keep. As children living in different cultures associate more or less frequently with different categories of people, their behavior profiles will be predictably different, too.

See also CARETAKERS, SECONDARY; DAILY ROUTINE; FATHERS; HOUSEHOLD COMPOSITION; INTEGRATION INTO ADULT LIFE; PEERS; SOCIALIZATION, AGENTS OF

Barry, Herbert, III, and Leonora Paxson. (1971) "Infancy and Early Childhood: Cross-Cultural Codes 2." *Ethnology* 10: 466–508.

Benedict, Ruth. (1946) *The Chrysanthemum and the Sword.*

Cohen, Yehudi A. (1966) *A Study of Interpersonal Relations in a Jamaican Community.*

Erchak, Gerald M. (1977) *Full Respect: Kpelle Children in Adaptation.*

Geertz, Hildred. (1961) *The Javanese Family: A Study of Kinship and Socialization.*

Goldman, Irving. (1963) *The Cubeo: Indians of the Northwest Amazon.*

Hara, Hiroko Sue. (1967) *Hare Indians and Their World.*

Hilger, M. Inez. (1951) *Chippewa Child Life and Its Cultural Background.*

Hitchcock, John T., and Leigh Minturn. (1966) *The Rajputs of Khalapur, India.*

LeVine, Robert A., and Barbara B. LeVine. (1966) *Nyansongo: A Gusii Community in Kenya.*

Maretzki, Thomas W., and Hatsumi Maretzki. (1966) *Taira: An Okinawan Village.*

Nydegger, William F., and Corinne Nydegger. (1966) *Tarong: An Ilocos Barrio in the Philippines.*

Powdermaker, Hortense. (1933) *Life in Lesu: A Study of Melanesian Society in New Ireland.*

Stephens, William N. (1963) *The Family in Cross-Cultural Perspective.*

Wagley, Charles. (1949) "The Social and Religious Life of a Guatemalan Village." *American Anthropologist* 51: 3–150.

Whiting, Beatrice B., and Carolyn Pope Edwards. (1988) *Children of Different Worlds: The Formation of Social Behavior.*

LANGUAGE ACQUISITION Virtually all children, even children with severe developmental handicaps, learn the language of their culture. Further, a child is already a relatively competent linguist by four years of age even though children make no overt effort to learn their language. This virtuosity impresses adults, in part no doubt because we remember the many hours we have spent trying to master the rudiments of a foreign language in school. Yet little children, who are surprisingly unsophisticated in their overall cognitive functioning, pick up language with seeming ease. What is more, any young child can learn any language equally well.

Theories of Language Acquisition

Early explanations of language acquisition attempted to explain the child's linguistic competence according to prevailing theories used to account for learning more generally. One of these theories assumed that children learned language because adults reinforced those sounds produced by an infant or child that happened to corre-spond to the spoken language of the culture. Thus, for example, if an English-speaking child produced a sound like "da" in the presence of its father, the positive response evoked by this noise would induce the child to say "da" again when the father was nearby. Linguistic sounds would then be fine-tuned as adults became fussier about the sounds that they would reward. Thus, for example, "dada" or "daddy" would evoke a clearer positive response from adults than would the earlier "da," and the child's linguistic output would more and more nearly approximate the language of its culture. The same sort of story was proposed for the learning of grammar. This theory of language development was quickly abandoned as it became clear that it could not adequately explain how children learned language. One problem had to do with the sheer inefficiency of the proposed mechanism. Thus, critics argued that children could never learn language as quickly as they do by this painstaking method. It is also the case that adults do not tend to correct a child's pronunciation or grammar. Rather, they tend to focus on whether what a child says is true or false. Even when adults do correct pronunciation or grammar, children do not take advantage of the corrections until they are spontaneously ready to do so.

A second theory of language acquisition proposed that children acquired language by imitating what they heard from the adults around them. This proposal was superior to the earlier theory because it allowed for vastly more accelerated learning. A child could learn words, sentences, and even strings of sentences at one time. And indeed, a child's vocabulary is learned by imitation. But imitation theory was viewed as suffering from a fatal flaw shared by reinforcement theory. Neither proposal could explain why children as well as adults are capable of producing what are called novel utterances, that is, sentences that they have never heard before but that conform perfectly well to the rules of their language.

Language Development and Brain Specialization

The fact that all language users regularly produce brand new utterances has led people interested in how children acquire language to be generally sympathetic to linguist Noam Chomsky's idea that human beings are biologically prepared to learn language. Chomsky proposes that all human beings are born with a specialized brain structure or structures, which he calls the "language acquisition device," dedicated to the understanding and production of human language. Chomsky models his language acquisition device on the computer. It is as if the brain takes the input of other people's linguistic utterances and extracts the rules underlying those utterances. The device can then understand what it has heard and also produce utterances of its own that remain loyal to the rules of the language that it has heard. This would explain why people can produce new sentences that they have never heard before but that are acceptable examples of their language.

No one knows the details of what specialized brain structures dedicated to language comprehension and production would look like, although brain structures specialized for language have been isolated. But there is evidence that children do extract the rules of their language and then apply them in the production of novel utterances. Thus, for example, a child will produce the grammatically appropriate plural for a nonsense word. In the case of English, the plural for "bik" becomes a soft "s," while the plural for "wug" becomes a "z" sound. This is taken to indicate that children are applying rules extracted from the language that they have heard because a child who produces the correct plural for "bik" or "wug" could never have heard it. The plurals are being created by the children who must, therefore, "know" the right grammatical rules to apply.

But what could be built into a language acquisition device that would allow children to extract the rules of their language? And what would such a device have to look like to allow a child to extract the rules of any language with equal ease and effectiveness? Chomsky's answer relies on the assumption that, while human languages clearly differ from one another, they also share core grammatical features in common. The language acquisition device then includes a kind of universal grammar onto which the universal rule-governed features of all languages map. The language acquisition device is also capable of transforming language-specific grammatical conventions in such a way that they map comfortably onto the universal grammar. Finally, the device can produce language-specific grammatical utterances through a kind of reverse transformation from the universal grammar to the particular language in which the person communicates.

Chomsky's notion of a universal grammar may initially appear improbable because human languages do seem to be so different from one another. But in fact, there are striking similarities in the structure of human language in all of its many forms. These structural similarities help language users to make sense of what they are hearing and make what they are saying comprehensible to hearers. It is easier to see the regularities across languages if we remember that language is a way of communicating something. Grammar allows meaning to be transferred from one person to the next. Language users often wish to exchange information about who did what to whom. A communication that performed this function would include what are known as agents, predicates, and patients. In a linguistic utterance, the agent does something or other, the predicate specifies what has been done, and the patient indicates to whom or what it has been done. In the utterance "John threw the ball," *John* is the agent, *threw* is the predicate, and *ball* is the patient. Moreover, across languages, predicates refer to the same kinds of things, for instance, actions, causation, location, motion, and possession. Language users might also wish to include information that specifies some property of an agent or patient, for instance, "John threw the *red* ball." A language user might wish to specify when something happened, and when it happened in comparison with when something else happened or in comparison with when the speaker is speaking. A communication might also include information about whether something has actually happened in fact, should happen, or just might happen. These are examples of the kinds of things that a user of language might wish to communicate, and all languages allow for these and other kinds of information to be exchanged between people. Part of the meaning of an utterance is captured in the meaning of the words of which the utterance is composed. But part of the meaning of an utterance depends upon the rule-governed relationships between words, and this is what is meant by the grammar of the language. All languages allow for the same sorts of information to be communicated because all languages have the grammar to do so. The particular grammatical conventions of languages differ, but all grammars do the same work of allowing people to talk about agents, patients, actions, modifiers, tense, and the like. From this perspective, the idiosyncratic differences in the details of the grammatical rules of different languages are trivial in comparison with the underlying regularities in the kinds of meaningful information that every grammar allows a speaker to communicate.

Stages of Language Development

The idea that language learning is underwritten by special brain structures dedicated especially to this job is supported by the observation that important details regarding how children learn their language are uniform across cultures. This regularity appears even before language proper makes its appearance. Thus, all human infants babble beginning at five to seven months of age.

Further, the appearance of the sounds uttered in babbling is the same across cultures. For instance, the first consonant sounds that appear in babbling are back-of-the-mouth consonants, for instance, "k," while the first vowel sounds are front-of-the-mouth sounds, for instance, the "i" sound in "sit." As babies grow older, they are able to produce a wider range of sounds, with the result that the babbling of a six- or seven-month-old infant reproduces all of the sounds found in human language. All human infants also initially distinguish between the same linguistic sounds and treat the same sounds as equivalent while still in the prelinguistic stage. Thus, human babies initially come prepared to learn any human language. By six months of age, an infant's babbling is beginning to be tailored to the language that the baby actually hears. Thus, infants at this age begin collapsing together whatever sounds the language of their culture treats as equivalent and distinguishing whatever sounds are treated as distinct. By ten months, babies are only reproducing the sounds that are used in their own language, although they continue to retain the ability to produce sounds exploited by other languages. It is only later on that individuals become less sensitive to hearing distinctions between sounds that are not used in their language and become less capable of making sounds that are not employed by their native tongues. Thus, a young Chinese child will continue to be able to hear the difference between the "r" in rice and the "l" in lice, whereas an older speaker of Chinese does not. Similarly, the young Chinese child can produce "r" and "l" while the older speaker of Chinese produces only an "l" sound. The capacity to hear and produce sounds foreign to one's own language appears to decrease dramatically by adolescence. Infants across cultures also employ the same kinds of consonants and vowels in the same order of acquisition as they begin to produce words in their language. Thus, for instance, American children say "tut" before "cut," Japanese children say "ta" before "ka," and Swedish children say "tata" before "kata."

Just as there is uniformity across cultures in how infants treat the sounds associated with human language, so is acquisition of language itself strikingly similar across societies. Thus, across cultures, children begin to produce their first words at about one year of age. At this stage of development, language consists of single-word utterances. Vocabulary typically refers to people, objects, animals, or social interactions and refers to familiar things in the young child's world. Infants begin to produce dozens of these one-word "sentences." The single-word utterances that children produce at this stage overlap strikingly from one society and language to the next.

Between 18 and 24 months of age, children the world over begin to string together two words at a time. The youngster's language at this stage is sometimes referred to as "telegraphic speech" because children are conserving the words that convey the most meaning and dispensing with the less contentful words, much as we do when we are sending telegrams and do not wish to waste money on throwaway words like "the." Moreover, the content of the two-year-old's language continues to be equivalent around the world. Thus, children who speak Russian, English, Finnish, German, Samoan, Turkish, and Luo all produce sentences such as "See doggie," "All gone thing," "Give papa," "My candy," "More milk," "Mama walk," and "Where ball?" And indeed, the speech of a child in one culture can be directly translated into the sentences produced by a child in another culture. The similarity in the content of children's language at this age reflects a similarity in the level of how children interact with the world and what in the world is important to them. Thus, across societies, the language of an 18-month-old is concerned with making claims on objects and services, commenting on sudden changes of state, pointing out locations, reporting the absence of objects, announcing intentions, and the

like. Further, the word order that children respect in telegraphic speech is also highly uniform across cultures in which language development in children has been explored. Thus, for example, youngsters speaking different languages will nevertheless all tend to place the word "more" first in a sentence, producing "more milk," "more cookie," "more ball," and so on. Similarly, the word "off" will be placed last in a two-word sentence, producing "shoes off," "clothes off," "kitty off," and the like. This is true regardless of the word order typical of adult language in that culture. This suggests that children are not forming telegraphic sentences by copying language of the adults in their culture. Rather, they are generating their own "grammar," suggesting that language acquisition is driven in important ways by unlearned developmental programs.

In the next stage of language development, linguistic competence explodes. Typically, the explosion begins with three-word utterances, so that children now begin to use filler words that were omitted in telegraphic speech. Three-word utterances predictably follow telegraphic speech in all of the cultures for which information is available. There is also evidence that new language elements emerge in a predictable sequence across children who speak English. For example, the present progressive (for instance, "he is speaking") is followed by plurals, and then irregular past verb tenses. A consistent succession of this sort has been discovered with respect to 14 language elements in all. It remains to be determined whether the same sequencing occurs as children in other cultures acquire language.

Promoting Language Development

Cross-cultural uniformities in language acquisition suggest that the acquisition of language is supported by a species-typical brain specialization of the sort represented by Chomsky's language acquisition device. The device allows infants and children to make sense of and produce the particular language that they hear. Often, an adult will make a conscious effort to produce a version of language that is especially accessible to babies and young children. Thus, in many cultures across the world, adults, and especially mothers, simplify their language when addressing infants or young children. In the resulting "motherese," sentences are shorter, words are uttered more slowly, and intonations are exaggerated. Once children are around 14 to 16 months old, mothers tend to alter their speech, now including more instructional content that directs the child's activities in some way (for instance, "Now you stir the pot."). Finally, the mother of an 18-month-old begins to alter her speech so that she is responding to the now meaningful utterances of the youngster.

Adults may also actively encourage speech on the part of infants. Among the Cubeo of the Amazon, parents encourage their babies to talk by playing lip-fluttering games with their infants. These games continue into late childhood. In North America, Chippewa adults believed that a child who began to use language early would be especially smart. Therefore, infants were fed the raw brains of small birds to get them to speak early. Parents also actively encouraged children to name objects. An adult would hold up an object and say its name until the child repeated it correctly. The youngster would then receive the object as a reward. When a North American Arapaho baby's fontanels began to harden, adults viewed the infant as "one that was just old enough to talk." A baby of this age was fed cooked meat and boiled meadowlark eggs so that it would talk early on and acquire much knowledge. Placing a meadowlark's bill between a baby's lips was also said to promote talking. In the past, a feast was thrown when a child said its first words. The guests included old men and women, who were told that the child had invited them so that they would pray for it. Parents actively attempted to teach their children words. The parent told the youngster to con-

centrate, showed some object, and then asked the child to say its name. In the evening, a Canadian Hare mother plays a game with her youngster in which she points to some part of the child's body, tickles it, and names it over and over. Thus she might tickle the youngster's nose, saying, "Your nose, your nose, your nose!" This game can last 30 or 40 minutes. Babies whose mothers have played this game with them can name a doll's body parts when someone points to them. Japanese babies are tutored in vocabulary and grammar and are taught, as well, to respect their language.

While adults in many cultures show an active interest in the language acquisition of children, the child's language development is not always a source of concern. Among the Guatemalan Chimalteco, adults do not actively track the progression of their children as they begin to use language. They do not pay much attention to the child's babbling, although some mothers think that a baby's jabbering means something to the baby. Adults expect children's first words to be *ta,* or "father," and then *na,* or "mother," but they have no specific expectations about when a youngster's language will begin to expand beyond these simple words. If a child fails to begin talking by four or five years of age, people will say that the parents or grandparents have committed some sin and that God is punishing them. For instance, perhaps one of the child's relatives has laughed at a mute person sometime in the past. Further, in some societies, adults do not talk directly to infants or young children, reasoning that it is a waste of time to talk to someone who has no idea of what you are saying.

Language Means Understanding

In some cultures, the appearance of language represents the appearance of "sense" in a child. The first stage of life recognized by the Semai is the stage of the "child." A newborn baby then becomes a "new child." New children know nothing and cannot be taught. They are, therefore, not responsible for what they do. The shift from the status of new child to child begins when the youngster "goes down the ladder to the ground" by itself and is completed when language appears. The child can now understand and becomes a target of correction and instruction. Similarly, the Arapaho used to say that a child who had begun to talk now had a little sense.

Benedict, Ruth. (1946) *The Chrysanthemum and the Sword.*

Blount, Ben G. (1981) "The Development of Language in Children." In *Handbook of Cross-Cultural Human Development,* edited by Ruth H. Munroe, Robert L. Munroe, and Beatrice B. Whiting, 379–402.

Brown, Roger. (1973) *A First Language: The Early Stages.*

Dentan, Robert. (1978) "Notes on Childhood in a Nonviolent Context: The Semai Case." In *Learning and Non-Aggression,* edited by Ashley Montagu, 94–143.

Gazzaniga, Michael. (1992) *Nature's Mind: The Biological Roots of Thinking, Emotions, Sexuality, Language, and Intelligence.*

Goldman, Irving. (1963) *The Cubeo: Indians of the Northwest Amazon.*

Hara, Hiroko Sue. (1967) *Hare Indians and Their World.*

Hilger, M. Inez. (1951) *Chippewa Child Life and Its Cultural Background.*

———. (1952) *Arapaho Child Life and Its Cultural Background.*

Munroe, Robert L., and Ruth H. Munroe. (1975) *Cross-Cultural Human Development.*

Pinker, Steven. (1994) *The Language Instinct: How the Mind Creates Language.*

Slobin, Dan I. (1990) "The Development from Child Speaker to Native Speaker." In *Cultural Psychology: Essays on Comparative Human Development,* edited by James W. Stigler, Richard A. Schweder, and Gilbert Herdt, 233–256.

Wagley, Charles. (1949) "The Social and Religious Life of a Guatemalan Village." *American Anthropologist* 51: 3–150.

LEARNING

In many societies, some kinds of learning occur in the formal setting of the school. But school learning is clearly not the only kind of learning that takes place even in the case of the child who spends a considerable proportion of time in school. In cultures without schooling, all learning obviously occurs in other contexts. But some of this learning consists of explicit training by adults of a sort that shares features in common with school learning. Thus, children across the world acquire knowledge and skills through a variety of means and in a variety of contexts, many of which overlap considerably from one culture to the next.

Learning through Lectures

In societies without schools, adults may teach children certain information through occasional or regular didactic lectures. Sometimes, children learn by listening to the stories and legends of their culture. In North America, Chippewa children were required to listen to legends every evening except during the summer. Some of the legends were for amusement, but some taught children about history and others about morality. It was often the grandparents to whom the children were sent to hear these stories. The old people received a gift of tobacco for their efforts. Similarly, among the Japanese Ainu, grandfathers recount stories and cautionary tales to their grandchildren in the evenings. A grandfather will also teach his most promising grandson the family history. North American Arapaho parents, grandparents, aunts, and uncles took every opportunity, day or night, to instruct and lecture any children to whom they were related about proper behavior. A father would make an object lesson out of some unacceptable action of some child or adult, warning youngsters that, if they misbehaved, they would be talked about. If a number of children happened to be collected in the tipi, some adult might use the occasion to preach some lesson to them. Or a grandmother might call all of her young relations around her for a lecture. A girl's aunts took a special interest in seeing to it that their nieces grew up to be respectable, and a boy's uncles participated in the training of boys. Sometimes, a parent might invite some successful older man to the tipi to describe his experiences to the children. The mother would prepare a meal of meat and bread, and everyone would gather about to listen. Or an old woman might be asked to come and talk to the girls in the family. Once a boy was about 15 years old, his father would spend a few hours teaching him what he would need to know when he was a man. The boy would learn about how to be a father and how to behave so as to preserve his good reputation. These lectures and instructions continued until the young people were in their twenties. Children who resisted listening to the advice of their elders were compelled to do so by their fathers. Parents were motivated to make sure that their children were properly trained because anyone who did not conform to the rules of good conduct would not be welcome in the tribe. In New Ireland, Lesu children are also explicitly taught the legends and folk tales of their culture. These are essentially morality tales about etiquette, taboos, customs, the importance of obedience to parents, and punishments for breaking any rules. Youngsters may have already heard these stories while sitting around the fire at night, but adults spend

each evening for three or four weeks recounting the tales to the children to make sure that they have been learned. A feast is then thrown to mark the end of this training period.

Training Skills

Adults explicitly teach not only knowledge but also skills. When he is around ten years old, a Guatemalan Chimalteco boy begins to spend his day with his father, who teaches the boy the various subsistence tasks that he will need to perform as an adult. Fathers consciously and explicitly show their sons the best way of preparing the soil, planting and harvesting the crops, finding and transporting firewood, and so on. In Mexico, Zinacanteco girls learn to weave through explicit instruction, and the same is true in the case of Liberian tailors in Africa. Teachers adjust their instructions to the growing competence of the student, systematically posing challenges of increasing difficulty along the way. In North America, Arapaho mothers tried to find the time to play with their daughters as a way of teaching them to acquire adult skills. The mother would show the girl how to treat her doll like a real baby, and when she was cutting and hanging meat out on a rack, she would give her daughter a bit of meat to dry on a small rack of her own. At around eight years of age, a Koaka boy in Guadalcanal begins to accompany his father or uncles on the evening fishing trips. He is given a small fishing rod, and the older men show him how to put bait on his hook. They also tell the boy where to find different kinds of fish and which are edible and which are poisonous.

Bush Schools

In some cultures, children attend what are called "bush" schools. Youngsters within some specific age range are tutored for an extended length of time in the skills and knowledge that will then equip them to take on adult roles. Initiation rites may also be integrated into the bush school "curriculum," so that the child is prepared for

In all cultures children learn by imitating adults, as with this Koryak boy practicing with his miniature bow and arrow.

adulthood practically and symbolically. In Liberia, Kpelle boys traditionally entered Poro school and girls entered Sande school when they were anywhere between seven and sixteen years old. Ideally, a boy remained in school for four years and a girl for three years. Nowadays, a child who is also attending a government school may sometimes only attend bush school during vacations. Boys are circumcised and girls undergo clitoridectomies, usually soon after entrance into the school. Boys learn tribal lore and skills, including house building, farming, crafts, mask carving, dancing, drumming, warfare, history, the classification of fish, animals, and so on, and the use of magic and medicines. A boy also learns how to behave in the presence of elders and chiefs

and how to treat and interact with women. The Poro school includes specialists who instruct boys with special talents in some field. For example, a boy with an excellent memory might be specially tutored in history. Members of the Poro school are tested at the end of their training. In the Sande school, girls are trained in singing, dancing, cooking, midwifery, witchcraft, and the use of poisons. A girl is also taught how to win a husband's affection. Girls are also given extra training in skills for which they have an aptitude. Before they leave the Poro or Sande school, members become privy to a number of tribal secrets that they promise never to reveal. On graduation, boys receive a new "bush" name. Both sexes are ritually dressed and washed, and members of the community throw a feast in which the graduates themselves do not participate.

Learning by Observation

While children learn some kinds of things because adults teach them in a formal and didactic manner, much learning on the part of a child is accomplished more informally. Learning through observation is a prime example of such informal learning. Mexican Nahuas expect most skills to be learned by observation. An adult will merely say to a child: "Watch carefully," and "Concentrate," and interference on the part of adults happens only when children are clearly unable to proceed on their own. When a young person fails to produce some object competently, people may laugh at the result. If a learner is successful, on the other hand, people will be called over to admire the good work. The ability to weave is very important for a Chimalteco girl, and a skillful weaver adds to her attractiveness as a potential wife. As a result, all Chimalteco girls begin to learn to weave when they are about nine years old. Daughters have watched their mothers weave for years, and when a girl begins to weave herself and makes mistakes, she is not corrected. Rather, she learns to weave properly by watching successful weaving. North American Arapaho boys learned to braid ropes from rawhide and make silver ornaments by sitting near their fathers and watching them at work. Among the communities of coastal Brittany, children do not receive explicit training for skills of any sort. Rather, children are immersed in the adult world and learn what is required of them by approximating the activities of their elders. Youngsters assume that if they are not scolded, they are performing correctly. There is never any modeling or any verbal explanation, nor can children simply imitate what they see when they see it because they are expected to perform particular tasks on their own and away from any models. The only task-related communications from

adult to child come in the form of commands, prohibitions, and, when the youngster's performance is inadequate, obscenities.

Learning by Doing

Children across cultures also learn by doing. The Semai of Malaysia do not train their youngsters because "our children learn by themselves." Children follow adults about, copying their activities. Soon, the child is really helping parents and grandparents with their tasks. In Micronesia, Palauan fathers make no effort to teach their sons the skills associated with adult work. Boys go out fishing, canoeing, and skin diving by themselves and learn by doing. Or they may tag along after their fathers and pick up this or that skill by observing the older men. A boy who wishes to become good at carving, making nets, building houses, and so on may also ask to be trained by some man who is well known as an expert. Neither do men tutor the next generation regarding the details of Palauan political or social life. When they turn six, small groups of African Swazi boys herd the calves together. Later, they are responsible for herding the cows, which takes them farther from home for longer stretches of time. In this manner, boys pick up considerable knowledge of their physical environment and also learn to manage on their own. Adults in many cultures assume that children will learn both information and skills by constant repetition. In Liberia, Kpelle adults assume that repeated commands have the effect of drumming the desired behavior into a child, so that, for example, if a young boy is consistently forced to give up his seat to elders, he will inevitably learn to show respect to those who are senior to him. Among the Chimalteco of Guatemala, a boy accompanies his father when the older man performs the ritual ceremonies associated with farming activities. Boys do not actively memorize these prayers; rather they learn them after years of hearing them repeated over and over.

A Japanese boy practicing calligraphy

Japanese adults do not typically rely on any overt strategies to induce proper behavior in children. Rather, they simply expect that children will do what is right. But in fact, children are trained in desirable skills or habits of mind by constant repetition, so that ways of thinking and doing become ingrained habits. Thus, learning is not left to chance. Training is detailed, meticulous, and repetitious. No adult assumes that desirable behavior will just be picked up along the way by a child.

Learning from Peers

Often, children pick up knowledge or skills from their peers. Among the Cubeo of the Northwest Amazon, a boy joins an all-male group when he is roughly six years old and spends most of his time in this pack past adolescence. The group is almost entirely independent of the adults. The boys choose their own leaders, who enforce rules of behavior and punish offenders. The leaders also help members of the group learn the skills that they will need as adults. Boys practice ceremonial songs and dances together. In Africa, Swazi children learn cultural lessons by solving riddles and playing verbal memory games, both of which are said to "sharpen the intelligence." Youngsters also learn songs and dances which "make a person into a person." And when the mother goes off to the fields, a Swazi toddler is left home with the other children and is usually supervised by some other youngster who is just a bit older. In these play groups, younger children learn accepted behavior from older ones and may be slapped sharply for failing to conform, although in general this kind of extreme discipline is not needed.

Native Theories of Learning

The styles of teaching children preferred by particular cultures are influenced by the theories of adults regarding how children learn. The Canadian Hare say that children learn as a result of their own intelligence. Teachers are not required for learning, and a Hare adult does not understand what role a teacher might play in helping a schoolchild to learn. Hare adolescents or adults who are asked from whom they learned this or that skill will say: "From nobody. I learned it myself." Rajputs believe that a child learns better from observation and imitation than from instruction. The Tarong of the Philippines believe that it is best to teach children while they are young. "Like the old tree which is already bent, you cannot unbend."

When it comes to teaching their children, adults do not always practice what they preach. Jamaican parents make no consistent efforts to model the behavior that they demand from their children. A youngster is always expected to say "thank you" for receiving some object or favor, but a parent never thanks a child. Children are harshly punished for lying and stealing, but adults will tell lies or cheat on financial transactions in the presence of youngsters, and a child who comments upon the parent's behavior is flogged.

Effects of Formal Schooling

While some strategies for teaching children in societies without formal schools overlap with teaching methods in a school setting, children who go to school differ from children who do not in important ways. Thus, schooled children perform better on formal tests of memory, logic, problem solving, classification, and similar cognitive skills than do unschooled children as well as unschooled adults. Part of the difference in performance may have to do with differences in familiarity with test taking and test materials.

A young child sits at the feet of a group of Santa Clara Pueblo women who are making pottery.

For instance, Kpelle adults do not tolerate questioning on the part of a child unless practical information is sought. For a youngster to question an adult is the ultimate sign of disrespect. This means that the give-and-take test format of questioning and answering upon which many cognitive tests rely is foreign to the Kpelle child. It may also be the case that schools teach certain skills and employ certain teaching strategies that are underemphasized outside of the school setting. For instance, Kpelle children are taught by nonverbal demonstrations. A youngster does not learn abstract skills or knowledge. Rather, children acquire information and competence that are relevant to concrete tasks. This would put the Kpelle child at a disadvantage on any test that focused on the ability to generalize.

See also COGNITIVE DEVELOPMENT; SCHOOL

Barnett, H. G. (1960) *Being a Palauan.*

Benedict, Ruth. (1946) *The Chrysanthemum and the Sword.*

Cohen, Yehudi A. (1966) *A Study of Interpersonal Relations in a Jamaican Community.*

Dentan, Robert. (1978) "Notes on Childhood in a Nonviolent Context: The Semai Case." In *Learning and Non-Aggression,* edited by Ashley Montagu, 94–143.

Erchak, Gerald M. (1977) *Full Respect: Kpelle Children in Adaptation.*

Goldman, Irving. (1963) *The Cubeo: Indians of the Northwest Amazon.*

Hara, Hiroko Sue. (1967) *Hare Indians and Their World.*

Hilger, M. Inez. (1951) *Chippewa Child Life and Its Cultural Background.*

———. (1952) *Arapaho Child Life and Its Cultural Background.*

Hitchcock, John T., and Leigh Minturn. (1966) *The Rajputs of Khalapur, India.*

Hogbin, Ian. (1964) *A Guadalcanal Society: The Kaoka Speakers.*

Kuper, Hilda. (1963) *The Swazi: A South African Kingdom.*

LeVine, Robert A., and Barbara B. LeVine. (1966) *Nyansongo: A Gusii Community in Kenya.*

Munroe, Robert L., and Ruth H. Munroe. (1975) *Cross-Cultural Human Development.*

Nydegger, William F., and Corinne Nydegger. (1966) *Tarong: An Ilocos Barrio in the Philippines.*

Piker, Steven. (1965) *An Examination of Character and Socialization in a Thai Peasant Community.*

Powdermaker, Hortense. (1933) *Life in Lesu: A Study of Melanesian Society in New Ireland.*

Segall, Marshall H., Pierre R. Dasen, John W. Berry, and Ype H. Poortinga. (1990) *Human Behavior in Global Perspective.*

Wagley, Charles. (1949) "The Social and Religious Life of a Guatemalan Village." *American Anthropologist* 51: 3–150.

the time they are crawling, if not earlier. Finally, in 11 percent of 129 cultures, even adults do not wear clothing.

In a number of cultures, modesty training is stricter for girls than it is for boys. In Kenya, Kikuyu boys do not typically wear much in the way of clothing. They may walk around completely naked in the village and perhaps throw a piece of goatskin around their shoulders when they are herding. Little girls, on the other hand, generally wear a small piece of material about the waist that covers their genitals as well as a larger skin for the upper body. Among the Gusii of Kenya, modesty training begins earlier and is treated more seriously for girls than for boys. Girls begin to wear dresses at an early age and are taught to cover their knees with their dresses and to keep their thighs together when they are seated. By the time that she is six years old, a little girl has already learned these lessons well. A boy, by contrast, need not cover his genitals in public until he is ten years old. A girl is also expected to sleep elsewhere at an earlier age than is her brother when their father is visiting for the night. In Polynesia, Tongan boys go swimming naked, but girls always keep their clothes on while swimming. In Thailand, the Banoi think that female genitals are disgusting, shameful, and ugly, and as a result, parents begin to enforce modesty training when a girl is as young as a year old. Thus, a little girl begins to wear a small apron around her abdomen. But boys as old as four or five years may be seen running about the house without clothes on, although they will put on pants to go out of doors. Until they are perhaps four years old, North American Omaha boys run around with nothing on but a small belt when the weather is warm. Girls are always clothed, even when quite small.

Modesty training in girls is clearly related to the idea that females must guard against making themselves objects of male sexual interest. In the Philippines, small Tarong girls are already wearing dresses that cover their genitals, and a

MODESTY

In 79 percent of 129 societies around the world, children begin to wear some kind of clothing once they have begun to walk. Thus, for example, in North America, Kaska children who can walk are warned to exhibit modest behavior in public and not to expose themselves in an indecent manner. In Mexico, Mixtecan parents are casual about modesty training for young children, and no one makes a fuss if a little boy or girl wanders about entirely naked. But an older child who goes about without clothes will be gently ridiculed. In 20 percent of 129 societies, youngsters begin to wear clothes at birth, even when they are home. Rural Irish adults are offended by nudity of any kind. People always dress and undress in private, often under the bed covers, and keep on their underwear during sexual relations. Even infants are covered in the presence of other people, including other babies. In an additional 13 percent of societies, clothing begins to be worn somewhere after six months of age but before the child is fully walking. Among the Konso of Ethiopia, girls begin to wear skirts by

caretaker will adjust a little girl's dress when she sits down. Girls are trained to keep their legs together when sitting, and adults will arrange the legs and skirts of a girl to conform to standards of modesty starting at birth. By the time she is four or five years old, a girl is accustomed to monitoring her own movements so as to remain modest whatever she is doing. Girls are further motivated to make sure that they are modestly covered because boys are permitted to pinch a girl's genitals whenever they are exposed. Among the Taira of Okinawa, modesty in a girl is more rigorously enforced than is modesty in a boy. A little girl learns to sit with her legs together, and even a small child who has not yet begun to wear pants must never allow her genitals to be seen. Boys sometimes show off by urinating in front of each other, but a girl will always go off by herself to urinate. A Japanese girl is taught not to lose control of her mind or body, even when she is asleep. She is instructed early on always to sleep with her legs together, and her mother may arrange her limbs in the proper position at bedtime. Boys, however, can be seen carelessly stretched out without attracting censure. And modesty is strictly enforced once a Tarong girl reaches adolescence. Girls use the buddy system when they go to bathe so that one can screen the other while she is bathing.

While in some societies children's dress habits anticipate the behaviors that will be expected of them in adulthood, child training does not always mimic adult modesty requirements. Among the Manus of New Guinea, adults are extremely reserved as regards nudity and will not be seen undressed even in front of another person of the same sex. But children go naked, and even when a little girl begins to wear a grass skirt at seven or eight years of age, she is apt to take it off in public and forget about it. Children only become embarrassed about nudity at puberty. So do North American Chiricahua adults avoid nudity in front of other people, but their children wear little or no clothing, especially when the weather is warm. In Madagascar, Tanala men and women are careful to avoid exposing themselves, but Tanala children run around naked until they are four or five years old.

Beaglehole, Ernest, and Pearl Beaglehole. (1941) *Pangai: Village in Tonga.*

Benedict, Ruth. (1946) *The Chrysanthemum and the Sword.*

Broude, Gwen J. (1975) *A Cross-Cultural Study of Some Sexual Beliefs and Practices.* Unpublished dissertation, Harvard University.

Dorsey, J. Owen. (1884) *Omaha Society.* Third Annual Report of the Bureau of American Ethnology, 1881–1882.

Hallpike, C. R. (1972) *The Konso of Ethiopia.*

Honigmann, John J. (1949) *Culture and Ethos of Kaska Society.*

Kenyatta, Jomo. (1961) *Facing Mount Kenya.*

LeVine, Robert A., and Barbara B. LeVine. (1966) *Nyansongo: A Gusii Community in Kenya.*

Maretzki, Thomas W., and Hatsumi Maretzki. (1966) *Taira: An Okinawan Village.*

Mead, Margaret. (1931) *Growing Up in New Guinea.*

Messenger, John C. (1971) "Sex and Repression in an Irish Folk Community." In *Human Sexual Behavior,* edited by Donald S. Marshall and Robert C. Suggs, 3–37.

Nydegger, William F., and Corinne Nydegger. (1966) *Tarong: An Ilocos Barrio in the Philippines.*

Opler, Morris. (1941) *An Apache Life-Way.*

Piker, Steven. (1965) *An Examination of Character and Socialization in a Thai Peasant Community.*

Romney, A. Kimball, and Romaine Romney. (1966) *The Mixtecans of Juxtlahuaca, Mexico.*

MORAL DEVELOPMENT

Moral thinking refers to evaluations that people make about right and wrong. A major task of parents in any culture is to teach children to make moral judgments. In societies the world over, adults appreciate that children under seven or so years of age are not capable of sophisticated reasoning, and this sometimes translates into the idea that young people are not capable of genuine moral thought or behavior. Thus, for example, the Mexican Mixtecans believe that the capacity to distinguish between right and wrong and to behave appropriately depends upon the ability to reason. As youngsters under six years of age are assumed to be without reason, no one makes moral judgments about the behavior of a small child.

Sooner or later, however, adults across cultures instruct their children in morality. Among the Chippewa of North America, children received evening instruction, usually by grandparents, on moral behavior. The instruction was in the form of legends. These stories dramatically affected the listeners, who played the legends over and over in their minds for days afterward. Among the Sanpoil of Washington State, adults regularly lectured their children on the moral virtues. Thus, children were admonished not to waste food, to be kind, to avoid speaking ill of anyone, to keep clean, to refrain from lying or stealing, and to remain loyal to all of the traditions of their culture. Old men and women drilled the youngsters on moral lessons every evening during the winter. Children were taught the customs, morals, and lore of the community, and they listened also as the myths and legends of the tribe were repeated in their presence. In the early mornings, when it was hard to sleep, older members of the household took the opportunity to instruct and advise the younger ones. In North America, Arapaho adults took pains to teach their children the difference between moral and immoral behavior. Parents, grandparents, aunts, and uncles all took every opportunity to lecture the children of the household about right and wrong, and a child was corrected by one or another adult on a continual basis. Adults would hold up others as examples of bad behavior, and children would be warned that everyone would talk about them and no one would want to be near them if they did not conduct themselves properly. Sometimes, an old man who had led a successful life would be asked to come and lecture to the children. Adults also stopped to give lectures to the younger members of the household if a number of children happened to be gathered in the same place. Or the children might be summoned to hear a lecture by the grandmother or some other relative. Even when children did not wish to listen to the teachings of an older person, the father would compel them to do so.

In some societies, moral thinking is not stressed. Rather, children are taught to base judgments about good and bad behavior upon other criteria, such as practical considerations. In Uganda, Sebei children are expected to work hard and to do the chores required of them competently. But a child is not taught that work is morally superior to idleness or that work brings its own rewards. Rather, the Sebei child comes to understand that work is simply something that must be done if one wishes to avoid punishment. More generally, Sebei adults do not place much emphasis upon morality. Adults do not tell children morality tales. A child is taught to obey rather than to be good. Similarly, among the North American Comanche, moral training focused a child's attention on the practical advantages of behaving in certain ways. Actions were not right or wrong. Rather, they were likely to draw the approval and respect or the condemnation of other members of the tribe. Thus, children learned to conduct themselves in ways that would win them praise and to avoid behavior that would earn them scorn. The North American Navaho were also concerned with the practical consequences of an action. Thus, according to one Navaho: "If you don't tell the truth, your fellows won't trust you and you'll shame your relatives. You'll never get along in the world that way."

Is there any uniformity in the progression of moral thinking with age across cultures? According to Lawrence Kohlberg, children of different ages make moral judgments in characteristic ways, based upon the cognitive level at which they are operating. Initially, in Level 1 of the Preconventional Stage of moral thought, moral evaluations are made according to the criterion of what actions seem to do the most harm and what actions will earn the most severe punishment. The intention of the actor is not taken into account. At Level 2 of the Preconventional Stage, somewhat older children can now take the perspective of other people and begin to make moral judgments based upon whether a person's actions will be reciprocated. Thus, for example, an individual should perform some particular good act for another person in order to earn a future favor in return. In Level 3 of the Conventional Stage of moral thought, children begin to make moral judgments based upon the intentions of the actor and the likely evaluations that others will make of the actor. A child at this stage of moral thinking is concerned with being thought of as a good boy or good girl. Eventually, in Level 4 of the Conventional Stage, the child's perspective broadens to include a consideration of the relationship of an action to the law. What is lawful is right and what is unlawful is wrong. Finally, in Levels 5 and 6 of the Postconventional Stage of moral thought, people come to appreciate that individual rights precede the law, so that an action can be moral even though it is against the laws of society.

Does Kohlberg's theory of moral development hold up? Studies suggest that moral thinking does proceed more or less in the manner described by Kohlberg. That is, children tend to pass through Kohlberg's stages in the order that

he predicts, although at different rates. Further, there is no guarantee that all people will eventually arrive at the final stage of moral thinking as described by Kohlberg, either within or across cultures. The modal level of moral thinking at which people operate also differs from one culture to the next. People who live in isolated peasant and tribal communities do not progress beyond Level 3 of the Conventioanl Stage of moral thought. High school and college adolescents and adults in both Western and non-Western societies advance farther than this. A possible reason for this difference may lie in differences in social and legal systems across cultures. In societies where the expectations and evaluations of other people are the primary means of social control, moral reasoning based upon concerns about being a "good girl" or a "good boy" might be emphasized. Once more formal systems of government emerge, moral judgments based upon ideas about law become relevant. Progression in moral thinking also depends in part upon the kinds of opportunities that children are given to participate in decision making and to take on the roles of other people. These opportunities are less common in some kinds of nonurban settings.

Berk, Laura E. (1989) *Child Development.*

Edwards, Carolyn Pope. (1980) "Development of Moral Judgment and Reasoning." In *Handbook of Cross-Cultural Human Development,* edited by Ruth H. Munroe, Robert L. Munroe, and Beatrice B. Whiting, 501–528.

Goldschmidt, Walter. (1976) *The Culture and Behavior of the Sebei.*

Henderson, Ronald W., and John R. Bergan. (1976) *The Cultural Context of Childhood.*

Hilger, M. Inez. (1951) *Chippewa Child Life and Its Cultural Background.*

———. (1952) *Arapaho Child Life and Its Cultural Background.*

Kluckhohn, Clyde, and Dorothea Leighton. (1958) *The Navaho.*

Ray, Verne. (1933) *The Sanpoil and the Nespelem: Salishan Peoples of Northeastern Washington.*

Romney, A. Kimball, and Romaine Romney. (1966) *The Mixtecans of Juxtlahuaca, Mexico.*

Shweder, Richard A., Manamohan Mahapatra, and Joan G. Miller. (1990) "Culture and Moral Development." In *Culture and Psychology: Essays on Comparative Human Development,* edited by James W. Stigler, Richard A. Shweder, and Gilbert Herdt, 130–204.

Wallace, Ernest, and E. Adamson Hoebel. (1952) *The Comanches: Lords of the South Plains.*

MOTHERS, CONSTRAINTS UPON

The daily experience of a child is importantly affected by the constraints upon the life of the mother. These constraints include what the mother does for a living and where her work takes her, what kind of contribution she makes to the welfare of her family, the form of household in which she lives, how free she is to move about and choose her own companions, and how much time she has to herself after her work is done. Across cultures, we find that mothers living under similar circumstances tend to manage their children in similar sorts of ways.

The mother's workload is an important factor in influencing the daily experience of her children. This includes the sheer amount of work that the woman is required to perform and also the amount of help that she can expect to receive from other adults. Across cultures, women who themselves have many chores to do each day are likely to recruit their children into the workforce. In Kenya, Gusii women are responsible for most of the routine agricultural as well as the household work. Women also take on any traditional men's tasks if male family members have left home temporarily to seek employment outside of the community. Further, Gusii men practice polygyny, and a wife typically lives in a hut of her own with her children. If co-wives get along, they may help each other with tasks and caretaking, but in comparison with women who live in extended families, the Gusii mother has little help. Gusii women solve the dilemma of how to get all of their work done by requiring their children to pitch in. Thus, Gusii children fetch wood and water, grind grain, garden, harvest, and prepare food. Further, boys herd the cattle and girls tend younger siblings. By contrast, in India, the Rajput mother has relatively little to do. Because the Rajputs enforce the seclusion of females, women are confined to the courtyards of their households. This restricts them to performing household tasks. As families are extended, a woman is also likely to have the help of her female housemates and well as servants. Thus, Rajput women have relatively little work to do and ask their children to do relatively few chores. As a result, a typical Rajput child may fetch water and do some sweeping and cleaning, but little else. The mother's workload also affects her expectations regarding the behavior of her children. Mothers with a heavy workload train and expect their children to be responsible and obedient and do not tolerate aggression directed at the mother. Women with lighter workloads are less diligent about training for responsibility and obedience and more tolerant of mother-directed aggression.

A child's life is also affected by where the mother's work takes her. If a woman works far from home where the presence of children is inconvenient, youngsters will find themselves under the supervision of substitute caretakers. Thus, for example, in Indonesia, an Alorese woman goes back to work in the fields around two weeks after she has given birth. The baby is

San mothers carry thier children on their backs while gathering wild plant foods.

left back in the village in the care of an older sibling or other relative for perhaps nine hours at a time. In some cultures, a woman's normal routine will be modified so that she can remain with her children. Sometimes, for example, gardens are far from home or are situated in potentially dangerous settings. In such cases, mothers may remain home to take care of the babies and young children, perhaps tending a small plot near the house, while men take over the other agricultural chores. This happens, for instance, in Guatemala and Mexico. In other cultures, a woman will sometimes take her children along when she is performing subsistence activities, in spite of the considerable inconvenience that the effort represents. Among the !Kung of the Kalahari Desert, women spend every other day

or so gathering vegetables to take home to camp. A round trip may mean a walk of 2/12 miles, and a woman will be carrying some 15 to 33 pounds of vegetables on the return trip. Nevertheless, mothers take any children under four years of age along with them on these gathering excursions, a baby being carried on the back and an older child straddling the hip. A child older than four years will probably be left back at camp, to be supervised by those adults who happen to be remaining home for the day.

The kind of contribution that a woman is making to the welfare of her family may also affect her performance as a mother. In most societies around the world, the division of labor by sex operates in such a way that the activities of men and women are complementary or cooperative. This means that women's work is not confined to maintenance or preparation chores such as cooking, cleaning, and baby tending. Rather, women the world over have traditionally produced things of value on their own. Often, women have access to their own cash resources. Thus, for instance, women may do agricultural work or they may tend animals. Often, they have gardens of their own. In many societies, a woman can sell some what she has produced to her neighbors or at market. Women who are producers may develop a sense of personal worth to a degree that is unlikely in women who produce nothing on their own and have no autonomous control over resources of any kind. In turn, levels of self-esteem may be related to how a woman interacts with her spouse and children. For example, across cultures, women who are producers are more likely to enforce obedience in their children and less likely to tolerate aggression or "back-talk" directed toward them by children. Women who make substantial contributions to the subsistence economy similarly insist upon obedience from their children. This makes sense given the further fact that mothers with a high workload usually recruit their children to do tasks. Once children are expected to perform serious chores, the mother needs to be able to depend upon the child to take orders and carry them out. But it may also be true that women who see themselves as competent and valuable contributors are less likely to put up with insubordination on the part of their children.

The degree of freedom and the kinds of company that a woman enjoys on a daily basis can also influence her management of her children. In traditional cultures, women typically come in contact with one another frequently in the course of a day. They may encounter one another while fetching water or wood. In foraging societies, they may go gathering in pairs. In agricultural cultures, they may prepare the soil, plant, weed, and harvest together. Women meet each other at market, or visit one another during the day between chores. In a large majority of societies, a single household includes a number of married couples, which means that women spend most of their time in the company of other adult females. And women in most cultures do not remain home for most of each day. Rather, they are away from the house doing productive work. Sometimes, however, a woman may find herself confined inside a house or courtyard alone or with the same people all day long. Mothers whose lives conform to this pattern are more irritable and more hostile to those with whom they are forced to interact, including other adults and children. This is true of American women who are confined to their homes for most of the day, and it is true for the Indian Rajput woman who is compelled to remain in the courtyard of her house along with her husband's mother and his unmarried sisters.

The number and identity of adults in a household affect the degree to which mothers show warmth toward their children. In households where a grandmother is present, mothers tend to display more warmth toward youngsters. This may be because the grandmother, who has no children of her own to raise, can help the mother with her chores, leaving the younger woman with more time to devote to her children. When a household is composed of many adults, however, the degree of warmth shown to a child by the mother actually decreases. This may be because people living in a crowded household are forced to restrain displays of emotion simply in order to keep the peace. This tendency to be emotionally subdued in general may spill over and affect the mother's style of interaction with her children. Women also tend to show less warmth to their own children in households with a relatively large number of children, either because the child has many siblings or because cousins share the same residence. Perhaps women who live in households with their own children and also their nieces and nephews are anxious to avoid showing favoritism toward their own youngsters and thus keep their displays of affection in check. Women who have many children of their own may find themselves spread so thin that they have little time to shower each child with affection. Interestingly, only children tend to receive relatively more warmth than do children with siblings, and youngest children tend to receive more warmth than oldest children. Thus, the same mother alters the amount of affection that she shows to her children, and even to the same child across time, indicating that displays of warmth depend in part upon external circumstances, for instance number of children in the household, and not only upon the personal characteristics of the mother herself.

A woman who has some time to herself on a routine basis treats her children differently from the woman whose workload monopolizes her time. In a majority of societies, women have some free time each day. A woman may work four or five hours for five days running or perhaps six to eight hours every other day. Further, a woman's schedule in traditional societies is generally flexible, allowing room for changes in routine when required. When most of a woman's time is eaten up by work, she is more likely to be harassed and exhausted and, therefore, less capable of holding up physically and emotionally when it comes time to deal with husbands and children.

In Okinawa, Taira women work long and demanding hours away from home and do not spend very much time with their children. Mothers are tired and short-tempered by the end of the day, and this is reflected in the impatience with which a woman will sometimes treat her child. Neither is the absence of work an unmixed blessing for women around the world. Kenyan wives who have left their farms to move to Nairobi with their husbands find themselves with time on their hands. They are no longer required to fetch water or fuel. There are no gardens to tend or animals to care for. Because women who live in cities are isolated from relatives and neighbors, Nairobi wives find themselves alone in their small apartments with no one but their children. This combination of boredom, lack of productivity, and isolation seem to affect the woman's interactions with her children. Thus, mothers who have moved to Nairobi from the country are more irritable and restrictive than their counterparts back home. Eventually, some of these women take jobs in the city, leaving their children with a relative or hired babysitter. But the children are bored in their tiny apartments, with no cousins or neighborhood children, no interesting adult activities going on, and no tasks to occupy them.

Lee, Richard B. (1979) *The !Kung San: Men, Women, and Work in a Foraging Society.*

Maretzki, Thomas W., and Hatsumi Maretzki. (1966) *Taira: An Okinawan Village.*

Minturn, Leigh, and William W. Lambert. (1964) *Mothers of Six Cultures: Antecedents of Child Rearing.*

Munroe, Robert L., and Ruth H. Munroe. (1975) *Cross-Cultural Human Development.*

Whiting, Beatrice B. (1972) "Work and the Family: Cross-Cultural Perspectives." Paper prepared for Women: Resource for a Changing World. An International Conference. Radcliffe Institute, Radcliffe College, April.

Whiting, Beatrice B., and Carolyn Pope Edwards. (1988) *Children of Different Worlds: The Formation of Social Behavior.*

Whiting, Beatrice B., and John W. M. Whiting (1975) *Children of Six Cultures: A Psycho-Cultural Analysis.*

MOTHERS, NEW

When a woman has had a baby, she is required to adjust to a variety of disruptions to her old life. Her body is undergoing a variety of physical changes. She is now responsible for a new baby. And she has to mediate whatever disturbances this addition to the household has caused in the relationships between family members, including her husband and any other children that she might have. Cultures around the world acknowledge that new babies mean adjustments, and new mothers are often given special dispensation of one kind or another until they are physically, emotionally, and logistically ready to resume their normal routines. These special arrangements also allow the mother to devote herself to her new baby and allow siblings to get to know the baby and become used to having it around. In cultures where birth is viewed as polluting, customs also exist for cleansing the new mother so that she will not contaminate her house or family.

Confinement as a Time for Rest

Sometimes, a woman is simply permitted to take it easy for a while until she has regained her strength. During her confinement, she may be entertained by visitors, who may bring gifts for her or the baby. In Okinawa, a new Tairan mother rests at home and receives visits from relatives and neighbors for some days after the birth. Everyone has tea and snacks, admires the new baby, offers the mother advice, and tells her the latest news. After a while, a woman will begin to show signs of restlessness as housework piles up and family resources become strained. Gradually, she begins to resume her normal work schedule, leaving the infant with a grandmother if possible. Even after they have returned to work, women will make sure to be home frequently to nurse the baby, and a mother with a baby younger than six months of age will try to devote herself to chores that can be accomplished near her own household. Among the Jivaro of Ecuador, new mothers are expected to take it easy for two weeks or so. Otherwise, the mother will become chronically ill because she will have to expose herself to cold water as part of her normal workload. During this resting period, the woman's husband will take over much of her workload if there is not another wife to help out. For instance, he will fetch the water and dig up and wash the manioc, which his wife will then cook. A woman will resume her garden work a few weeks after the birth. In Micronesia, after her baby is born, a Truk woman rests for a while and then begins to receive visitors, a few at a time. Everyone comments on the beautiful baby and most people bring small gifts, such as perfume or soap. The Truk believe that eating helps women to regain their strength and produce milk more quickly. Thus, new mothers are fed whatever they wish. A new Truk mother and baby are visited by relatives, and the woman is expected to take it easy for as long as it takes for her to regain her strength. This may take a number of weeks, and even then, new mothers refrain from doing heavy work until the baby can crawl, if not longer. The idea here is that the mother should be devoting herself to the new infant and not to other routine chores. Among

the Takashima of Japan, a woman is ideally required to rest for 33 days after a birth. She stays in bed for at least seven days, after which she is allowed to get up for brief periods of time and do a small number of chores. She continues to rest periodically for at least another week. New mothers drink sugar water and an herb decoction until they are ready to nurse and eat sea bass and rice with beans for a week after delivery to help along the postpartum recovery. A new mother must not eat persimmons or walk under a persimmon tree or else something bad will happen. In Polynesia, a Tongan mother is confined to her house for ten days following the birth of her baby. The mother lies on a bark cloth bed, covered with layers of bark cloth, her head wrapped in a bark cloth headdress. The baby lies close by on its own bark cloth bed overhung by a light piece of cloth to keep flies away. For the first three days of confinement, the mother's kin congregate in the public section of the house, which is separated from the new mother's private quarters. Male relatives bring gifts of kava each day, while female relatives make presents of baby clothes. On the first day, the new father prepares a big feast. A designated man enters the house, throws a present of kava on the floor, and declares: "Thank you for the child's birth." Everyone then chats and drinks kava all day long. Toward the end of the ten-day confinement, the father's relatives also come to call. They are also offered food and kava during their visit. Greater attention is paid to the woman's relatives during confinement because the Tongans see the new mother as presenting a valuable gift to her husband's family. It is her family, therefore, that should be honored when a baby is born. Sometimes, a relative of the husband or wife is imported into the household for some period of time to relieve the new mother of her normal workload and to allow her to recover or to devote her attention to the new baby. When a Jamaican woman gives birth, her own mother attends the delivery and then stays with the woman for at least another nine days to do all of the housework normally performed by a wife. A mother will sometimes stay for some weeks beyond the required nine days if she is especially fond of the daughter. Men will not eat food cooked by their mothers-in-law. Therefore, a new father cooks his own meals or gets an older child to do so while his wife's mother remains in his house. New mothers remain in bed for three days and do not leave the house for another six days. They will not cook or wash for three months if their mothers remain with them for that long. A woman who has just had a baby only eats porridge and bread for nine days after the delivery. She may not eat "hard food" or "ground provisions."

Obligatory Activities

In some cultures, a new mother is required to perform a set of activities meant to promote her return to good health or to guarantee the future of the baby. A Taira mother and her new baby are confined for four days in the darkened back room where she has given birth. The seclusion ends with a ceremony at which the woman's female relatives offer food to the ancestors in return for the good health of the baby. The mother is allowed to have her first bath six days after the delivery. Among the Mixtecans of Mexico, a woman is supposed to take it easy for 40 days after she has given birth. Ideally, she will remain in bed with her infant. In fact, women gradually begin to move around during this period, but they do not generally leave the house and they never do any strenuous work. A few days after her baby has been born, the new mother washes herself with an herbal brew, and six days after the birth, accompanied by two female relatives, she takes a sweat bath. She must take from 12 to 15 more baths before she is thought to be entirely recovered. During her confinement, other women come to visit the new mother, bringing her gifts such as chocolate or bread. A person may also give the mother some money

or baby clothing, but no one actually looks at the infant for fear of being accused of the evil eye. After she has given birth, a Tarong woman will be given some warm water to drink as well as a cigar. She will also chew on a bitter root in an attempt to alleviate nausea. The new mother is then washed and goes to lie in the inclined bed that has been placed in the living-bedroom for her use. A woman is expected to remain in bed for 11 to 30 days. This is the *dalagan* period, or the time of the "roasting" of the mother. Its length depends upon the woman's health, the size of her family, and her ability to withstand the daily roasting that she will be required to endure. Neither she nor her baby can be touched by anything that is cold. Food and drink are warmed, and there is always a fire in the room where the two are confined. Neighbors and relatives visit the mother and baby often, and a female member of the household or other relative remains with the woman whenever possible, although during the busier seasons everyone may be preoccupied with subsistence chores so that the new father may have to take over the chores normally performed by his wife. Every morning, the woman receives a massage by the "*ilot* of childbirth," the masseuse who attends new mothers. Women will also begin to expose their bodies, a bit at a time, to the hot stove in order to "stop the blood." After nine days of such gradual exposure, the woman washes her hair in warm water and begins the "roasting" procedure, which is thought to diminish soreness and help the uterus to maintain its proper position. During the period of roasting, the woman sits on a chair draped in a blanket. A bowl of glowing coals is placed under the chair, and the woman remains there to roast until the coals become cold. This procedure is repeated each day until the *dalagan* is over, a minimum of 11 days. The roasting is considerably more oppressive to Tarong women than is the birth itself. At the end of the roasting period, a woman will dress warmly for three days and will continue to remain indoors. This is the cooling-off period. She then takes a cold bath, washes her hair, and perhaps pounds a bowlful of rice. Women do not resume their normal workloads for another month or so, nor may they lift heavy loads. A woman will also wear a band around her hips and perhaps another around her chest while she is working. Similarly, in Thailand, a new Banoi mother is put "on the fire." She is placed on a platform that has been erected over a low-burning fire, acting as a kind of steam bath. The woman remains there for around two weeks. The heat and perspiration from the fire is supposed to rid the new mother of the dirty blood in the uterus and to relieve whatever discomfort she is experiencing from the birth. While a woman is on the fire, her husband and older children and perhaps a few relatives perform all of the household tasks. Once the steam treatment is over, the woman begins to resume her normal work schedule. In Indonesia, a Javanese woman gives birth in a sitting position, and she is supposed to remain sitting for 35 days after the baby is born. She leans against pillows or a backrest and does not lie down even to sleep. New mothers are also exhorted to stand up and move around as soon as they can to get the blood flowing out. This will make them clean again. A Javanese woman is also expected to greet the guests that come to attend the ritual meal prepared for the baby on the day of its birth. The entertaining of visitors then continues for five additional days and nights, taxing the strength of the woman who has just given birth and sometimes leading to her death. New mothers and their babies are also bathed and massaged every day by the midwife for 35 days. While she is washing the infant, the midwife recites a spell to make the baby healthy and beautiful. The mother washes according to a precise recipe, pouring water all over herself, keeping her eyes open, and blowing air out of her mouth. A woman can become ill if she does not bathe in the proper way. While the mother is bathing, the midwife announces to the guardian spirit of the village that the impure blood from the birth is being washed away. The baby is also massaged twice a day for 5 days at a minimum and ideally for 35 days. The purpose is to shape the infant's body correctly and to exercise it to make it soft instead of stiff. A mother also receives massages so that her body will return to its original state. Mothers also apply salves to their bodies and take two potions, one to make the mother feel "cool" and the other to cause her milk to be good-tasting and plentiful. A salve is also applied to the baby, who is then sprinkled with white rice-flour powder, giving it a gray coloring. In Guatemala, Chimalteco women are required to remain in confinement for 20 days and to stay in bed for the first 15 days after the birth. This period of time is understood to be a dangerous one for the new mother, who is seen as in a weakened state. Her husband finds a diviner to pray for her every fifth day during her confinement, and the midwife visits her in the morning and the evening, giving her a sweat bath and massaging her stomach with a warm rock. The woman's mother-in-law or sister-in-law come to take care of the house every day, and other relatives of the husband, and sometimes of the wife, visit each day bringing tortillas for the family to eat. After the first 15 days have passed, the midwife comes only once a day and the new mother can do some light work. She can begin to take on more strenuous chores when the 20 days are over. During the confinement, husband and wife may sleep together but may not engage in sexual intercourse. To do so would invalidate the prayers of the diviner. At the end of the confinement, the husband, wife, and baby are given a sweat bath by the diviner while he burns candles and says prayers for the long life and health of the child.

Minimal Confinement

In a number of societies, the confinement period is minimal. A new mother rests for a brief period of time and then things in her household return to normal. A North American Chippewa woman might take it easy for two or three days after delivering a baby, but some resumed their normal schedules within a day after a birth. A new mother drank three or four cups of tea for 10 to 14 days after her baby was born. In Mexico, the new Tarahumara mother returns to her normal routine soon after she has given birth, but she must not take a bath for four days; otherwise the flow of blood may stop. New mothers avoid eating apples and calabashes for two or three weeks.

New Mothers as Polluted

When birth is viewed as polluting, a new mother may be removed from her house or isolated from other members of her family until she is no longer dirty. In North America, a Fox woman gave birth in a lodge that was separated from the main living quarters of the family. She was required to stay there for ten days after her baby was born. During this period, she was waited on by the other women. When the ten days were up, the new mother bathed and was then allowed to sleep alone with her baby in the main house. However, she still had to eat in the separate lodge for an additional 20 days; 30 days after the delivery of her baby, the woman returned to the main house and to her normal life. During her seclusion, a woman had nothing to do with any men. A North American Sanpoil woman drank an herb mixture immediately after she had given birth to guard against excess bleeding. She then rested in bed for a few hours, or a day at most. The mother then began to take care of the baby, resting when she could. New mothers continued to take it easy for a week. A woman was not permitted to cook during this time for fear of contaminating the food, as she was still bleeding. Nor was she allowed to pass in front of a man. A woman who had just given birth was supposed to stay away from the fire so that she would not perspire and begin to hemorrhage.

She drank a tonic twice a day for a month to help her regain her strength and she avoided meat for ten days. Women did not bathe or sleep with their husbands for the first month after delivery. After that, the new mother took a bath and resumed her normal life.

New Fathers

In a number of cultures, certain behaviors are required of the new father as well as the new mother. A new Tarahumara father does not return to work for three days after the birth of his child. Among the Sanpoil, the father of a newborn baby had to catch a horse or dog and beat it severely, or he was required to ride the horse until it became exhausted. If the man had no access to a dog or horse, he had to run to exhaustion himself. Otherwise, the baby would be fussy, cry a lot, and have convulsions. Among the Cubeo of the Northwest Amazon, after a baby is born, the father as well as the mother respect a three-day resting period. The two remain in their hammocks all day and night, only leaving the house for excretion. They eat and drink sparingly and avoid engaging in activities of any kind because virtually anything that the parents do during this dangerous time can have terrible consequences for the baby. If a parent stubbed a toe, the baby's toe would be damaged. If the mother or father ate papers, the baby's internal organs would be burned. The grandmother looks after the newborn infant, handing it over to the mother only for nursing. The end of the three-day resting period is marked by three magical ceremonies. The first two rites make food and the river safe for the infant and its parents. At the last rite, the baby's body is painted. The painting is seen as a means of removing the fetal skin which, if it were to remain on the baby, would interfere with its growth.

Prohibited Behaviors

Cultures can also place restrictions upon the behavior of the new parents. A new Mixtecan mother may not touch a needle, hold a broom, or lift anything. She is allowed to drink only chocolate, warm tea, atole, and broth and to eat chicken or special tortillas. A woman cannot eat chiles, pork, green or black beans, grease, or any cold foods. If she cuts her hair at any time during the first 40 days after the birth of her baby, it might "go inside" and kill her. New Jivaro parents avoid eating certain birds or animal entrails. If the parents of a newborn engage in extramarital sex, the baby will die from vomiting. Tarong women are required to observe the *tangad*, a period of five months or so after the birth of a child during which the new mother observes a set of customs designed to protect her milk supply. The woman's mother-in-law is responsible for seeing to it that the new mother follows these rules for her first two or three births. Most *tangad* rules have to do with the woman's diet and restrict her intake to a few plain, wholesome foods. For instance, food that is sour, strong tasting, or slippery is prohibited. Some mothers-in-law also prohibit sweet foods, and some daughters-in-law are annoyed by the practice. A mother and baby are also prevented from staying in the sun for too long for fear that the infant will "suck in the heat" and develop a fever. The period of *tangad* limits a woman's activities, and a new mother will occasionally complain that she has missed some party in another neighborhood or that she has not been to market for months. A woman who is observing the *tangad* does, however, have opportunities to socialize with other women who live nearby, and many women will pay less and less attention to the *tangad* restrictions as time goes by, resuming their normal schedules as soon as they can.

———

Beaglehole, Ernest, and Pearl Beaglehole. (1941) *Pangai: Village in Tonga.*

Bennett, Wendell, and Robert Zingg. (1935) *The Tarahumara: An Indian Tribe of Northern Mexico.*

Cohen, Yehudi A. (1966) *A Study of Interpersonal Relations in a Jamaican Community.*

Geertz, Hildred. (1961) *The Javanese Family: A Study of Kinship and Socialization.*

Gladwin, Thomas, and Seymour Sarason. (1953) *Truk: Man in Paradise.*

Goldman, Irving. (1963) *The Cubeo: Indians of the Northwest Amazon.*

Goldschmidt, Walter. (1976) *The Culture and Behavior of the Sebei.*

Harner, Michael J. (1973) *The Jivaro: People of the Sacred Waterfalls.*

Hilger, M. Inez. (1951) *Chippewa Child Life and Its Cultural Background.*

Jones, William. (1939) *Ethnography of the Fox Indians.*

Maretzki, Thomas W., and Hatsumi Maretzki. (1966) *Taira: An Okinawan Village.*

Norbeck, Edward. (1954) *Takashima: A Japanese Fishing Community.*

Nydegger, William F., and Corinne Nydegger. (1966) *Tarong: An Ilocos Barrio in the Philippines.*

Piker, Steven. (1965) *An Examination of Character and Socialization in a Thai Peasant Community.*

Ray, Verne. (1933) *The Sanpoil and the Nespelem: Salishan Peoples of Northeastern Washington.*

Romney, A. Kimball, and Romaine Romney. (1966) *The Mixtecans of Juxtlahuaca, Mexico.*

Wagley, Charles. (1949) "The Social and Religious Life of a Guatemalan Village." *American Anthropologist* 51: 3–150.

Every member of the human species goes by a name. However, who confers the name and when it is conferred, how many names are given to a person and how a name is chosen, and whether a naming is or is not transformed into a formal occasion depends upon the culture into which an individual happens to be born.

NAMING

In a survey of 60 cultures, 75 percent require that babies be named at birth or within the following month, 10 percent require naming in the first year after birth, and in 15 percent parents wait until over one year after the birth. Among the Cubeo of the Northwest Amazon, a baby is not named until it is a year old. A baby named earlier than this would die. Until the baby has a name, it is not viewed as a full member of its kin group. The child is named at a naming ceremony led by the father's father and lasting for several hours. Once the baby is named, it can be influenced by the Ancients and their growth magic, allowing the infant to grow large and strong, valued characteristics among the Cubeo.

Children are named by certain designated people. However, the identity of the person assigning the name differs from one society to the next. Across cultures, it is more likely that the father rather than the mother picks the name, and in some cultures the grandparents, an aunt or uncle, religious leader, or an old and wise person may pick or help pick the name. In Ecuador, a Jivaro baby is named a few days after it is born. Sometimes, the father will name all of the children and sometimes boys will be named by the father and girls by the mother. If a boy's paternal grandfather is alive, he may be asked to name his grandson. Granddaughters, similarly, may be named by the mother's mother. Children are named after some deceased relative who had earned a reputation for being a hard worker and, if the namesake is male, a good hunter. In Polynesia, a Tongan baby is named by the father's sister or one of her close relatives. She asks the father for permission to name the baby, and presents the infant with a gift of clothing or a baby mat at the time of the naming, a few hours after its birth. In return, the father throws a feast for the name-giver three days later and presents her with mats and bark cloth donated by the baby's grandmothers. The gift exchange is more extensive for a firstborn child and most elaborate for a first son. Among the Banoi of Thailand, a father takes his three-day-old infant to a monk who decides on the right name for the baby based upon astrological calculations. In Micronesia, Truk parents ask one of the friends or relatives who come to visit after a birth to suggest a name for the baby. If they want a name that is connected to spells of magic or divination, they may ask someone who knows of these things. Such names do not give children any special powers. When its umbilical cord drops off, a Kenyan Gusii baby is named by the women who had attended its birth. Until then, babies are called *Mosamba Nwaye,* or "burner of his own home," based on the idea that the baby is now out of the womb and can never go back there. The child will be given a name or two, to be approved by its mother and its father's mother. An Australian Tiwi infant receives its first name from its father, or from the current husband of its mother, a few weeks after birth. But if the mother's spouse dies and she remarries, any names given to a person by the dead man become taboo. The mother's new husband then renames her children. In this way, he establishes his status as the exclusive father of his wife's children, giving him authority over them, although not the right to cancel any former obligations made for them by former fathers. Tiwi women usually remarry a number of times, with the result that most youngsters are renamed a number of times. A person technically has to abandon old names for new ones until the mother dies. However, adults generally retain their current names in the long run, taking on new names from the mother's current husband only temporarily and then reverting to the use of their former names. This is especially the case once a man is in his late twenties or thirties and when a woman is married for the first time, usually when she is a young adolescent.

The criteria for choosing names vary considerably across cultures. Children may be named after some family member. Sometimes, a name represents some special place or event associated with the child's birth. In some cultures, a child is named after people with desirable characteristics in the hope that the namesake will inherit the valued traits as well as the name. Children often also take on nicknames, which they may or may not retain into adulthood. A North American Comanche child who was frequently ill would be given a new name because the Comanche believed that names were connected to an individual's personal characteristics. Thus, a physically fragile child could be made healthy by naming him after a brave warrior. By the same reasoning, a child who was named after someone who had committed some blameworthy deed would suffer as a consequence. North

American Chippewa babies were named by an older person who had enjoyed good health. But a sick infant might be given a second name by someone who had lived for a long time and a third name and so on if the baby remained ill. Youngsters also had pet names and, later, nicknames, usually referring to some characteristic of the child or some event that had occurred on the first day of the youngster's life. The names were usually funny. Comanche families who owned property might name a youngster after a close relative who would then be expected to give the child a gift. People also went by nicknames, which might describe some action, characteristic, or idiosyncrasy of the person or of someone in his family. A boy's nickname was usually changed when he had been successful at hunting, in war, or the like. Then, the boy himself or else a close associate would provide a new nickname. In Okinawa, a Tairan infant is named when it is four or five days old. The name is carefully chosen to include the right combination of Japanese symbols necessary to insure a fortunate personality for the child. Traditionally, the baby was given a temporary name to hide its identity from any malevolent spirits who might wish to do the child harm. Among the Gusii, the choice of a name is influenced by such things as evil omens observed before the birth of the child, weather and other circumstances surrounding the birth, and the mother's condition during delivery. Or more likely, a child may be given the names of people in each parent's family who have recently died. The more important name will come from a relative of the father. The less important name, which comes from the mother's family, can eventually be dropped. North American Arapaho babies were often named after some unusual event, such as a brave or kind deed or a yellow bear or white squirrel. Or they might be named after some event occurring during a war, such as a difficult siege. In choosing names, no distinction was made on the basis of sex, although the word "woman" could be tagged onto the name of a female. Most children were initially named soon after they were born, but sometimes a youngster would remain without a name for two or three years, and people could be found who had no name until they were ten. Jamaican names are chosen for their uniqueness, and two people rarely have the same first name as a result. Anyone can propose a name for a child, but usually it is the mother who makes the final choice. Some people say that it is bad luck to pick a name before the baby is actually born.

In some cultures, a youngster is named a number of times. A former name may be retained or it may be dropped in favor of the newest one. In Uganda, Sebei children are given a number of names. An infant first receives a name that is associated with some circumstance surrounding its birth, such as the place where it was born, the time of its birth, a special event that happened during its birth, and so on. Later on, the baby is also named after an ancestor. This name may be changed later on in life. Another name is given at the time of circumcision. A woman is also known as the mother of her oldest child. When she becomes a grandmother, she is called after her oldest grandchild. A man may also be named after a child, and sometimes a man will also take the given name of his father, preceded by "son of." A Sebei will, thus, be called by any of a number of different names depending upon the individual's age as well as the context. In North America, a Sanpoil baby was given a name sometime before it was a year old. Infants were usually named by some elderly relative, often a grandparent, at the parents' request. Parents themselves rarely named their children. The name chosen for the baby was usually that of a recently dead relative. Most individuals continued to take on other names in the course of their lives. These might be family names or they might be names given by the person's guardian spirit. People often used one of each of these kinds of names at the same time. A child or adult might take on the name of a deceased relation a few years after the death. If the name was being conferred on a child, a small ceremony was performed in which the dead person was eulogized and the child lectured. Among the Semai of Malaysia, a baby initially receives one or more names designating its general status and identity. One name specifies the baby's birth order and another may refer to its gender. These first names are taken to be tentative and not very serious because infants often die. Once it becomes likely that a baby will live, it receives a personal name, which is based on some characteristic of the child, such as its first word or some idiosyncrasy of the youngster. As people grow older, they often become embarrassed about their personal names and may change them. Adults also take on additional names incorporating the names of their children into their own names. An Arapaho child might be given a name that had already been used by someone else, especially a relative and especially a person who had lived to a ripe age. Or the name might be a new one. People usually changed their names in adolescence or adulthood, and some individuals did so often, although it was possible to find people who retained their original names for life. Names were changed for a number of reasons. Someone who had performed an extraordinary act typically took on a new name, as did a child or adult who was quite sick. People changed their names when a beloved relative died. And a man always took a new name when he had killed or attacked an enemy in a war. Sometimes, a person was forced to change names because someone took the name that the individual was currently using. When a new name was adopted, this was the only one that the person used. Former names were retired.

Naming is sometimes the occasion for a formal ceremony, and in 53 percent of 60 cultures the ceremony typically involves some expense by the family. Community members are also present at the naming in many cultures. Among the Japanese Takashima, a baby is named when it is seven days old, unless that day is unlucky. The infant is dressed in a red kimono and it is ceremonially offered dishes of special food, which are later eaten by members of the family. Sometimes, a smooth round stone is also placed on the tray along with the food so that the baby will grow up to be strong and firm like the stone. The baby may be named after some traditional hero, or an elder may be asked to help choose a name. Or if there are a number of candidate names, they may be written on pieces of paper and one of them chosen from the pile. In North America, a Comanche baby would be called by some pet name until a permanent name was chosen, perhaps by the father but more commonly by some other person at the father's invitation. The same name was equally appropriate for a girl or boy. If an infant was named by a medicine man, a public ceremony conducted inside a tipi accompanied the naming. The medicine man would light his pipe, blowing smoke toward the sky and earth and east, west, north, and south. He offered a prayer for the baby's well-being and lifted the infant high up four times in a row as a sign that it would grow to adulthood. The baby was then given a permanent name. The Comanche said that a person who had been named by a medicine man was likely to have a longer and more productive life. A Gusii baby's head is shaved at the time of its naming, with a small topknot being left on its head until its initiation if the mother has already lost a number of children.

———

Alford, Richard D. (1988) *Naming and Identity: A Cross-Cultural Study of Personal Naming Practices.*

Beaglehole, Ernest, and Pearl Beaglehole. (1941) *Pangai: Village in Tonga.*

Cohen, Yehudi A. (1966) *A Study of Interpersonal Relations in a Jamaican Community*

Dentan, Robert. (1978) "Notes on Childhood in a Nonviolent Context: The Semai Case." In *Learning and Non-Aggression*, edited by Ashley Montagu, 94–143.

Gladwin, Thomas, and Seymour Sarason. (1953) *Truk: Man in Paradise.*

Goldman, Irving. (1963) *The Cubeo: Indians of the Northwest Amazon.*

Goldschmidt, Walter. (1976) *The Culture and Behavior of the Sebei.*

Harner, Michael J. (1973) *The Jivaro: People of the Sacred Waterfalls.*

Hart, C. W. M., and Arnold Pilling. (1960) *The Tiwi of North Australia.*

Hilger, M. Inez. (1951) *Chippewa Child Life and Its Cultural Background.*

———. (1952) *Arapaho Child Life and Its Cultural Background.*

LeVine, Robert A., and Barbara B. LeVine. (1966) *Nyansongo: A Gusii Community in Kenya.*

Maretzki, Thomas W., and Hatsumi Maretzki. (1966) *Taira: An Okinawan Village.*

Norbeck, Edward. (1954) *Takashima: A Japanese Fishing Community.*

Piker, Steven. (1965) *An Examination of Character and Socialization in a Thai Peasant Community.*

Ray, Verne. (1933) *The Sanpoil and the Nespelem: Salishan Peoples of Northeastern Washington.*

Wallace, Ernest, and E. Adamson Hoebel. (1952) *The Comanches: Lords of the South Plains.*

NURSING

All mammals nurse their young. However, it is possible to distinguish two patterns of nursing across mammalian species. Thus, among "continuous" feeders, the infant clings to or follows its mother. This means that, in the case of continuous feeders, the mother is always close by. Further, the milk content of continuous-feeder females is relatively diluted and low in fat and protein content, and infants in continuous-feeding species suck at a relatively low rate. It is no doubt the composition of the mother's milk in continuous-feeding species that pressures infants to be continuous feeders. These infants require a more or less constant supply of milk if they are going to receive adequate calories and nutrition. Thus, a continuous-feeding infant nurses on and off all day and night. The fact that continuous-feeding infants remain near their mothers at all times allows them to nurse more or less constantly. In contrast to continuous feeders are "spaced" feeders. In these species, the mother's milk is relatively concentrated and high in fat and protein, and infants suck quickly and nurse on an irregular basis. Spaced-feeding infants are often left behind by their mothers. They can afford to nurse at spaced intervals because they are able to obtain adequate nutrition without constant feeding. Spaced feeders include rabbits, tree shrews, and eland. Bats, marsupials, and some ungulates are continuous feeders. Human infants and their mothers also display many of the traits associated with continuous feeding. And indeed, mothers in many cultures treat their infants as continuous feeders, nursing a baby throughout the day and night whenever it cries.

Frequency of Nursing

Frequent nursing is common across cultures. In Mexico, for example, Mixtecan infants nurse at will, and a baby will fall asleep while nursing. Among the Chimalteco of Guatemala, a baby is nursed whenever it cries, and a woman will stop whatever she is doing to tend a fretting infant. Babies are always fed first thing in the morning, as they cry immediately upon waking up. Chimalteco women say that babies are fed more frequently at night because that is when they cry

the most. In rural Kenya, infants nurse perhaps 20 times a day for the first four months of life. And Kalahari !Kung babies nurse multiple times per hour.

While babies in many cultures are nursed many times an hour, in other societies babies may have to wait a while before nursing. In part, frequency of nursing depends upon whether or not the baby is constantly held by the mother. Thus, for example, among the Tarong of the Philippines, an infant is slung on the mother's hip and supported by an arm while the woman works. As a result, the mother is able to nurse her baby while she is performing chores. And indeed, the baby is nursed whenever it cries for as long as it likes. Similarly, in the Northwest Amazon, a Cubeo baby is nursed whenever it cries, and even when a woman is engaged in some delicate task, she will nevertheless stop and adjust a crying baby so that it can easily reach a breast. By contrast, a young Rajput baby, who spends a good deal of time in its crib, is nursed perhaps every half hour, while older infants nurse three or four times a day.

When cultural nursing patterns tilt in favor of treating babies like continuous feeders, nursing is likely to take place whenever a baby happens to show signs of fussing. Among the Tairans of Okinawa, an infant is nursed whenever it seems hungry or unhappy, and a mother will nurse her infant while carrying on a conversation or attending a village meeting. Babies are nursed at market, on buses, or at gatherings of members of different villages. In North America, a Chippewa mother might nurse a baby while it lay in its cradleboard. Older children might nurse while standing.

Constraints on Continuous Nursing

The nature of the mother's workload influences the frequency with which a baby nurses. If the woman's work takes her away from home, and if it is impossible for her to take her baby along with her, then the number of nursing episodes

A Cherokee woman nurses her infant on a North Carolina reservation.

will clearly decrease. In Indonesia, an Alorese woman returns to the field two weeks or less after the birth of her baby, and she may be gone for nine hours. Meanwhile, the infant is left with an older sibling or other relative. When the infant becomes hungry, it may be fed prechewed food, and sometimes another woman may try to nurse the baby. But babies often try to spit out the food that they are given, searching instead for a nipple. When she finally comes home, the mother nurses her infant and spends the rest of the evening with the baby. Sometimes, a woman whose chores take her away from home will try to juggle her schedule so that she can perform her tasks and also nurse her baby when it is hungry. Among the Gusii of Kenya, women work in the fields during the day. A mother gets up early in the morning and tends to her chores

until the baby wakes up and starts fussing. The infant is then nursed, after which the mother goes off to the fields. If her work is not too vigorous, a woman will strap her baby to her back and take it along, nursing it immediately when it cries insistently and waiting a few minutes if the crying is not urgent. However, no woman will allow a baby to cry for even as much as five minutes without allowing it to nurse. If a mother's work prevents her from carrying the baby in this way, she will entrust the infant to a child nurse for the day. If a baby is not yet eating supplementary foods, the baby tender may accompany the mother so that the baby can still nurse. Or the child nurse may keep the baby at home, calling the mother back from the fields or taking the infant to its mother to be nursed if nothing else works to quiet the baby's cries. Women come home at noon to feed the older children and tend to chores around the house. An infant will continue to be supervised by the child baby tender but will be handed over to the mother when it is hungry. Thus, no Gusii infant will go for any length of time without being nursed once it has begun to cry. Infants also sleep with their mothers, so a baby can often nurse without waking up its mother.

Scheduled Nursing

In some societies, babies are fed on schedule. Jamaican babies are nursed an average of four times a day for the first two or three months. A mother will nurse for about five minutes. A baby almost always cries when its mother removes it from the breast, and women say that this is because the infant is still hungry and wants more food. Babies often cry for an hour before it is time for their scheduled feeding. Beginning at the end of the second or third month of life, an infant is nursed only three times a day, again for about five minutes. The schedule is cut back after another few months to twice a day. The baby is then offered black tea, usually with sugar, for its third feeding. An infant is not fed at night, and a baby who wakes up and cries to be fed will get no response.

The Jamaican schedule is similar to the one followed by American women who feed their babies on schedule. But most American mothers who say that they nurse on demand are also using a schedule, although a more liberal one. Thus, recent advice on frequency of nursing recommends perhaps a 20-minute nursing about every two hours. A schedule of this sort still differs from the pattern characteristic of demand feeding in other cultures and of the feeding regime of other continuous-feeder mammals. Some investigators speculate that feeding problems and "colic" commonly reported by American mothers may be caused by the feeding schedules that American babies follow. Disruption of infant sleep patterns and infant blood sugar levels as well as maternal problems with milk production and mood swings may also be the result of placing infants on feeding schedules that depart dramatically from what the physiology of continuous-feeder species expects. These problems, which are common complaints among American infants and their mothers, are virtually unknown in other cultures.

Nighttime Nursing

Regardless of whether or not a baby nurses on demand during the day, mothers in virtually all societies around the world allow their infants to nurse on demand at night. Across cultures, infants sleep with their mothers, making it easy for them to nurse at night. In 69 percent of 89 societies around the world, babies sleep in the same bed as their mothers. In the remaining 31 percent, they sleep in different beds, but in the same room. In none of these cultures does a baby sleep in a separate room, and in fact, placing a baby in a room of its own is very rare across societies. Here, too, the American case is extreme.

Nursing To Pacify the Baby

In many cultures, mothers will nurse a baby even when the infant seems perfectly content, or nursing may be used as a way of quieting a baby. In Thailand, a Banoi woman often offers her baby a breast even when the infant shows no sign of upset or hunger. The baby may then nurse for a few minutes. Banoi women also immediately offer a breast to a baby who is fussing for any reason. A Tairan mother will nurse her infant whenever the baby cries or is distressed, so that the breast becomes not only a source of nourishment but also a pacifier.

Substitute Nursers

Many women who cannot always be present to nurse their own babies will find another nursing mother to act as a substitute. Mixtecan mothers recruit other women to nurse their babies. It is almost always a close relative who acts as substitute, aunts being the most frequent choice. Substitute nurses are used by Mixtecans when a woman has to be away from the house for a short time and needs to leave her baby behind. A Tarong infant is nursed by a neighborhood woman until its own mother's milk begins to come in. Some women will continue to use substitute nurses, especially if the mother's family is poor and she is needed in the fields. One group of four sisters-in-law took turns watching each other's children and nursing each other's babies so that the remaining women could go off to work. A Tairan mother who has enough milk for two infants may help to nurse a baby whose own mother is producing insufficient milk to satisfy the infant. Mothers with an abundant milk supply will also nurse a baby whose mother is working too far from home to come back and feed the infant. One woman whose baby has been nursed by another mother while she was away from home will return the favor at a later date. About one-third of Banoi mothers occasionally recruit relatives to nurse their babies.

Where a mother is permanently unable to nurse, another woman may take on the responsibility of nursing her baby. Among the Truk of Micronesia, if a mother is unable to produce milk, or if she dies, a relative is sought to function as a wetnurse. If no relative can be found, some unrelated woman may be asked to nurse the baby, but in this case, the woman is likely to want to adopt the baby, a circumstance that is resisted by the parents. A Chimalteco mother who cannot provide adequate milk for her baby will look for some other woman to nurse her baby. Whenever her infant cries, the mother takes it to the substitute nurse, even though this entails many trips each day and some of them at night. A substitute nurse should be given presents by the mother, but there is no formal payment for her help. Chimalteco women appear to like taking care of children, and nursing is one component of caretaking. Even if a woman is able to provide enough milk for her own baby, another one may take over for a nursing session if the mother happens to be busy. If a North American Sanpoil mother died, some other woman would temporarily take on the care of the baby. When the infant was weaned, at about two years of age, the grandparents would take over as the guardians.

In some cultures, only the mother will nurse a baby. The Toba of Bolivia say that an infant cannot be nourished by any milk except for what is produced by its own mother. Therefore, if a woman dies in childbirth, the baby is buried along with her. Similarly, if a woman has twins, the first to have been born is often killed because the mother will not have an adequate milk supply to feed them both. While many Tarong women use substitute nurses, other mothers do not like the idea of having other women nurse their babies. And if a Chippewa mother was unable to nurse, the baby was fed wild rice or cornmeal porridge boiled with fish broth or meat. The food was put in a clean animal bladder and a small hole was made from which the baby could suck.

Special Diets

A woman who is nursing an infant will often follow special diets and routines. Tairan women who are nursing infants eat special foods and avoid others in an effort to insure that they will produce enough milk. They are also warned not to tire themselves out. Chippewa mothers were supposed to eat porridge made of fish or meat broth mixed with cornmeal or wild rice to increase the supply of milk. A nursing woman was in general given the best foods so that her milk would flow and the baby would grow, and a drink made of raspberry roots was thought to be particularly powerful in producing milk. Corn soup and other thick soups were also recommended so that the baby would become strong. By contrast, hominy, choke cherries, potatoes, and bread were thought to dry up a woman's milk supply. Chimalteco women say that if a baby continues to cry after it has been nursed, it is because of something that the mother has eaten. Nursing women are supposed to avoid turkey and beef, and vegetables that are considered "hot" will also make a mother's milk bad for her baby. Arapaho women drank broth or else a decoction made of certain plants to increase their flow of milk. A nursing woman was prohibited from drinking coffee because it would cook the milk. She was also supposed to keep her breasts, and sometimes her back, covered to protect her milk from the heat of the sun or of the fire.

Number of Nursing Infants

Typically, a woman will only nurse one child at a time, and indeed, the most common reason for weaning one baby is that the mother is pregnant with another. Nevertheless, women will occasionally nurse two children simultaneously. A Chippewa mother might allow an older child to continue nursing even though she had a new baby. But women did not nurse while they were pregnant.

See also WEANING

Barry, Herbert, III, and Leonora M. Paxson. (1971) "Infancy and Early Childhood: Cross-Cultural Codes 2." *Ethnology* 10: 466–508.

Cohen, Yehudi A. (1966) *A Study of Interpersonal Relations in a Jamaican Community.*

Gladwin, Thomas, and Seymour Sarason. (1953) *Truk: Man in Paradise.*

Goldman, Irving. (1963) *The Cubeo: Indians of the Northwest Amazon.*

Hilger, M. Inez. (1951) *Chippewa Child Life and Its Cultural Background.*

———. (1952) *Arapaho Child Life and Its Cultural Background.*

Hitchcock, John T., and Leigh Minturn. (1966) *The Rajputs of Khalapur, India.*

Karsten, Rafael. (1923) *The Toba Indians of the Bolivian Gran Chaco.*

Konner, Melvin J. (1981) "Evolution of Human Behavior Development." In *Handbook of Cross-Cultural Human Development,* edited by Ruth H. Munroe, Robert L. Munroe, and Beatrice B. Whiting, 3–52.

LeVine, Robert A., and Barbara B. LeVine. (1966) *Nyansongo: A Gusii Community in Kenya.*

Maretzki, Thomas W., and Hatsumi Maretzki. (1966) *Taira: An Okinawan Village.*

Munroe, Robert L., and Ruth H. Munroe. (1975) *Cross-Cultural Human Development.*

Nydegger, William F., and Corinne Nydegger. (1966) *Tarong: An Ilocos Barrio in the Philippines.*

Piker, Steven. (1965) *An Examination of Character and Socialization in a Thai Peasant Community.*

Ray, Verne. (1933) *The Sanpoil and the Nespelem: Salishan Peoples of Northeastern Washington.*

Romney, A. Kimball, and Romaine Romney. (1966) *The Mixtecans of Juxtlahuaca, Mexico.*

Super, Charles M. (1981) "Behavioral Development in Infancy." In *Handbook of Cross-Cultural Human Development,* edited by Ruth H. Munroe, Robert L. Munroe, and Beatrice B. Whiting, 181–270.

Wagley, Charles. (1949) "The Social and Religious Life of a Guatemalan Village." *American Anthropologist* 51: 3–150.

NURTURANCE TRAINING

A child who offers help or support to another individual can be said to be exhibiting nurturance. Children can and do offer food, toys, tools, information, comfort, and other material and emotional resources to other people. On the other hand, children in some cultures are more likely to exhibit nurturance, and adults in some societies are more inclined to encourage nurturance in their children. Thus, for instance, in Okinawa, Tairan adults are consistently nurturant to babies and consciously model and reinforce such behavior in children. If a number of mothers and children are gathered together, one woman may pat a baby's head and then encourage her own child to do the same. A youngster who is spontaneously nurturant to another child will be praised by any witness. By contrast, in India, Rajput children cannot be relied on to help each other. When asked what they would do if a friend got hurt, some children said that they would help or get help, but almost as many said that they would not do anything. Nor do Rajput children typically help their younger siblings, and one father said that only a good-natured child could be expected to help a younger one. Children are not punished for failing to help other people and they are not praised for being helpful. In fact, children are only likely to help someone if they are worn down by persistent

A very young Cherokee girl poses with a tame bird. Most cultures encourage and even require nurturing behavior in girls, though not as often in boys.

without exception, showed more nurturant than egoistic behavior in daily observations of the children over an extended period of time.

Why does the assignment of chores induce a child to be nurturant? The kinds of tasks that children in many cultures are asked to perform have a clear connection to the welfare of the family. Thus, the very activities in which youngsters are asked to engage encourage a nurturant attitude on the part of the child. By contrast, children in some cultures are assigned tasks that do not have this kind of obvious connection to the welfare of the family. An American boy who is asked to make his bed or pick up his toys is doing chores that are more for his own benefit than for the good of the family. And in fact, in one long-term study of children in an American neighborhood, only 8 percent of the youngsters displayed a higher proportion of nurturant than egoistic behavior.

The relationship between task assignment and nurturance in children becomes especially clear in the case of baby tending. Across cultures older children are expected to act as nurses for their younger siblings and cousins. The role of nurse is an inherently nurturant one. Further, young children, and especially infants, naturally elicit nurturant responses from other people. This power on the part of infants to evoke nurturance is so strong that even toddlers as young as two years old are predominantly nurturant to babies. Thus, in one study, 80 percent of the responses of two-year-olds toward infants were nurturant, while only 8 percent were negative. The implication is that nurturance is encouraged in children who are recruited as baby tenders in part because the supervision of infants and toddlers requires nurturance and in part because babies and small children naturally call out nurturance in others.

The effects of baby tending on nurturance in children may account in part for observed sex differences in nurturant behavior. Thus, in one study, girls and boys of three to five years of age

nagging, a pattern that is also typical for adults. Sometimes, a child will simply ignore a peer or sibling who is in need of assistance, even if the other child is crying.

The propensity on the part of a child to offer help and support is related to the activities the children are expected to perform on a daily basis. Where children are expected to contribute to the family's welfare by doing chores, nurturant behavior in youngsters is common. Further, the more chores a child is expected to do, the more likely we are to see nurturance. In Kenya, Gusii mothers assign their children an unusually high number of tasks at an especially early age. Thus, over half of Gusii three- and four-year-olds are fetching wood and water, preparing food, cleaning, gardening, and caring for animals. A three- or four-year-old Gusii child typically performs five tasks each day. Further, all Gusii children, are equivalent in their displays of nurturance, which are relatively low for both sexes. With increasing age, however, boys continue to show little nurturance, but nurturant behavior in girls increases dramatically. This pattern may reflect the tendency of mothers across cultures to recruit girls instead of boys as child nurses. But it is also the case that girls seem to be more enthusiastic about baby tending than arc boys, suggesting perhaps a prior inclination on the part of girls to take on roles that demand nurturance.

See also CHILD NURSES; CHORES; RESPONSIBILITY; SEX DIFFERENCES

Hitchcock, John T., and Leigh Minturn. (1966) *The Rajputs of Khalapur, India.*

Maretzki, Thomas W., and Hatsumi Maretzki. (1966) *Taira: An Okinawan Village.*

Whiting, Beatrice B., and Carolyn Pope Edwards. (1988) *Children of Different Worlds: The Formation of Social Behavior.*

Whiting, Beatrice B., and John W. M. Whiting. (1975) *Children of Six Cultures: A Psycho-Cultural Analysis.*

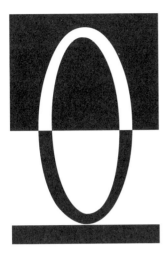

their children, and in fact, children do not tend to respond quickly to the mother's requests. From the mother's point of view, however, a youngster who eventually does what he or she is told is an obedient child. Children will sometimes simply avoid doing a chore by busying themselves with some other tasks or disappearing altogether. But it is only when a youngster outright refuses to do what he or she is told to do that punishment for disobedience is likely to follow. North American Kurtachi children disregard the commands of their fathers with impunity. A man might ask his five-year-old daughter to fetch him some fire to light his pipe. The little girl might retort "Tsuga," that is, "I don't want to," and nothing will happen to her. Rather, her father will get the fire himself. If a southern Indian Gopalpur mother tells a daughter to rock a baby sibling in its cradle, the older child will just as likely refuse and go out to play instead of obeying the command. Or the sister may insist upon being fed before she takes care of the baby. When a New Ireland Lesu boy or girl runs away from home, the parents can do nothing about it. Children go back to their own houses when they feel like it.

Even where obedience is valued in the abstract, parents may not vigorously enforce obedience in their children. In Mexico, Mixtecan mothers say that they would scold or punish a child who disobeyed them. In fact, however, children are not pressured to be obedient before seven years of age. Thus, disobedience in a younger child is ignored by parents, and children are rarely physically punished. Most mothers say that their daughters are obedient, although boys are described as less so. In India, Rajput mothers value obedience and passivity in their children above other qualities, and the good child is the one who obeys. However, Rajput children are not very obedient in fact. Children must often be nagged by adults before they do what they are told. Mothers often get mad at their disobedient children, but then calm

OBEDIENCE If parents wish to be effective as socializers, they must demand at least minimal obedience from their children. Different cultures, however, place greater or less stress on obedience in youngsters. In Liberia, all Kpelle parents say that a child should, above all, show "full respect" toward any older person in general and toward parents in particular, and disobedience toward a parent is the most severely punished form of bad behavior among the Kpelle. Similarly, Jamaican children are not expected to take the initiative for engaging in any activity on their own. All of their behaviors should be at the direction of the mother, and whenever children do show initiative, they are accused of being "rude." While they are young, the favorite children of their parents are those who are submissive and subservient. In Uganda, a Sebei child is expected to show deference, not only to parents but also to all older people. And among the Polynesian Tonga, children who fail to obey will be severely beaten by their mothers. By contrast, Philippine Tarong mothers value eventual rather than immediate compliance in

down and let the matter drop with the result that the youngsters get away with ignoring their commands. Because Rajput women are confined to their courtyards by the custom of purdah, or seclusion, children can easily disregard their mothers' requests by leaving the courtyard, and virtually all children employ this tactic on occasion. Among the Banoi of Thailand, parents say that the best way to achieve compliance from young children is to treat them with indulgence and affection. Similarly, they say that an older child is most likely to be obedient when gentleness and flattery are mixed with clear explanations regarding appropriate behavior. In fact, parents are prone to mix indulgence with threats of punishment as the typical way of encouraging obedience in children. And young children frequently disobey their parents. By the age of ten or twelve, however, youngsters are rarely disobedient, and girls tend to be even more compliant than boys.

In many cultures, parents recognize that obedience is hard to enforce in younger children and they will sometimes be more lenient with children under seven years of age because a child who is younger than seven cannot be expected to reason. Korean parents are extremely lenient when a young child misbehaves. A small child who breaks some object or causes a sibling to cry is not punished because, as the parents says, "he is only a child and doesn't know any better." By contrast, an older child is expected to obey a command immediately, and a youngster who disobeys is slapped or beaten. Among the Tairans of Okinawa, parents do not expect obedience on the part of children younger than seven years of age except with regard to safety rules. As a result, mothers, fathers, and grandparents can regularly be heard nagging children, who regularly ignore them. Mothers acknowledge that they allow their children to disobey them. Once a child approaches seven years of age, adults are more consistent in their demands for obedience regarding rules of safety. They are less so regard-

ing the willingness of children to do chores or run errands when they are told. And children become adept at predicting when a parent is likely to enforce a command and when the youngster can disobey the parent with impunity. Thus, a child obeys the orders of a tired or irritable parent but may ignore the demands of a parent who appears to be in a good mood. This inconsistency in parental enforcement of commands has the consequence of promoting disobedience on the part of children. The same child who ignores a parent's requests, however, listens to high-status adults such as teachers or the village headman. A child who is obedient is praised by adults, who say that the youngster has a "good head." Parents like their own children to play with a youngster who predictably obeys commands. In some cultures, parents also appreciate that young children are predictably stubborn at particular stages of life. Thus, in Canada, Hare mothers observe that children between the ages of two and four are prone to be disobedient and they tend to ignore contrariness in youngsters of this age unless matters threaten to become serious.

Parental attitudes toward obedience are influenced in part by the patterning of social relationships in their culture. Thus, for example, among the Gusii of Kenya, human relationships in general are defined in terms of dominance and obedience. The old, wealthy, and dominating are adopted as leaders and deferred to by other members of the community, and men who want to advance themselves try to curry favor with people in power instead of depending upon their own skills and effort as the means of achieving status. This emphasis on obedience extends to child rearing, and children are pressured to be obedient beginning at a very early age. Obedience to the teacher is understood to be the best way to succeed in school and is also expected of adult sons toward their fathers.

Expectations regarding obedience in children are also affected by the mother's lifestyle.

Across cultures, women who have heavy workloads usually recruit their children to do chores. Because these children are being asked to do important work, it becomes important for them to follow directions, and their mothers strictly enforce demands for obedience. A woman who is contributing to the welfare of her family by producing goods or bringing home money may also have high self-esteem and may, therefore, be more willing to punish insubordination in her children.

Parents do not necessarily take the child's motivation into account when deciding whether or not to enforce demands of obedience. Tarong parents do not dole out punishment on the basis of the underlying motives of an act. It is the consequences of a behavior that matter. Thus, when two children are fighting, both are punished, and it makes no difference who began the fight. Tarong children, therefore, rarely bother to attribute blame to someone else when they are caught doing something wrong.

Across cultures, obedience tends to be emphasized more for girls than for boys. Thus, for example, while Rajput adults value obedience in both sexes, it is slightly more important for a girl to obey and for a boy to be brave. Similarly, Jamaican mothers do not punish a son who refuses to do work around the house. A daughter who resists doing her chores, by contrast, is flogged, and in fact, girls are physically punished twice as often as boys. This may explain the claim by Jamaicans that daughters are more obedient than sons.

It is also the case that mothers across cultures have trouble convincing their children, and especially their sons, to obey them. For this reason, mothers often leave the job of punishing children, especially for serious offenses, to their husbands. Tairan children obey their fathers more readily than their mothers, and among the Mixtecans, children are on their best behavior when their father is at home. Rajput men expect children to obey them, and indeed, children do listen to men more than to women, although youngsters may also ignore the requests of men by making themselves scarce when asked to do something.

See also CHORES; PARENTING, STYLES OF; PARENTS, CHILDREN'S TREATMENT OF; RESPECT; RESPONSIBILITY

Barry, Herbert, III, Lili Josephson, Edith Lauer, and Catherine Marshall. (1976) "Traits Inculcated in Childhood: Cross-Cultural Codes 5." *Ethnology* 15: 83–114.

Beaglehole, Ernest, and Pearl Beaglehole. (1941) *Pangai: Village in Tonga.*

Beals, Alan R. (1962) *Gopalpur: A South Indian Village.*

Blackwood, Beatrice M. (1935) *Both Sides of Buka Passage.*

Brandt, Vincent. (1971) *A Korean Village.*

Cohen, Yehudi A. (1966) *A Study of Interpersonal Relations in a Jamaican Community.*

Erchak, Gerald M. (1977) *Full Respect: Kpelle Children in Adaptation.*

Goldschmidt, Walter. (1976) *The Culture and Behavior of the Sebei.*

Hara, Hiroko Sue. (1967) *Hare Indians and Their World.*

Hitchcock, John T., and Leigh Minturn. (1966) *The Rajputs of Khalapur, India.*

LeVine, Robert A., and Barbara B. LeVine. (1966) *Nyansongo: A Gusii Community in Kenya.*

Maretzki, Thomas W., and Hatsumi Maretzki. (1966) *Taira: An Okinawan Village.*

Minturn, Leigh, and William W. Lambert. (1964) *Mothers of Six Cultures: Antecedents of Child Rearing.*

Nydegger, William F., and Corinne Nydegger. (1966) *Tarong: An Ilocos Barrio in the Philippines.*

Piker, Steven. (1965) *An Examination of Character and Socialization in a Thai Peasant Community.*

Powdermaker, Hortense. (1933) *Life in Lesu: A Study of Melanesian Society in New Ireland.*

Romney, A. Kimball, and Romaine Romney. (1966) *The Mixtecans of Juxtlahuaca, Mexico.*

Whiting, Beatrice B., and Carolyn Pope Edwards. (1988) *Children of Different Worlds: The Formation of Social Behavior.*

societies, women offer their children help and support, train them, control and restrain them, and enjoy friendly positive exchanges with them. However, one kind of interaction tends to dominate over others in particular kinds of cultures, leading to a predominant style of interaction between mother and child. In turn, different styles of parenting may help to produce different behavior and personality profiles in the children themselves.

In some societies, the mother's style of interaction with her children is dominated by training. In these cultures, mothers are concerned with teaching their youngsters appropriate skills and social behavior and with preventing them from engaging in dangerous or undesirable behavior. The mother who spends most of her time training her children also expends considerable effort in attempting to control their behavior. Training mothers are women whose own workload is relatively demanding. As a result, children are recruited to help their mothers with chores. A child who is expected to make real contributions to the work force needs to be taught how to perform chores properly and also needs to learn how to avoid dangerous situations. Thus, the mother finds that a high proportion of her interaction with her children is devoted to training them. In cultures where mothers are predominantly trainers, women believe that children are capable of being both obedient and responsible at an early age. Among the Ngeca of sub–Saharan Africa, where women often perform all of the agricultural work, mothers begin to assign children tasks at two years of age, and children are punished if they refuse to do their chores. A young child may be asked to peel the potatoes or fetch a spoon or pan. Older girls fetch water and tend babies, while boys pasture and milk the cattle and take the milk to the dairy. In Liberia, Kpelle women farm and are responsible for providing their children's food, and mothers train their young children to perform chores, respect property, conserve food, and follow rules

PARENTING, STYLES OF

The job of a parent is strikingly similar across cultures. Thus, in societies around the world, parents, and especially mothers, take care of the physical needs of their children, both feeding them and protecting them from physical dangers. Mothers provide emotional support for their youngsters, toilet train them, and teach them proper hygiene. Children across cultures are trained to conform to the social norms of their culture by their mothers. And parents everywhere teach their youngsters various skills. It is not surprising that the job description for parents is so uniform across cultures. All children have the same general needs regardless of the culture in which they happen to live, and all societies insist upon what they take to be civilized behavior on the part of their members. Therefore, all parents are interested in meeting the needs of their children and in teaching them the norms of their culture.

The content of the interactions between parents, and especially mothers, and their children also overlaps across cultures. Thus, across

regarding health, safety, and cleanliness. In general, training mothers exploit the natural inclination of young children to want to be competent actors. Across cultures, we hear of small children trying to imitate the activities of adults or older brothers and sisters. The woman who emphasizes training in her interactions with her children encourages and directs this autonomous motivation on the part of the child to be an effective agent.

In other cultures, most of a mother's time is taken up in attempts to control her children. Controlling mothers have a less demanding workload than do training mothers, with the result that children are not recruited to do specific chores as they are by training mothers. Controlling mothers also tend to live in extended families, which means that a number of adults and children are housed under one roof. Such households are relatively noisy and confused, and children are often underfoot, interfering with the work and conversation of the adults. As a result, mothers find themselves reprimanding, correcting, threatening, commanding, and punishing children who have gotten into trouble. Controlling mothers may insist that a child stop misbehaving without giving the youngster any productive activity to do. By contrast, the training mother will assign some task to a child who is getting into trouble or who even shows signs of restlessness, and often youngsters who are too exuberant will be recruited to do some chore even before they have the opportunity to misbehave.

In some cultures, many of the interactions between mothers and their children are friendly in nature. While sociable exchanges are never the predominant form of interaction between women and children, in a small number of cultures the mother-child relationship is unusually friendly. Sociable mothers are typically isolated from other adults for much of the day. Thus, they spend their time largely with children and turn to their children for company. Further, the workload of sociable mothers is light by cross-cultural standards, so there is no pressing need to require children to do tasks. Sociability is characteristic of some American mothers who are not employed outside the home during the day. These mothers assign few chores to their children, depending on their youngsters more for social interaction than for work. The relationship between a sociable mother and her children is characterized by positive, friendly interaction, including talking, teasing, laughing, touching, and exchanges of information.

Parents within and across cultures can also be distinguished regarding their disciplinary styles. *Authoritarian* parents emphasize obedience as a virtue. Their word is law, and a child who disobeys an authoritarian parent is forcefully punished, usually by physical means. Jamaican parents typify the authoritarian attitude. Children are flogged for disobeying their parents, and girls more so than boys. Children are never asked what they think about anything, nor can they offer their opinions spontaneously. A child who asks the mother for some of her food will be told "No, it is mine." But the same youngster will be required to share food with a mother who wants some. A youngster who comments on a parent's behavior will be flogged, and the ideal parent is the one who is strict and rigid. Jamaican children are required to exhibit unquestioning obedience to their parents as long as they are supported by them. Jamaican parents and children do not participate in social activities together. They do not relax or play together, in part because children must always treat their parents as the dominant figures in their joint interactions.

By contrast, some parents adopt an *authoritative* style of discipline. The authoritative parent emphasizes rational thought and behavior in children. Parents who conform to this style of discipline value conformity to cultural standards, but they also encourage independence. Thus, the child of the authoritative parent appreciates that there are limits regarding what is acceptable behavior but also enjoys a certain degree of freedom within the constraints of those limits. Authoritative parents encourage their children to participate in making decisions that affect the family. They expect their children to behave in a mature manner and they firmly enforce those expectations. Authoritativeness is typical of some American middle-class parents.

Finally, some parents adopt a *permissive* style of discipline. Permissive parents view themselves more as resources and facilitators than as trainers or controllers of their children. The permissive parent believes that children should be allowed maximum freedom of movement and expression, with the result that the parent does not restrain the child. The child of a permissive parent is not assigned chores, need not display good manners, and may interrupt parents and other people with impunity. Permissiveness as a form of discipline is unknown in cultures where parents rely on their children to make real contributions to the workload or, at a minimum, to refrain from interfering with the activities of busy adults. Parents are free to shift from an authoritarian to an authoritative or permissive style of parenting once the economic circumstances or household structure of the family mean that demands upon the child can be relaxed. We see this dynamic operating in Tepoztlán, Mexico, as the community shifted from a rural to an urban base. In 1943, Tepoztlán families depended upon farming to make a living, and parents were restrictive and punitive. By 1956, the community had become urbanized, and parents were now more permissive and indulgent.

Different styles of discipline tend to be associated with different behavior and personality in children. Children of authoritarian parents are described as typically withdrawn, unhappy, anxious and insecure with their peers, and dependent. These are children who are likely to become hostile when they are frustrated. They do not tend to explore and they are not motivated to achieve. The children of authoritative parents,

by contrast, are often self-reliant, achievement-oriented, friendly, cooperative, and happy. They persevere even in the face of challenges and inhibit potentially disruptive behavior. These are children who have high self-esteem and internalized moral standards. They also do well in school. Finally, the children of permissive parents are typically immature, dependent, and demanding. They have trouble controlling their impulses and remaining involved in activities. These are disobedient children who may explode when asked to do something that conflicts with their own desires.

Across cultures, mothers also differ regarding the extent to which their interactions with their children are physical in nature. Thus, for instance, Japanese mothers soothe, lull, and rock their babies more than do American women. Mothers in America, by contrast, spend more time interacting verbally with their infants. Differences in the baby's behavior are consistent with these differences in maternal behavior. Thus, American infants as young as three or four months of age vocalize more than Japanese babies and also display a greater amount of activity and play. It is tempting to infer that the differences in infant behavior are attributed to divergences in how mothers from these two cultures treat their babies. But it is also the case that initial temperamental differences between American and Japanese babies may tend to elicit different kinds of maternal behavior and to lead to different patterns of behavior in the babies themselves.

Babies in African cultures typically remain in close proximity to their mothers for most of the day as well as the night. But in some African societies, women do not hug, kiss, or smile at their infants as a general rule. Rather, the mother holds the baby passively, often attending to other things instead of devoting her attention to the infant. The relationships between both Gusii and Sebei mothers and their infants are described as aloof, and Gusii women seem to actively avoid face-to-face interaction with their babies. Gusii, Maragoli, and Luo mothers say that it is "silly" to talk to a baby who cannot understand language or talk back. It has been suggested that the emotional flatness said to characterize mother-infant relationships in some African cultures is then the cause of relatively distant relationships formed between adults. The proposed connection, however, is only speculative. It is, again, equally possible that both patterns of mother-infant interaction and adult relationships are influenced by basic temperamental characteristics of the people. Or aloof styles of maternal behavior may have a cause that is entirely different from the causes of aloof adult relationships. Maternal aloofness is not the rule in all African societies. Thus, for example, a Nigerian Igbo infant is held so that it can have face-to-face contact with an adult, who then talks and babbles to the baby for extended periods of time. Similarly, Ugandan adults, as well as children, will often talk with and smile at a baby and try to make it smile back.

See also CHORES; COACTION; OBEDIENCE; RESPONSIBILITY

Berk, Laura E. (1989) *Child Development.*

Cohen, Yehudi A. (1966) *A Study of Interpersonal Relations in a Jamaican Community.*

Goldschmidt, Walter. (1975) "Absent Eyes and Idle Hands: Socialization for Low Affect among the Sebei." *Ethos* 3: 157–163.

Henderson, Ronald W., and John R. Bergan. (1976) *The Cultural Context of Childhood.*

LeVine, Robert A. (1973) "Patterns of Personality in Africa." *Ethos* 1: 123–152.

Munroe, Ruth H., and Robert L. Munroe. (1971) "Household Density and Infant Care in an East African Society." *Social Psychology* 83: 3–13.

Super, Charles M. (1981) "Behavioral Development in Infancy." In *Handbook of Cross-Cultural Human Development*, edited by Ruth H. Munroe, Robert L. Munroe, and Beatrice B. Whiting, 181–270.

Whiting, Beatrice B., and Carolyn Pope Edwards. (1988) *Children of Different Worlds: The Formation of Social Behavior.*

PARENTS, CHILDREN'S TREATMENT OF

In many societies around the world, grown children are expected to treat their aging parents with respect and consideration and to see that the needs of their parents are met when they can no longer provide for themselves. Ideally, a Philippine Tarong adult should take care of elderly parents as if they were babies. In the words of one man: "When you are older, even should you feed your mother from the palm of your hand, you could never repay her for the trouble you caused her." In North Africa, a Teda child is expected to refrain from quarreling with his or her mother, and if a fight occurs, the neighbors will take the mother's side.

Often, however, the ideal of a child who cheerfully takes care of old parents is different from the reality. Usually, this is because it is hard if not impossible for children to afford the burden of an extra mouth to feed. Thus, for example, if elderly Teda parents can no longer support themselves, they often separate. The father then goes to live with a son and the mother with a daughter. The separation is necessary because it is too hard for one household to provide for two unproductive individuals. Among the Tarong, infirm parents are a burden to poor families, who cannot afford the extra rice for a person who cannot contribute materially to the household.

Old people who are no longer able to make themselves useful are viewed as a nuisance. Even families who can afford to care for a dependent parent may not take on the responsibility gracefully. The North American Chippewa emphasized respect for older people, but the aged were not materially helped by the more able bodied. Sons did not show any sense of responsibility for their elderly parents. Daughters showed a bit more. The parents themselves did not complain about the treatment that they received at the hands of their children. In Jamaica, a husband may actually forbid his wife from giving food or money to her parents, but she may do so behind his back, even though she risks a flogging. Jamaican sons are not as willing to provide for their aged parents.

Parents in many cultures understand that old age means increased dependence upon grudging children, and they do not look forward to their fate. In Micronesia, Truk men and women do not surrender happily or easily to the inactivity that aging implies for them. Self-sufficiency, especially in providing themselves with food, as well as the ability to contribute to the welfare of the lineage, are extremely important to the Truk, and no one looks forward to depending upon others for meeting basic needs. Once parents do become dependent, they cannot count on their children or other kin for anything more than food, and there is no guarantee that enough of that will be provided to them. Aging parents, sensitive about their dependent status and guilty about using up the family's resources without being productive themselves, often try to restrict their eating to what they absolutely need. They also display considerable deference to their children and other youthful relatives and try to be helpful around the house. Women have greater success than men in performing useful services, as there is little to do at home that is not defined as women's work.

Some societies are sensitive to the feelings of older people who do not want to be dependent upon others and try to minimize the embarrassment of the old person. Elderly Javanese parents live with their children, grandchildren, or perhaps a niece or nephew. Ideally, old people are accorded great respect, and those individuals who have special skills or knowledge are respected in fact. Although the parent actually moves in with some member of his or her family, people say that the younger person has moved in with or is being taken care of by the elderly parent. Otherwise, it might sound as if the parent were a servant in another person's house, and this would be damaging to the old person's feelings and reputation. In general, old parents live tranquil lives, taking care of the children of the household and enjoying a warm and informal relationship with them. Some Tarong grandparents solve the dependency problem by inviting a grandson to live with them as a "second son" while he is still a youngster. They provide for him a more comfortable existence than he can hope for at home, and in return he assumes the responsibility for farming the old people's fields. The boy will eventually inherit any of his grandparents' property. Grandsons usually treat their grandparents well.

In cultures where older people retain control of property, power, or other resources, children are more likely to treat their parents well. But grown children, and especially sons, in societies of this sort may also resent their still-powerful parents for standing in the way of their own advancement. In farming communities, older men are often the owners of the land, making younger men dependent upon them for its use and ultimately its transfer. In herding communities, elderly men often own the livestock. In societies that require transfers of wealth from the groom's to the bride's family at marriage, young males frequently depend upon older ones in meeting the bride-price payments. And it is often the older men in the bride's family who receive the marriage gifts, adding to their power base. In these cultures, conflict between the old and the young is likely to be pronounced. Especially in societies where power and property is vested in male relatives, the relationship between a father and son may be tense. In these cultures, sons are dependent on their fathers economically, which means that the younger man is beholden to his father for his livelihood and even his ability to marry. When a married couple moves into the household of the new husband, a grown son is also under his father's thumb in regard to his domestic life. Often, a father will try to retain his power in the household for as long as he can, while his sons wait impatiently for the older man to hand over the reins. In the Indian village of Gaon, a man, although full grown and married, is still expected to wait on his father and obey him in all matters, relegating the son to something like the status of servant. In some societies, a son, even if he does not live in his father's house, is still expected to work for him. Among the Anlo Ewe of southern Ghana, a married man establishes his own household near to his father's and at a place of the older man's choosing, and then works a parcel of land that his father has given him to use. The son is expected to weed, sow, and hoe for his father. In societies where a man owes payments to or is required to work for his father-in-law, the relationship between the two may also be strained. Among the Kpelle of Liberia, bride-price payments are drawn out for many years, during which time a husband remains obligated to his wife's father. Kpelle fathers-in-law, therefore, feel justified in asking for financial assistance from the daughter's husband any time they need it. Strains between mothers and sons are not commonly reported, perhaps in part because women are rarely in control of the kinds of resources or in the kinds of positions of power that threaten sons. Similarly, the mother-daughter relationship is usually described as warm even when a daughter is living in her mother's household and is therefore to some extent under her influence.

Cohen, Yehudi A. (1966) *A Study of Interpersonal Relations in a Jamaican Community.*

Foner, Nancy. (1984) *Ages in Conflict.*

Geertz, Hildred. (1961) *The Javanese Family: A Study of Kinship and Socialization.*

Gladwin, Thomas, and Seymour Sarason. (1953) *Truk: Man in Paradise.*

Hilger, M. Inez. (1951) *Chippewa Child Life and Its Cultural Background.*

Kronenberg, Andreas. (1981) *The Teda of Tibesti.*

Levinson, David, and Martin Malone. (1980) *Toward Explaining Human Culture.*

Murphy, Yolanda, and Robert F. Murphy. (1985) *Women of the Forest.*

Nydegger, William F., and Corinne Nydegger. (1966) *Tarong: An Ilocos Barrio in the Philippines.*

Simmons, Leo W. (1945) *The Role of the Aged in Primitive Society.*

PARENTS' PREFERENCE FOR BOY OR GIRL

Of a sample of 170 societies around the world, 54 percent value boys and girls equally, 38 percent value boys more highly than girls, and 13 percent value girls more highly than boys. Among the Rajputs of India, when a couple is expecting a baby, the parents hope to have a boy, and this preference for males is reflected in the elaborate birth rituals that accompany the birth of a son. The bias toward boys is also translated into the inferior medical care given to female children, resulting in a higher death rate for girls. A midwife is paid twice as much for delivering a male baby. Mothers who are worried about the health of a son may promise gifts to one of the goddesses if the boy lives to some specified age. Similar deals are not struck on behalf of a sickly daughter. North American Chippewa parents did not prefer one sex over the other. But women liked to have a number of daughters since it was girls who took care of their parents when they were old. In North America, Arapaho mothers liked to have some daughters and fathers liked having some sons. A mother wanted have a girl to help her with her chores and a father wished to have a son for the same reason. Indeed, many mothers preferred the first child to be a girl so that they would have help around the house. But parents did not want to have one sex to the exclusion of the other.

Although parents in most societies say that they want children of both sexes, where a preference is stated, the bias is heavily toward males. This preference for boys is reflected in the differential treatment of the sexes, and this shows up in a variety of ways from one culture to the next and beginning at the birth of the baby. Thus, if a North American Comanche woman gave birth to a boy, the family might paint a black spot on the tipi door to inform neighbors that the tribe now had a new "brave." Both mother and father were more indulgent of sons than of daughters. Among the Rajputs, a drum is beaten in front of the house of the new parent, and special songs are sung by women of the Brahman caste when a boy is born. This ceremony is repeated for ten days.

Differential treatment also shows up in the day-to-day lives of male and female children. Among the Tairans of Okinawa, boys are accorded privileges in school that are denied to girls. The boys are allowed to leave the classroom first. Boys are first when children line up at school. Boys are allowed to choose equipment before the girls. And girls complain that the teacher always calls on the boys in class. Similarly, in comparison with their sisters, boys are treated indulgently by their mothers among the Cubeo of the Northwest Amazon. Once they

are able to take on serious tasks, girls are more severely disciplined than are boys.

Biases in favor of boys even show up in relative death rates of male and female children across cultures. The Rajput preference for males is reflected in the fact that mortality is 25 percent for boys and 41 percent for girls, and until the beginning of the twentieth century, the Rajputs practiced female infanticide. Parents tend to give up hope sooner if a girl becomes ill and does not quickly recover, and sick female babies are more likely to stop receiving medical aid than are boys, especially if the family is poor. Preferences for boys also show up from place to place in differential rates of infanticide. Cubeo women practice infanticide when they do not want a child, but if the baby is a boy, it will almost certainly be spared. Males and females both say that girls are less important than boys.

Sometimes, a husband's treatment of his wife depends upon whether or not she gives him a son. Tairan men show a slight preference for male children, and if a woman does not produce a son, her marriage may be annulled or else she may be demoted to the status of co-wife. Ideally, a man wants three sons. A husband tends to be more solicitous of his wife and the baby when he is male, and he may be willing to carry the baby about for a little while even though men think of baby tending as women's work. Women, however, like to have daughters because girls will help them with household chores.

The preference for boys in a substantial number of societies reflects the fact that, in these cultures, male children are useful to their parents in ways that daughters are not. Boys are important to a Rajput family for a number of reasons. Males work the farms and serve as protectors of the family's reputation. Further, the family line is perpetuated through males. Sons are indispensable in the performance of particular rituals at a man's death, and the salvation of a man may be in danger if he has no son. Among the Kalderas of Canada, parents prefer sons over daughters because a boy brings home a daughter-in-law for his mother to order around. Their children will then perpetuate the family. A Kalderas man's own political power is also influenced by the number of his sons and grandsons. A son also helps in his father's business, while his wife makes money by telling fortunes. In Thailand, almost all Banoi men and women prefer sons over daughters. This is because, for the Banoi, men are more important in the cosmic scheme of things. Males also have a better chance of acquiring a standing in the community that will do credit to their parents. Sons are also easier to raise because a parent is not as concerned with a boy's sexual activities. A married couple, however, also wishes to have at least one daughter, preferably early on, because daughters help their mothers with household chores, including the tending of younger children. And as a girl remains in the household of her parents, living there with her husband after she is married, it is the daughters who are responsible for caring for parents when they become old. Most Jamaican parents prefer boys because they can work harder and help in the fields. They also contribute some of their income to the family when they take on outside jobs in adolescence. Parents also say that boys are easier to raise, less troublesome, smarter, and more courageous than girls. They cost less because they need less clothing, and if they father illegitimate children, it is the girl's family who has to take on the economic and logistic burden of raising the child and not the boy's. Women also say that it is easier to deliver boy babies. Among the Sebei of Uganda as well as the Gusii of Kenya, men prefer sons because it is males who carry on the lineage and guarantee the perpetuation of its property. The same is true for the Japanese Takashima household. Further, Gusii mothers achieve status through their sons.

Preferences for boys also reflect the liabilities that girls represent in some societies. Among the Rajputs, girls are costly to their families. A girl is expected to bring a dowry with her when she marries, and a bride's family is also responsible for presenting the girl's in-laws with a series of gifts. All of this means substantial financial expenditures for the parents of a daughter. Since women are lower in status than the men that they marry, a girl's relatives also find themselves placed in a position of inferiority relative to the groom's family. A mother, nevertheless, sometimes expresses a greater liking for a daughter than for a son because girls leave home to live with their husbands while boys remain with their parents even after marriage. Parents also want to have a daughter because, according to Hindu tradition, every man should give a daughter in marriage. The Takashima prefer boys in part because girls cost their parents a considerable amount of money when they marry. The Kalderas recognize that girls contribute to the income of the family while they remain with their parents and bring in a bride price at marriage. But parents also have to watch their daughters closely to insure that they remain virgins before marriage, so daughters are also a great inconvenience. Further, once she is married, the relationship between a daughter and her parents might be virtually severed.

Where daughters are preferred, this often reflects the concrete advantages that they symbolize for parents. Some Jamaican parents prefer daughters because they "get more out of girls." Daughters help with the household chores. A girl also tends to take better care of her parents in their old age than sons do. Sebei men also like to have daughters because girls bring in payments from the groom's family when they get married. Among the North American Hopi, parents want children of both sexes, but it is essential to have a daughter because, as kinship is traced through females, only she can perpetuate the clan.

In a number of societies, parents agree that the ideal family includes sons and daughters, but they still state a preference for boys. Thus, while many Ugandan Sebei adults hope to have children of both sexes, when a preference is stated, it is usually for a boy. Similarly, in Ecuador, Jivaro couples prefer their first baby to be a male, as a boy will be able to hunt with his father. The second baby should ideally be a girl. The Guatemalan Chimalteco say that the ideal family consists of four boys and four girls. Most parents, however, would like to have more sons than daughters. In fact, families rarely have as many as eight children, and a father who had more than two or three sons would not have enough land to divide between them. In North Africa, Teda parents prefer sons, but they are most pleased if they have the same number of sons and daughters. If a couple has more girls than boys, then the parents may remind themselves that girls are more attached to their parents than boys are and that boys face more dangers. Tarong parents like to have an equal number of sons and daughters. Some people prefer to have a girl first so that she can help around the house when new babies arrive. Others prefer to have a son first to help with the farmwork so that their growing family will be more securely provided for. Overall, there is a slight bias toward wishing for the first child to be a boy.

Where parents have no exaggerated bias for one sex over the other, this is often because both boys and girls prove to be valuable contributors to the welfare of the family. Gusii parents value both sons and daughters. Boys are desired because, as permanent members of the household, they will make a continuing contribution to the welfare of the family. And when a daughter marries, the family of her new husband presents her family with a gift of cattle. Sometimes, a mother will say that she prefers a boy to bury her when she dies, to take care of her in her old age, to bring a wife into the household to help her with her work, or to help her to grow food and do chores. But preferences are also sensitive to the unique composition of a household. If a family owns cattle but there is no one to herd them, a woman is likely to want sons. But if there is no one to fetch water and wood, the preference may be for a daughter.

Sometimes, adults in a particular culture claim a superiority of one sex over the other even when children of both sexes are desired. The Kpelle say that boys are "smarter" than girls, as reflected in the fact that they are braver and have more power than girls and do not cry. They are also "ahead in things."

Barry, Herbert, III, and Leonora M. Paxson. (1971) "Infancy and Early Childhood: Cross-Cultural Codes 2." *Ethnology* 10: 466–508.

Cohen, Yehudi A. (1966) *A Study of Interpersonal Relations in a Jamaican Community.*

Erchak, Gerald M. (1977) *Full Respect: Kpelle Children in Adaptation.*

Harner, Michael J. (1973) *The Jivaro: People of the Sacred Waterfalls.*

Goldman, Irving. (1963) *The Cubeo: Indians of the Northwest Amazon.*

Goldschmidt, Walter. (1976) *The Culture and Behavior of the Sebei.*

Hilger, M. Inez. (1951) *Chippewa Child Life and Its Cultural Background.*

———. (1952) *Arapaho Child Life and Its Cultural Background.*

Hitchcock, John T., and Leigh Minturn. (1966) *The Rajputs of Khalapur, India.*

Kronenberg, Andreas. (1981) *The Teda of Tibesti.*

LeVine, Robert L., and Barbara B. LeVine. (1966) *Nyansongo: A Gusii Community in Kenya.*

Maretzki, Thomas W., and Hatsumi Maretzki. (1966) *Taira: An Okinawan Village.*

Norbeck, Edward. (1954) *Takashima: A Japanese Fishing Community.*

Nydegger, William F., and Corinne Nydegger. (1966) *Tarong: An Ilocos Barrio in the Philippines.*

Piker, Steven. (1965) *An Examination of Character and Socialization in a Thai Peasant Community.*

Salo, Matt, and Sheila Salo. (1977) *The Kalderas in Eastern Canada.*

Thompson, Laura, and Alice Joseph. (1947) *The Hopi Way.*

Wagley, Charles. (1949) "The Social and Religious Life of a Guatemalan Village." *American Anthropologist* 51: 3–150.

Wallace, Ernest, and E. Adamson Hoebel. (1952) *The Comanches: Lords of the South Plains.*

PEERS

Psychologists interested in human development have speculated that children do best when they have the opportunity to form relationships with peers. And friendships are, in fact, highly valued in many societies the world over. Thus, for example, the Tarong of the Philippines place enormous value on sociability. A child who is alone is assumed to be lonely, and adults strongly encourage children to play together. Indeed, Tarong adults desire companionship and imagine that children do too. And in fact, it is rare for a child to be found playing alone. Similarly, in Okinawa, Tairan parents do not like their children to be alone and a parent will tell a youngster to go play with the other children so that people will not think that the child is disliked. Adults also think that children are less liable to get into trouble if they are with other youngsters. And in India, Rajput mothers like their children to play with other youngsters rather than remaining by themselves, although a woman does not want her children to play with other youngsters

who are aggressive. Nevertheless, youngsters living in some cultural settings do not always have the chance to interact regularly with other children, and ties to chums are not understood to be very important in cultures of this sort. For instance, in Kenya, Gusii children have relatively little opportunity to form close peer relationships. Youngsters do not generally stray far from their own homesteads, and it is hard for children to develop stable play groups because they are often busy doing the chores that have been assigned to them by their parents. Friendships among children are not greatly valued by the culture.

The composition of peer groups depends in part upon the structure of the child's family and community. All of the children in a Tairan village know each other and have spent most of the day together for much of their lives. Individual children form special friendships because they live near each other, or are related, or are the same age or sex, or simply like one another. But two friends will be joined by other children who want to play with them. North American Chippewa children lived in small camps, with the result that a youngster was forced to play with other children in the family or with any children of a neighbor's household. And in Micronesia, small Truk children often play alone or with other children who happen to live in the neighborhood. Older children play with youngsters their own age, and the play group becomes more predictable in its organization. A child's peer group often consists wholly or in part of relatives. Indeed, Truk children learn early on that kin form a special category of playmate and they tend to choose children who are related to them as companions. Youngsters know that related children will stick up for them in a dispute with other children. Jamaican children younger than five years of age are not allowed to wander from home, and as a result, they never play with anyone but siblings. Jamaican adults tend to believe that other parents do not know how to raise their children properly. Therefore, they fear that their own children would be "spoiled" by contact with other youngsters, especially since young children like to imitate other people and are likely to pick up the bad habits of other youngsters who have not been brought up in the right way. Parents also isolate their children from those of neighbors with whom they themselves do not get along. The Chimalteco of Guatemala live in villages composed of a number of extended families. The typical family is composed of perhaps three generations, so that an older husband and wife may live with their married sons and their wives and children as well as their unmarried daughters. The extended family members live in close proximity, often in a number of houses circling a common yard. As children are forced to stay near home, their only playmates until they go to school are often other youngsters in the extended family, including brothers, sisters, and cousins on the father's side. Little children visit the houses of their relatives whenever they wish and are greeted warmly by everyone. Children who are six or seven years old are allowed to wander farther from home to play with other youngsters of their own age. Usually, it is not until they go to school that their play groups include nonrelatives.

The world over, children begin to break up into same-sex peer groups at around six years of age. In North America, little Comanche boys might join a girl's group where they played house, but older children played in same-sex groups. The youngsters would build a windbreak and choose a chief. The boys chose wives, and everyone went swimming or riding for a while. The boys would then hunt squirrels and bring them back to be cooked by the girls. Meanwhile, the girls were out gathering berries, roots, eggs, and the like. Boys and girls also sometimes played games together. Similarly, North American Chippewa children played in mixed-sex groups when they were little, but then refused to play with anyone of the opposite sex when they were

older. Same-sex groups would have nothing to do with a member of the other sex. North American Comanche boys spent the greater part of a day playing with other boys. A typical day would be spent in following and catching birds and insects, and as a result boys honed their tracking and shooting skills. Similarly, Canadian Hare children prefer to congregate with children of their own age. When they move into smaller camps during some seasons of the year, they miss their peers who have gone off to live in different camps and are anxious to see their friends again when they return to the larger camps. Once they begin to attend school, Tairan children tend to play with other youngsters of the same age and sex. The composition of a play group changes from moment to moment. But regardless of the particular identities of the children, boys prefer to be with boys and girls with girls. Sometimes, however, an older girl will be watching a number of younger siblings. In this case, the baby tender will often remain with a group of younger children. Older Truk boys and girls play many of the same games, but they do so in different groups, boys congregating only with other boys and girls with girls. Males and females do play together, along with adolescents, at well-organized games in the night on the sandspit. Once they are initiated, North American Hopi children form separate play groups from which both the uninitiated and children of the opposite sex are excluded. Youngsters gather together in groups in the late afternoon and evening after they have finished their chores for the day. Parents may actually prefer their children to play in same-sex groups. In Thailand, Banoi parents urge daughters who are ten years of age or older to play exclusively with other girls of their own age. The idea is to maintain a separation between the sexes and, therefore, to increase the likelihood that daughters will not become involved in sexual entanglements. Mothers would, in fact, prefer if their daughters kept away from boys at an even younger age, but they do permit cross-sex play between young children.

Across cultures, younger children prefer to play with somewhat older children of their own sex. Rajput three- and four-year-olds tag along after the older children when they go off to play. The younger child is more of an observer than a participant, watching a game in progress or rooting for an older sibling. As the children get older, they begin to join the activities of the play group. Often, younger Truk children will follow the play groups of the older children as they wander from here to there. Everywhere, the desire of the four- and five-year-old boy to be accepted into the peer group of the six- to ten-year-olds is so strong that younger children will put up with bullying of all sorts by the older boys just to remain with them.

Children across cultures are often allowed to play on their own without any adult supervision. Rajput play groups are left to their own devices unless the children are being disruptive. And in Melanesia, Trobriand children of four or five can go off to play in the children's group if they wish, and all of the youngsters may go off an a day's expedition without adult supervision or permission. In Guatemala, Chimalteco children are free to visit any of the houses in the family compound, and a mother will not worry about the whereabouts of her child if she has a sense of where the youngster is likely to be found. Mothers will go out to look for any children who have not returned home by the evening.

Peer pressure can be as powerful an influence in the lives of children in other cultures as it can be in contemporary American culture. By the time they are preadolescent, Tarong boys and girls are highly susceptible to ridicule, shaming, and teasing by peers. Among the Taira, peers are effective socializers. A child who originally tries to get his way by bullying his friends soon learns to abandon such aggressive tactics because the other children begin to avoid him. As a result, even pushy children learn to ask for what

they want, share, and wait their turns. Tairan children are likely to go along with their peers even against the wishes of their parents and even when they risk punishment for their behavior. Perhaps this is because children spend most of their time with their peers and are less willing to risk their disapproval than that of parents, with whom the Tairan youngster spends less time. Peers also keep an eye on each other. An older child will chastise a younger caretaker for ignoring a crying baby. When a disagreement occurs, the children manage to resolve things without parental interference, and youngsters do not hold grudges.

See also FRIENDSHIP

Cohen, Yehudi A. (1966) *A Study of Interpersonal Relations in a Jamaican Community.*

Gladwin, Thomas, and Seymour Sarason. (1953) *Truk: Man in Paradise.*

Hara, Hiroko Sue. (1967) *Hare Indians and Their World.*

Hilger, M. Inez. (1951) *Chippewa Child Life and Its Cultural Background.*

Hitchcock, John T., and Leigh Minturn. (1966) *The Rajputs of Khalapur, India.*

LeVine, Robert A., and Barbara B. LeVine. (1966) *Nyansongo: A Gusii Community in Kenya.*

Maretzki, Thomas W., and Hatsumi Maretzki. (1966) *Taira: An Okinawan Village.*

Munroe, Robert L., and Ruth H. Munroe. (1975) *Cross-Cultural Human Development.*

Nydegger, William F., and Corinne Nydegger. (1966) *Tarong: An Ilocos Barrio in the Philippines.*

Piker, Steven. (1965) *An Examination of Character and Socialization in a Thai Peasant Community.*

Thompson, Laura, and Alice Joseph. (1947) *The Hopi Way.*

Wagley, Charles. (1949) "The Social and Religious Life of a Guatemalan Village." *American Anthropologist* 51: 3–150.

Wallace, Ernest, and E. Adamson Hoebel. (1952) *The Comanches: Lords of the South Plains.*

PHYSICAL DEVELOPMENT

The development of the human being, as well as of any other organism, is a product of the individual's genetic endowment, or genome, and the environment in which the individual is growing and functioning. Genes provide the "directions" for constructing the individual, but genes need environmental cues in order for the directions to be translated into a person. What is more, different environmental cues can trigger the genetic directions to produce somewhat different organisms. Conversely, the same environment will produce a different person when it acts upon different genomes. This idea that the individual is a product of genes acting in environments is called coaction. The principle of coaction tells us that any cross-cultural differences that we find in developmental trajectories and outcomes can be accounted for by similar genomes acting in different environments or by different genomes acting in different environments. This means that it is difficult to tell precisely what accounts for any cross-cultural differences that we find. We do know, however, that numerous environmental factors can affect developmental outcomes. These include the mother's age and health during her pregnancy as well as the course of the pregnancy itself. The birth process, including medication taken by the mother and other interventions, can also affect the physical condition of the baby as can the baby's birth order. Feeding schedules, including whether or not the baby is breast-fed and when and what kinds of supplementary food are fed to an infant and child, affect development. So do levels and kind of stimulation and stress in the baby's environment influence developmental outcomes. Although it is hard to untangle genetic and environmental influences on development, certain cross-cultural differences are sufficiently robust to allow us to hypothesize constitutional differences in babies from different cultures over and above any environmental influences that we might observe.

Temperament Differences

A small number of temperamental differences between babies from different cultures have been reported. Thus, American babies of European ancestry are easier to upset and harder to calm than are Japanese-American, Chinese-American, and Navaho babies. Chinese infants tend to be less changeable than American babies. They also become used to new stimuli more readily.

Physical Differences

Some physical differences between babies from different cultures are also evident. African babies have a somewhat shorter gestation period than do American newborns and exhibit more advanced skeletal development at birth, with the trend perhaps lasting through middle and late childhood. Nail growth, skin texture, and hair growth are also more advanced in African infants, and some permanent teeth also erupt earlier among African children. Western newborns also weigh a bit more on an average than non-Western infants, and the trend continues with age. Thus, Western one-year-olds continue to be larger, to weigh more, and to have larger head and chest circumferences than do non-Western babies. And even at eight years of age, American and European children are taller and heavier than other youngsters the world over. Thus, for example, the average height for a white American child of this age is four feet and two inches, while a New Guinea Marind-Anim child of the same age is an average of four feet tall and an African Bantu Wadigo youngster is three feet and ten inches. Similarly, the average weights for children in these three cultures are 59 pounds, 49 pounds, and 44 pounds, respectively. According to some studies, African American babies remain advanced over white American babies with respect to sitting, standing, head control, and turning from the side to the back. The same is true for black babies living in Jamaica and in England. However, black babies living outside of Africa are not so precocious as are infants from African societies. If these findings are valid, we see the joint effects of genome and environment in producing physical and behavioral profiles. Physical maturation is also affected by diet. This is especially true for height. Thus, Japanese children reared in America are taller, weigh more, and show more advanced skeletal growth at every age in comparison with Japanese children living in Japan, and this is assumed to be in part the product of dietary differences between the groups of youngsters.

Motor Development

Motor development is less advanced in Western babies for the first two years of life. For example, at birth, Ugandan babies can already prevent their heads from falling back when they are seated upright. They can hold their backs straight, control their heads, sit up without help, and stand at an earlier age than Western babies. A Ugandan baby also typically walks by ten months of age, two months sooner than the average Western baby. West Indian babies show superior general tonus and postural control in comparison with London babies.

Promoting Development

Adults in some cultures take pains to encourage motor development of various sorts in their infants. When a New Mexican Zuni baby was born, the woman in charge of the delivery shaped the infant's nose and head and pulled its arms and legs to give them the proper shape. Babies were also rubbed with finely powdered wood ashes to prevent the growth of body hair, which was considered ugly. The North American Sanpoil were actively concerned about the physical development of children and instituted a number of customs designed to promote strength. Children were expected to rise at dawn and run to the river, where they would plunge into the water a number of times. This was required in both summer and winter. Swimming was viewed as a critical skill, and children learned to swim into the swift river currents. The goal was to increase strength, to build up resistance to disease, and to guarantee that a child would not drown if a canoe capsized. Children also ran on a regular basis, sometimes right after a swim. They also practiced running uphill for as long as possible without breathing. The North American Arapaho splashed cold water on an infant every day, including in the cold of winter, from the time that its cord stump fell off until it was able to walk. And because the infant jumped back and tried to hold up its head when it felt the dash of water, these baths were believed to make the baby strong. By the time he was 12 years old, much of the play of an Arapaho boy was directed toward the development of physical fortitude. Boys swam early in the morning while the sun was still rising. They ran competitive races and walked or ran for long distances, sleeping out in the open at night. They climbed trees and wrestled with boys from other tribes. Girls also occasionally ran races or played a game in which a ball was kicked toward a goal. Kalahari !Kung mothers do not allow their infants to lie down when they are awake because they believe that this would impede motor development. The Kipsigis of Kenya do not allow any infant to travel for very long in a sling or shawl draped on the mother's body. To do so would mean that the baby's legs would have to be stretched in a way that would hamper proper development. The African Swazi focus on the promotion of physical strength once a boy has turned six, and youngsters are encouraged to participate in social and economic activities as much as their physical capacity permits. In Africa, adults from a number of cultures including the Acholi, Teso, and Somali encourage babies to crawl. The infant is placed in a crawling position and then some desirable object is offered while some older child shows the baby how to crawl toward the bait. Adults in many African societies deliberately encourage their infants to sit and walk. The African Igbo build a wooden railing for an infant to hold onto as it practices walking. In the Pacific, Fiji adults take note of a child's progress in learning to crawl and walk, and a baby who seems to be delayed in standing will be buried up to the chest in sand for a brief period of time each day to help it learn to maintain an upright position. A Japanese adult who wishes to teach a youngster how to sit, write, and so on actively guides the child's body into the proper position. A father will fold a son's legs into the correct sitting position. Similarly, adults teach children to write, to use chopsticks, and to bow by physically moving their hands or bodies in the correct manner.

The fact that people in some cultures take the time to train basic motor skills in children invites the question of whether training has any effect upon the acquisition of motor skills. Some studies suggest that basic physical skills are not significantly affected by increased experience. Thus, for example, a group of two-year-old children given 12 weeks of practice with climbing ladders, buttoning and unbuttoning, and cutting with scissors were no more proficient at these skills than another group of two-year-olds who had practiced the same skills for only one week. Similarly, a study demonstrated that North American Hopi babies who were confined to cradleboards began to walk at the same age as infants from the same culture who were not confined to cradleboards. Babies who are swaddled during some

portion of infancy nevertheless make normal use of arms, hands, fingers, and legs when their wrapping is off, and sit, crawl, and walk normally.

There is also evidence that experience does matter to physical development in a number of ways. Children whose opportunities to practice motor skills are minimal tend to be retarded in performance. Thus, for example, institutionalized infants who have been confined to cribs and prevented from moving do not crawl or walk at the normal time. Similarly, differences in the chance that children have to practice motor skills can show up in differences in virtuosity of performance. For instance, in one study, a twin who had a greater opportunity to move around displayed more grace and fluidity in walking upstairs than the other twin, even though both began to climb stairs at the same age. Similarly, while the primitive walking reflex, in which an upright newborn makes walking movements with its legs, normally disappears at about two months of age, the reflex remains apparent in babies who are allowed to practice it every day. Further, these babies then begin to walk at about ten months of age, two months earlier than the average onset of walking. Some studies suggest that the age of onset of turning over and crawling are strongly related to the child's opportunity to practice these skills. In Mexico, Mestizo and Mayan babies exhibit advanced fine motor coordination relative to other infants, but they begin to walk later than other babies. It is also true that these infants are carried around when awake because the floors of the houses in which they live are made either of dirt or cold tile. Thus, the delay in walking may be affected by the absence of any real opportunity to practice the skill.

Stress in infancy may also affect growth. Thus, people in cultures where infants are immediately separated from their mothers or where they are tattooed, scarified, bathed every day in scalding water, inoculated, or exposed to other stresses are taller in adulthood than are individuals who are raised in societies where such infantile stressors are absent. In order for a stressor to affect height, it must be experienced in the first two years of the child's life. Age of menarche is similarly influenced by stress in early childhood.

No Interventions

Whereas adults in some cultures consciously attempt to promote physical and motor development, parents in other societies let nature take its course. Guadalcanal Kaoka adults view walking as a natural accomplishment that needs no encouragement, and children are left to follow their own schedules. The same noninterventionist attitude is extended to swimming. Parents will take an infant to one of the brooks near home and permit the baby to splash around in the shallow water, and a two-year-old is allowed to play at the edge of a village creek. No one shows a child how to swim, but every child can float and move about in the water without touching bottom by three years of age. In Malaysia, Semai adults pay a good deal of attention to the progress of a child's motor development because they view such advances as a measure of the youngster's overall health. However, children are not hurried, nor is there any explicit effort to teach them motor behavior, although an infant may be coaxed into a sitting position or held erect. The older a child gets, the less physical progress is monitored because the parents do not worry so much about the youngster's well-being. In some cultures, parents actually prevent children from practicing motor skills. Japanese adults traditionally discouraged crawling, and people felt that a baby should not be standing or taking steps until it was a year old and that mothers should prevent infants from walking any earlier than this. Similarly, Balinese adults discourage crawling in children because crawling reminds them of the kind of activity than an animal performs.

First Tooth

In some cultures, the eruption or loss of a child's first tooth is cause for celebration. Among the Arapaho, a feast was held when a child's first tooth came in. The parents always made sure to invite an old man who had been to many wars, and it was he who pierced the baby's ears if they had not already been pierced. He received one of the family's best horses in payment. And when an Arapaho child lost his or her first tooth, it was hidden in the youngster's hair at the crown of the head and left there until it fell out and disappeared. The idea was that the new tooth would then grow in quickly. Some children did this with all of their upper teeth. Sometimes, the lower teeth were thrown under the bed. The New Ireland Lesu hold a ritual feast when a baby cuts its first tooth. If the baby is a boy, only the men eat at the feast; if it is a girl, only the women eat. Someone may make a brief speech to the following effect: "We have come here because Ongus has a tooth. It is a very small feast, and there is not much food. Now we have finished."

See also COACTION; WALKING

Benedict, Ruth. (1946) *The Chrysanthemum and the Sword.*

Dentan, Robert. (1978) "Notes on Childhood in a Nonviolent Context: The Semai Case." In *Learning and Non-Aggression,* edited by Ashley Montagu, 94–143.

Freedman, Daniel G. (1974) *Human Infancy: An Evolutionary Perspective.*

Henderson, Ronald W., and John R. Bergan. (1976) *The Cultural Context of Childhood.*

Hilger, M. Inez. (1952) *Arapaho Child Life and Its Cultural Background.*

Hogbin, Ian. (1964) *A Guadalcanal Society: The Kaoka Speakers.*

Kuper, Hilda. (1963) *The Swazi: A South African Kingdom.*

Landauer, Thomas K., and John W. M. Whiting. (1981) "Correlates and Consequences of

Stress in Infancy." In *Handbook of Cross-Cultural Human Development*, edited by Ruth H. Munroe, Robert L. Munroe, and Beatrice B. Whiting, 355–387.

Lee, Richard B., and Irven DeVore. (1976) *Kalahari Hunter-Gatherers: Studies of the !Kung San and Their Neighbors.*

Leighton, Dorothea, and John Adair. (1966) *People of the Middle Place: A Study of the Zuni Indians.*

Munroe, Robert L., and Ruth H. Munroe. (1975) *Cross-Cultural Human Development.*

Powdermaker, Hortense. (1933) *Life in Lesu: A Study of Melanesian Society in New Ireland.*

Ray, Verne. (1933) *The Sanpoil and the Nespelem: Salishan Peoples of Northeastern Washington.*

Super, Charles M. (1981) "Behavioral Development in Infancy." In *Handbook of Cross-Cultural Human Development*, edited by Ruth H. Munroe, Robert L. Munroe, and Beatrice B. Whiting, 181–270.

Thompson, Laura. (1940) *Fijian Frontier.*

Wallace, Ernest, and E. Adamson Hoebel. (1952) *The Comanches: Lords of the South Plains.*

Whiting, John W. M. (1981) "Environmental Constraints on Infant Care Practices." In *Handbook of Cross-Cultural Human Development*, edited by Ruth H. Munroe, Robert L. Munroe, and Beatrice B. Whiting, 155–179.

Zelazo, N. A., P. R. Zelazo, and S. Kolb (1972) "Walking in the Newborn." *Science* 176: 314–315.

PLAY Psychologists speculate that play is an enormously important activity because it permits children to rehearse skills and roles in anticipation of adulthood. And indeed, play is characteristic not only of young members of our own species but also of immature animals in other species with complex social roles and relationships. However, children in different cultures have vastly different opportunities for play, and the amount of time that a youngster can devote to playing is largely a function of how busy the child is kept doing daily chores. For instance, until they are around ten years old, Micronesian Truk youngsters spend virtually all of their time playing. Small children play alone in the sand close to home while older children stray farther afield. The children may engage in various games, or they may while away the hours watching some particularly interesting adult activity. By contrast, in Kenya, Gusii children have relatively little opportunity for playing. Youngsters do not generally stray far from their own homesteads, and it is hard for children to develop stable play groups because they are often busy doing the chores that have been assigned to them by their parents. And in Ecuador, Jivaro adults actually discourage children from playing, in part because they think that play leads children to dislike working. Parents do not like their own children to be around another youngster who has a reputation for liking to play. Even jesting is disapproved of, because adults believe that it leads to lying later on in life. Jivaro children, in any event, have relatively little opportunity to play with anyone who does not live with them because households are geographically isolated from each other.

Composition of Play Groups
The composition of children's play groups is often dictated by practical considerations having to do with who lives where, and with or near whom. The fact that many children across cultures act as child nurses means that they must cart their young charges along while playing. In the Philippines, Tarong play groups consist of the neighborhood children. This means that perhaps as many as 36 boys and girls of various

ages are playing together. Most of the children in a play group are under ten years of age, and many are babies who are being supervised by the older children. Usually, children who play together are also related. They walk to and from school together, do chores together, and play with each other. Parents prefer their children to play with siblings and cousins, so that children from other neighborhoods begin to be viewed as "others." In Polynesia, Tongan children play in mixed-age groups, in part because older girls are generally accompanied by the younger children whom they supervise during the day. Play groups, as a result, include youngsters from 16 months to seven years of age. Children spend most of their time playing and exploring on the beach or in the bush. The play group may engage in much shouting and laughing one moment only to degenerate into an aggressive attack by an older child on some misbehaving charge a moment later.

Play groups universally become confined to children of the same sex once youngsters are around six years old. This occurs spontaneously because children of this age simply prefer to play in same-sex groups. In the Northwest Amazon, Cubeo boys begin to spend their time in a single, same-sex group when they are around six years old. The boys are virtually independent of adults, finding their own food and playing in the bush or at the river by themselves. They choose their own leaders, who are responsible for enforcing rules and disciplining bad behavior on the part of group members. The boys' group may join the men when they are engaged in some collective activity. Boys also rehearse ceremonial songs and dances together. Membership in the male group lasts beyond adolescence. In North America, older Comanche boys did not play with girls. Instead, they formed all-male gangs and spent their time racing, wrestling, hunting, and swimming. In the evening, they would sometimes corral some horses for a joyride on the prairie. Japanese Takashima children play only with

children of their own sex by the time they are ten years olds. A folk saying asserts that boys and girls should be separated by the time they reach this age, but in fact no one needs to separate them—they do so on their own. Guadalcanal Kaoka children play in mixed-sex groups, but by the time they reach adolescence, boys avoid girls, and if they see a girl approaching, they will call her names, push her, and throw stones at her.

Toys

Toys are not ubiquitous across cultures as they are among American children. Tarong children do not typically play with toys. Adults expect a child's playtime to focus on interactions with other youngsters and not on toys, and even young infants who have just begun to crawl are told to go and play with the other children. Youngsters might amuse themselves with sticks, stones, or broken household equipment. Or sometimes a gourd will be made into a rattle. Children like to play with the three-inch coconut beetles that are found in the coconut trees, attaching a string to the creatures for use as a leash. Similarly, in Okinawa, there are no toys in the Tairan kindergarten. Rather, children play games, sing and dance, and draw in the sand with their fingers or with sticks. Children collect shells or investigate washed up fish or seaweed at the shore of the river outside the school. In after-school play groups, youngsters use any objects that they can find as playthings. Peas or stones become marbles, cabbage leaves are turned into helmets, and a carton becomes a car.

Where store-bought toys are unavailable, children often make their own toys. Cubeo boys make tops out of fruit and balls out of corn husks. They also play cat's cradle and sometimes walk about on stilts. In Uganda, Sebei children make many toys, including hoops, push-toys, dolls, wagons, hats, and tiny houses. African Baoule youngsters make bicycles and also cars that have steering devices, movable wheels, and company trademarks. Toymaking, at least in African societies, is more common among boys than girls, and boys are also more likely to help fix things than are girls.

Children in other cultures are, however, sometimes given toys by adults. North American Chippewa parents attached various objects to a baby's cradleboard to be used as toys. These included a small bag holding the infant's umbilical cord and strings of beads, animal claws, or skulls of small animals. Chippewa girls had dolls and boys played with small bows and arrows. Dolls were a girl's primary plaything among the North American Arapaho. A doll was a very rough version of a person, with a stuffed head and a limbless body wrapped in a piece of cloth fashioned like a shawl. Dolls were not treated as babies. Rather, they were meant to represent grownups, and they were made to imitate adult activities such as riding horses.

Games

Children in many cultures spend at least some of their leisure time playing games. Games come in different varieties, and people who study games like to make a distinction between games of physical skill, games of strategy, and games of chance. In games of physical skill, the outcome depends upon the strength, dexterity, or agility of the players. In games of strategy, the winner is the participant who makes the better rational decisions as the game progresses. Games of chance depend upon fortuitous circumstances beyond the control of the players. Any particular game may depend purely upon physical skill, strategy, or chance. Or a game may be some combination of physical skill, strategy, and chance. In some cultures, such as the Bolivian Siriono and the central African Pygmies, people play only games that involve physical skill. The North American Chiricahua and the Truk of Micronesia play games of chance and physical skill. In some societies, such as the African Azande, all three kinds of games are common.

Particular game categories tend to be found in particular kinds of cultures. Games of chance are most often played in societies where the economic base is uncertain, cultures that depend upon hunting and gathering for their subsistence being a prime example. Games of this sort also tend to occur where warfare is frequent, again emphasizing the connection between games of chance and cultural events that are likely to make people feel insecure. By contrast, games of chance are absent or actually outlawed in agricultural or herding societies. Rather, in cultures of this sort, games of strategy are emphasized. Interestingly, games of strategy require planning as well as adherence to the rules, as does success in farming and herding. Thus, we see a parallel between the kinds of games that people play and features of their culture's economy. Games of strategy are also found in societies where social stratification is present and where parents place great emphasis on obedient behavior in their children. Games of skill are often found in cultures that emphasize individual achievement in children.

Examples of Games

Tarong caretakers play the kinds of games with their infants that are most likely to provoke delighted responses. Peek-a-boo is a favorite, and as an infant grows older, other children in the household play a more complex version of the game, popping up out of hiding places to surprise the baby. Later on, hide-and-seek becomes a popular pastime. Children also like to play hand games. Tairan preschoolers and kindergartners, that is, children between two and six years of age, like games that involve racing and choosing partners. They also play at something like the American "rock, paper, and scissors" finger game. Older children enjoy games that demand some skill, such as jacks and hopscotch. Even when a game produces winners and losers, the winner doesn't strut or boast in front of the other children. School children also congregate after

Children on a slide in Guatemala

classes to play group games such as kick the can. In the Northwest Amazon, a favorite game among Cubeo children pits the "forest ogres" against the "tem bird." A group of youngsters, acting as the forest ogres, forms a circle around a grown boy, who represents the tem bird. The "forest ogres" dance around the "bird," stopping from time to time to pinch the "tem tem" in order to determine whether he is ready to be eaten. Eventually, the "bird" begins to try to break loose from the circle, making sure, however, not to breach the circle at a point where a toddler will not be able to restrain him. Some of the children shout encouragement to the "bird" while others try to inspire the circle to hold firm against the "bird." Once the "bird" has broken free, he returns to the center of the circle and attempts to get loose again, this time by verbal challenges at the circle of children. The "bird" points to some body part of a child, who must then name that part of the body, adding "of the forest ogre." When a few of the children fail to give the right answer, usually by forgetting to say that the body part belongs to the ogre, the "bird" is free again. The game then begins again with the capture of another "bird." The game is related to a myth known to Cubeo children. The story tells of a group of children whose father is dead and whose mother is too poor to feed them. The youngsters slowly turn into birds and are cared for by their elder brother, who is eventually captured by the forest ogres but who manages to free himself so that he can continue to care for his younger siblings. Comanche boys and girls played a number of games together. In the game of "grizzly bear," a group of children formed a line circling around another child, who played the grizzly bear. The grizzly bear tried to capture one of the other children. The "mother," who was the first youngster in the line, protected the other children from the grizzly by causing the line to veer back and forth. Eventually, a child would be captured by the grizzly and "eaten," that is tickled, by the bear. The remaining children would then run to a mound of sand, which represented the bear's sugar. Each child would try to steal some of the sugar. Each of the children was eventually caught and tickled until all of the sugar was stolen or all of the children were captured by the bear. Comanche children also played a hide-and-seek game. A number of youngsters would hide under blankets or robes and an older boy would try to guess the identity of each child. Truk children play guessing games, such as guessing which hole contains a shell. Or a child with his back turned may have to guess how many holes have been made in the sand. Truk children also play a number of nighttime games. Their favorite, played in mixed-sex groups and including young adolescents, is a variation of hide-and-seek. One child, designated the ghost, looks for the other children. The first child who is discovered is "eaten," which means that the ghost digs his knuckles into some part of the body of the exposed child, who now becomes the ghost. The search is repeated until all but one of the children are discovered. The last child then becomes the ghost and the game begins all over again. The ghost game may continue for the better part of the night. As the evening progresses, the smaller children begin to become tired and giddy, either giggling or simply dropping out of their hiding places so that their discovery becomes inevitable and the game begins to be less exciting for them. Eventually, only the older children are left to play the game. Arapaho children played a number of games of chance, including dice and hand games. They also

played a number of games of skill. These included archery, hoop and pole, and ring and pin.

Developmental Aspects of Play

Psychologists who have studied children's play activities have noticed that the play of young children in our contemporary American culture is different from that of older ones. Thus, for example, young children in America do not tend to engage in cooperative play even when they seem to be playing with other children. Two young children sitting in a sandbox together will not play the same game. Rather, each will build his or her own castle, mud pies, or the like. The same trend can also be witnessed in other cultures. Thus, for example, in Mexico, Mixtecan children spend part of each day in the central courtyard shared by the members of their extended family household, and youngsters below the age of seven pass most of their waking hours there. Younger children, while they play together in the same place, do not really play together. They do not talk to each other very much, and each child is preoccupied with his or her own activities, even when children are playing with the same materials. Psychologists have also observed that young children in America have trouble understanding the games that they play, partly because they do not understand the rules although they think that they do. We see the same dynamics operating in other cultures. Thus, young Truk children spend their playtime wandering and idling about. Older children begin to play more organized games with recognizable themes. Some child suggests a particular activity, and the group follows the lead until some idea for a new game captures their attention. Similarly, in the South Seas, Javanese boys play a number of games, some of which are competitive. But the rules are vague and no one argues about what is and is not allowed in a game. And among the Liberian Kpelle, games with rules are uncommon. But older children begin to play games that have some structure.

Young children in America also have trouble understanding what it means to compete and to win. This problem is also echoed in other cultures. Thus, while the games of Tairan youngsters below six years of age include the idea of winning and losing, children of this age do not really compete. For instance, the mother of one Tairan boy who always came in third in races encouraged him to try harder. The child, however, insisted that his mother simply did not understand. He always came in third and that was his normal ranking in races. To try to change his rank seemed to him to be a funny idea.

Imitating Adult Roles

A major focus of the play of children across cultures has to do with imitating adult activities. Tarong children play at building twig houses, cooking, stringing tobacco, and cutting cane, all of which are imitations of adult roles, and the children's play activities are likely to mirror the current work in which the adult happens to be engaged at the time. Youngsters will also recreate the tools used by adults in their daily activities out of what is available. Some inner tubing from a tire and a jar cover may be fashioned into a stethoscope. Or strips of bamboo may be tied together to make a sled. In India, the imitation of adult work is an important part of Rajput children's play. Because Rajput males and females live largely separate lives, there are few adult activities for youngsters to copy that include both sexes, and when boys and girls play at adult roles, they play separately. Boys pretend to farm and girls to cook. Little girls are especially fond of making pretend bread out of mud, and the script that they follow remains very loyal to the steps that women follow when they make bread. Boys pretend to plow and to sow wheat. Sometimes, their play is a very detailed imitation of farming activities, with elaborate facsimiles of fields, which the boys then irrigate. Sebei children play house and also pretend to bargain for cattle or wives. They use stones of various colors as stand-ins for the cows that they trade and they pretend to drink beer as they barter. Boys also frequently hunt birds, rodents, and so on with primitive but effective bows and arrows. The children cook and eat the animals on their own. Young Comanche boys and girls sometimes played house together. The youngsters would build a windbreak and choose a chief. The boys chose wives, and everyone went swimming or riding for a while. The boys would then hunt squirrels and bring them back to be cooked by the girls. Meanwhile, the girls were out gathering berries, roots, eggs, and the like. Older boys played in same-sex groups. Their favorite passion was to follow and catch birds and insects in imitation of the tracking and hunting activities of the older males. Chippewa children played at housekeeping, baby tending, cooking, hunting, fishing, and dancing in imitation of adult activities. Youngsters played in diminutive one-room "houses" consisting of inch-high walls made of soil along with miniature furniture made of clay. The furniture was detailed and realistic, but was likely to be discarded after a day's play, with new furniture made all over again for the next play session. Truk children enjoy copying the behavior of adults. For instance, one child will suggest that the group take a trip, and everyone will then engage in a long discussion about where to go, who will go, what canoe to use, and how to prepare for the excursion. Or the children may throw a "feast," while some "chiefs" harangue the other "adults" or try them for this or that misdeed. If any adults are about, they are likely to be amused by the children's games and to join in on the fun. But children also like to play at grownup activities when there are no adults around, and if some older person shows up, the group will suspend its activities for fear of being laughed at. Truk children do enjoy a degree of privacy when they play in the sand spit, a spot that is hidden from the village by thick bushes and is rarely visited by adults. In Mexico, small Tarahumara girls make miniature tortillas from dirt and water using miniature utensils, while little boys cut down young trees with their fathers' axes and then build corrals and so on with the wood. Girls play at being mothers to their dolls, or children may imitate the drinking parties of adults by having their dolls get drunk and behave in the manner of grownups on similar occasions. Or a group of youngsters might build a small replica of a house and livestock enclosure, populated by stones representing people and animals, and then throw a mock party to celebrate the construction of the buildings. Boys also have footraces imitating those of their fathers. They paint their legs and wear leather belts as the men do when they are racing. In Guatemala, every little Chimalteco girl plays house, recruiting a younger brother or cousin as "husband" whether he likes the game or not. A girl might force her little relative to eat the miniature tortillas that she has made. A girl who is helping her mother sweep the house, fetch water, or grind maize will pretend that she is doing these chores for her "husband." Japanese children pretend that they are going to a festival or getting married, and children also play house. Youngsters try to model their play activities after the real actions of adults, and if they disagree about what constitutes correct adult behavior, they may go and ask someone's mother. Sometimes, children will imitate adult roles down to the last detail. Kpelle boys can be seen sweeping their way through town swinging their arms as if they held cutlasses clearing the bush, while the girls bend over invisible rice with invisible hoes. Both mop their brows and pretend to be tired according to the custom of adults.

Sometimes, adults plan the leisure activities of children with the goal of preparing them for adult roles. By the time he was 12 years old, a Comanche boy's play activities placed considerable stress on physical training. Boys swam, ran races, climbed trees, and walked and ran long distances, sleeping outside at night for the duration of the trek. Adults also encouraged boys to carry heavy weights such as a turkey or a log of firewood on their backs. Boys from different tribes also wrestled with each other. Girls also occasionally ran races or played a game in which a ball was kicked toward a goal.

Sex Differences

Across cultures, boys and girls not only prefer to play in different groups but also like to play at different activities. Sometimes, the play activities of girls are constrained by the kinds of chores that they are assigned. Older Tarong boys and girls continue to play in the same group, but by the time they are eight or nine years old, the girls are beginning to play quieter games such as jacks and hopscotch. Boys are playing at marbles, pitching pennies, bolo tossing, wrestling, tag, and so on. Boys also hunt about for wild fruits and edible insects, and, if they catch a beetle, they may attach it to a string and swing it about so that it will make a whirring noise. A Cubeo boy spends much of his childhood in the boys' pack. The boys roam around on their own without adult supervision and unfettered by adult demands or restrictions. They work when they wish and play when they wish. Girls, by contrast, are required to remain close to home minding infants. Their company consists of other child nurses, and young girls and their charges can be seen collecting in small groups to gossip and to comment on each other's adornments. A girl is not allowed to join the boys' group unless explicitly invited to join in some game. Girls do not play any games by themselves. Tarahumara children respect a more extreme division of labor in their play than exists in fact in the daily lives of adults. Thus, while it is indeed the man's job to fetch more wood for a fire, a woman will perform the task if no men are around. But only boys play at fetching wood. Javanese girls play by themselves. Boys play a variety of games with each other, some of which are competitive.

See also FRIENDSHIP; PEERS

Barry, Herbert, III, and John M. Roberts. (1972) "Infant Socialization and Games of Chance." *Ethnology* 11: 296–308.

Beaglehole, Ernest, and Pearl Beaglehole. (1941) *Pangai: Village in Tonga.*

Benedict, Ruth. (1946) *The Chrysanthemum and the Sword.*

Bennett, Wendell, and Robert Zingg. (1935) *The Tarahumara: An Indian Tribe of Northern Mexico.*

Erchak, Gerald M. (1977) *Full Respect: Kpelle Children in Adaptation.*

Geertz, Hildred. (1961) *The Javanese Family: A Study of Kinship and Socialization.*

Gladwin, Thomas, and Seymour Sarason. (1953) *Truk: Man in Paradise.*

Goldman, Irving. (1963) *The Cubeo: Indians of the Northwest Amazon.*

Goldschmidt, Walter. (1976) *The Culture and Behavior of the Sebei.*

Harner, Michael J. (1973) *The Jivaro: People of the Sacred Waterfalls.*

Hilger, M. Inez. (1951) *Chippewa Child Life and Its Cultural Background.*

———. (1952) *Arapaho Child Life and Its Cultural Background.*

Hitchcock, John T., and Leigh Minturn. (1966) *The Rajputs of Khalapur, India.*

Hogbin, Ian. (1964) *A Guadalcanal Society: The Kaoka Speakers.*

Levinson, David, and Martin J. Malone. (1980) *Toward Explaining Human Culture.*

Maretzki, Thomas W., and Hatsumi Maretzki. (1966) *Taira: An Okinawan Village.*

Norbeck, Edward. (1954) *Takashima: A Japanese Fishing Village.*

Nydegger, William F., and Corinne Nydegger. (1966) *Tarong: An Ilocos Barrio in the Philippines.*

Roberts, John M., and Brian Sutton-Smith. (1962) "Child Training and Game Involvement." *Ethnology 1: 166–185.*

Roberts, John M., and Herbert Barry, III. (1976) "Inculcated Traits and Games Type Combinations: A Cross-Cultural View." In *The Humanistic and Mental Health Aspects of Sports, Exercise and Recreation,* edited by T. T. Craig, 5–11.

Romney, A. Kimball, and Romaine Romney. (1966) *The Mixtecans of Juxtlahuaca, Mexico.*

Segall, Marshall H., Pierre R. Dasen, John W. Berry, and Ype H. Poortinga. (1990) *Human Behavior in Global Perspective.*

Sutton-Smith, Brian, and John M. Roberts. (1981) "Play, Toys, Games, and Sports." In *Handbook of Cross-Cultural Psychology, vol. 4. Developmental Psychology,* edited by H. C. Triandis and A. Heron, 425–471.

Wagley, Charles. (1949) "The Social and Religious Life of a Guatemalan Village." *American Anthropologist* 51: 3–150.

Wallace, Ernest, and E. Adamson Hoebel. (1952) *The Comanches: Lords of the South Plains.*

PREGNANCY

In virtually every society around the world, most women become mothers more than once. This is one fact of life that unites the female of the species. But the cultural management of pregnancy varies dramatically from place to place in a number of ways. Pregnancy may be treated in a matter-of-fact manner. Or the pregnant woman may be regarded as in a dangerous or delicate state. In some societies, women announce the anticipated birth of their babies to the entire community, while in others, even the expectant father is presumed to be ignorant of the coming event. Sometimes, a pregnant woman conducts herself much as she has always done, but often a variety of prescriptions and prohibitions are enjoined upon a woman who is expecting a baby, so that her life as a pregnant woman is significantly different from her life before she became pregnant. Whatever differences exist in the treatment of pregnant women across cultures, the array of customs surrounding pregnancy are erected for the same universal reason, and that is to preserve the lives and health of the expectant mother and her baby at a time when things have the potential of going very wrong.

Recognition of Pregnancy

Across cultures, women interpret similar physical changes and symptoms as signs of pregnancy. Among the Mixtecans of Mexico, a woman knows that she is pregnant when she stops menstruating. She will then inform either her own mother or her mother-in-law if she is living with her husband's family. Similarly, in North America, Chippewa women assumed that they were pregnant when they missed a menstrual cycle. The woman then noted the phase of the moon and counted nine moons of the same phase to pinpoint the likely day of delivery. Some women marked a stick to keep track of the passage of moons, while others relied on memory. In the Philippines, a Tarong woman also assumes that she is pregnant if she has missed her last menstrual period. If she has not begun to menstruate again after her last baby, a woman will guess that she is pregnant again if she experiences nausea or cravings or if her abdomen begins to become larger. In Okinawa, the cessation of menstruation combined with food craving persuade a Tairan woman that she is pregnant. And among the Tongans of Polynesia, a woman suspects that she is pregnant when she loses her appetite and becomes more sensitive to odors, although physical weakness and the cessation of menstruation are also signs of pregnancy. Among the North American Arapaho, a woman became aware that she was pregnant through a dream. Or else, she might sense the presence of another being sometime during the day in the course of her routine activities. This was said to happen less than two weeks after the baby had been conceived.

Announcing a Pregnancy

In some cultures, a woman who finds that she is pregnant announces the good news to husband, relatives, friends, and neighbors. But in other societies, an expectant mother keeps her condition to herself, and even the future father remains ignorant that he will soon have a child. In India, a Rajput woman's husband is not supposed to know that she is pregnant. When she discovers that she is pregnant, a Jamaican woman keeps the news to herself. Her husband assumes that she is pregnant when she begins to avoid lifting heavy objects, usually two or three months into her pregnancy. Since a woman does not go out in public when her condition becomes obvious, neighbors remain unaware that she is going to have a baby. A pregnant Tarong woman will tell her husband and probably her mother, but no one else is notified. The Canadian Kalderas tried to avoid mention of a pregnant woman's condition, especially between males and females or people of widely different ages. A woman was also ashamed to talk about her pregnancy in front of her mother-in-law. Among the Mixtecans, the pregnant woman's mother or mother-in-law is responsible for informing the expectant father and grandfathers that the woman is going to have a baby. Women tend to be embarrassed when other people find out about their condition, especially if it is a first pregnancy. By contrast, a Canadian Hare woman who discovers that she is pregnant should inform her husband and relatives. If she fails to do so, one of her parents, siblings, or children will die.

Cravings

Food and other cravings are common during pregnancy. Among the Gusii of Kenya, many women suddenly want foods such as bananas and certain grains when they are pregnant, and these cravings are expected and indulged. Some pregnant Rajput women have cravings for, and eat, mud, perhaps because of a calcium deficiency. Among the Jivaro of Ecuador, pregnant women may having a craving for dirt, and some will eat small amounts of unfired clay pottery. In Thailand, Banoi women experience a number of cravings, most frequently for sour foods, and a husband will go out of his way to procure whatever food his wife desires. Among the Chimalteco of Guatemala, some women develop a desire for clay, which they then continue to eat even after the birth of the baby. People worry when this craving appears because it is thought to be deadly. The habit may be broken if the woman eats *max*, tobacco mixed with lye. All Jamaican women find some particular food especially attractive while they are pregnant, and cravings for fish and meat are common. In Indonesia, pregnant Javanese women crave a number of foods, and especially extremely peppery food, and husbands are expected to find the desired foods no matter how hard this may be to accomplish. And Tarong women experience intense and persistent cravings for the first four or five months of pregnancy, usually for specific foods but sometimes also for places, people, pictures, or other things. Cravings are thought to "come from the child" and can be different across pregnancies. A woman should make sure that she satisfies any cravings for the good of her baby. If a baby has a deformity, the problem is always seen as a result of the mother's cravings.

Physical Symptoms

Mood swings, morning sickness, and other physical symptoms are also commonly experienced by pregnant women. The Gusii say that some women are more quarrelsome when they are pregnant, and some wives insist that their husbands remain at home for the entire period of pregnancy. Gusii women also experience morning sickness, and some are said to vomit at the sight of their husbands or even the clothing of their husbands in the morning. Tarong women may become temperamental when pregnant. These outbursts are ignored by anyone who witnesses them. A pregnant Mixtecan woman often becomes nauseous during the first three months of pregnancy, and this is considered normal. A Tarong woman is often nauseous during the first trimester of her pregnancy, especially just after she gets up in the morning. Most Jamaican women are chronically nauseous for some part of their pregnancies, and some remain sick for the entire period. Chimalteco women are said to lose their appetites and become very sick when the baby begins to move. Some Tairan women experience swollen hands and feet during pregnancy. By contrast, in some societies, physical nausea and other physical complaints are not usually associated with pregnancy. Among the Taira, pregnancy is not typically accompanied by morning sickness. Among the Truk of Micronesia, many women make it through their pregnancies without experiencing morning sickness, and those who do are only ill for the first trimester. Some Hare women feel especially sleepy and "lazy" during the second and third months of pregnancy. But many women pass through these first months with no physical symptoms.

Pampering

In a number of cultures, pregnant women can expect to be pampered by their spouses. Mixtecan husbands are supposed to treat their pregnant wives with special consideration. And men are usually more thoughtful and affectionate to their spouses, at least for a first or second pregnancy. A Mixtecan husband provides his wife with whatever foods she wants when she is pregnant for fear that, if her whims are not satisfied, something will go wrong with the pregnancy. But as more children arrive, a woman is likely to be regarded in the same way by her husband whether or not she is expecting a baby. A Truk husband is expected to humor his wife and to satisfy any of her food cravings. Indeed, one of the attractions of having a baby for a Truk woman is the special attention that she receives while pregnant in contrast to the normal submissive role that she is expected to play in her everyday life.

Restrictions on Activities

Cultures also differ regarding the degree to which they restrict the everyday activities of pregnant women. Sometimes, the workload of an expectant mother is decreased. But it is quite common for a woman to follow the same daily routine whether or not she is pregnant. Among the Gusii, pregnant women are not treated specially, and a woman will continue to perform her normal strenuous physical activities until she feels unable to do so any longer. Thus, women persevere in their normal household and subsistence activities until perhaps a week before they go into labor, although an expectant mother who did not feel up to doing her work would be helped by her husband and her female kin. A pregnant Tairan woman will continue to make a number of trips a day to the mountains to cut firewood, transporting each load of wood down the mountain on her back, and she may do so up to the day that she gives birth. And Cubeo women follow their usual routines until the moment that they go into labor, and a woman may start off for her manioc garden one morning as if it were a normal workday and return in the afternoon with a baby. In some societies, work is actually viewed as necessary for a normal pregnancy and delivery. Thus, Chippewa women were admonished to continue working hard while pregnant. Otherwise, the placenta would not be properly expelled after the birth of the baby. Strenuous work during pregnancy was also thought to loosen the fetus and make delivery less difficult. Among the Tarong, work is thought to be good for a woman who is expecting a baby. Work is said to make a delivery easier, while siestas produce more water and, therefore, make for a harder labor.

In some societies, women continue to work as usual but ease up when it comes to strenuous activities. For example, Mixtecan women perform their normal household activities, grinding corn for tortillas, washing clothes, and so on. A woman who is going to have a baby, however, avoids carrying heavy loads. Similarly, a Rajput woman who is expecting a baby follows her normal routine but avoids overexerting herself. A pregnant Tarong woman should not carry anything that is too heavy and she should avoid working when it is very hot so that she will not "cook the fetus." Otherwise, there are no prohibitions concerning a pregnant woman's workload, and one Tarong woman was still harvesting rice two days before she delivered twins.

In some societies, the work activities of a pregnant woman are more severely constrained. A Banoi woman typically experiences nausea, dizziness, weakness, and vomiting at least during the early months of pregnancy and sometimes until she gives birth. These symptoms can become severe enough to disrupt her work schedule and send her to bed. Her husband and children will do much of the housework during a woman's pregnancy, although she will continue to perform some tasks if she is not ill. And as soon as she discovers that she is pregnant, a Truk woman is expected to do only very undemanding work.

Fear during Pregnancy

Where cultures do not have the means of handling complications associated with pregnancy and birth, a woman who is expecting a baby has good cause to worry about her own welfare as well as that of her baby, and in many societies, a pregnant woman does express concern that she or her baby will die. Thus, for example, pregnancy represents a genuine danger to the life of a Truk woman, and many will say that they are frightened of what will happen to them, especially in the case of a first pregnancy. In former times, a "farewell" feast was held by the close kin of a woman in her final stages of her first pregnancy in case she died delivering her baby. The woman received some cloth that would be used for her shroud if she failed to survive the birth. If she lived, the cloth would be preserved in case she died during a subsequent labor or in case her baby was born dead. When a Chimalteco woman realizes that she is pregnant, a soothsayer is summoned to pray for the mother's health. The soothsayer will also pray for a boy or girl baby, depending upon the parents' preferences. He also discovers by divination whether the parents have committed any sins that will complicate the delivery. The soothsayer kills a turkey, mixes its blood with incense, and prays at various churches and shrines on behalf of the mother and baby. Some families will call in the diviner a number of times if they are fearful of a difficult birth. During her first pregnancy, a North American Sanpoil woman was unhappy and fearful. She was constantly warned that she would die if she broke any of the numerous taboos on her behavior. Hare women are fearful about having babies, but after the first birth, they come to see that the process is easier than they had expected. The first birth is also frightening for Jamaican women. Once she has had a baby, a woman then knows what to expect, but subsequent births are no easier than first deliveries.

Regulations on Behavior

The legitimate anxiety that pregnant women experience the world over is reflected in the numerous behavioral restrictions and prescriptions that are applied to expectant mothers across cultures. These rules are understood to protect the expectant mother or her baby. Some of these regulations have a practical or quasi-practical basis. Thus, for instance, a pregnant Tairan woman will wind a sash about her abdomen to hold the baby in the right position. And among the Sebei of Uganda, an old woman who is an expert on birth may rub butter on the stomach of an expectant mother during the last months of the pregnancy. She may also try to reposition the fetus by manipulating the mother's abdomen if this appears to be necessary.

Other rules regarding the behavior of pregnant women are magical in nature. Women are especially likely to resort to sympathetic magic, in which like is assumed to produce like. The special association between magic and pregnancy is perhaps accounted for by the special circumstances in which a pregnant woman finds herself. A pregnant woman is in a precarious position, as pregnancies always have the potential of going wrong. Further, the woman's own life as well as the life of her baby hang in the balance. The fate of her pregnancy is to some degree beyond her control. No matter how vigilant she may be, some disaster can occur. Across time and place, human beings have resorted to magic when they could not control the outcome of extremely important events. Pregnancy magic is probably an example of this more general tendency. When pregnant Tarong women avoid staying in water for any length of time, they are practicing a kind of sympathetic magic. This is because they believe that overlong baths will mean that there will be "too much water" during delivery, making for a difficult birth. The Tarong also say that lying in doorways or lying in certain positions will lead to difficulties during delivery. A pregnant Tongan woman is prohibited from tying anything around her neck. Otherwise, the baby will be strangled by the umbilical cord. If a woman removes the buttons from her husband's shirt, the baby's ears or mouth may be injured during delivery. If she eats on her husband's sitting mat, the infant's head will be soft and swollen. If she talks about or criticizes someone with a physical defect, her baby will be born with the same defect. And a woman who remains in the same position for any length of time will have a hard delivery. A Chippewa woman was warned that if she looked at a human corpse her baby's eyes would be dazed and queer-looking or cross-eyed. A child would be physically deformed if the mother looked at a deformed person or animal. Neither Sanpoil spouse could kill a rattlesnake or else the baby would cry and wriggle like a rattlesnake. The infant might also might swell up and turn green. If a Chippewa mother had been frightened by a lizard when she was pregnant, the baby would be born with a head shaped like a lizard's and with short arms and legs like a lizard. Chippewa women were also warned not to turn over in bed or else the umbilical cord might twist around the baby's neck or body. As a result, pregnant women were expected to sit up or at least to rise on their knees if they wished to change position. In Japan, a pregnant Takashima woman should place water in a cooking pot first and then the food; otherwise, she will have a dry delivery. If a pregnant Arapaho woman dropped a skunk down her dress, she would have an easy delivery, just like skunks.

Expectant mothers may also avoid other activities that seem likely to court trouble. In many societies, pregnant women are careful to stay away from anything associated with dying. A pregnant Tarong woman leaves her house if someone is near death or has died there. She may attend the funeral if she leaves the house before the dead person, but she must have no contact with the body and she should not wash her hair on the next Tuesday or Friday, both of which are unlucky days. It is especially dangerous for her to hear about the death of another pregnant woman, and she must try to prevent herself from following the deceased woman to her grave by washing her hair in lye and wine. If a Sanpoil woman went near anything that had

been killed recently or if she stepped over blood, her infant would be harmed and her husband would have bad luck. Mixtecans say that a baby may "lose moisture" and be born with some kind of defect if its mother has seen a moon in eclipse, and harelips as well as deformities of the limbs are attributed to this experience on the part of the woman. An expectant mother's gossip can affect an unborn child, so that, for example, if a pregnant woman tells someone that he has the face of a fox, the baby may be born looking like a fox. If an Arapaho woman worked too hard and carried loads on her back that were too heavy, her baby would be born with a blue birthmark on its back. Kalderas women avoided tempting fate by not accumulating many baby clothes before the baby was born. And a pregnant Sanpoil woman tried to avoid insulting or angering anyone in case the person had the power to jinx the child. Chippewa women were warned not to visit the tipi of or receive gifts from anyone but a close relative for fear that some unknown enemy might use "bad medicine," that is, magic, to harm the baby.

Some of the restrictions placed upon the pregnant woman are meant to protect her and her baby from harmful supernatural influences. Pregnancy can be a dangerous time for a Tarong woman because of the jealousy of nonhumans, or the supernatural spirits, who may cause her to miscarry or even to die by striking her. Pregnant women, therefore, avoid going out at night.

In many places, women who are pregnant try to avoid stressful situations. A pregnant Truk woman should not become upset. Thus, people are prohibited from speaking to her in an angry voice, or even exhibiting anger in her presence.

Restrictions on Sexual Activity

Cultures vary in the extent to which they restrict the sexual activity of pregnant women. A Mixtecan couple can continue to have sexual intercourse until the baby is born, and nothing special is done to avoid hurting the fetus. There are no taboos on sexual intercourse for a pregnant Tarong woman, although people think that it is best to avoid sex for the last two months or more of the pregnancy. And Tairan couples can continue to engage in sexual relations throughout a pregnancy and may resume having sexual intercourse a week after the birth.

By contrast, the Sebei believe that semen is harmful to the fetus. As a result, sexual intercourse is restricted during pregnancy. Similarly, Rajput couples are supposed to avoid sexual intercourse during a pregnancy. Sexual intercourse is prohibited for a pregnant Truk woman for the first few months of a pregnancy until the fetus takes secure hold in the uterus. Nor can her husband engage in sexual activity with any other women or else his wife will become ill and may even lose the child. A Javanese couple who are expecting a baby are supposed to refrain from engaging in sexual intercourse for fear of causing the infant to be deformed. In fact, however, many husbands do not honor the taboo.

In some societies, sexual intercourse is required while a woman is pregnant. Some Chippewa believed that the husband and wife should engage in sexual intercourse for the duration of a pregnancy so that the fetus would continue to grow. Jamaican couples generally continue to have sexual intercourse throughout a pregnancy, and many people say that the more often the woman has coitus the easier the delivery will be.

Food Taboos

In some cultures, the diet of a pregnant woman is not restricted. There are no constraints on a Mixtecan or Chippewa woman's diet while she is pregnant, although people in both cultures say that if an expectant mother eats too much, labor will be painful. However, in many cultures, there are specific foods that a pregnant woman is prohibited from eating. An expectant Tarong mother should not eat bitter substances, or else she may have a miscarriage. Some women also

avoid eating sweet foods for fear of making the baby fat and, therefore, harder to deliver. Pregnant Rajput women avoid eating milk, cold rice, spicy food, and anything that is very hot or very cold. Women in some cultures think that milk is bad for a pregnant women because it poisons the Fallopian tubes, while others say that if a woman drinks milk, the baby will become too large. Sebei women are not permitted to eat meat from an animal that has died on its own, but they may eat from the hind legs of one that has been slaughtered. During the last few days before she expects to deliver her baby, a Jivaro woman is prohibited from eating the meat of particular wild birds. If a Tongan woman ingests hot foods, her baby will have raw, reddish skin. An infant will be born with spotted skin if the mother eats octopus or reeffoods and without pubic hair if the mother eats certain kinds of fish. Takashima women are told to avoid tea and pepper while pregnant. A Sanpoil woman was expected to eat lightly while pregnant. If a woman ate too much, she would make herself ill and her baby would be big and the delivery difficult. Some food prohibitions function as a kind of sympathetic magic. Sanpoil husbands and wives were required to observe a variety of food taboos during the woman's pregnancy. For instance, if either spouse ate speckled trout, the baby would cry a lot and shake like a trout. If they ate rabbit, the baby would have weak legs. The Chippewa said that neither husband nor wife should eat turtle when a women was pregnant. Otherwise, the baby would always be stretching just as a turtle is always stretching. If either parent ate catfish, the infant would be born with rings of sores around its head. A pregnant Takashima woman who eats octopus will give birth to a baby with no bones, and if she sees a fire, her infant will have a red birthmark.

Preparations for Birth

A woman often makes special preparations for the birth of her baby during the last months of her pregnancy. A month or so before she is due to have a baby, a Mixtecan woman will undergo some special procedures once each week to insure a successful delivery. A midwife will massage the woman's abdomen with warm almond oil. She will also blow catalan from her mouth onto the buttocks and hips of the expectant mother. If a Mixtecan woman has reason to believe that she may go into premature labor, she will drink a preparation made of a mixture of various herbs. The concoction is believed to make the fetus stick more securely in the uterus so that it will not "fall out early." Both treatments are supposed to loosen the fetus and to make childbirth less painful as a result. A Takashima woman begins to wear an abdominal band on the Day of the Dog during her fifth month of pregnancy to guarantee a safe, easy birth. She also receives a number of amulets, one of which predicts the sex of the baby, and a bottle of water, said to remove birthmarks on a newborn infant.

Sometimes, a pregnant woman returns to the home of her parents for some length of time and then has her baby there. For the final months of her pregnancy, a Sanpoil woman stayed close to her mother. Since wives lived in the communities of their husbands, this meant that the pregnant woman had to move out of her own household and in with her mother. The husband remained in his own village until the end of the pregnancy. A mother instructed her daughter about how to take care of her baby, gave her encouragement, and made sure that she respected the various taboos placed upon a pregnant woman. Beginning in her eighth month of pregnancy, a North African Teda woman goes to stay with her mother. If for some reason she is forced to remain at home, however, then a separate hut is built for her husband and children, where they live until 40 days after the birth. Until then, a husband may not touch or sleep with his wife or see the baby. By contrast, a Tairan woman who is close to her delivery date will make sure that her work does not take her far from her own home. The woman does not make any elaborate preparations in anticipation of giving birth. She will clean an old mat and some rags and will make sure that a bamboo-slat bed is ready for her to sleep on after her baby is born. Women will also make some baby clothes unless hand-me-downs from older children are already available.

Predicting the Sex of the Baby

Methods of predicting the sex of a baby are found in many cultures. Among the Hare, old people claim to be able to predict the sex of a baby. A girl faces toward you and a boy faces away. Some people also say that a woman can tell that a baby is a boy because boys kick. Jamaicans say that if an infant urinates on a woman who has not yet had children, her first baby will be a boy.

See also BIRTH; INFANTS, TREATMENT OF NEWBORN; SEX TABOO, POSTPARTUM

Ayres, Barbara. (1967) "Pregnancy Magic: A Study of Food Taboos and Sex Avoidance." In *Cross-Cultural Approaches: Readings in Comparative Research*, edited by Clellan S. Ford, 111–125.

Beaglehole, Ernest, and Pearl Beaglehole. (1941) *Pangai: Village in Tonga.*

Cohen, Yehudi A. (1966) *A Study of Interpersonal Relations in a Jamaican Community.*

Geertz, Hildred. (1961) *The Javanese Family: A Study of Kinship and Socialization.*

Gladwin, Thomas, and Seymour Sarason. (1953) *Truk: Man in Paradise.*

Goldman, Irving. (1963) *The Cubeo: Indians of the Northwest Amazon.*

Goldschmidt, Walter. (1976) *The Culture and Behavior of the Sebei.*

Hara, Hiroko Sue. (1967) *Hare Indians and Their World*.

Harner, Michael J. (1973) *The Jivaro: People of the Sacred Waterfalls*.

Hilger, M. Inez. (1951) *Chippewa Child Life and Its Cultural Background*.

———. (1952) *Arapaho Child Life and Its Cultural Background*.

Hitchcock, John T., and Leigh Minturn. (1966) *The Rajputs of Khalapur, India*.

Kronenberg, Andreas. (1981) *The Teda of Tibesti*.

LeVine, Robert A., and Barbara B. LeVine. (1966) *Nyansongo: A Gusii Community in Kenya*.

Maretzki, Thomas W., and Hatsumi Maretzki. (1966) *Taira: An Okinawan Village*.

Norbeck, Edward. (1954) *Takashima: A Japanese Fishing Community*.

Nydegger, William F., and Corinne Nydegger. (1966) *Tarong: An Ilocos Barrio in the Philippines*.

Piker, Steven. (1965) *An Examination of Character and Socialization in a Thai Peasant Community*.

Ray, Verne. (1933) *The Sanpoil and the Nespelem: Salishan Peoples of Northeastern Washington*.

Romney, A. Kimball, and Romaine Romney. (1966) *The Mixtecans of Juxtlahuaca, Mexico*.

Salo, Matt, and Sheila Salo. (1977) *The Kalderas in Eastern Canada*.

Wagley, Charles. (1949) "The Social and Religious Life of a Guatemalan Village." *American Anthropologist* 51: 3–150.

PROTECTION OF CHILDREN FROM DANGER

Parents in every culture are interested in preventing their children from coming to harm, and all parents take measures of some sort to keep their children safe. This is one of the universal roles of parenting, and especially of mothering. Adults are more vigilant while children are young because they recognize that a small child is more apt to get into trouble. Thus, for instance, the Tarong of the Philippines view children below the age of two or three as creatures without sense. Adults, therefore, emphasize the protection of children from potential danger as the primary responsibility of the caretaker of a young child. In an effort to keep youngsters safe, caretakers will remove the child from any potentially unsafe situation. This means that someone must constantly supervise a small child. It also means that children are prevented from exploring as much as they might with less protective caretakers. In Thailand, Banoi parents discourage children from engaging in dangerous activities as soon as they become mobile. Thus, youngsters are prevented from playing with dogs as well as with hot or sharp objects, or from going near the edge of the house. As they become older and range farther from home, children are also prohibited from swimming without supervision, climbing trees, or behaving raucously when in a boat. Parents also say that "too much activity" on the part of children is likely to lead to broken objects, fighting, excessive noise, and injury. For this reason, they discourage noisy or wild play, running around the house, and the like. On the other hand, adults say that an active child is preferable to a passive one, as an active youngster is more liable to be a good worker. The annoyance of having an overly active child around, however, encourages parents to try to rein in their children, although without much effect. Parents, and especially mothers, also worry when their children wander off because this is taken as a sign that the youngster will, when grown, become a ne'er-do-well son or a wayward daughter. Both outcomes mean that the child has abandoned the parents, and this concern about abandonment by one's offspring is a prominent theme among the Banoi. A Jamaican youngster who approaches a fire for the first time is threatened with a flogging. The second time around, the child is flogged in fact. Jamaican children always try to go near the fire twice, but none goes back a third time.

Adults may actually prevent children from functioning effectively because of fears that the youngster might get hurt. Tarong children are prevented from exercising their full abilities as a result of the protective measures taken by adults. A caretaker who has something else to do will put a child on her hip and cart the youngster off, interfering with his or her activities. A child who protests is offered a breast or bounced around by the caretaker. Children may be encouraged to walk or climb a ladder, but only when there is little chance of harm. A child is more likely to be put down and allowed to crawl around if the caretaker is a sibling, as the older child eventually becomes tired of carrying the younger one about. A youngster who is being tended by siblings can also become incorporated into the peer group of the older children and may watch or play with them for a while before becoming fussy. Thus, the Tarong youngster enjoys a bit more freedom when being supervised by another child.

Adults from different societies clearly differ in the extent to which they worry about the safety of children. Thus, while the Micronesian Truk assume that small children are unteachable, this belief does not cause adults to rein in their children. Rather, youngsters are allowed to do whatever they wish. As a result, infants often end up playing with sharp knives and the like without intervention from adults. Babies, however, are more likely to lose objects of this sort than to do serious harm to themselves. The three- and four-year-old is already used to climbing coconut trees and other treacherous objects without the interference of adults. In Okinawa, Tairan parents are not overly anxious about the physical safety of their children. Young Tairan children are taught to avoid the occasional car that drives through town, and parents do not prohibit them from playing near the main road. Similarly, youngsters know about the steep hills, slippery grounds, and other dangerous spots around home and are allowed to negotiate these obstacles on their own. Little children as young as three years of age will scurry across a frail bridge and slippery trails and over rocky ground without encountering any problems. Four-year-olds are able to use sharp knives without hurting themselves, and hatchets, hoes, rakes, and so on are left within easy reach of small children. Kindergartners are often yelled at for playing with dangerous implements, but a parent whose child still insists on handling the tool will probably be permitted to do so. Tairan parents instruct their children about the dangers associated with the wells, river, beach, main road, and rice paddies that the children are bound to encounter in their daily lives, and an adult who comes across a child doing something dangerous is sure to chastise the youngster. Nevertheless, young children are permitted to tag along after their older siblings who play in dangerous places, with the result that little children are likely to find themselves in harm's way.

Adults in any given culture often single out particular targets as dangerous while ignoring other targets that can do children equal harm. Among the Canadian Hare, babies may be permitted to crawl or walk around the house at eight months of age. No precautions are taken to remove dangerous objects, and children do have accidents such as poking an eye with a pair of scissors. Mothers also give children household items to play with when they are not being used, so youngsters end up adopting scissors, knives, and axes as playthings. Hare mothers are careful, however, to keep their children away from freezing water, and a woman may pitch her tent up on a hill to prevent the children from going near the water. And small children are warned over and over not to touch guns, stoves, or traps. Mothers also put scissors and knives out of reach of young children when they are planning to be away from the house. Similarly, whereas Truk adults are generally unconcerned about the possibility that their children might be harmed, they show considerable concern when it comes to the potential for drowning. Truk communities are built close to the water, and older children spend a good deal of their time swimming while younger ones play on the beach. Mothers are terrified that their children may drown and, in fact, there have been a number of near catastrophes of this sort. Nevertheless, Truk youngsters can usually swim well by six or seven years of age, and they swim without any serious interference from parents.

In some cultures, children are relatively free from constraint by adults simply because their surroundings are generally safe. There are few dangers in the environment of Mexican Mixtecan children. The only real threats to their safety are the oxen, sheep, and goats who can trample a child as they make their way down the street. Adults and older children will always take care to warn youngsters to move out of the way when the animals are about. Or they will physically remove the children from their vicinity.

In some cultures, children are warned against imaginary dangers by adults in an effort to prevent them from being harmed by real ones. The floors of Japanese houses are covered with small mats bordering each other. Children are told that the ancient samurai used to stab people by thrusting their swords up through the floors where the mats touched, and youngsters are persistently warned that it is dangerous to sit or step where the mats join. Houses are supported on joists that raise the structures off the ground, and adults also believe that a child can knock an entire house out of shape by stepping on the threshold. Thus, youngsters are also cautioned that it is dangerous and therefore forbidden to do so.

Benedict, Ruth. (1946) *The Chrysanthemum and the Sword.*

Cohen, Yehudi A. (1966) *A Study of Interpersonal Relations in a Jamaican Community.*

Gladwin, Thomas, and Seymour Sarason. (1953) *Truk: Man in Paradise.*

Hara, Hiroko Sue. (1967) *Hare Indians and Their World.*

Maretzki, Thomas W., and Hatsumi Maretzki. (1966) *Taira: An Okinawan Village.*

Nydegger, William F., and Corinne Nydegger. (1966) *Tarong: An Ilocos Barrio in the Philippines.*

Piker, Steven. (1965) *An Examination of Character and Socialization in a Thai Peasant Community.*

Romney, A. Kimball, and Romaine Romney. (1966) *The Mixtecans of Juxtlahuaca, Mexico.*

Whiting, Beatrice B., and Carolyn Pope Edwards. (1988) *Children of Different Worlds: The Formation of Social Behavior.*

with or speak to the infant. It is only when they arc about 15 months old that Guatemalan infants begin to spend their time outside of the hut and in the company of other children. A comparison of young children with American babies of the same age shows that the Guatemalan infants are less active and more fearful. They smile very little and are extremely quiet. Even at 3 years of age, Guatemalan children remain quiet, timid, and passive. By the time they reach 11 years of age, these same youngsters are happy and active children. Similarly, while younger Guatemalan children lag behind American youngsters of the same age on tests of memory, perceptual analysis, and conceptual inference, they perform as well as their American counterparts by the time they are 11 years old. Examples like this suggest that experience may affect the rate of cognitive development but not so much the final outcome. Human beings are thus strongly selected to understand the world in uniform ways and resist straying from this universal cognitive attitude even in the face of widely different experiences. There are also limits to what the human being can tolerate while still remaining on course, so that in cases of extreme deprivation a child may remain cognitively arrested. But no culture arranges the experiences of the majority of its children in such a way as to produce this result. Extremely deprived environments occur in individual families, not in entire societies. The idea that human beings are selected to exhibit some fundamental species-wide cognitive skills regardless of variable cultural experience is supported by evaluations of intelligence across a number of societies. Thus, in Guatemala and in Botswana, children who have scored well on tests of cognitive skill also happen to be the children whom other people in their culture judge as highly intelligent. This suggests that people across cultures agree about what constitutes intelligence and that this shared definition of intelligence is being captured by formal tests of cognitive capacity.

RESILIENCY The challenges and opportunities that a human being's environment offers are never entirely predictable. This means that human beings must be plastic enough to be changed by their surroundings if they are going to be able to thrive in the particular culture in which they happen to live. On the other hand, all human beings need to be able to meet certain universal challenges, and people, as well as other organisms, are thus predisposed to exhibit traits that allow them to do so regardless of the vagaries of environmental influence. Developmental resiliency refers to this tendency for the developmental trajectory of an individual to remain "on course" in spite of environmental fluctuations. Resiliency is evident across a variety of traits in the physical, cognitive, and behavioral realms.

Cognitive performance appears to be quite resilient in spite of large differences in the child's early environment. An infant raised in a Guatemalan village spends the first 10 or 12 months of life in its cradle. The baby remains in a small, dark, windowless hut. Other people rarely play

Resiliency is also exhibited in physical growth patterns. For example, if a child's diet is inadequate for some period of time, there will be a decrease in the youngster's growth rate. As soon as the child's diet improves, the rate of growth speeds up as if the child were making up for lost time. Again, there are limits to resilience in physical growth. If a child's diet is persistently inferior, the youngster will never attain the level of growth that would have occurred with an adequate diet.

Resiliency in human development makes good sense from the point of view of evolution. Evolutionary theory reminds us that organisms existing today tend to exhibit characteristics that have helped their ancestors to survive and reproduce in the past. Resiliency in the face of environmental vagaries is one trait that is likely to have promoted survival and reproduction and is, therefore, predicted to be typical of members of our own and other species who are living today. This proposal is captured in the idea of canalization, which postulates that organisms will develop toward a predictable final outcome in spite of environmental variations. Canalization does not claim that environments are irrelevant to development. Rather, it specifies that the organism can arrive at some final outcome by a number of different routes, and that the developmental route that is followed depends upon the particular environment in which the organism is embedded. Clearly, a sufficiently bizarre environment can knock an organism off track. Thus, for example, if one of a kitten's eyes is covered at birth, the kitten will be blind in that eye for life even after the eye patch has been removed. The kitten's visual system is not capable of switching routes in the absence of normal environmental stimuli so as to produce an eye that still sees. The failure of a trait to develop normally under extraordinary environmental conditions of this sort is understandable. Because the environmental circumstances are so unusual, natural selection has never had the opportunity to select a developmental path that will respond to the circumstance so as to produce the desired trait. In the normal course of evolution, cats would not have experienced a total absence of light. As a result, even if some mutation had produced a cat visual system that could develop normally in the absence of light, no advantage would have accrued to the possessor of such a system and the mutation would not have spread through the cat population.

It is also true that resiliency does not apply equally well to all characteristics of an organism. For instance, in the case of facultative adaptations, that is, adaptations that differ according to environment, an organism might develop in a number of alternative ways depending upon what the environment has to offer. Thus, for instance, the brains of rats and other animals enlarge in a number of important ways when the environment is relatively stimulating. Similarly, we all know that muscles become larger with use. These effects, however, are also consistent with an important feature of resiliency, which is that developmental programs are biased to produce organisms that function effectively in the environments in which they find themselves. In the case of canalization, the organism arrives at the same final outcome regardless of environmental exigencies. In the case of facultative adaptations, variations in outcome that depend upon environmental circumstances produce a tailored fit between the organism's traits and the environment in which the trait must be expressed. If the ideas of canalization and of facultative adaptations turn out to be correct versions of developmental processes, then it becomes important to determine what kinds of traits are best described as the product of canalization and what kinds are the result of facultative adaptation.

See also CANALIZATION; COACTION

Henderson, Ronald W., and John R. Bergan. (1976) *The Cultural Context of Childhood.*

Kagan, Jerome, and Robert E. Klein. (1973) "Cross-Cultural Perspectives on Early Development." *American Psychologist* 28: 947–961.

Konner, Melvin J. (1981) "Evolution of Human Behavior Development." In *Handbook of Cross-Cultural Human Development,* edited by Ruth H. Munroe, Robert L. Munroe, and Beatrice B. Whiting, 3–52.

RESPECT

In cultures around the world, children are taught to show respect in the company of certain categories of people. Often, a child is required to be respectful toward older people. Among the Palauans of Micronesia, younger people are expected to show respect for their elders, and young people will show outward deference to an older person who is lecturing or scolding them regardless of their private feelings. In North America, an older Comanche boy who was insolent to an adult male would be greeted by the man with cutting sarcasm, and boys soon learned to be respectful to their elders. Old people were greatly respected among the North American Arapaho. They contributed importantly to the instruction of children, and young people who were approaching 20 years of age were still lectured by older members of the tribe.

Children may also be expected to show respect to a particular category of relative. Once he reaches puberty, a Micronesian Truk boy is required to be respectful toward his older brothers. He may not tell vulgar jokes in their presence, nor may he interrupt their activities, especially outside of their own household. An adolescent North American Arapaho girl is required to show reserve in the presence of her brothers and all other relatives whom she calls "brother." She should not look at a brother and should leave or refrain from entering a room that he is occupying. Sisters are not allowed to talk to their brothers unless it is absolutely necessary, and then they must do so with lowered eyes. A Hindu saying reflects the degree of respect that children are expected to display toward their older relatives: "If my father or elder brother tells me to stand in one place, I'll stand there, dammit, all day if need be, until they tell me I can move."

In many societies, children are expected to be respectful toward their fathers. An African Nyoro son calls his father "my master" or "sir," terms that are also reserved for addressing a chief, and is expected to be respectful to the older man at all times. Even as a man, a son does not sit on a stool or chair in his father's presence. Rather, he squats on the floor. A man does not use his father's spear or borrow his clothes. A male may not shave or smoke for the first time until he has made a token payment to his father. Similarly, a father is said to rule his daughter, and girls are even more subordinate to their fathers than are sons because of their status as females. This deferential relationship between fathers and children extends to a youngster's demeanor toward the father's brother, who is called the "little father," and also toward the paternal aunt, or "female father," whom children often regard as a severe individual. By contrast, a child feels more intimate toward maternal aunts, whose relationship to the child is much like the mother's.

Sometimes, children are expected to be respectful to visitors or strangers. In the Philippines, Tarong preschoolers are taught not to pass in front of a guest or to interrupt a conversation except in an emergency. A youngster should "be ashamed" in the presence of guests, and should be seen but not heard. These expectations are most likely to be enforced when a visitor is an important person or a stranger. Sometimes, respect is viewed as a generally desirable attribute in children. North American Chippewa children were taught to respect everyone with whom they came in contact. They were to avoid looking at anyone for a long time or making fun of another person. A child was instructed not to look into a neighbor's wigwam or to visit anyone during a meal. Youngsters were also taught to respect older people in particular. They were given tobacco to present to an elder person as an expression of goodwill and were expected to speak to older individuals respectfully and listen to them with attention.

In some societies, respect is expressed by outright avoidance of the respected person. From the time that he was an adolescent, a North American Comanche boy was required to avoid his sister, and at this age, an unmarried brother began to live in a tipi behind the house of his parents to insure that he and his sister did not meet. Brothers and sisters could not touch or sit near each other, and a boy whose sister failed to observe these rules could kill her with impunity. Similarly, among the Truk of Micronesia, brothers and sisters are expected to avoid talking about sex or elimination in each other's presence or to sleep in the same house once they reach puberty. The boy will ideally live with some other relative until he marries, although brothers sometimes sleep in another room or at the opposite end of the house in which their sisters live. In former times, Truk brothers were not allowed to stand in the presence of a seated sister. Nor could his sister stand when he was seated. Thus, one sibling was forced to crawl or crouch when the other was sitting down.

In contrast to rules that require respectful treatment of certain people are customs permitting or even dictating informality between a child and particular other individuals. For instance, the relationship between a North American Comanche boy and his mother's brother was relatively informal and usually friendly and easy-

going. The two called each other by the same name, and a boy could borrow some article from his uncle without asking permission and could rely on the older man for help.

See also SENIORITY

Barnett, H. G. (1960) *Being a Palauan.*

Beattie, John. (1960) *Bunyoro: An African Kingdom.*

Carstairs, Morris. (1958) *The Twice-Born.*

Gladwin, Thomas, and Seymour Sarason. (1953) *Truk: Man in Paradise.*

Hilger, M. Inez. (1951) *Chippewa Child Life and Its Cultural Background.*

———. (1952) *Arapaho Child Life and Its Cultural Background.*

Nydegger, William F., and Corinne Nydegger. (1966) *Tarong: An Ilocos Barrio in the Philippines.*

Piker, Steven. (1965) *An Examination of Character and Socialization in a Thai Peasant Community.*

Stephens, William N. (1963) *The Family in Cross-Cultural Perspective.*

Wallace, Ernest, and E. Adamson Hoebel. (1952) *The Comanches: Lords of the South Plains.*

RESPONSIBILITY Parents in different societies vary in the degree to which they train their children to be responsible. Responsibility training is emphasized in societies that recruit children into the work force. Thus, for example, both obedience and responsibility in children are highly valued among the Gusii of Kenya, who begin to recruit their youngsters to do household chores at a very early age, and no adult or older child will think twice before sending a youngster off on an errand. A child may at first be required to carry food from house to house in the family homestead. Soon, the youngster will also be expected to fetch coals to light the father's cigarette or the mother's pipe or to bring a visitor a stool on which to sit. Youngsters are sent around the neighborhood to invite guests to beer parties and to collect utensils for the gathering. Somewhat older children are expected to perform more demanding tasks. Boys begin to herd the animals and girls to carry pans or pots of water from the river. A five-year-old girl will also begin to tend babies. Children who neglect their duties, or who do them carelessly, will be scolded and often caned. A girl who left an infant untended would be severely punished, perhaps receiving a beating from her mother. Similarly, the Tarong of the Philippines view responsible behavior as very important in adults and children, and training to be responsible begins when a youngster is around five years of age. Children of this age are carrying small jars of water, keeping up the stove fire, supervising infants, fixing the tether to which the family goats are tied and guiding them home at night or in bad weather, feeding the chickens, picking vegetables, cutting rice, and bathing themselves. Initially, preschool children are closely watched as they perform these chores. As children become older, they are assigned a greater number of tasks. While youngsters are expected to perform these chores responsibly, and while they are in fact making useful contributions to the household, adults do not think that preschoolers can do these tasks on their own. Rather, adults need to tell them what to do and when to do it. Adolescence brings with it increasing responsibility and also increasing autonomy for the Tarong boy and girl.

Conversely, where responsibility is not stressed, children are not incorporated into the work force. The Tairans of Okinawa say that a child under seven years of age has no sense.

Youngsters of this age are not viewed as very reliable, and parents try to discourage them from taking on serious chores such as baby tending. Indeed, youngsters are not viewed as capable of taking on serious responsibility until they are approaching adolescence. Similarly, a four- or five-year-old Indian Rajput child is given very little responsibility, and youngsters of this age spend most of their waking hours playing. Five-year-olds may be sent to the store to shop for their mothers, who cannot leave home because they follow the custom of purdah, or seclusion. The store is a few hundred yards away from the neighborhood in which the Rajputs live. Little girls may also be asked to wash a few dishes, and both sexes will fetch water if the day's supply has run low. Children may also take messages from the women's courtyard to the men's platform. These are not regularly assigned tasks, however. Rather, children will be asked to perform some task when their help is genuinely needed. Among a group of Mormons in New Mexico, children who are assigned chores are viewed as "helping" their parents rather than as making independent contributions to the household. Some mothers think that eight-year-old children are too young to be given much responsibility, and even a thirteen-year-old may not be expected to do regularly assigned chores.

Children across cultures are highly motivated to do the kinds of work that they observe adults doing. As a result, they are often thrilled to be given responsibilities by adults. Little Gusii children as young as three years old will ask to help adults who are hoeing a field, and they enjoy working alongside their elders. Two Gusii six-year-old girls planted and harvested their own garden plots without prompting or help from any adults. In Mexico, Mixtecan children are expected to do a greater number of chores, and more important chores, as they enter middle childhood, and they are excited because they can now participate in the same activities that older people perform. Tarong children, after they have begun to be assigned tasks by their parents, start to take on new chores at their own initiative, and four- and five-year-olds regularly try to do chores that their elders think are too ambitious for them. Indeed, young children may be punished for attempting a task that a parent has forbidden them to do. A child, nevertheless, may persist in trying to do the task. Tarong children of about six years of age are given additional responsibilities. They welcome the extra work, because they view it as a sign that their parents think of them as more grown up. Children of this age say that chores are their favorite activities, especially those that require adult assistance because they are especially taxing. Similarly, adolescents are anxious to be viewed as adults and are happy to take on the responsibilities and enjoy the privileges that accompany the entrance into the adult world. Tairan children under seven years of age want to help out mopping the floor and setting or clearing the table even though adults do not view young children as reliable. Parents say that youngsters of this age are only allowed to help out with tasks because they like to do them. Kindergarten children are happy to help their mothers in the potato fields, cleaning the dirt off the potatoes or putting potato seeds in the holes that are dug by an adult during the planting season. First-graders want to help their older siblings gather snails after a rainfall or hunt frogs, grasshoppers, and dragonflies and are, in fact, more enthusiastic about doing these chores than are the older children. Adults don't view any of these activities as real work and don't encourage their young children to take on responsibilities of this sort. But the children are proud when they are permitted to do such chores. And if the household happens to be low on chicken feed, a mother may admonish a young child for "thinking only of play and not of the hungry chickens." The desire of children to take on responsibilities is clearly related to their interest in feeling grown up rather than to any enthusiasm about the tasks themselves. A Guadalcanal

Kaoka father usually gives his son a pig to care for by the time the boy is eight years old. Youngsters are at first very enthusiastic about this new privilege, but soon they may become careless about collecting food for their animals and have to be warned not to forget their responsibilities. Similarly, Tairan children want to be allowed to plant rice or cook or do other chores that the older children are expected to do because they want to feel grown up. The same children are less enthusiastic about performing the routine tasks that have been assigned to them, especially when their chores interfere with other activities that are more fun.

Across cultures, children are expected to take on more responsibility as they get older. When he was eight years old, a North American Hopi boy was expected to kill his first rabbit. He then acquired a "hunt father" and was initiated as a hunter. Now, instead of helping his female relatives with their chores, he often went to the fields and sheep camps with his father and grandfather. At first, he guarded the fields and orchards, but as he became more skilled at subsistence activities, he began to help plant, harvest, and herd. By the time he was around fourteen years old, a boy was probably herding his own animals and taking charge of his mother's fields. In the winter, a boy of this age would also practice men's crafts, including carding, spinning, and eventually weaving and moccasin making. In Guatemala, a Chimalteco boy under ten years of age spends most of his day doing what he wishes. On occasion, he will be asked to do small chores, such as carrying light piles of wood. Beyond this, his time is his own. When he is ten, however, he becomes the constant shadow of his father. He is now treated almost as an adult, putting in adult work hours as he works alongside the older man. Boys of this age now farm, find and transport firewood, attend ritual ceremonies, and travel to the markets with their fathers. The Truk of Micronesia expect people to gradually take on more responsibility as they grow older, and this remains true through middle age. But it is at adolescence, the stage of life when a Truk assumes the status of adult, that a person is first thought to be really responsible for his behavior, and an adolescent who behaves inappropriately and gets caught may end up the target of the victim's anger.

In Malaysia, little Semai children begin by following their parents and grandparents about, copying their activities. Adults, noticing the child's interest, may make a miniature version of a tool or show the youngster how to do this or that properly. Gradually, the child is no longer just imitating but, rather, helping out. When he was around nine years old, a New Mexican Zuni boy began to help with the hoeing and planting. He also went to the sheep camp with some older male relative, but boys of this age acted more as companions to the shepherds. Older boys were given more herding responsibilities, and by late adolescence, a male was taking the sheep out on his own. When a boy began to take a more active role in herding, he was given a lamb of his own, and an adolescent who was tending to the sheep by himself was given his own small flock.

Across cultures, responsibility training is stressed more for girls than for boys. And girls often take on more responsibility than boys in fact. For instance, among the Tairans, firstgraders clamor to be allowed to help their mothers with household chores, and girls are more eager than boys to be included in the work force. Girls also begin to act as child nurses earlier than their brothers and take their responsibilities as caretakers more seriously besides. In Thailand, preschool Banoi boys are not expected to take on any responsibilities. Girls of the same age begin to contribute in important ways to household work. Thus, a girl of this age may be asked to carry water, clean the house, wash the floor, help make hats, work in the kitchen garden, wash clothes, run errands, and tend the baby. And in Guatemala, a Chimalteco boy is expected to do only small chores until he is ten years old, but a girl is recruited into the work force by the time she is six or seven. She learns to make tortillas and helps her mother grind meal, sweep the house and fetch water. Similarly, a Brazilian Yanomamö girl is expected to help her mother do serious work while her brother is still filling his time by building play huts in a pretend camp of his own. By the time that she is ten years old, a daughter is an actual economic asset to her mother. Boys, on the other hand, might continue to do little but play well into their teen years. Sometimes, however, responsibility training is more severe for boys. Task assignment is very light for Rajput children, but girls are asked to do even less than boys because a mother views her daughter as a guest in her house since girls leave home to live with their husbands when they are married. Women also say that, since a girl works very hard once she is a wife, she should be treated with indulgence while she is still a child. Some families train the oldest son to take on extra responsibility so that he will be able to manage the farm and head the household when he is grown. His younger brothers are also trained to obey him. Other families, however, treat all of their sons equivalently, which means expecting little in the way of responsibility from any of them while they are young.

See also CHILD NURSES; CHORES

Barry, Herbert, III, Lili Josephson, Edith Lauer, and Catherine Marshall. (1976) "Traits Inculcated in Childhood: Cross-Cultural Codes 5." *Ethnology* 15: 83–114.

Chagnon, Napoleon A. (1983) *Yanomamö: The Fierce People.* 3rd ed.

Dentan, Robert. (1978) "Notes on Childhood in a Nonviolent Context: The Semai Case." In *Learning and Non-Aggression,* edited by Ashley Montagu, 94–143.

Gladwin, Thomas, and Seymour Sarason. (1953) *Truk: Man in Paradise.*

Hitchcock, John T., and Leigh Minturn. (1966) *The Rajputs of Khalapur, India.*

Hogbin, Ian. (1964) *A Guadalcanal Society: The Kaoka Speakers.*

Leighton, Dorothea, and John Adair. (1966) *People of the Middle Place: A Study of the Zuni Indians.*

LeVine, Robert A., and Barbara B. LeVine. (1966) *Nyansongo: A Gusii Community in Kenya.*

Maretzki, Thomas W., and Hatsumi Maretzki. (1966) *Taira: An Okinawan Village.*

Nydegger, William F., and Corinne Nydegger. (1966) *Tarong: An Ilocos Barrio in the Philippines.*

Piker, Steven. (1965) *An Examination of Character and Socialization in a Thai Peasant Community.*

Romney, A. Kimball, and Romaine Romney. (1966) *The Mixtecans of Juxtlahuaca, Mexico.*

Thompson, Laura, and Alice Joseph. (1947) *The Hopi Way.*

Wagley, Charles. (1949) "The Social and Religious Life of a Guatemalan Village." *American Anthropologist* 51: 3–150.

Whiting, John W. M., Eleanor Chasdi, Helen Antonovsky, and Barbara Ayres. (1966) "The Learning of Values." In *The People of Rimrock: A Study of Values in Five Cultures,* edited by Evon Z. Vogt and Ethel M. Albert, 83–125.

In Western societies, learning tends to be equated with schooling.

Clearly, however, the human species is highly dependent upon learning, and human beings are continually learning outside of the school setting. Indeed, school is a very recent human invention to which a minuscule number of the children of the human species have been exposed, yet children and adults have always learned from their environments and from the people around them as well as by thinking things through. Nevertheless, schooling does appear to affect performance, especially in the realms of memory and thinking. Thus, across a variety of tasks, children and adults from one culture to the next who have attended school perform differently from children and adults who have never gone to school.

Differences between schooled and unschooled children show up in memory skills. For example, schooled people can remember more words from a list that has been read to them than can unschooled individuals. Further, schooled individuals will remember more of the words on a list if it is repeated to them, while unschooled people benefit less from repetitions of words on a list. Schooling also affects the way in which people classify objects. Children who have gone to school are more likely to classify objects by form or function as opposed to surface appearance, for instance, color. They are also more willing to classify the same array of objects in a number of different ways. Youngsters who are schooled are superior at verbally explaining the basis for their choice of classifying scheme. Individuals who have been schooled are also better at solving problems from a purely logical perspective. By contrast, a person who has not attended school tends to resist solving puzzles when he has not had direct experience with the problem at hand. Thus, for example, in one famous case, an unschooled individual who was asked to judge the validity of a syllogism that focused on white bears in the far north refused to assess the logic of the syllogism because he had never been to the far north and, therefore, did not know what color the bears were there.

Schooled children and adults also perform better on tests measuring the concept of conservation of physical properties such as number, volume, and weight. In a famous conservation task, a subject initially stands in front of three beakers, two of which are identical and the third of which is taller but also thinner than the others. Milk has already been poured into the first of the two identical beakers. With the subject watching, the experimenter begins to pour milk from a pitcher into the remaining identical beaker until the subject agrees that there is now the same amount of milk in the two identical beakers. The experimenter then pours milk from one of the identical beakers into the taller but thinner beaker. The subject now has to judge whether or not there is the same amount of milk in the two filled beakers and why. People who understand the law of conservation appreciate that there must be the same amount of milk in the two beakers because the milk has been

Young Korean children arrive for school, having removed their shoes before entering the building.

conserved, or preserved, even though it has changed locations. In Western cultures, conservation begins to be appreciated once a child is around seven years old. Younger children do not understand conservation. Thus, on the conservation task, they say that there is more milk in the taller but thinner beaker because the milk makes a taller column. In societies where children are not schooled, subjects are considerably older than seven before they give the correct answers on conservation tasks, and sometimes even adults do not respond correctly.

While schooling has demonstrable effects upon formal tests of learning and thinking, in a

Penobscot children in their classroom in Oldtown, Maine, in 1921.

small number of studies, unschooled children have matched the cognitive performance of children who went to school. Thus, in Africa, seven-and-one-half- to eight-year-old Tiv youngsters easily solved conservation problems even though they had not attended school, and even the seven- and seven-and-one-half-year olds who were tested got about half of the problems right. Moreover, the Tiv children appreciated that conservation is a logical proposition. If you pour some substance from one container into another, the amount of the substance must remain the same. Children also tried to demonstrate that the amount of the substance (sand) had been conserved by reversing the process, pouring the sand back into the original container. Similarly, while Westerners are usually more successful at finding hidden figures in a picture than non-Westerners, unschooled Eskimo children do as well on these tests as Scottish youngsters who have gone to school for ten years. We do not know what accounts for the excellent performance of unschooled children in either of these cultures.

Why does schooling have a positive effect on tests of memory and thinking? Many researchers have observed that unschooled children and adults are simply unfamiliar with test taking, which is a skill specifically learned and rehearsed in school. Thus, their performance may have less to do with memory and thinking skills than with the test-taking situation itself. Children from traditional cultures may face additional problems because they are not used to seeing adults perform activities that have no practical outcome. On the conservation task, a child might not believe that an adult would pour milk from beaker to beaker for no reason. The adult, therefore, must think that she was changing the amount of water, and a child raised to show adults respect would certainly not disagree. The materials used in tests may also be unfamiliar to unschooled children and adults. The idea that familiarity with materials matters to

A teacher in northern Nigeria helps his eight-year-old student solve a reading problem.

performance has been supported by testing both schooled and unschooled subjects with unfamiliar materials. Thus, adult Liberian subjects with no school experience sort kinds of rice by function. Further, they can sort the same rice using different criteria. The same adults have difficulty sorting geometric shapes. By contrast, schooled subjects from America can sort geometric shapes easily, but the same subjects are bewildered when asked to sort kinds of rice. As schooled Americans have more experience with geometric shapes than with rice, and Liberian adults have more experience with rice than with geometric shapes, the performance of the subjects seems to parallel their familiarity with the objects with which they are working.

One question is whether inferior performance on tests of memory and thinking really reflects the capabilities of unschooled children

A group of preschoolers makes its way across a street in Beijing in 1988.

and adults. The problem is dramatized by a well-known case in which the experimenter was attempting to test classification skills in a group of unschooled Liberian Kpelle individuals. Over and over, subjects kept sorting objects into functional groups, placing the knife with the orange, the potato with the hoe, and so on, and observing that this was how a wise man would do things. Finally, the experimenter asked one subject how a fool would sort the objects. The subject constructed four piles of objects sorted by kind so that the foods were placed in one pile, the tools in another pile, and so on. This is the kind of sorting that Western researchers regard as the most sophisticated. Clearly, the Kpelle subjects were capable of classifying by type but did not prefer to do so when given a choice.

Even when children have attended school, the style of teaching to which they are exposed can influence what they take away from the schooling experience. Among the Kpelle, individuals are expected to show respect for their seniors. This means that a school child will defer to a teacher, learning whatever is taught because whatever the teacher says is assumed to be true. One Kpelle child was beaten by his teacher for insisting that insects had six legs, not eight. There is no attempt to analyze problems or to discover generalities across subject matter, and children should not try to discover answers on their own. Children are not expected to ask why something is true, and another instructor beat any youngster who asked too many questions. This is obviously very different from the school experience of many Western children, and these differences are likely to have different consequences for the thinking styles of children.

While school is a recent innovation for our species, across cultures schools are becoming more and more accessible to children whose parents had never dreamed of entering a school building when they were young. Parents in some societies welcome the opportunity to send their children to school, appreciating the advantages that an education can offer. In Thailand, all Banoi children go to school for at least four years, and Banoi parents pressure their children to do well and punish youngsters who fail to apply themselves. Success at school is important to parents because the child's future occupational success depends upon it. Similarly, Jamaican parents say that only intelligent people can make a lot of money quickly. As school breeds intelligence, they pressure their children to get a formal education. Children may also welcome school for one or another reason. Until they enter school, the freedom of Jamaican children is highly constrained by parental demands that they remain close to home. Children under five years of age spend their days in the house or backyard in the company of siblings. Older children may be sent off to do errands, but they are expected to return home without dawdling and are flogged if they linger. As a result, youngsters like to go to school, in part because this is their first chance to get away from the house without having to pay a price afterwards. This is also their first opportunity to make friends with children outside of the family. Most youngsters are expected to come home right after school, but sometimes a child is permitted to play at the post office for a few hours. Often, they engage in a considerable amount of rough-and-tumble play, activities for which they are flogged if carried out in the presence of parents.

Across cultures, the existence of the school can also create a considerable amount of disruption for families who are not used to this intrusion in their lives. In Guatemala, Chimalteco children are supposed to attend government schools beginning at six cr seven years of age. Here, they learn to speak, read, and write Spanish and to do simple arithmetic. In fact, the appearance of the children at school is irregular.

Youngsters may skip class because parents do not approve of their going to school or because they are needed at home to perform chores. Some fathers say that school only teaches children to be lazy. Men often prefer it if their sons go to the fields with them to learn farming. A boy who is going to school while his brother is home working may feel guilty for sitting around all day while his sibling is doing chores. Even when particular children have become proficient in Spanish at school, they typically forget everything that they have learned once their schooling is over and revert exclusively to using their Indian dialect. The Canadian government expects Hare children to attend school, but parents do not always cooperate in this regard. They miss their children as companions and they miss their help around the house. Sometimes, the entire family may have stayed up late at a drinking party, with the result that the children cannot get up early enough to go to school the next day. Or the family may decide to go out to the bush, bringing the children along. Sometimes, a parent will recruit a child to do some chore instead of going to school. Jamaican children, who begin school at seven years of age, may stay home on a particular day for a variety of reasons. A youngster who has been sent off on an errand in the morning may then balk at going to class and being flogged for lateness. Children will be kept home if they do not have clean clothes to wear or if their assistance is needed in doing chores. Some Kpelle children attend a school run by a man with a few years of education. Some youngsters learn to read, but attendance is irregular, school material is irrelevant to the everyday lives of traditional Kpelle, and not much is accomplished in the way of learning. Adults recognize that schooling disrupts the course of life for everyone, children and adults alike. Thus, parents say that a youngster who attends school becomes "foreign," "strange," "educated," or "American," that is, non-Kpelle and non-African. In fact, schoolchildren are

For most children in developed nations and more and more children in developing nations, much time is spent in school, as with these Muslim girls and boys in Afghanistan.

caught between two cultures. Adults are often ambivalent about sending their children to school. On the one hand, children with a Western education no longer respect their elders and are no longer motivated to become rice farmers. On the other hand, a child with some schooling might get a job that then provides the income to raise the standard of living of his family. Many children end up going to school long enough to make farming unattractive but quitting by fourth or sixth grade, with the result that they can't really succeed in the outside world. They thus become marginal, returning to something approximating traditional life or moving to a town where they can find a job. Traditional Kpelle are contemptuous of such people. In the 1940s, most Hopi children went to school for six to ten years. Attendance was more regular among children whose families had become ac-

culturated. Parents were not interested in the components of the curriculum that focused on white American culture, and some aspects of the curriculum were positively disliked. Thus, for example, some parents thought that arts and crafts should be taught by Hopi clans and ceremonial groups and not in school. Similarly, some parents objected to coeducational schooling. Most Hopi children viewed their school experiences as disconnected from the rest of their lives. Hopi boys, further, found themselves forced to go to school at precisely the time that they had begun to accompany their fathers to the fields and to be accepted into the world of males. For a Hopi girl, by contrast, school actually represented freedom from household chores and baby tending and gave her a chance to interact with other children of her age in a way that would not have been possible if she remained at home.

See also COGNITIVE DEVELOPMENT; LEARNING

Cohen, Yehudi A. (1966) *A Study of Interpersonal Relations in a Jamaican Community.*

Erchak, Gerald M. (1977) *Full Respect: Kpelle Children in Adaptation.*

Hara, Hiroko Sue. (1967) *Hare Indians and Their World.*

Hilger, M. Inez. (1951) *Chippewa Child Life and Its Cultural Background.*

Munroe, Robert L., and Ruth H. Munroe. (1975) *Cross-Cultural Human Development.*

Piker, Steven. (1965) *An Examination of Character and Socialization in a Thai Peasant Community.*

Rogoff, Barbara. (1990) *Apprenticeship in Thinking: Cognitive Development in Social Context.*

Thompson, Laura, and Alice Joseph. (1947) *The Hopi Way.*

Wagley, Charles. (1949) "The Social and Religious Life of a Guatemalan Village." *American Anthropologist* 51: 3–150.

SEGREGATION OF CHILDREN FROM PARENTS

In some cultures, parents and their offspring begin to be segregated at some point during childhood or adolescence. Most commonly, children begin to sleep apart from the parents' household but may come home to eat, do chores, or just hang around. Sometimes, the segregation is more extreme, as is the case with Nyakyusa age-villages in Africa and Murngin bachelor camps in Australia. When Nyakyusa boys reach the age of about ten or eleven, they move out of their parents' houses and into a village of their own. This settlement is built on the outskirts of the community in which their parents live. As the boys reach adulthood, their wives also come to live in the village and eventually this boys' town evolves into the new center of Nyakyusa society. Similarly, after his first initiation rites at puberty, a Murngin boy leaves his parents' home and goes to live in the camp reserved for single males.

The segregation of parents and children at night is a common practice across cultures. But the separation is much more likely to apply to boys than to girls. Of 57 societies, 44 percent require boys to sleep in a different house. When he remains in the same house as his parents, a boy often sleeps in a separate part of the house by himself or with other men and away from his mother and other females. By contrast, it is uncommon for girls to sleep separately from both parents. In 61 percent of the same 57 cultures, unmarried girls sleep with their parents. Thus, the common pattern across cultures is for a boy to be removed from the immediate vicinity of both parents or his mother but for a girl to remain with both parents or her mother. The Chinese reflect this pattern. A married couple sleeps in the same bed along with their young children. A youngster who turns seven or eight years old begins to sleep in another bed in the same room as the parents. Unmarried girls remain in the parents' room, but older unmarried boys begin to sleep in a front room apart from the rest of the family. Similarly, in Canada, unmarried Ingalik males sleep in the men's house, but women all sleep on the family bench, with a daughter between her mother and the wall. In East Asia, a Lakher bachelor does not sleep at his parents' house; rather, two or three unmarried men go to sleep in a girl's house. But an unmarried daughter sleeps at home, often near the bed of her parents. And in New Ireland, Lesu boys are sleeping in the men's house by the time they are nine or ten years old, but Lesu girls stay at home until marriage.

Nevertheless, girls do sometimes sleep away from their parents' house just like their brothers. Unmarried females spend the night in a dwelling different from that of their parents in 1 percent of 57 societies. In southern Africa, Bemba girls generally go to the hut of an unmarried or widowed woman to sleep. Girls among the West African Fon may sleep with their mothers but, more typically, they spend the night at their paternal grandmother's house. In Uganda, Ganda girls stay with their married brothers. And by seven or eight years of age, Kalahari !Kung girls are likely to be sleeping with a grandmother or a widowed relative or friend.

The tendency for boys to be separated from their parents at night but girls to stay at home means that parents can supervise the activities of their daughters at night. Even when children of both sexes are separated from their parents, sleeping arrangements may allow parents some opportunity to keep an eye on a daughter. In the insular Pacific, Iban boys and bachelors sleep on the veranda, while unmarried girls often sleep in the loft. The loft, however, is accessible to the sleeping quarters of the parents by a ladder. Thus, the activities of the daughters of the house are easily monitored by the mother and father. This tendency to be more vigilant of daughters than of sons is in keeping with the fact that parents around the world are often more concerned about the premarital sexual behavior of their female than of their male children.

In a few societies, youngsters are sent to live away from their parents beginning at an early age. Among the Hehe of Tanzania and Thonga of South Africa, children usually go to live with their grandmothers when they are weaned. Bemba parents also send their children to live with their grandparents at around two or three years of age, and an elderly couple may have as many as five or six youngsters to tend.

Why do children sleep apart from their parents in so many cultures? The Nyakyusa say that they send their sons to live in age-villages so that the boys will not hear or see anything having to do with the sex lives of their parents. Indeed, the tendency for parent-child segregation to begin when a youngster reaches puberty suggests that the custom is associated with the emerging sexuality of the children. In particular, such separations may help household members to obey the various incest prohibitions dictated by their culture. People are less likely to yield to temptation when they are physically separated from each other. The customs of the African Igbo support the idea that parent-child segregation is related to sexual temptations and restrictions. When young, Igbo brothers and sisters sleep together in the same room apart from their parents. Eventually, an older unmarried son will move into a "single" house, while unmarried daughters continue to sleep in the house of their parents. However, a grown girl will not sleep at home if her father is there. Even while keeping their daughters at home, then, the Igbo prefer to keep sexually mature females and their fathers apart.

See also SEGREGATION OF BOYS AND GIRLS; SLEEPING

Fei, Hsiao-Tung. (1939) *Peasant Life in China.*

Frayser, Suzanne. (1985) *Varieties of Sexual Experience.*

Gomes, Edwin H. (1911) *Seventeen Years among the Sea Dyaks of Borneo.*

Herskovitz, Melville. (1938) *Dahomey: An Ancient West African Kingdom,* v. 1.

Junod, Henri A. (1927) *The Life of a South African Tribe,* v. 1.

Marshall, Lorna. (1959) "Marriage among the !Kung Bushmen." *Africa* 29: 335–364.

Osgood, C. (1958) *Ingalik Social Culture.*

Parry, N. E. (1932) *The Lakhers.*

Powdermaker, Hortense. (1933) *Life in Lesu: A Study of Melanesian Society in New Ireland.*

Richards, Audrey. (1940) *Bemba Marriage and Present Economic Conditions.* Rhodes-Livingstone Papers 4.

Roscoe, John. (1911) *The Baganda: An Account of Their Native Customs and Beliefs.*

Stephens, William N. (1963) *The Family in Cross-Cultural Perspective.*

Uchendu, Victor C. (1965) *The Igbo of Southeast Nigeria.*

Warner, W. Lloyd. (1937) *A Black Civilization: A Social Study of an Australian Tribe.*

Wilson, Godfrey. (1936) "An Introduction to Nyakyusa Society." *Bantu Studies* 10: 253–292.

SEGREGATION OF GIRLS AND BOYS

In many societies around the world, customs require that boys and girls begin to be segregated sometime during childhood. Seventy percent of 54 societies separate the sexes by adolescence, providing at a minimum different sleeping quarters for the two sexes. In New Guinea, a small Kwoma boy receives a tool kit for betel chewing from his father and a small bag in which to keep his betel from his mother. Henceforth, he is viewed as a little man and can no longer play with girls. Once he arrives at puberty, a Melanesian Trobriand boy begins to sleep in the bachelors' hut along with a few other males of his age. Boys still eat at home, however, and also perform chores for the family.

Often, the separation of children from one household by sex is simply a by-product of the desire of parents to establish their own living quarters apart from their children. When a number of related nuclear families live together, sisters and their female cousins and young unmarried aunts may be housed in one place apart from parents, while brothers, male cousins, and young unmarried uncles are housed in another location. Sometimes, the sexes live in the same household but in different rooms, while sometimes they live under different roofs entirely. Brothers and sisters are segregated in 74 percent of 57 societies as a result of customs that require children to sleep apart from their parents. Usually, the separation occurs because a girl sleeps in the same house as her parents, while a boy sleeps somewhere else.

In some societies, adults prefer to separate boys and girls in order to protect the reputations of unmarried girls. African Mbundu parents tell their young daughters: "A girl does not play with boys, for boys are sharp ones. Don't play with them." The goal of the adult is to minimize the likelihood of sexual activity. The South American Yahgan place a high value on premarital chastity for girls and separate boys and girls before puberty so that they will adapt to same-sex activities. If a North American Gros Ventre bride is not a virgin, her family is disgraced. Thus, parents send their young daughters to live with a female relative because they do not want the girl to be around her father, brothers, or male cousins. Beginning at puberty, southern African Fon girls are removed from the company of boys and warned about what will happen to them if they lose their virginity before marriage. However, many societies that disapprove of premarital sex find other ways of enforcing chastity that do not require the sexes to live apart from each other.

Sometimes, the separation of the sexes is reserved for males and females who bear a specific relationship to each other. According to Samoan custom, brothers and sisters as well as cousins of the opposite sex must refrain from engaging in a wide variety of activities in each other's presence. They must not sit or eat together, or talk with each other in an informal manner. They may not touch each other, or use one another's possessions. They cannot dance on the same floor or be in the same place unless

Young girls after a church service in Mexico

they are at home or in a crowded setting. By the age of nine or ten, Samoan boys and girls are avoiding each other according to the prescribed rules. The avoidances also apply to the children of a brother or sister and to relationships resulting from marriage or adoption.

Across cultures, boys and girls tend to separate spontaneously even when there are no cultural customs mandating segregation of the sexes. In the Philippines, Tarong boys and girls congregate in mixed-sex and mixed-age play groups from the time that they are babies. But as they grow older, boys and girls begin to become segregated, first playing separately in the same group when they are eight or nine years old and eventually forming single-sex cliques in

preadolescence. The girls try to act like young ladies and enjoy being teased by the boys. North American Chippewa children played in mixed-sex groups when they were little, but then refused to play with anyone of the opposite sex when they were older. Same-sex groups would have nothing to do with a member of the other sex.

See also Peers; Segregation of Children from Parents

Childs, Gladwyn. (1949) *Umbundu Kinship and Character.*

Flannery, Regina. (1953) *The Gros Ventre of Montana,* part 1.

Gladwin, Thomas, and Seymour Sarason. (1953) *Truk: Man in Paradise.*

Gusinde, Martin. (1937) *The Yahgan: The Life and Thought of the Water Nomads of Cape Horn.*

Herskovitz, Melville. (1938) *Dahomey: An Ancient West African Kingdom,* v. 1.

Hilger, M. Inez. (1951) *Chippewa Child Life and Its Cultural Background.*

Murdock, George P. (1936) *Our Primitive Contemporaries.*

Nydegger, William F., and Corinne Nydegger. (1966) *Tarong: An Ilocos Barrio in the Philippines.*

Whiting, John W. M. (1941) *Becoming a Kwoma.*

SELF-ESTEEM

Self-esteem refers to the judgments that individuals make about their own worth. People with high self-esteem are relatively satisfied with themselves as individuals, while people with low self-esteem are relatively dissatisfied with themselves.

Self-evaluations depend upon assessments of one's own qualities and accomplishments as well as comparisons of one's qualities and accomplishments with those of other people. This has implications regarding how child-rearing environments may influence a child's self-esteem. As different societies offer children vastly different opportunities to exercise their talents and capabilities, children in different cultures will have different kinds of experiences upon which to base self-evaluations. Thus, for example, in subsistence economy societies around the world, children are recruited to perform chores at an early age and are expected to do real work and to make genuine contributions to the welfare of their family. A seven-year-old Canadian Hare child already uses knives, scissors, and axes, and ten-year-old girls are embroidering, baking, preparing meals for the family, cleaning and laundering, and fetching water, while twelve-year-old boys are fishing and hunting with the men. In Uganda, a four- or five-year-old Sebei boy is taught to herd the family's cattle, while in Kenya, a five-year-old Gusii girl is tending her infant siblings without adult supervision. Children of the same age in American kindergartens are only expected to pretend to perform the very activities that children in other cultures are performing in earnest. This means that children in some cultures have ample evidence of their own accomplishments, while the message communicated to children of the same age in other societies is that they are incapable of engaging in adult activities and are only fit for play. In subsistence economy cultures, children who are performing serious chores also have the experience of making a difference to the family's welfare, and this sense that they matter also has the potential to influence self-esteem.

Self-evaluations also depend upon comparisons of one's own attributes and accomplishments with those of others. A child whose reference group is comparatively small has less of a chance of fading into the background in comparison with other youngsters. Thus, in societies where children aggregate in small peer groups, any individual youngster has a greater chance of preserving a relatively positive self-assessment. The idea that size of reference group can affect self-esteem is supported by trends in self-assessment as a function of age in American children. Thus, youngsters in America experience a drop of self-esteem in the early school years, precisely the time at which they find themselves thrown together with a large number of other children. This is in sharp contrast with their previous experience with a small circle of siblings and small preschool play groups. It is not until fourth grade that self-esteem begins to rise again. Where youngsters continue throughout childhood to interact in small groups, this dip in self-esteem may not occur.

Variations in the nature of children's activities from one culture to the next may also differentially tap into a fundamental human motivational system. Some psychologists have proposed that human beings are motivated from very early on in life to feel that they are effective actors in the world. This shows up even in infancy, where babies exhibit far more delight when allowed to manipulate mobiles and similar toys on their own than they do when required to watch passively the same toy automated by its own motor. Similarly, babies continue to maintain interest when presented with problems to solve, but then become bored once the solution has been found. It is as if the infant enjoys challenges. Anyone who has endured the ordeal of feeding an infant knows that babies prefer to feed themselves in spite of the fact that the process is initially messy and inefficient. Psychologists view the baby's persistence as a reflection of the human need to become competent at doing things. If human beings are motivated to be competent and effective, then differences in opportunities to perform activities that are challenging may have important effects upon children. In particular, competence motivation may be satisfied to a greater degree for children in some cultures than for children in other societies. It is also the case that different cultures provide opportunities for effectiveness in different realms. Thus, children who are assigned few chores but who go to school may evaluate themselves positively with respect to their intellectual competencies but less favorably with respect to practical skills or ability to be useful to other people. Children who perform many important chores in the household but do not go to school may exhibit the reverse self-esteem profile.

See also CHILD NURSES; CHORES; RESPONSIBILITY

Berk, Laura E. (1989) *Child Development.*

Goldschmidt, Walter. (1976) *The Culture and Behavior of the Sebei.*

Hara, Hiroko Sue. (1967) *Hare Indians and Their World.*

Kagan, Jerome. (1984) *The Nature of the Child.*

LeVine, Robert A., and Barbara B. LeVine. (1966) *Nyansongo: A Gusii Community in Kenya.*

White, Robert W. (1959) "Motivation Reconsidered: The Concept of Competence." *Psychological Review* 66: 297–333.

SELF-RELIANCE AND AUTONOMY

In many cultures around the world, children are expected to be self-reliant at an early age. In other societies, self-reliance in children is less highly valued and sometimes parents actually attempt to prevent their children from becoming independent. The Canadian Hare stress self-reliance, and by the time they are four years old, Hare children are dressing on their own, except during the winter when they need some help with heavy outerwear. A four-year-old may be sent to the store to fetch some items for a parent. And a child of four or five may take a younger sibling off to the neighbor's for a visit. When a three- or four-year-old falls down, no one comes to the youngster's aid. A child who cries will be ignored, or the mother might say: "You are careless. You are stupid." Hare children as young as three years of age are expected to make their own decisions about what they want to do, where they want to go, and so on. A little girl may be asked whether she wants the last piece of meat, and she must decide immediately, because if she says "no" her mother will eat the food herself. Similarly, children of this age may also decide whether they want to go to church with the family or stay at home. In Mexico,

Mixtecan parents assume that their children will be self-reliant and make no special effort to teach them to be independent. Each morning, little girls will shake out their own rebozos and a boy will shake out his hat, and children are dressing themselves by four years of age.

By contrast, in some societies, independence is not stressed, and sometimes adults consciously impede self-reliance in their children. Among the Tarong of the Philippines, adults do not think that young children can perform routine tasks on their own. Rather, youngsters are closely supervised. Adults say that the preschooler "has to be told—he cannot just do it yet." Tarong parents worry when children begin to do tasks on their own because initiative on the part of a youngster can result in disasters of one kind or another. Further, self-reliance pushed too far can lead a child to become stubborn and uncooperative. Tarong preschoolers are assigned a number of chores, and even at this age they are making useful contributions to the household. However, they also readily ask for help instead of persisting on a task that is difficult for them to do, and a child who is facing some new challenge is unlikely to try to confront it alone. Nevertheless, Tarong children are constantly trying to do things that their parents do not think them capable of doing. In Okinawa, a Tairan child is carried about on the back of one or another caretaker for the first two years of life. Therefore, the youngster has little opportunity to develop self-reliant behavior. Among the Rajputs of India, children are typically able to eat by themselves before the second birthday, but some mothers still feed their youngsters. Adults also bathe and dress children until they are five or six years of age. When Rajput children are faced with some problem, they will seek help from an adult or simply give up instead of finding a solution on their own. One youngster is unlikely to ask another for assistance, and in fact children cannot be counted on to help one another. Rajput children also persistently nag for anything

that they want anytime that they can get away with it. Children who attempt to do things for themselves may be discouraged by the impatient responses of their parents. Thus, for example, a boy who is attempting to feed himself may be punished by his mother for dropping the food. Or a girl who is attempting to embroider a petticoat may be stopped by her aunt because she is ruining the garment.

Among the Banoi of Thailand, parents do not pressure their young children to be self-reliant and in fact, Banoi parents, and particularly mothers, show concern when their children attempt to go off on their own, in part because the tendency to wander off in childhood is understood as a signal that the child will abandon the parents in adulthood. Children from five to ten years of age begin to bathe, eat, dress, and go to bed by themselves. Thus, the achievement of self-reliant behavior is gradual and applies to very basic kinds of routine activities. Similarly, Jamaican adults expect children to be passive and unobtrusive, and youngsters are not supposed to perform activities at their own discretion. Rather, all of their activities should be directed by the mother, and children who show initiative or independence are criticized for being "rude." Even childish behaviors that amuse adults are viewed as signs of "rudeness." Regardless of the attitudes of adults concerning independence in children, self-reliance inevitably comes with the acquisition of skills that allow a child to become somewhat independent from adults. Among the Truk of Micronesia, adolescents begin for the first time to be able to prepare their own food and are, therefore, no longer at the mercy of their mothers or other relatives when they are hungry. Boys and girls take great pride in this new self-reliance and like knowing that other members of the community are also aware of their new competence.

Even where children are expected to be self-reliant, parents may only accord youngsters freedom when they are at or near home. In

Guatemala, Chimalteco children are permitted to wander freely from house to house within the family compound, and mothers do not worry about the whereabouts even of their toddlers if they have a good sense of where the children are likely to be found. A mother will begin to look for a child who has not returned home by evening. In contrast to the freedom granted to children within the compound, youngsters under six or seven years of age are not generally allowed to stray very far outside the compound. Until they are around five years old, Jamaican children are not allowed to wander from home, and youngsters, therefore, spend their time in the backyard in the company of siblings. Even when children are older and begin to be sent off on errands, parents know how long it should take a child to perform a given chore, and youngsters who are away from home longer than expected are severely flogged for dawdling when they finally return. All Jamaican children are tempted to do some exploring on the way home from an errand, and all Jamaicans can remember being flogged often for lateness. Similarly, by the time they are four or five years old, Hare children are left to themselves to do as they please as long as they stay close to home.

In some societies, girls have less freedom because parents are interested in making sure that their daughters stay away from men until they are married. Banoi parents constantly worry that a daughter might be seen in the company of a man, as her reputation would be ruined along with her chances of making a good marriage. Girls, therefore, are always supervised by a parent or some other responsible adult. Similarly, Jamaican girls are punished more severely than their brothers for staying away from home longer than their tasks require.

Across cultures, training for self-reliance tends to be associated with specific kinds of economies. Thus, children are encouraged to be independent and to try new ways of doing things in societies that depend upon hunting and fish-

ing for their subsistence. By contrast, in cultures that practice agriculture or animal husbandry, self-reliance tends not to be encouraged. Rather, the emphasis is on obedience. Perhaps the tendency to be independent and innovative can be harmful in farming and herding economies where mistakes made can wipe out food and cash resources for an entire year. Where innovation and independence can produce an especially good kill or catch if successful and only a temporary economic hardship if unsuccessful, these traits may turn out to be useful in the long run. Differences in patterns of self-reliance and dependence are also related to variations in household composition. Where youngsters are raised in nuclear families composed of a mother and father and a small number of closely spaced brothers and sisters, children are likely to depend upon their parents, and especially the mother, to meet their needs and to compete with their siblings for the mother's attention. In cultures where a number of families live in one household, children do not tend to be dependent upon particular adults to meet their needs. And in fact, a youngster is as likely to depend upon older children instead of adults where there are a number of children of different ages within easy reach.

Ironically, while American parents tend to value independence in their children, their youngsters do not typically have the same kind of opportunity to practice autonomy as do children in some other cultures. Thus, while American youngsters are encouraged to dress, feed, wash, and entertain themselves at a relatively early age, these same children exhibit a dependence upon the mother that is expressed in habitual demands for attention. In cultures where children become part of a peer group instead of spending most of their time with their mothers, this kind of dependence is not seen. Rather, children restrict themselves to asking for practical help from the mother. American children spend a considerable amount of their time with adults by cross-cultural standards. Thus, for example, in one observational study of children living in an American community, 60 percent of a child's interactions were with an adult. This is in contrast, for instance, to a Kenyan community, where only 13 percent of a youngster's interactions were with adults.

Cubeo boys congregate in a single group of males ranging in age from perhaps six years through adolescence. The youngsters roam around on their own without any supervision from adults. The boys choose their own leaders and find their own food. Sometimes, the pack will help the men when they are engaged in some collective project. But it is the leaders of the boys' group who are responsible for enforcing rules and disciplining misbehavior. Cubeo boys become more independent from their mothers in childhood. By contrast, a girl at this stage of life is linked more and more closely to her mother as she begins to be assigned a greater number of chores. The Seminole place a high value on personal autonomy, and this begins to appear in the treatment of even very young children. A mother encourages a youngster to be independent, and parents treat their children more like peers than like dependents. The property and rights of children are respected, and youngsters are given pigs, chickens, fruit trees, and vegetable gardens as soon as they are able to care for them. These are then the property of the child. This emphasis upon individual autonomy has consequences for the parent-child relationship. Adults may give advice to children, but a grown-up is not supposed to tell a child what to do. Neither do children go to their parents with problems. Korean children are taught to be dependent, cooperative, and obedient. Youngsters are encouraged to appreciate that they are inferior in status to adults and subordinate to the group. And in fact, children past infancy are unlikely to be assertive. Comanche boys were given considerable freedom, and most of their time was spent playing in same-sex groups. Truk children begin to

be expected to take care of themselves as soon as they begin to understand and use language. This means that youngsters as young as two and three are expected to go to sleep on their own when tired, fetch food for themselves when hungry, and eliminate in the appropriate place. Children who forget to attend to their own needs in a timely manner will be prodded by some adult, but in a way that clearly suggests that the youngster should not have needed reminding.

Barry, Herbert, III, Irvin L. Child, and Margaret K. Bacon. (1967) "Relation of Child Training to Subsistence Economy." In *Cross-Cultural Approaches: Readings in Comparative Research*, edited by Clelland S. Ford, 246–258.

Brandt, Vincent. (1971) *A Korean Village*.

Cohen, Yehudi A. (1966) *A Study of Interpersonal Relations in a Jamaican Community*.

Gladwin, Thomas, and Seymour Sarason. (1953) *Truk: Man in Paradise*.

Goldman, Irving. (1963) *The Cubeo: Indians of the Northwest Amazon*.

Hara, Hiroko Sue. (1967) *Hare Indians and Their World*.

Hitchcock, John T., and Leigh Minturn. (1966) *The Rajputs of Khalapur, India*.

Lefley, Harriet Phillips. (1973) *Effects of an Indian Culture Program and Familial Correlates of Self-Concept among Miccosukee and Seminole Children*. Unpublished dissertation, University of Miami, Coral Gables, Florida.

Maretzki, Thomas W., and Hatsumi Maretzki. (1966) *Taira: An Okinawan Village*.

Nydegger, William F., and Corinne Nydegger. (1966) *Tarong: An Ilocos Barrio in the Philippines*.

Piker, Steven. (1965) *An Examination of Character and Socialization in a Thai Peasant Community*.

Romney, A. Kimball, and Romaine Romney. (1966) *The Mixtecans of Juxtlahuaca, Mexico.*

Wallace, Ernest, and E. Adamson Hoebel. (1952) *The Comanches: Lords of the South Plains.*

Whiting, Beatrice B. (1978) "The Dependency Hang-Up and Experiments in Alternative Life Styles." In *Major Social Issues: A Multidisciplinary View,* edited by S. Cutler and M. Winger, 217–226.

Whiting, Beatrice B., and John W. M. Whiting. (1975) *Children of Six Cultures: A Psycho-Cultural Study.*

SENIORITY

In many cultures around the world, relative age dictates the tone of relationships between individuals, with younger people deferring in a variety of ways and a variety of contexts to older ones. Among the Tongans of Polynesia, age confers status, even among children. Thus, an older child has the authority to beat a younger one for some misdeed, and the younger child is entitled to hit an even smaller one in turn. Similarly, anyone can be recruited to do some task by an older person, and an individual who has some chore to perform will generally look around for someone younger to press into service. In Japan, an older Takashima sibling is superior in status to a younger one, and younger brothers also defer to older sisters in childhood, although by the time a boy is ten years old, he no longer pays much attention to his sisters, reflecting the generally higher status of males over females. Age-based seniority also extends to the spouses of siblings, so that the wife of a younger brother is junior to the wife of an older brother and especially to the oldest son in the family. Among the Semai of Malaysia, a parent's younger brother is referred to as *Bah* and a younger sister as *Wa'*. A person need not heed anyone with either title, and putting the term *Bah* before someone's name during a disagreement is considered to be a dirty trick. Among the Nayar of India, dominance and submission between males are determined by relative age. A male must show respect and obedience to anyone older than he is and can command and discipline anyone younger. This means that a male may dominate an uncle who happens to be younger than he is and may be forced to obey a nephew who happens to be older. One male may not touch another, older male and must remove a specific piece of clothing, the upper cloth, before approaching the senior man. A younger male must hide himself behind a pillar when talking to an older one and must cover his mouth to prevent his breath from reaching someone who is of superior status. For the Liberian Kpelle, the male elders are the keepers of cultural tradition and cannot be questioned by children or even by other adults. Elders have a more profound understanding of Kpelle tradition both because of their extensive experience and because they are closer to the ancestors, and it is inconceivable that a child could know as much as an elder. Children are expected to show respect not only to elders but to any older person, and disobedience, particularly toward parents, is punished more harshly than any other behavior. In Kenya, a Gusii child between the ages of three and eight probably has the lowest status of any member of society. Infants receive attention and affection from their mothers and no demands are made on them, and the initiated girl and boy have not only responsibilities but also certain privileges, as do adults. But the uninitiated child is required to do everyone's bidding and has no younger one who can be bossed around in turn. Children of this age are the targets of the most severe physical punishments as adults attempt to teach them proper behavior. Nor are they accorded any rights that would require other people to show them some respect.

Across cultures, bigger and stronger children assert dominance over younger ones. The way in which this dominance is expressed differs to some extent from one society to the next. For example, where older children are expected to take care of younger siblings and cousins, the bigger child may order the younger one to do some chore. In other cultures, older children may force younger ones to do them favors. In both cases, however, a clear "pecking order" emerges. Younger children between four and five years of age, however, typically put up with the dominance of six- to ten-year-olds in order to be able to join their play groups. Thus, a younger child, and especially a smaller boy, will tolerate bossiness, roughhousing, and even physical injury at the hands of an older child if this means being included in the activities of the big boys.

Sometimes, youth confers certain privileges. In Micronesia, Truk adults are extremely permissive as regards the behavior of young children. Behavior that is considered unacceptable in older children is tolerated in younger ones. This indulgence is attributable to the attitude that small children are not really full-fledged people; rather, they are more like family pets.

See also RESPECT

Beaglehole, Ernest, and Pearl Beaglehole. (1941) *Pangai: Village in Tonga.*

Dentan, Robert. (1978) "Notes on Childhood in a Nonviolent Context: The Semai Case." In *Learning and Non-Aggression,* edited by Ashley Montagu, 94–143.

Erchak, Gerald M. (1977) *Full Respect: Kpelle Children in Adaptation.*

Gladwin, Thomas, and Seymour Sarason. (1953) *Truk: Man in Paradise.*

LeVine, Robert A., and Barbara B. LeVine. (1966) *Nyansongo: A Gusii Community in Kenya.*

Norbeck, Edward. (1954) *Takashima: A Japanese Fishing Community.*

Stephens, William N. (1963) *The Family in Cross-Cultural Perspective.*

Whiting, Beatrice B., and Carolyn Pope Edwards. (1988) *Children of Different Worlds: The Formation of Social Behavior.*

SEX DIFFERENCES

Across cultures, children display a number of characteristics that appear to vary with sex. Thus, girls exhibit behavior profiles that are to some extent similar from one society to the next and that are also different from the profiles exhibited by boys across cultures. These sex differences are the result of the interaction between the genes with which children come equipped and the environment in which the children find themselves. Thus, we find initial differences in genetically grounded biology and brain functioning between boys and girls that influence behavior and that appear in all societies. The biology and brain function of any boy or girl is also affected by environment, including the daily experience of the youngster and the child-rearing practices to which the youngster is exposed. This means that culture can deflect sex-typed behavior in one or another direction. But cultural influences can go only so far because the biology of the child is not infinitely flexible. After all, cultural influences are really influences on the biology of the child, that is, on the body and brain of the child which, in turn, underwrite the youngster's cognitive and behavioral functioning. Further, genetically grounded human sex differences are predicted to be somewhat resistant to major influences by the environment because sex differences are fundamental evolutionary human adaptations and, therefore, fundamental to the Darwinian fitness of the individual.

Infancy

Sex differences already begin to appear in the newborn. Male infants are typically larger and more muscular and have higher basal metabolism rates. They are more active and have a higher pain threshold. Boys remain awake longer and are harder to calm when fussy. Infant girls are more sensitive to touch than boys. Boys have slightly more acute vision, while girls have slightly better hearing at birth. Rates of development also differ for boys and girls, with females reaching puberty earlier than boys across cultures. Thus, for example, in Kenya, Gusii girls are two or three years younger than boys when they are initiated because girls "grow up more quickly" and are, therefore, ready to accept adult roles earlier. As a result, girls are already taking on adult chores by the time they are eight years old, while boys who have passed their tenth birthdays are still behaving like children.

Childhood

A number of sex differences in childhood also appear more or less predictably across cultures. Perhaps the most well-documented sex difference both in America and in other cultures is the greater degree of both verbal and physical aggression that is exhibited by males. The difference shows up in boys and girls at least by three years of age. In the Philippines, Tarong parents say that aggression is natural in boys but that girls should be better behaved than their male counterparts. Similarly, among the Palauans of Micronesia, adults say that girls are more even-tempered than boys. Thus, when a Palauan woman begins to show less indulgence toward her older children, she can expect her daughters to have fewer tantrums than her sons, and fits of temper are viewed as characteristic of males but not females in this society. In a number of cultures, boys also display more domineering behavior than do girls. They are also more likely than girls to respond to aggression with aggression and to seek attention and material goods. By contrast, girls are more inclined than boys to seek help and to seek and offer physical contact. Among the Banoi of Thailand, adults agree that boys are more frequently the targets of physical punishment because they are more stubborn and obstinate than girls. Similarly, men are viewed as the real troublemakers in Banoi society. By the time they are eight or nine years old, Tarong boys and girls respond differently to aggression on the part of peers. When asked what they would do if hit by another boy, males are likely to say that they will hit back. Females sometimes say that they would tease back in response to teasing from another girl, but they may also simply retreat and tell some adult about the incident. If a girl teases a boy, he will simply ignore her. And girls say that they would either ignore the teasing of a boy or tell on him.

Girls older than seven years are also more nurturant than are boys. For instance, Gusii females are more sociable, warm, and expressive than are males. And parents prefer to recruit girls as child nurses to care for younger infants. It may be that the young girl's experience as a caretaker contributes to the female profile of greater friendliness and nurturance. It may also be that an initial tendency on the part of girls to be nurturant is what makes them attractive to their mothers as baby tenders. Girls typically stay closer to their parents and other adults and remain closer to home than boys.

Across cultures, we also find that boys tend to be more self-assertive than girls, while girls, in turn, are more socially passive and submissive. Boys are often also more motivated to achieve. Girls tend to conform to the demands of others, and especially to those of adults. The Gusii observe that boys are more difficult for mothers to control than are girls. In Mexico, a Mixtecan girl will comply with her mother's request more quickly and consistently than her brother. A boy sometimes avoids obeying his mother's commands at all, and a mother will occasionally recruit her husband to discipline a recalcitrant son. While most Mixtecan mothers say that their daughters are obedient, most mothers also say that their sons do not obey them immediately if they obey at all. Tarong grandmothers are more likely to take a little granddaughter on a trip away from the neighborhood because "they behave better than the boys." Jamaican parents say that girls obey directions better than boys and that boys are harder to teach.

Sex differences are also evident in children's play patterns. Girls generally prefer to play with other girls and boys with boys. Girls tend to interact in small groups of two or three children, while boys prefer large groups. When girls play, they confine themselves to a relatively small area, while boys range more widely. Boys also maintain more personal space among themselves and other youngsters, and girls stand farther away from boys than from other girls.

Girls are often reported to be more responsible than boys. The Gusii make this claim with the result that, while herding is usually a boy's job, parents with no sons will recruit a daughter as a herder. Girls who look after the animals are much more responsible than boys, who are likely to run off to fish or catch birds when they should be tending the cattle. Girls are also more likely than boys to want to help their mothers in the garden.

In some cultures, sex differences are not salient. Thus, for example, the behavioral profiles of Mixtecan boys and girls are quite similar. Little girls are more nurturant than are boys, but even this difference begins to disappear as the children become older and boys start to display frequent nurturant responses.

Socialization of Sex Differences

We find some evidence that parents in different societies value and train different traits in girls and boys. For instance, Palauan parents keep a tighter hold on their daughters, and while mothers show considerably less indulgence to all children over five or so years of age, the separation of a girl from her mother is less abrupt than it is for her brother. In Liberia, Kpelle girls are expected to take on more responsibility than are boys of the same age, and they are also expected to control their impulses at earlier age. By contrast, everyone assumes that boys through six years of age will be aggressive and roughhouse with their peers. However, these differences are modest in comparison with the actual differences in sex-typed behavior that are also reported. Thus, across a variety of behaviors, including fortitude, aggression, self-reliance, industry, responsibility, and obedience, a majority of societies, and sometimes a very large majority, do not distinguish between boys and girls in their training practices. Where the sexes are treated differently, fortitude, aggression, and self-reliance are favored in boys, while girls are trained to be industrious, responsible, and obedient. Boys are pressured to achieve in a majority of cultures, while nurturance is stressed for girls.

In fact, we sometimes find that parents more strongly discourage children of a particular sex from engaging in just the behaviors that are more typical of their sex in fact. Thus, Gusii boys are more aggressive than are girls and are also punished more frequently for aggressive behavior. Nevertheless, in adulthood, women are less likely to be physically violent, although they are more verbally hostile than are males. The relatively high incidence of homicide and assault among Gusii males suggests that punishment for aggression in early life is not a dramatically effective way of curbing aggressive impulses. Among the Philippine Tarong, the Okinawan Taira, the Indian Rajputs, and the Mexican Mixtecans, no distinctions are made between boys and girls when it comes to training for responsibility, obedience, or aggression, but boys are more aggressive in these cultures, while girls are more responsible and obedient. In American culture, boys are punished more for aggression than are girls, but boys remain the more aggressive of the sexes. Among the Kalahari !Kung, parents do not expect girls to remain closer to home than boys, but girls, nevertheless, do not wander off the way that boys do. And across cultures, regardless of the attitudes of adults concerning independence in children, self-reliance inevitably comes with the acquisition of skills that allow a child to become somewhat independent from adults. Among the Truk of Micronesia, adolescents begin for the first time to be able to prepare their own food and are, therefore, no longer at the mercy of their mothers or other relatives when they are hungry. Boys and girls take great pride in this new self-reliance and like knowing that other members of the community are also aware of their new competence.

Where differences in the treatment of boys and girls do occur, they have further effects upon the daily experience of children. Kpelle girls have less freedom and are assigned more chores than are boys. They are also required to stay home with their mothers for a greater proportion of the day. As a result, girls are excluded from activities that involve leaving the house, and they play less with toys that demand mobility. Thus, boys ride in or pull homemade cars, but girls do not. Rather, they play at games that anticipate the chores that they will later do in earnest. Because Kpelle girls are assigned tasks at five or six years of age, they remain around adults to learn and then to help with chores. Boys, by contrast, are free from serious responsibility until they are ten or eleven. As a result, they spend much of their time in the company of peers. Similarly, in Africa, Swazi boys begin to herd the cattle at the age of six, and as they get older, bands of boys range far from home for much of the day while tending the animals. Girls, by contrast, draw water, gather wood, or plant in the fields with their mothers or age-mates and spend much of the day tending to household chores.

Companions

Across cultures, the behavior of children is in part influenced by the company that they keep.

A child who is interacting with a baby is likely to be nurturant. A child who is interacting with an adult is prone to display dependence. Finally, interactions with peers tend to evoke aggression in children. Further, certain behaviors are predictably inhibited in the presence of particular kinds of people. Children rarely exhibit aggression toward adults, nurturance toward peers, or dependence and aggression toward babies. If boys and girls tend to keep company with different categories of people, then sex differences may in part be a function of this difference. And in fact, girls are more frequently in the company of babies and younger children and of adult women. And as boys across cultures spend more time away from home, they may find themselves more often in the company of peers. These sex differences in targets of interaction may account in part for why boys are more aggressive than girls, while girls ask adults for help more often and display more nurturance toward others.

Correlates of Differential Training

Societies are most likely to socialize boys and girls for dramatically different traits when the subsistence base requires superior strength and superior development of motor skills requiring strength. In societies that accumulate food to be consumed later on, for instance in agricultural societies, the pressure on girls to be compliant is very strong. Further, the difference in expectations for boys and girls as regards compliance is large. In contrast, where the population does not accumulate food, for instance where the economy depends upon hunting and gathering, compliance is not stressed for either sex. Where women make a large contribution to the subsistence economy, as is true, for instance, in gathering and some kinds of farming societies, girls are trained to be industrious.

See also CHILDREN'S ACTIVITIES; CHORES; PARENTS' PREFERENCE FOR BOY OR GIRL; SEGREGATION OF GIRLS AND BOYS

Barnett, H. G. (1960) *Being a Palauan.*

Barry, Herbert, III, Margaret K. Bacon, and Irvin L. Child. (1957) "A Cross-Cultural Survey of Some Sex Differences in Socialization." *Journal of Abnormal and Social Psychology* 55: 327–332.

Barry, Herbert, III, Irvin L. Child, and Margaret K. Bacon. (1959) "Relation of Child Training to Subsistence Economy." *American Anthropologist* 61: 51–63.

Barry, Herbert, III, Lili Josephson, Edith Lauer, and Catherine Marshall. (1976) "Traits Inculcated in Childhood: Cross-Cultural Codes 5." *Ethnology* 15: 83–114.

Cohen, Yehudi A. (1966) *A Study of Interpersonal Relations in a Jamaican Community.*

Draper, Patricia. (1975) "Cultural Pressure on Sex Differences." *American Ethnologist* 2: 602–616.

Ember, Carol R. (1973) "Feminine Task Assignment and the Social Behavior of Boys." *Ethos* 1: 424–439.

Ember, Carol R. (1981) "A Cross-Cultural Perspective on Sex Differences." In *Handbook of Cross-Cultural Human Development,* edited by Ruth H. Munroe, Robert L. Munroe, and Beatrice B. Whiting, 531–580.

Erchak, Gerald M. (1977) *Full Respect: Kpelle Children in Adaptation.*

Kuper, Hilda. (1963) *The Swazi: A South African Kingdom.*

LeVine, Robert A., and Barbara B. LeVine. (1966) *Nyansongo: A Gusii Community in Kenya.*

Munroe, Robert L., and Ruth H. Munroe. (1975) *Cross-Cultural Human Development.*

Nydegger, William F., and Corinne Nydegger. (1966) *Tarong: An Ilocos Barrio in the Philippines.*

Piker, Steven. (1965) *An Examination of Character and Socialization in a Thai Peasant Community.*

Romney, A. Kimball, and Romaine Romney. (1966) *The Mixtecans of Juxtlahuaca, Mexico.*

Schlegel, Alice, and Herbert Barry III. (1986) "The Cultural Consequences of Female Contribution to Subsistence." *American Anthropologist* 88: 142–150.

Segall, Marshall H., Pierre R. Dasen, John W. Berry, and Ype H. Poortinga. (1990) *Human Behavior in Global Perspective.*

Whiting, Beatrice B., and Carolyn Pope Edwards. (1963) "A Cross-Cultural Analysis of Sex Differences in the Behavior of Children Aged Three through Eleven." *Journal of Social Psychology* 91: 171–188.

SEX (GENDER) IDENTITY

Sex identity refers to the individual's self-perception as a male or female. Related to sex identity is sex role acquisition, which refers to the taking on of traits identified with one or the other sex. The connections between sex identity and sex role acquisition are complicated. Thus, an individual may retain a solid sex identity as male or female but nevertheless display behaviors that are atypical of his or her own sex. Conversely, a person whose behavior profile matches the cultural prototype of his or her sex may, nevertheless, also display a shaky sex identity. Indeed, some theories propose that a male who is anxious about his sex identity may overcompensate by displaying hypermasculine behavior. Other theories predict a good fit between sex identity and sex-typed behavior.

Children do not initially form stable sex identities. That is, youngsters do not appreciate that gender is a permanent characteristic of individuals, including themselves. Two- and three-year-olds have already learned sex-typed linguistic labels such as boy, girl, man, and woman and can apply them correctly, but a youngster below three-and-one-half years does not yet understand that gender is constant. Thus, a young boy imagines that he can become a girl, and children of this age may think that alterations in clothing or hair style are enough to alter gender. Even an older child tends to believe that irrelevant characteristics of an individual such as hairstyle or behavior determine gender. It is not until children are around seven years of age that they come to appreciate that sex is determined by primary sex characteristics and that it is immutable across time and situation.

How do children eventually come to identify themselves as male or female? Some theorists propose that children acquire sex identities by imitating the behaviors of other people of their own sex and then being rewarded for displaying appropriate sex-typed behavior. The child then identifies with the sex whose behavior he or she has imitated. A related theory speculates that a child acquires a sex identity by imitating the behavior of people who are perceived to control desired resources. In this view, a child of either sex can identify with and adopt the behavior of either gender depending upon who is perceived as having power. A third theory claims that children first cognitively identify themselves as male or female independent of any behavior that they happen to display. Once a child has labeled himself or herself with the appropriate gender label, sex-typed behavior is adopted.

Theories that focus on imitation as the moving force behind sex identity acquisition emphasize the role of the father, especially as this affects the sex identity of boys. In particular, father-absence has been viewed as leading a little boy to identify initially with his mother as the most important model and also as the most powerful person in his life. As the boy grows older, he recognizes that he has misidentified with females. The mistake is regarded by him as especially serious if he lives in a society where males

have control over desired resources. Boys from father-absent households, and especially in cultures where men have the power, will then, according to this view, form a new identification with males. But because their first identification has been with females, they unconsciously overcompensate for the initial error by displaying hypermasculine behavior, including aggression, drinking, theft, crime, and emphasis on glory in warfare. In societies or families where males are not perceived as powerful, or where the roles of males and females are not different, father-absence is not predicted to lead to hypermasculine behavior. Rather, boys who have been raised without male role models in environments of this sort will retain a female sex identity as well as feminine behavior profiles, including high dependence, low assertiveness, low physical aggression, high verbal aggression, feminine game and sex-role preferences, and avoidance of activities involving physical contact.

It may be the case that boys who are raised without male role models display feminine behavior in their early childhood and then, in certain circumstances, begin to adopt extreme male sex-typed behaviors later on. However, the psychological mechanisms proposed to underlie these trends are not consistent with what we know about the cognitive functioning of young children. We have already established that very small children have no appreciation of gender constancy and do not identify themselves as having permanent membership in either sex. Therefore, at the time when boys are assumed to be forming an initial identification with females, young children are, in fact, forming no stable identification at all. More likely is the proposition that young boys are imitating the behavior of the model who happens to be most salient in their lives in the absence of a father. This is the mother. Later on, as boys get older, father-absence may lead to excessive aggression and the like simply because mothers have a harder time controlling the aggression normally displayed by boys. The world over, mothers complain that they are ineffective in obtaining obedience from their sons, and the world over, women warn their male children to "wait until your father gets home." The idea that sex-typed behavior is related to maternal behavior is supported by the finding that the manner in which the mother treats a boy in a father-absent household has an affect on the youngster's behavior. Thus, for example, where mothers pressure their sons to exhibit behaviors typically identified as masculine, boys do not exhibit the feminine profiles normally associated with father absence.

Sex-typed behavior appears to be the result not only of imitating available models, but also of the kinds of activities in which children are required to engage. In a study of the Luo, a community in Kenya, families that had more sons than daughters assigned boys tasks that were usually delegated to girls. These included baby tending, housekeeping, fetching water and wood, and milling flour. Boys who regularly undertook such chores were less likely to demand attention and were more likely to be sociable than other Luo boys. These are traits normally displayed by girls. The effect was especially apparent when a boy's tasks kept him inside the house. Baby tending was most likely to decrease aggressive attention seeking in boys. Moreover, this moderating affect of performing feminine chores showed up even when the boys were not specifically doing these tasks, so that the behaviors generalize, becoming an integral part of the child's behavior profile. While boys who were assigned to do work normally performed by their sisters were less egoistic and more sociable than other males, they were less so than the typical Luo girl.

See also SEX DIFFERENCES

Berk, Laura E. (1989) *Child Development.*

Burton, Roger V., and John W. M. Whiting. (1963) "The Absent Father and Cross-Sex Identity." In *Studies in Adolescence,* edited by Robert E. Grinder, 89–106.

Ember, Carol R. (1973) "Feminine Task Assignment and the Social Behavior of Boys." *Ethos* 1: 424–439.

Hitchcock, John T., and Leigh Minturn. (1966) *The Rajputs of Khalapur, India.*

Munroe, Robert L., and Ruth H. Munroe. (1975) *Cross-Cultural Human Development.*

Stephens, William N. (1962) *The Oedipal Complex: Cross-Cultural Evidence.*

SEX TABOO, POSTPARTUM

In a number of places the world over, cultural tradition prohibits a woman from engaging in sexual intercourse for a designated period of time after the birth of a baby. This prohibition is known as the postpartum sex taboo and occurs in 85 percent of 151 societies. The length of the postpartum taboo varies across cultures. In 69 percent of the 151 societies, the postpartum sex taboo lasts for a year or less. An additional 14 percent of societies with a postpartum sex taboo prohibit sexual intercourse for a husband and wife for from one to two years. The remaining 17 percent restrict sexual activity for more than two years. In Canada, a Hare husband should not sleep with his wife while she is pregnant or for eight days after she has given birth. Otherwise, he will have bad luck when hunting. Jamaican couples are expected to wait eighteen days after a birth before resuming sexual intercourse. In fact, most husbands and wives wait longer than this, the average period of abstention being from one to three months. This is partly because women become pregnant quickly, and worry that "it won't look good" when a new baby appears nine months after the last one. A couple that already has more children than desired tries to wait much longer, and perhaps as much as a year, before having sexual intercourse. In Micronesia, Truk mothers are supposed to refrain from engaging in sexual intercourse until the baby is weaned or can walk, but many women only wait until the baby can crawl around a bit. The husband and wife still sleep together during the taboo period. Some societies have no explicit postpartum sex taboo. Thus, for example, there is no formal postpartum sex taboo among the polygynous Gusii of Kenya, although a husband who has more than one wife is likely to stay with a spouse who is not nursing an infant. In some societies with no formal taboo, a woman is actually expected to engage in sexual intercourse soon after the birth of her child.

Extended prohibitions on sexual intercourse for women who have had a baby tend to be found in societies that depend upon root crops for their primary food source. This means that the diets of people in cultures with a long taboo are low in protein. One explanation for a long taboo suggests that the prohibition allows women to provide a high-protein food supply for their babies. As a woman who abstains from sexual intercourse for an extended period of time will not have to nurse babies in rapid succession, her newest infant will have exclusive access to protein-rich milk for a few years. In this view, the long postpartum sex taboo may be a response to a society's ecological, and thus dietary, profile.

The idea that sexual abstinence on the part of a new mother is good for the baby is reflected in the beliefs of cultures that enforce the postpartum sex taboo. Among the Rajputs of India, women are supposed to observe a postpartum sex taboo of from two to three years because the resumption of sexual intercourse will make the mother's milk go bad, causing her baby to become sickly. The habits of older couples appear to conform to this rule, but younger couples are less likely to avoid having sexual relations for the entire two-year period. In Guatemala, a Chimalteco husband and wife may sleep together for the twenty days of a woman's confinement after the birth of their baby. But they cannot have sexual intercourse. To do so would invalidate the prayers that the diviner says during this period on behalf of the health and long life of the baby.

Barry, Herbert, III, and Leonora M. Paxson. (1972) "Infancy and Early Childhood: Cross-Cultural Codes 2." *Ethnology* 10: 466–508.

Cohen, Yehudi A. (1966) *A Study of Interpersonal Relations in a Jamaican Community.*

Gladwin, Thomas, and Seymour Sarason. (1953) *Truk: Man in Paradise.*

Hara, Hiroko Sue. (1967) *Hare Indians and Their World.*

Hitchcock, John T., and Leigh Minturn. (1966) *The Rajputs of Khalapur, India.*

LeVine, Robert L., and Barbara B. LeVine. (1966) *Nyanongo: A Gusii Community in Kenya.*

Levinson, David, and Martin J. Malone. (1980) *Toward Explaining Human Culture.*

Wagley, Charles. (1949) "The Social and Religious Life of a Guatemalan Village." *American Anthropologist* 51: 3–150.

SEXUAL BEHAVIOR Cultures differ widely in the degree to which they tolerate sex play on the part of children. Adults may encourage or at least tolerate sexual experimentation, and they may even play with a baby's genitals while the infant is being nursed, bathed, or held. In other cultures, sex play is discouraged, and boys and girls may even be kept apart as insurance against sexual experimentation. Societies also differ regarding how children learn about sex and how much sex education they receive. Children in some cultures grow up largely ignorant of biological and sexual functions, while in others they are explicitly instructed about sex. Because the living arrangements in many cultures do not afford a married couple any privacy, children in many societies learn about sex simply by observing the activities of older people.

Sex Play

Among the Cubeo of the Northwest Amazon, mothers encourage babies to play with their own genitals, and a woman often pats a boy infant's genitals "to give him pleasure." Similarly, in Thailand, a Banoi mother habitually strokes her son's genitals while he is nursing, when he is fussy, or just because she wishes to show him affection, as do other female relatives, although less often. Touching of a boy's genitals usually stops when the child is around three years and more certainly by the time he is seven or eight. A woman will less commonly pat the genitals of a daughter, in part because mothers think that it will cause a girl to become a prostitute. Men never play with a baby's genitals. In Micronesia, Truk adults play with an infant's genitals, and touching of their own genitals by young children is ignored or regarded with amusement, even when it is done in front of other people who will later become sexually taboo to the youngster. This permissiveness derives from a more general attitude on the part of the Truk that little children are not yet full-fledged individuals. In China, Manchu mothers tickle the genitals of their little daughters and suck the penis of a small son.

Just as adults in some cultures think nothing of playing with the genitals of an infant, grown-ups may also be permissive about the sex play of children themselves. In India, Baiga adults may tell children who are engaging in sex play to wait a while. But they regard such behavior as harmless. Children play games like Pig and Sow, Cow and Bull, and Horse and Mare when they are in the fields or forest, and a youngster's first sexual experience may occur in the course of playing Houses, a game in which a boy and girl pair off and build a small hut of leaves and branches in the jungle. Similarly, Lesu children imitate the sexual behavior of adults in public, standing face to face with their genitals touching. Adults view such play as natural. Sometimes, youngsters will go off into the bush, which they know to be the preferred setting for sexual activity among their elders. Among the Javanese of Indonesia, no one minds if young children handle their own genitals. North American Navajo adults regarded sex as a natural function. They were not bothered when little boys and girls touched their own bodies. In Polynesia, Pukapuka children up to 12 years of age can regularly be seen handling their genitals in public, and adults regard this behavior as a game that comes naturally to children. Masturbation or sex play on the part of young Mexican Mixtecan children is treated casually, although by the time a child is seven years old, these behaviors are ridiculed by an adult who happens to witness them.

In other cultures, sex play is not tolerated. Sometimes, adults who disapprove of sexual experimentation on the part of children are the same adults who approve of playing with a child's genitals in infancy. Among the Truk, genuine masturbation is not tolerated even in little children, and it becomes more harshly punished in older ones. In Kenya, Gusii children are punished for showing any interest in sex. But youngsters still use obscene language when adults are not around and engage in other kinds of sex play. Similarly, Irish adults condemn any behaviors in children that are even indirectly sexual in nature. Touching of one's own or another person's body is forbidden, nor is a child allowed to use any word that refers to a sexual organ or function.

While Banoi adults play with the genitals of infants, they also say that it is shameful for children to touch themselves, and parents say that they would move or slap the hand of the offending child, although they rarely do so in fact. Among the Taira of Okinawa, children do not appear to engage in sex play of any sort, although little boys may show off by urinating in front of each other. Adults do not approve of this kind of behavior. Little girls are trained to avoid exposing their genitals, and a boy may tease some little girl by yelling at her that her vagina is showing. By the time children are old enough to attend school, any mention of genitals is embarrassing. As they get older, boys and girls begin to congregate more exclusively in same-sex groups, so that opportunities for heterosexual sex play in any event diminish. Most Truk children begin to experiment with sex when they are approaching adolescence. Such experimentation is regarded with disapproval because sexual activity at this age is assumed to make a child sick. By contrast, it is all right for children past puberty to engage in heterosexual behavior.

Sex Education

In some cultures, children do not receive any sex education from adults. Gusii parents do not educate their children about sex. Boys are punished for attempting to have sexual intercourse with a girl, and parents, perhaps because of their reluctance to talk explicitly about sex, treat sexual misdemeanors essentially as acts of aggression. In the Philippines, Tarong parents are not self-conscious about sexual matters, but neither do they instruct their children about sex. Children with questions are likely to be ignored or told that they should not be asking about "foolish things." Adults say that it is not necessary to teach children about sex because they all know about it anyway. Banoi parents say that they would be ashamed to talk about sex with their children, nor do they think that youngsters need to be taught about sex. Rather, they believe that

children have innate knowledge about sexual matters and that adolescents begin to act upon this knowledge without any help from adults. A mother may inform her young daughter that she will eventually grow up, become pregnant, and have children, but this is the extent of the information that she provides. As a result, Banoi adolescents do not know much about sex, and a girl may be entirely ignorant about menstruation until she starts to menstruate herself or notices blood on the skirt of another girl and begins to ask questions. Youngsters may pick up some details about sexual matters by actually watching their mothers having babies, but children nevertheless misunderstand basic facts about childbirth, some thinking that babies are born though the navel or anus. If a youngster asks a direct question about childbirth, a parent will answer truthfully, but children do not discuss sexual intercourse with their parents. In Japan, Takashima adults do not teach their children about sex, and people say that a girl's first menstrual period comes as a surprise. Youngsters pick up bits and pieces of information and misinformation about sex from other children starting in early childhood. As children sleep in the same room as their parents and as houses are crowded, they also learn by observation. Many Jamaican parents want to inform their children about sexual matters but find that they are too embarrassed to do so. Sometimes, pairs of women agree to instruct each other's daughters, and women discover that the embarrassment about sex that they experience with their own children disappears. No one thinks to tell a boy about sex. Sons only need to be warned about the consequences of sexual activity.

By contrast, in some cultures, children pick up information about sex by listening to the conversation of adults. And in some cultures, there is a conscious attempt to transfer information about sex to young people. Lesu adults discuss sex, tell obscene stories, and exchange gossip in front of children, who come to have a good understanding of sexual matters as a result. North American Papago children learned a good deal about sex from the constant chatter and joking about reproductive processes that buzzed around them. In North America, Navaho girls were explicitly instructed and advised about sex by older female relatives sometime before puberty, and the father or mother's brother would also talk to a boy.

Children in many cultures also acquire an education about sex from other children. In India, Gond youngsters learn about sexual techniques in the *ghotul,* the mixed-sex sleeping quarters where young people reside. Older boys teach younger boys and older girls younger ones, but sometimes a big girl will show a younger boy of whom she is fond the skills associated with sexual intercourse. Haitian children similarly learn about sex by experimenting with one another, despite the disapproval of parents. African Mbuti children play house as soon as they can walk. They imitate the typical household routine and, when their pretend chores are done, the playmates lie down and act out sexual intercourse. Among the Alor of Indonesia, groups of boys and girls sometimes play in the field houses together, copying the sexual activities of their parents.

Children also engage in sexual sport with other youngsters of their own sex. Among the games that New Guinea Kwoma boys play together is one in which one youngster throws the other down and pretends to copulate with him. Another boy will then climb onto the original aggressor and simulate copulation, and more boys will line up and pile onto the heap, all the while laughing and screaming gleefully. One boy will call another his wife and say that he has made 'her' pregnant. Adolescents also like to join the game.

Cohen, Yehudi A. (1966) *A Study of Interpersonal Relations in a Jamaican Community.*

DuBois, Cora. (1944) *The People of Alor.*

Elwin, Verrier. (1939) *The Baiga.*

———. (1947) *The Muria and Their Ghotul.*

Geertz, Hildred. (1961) *The Javanese Family: A Study of Kinship and Socialization.*

Gladwin, Thomas, and Seymour Sarason. (1953) *Truk: Man in Paradise.*

Goldman, Irving. (1963) *The Cubeo: Indians of the Northwest Amazon.*

Herskovitz, Melville. (1937) *Life in a Haitian Valley.*

Leighton, Dorothea, and Clyde Kluckhohn. (1969) *Children of the People.*

LeVine, Robert A., and Barbara B. LeVine. (1966) *Nyansongo: A Gusii Community in Kenya.*

Maretzki, Thomas W., and Hatsumi Maretzki. (1966) *Taira: An Okinawan Village.*

Messenger, John C. (1971) "Sex and Repression in an Irish Folk Community." In *Human Sexual Behavior,* edited by Donald S. Marshall and Robert C. Suggs, 3–37.

Munroe, Robert L., and Ruth H. Munroe. (1975) *Cross-Cultural Human Development.*

Norbeck, Edward. (1954) *Takashima: A Japanese Fishing Village.*

Nydegger, William F., and Corinne Nydegger. (1966) *Tarong: An Ilocos Barrio in the Philippines.*

Piker, Steven. (1965) *An Examination of Character and Socialization in a Thai Peasant Community.*

Powdermaker, Hortense. (1933) *Life in Lesu: A Study of Melanesian Society in New Ireland.*

Romney, A. Kimball, and Romaine Romney. (1966) *The Mixtecans of Juxtlahuaca, Mexico.*

Shirokogoroff, S. M. (1924) *The Social Organization of the Manchus.*

Turnbull, Colin M. (1965) *Wayward Servants: The Two Worlds of the African Pygmies.*

Underhill, Ruth. (1936) *The Autobiography of a Papago Woman.*

Underhill, Ruth. (1939) *Social Organization of the Papago Indians.*

Whiting, John W. M. (1941) *Becoming a Kwoma.*

Whiting, John W. M., and Irvin L. Child. (1953) *Child Training and Personality.*

SHARING

Sharing is viewed as a desirable trait in both children and adults in many cultures around the world. Therefore, parents are motivated to teach their children to share possessions, food, and other resources that the youngsters themselves value and would rather keep. Nevertheless, parents across cultures find that it is hard to persuade children to share. Apparently, the need to be generous with one's own prized possessions is a hard lesson for children to learn.

The Tarong of the Philippines depend upon the good will and concrete help of other people on a daily basis, so that cooperation and sharing are highly valued traits. Children, therefore, are taught early to share, and adults will tease a youngster mercilessly until the child finally capitulates and shares some desired item with playmates. Tarong youngsters quickly learn that sharing is a necessary part of life, but children also learn to squirrel away any treasured object that they do not wish to share. Similarly, in Micronesia, the Truk social system depends upon sharing between members of the same lineage, with the result that children begin to be taught to share items of food and so on. Youngsters do this grudgingly, and sometimes they will lie about having food to avoid sharing. Thus, when one boy asked his younger brother whether there was any food in the house, the smaller boy said no.

Later, when the elder sibling discovered that his brother had been lying and asked him why he had said that there was no food, the younger child said that he had wanted to eat it all by himself. For that response, he got a beating from the older boy. Truk children cannot be trusted to share voluntarily with each other. One child may eat all of the prized coconut meat, leaving the other child only some of the milk. The Guadalcanal Kaoka regard generosity as one of the cardinal virtues, and parents attempt to train children to share even before the youngsters can understand what is being asked of them. Thus, a two-year-old will be given a piece of fruit and then commanded to give half of the food to this or that person. The lesson is not easily learned, and even after two years of persuasion, a child still gives up possessions reluctantly. A youngster may, for instance, hide nuts that his mother has given him so that another child will not see them. A parent who witnesses this kind of behavior will try to reason with the child, telling him not to be greedy and explaining that a person must think of others if he wants to be respected by the rest of the community. At meals, children may be asked to face everyone else while eating to insure that they are not taking too much for themselves. One child may be sent off to invite another in to a meal, and adults regularly require children to serve food to some visitor, the idea being that a child who habitually served as a waiter would learn to be generous. Older children do learn the lesson and typically share food without thinking about it. But even years of training are not sufficient to make a child who is hungry or who has become the owner of some treat happily share with some other person. In Japan, Takashima children who live in the same household often quarrel over toys or other possessions. Adults expect the older child to give in on such occasions. Many American parents regard sharing as an important quality in children because sharing is consistent with the sense of fairness and egalitarianism that American adults also value and wish their children to respect. Nevertheless, parents find themselves mediating battles between siblings who are acting selfishly by refusing to share toys, take turns, and so on.

The difficulties experienced by parents across cultures as they attempt to instill a sharing ethic in their children have been replicated by psychologists in the laboratory. Studies have shown that young children will not willingly share in return for praise, pats and hugs, and other nonmaterial reinforcements unless they are being asked to give up something of minimal value. By contrast, three- and four-year-olds will share such items as marbles if they are given something of value, such as bubble gum. It is not really surprising that children do not like to share without good reason. Sharing confers a benefit on some other person that he or she would otherwise not enjoy. Evolutionary theory reminds us that natural selection would not favor organisms, including human beings, who sacrificed for the benefit of others. Given two individuals, one who made such a sacrifice and one who did not, the individual who avoided sacrifices would have a better chance of surviving and reproducing and, therefore, of passing down those genes that underwrote the tendency to withhold valued resources from others. Evolutionary theory also tells us that individuals will make short-term sacrifices for a net gain. And even children will give in order to get. Thus, parents across cultures would have an easier time persuading their children to share if they did not expect the sharing to mean a net loss for the child.

Fischer, W. F. (1963) "Sharing in Prechool Children as a Function of Amount and Type of Reinforcement." *Genetic Psychology Monographs* 68: 215–245.

Gladwin, Thomas, and Seymour Sarason. (1953) *Truk: Man in Paradise.*

Harper, Lawrence. (1989) *The Nurture of Human Behavior.*

Hogbin, Ian. (1964) *A Guadalcanal Society: The Kaoka Speakers.*

Norbeck, Edward. (1954) *Takashima: A Japanese Fishing Village.*

Nydegger, William F., and Corinne Nydegger. (1966) *Tarong: An Ilocos Barrio in the Philippines.*

Whiting, Beatrice B., and Carolyn Pope Edwards. (1988) *Children of Different Worlds: The Formation of Social Behavior.*

SIBLING RIVALRY

With the exception of last-born children, most youngsters the world over eventually find themselves supplanted by a newborn brother or sister. Older siblings typically resent this displacement and they may express their anger and jealousy by becoming demanding and clingy and by physically assaulting the new baby. Mothers may make efforts to minimize the strain placed upon older siblings when a new baby arrives. Or a woman may show little sympathy when children display jealousy of a new sibling.

Among the Gusii of Kenya, children display their distress at being displaced by a new baby. Suddenly, there is an infant in bed with mother, where the older child is used to sleeping. The older sibling may then refuse to sleep in the mother's house and find another place to stay for a few nights. When she is going on a long trip, a mother prepares to take along the new baby but leave the older sibling behind. When the displaced child cries bitterly and insists on going along too, as will typically happen, the mother is very likely to cane the protesting youngster. Gusii mothers punish an older sibling who cries while a new baby is being held or carried because the protest is taken as a display of *okoema*, or murderous jealousy, which is strongly condemned in Gusii society. Because Gusii mothers are irritated by children who cry when they are neither hurt nor hungry, persistent weeping or tantrums in the sibling of a newborn infant is met with serious punishment or threats that are soon successful in silencing children. Gusii mothers also try to distract older siblings and therefore diminish the distress that the older child feels at the appearance of a new baby by recruiting them to do various chores. The oldest child will bring food prepared by a co-wife or mother-in-law to the mother during her lying-in period. Youngsters will also be asked to chase chickens away from drying foods, to carry things from one adult to another, or to help the older boys with the herding. Among the Tairans of Okinawa, the arrival of a new baby is enormously trying for an older sibling. Formerly, the youngster has been carried on the backs of his or her caretakers. Suddenly, the same child is ridiculed and punished for wanting to be picked up. Children now turn whiny, tyrannical, and sullen. Weaning from the back takes place at the same time as does weaning from the breast, so the youngster has to adjust to simultaneous dethronements. Such children may be seen screaming and throwing stones and dirt at family members or other adults who have approached them. This kind of behavior, however, no longer evokes the nurturance from others that it once did. Instead, the child is told to stop crying and is left behind by irritated and impatient caretakers. People ridicule such youngsters for their babyish behavior. These attempts to gain attention, which prove in any case to be ineffective, diminish after a few months. Jamaican mothers rarely show physical affection to their youngsters, and even what occasional contact a child does receive is cut off by the arrival of a new infant. Parents are aware that older siblings "feel neglected" when attention is diverted to a baby brother or sister.

The appearance of a new infant in the household can disrupt the lives of older children in a variety of practical ways. In Taira, visitors steadily stream in and out of a household where there is a new baby. An older child feels special during this time and goes out of the way to announce to everyone that he or she has a new sibling. Friends are jealous when the older brother or sister is finally allowed to carry the baby around and play with it. As the household settles down to its normal routine and the older sibling is expected to help with routine baby tending, however, the excitement and pride associated with having a new baby in the house begins to fade and the older child may try to avoid having to take care of the infant. In Thailand, a new Banoi baby gets clearly preferential treatment from adults, who shower the infant with attention and attempt to satisfy any of its desires. Older siblings, by contrast, receive little attention and are themselves expected to indulge the whims of their youngest sibling. An older sister who is playing with a toy is required to give it up to her baby brother if he indicates a desire for it. A child whose mother is busy tending to an infant will typically be ignored despite repeated attempts to get her attention. Older children often have to repeat requests a number of times before being acknowledged by a parent, in contrast to babies, whose fussing attracts immediate responses on the part of caretakers. The frustration of the older child is reflected in numerous aggressive acts toward the youngest sibling. The problem is especially acute for second youngest children, who continue for some time to try to reinstate their former status as the center of attention. Older siblings have usually given up any hope of being coddled and have begun, instead, to adopt more adult roles. This is especially true of older sisters who, instead of interfering with a baby sibling, will exhibit a good deal of indulgence toward the baby. Older sisters also frequently try to comfort younger siblings whose attempts to get attention from the mother have been rebuffed.

Jealous older siblings may express their anger through violence directed at the new baby. An older Guatemalan Chimalteco child will often hit a new sibling and throw things at it. Some mothers do not like to punish this kind of behavior. They may simply slap the older child gently on the back of the head. In Japan, a Takashima child commonly throws temper tantrums when a new sibling arrives, and the older child may try to push the baby off the mother's lap. Takashima women expect this kind of behavior and regard it as natural. If the older child has a grandmother or older sister, one of these may be recruited to take over the care of the youngster for a while, and the jealousy of the older sibling more or less disappears. But sibling jealousy does not always end in aggression toward the younger child. In spite of the anger and anxiety that Tairan youngsters feel at the introduction of a new baby into the household, an older sibling does not display aggression toward a baby brother or sister and, in fact, the infant is treated with affection and nurturance even by a youngster who has just been weaned because of the arrival of the new sibling. Rather, any resentment that the displaced child feels is directed toward the mother. Similarly, when Tarong children show frustration at being weaned, they do not direct their anger at the new baby who has displaced them. Rather, their anger is reserved for the mother herself. Indian Rajput children do not typically exhibit any hostility toward a new baby. This may be true for a number reasons. First, adults do not display much affection to children, so older children are not likely to feel that they are suddenly being deprived of attention. Further, when not actively fussing, an infant is placed out of the way in a crib to sleep, so there is not much cuddling and attention directed toward babies for older sibling to envy. Finally, as Rajput households consist of parents, aunts, uncles, siblings, and cousins, there are many people who can fill in for a busy new mother, and there are many other children who have also had the experience of being displaced by a new baby. So older siblings have a number of sources of practical and emotional support when a new brother or sister arrives on the scene.

Hostility resulting from jealousy over a new baby can be ongoing. When a Jamaican family has multiple children, any child is likely to be in an aggressive relationship with some of his or her siblings. But siblings do not form larger coalitions against each other. Thus, rivalries only tend to occur between a child and the next oldest and next youngest brother or sister. Children who are in a rivalrous relationship can be openly aggressive toward each other. Siblings may try to poke out each other's eyes, take things from one another, or simply engage in fist fights. These disputes are quickly disrupted by a parent, who flogs the children. A sibling will remain silent while another takes the blame and punishment for the bad behavior of the first one. In contrast to these hostile relationships, siblings who are not adjacent to each other in age display a good deal of affection for each other, and the greater the number of other siblings that separate them, the more this fondness shows up.

In some cultures, mothers take pains to minimize sibling jealousy when a new baby is expected. Japanese mothers know that the birth of a new baby can lead to jealousy and resentment on the part of siblings, and they work hard before the arrival of the infant to minimize the problem. Children are told that they will soon have a real doll in the house instead of a pretend baby. The mother reminds them that they will now be able to sleep with their father. Youngsters help to prepare for the new baby. As a result of these efforts on the part of the mother, children are generally excited about the coming of a new sibling. Occasional bouts of jealousy, however, still occur, so that a youngster may pick up the new baby and walk off with it with the intention of giving it away. Mothers expect scenes of this sort, and persist in trying to change a jealous child's attitude. Thus, a woman might remind older siblings that the baby likes them and that they are needed to help care for the infant.

See also SIBLINGS

Benedict, Ruth. (1946) *The Chrysanthemum and the Sword.*

Cohen, Yehudi A. (1966) *A Study of Interpersonal Relations in a Jamaican Community.*

Gladwin, Thomas, and Seymour Sarason. (1953) *Truk: Man in Paradise.*

Hitchcock, John T., and Leigh Minturn. (1966) *The Rajputs of Khalapur, India.*

LeVine, Robert A., and Barbara B. LeVine. (1966) *Nyansongo: A Gusii Community in Kenya.*

Maretzki, Thomas W., and Hatsumi Maretzki. (1966) *Taira: An Okinawan Village.*

Norbeck, Edward. (1954) *Takashima: A Japanese Fishing Community.*

Nydegger, William F., and Corinne Nydegger. (1966) *Tarong: An Ilocos Barrio in the Philippines.*

Piker, Steven. (1965) *An Examination of Character and Socialization in a Thai Peasant Community.*

Wagley, Charles. (1949) "The Social and Religious Life of a Guatemalan Village." *American Anthropologist* 51: 3–150.

SIBLINGS

Virtually all children the world over have brothers and sisters. Sometimes, siblings serve as a child's primary playmates along with cousins who may happen to live close by. Parents across cultures face the common dilemma of how to promote amiable interactions between siblings in the face of the inevitable fights in which brothers and sisters engage. Sibling relationships are often close and sometimes represent a person's closest tie during an entire lifetime. In some cultures, however, customs require that siblings remain distant from one another. Older brothers and sisters may torment younger ones, but they also tend to be protective of their smaller siblings when strange children threaten them, reflecting the special connection that prevails between siblings in societies around the world.

Fighting

Fighting between siblings is frequently reported across cultures. Jamaican youngsters are not allowed to play with neighborhood children, nor are they permitted to range far from home. This means that their only companions are siblings, all of whom spend most of the day in the back yard. In the course of the day, siblings inevitably get into quarrels, chasing each other, stealing things from one another, and starting fistfights. Parents are quick to stop these squabbles, and siblings, as a consequence, end up off on their own instead of playing together. North American Chippewa parents might ignore a quarrel between siblings, or they might whip the children or send them away from the house.

Younger and Older Siblings

In some cultures, older siblings are expected to be indulgent toward smaller brothers and sisters. For instance, Javanese parents in Indonesia expect an older sibling to give in to the whims of a younger one, and in a quarrel between siblings, the older one is held accountable, even if the difference in age between the two is not large. Among the Banoi of Thailand, siblings habitually fight with each other until sometime during adolescence. Parental attempts to mediate these squabbles are for the most part ineffective. Mothers interpret these fights as reflections of temporary hatred between the children. Women also acknowledge that it is usually the younger child who begins the fight by attempting to boss around the older sibling. But the older children bear the brunt of the blame anyway because, as mothers say, they should know better. Thus, older children should have enough self-restraint to give in to the demands of the younger child in the same way that adults respond to the imperious behavior of young children with indulgence. In other cultures, mothers expect older children to enjoy more privileges than their younger siblings. This is especially likely in families where the mother's workload is heavy and older siblings are responsible for tending younger ones. Among the Gusii of Kenya, an older sister may slap a younger one, kick dirt in her face, and insult her without interference even though the mother is present. Truk siblings sometimes exhibit antagonism toward one another. Older siblings may beat up younger ones, and a child may withhold food from a hungry brother or sister. Often across cultures, older children are also expected to stick up for smaller brothers and sisters. Among the Truk of Micronesia, siblings can be aggressive and selfish with one another. But they also understand that siblings stick up for each other and help each other out in the face of trouble from other children.

Close Relationships between Siblings

In many societies, the relationship between siblings is close, with each sibling depending upon the other for emotional as well as concrete support throughout life. Among the Javanese, older brothers and sisters are recruited to take care of the baby in the family, and the child nurses display considerable fondness for their younger siblings. In the Philippines, a Tarong man will depend upon his older siblings, and especially his oldest brother or sister, in the same way that

he would depend upon a parent. A man who does not have a brother will establish an equivalent relationship with a near relative who is a leader of his kin group. A North American Comanche boy typically formed a very close relationship with one of his brothers. The two regularly helped each other, and the elder brother watched over the younger one and gave him advice. The connection between the brothers remained intact during adulthood, even to the extent that one man would lend the other his wife and expect the favor to be returned at a later date. Sometimes, friends formalized their relationship as one between brothers, in which case they were expected to treat one another as real siblings. A Jamaican child typically becomes embroiled in hostile relationships with the next oldest and next youngest sibling. But other siblings are openly fond of each other, and the more separated in age the youngsters, the greater the show of affection. This affection is demonstrated by gifts of food from older brothers and sisters to younger ones in a society where children are chronically underfed. Among the Arapaho, brothers were felt to be responsible for their sisters. A girl's eldest brother consented to her marriage and gave her advice. In turn, a brother looked to his mother's eldest brother for guidance. If an Arapaho girl did her brother a favor, he was expected to give her a gift in return. A sister who wanted a tent or a horse might do something for her brother, causing him to be indebted to her. Girls might also make important sacrifices for a brother. The story is told of a sister who, at the age of 16, cut off the first joint of her little finger to get her brother released from jail. Among the Javanese, older siblings take care of younger ones as soon as they appear responsible enough to do so, and the relationship between a sister and the younger brother to whom she has tended in childhood remains close when they are grown. Indeed, the Javanese say that older sisters, like mothers, love their younger brothers unconditionally. Among

A young Indian girl holds her baby brother.

the African Nyoro, brothers form corporate groups in adulthood, and brothers are expected to stick together and help each other out. Sisters do not form any kind of corporate group in adulthood, and as a result, while sisters often remain friends as adults, there is no sense of "sisterhood" as there is of "brotherhood." Nyoro brothers and sisters also remain close as adults. They confide in each other, including about sexual matters, and a brother may call his sister "wife" in jest as it may be the bridewealth paid at her marriage that pays for his bride. Cultures may also adopt customs that promote a sibling like relationship between children living in the same household who are not true siblings. In Uganda, when two of a Sebei man's wives give birth to boys at more or less the same time, a ceremony is conducted to cement a friendship between the children. Half-brothers who are about the same age are viewed as similar in many ways to twins.

Avoidance between Siblings

In some societies, a close relationship between siblings is prohibited. In Polynesia, Tongan brothers and sisters are expected to avoid each other as a sign of respect. This avoidance relationship is also maintained by people who call each other brother and sister. Siblings of the opposite sex may not gossip or quarrel between or about each other. They are prohibited from sleeping in the same house, drinking from the same coconut, eating the same dish of food, or wearing one another's clothing. Restrictions on the behavior of brothers and sisters were formerly even more extreme. Avoidance customs are first observed when a girl begins to menstruate and remain in place until the siblings reach an advanced age. Similarly, at sexual maturity, Truk brothers and sisters are expected to avoid references to sexual matters or to elimination, and even other people are prohibited from speaking of such things when a brother and sister are present. Brothers and sisters cannot sleep in the same house, which means that boys move

out of their natal household sometime around puberty. Sometimes, the brother remains in the same house as his sister, but in that case, he sleeps at the other end of the house or in a separate room. But ideally, he should find some other place to live, for instance with some relative, until he marries. And beginning at puberty, Truk boys are expected to be respectful toward their older brothers. A male cannot use vulgar humor in front of an elder brother nor can he intrude upon the older man. Among the North American Arapaho, small brothers and sisters bathed and swam together and teased and fought with each other. They were each other's friends and playmates. At puberty, all of this changed. Brothers and sisters no longer spoke except when required to do so, and then only in a respectful manner. Sisters were prohibited from looking at their brothers, so a girl cast her eyes downward when talking to a brother. If one sibling had to communicate something to another, the preferred method was to find a younger child to act as go-between. Brothers and sisters now played separately. Nor were they allowed to be in the same room, and a sister left any room or refrained from entering if a brother of hers was there. These restrictions were finally lifted in old age. As the Arapaho referred not only to siblings but also to cousins as "brother" and "sister," cross-sex avoidance was extended to cousins of the opposite sex. In Liberia, Kpelle brothers and sisters are also expected to avoid each other while they are still living under the same roof. A boy who is approaching puberty cannot play with his sister, sit on her bed, hold her hand, enter her room, or shout at her.

Sibling relationships can be aloof even when there are no formal customs prohibiting a close connection. The relationship between Kpelle brothers is strained. Brothers compete for their father's attention, and the oldest brother inherits his father's wives, resulting also in sexual jealousy between the boys. Similarly, once they leave home, Jamaican siblings do not interact with each other any more than they do with unrelated neighbors, and contact between neighbors is in fact minimal.

Beaglehole, Ernest, and Pearl Beaglehole. (1941) *Pangai: Village in Tonga.*

Beattie, John. (1960) *Bunyoro: An African Kingdom.*

Cohen, Yehudi A. (1966) *A Study of Interpersonal Relations in a Jamaican Community.*

Erchak, Gerald M. (1977) *Full Respect: Kpelle Children in Adaptation.*

Geertz, Hildred. (1961) *The Javanese Family: A Study of Kinship and Socialization.*

Gladwin, Thomas, and Seymour Sarason. (1953) *Truk: Man in Paradise.*

Goldschmidt, Walter. (1976) *The Culture and Behavior of the Sebei.*

Hilger, M. Inez. (1951) *Chippewa Child Life and Its Cultural Background.*

Nydegger, William F., and Corinne Nydegger. (1966) *Tarong: An Ilocos Barrio in the Philippines.*

Piker, Steven. (1965) *An Examination of Character and Socialization in a Thai Peasant Community.*

Wallace, Ernest, and E. Adamson Hoebel. (1952) *The Comanches: Lords of the South Plains.*

Whiting, Beatrice B., and Carolyn Pope Edwards. (1988) *Children of Different Worlds: The Formation of Social Behavior.*

SLEEPING

In vast the majority of societies around the world, children do not sleep in a room of their own. Often, children share a bed with other members of the family. It is even more unusual for an infant to sleep alone. Thus, of 139 societies, none places a baby in a room of its own. An infant sleeps in its mother's bed in at least 45 percent of these cultures and in the same room as its mother in the remaining societies. The father also shares a bed with a baby in at least 14 percent of the 139 societies and sleeps in a different room or house in only 12 percent of the cultures. Typically, other members of the family also share a bed or room. Mothers and babies are more likely to sleep in the same bed where the climate is consistently warm. Where the temperature falls below freezing, a baby more commonly sleeps in a crib, cradleboard, bag, or the like of its own. Thus, where an infant may become cold at night, separate bundling allows it to stay as warm as possible while it sleeps.

In Kenya, a Gusii husband, wife, and children all sleep together, unless the man is visiting another of his wives. If the family has a traditional dried mud bed, some of the younger children will also crowd close to their mother. Or if the parents sleep in a rope-spring bed, the children will sleep on the floor beside the bed or in a separate children's house nearby. Everyone sleeps naked under blankets and close to the cooking fire. Girls of five or six and boys of seven or eight are sent off to sleep apart from their parents, as the father becomes embarrassed to have sexual relations with his wife when older children are about. A daughter may go to sleep with a co-wife of her mother or, even more likely, with her grandmother. Boys may also go to their grandmother's house, but more frequently they will sleep in the children's house. Little boys are especially likely to be afraid of the witches and animals that are lurking in the darkness, so that the experience of sleeping away from their mothers is initially terrifying. Among the Mixtecans of Mexico, an infant sleeps with its parents, usually in the same bed or perhaps in a cradle alongside the bed. But when youngsters enter the stage of early childhood, at one or two years of age, they begin to sleep with their siblings. Among the Taira of Okinawa, sleeping arrangements differ from one family to the next. People curl up in some corner of the living room to sleep, with two or three family members sharing a single cover. If a husband and wife sleep next to each other, there is also likely to be an infant sleeping between them. Perhaps, too, another child will settle down next to the father. Other youngsters may sleep alongside a grandmother, and pairs of same-sex or opposite sex siblings may also sleep together. In India, Rajput men and women sleep in separate rooms. A child sleeps with the mother for a number of years. When a new sibling arrives, the next youngest child may sleep elsewhere for a while, but eventually returns to the mother's bed along with the baby, and women commonly sleep with two or three children at a time. Among the Banoi of Thailand, a mother and her youngest child, or perhaps two or three of her smallest children, will sleep together under a mosquito net. In the same room, the father and his older sons may sleep under another mosquito net together. Or, if there is a side room in the house, other family members may sleep there. A North American Fox family lived in a wigwam in the winter and a bark house in the summer. Both kinds of dwellings contained only one room, where the whole family slept, women and children on one side and men on the other. Boys between eight and twelve years of age slept with the men. In Jamaica, three to five children or adults sleep in the same bed. People, including children, try to make up for an uncomfortable night's sleep by taking a nap during the day when a person can sleep in the bed alone. A young Javanese child in Indonesia sleeps with the mother and often also with the father. When older, children sleep in the same room as the parents on their own bench or mat. Or they may move into an adjoining room. Neighborhood children will sleep together. Young adolescent males sometimes spend the night at the house of a close friend.

In many cultures, a child does not have a regular bedtime. The Gusii tend to be afraid of the dark, the women and children more so than the men, but no one likes to be out at night. Thus, Gusii families go to sleep in the early evening unless there is a beer party. Youngsters are then allowed to stay up late, but the smaller children end up falling asleep on the floor or in someone's arms. Micronesian Truk children go to sleep whenever and wherever they feel tired, and no one tries to impose a regular sleep schedule even on a young baby. By the time children can speak and understand language, they are expected to put themselves to bed when they are tired, and a youngster who is obviously sleepy will be told to go to sleep in a tone that suggests that the child should have known enough to do so without being told. There are no regular bed or nap times for a Canadian Hare baby. Rather, infants just sleep whenever they wish. As a baby is left in a hammock all day for the first ten months of its life, it is easy for the infant to just drift off to sleep when it is tired.

Javanese children can stay up late if they wish. A mother simply asks a youngster whether he or she is ready for bed, and keeps asking every so often until the answer is "yes." Sometimes, a child will stay up all night watching the activities of the adults and dozing off for a while just to wake up again. In New Mexico, Zuni children were permitted to stay up until they became tired. Youngsters who were taken to the night dances feel asleep in a parent's lap, and older children who sat up to listen to their parents chatting together just fell asleep on the bed in their clothing. In some cultures, bedtime is more regular. The North American Fox typically went to sleep before eight o'clock in the evening and rarely after ten o'clock. Smaller children went to bed at dusk, when it was too dark to play any longer. Older children retired along with the adults, sometimes staying awake past ten. Typically, the last to go to bed were the men. Nor do mothers across cultures expect babies to fall asleep in bed. In Kenya, a Gusii infant generally goes to sleep in someone's arms or on a caretaker's back. In both cases, the baby remains in physical contact with some other person. A Japanese mother allows the baby to fall asleep in her arms, but she then attempts to place it in a bed. The infant then wakes up, and the process is repeated all over again.

Infants or children in different cultures may get the same amount of sleep each day, although the rhythm of sleep may differ from place to place. American and rural Kenyan babies sleep the same amount of time. But American babies, who sleep continuously for about four hours as newborns, often remain asleep for eight-and-one-half hours during the night by the time that they are four months of age. By contrast, Kenyan babies, who nurse at will and are not pressured to remain asleep through the night, continue to sleep uninterrupted for only four hours at most. Tairan kindergartners, who may be between two and six years of age, get around eight hours of sleep. They are in bed by 8:30 or 9:00, although the bedtime of any individual child will depend upon how tired the youngster happens to be, so that a very sleepy child may be asleep not too long after dinner. Older children may stay up later, especially if there is a good deal of moonlight. A village bell signals the end of the day for everyone in the village. Rajput children may go to sleep a bit earlier than adults. And mothers prefer their youngsters to stay in bed until the fire has warmed up the room and breakfast is ready. But otherwise, bedtime is about the same for adults and children. A tired Hare youngster will be put to bed right after supper. Perhaps someone will sing the child a lullaby. On other nights, bedtime may be midnight. Children are not awakened at any specific time in the morning. Rather, they are allowed to sleep as long as they wish. Usually, a child gets ten to twelve hours of sleep at night.

Children in many societies are not expected to take naps. Tairan children do not generally take naps unless the day is particularly hot. Rajput adults think that too much sleep makes a person lazy. As a result, children are not expected to take naps. By the time they are three years old, Hare children can manage to stay awake all day without taking a nap.

———

Barry, Herbert, III, and Leonora Paxson. (1971) "Infancy and Early Childhood: Cross-Cultural Codes 2." *Ethnology* 10: 466–508.

Cohen, Yehudi A. (1966) *A Study of Interpersonal Relations in a Jamaican Community.*

Geertz, Hildred. (1961) *The Javanese Family: A Study of Kinship and Socialization.*

Gladwin, Thomas, and Seymour Sarason. (1953) *Truk: Man in Paradise.*

Hara, Hiroko Sue. (1967) *Hare Indians and Their World.*

Hitchcock, John T., and Leigh Minturn. (1966) *The Rajputs of Khalapur, India.*

Jones, William. (1939) *Ethnography of the Fox Indians.*

Leighton, Dorothea, and John Adair. (1966) *People of the Middle Place: A Study of the Zuni Indians.*

LeVine, Robert A., and Barbara B. LeVine. (1966) *Nyansongo: A Gusii Community in Kenya.*

Maretzki, Thomas W., and Hatsumi Maretzki. (1966) *Taira: An Okinawan Village.*

Munroe, Robert L., and Ruth H. Munroe. (1975) *Cross-Cultural Human Development.*

Piker, Steven. (1965) *An Examination of Character and Socialization in a Thai Peasant Community.*

Romney, A. Kimball, and Romaine Romney. (1966) *The Mixtecans of Juxtlahuaca, Mexico.*

Super, Charles M. (1981) "Behavioral Development in Infancy." In *Handbook of Cross-Cultural Human Development,* edited by Ruth

H. Munroe, Robert L. Munroe, and Beatrice B. Whiting, 181–270.

Whiting, Beatrice B. (1971) "Folk Wisdom and Child Rearing." Paper presented at meetings of the American Association for the Advancement of Science, December.

Whiting, John W. M. (1964) "Effects of Climate on Certain Cultural Practices." In *Explorations in Cultural Anthropology*, edited by Ward E. Goodenough, 511–544.

SOCIABILITY

Sociable children are children who make friendly responses to the overtures or prospective overtures of other children or adults. The sociable child also tends to engage in activities with other people and to cooperate in order to promote social interaction. Sociability is valued and encouraged in some cultures. Thus, for the Tarong of the Philippines, a good baby is the one who takes pleasure in the company of other people. An infant who has just begun to crawl will be sent off to play with the other children, and youngsters of all ages are expected to find their greatest amusement in playing with one another. Toys, therefore, are scarce. Games, which promote interaction between people, are much more important. A Tarong adult assumes that a child who is alone must be lonely. If children do not form a play group on their own, adults will attempt to get one organized so that a Tarong child is virtually always in the company of other children. Similarly, in Okinawa, Tairan parents want their children to be friendly and well liked, and adults as well as children work hard to get their babies to laugh and smile. Men and women talk to and make faces at infants in order to evoke a positive response, and youngsters will clap their hands at a baby in the hope of earning a smile. Kindergartners are encouraged to play with other children, and parents warn children who go off by themselves that other people will think of them as unlikable. Adults also believe that a child who is alone is more likely to get into some kind of trouble or to do something dangerous. In South India, Gopalpur children do not have toys, and the result is that a child's most interesting playthings are other children and small animals. The favorite game of Gopalpur children is house. One child plays mother and the other plays father. Cakes are made of sand and chickens stand in for sheep and cows. Little boys are yoked together to pull carts or plows, and infant siblings take the place of dolls. A good deal of the children's play activities consists of handing around peanuts, green grain, small pieces of bread, and semi-edible green fruits.

Children are more likely to be sociable in cultures with nuclear families, especially when the father eats with the family, sleeps in the same bed as his wife, attends the births of his children, and helps care for infants. Households of this sort are characterized by an egalitarian ethic, and this may be contributing to the friendly, egalitarian style of the children who are raised in this kind of setting. Sociable children are also likely to be home during the day with their mothers. The mother, because she has no other adults with whom to associate during the day, turns to her children for companionship. As a result, the sociable child raised in a nuclear family learns friendly, playful behavior while interacting with an adult. This is unusual across cultures. More typically, children learn to display playfulness while interacting with other children, and especially with siblings, half-siblings, and cousins. A child's tendency to display sociability is also affected by the status of the people with whom the youngster is interacting. Thus, the behavior of children is predominantly sociable when a child is in the company of peers, while a youngster is unlikely to exhibit sociability in the presence of an infant. Sociability is the second most frequently displayed behavior of children in the presence of adults, preceded by dependency. Sociability is not sex-typed. Boys and girls are equally sociable across cultures.

Beals, Alan R. (1962) *Gopalpur: A South Indian Village.*

Maretzki, Thomas W., and Hatsumi Maretzki. (1966) *Taira: An Okinawan Village.*

Nydegger, William F., and Corinne Nydegger. (1966) *Tarong: An Ilocos Barrio in the Philippines.*

Whiting, Beatrice B., and Carolyn Pope Edwards. (1988) *Children of Different Worlds: The Formation of Social Behavior.*

Whiting, Beatrice B., and John W. M. Whiting. (1975) *Children of Six Cultures: A Psycho-Cultural Analysis.*

SOCIALIZATION, AGENTS OF

Socialization refers to the process of raising a child to think and behave in ways that conform to cultural standards. An agent of socialization is a person who helps to rear a child toward these ends. In all cultures, parents participate in the socialization of their own children. However, in most societies, parents are assisted in this process by what we can call secondary socializers. These secondary socializers usually include relatives and other members of the community, including teachers and paid caretakers. The degree of help that parents receive from other people in socializing their children to be civilized members of their society differs from one place to the next. However, it is uncommon for someone besides the mother to have the primary responsibility for taking care of a young child. In 44 percent of 116 cultures, infants are cared for almost exclusively or primarily by the mother. A mother remains the principal caretaker but receives significant help from other people in 46 percent of 116 cultures. Around half of the responsibility for taking care of infants is retained by the mother in an additional 8 percent of these societies, and in the remaining 2 percent, the mother's role in caretaking is less significant than is the combined role of other caretakers. In childhood, the role of the mother tends to become somewhat less significant, and children begin to spend more time with other people. Thus, in 88 cultures around the world, the caretaking of young children is never managed exclusively by the mother, and mothers retain major responsibility for the caretaking of young children in only 26 percent of these 88 cultures. Children spend around half the time under the supervision of their mother in 36 percent of the 88 societies, and a majority of the young child's time is spent away from the mother in the remaining 38 percent of these societies.

In most cultures, the mother has exclusive or primary responsibility for socializing a young child. Among the Okinawan Taira, it is the mother who has control over the daily life of a youngster. She decides when a child will get new clothes, go to the doctor, or accompany her to town. And it is primarily the mother who supervises her children's school activities. In North America, a Comanche girl begins to follow her mother around everywhere as soon as she can walk, imitating her mother's activities all day long. Jamaican mothers are also primarily responsible for overseeing the behavior of children under the age of ten, and it is they who punish minor infractions. Older children whose misbehavior is viewed as more serious are flogged by the father when he gets home from work. But fathers have nothing else to do with their children for the first ten or so years of a youngster's life, and a young boy who tries to become a companion to his father is harshly reprimanded.

In polygynous societies, a woman can often depend upon her husband's other wives to help tend her children. In Liberia, a Kpelle child refers to all of the father's wives as "mother," and in a smoothly functioning household, women will leave their own youngsters with a co-wife or an older daughter of a co-wife. All of the co-wives in a Kpelle household are expected to discipline one another's children whether or not the mother herself is present. Wives also take turns doing some of the household chores, and this can lighten a mother's workload a bit, allowing her to spend more time tending to her children. When co-wives do not get along, or where they do not live under the same roof, a woman cannot count on her husband's other wives for this kind of help.

In most societies, the mother can depend upon other members of the family to help her with the task of socialization. A North American Comanche woman could count on a variety of relatives to perform a variety of socializing functions on her behalf. For instance, a Comanche girl was very close to her mother's sisters and called them "pia," or mother. An aunt, in turn, thought of her niece as her own child and helped to instruct the daughters of her sisters. Comanche grandparents also helped raise their grandchildren and in fact were likely to spoil them. This was especially the case regarding the behavior of a grandmother toward her own daughter's daughters. Grandparents, however, also performed more constructive roles. For instance, because a Comanche boy's father was often away at war or on a hunting trip, it therefore fell to the mother's father to train young males. Grandfathers taught their grandsons to hunt and shoot and to make a bow and arrows. A boy also learned tribal tradition, history, legend, and religion from his mother's father. Boys were also instructed by their fathers, older brothers, and paternal uncles.

It is also very common across cultures for older children to have an important role in so-cializing younger ones. We see this in the ubiquitous custom of recruiting older siblings or cousins as child nurses. A more extreme example of peer-based socialization is found among the Cubeo of the Northwest Amazon. Here, boys form an autonomous group, the membership of which ranges from six years of age to past adolescence. The group chooses its own leaders, who then become responsible for enforcing rules and disciplining bad behavior. Adults rarely punish children of either sex, even if the actions of a youngster cause serious damage.

In a number of societies, the socialization of every child is at least in part the responsibility of the community. In the Philippines, a Tarong child is likely to be scolded by any adult who happens to witness a naughty act. Adults agree that everyone helps to raise everyone's children. Among the Tairans of Okinawa, any adult who sees a child misbehaving or engaging in some dangerous activity will stop to shout a warning to the youngster. But these intrusions of the community at large into the life of a child are only verbal and do not extend to actual punishment. Similarly, an older Indian Rajput child thinks nothing of slapping a younger sibling, and a neighbor will also yell at a child who is misbehaving.

When everyone in the community has some hand in socializing children, a youngster may also find refuge with some other adult when there is a threat of punishment from the parents. Among the Gusii of Kenya, an adult who observes a child engaging in serious misbehavior will feel obligated to tell the parents. On the other hand, youngsters who are attempting to escape some punishment from their parents can realistically hope to find a welcome in another adult's home. A Samoan child is the charge of the community at large. When youngsters in this culture are at odds with their parents, they simply pack up and move in with a neighbor for a while.

When people other than the parents have some role in socialization, there are often implicit rules regarding who is allowed what kinds of authority over the child. Among the Rajputs, the oldest person who is present should theoretically be the one to discipline a naughty child. As children spend most of their time in the enclosed outdoor courtyard with the women of the family, this will usually be the grandmother, great-aunt, or oldest aunt. But another woman will not discipline a child whose mother is present and no woman will approach the child of a woman who outranks her. Neither will a woman hit a child who is not her own. In reality, then, a child can expect a mild scolding from a woman other than the mother, but nothing more serious than that. Men are also sensitive to issues of rank when it comes to punishing a child, and a man may refrain from scolding his child when his own father or an uncle is present. Similarly, Gusii children are expected to show respect toward anyone of their parents' generation, and any adult may correct a child who has been caught misbehaving. But the severity of the punishment that a socializer will administer to a child depends upon the nature of the relationship between the individual and the youngster's parents. For instance, co-wives will discipline one another's children without hesitation if the women themselves are on good terms. But if the relationship between the two women is strained, neither will discipline the children of the other for fear of being charged with witchcraft if the punished youngster becomes sick.

Even though child rearing is a shared task in many cultures around the world, children as a rule still maintain a special relationship with their mothers. Tairan children spend relatively little time with their mothers, who spend much of the day away from home engaged in subsistence activities. Children between five and twelve years of age also act as child nurses, and younger children spend a good deal of time on the backs of older siblings while the adults are away at work. Grandmothers also play an important role as caretakers of children in the mother's absence.

Nevertheless, it is the mother to whom a child is closest throughout the childhood years. Tairans think of the mother as the person most responsible for the rearing of children, and the mother takes the blame if a child is misbehaved. A child will go to the mother for support and thinks of her as the cornerstone of the family. This is reminiscent of the special attachment that American children show toward their mothers even when the youngsters spend much of each day in a day-care setting.

In many cultures, fathers do not take on any significant responsibility for raising children. Often this is because child rearing is viewed as women's work. This is the view of the Tairan male and, as a result, men in this culture have little to do with children unless some decision needs to be made about a youngster's future. In Thailand, Banoi fathers spend more time with their children than do Tairan men, but here, too, it is the mother who coaxes, threatens, and punishes badly behaved children.

Fathers do, however, often have a particular role in the lives of their children, and the role is similar across societies. That is, fathers act as disciplinarians, especially when the mother has trouble controlling a child. And in fact, mothers across cultures commonly find that their children do not always submit to their authority. The major role of a Tairan father is that of disciplinarian, and a mother will send a child who refuses to obey her to the father. Tairan mothers can persuade their children to behave by warning that if they do not they will have to "report to father." In fact, the very presence of the father at home alters the behavior of the children, who make an effort to be quiet and to do their chores and schoolwork when he is around, even though they are not explicitly told to do so. Tairan mothers do most of the scolding and spanking, but children are, nevertheless, more fearful of their fathers. Similarly, in India, Rajput women are not very effective disciplinarians of their sons, who are both disobedient and rude toward their mothers. Fathers and uncles become the disciplinarians when boys no longer listen to their mothers. Gusii fathers are generally harsher disciplinarians than are mothers. Thus, a woman may give her child food on the sly even though her husband has ordered her not to feed the youngster as punishment for some misdeed. Children understand that their mothers are more lenient than their fathers. And as a son grows older and becomes harder for his mother to manage, she threatens to tell his father, who will then beat him if he continues to misbehave. Thus, mothers contribute to the perceptions of children that fathers are to be feared. In Mexico, Mixtecan children always obey their fathers more quickly than they obey their mothers. In part, this may be because fathers consistently punish noncompliance, whereas mothers do not. Mothers are also more permissive with their sons than they are with their daughters, while fathers insist upon equal obedience in all of their children. Tarong mothers are likely to scold or slap children who have not done their chores with care. Fathers, by contrast, punish their children less frequently and with less emotionality, and mothers say that punishment by the father is more dreaded by children and also more effective. A North American Chippewa mother who had trouble getting her children to obey even after striking them across the shoulders would threaten to turn them over to their father. The children then complied because they were afraid of him. Jamaican mothers discipline children for minor offenses. The father is called in when the offense is more serious. Every day, when he comes in from the fields, the father asks whether any of the children need flogging. In Japan, Takashima youngsters are less respectful toward their mothers than toward their fathers, whom they see less frequently because the men are often away fishing. Rajput mothers may need to resort to threats about ghosts because children are not likely to listen to women who do not use fear tactics of this sort. Rajput men do not

threaten their children in this way, nor do they need to, as their authority is enough to frighten a child into obedience.

Agents as well as techniques of socialization can differ depending upon the sex of the child. Rajput men are not supposed to discipline their older daughters, and some men avoid punishing even a young girl. The appropriate socializer of girls is a woman, and in fact, men are more severe with their sons than with their daughters. Banoi parents hit their sons more frequently and boys, they say, are more obstinate than girls. Takashima boys are treated with more indulgence than are girls, and it is boys who have temper tantrums. While it is the job of a Jamaican mother to raise both sons and daughters under the age of ten, a boy begins to spend significant time with his father once he is ten years old and fathers then exert as much control over sons as do mothers. A girl, however, remains under the thumb of her mother. So will the age of the child have an influence on who is responsible for socializing the youngster. In Micronesia, as the Truk child becomes an adolescent, the parents, who frequently slap and beat their youngsters, will no longer use physical punishment as a method of discipline unless they are quite angry. They will still advise or chastise their children. Parents may call in a brother to handle the matter since the misbehavior of an adolescent, who is now considered an adult among the Truk, generally also affects his brother, who will be expected to help him out when he gets into trouble.

Where persons other than the parents help to socialize children, some categories of secondary caretaker are more common than others across cultures. In a sample of 186 societies around the world, sibling caretakers are more common than any other kind of secondary socializer, with grandparents following closely behind. Nonrelatives act as secondary caretakers in 15 percent and relatives other than siblings and grandparents act as secondary socializers in 9 percent of these cultures.

See also CHILD NURSES; FATHERS

Barry, Herbert, III, and Leonora Paxson. (1971) "Infancy and Childhood: Cross-Cultural Codes 2." *Ethnology* 10: 466–508.

Cohen, Yehudi A. (1966) *A Study of Interpersonal Relations in a Jamaican Community.*

Erchak, Gerald M. (1977) *Full Respect: Kpelle Children in Adaptation.*

Gladwin, Thomas, and Seymour Sarason. (1953) *Truk: Man in Paradise.*

Goldman, Irving. (1963) *The Cubeo: Indians of the Northwest Amazon.*

Hilger, M. Inez. (1951) *Chippewa Child Life and Its Cultural Background.*

Hitchcock, John T., and Leigh Minturn. (1966) *The Rajputs of Khalapur, India.*

LeVine, Robert A., and Barbara B. LeVine. (1966) *Nyansongo: A Gusii Community in Kenya.*

Maretzki, Thomas W., and Hatsumi Maretzki. (1966) *Taira: An Okinawan Village.*

Norbeck, Edward. (1954) *Takashima: A Japanese Fishing Village.*

Nydegger, William F., and Corinne Nydegger. (1966) *Tarong: An Ilocos Barrio in the Philippines.*

Piker, Steven. (1965) *An Examination of Character and Socialization in a Thai Peasant Community.*

Romney, A. Kimball, and Romaine Romney. (1966) *The Mixtecans of Juxtlahuaca, Mexico.*

Wallace, Ernest, and E. Adamson Hoebel. (1952) *The Comanches: Lords of the South Plains.*

SOCIALIZATION, TECHNIQUES OF

In every culture around the world, adults have certain expectations regarding what constitutes appropriate behavior in children. This means that youngsters need to be persuaded one way or another to conform to these expectations. Socialization is the process of "civilizing" children so that they will behave in ways deemed desirable by their culture. Socializers across cultures use a variety of techniques to try to shape children's actions to coincide with cultural standards. These include frightening, physically punishing, teasing, scolding, embarrassing, or withholding desired resources from a misbehaving child. Socializers may also attempt to mold the behavior of children by praising or materially rewarding a youngster who has been good or by relying on reason.

Of the variety of socialization techniques practiced across societies, the most frequent are physical punishment and rewards, the latter including both gifts and the granting of some privilege in return for good behavior. In decreasing order of frequency come lecturing, scolding, teasing, and reliance on public opinion. Adults in any particular society will generally depend upon multiple strategies in trying to promote desirable behavior. The choice will depend in part upon what behavior the adult is attempting to promote or discourage. Different strategies will also be chosen depending upon the temperament of the adult doing the training and the sex, history, tractability, and other emotional and behavioral characteristics of the child.

Instilling Fear

In a number of cultures, adults attempt to discourage undesirable behavior in children by employing fear tactics. For instance, the adult warns misbehaving youngsters that they will be taken away or killed by some terrifying creature. A favorite strategy encourages and then exploits the young child's fear of animals. Among the Gusii of Kenya, adults call any animal that appears before a child *ekuku*, who "will bite you." When a youngster begins to cry, someone will pretend to call over a dog, frightening the youngster into silence. Beginning when they are very young, Gusii children are warned that domestic animals, imaginary hyenas, and witches will hurt or eat anyone who has behaved badly. Children also become convinced that a similar fate awaits them at the hands of their fathers. The Gusii continue to believe in malevolent beings who are waiting to punish any small wrong. Adults remain afraid of the dark and prefer to stay at home in the evening if there is no moonlight.

Similarly, in Thailand, as soon as a Banoi child is old enough to understand language, parents begin to use threats as a means of attempting to get compliance from youngsters. A mother may warn her child that a cat will bite him or that a lizard will eat his insides in order to persuade the youngster to go to sleep, to stop crying, to play calmly, to stop fighting with siblings, and the like. Or a child who tries to follow his mother out of the house or who tends to wander from her side may be warned that a mad dog will attack him. Descriptions of what will happen to the child are extremely graphic. One Banoi father was able to frighten his children into behaving properly by relating how he would kill them, cut them up, and make them into a curry that he would eat for dinner. If a child is too young to understand verbal threats, a mother may suddenly appear and imitate animal noises and facial gestures in an effort to frighten the baby into compliance. A Banoi child can expect to be the target of a number of threats every day, and a youngster may be genuinely frightened by some of them.

Parents in some cultures threaten their children with harm at the hands of some unknown person if they are bad. Sometimes, threats about the bogeyman are invoked. For instance, among the Javanese of Indonesia, parents teach children early on to distinguish between familiar people, who are to be trusted, and strangers, who are not. Adults then exploit the child's fear of the unfamiliar to persuade them to behave. Thus, a child is warned that some soldier will shoot him unless he is quiet. Or the bogeyman will

come and fetch a youngster if she does not go to sleep. Indeed, children come to be so afraid of strangers that they burst out crying at the sight of someone whom they do not know. Similarly, Gusii adults threaten to send children away with strangers if they cry. Among the Tarong of the Philippines, youngsters are warned that *Wawak,* the bogeyman who kills and eats bad children, will come to get them if they are bad. The strategy works because a Tarong woman who owns a *Wawak* mask wanders around the neighborhood at dusk once or twice a year, terrifying the children with her charade and managing to elicit promises of good behavior from the youngsters. Subsequent creaks and noises attributed to *Wawak* are effective in scaring children for months after the visit. Mothers who wish to convince their children to behave properly borrow the mask and act out the role of *Wawak* themselves. One mother who was weaning her baby draped a dark cloth over a chair during the night and, pointing to the resulting silhouette, threatened the infant that *Wawak* forbade the baby to nurse. Tarong parents will also try to scare a child who has been bad by telling some important visitor about the youngster's misdeeds while the unfortunate child is present. The guest, who is in on the conspiracy, will then scold the youngster, who is embarrassed and frightened by the episode. When the youngster begins to show unmistakable signs of misery, all of the adults begin to laugh, and the parent attempts to comfort the child. The result is a youngster who is more impressed with the parents' power as disciplinarians. This use of fear as a tactic for socialization begins to be used by adults once a child has been weaned.

In Okinawa, Tairan mothers regularly depend upon a child's fear of the supernatural as a way of controlling behavior. Children are reminded that God is everywhere and always knows what a person is doing and will punish a naughty child. Threats about an omnipresent supernatural are particularly useful as a technique of socialization because Tairan children are often off by themselves and out of earshot of adults. Similarly, in India, a Rajput mother may threaten misbehaving children that they will be taken away by ghosts. Guadalcanal Kaoka elders tell children stories about the *umou*, or giants, who live in the faroff mountains and gather up naughty children, taking them to a cave to be cooked and eaten. Recalcitrant children are warned that an *umou* is behind the tree, watching and listening to them, and parents threaten to hand misbehaving youngsters over to the *umou*.

Sometimes, fear tactics are only used as a last resort if nothing else seems to persuade a child to be good. Banoi adults explicitly state that children will not obey their parents unless they have been taught to fear them. However, parents also believe that children should be treated with affection and indulgence. As a result, Banoi parents first attempt to gain compliance from their children with praise, affection, and sweet words, but then turn to threats if the youngster fails to obey. Thus, for example, a mother may initially try to get a small child to go to sleep by rocking, nursing, and talking softly to the youngster. If these tactics fail, she may warn him that unless he goes to sleep a lizard will eat out his insides or a cat will come and claw him.

Physical Punishment

Physical punishment is employed in a large majority of societies around the world as a technique of socializing children. Jamaican children are flogged with a strap or a switch. Parents say: "If you don't hit your child when he is young, he gets hard, and you cannot bend him as you would like to bend him." Children are flogged for a variety of reasons. Infants will be hit for getting underfoot, for damaging something of the mother's, for fighting with a sibling, for disobeying, or for crying. The most severe punishment is for taking food that is meant for another person. Gusii mothers say that if you want to teach a child anything you must cane him, and women frequently hit disobedient children, sometimes to teach them a lesson and sometimes simply out of irritation or frustration. Children learn that a casual slap from the mother only means that she is temporarily annoyed, and the smack is quickly forgotten by both mother and child. A mother who is more seriously upset by a child's behavior may stop what she is doing to whip the offender with a stick. This occurs much less frequently than the absent-minded swat, but all Gusii children are the targets of at least a few such painful beatings. A Gusii father will also beat his children for a variety of offenses. Among the Jivaro of Ecuador, a father may spank a child with a nettle for fighting with another youngster over food, repeatedly grabbing at breakable objects, taking meat or peanuts without permission, and so on. A more severe punishment consists of dropping a supply of hot peppers into a fire and then forcing the child to remain over the fire under a large cloth until he faints. If a youngster continues to misbehave even after this punishment, his father may threaten to burn off the child's hair, although no one has ever actually carried out such a threat. In Micronesia, Truk parents or grandparents may beat a child who has misbehaved. Often, this is just a matter of slapping the youngster with a hand, or perhaps with a stick. A parent who is particularly angry with a child will use a thick stick with which to smack the youngster on the backside while repeatedly asking: "Why did you do it?... Do you hear me?... Why did you do it?" The effect of this punishment, which may go on for a few minutes, is to reduce the child into a sobbing fit. Children may be physically punished for a number of reasons. A small child will be hit for going out into the water and an older one for using vulgar language. A youngster who disrupts some important activity of the adults may also receive a beating. In Guatemala, Chimalteco mothers slap disobedient children on the back of the head. Some women say that youngsters will not learn their lesson if they are hit on any other part of the body. A North American Arapaho adult sometimes poured water on the head of a naughty child. If that did not persuade the youngster to behave, the adult would threaten to get more water. That usually convinced the child to mind the adult. Jamaican parents use a switch to flog a small child and a strap to flog an older one. The strap hangs in the sitting room, and a brave child who knows that a flogging is imminent may hide the strap. If caught, the youngster will now be punished twice, once for the original deed and once for the second.

In some cultures, parents recruit some other person to administer physical punishment to a misbehaving child. In North America, if a Sanpoil child misbehaved, punishment was administered not only to the guilty youngster but to all of the other children in the community. An old man went from household to household, ordering the children in each house to lie face down on a blanket in the middle of the room. Each youngster received a few light swats with a whip. The parents themselves rarely physically punished their children. Rather, they recruited a particular individual as community disciplinarian. Mild whipping of children occurred in response to small misdeeds. In the case of more serious misconduct, parents warned the child that "the old man from up the river" was coming. The community disciplinarian, who had been secretly summoned by the parents, then showed up in disguise. He had whips with him, and the child was told to lie down to be punished before the whips became even coarser than they were. The youngster received a more severe whipping in cases of this sort, and a crying child got additional lashes. The old man then warned the child not to misbehave again. Otherwise, the youngster could expect a visit from the other man from up the river, who was much stronger and could hit children much harder. A North American Comanche parent whose child required physical punishment would assign a classificatory or real sister to do the job. Children typically resented the bossiness of these older child disciplinarians.

While children in virtually all human cultures can expect to be punished physically at some point in their lives, adults in some societies disapprove of physical punishment. In Japan, this is true of Takashima parents and people say that if a mother hits a child, the child will hit other people. Children are usually scolded instead of being hit. When physical punishment does occur, it consists of pinching the youngster or pricking the child's fingers with a needle. Adults do not believe in striking or slapping children. Arapaho adults do not like to resort to physical punishment, although children may occasionally be whipped. Some older people said that scolding or slapping a child just made him worse. A North American Chippewa child older than five years might be slapped or switched once or twice by either parent for serious offenses such as lying, fighting, refusing to obey, stealing, or staying away all day without permission. But some Chippewa parents disapproved of physical punishment, saying that children who were hit would have the spirit knocked out of them. They preferred to point out examples of good and bad behavior in other people as object lessons for their children.

Sometimes, physical punishment is only used a last resort. Tairan mothers say that they always try to talk to or simply scold a naughty child before they spank a child. But almost all mothers do administer a spanking, either with the hand or with a piece of firewood or bamboo, and often the talking and spanking occur simultaneously. Older children who are supervising a younger sibling are quicker to hit a disobedient child than is the mother, and youngsters are also more likely to mind their child nurses than they are their mothers. Children may also have their hands or feet tethered for a few minutes or perhaps as long as an hour for straying into some forbidden place or for engaging in some prohibited and dangerous activity. Grandmothers use painful pinches to punish bad behavior, and once a child has been pinched the grandmother need only make motions to pinch the youngster again to see the undesirable behavior halted. A Tarong preschooler might be slapped with a twig, slipper, or hand for clear examples of bad behavior, and the youngster will then be left to cry angrily. But teasing and gentle scolding are usually enough to persuade a child to behave properly. Among the Mixtecans of Mexico, mothers claim that hitting a child is one acceptable way of punishing disobedience. But children are rarely if ever physically punished in fact.

Teasing

Teasing and ridicule are also employed to persuade children to stop engaging in some behavior of which adults in a culture disapprove. The Tarong use teasing as a method of influencing children and adults alike. The teasing is friendly, but it is also brutally accurate and has the effect, therefore, of embarrassing the targets and of changing their behavior in the future. Ridicule is an especially effective strategy for controlling the behavior of adolescent Tarong boys, who would rather be beaten in a fight than made fun of. Rajput adults often make fun of a child who is behaving badly. And many children the world over learn to eliminate in the place and manner dictated by their culture when older children and adults call them "babies" because they are not toilet trained.

Scolding

Most Mixtecan mothers say that they prefer scolding to hitting as a way of punishing the misbehavior of a child. Rajputs frequently scold their children for doing something wrong. A scolding is often a simple curse or expletive, such as "Go away," "Go to hell," "sister seducer," and the like. Among the Arapaho, a naughty child might be called "crazy." This was

the worst thing that one person could call another one.

Public Opinion

Sometimes, children are warned that they will get a bad reputation if they continue to misbehave. Tairans are particularly sensitive about the opinions of others and as a result, threats about what other people will think are effective in influencing the behavior of children. For instance, an adult may say to a child: "People will think that you are unpopular if you play alone," and that will be enough to persuade the youngster to seek out a peer. Or a child will be reminded that he will get a bad reputation if he picks fights. Rajput parents may tell naughty children that other adults will think badly of them. A woman may tell her son that other mothers will think he is a dirty boy if he plays in the dusty street without washing up afterward. Or a father may tell the other men on the men's platform about his son's misbehavior, perhaps praising some other child to boot. An Arapaho child soon learned that the tribe had no use for people who behaved in ways that were not approved. The realization persuaded some youngsters to mend their ways for fear of being ostracized by the community.

Banishing a Child

In some cultures, adults will isolate a child or threaten to send away the youngster who misbehaves. Rajput men sometimes punish bad behavior by sending a child to the corner of the men's platform or into one of the men's cubicles, thus isolating the child. Sometimes, a man will banish a naughty youngster to the women's courtyard, and a woman will send a bad child to the men's platform. A particularly recalcitrant child may be shuttled back and forth from courtyard to platform all day long. Sending a child away in this manner is not so much a punishment as it is a way of being rid of the youngster. Jamaican children are sometimes locked in an empty room. Rajput women also sometimes lock bad children up in a room of the house. As rooms are completely dark when the door is closed, this tactic genuinely frightens children. Locking a child up is viewed as an especially harsh punishment and is not commonly used. Men do not approve of their wives' fear tactics and do not use fear as a form of punishment themselves because they believe that instilling fear in children makes them timid. A Mixtecan mother may isolate a disobedient child, but this is viewed as an extreme form of punishment and a woman is not likely to resort to isolation unless, for instance, a child who is being chastised fights back.

A Rajput mother who is genuinely angry with a child may refuse to speak to the youngster. Refusal to speak to someone is considered to be a major breach of etiquette in Rajput society, and is used by adults who have had a serious quarrel with each other. Arapaho adults would sometimes ignore a child who failed to obey.

Withholding Food

Sometimes, a child will be deprived of a meal as punishment for being bad. Some Truk parents withhold food from a child, for instance if the youngster has wandered off from home without permission or stayed out too late. Or a child who neglected to do some assigned task or used vulgar language might be refused food. Jamaican children are often flogged for bad behavior, and other punishments may also follow some misdeed on the part of a youngster. But the worst punishment that a parent can administer is the withholding of food. Thus, a naughty child may have to wait to eat until the rest of the family has had its meal and the dishes are washed, and youngsters, who are always hungry, find it very hard to watch other people eating before they can have any food. A Gusii father will insist that the mother withhold food from a child who has somehow misbehaved.

Psychological Tactics

Tairan parents depend more upon the with-drawal of love than upon any other technique to socialize their children, although they also use physical punishment, shaming, and threats that a naughty child will be deprived of food. Thus, for example, the mother of a disobedient boy may threaten to sell him to a fisherman from some other village. Or a little girl is told that she will be sold to strangers as a slave. These threats are taken seriously by children because they refer to actions that are known to have taken place in the past. A mother may also threaten a misbehaving child that she herself will run away and leave the naughty youngster with the father. Similarly, an Arapaho mother told her disobedient children she felt bad because of their naughty behavior. Guadalcanal Kaoka parents sometimes try to ignore a child who has misbehaved, and a youngster may be slighted for two hours or more. Children who receive the cold shoulder from a parent first protest, but when they discover that no one is paying attention to their tears, they usually try to make it up with the parent by helping out with some chore or the like.

Praise

Adults in some societies will depend upon praise as a way of encouraging children to continue to behave in desirable ways. A parent who uses praise when a child is good may also make negative comments when children are not meeting the parent's expectations. A Tairan adult begins to use the terms "good child" and "naughty child" to refer to youngsters when they are still very young and cannot even understand the words that are directed at them. Grownups also enthusiastically praise or reward virtually any instance of good behavior on the part of a toddler. Older children are praised less extravagantly and less consistently. Arapaho adults regularly let a child know that they were pleased with the youngster's good behavior. They believed that praise encouraged children to be good. A parent might praise a child for using good judgment, for being alert, for offering to run an errand, or for pursuing some desirable activity. When a Canadian Hare child performs a task well, the mother may say: "Oh, you are smart," and an adult may encourage a youngster who is attempting some ambitious project by repeatedly telling the child that he or she is very smart. When youngsters fail to do something properly, they may be told: "Gee, you are stupid." A Tarong child who shares with another youngster will be lavishly praised.

Adults in other cultures do not like to praise children and some believe that praise is positively bad for a child. The Gusii say that praise causes a youngster to be conceited and disobedient. As a result, children are not praised and do not expect to be rewarded for good behavior. Mixtecan mothers may sometimes hug or praise a young child who has behaved well. But children past the age of five or six, who are by now performing numerous tasks throughout the day for the benefit of the household, cannot expect their parents to praise or thank them for their efforts. The Rajputs believe that children who are praised to their faces will think that their parents love them too much and will end up spoiled and disobedient. Rajput men say that children obey their fathers more than their mothers because the women love their children too much. And in fact, the Rajputs seldom praise their children. Adults living in the same household also avoid praising their own or another parent's children because they do not wish to be accused of favoritism or of spoiling a child. Jamaican parents avoid rewarding or praising children who do their chores well because both rewards and acclaim "will make them bad." Even the work of children who have done a fine job is criticized as being mediocre, and a mother will hold up the superior efforts of some absent sibling as a comparison. After all, there is always the possibility of improvement. Children become depressed at this kind of criticism, but parents say that there is no reason to praise children for doing well because this is merely what is required of them. In Uganda, Sebei children are punished when they perform poorly. But a child does not receive praise for doing well.

Material Rewards

Children in some places around the world can expect to receive gifts or other kinds of rewards if they are good. Mixtecan mothers say that they will sometimes give an obedient child a present of some sort. Arapaho children sometimes received fried bread as a reward for good behavior. Sometimes, a parent promised a child some treat in return for being good. For instance, a mother might promise her daughter a little shawl for doing what she was told. Adults, however, did not consistently depend upon rewards as a way of promoting desirable behavior in children. Some Rajput mothers say that they may give a child food, money to buy candy, or promise a trip to another town or to visit relatives as a reward for good behavior. But in fact, children are rarely given material rewards for behaving themselves.

It also happens that a child may be promised some reward that never materializes. This appears to be a typical pattern in some cultures. Tarong adults will sometimes give a child a cookie or piece of fruit as a reward for good behavior. But material rewards are not frequent, and adults often fail to deliver, so that youngsters soon come to regard promises that they will be rewarded with a degree of skepticism. As a Tairan child gets older, adults are likely to promise some kind of material reward such as a food treat or some new piece of clothing instead of using praise in response to good behavior. But they frequently forget their promises and have to be reminded repeatedly by the child before the reward materializes. Children soon come to regard these promises with suspicion and often forget about an anticipated reward themselves. Similarly, Banoi mothers promise their children some reward, such as a bit of candy or cake, for good behavior. Often, they keep their word, but mothers admit that they frequently make such promises simply to persuade their children to behave without meaning to make good the promise. As a result, youngsters often eagerly await a promised reward only to cry in disappointment when their mothers return empty-handed.

Persuasion

Adults in some societies try to persuade children to be good by making object lessons out of the bad behavior of other children and of grown men and women as well. When someone committed some unacceptable act in front of a Chippewa child, parents would use the occasion to point out the bad behavior and to demonstrate what happened to people who did bad things. Adults felt that children should not be ridiculed and that even too much scolding just made them worse. Tarong parents hold up failed adults as examples of what can become of a person who does not behave properly. To a child who has been wasteful, an adult might warn: "So you are deaf to what I say? Do you want to become like Adriano and sleep in the fields?"

Reason is employed by Japanese parents, for instance, when they are arbitrating a dispute. A mother often tries to persuade an older child to give in to a younger one, and children are consistently reminded that it is sometimes better to "lose to win." Sometimes this means, for instance, that the younger child who is given a disputed toy will very soon tire of it anyway. Or it might mean, for instance, that the youngster who concedes a point in a game will nevertheless win by enjoying the fun that follows. Losing to win is also a favorite strategy employed by adults in ending disputes.

Adults who depend upon object lessons as a way of socializing their children may also explain to their children why some actions are approved of while others are not. By contrast, adults in other cultures are not interested in offering explanations for why some behavior is bad. A Korean mother will tell a child to stop engaging in some specific activity that she considers inappropriate. Thus, a youngster who continues to lie on the porch when an elderly man wishes to sit there or a child who is playing near a boat that is being prepared for a trip will be shooed away. But adults do not try to explain why the child's behavior is wrong or what general rules of good behavior are expected. As a result, youngsters pick up specific information about what kinds of actions are likely to be punished in what specific situations by which particular individuals. Rajput adults do not explain why the child's behavior is wrong or what constitutes good behavior because they believe that children learn from observation and not by direct instruction.

Changes in Tactics with Age

Parents across cultures often tailor their socialization strategies to the age of the child. Mixtecan mothers will hug and praise a younger child for good behavior and perhaps offer some kind of material reward. But in the case of older children, punishment for bad behavior is the major technique for training a child. A child who is good or who performs a task properly is not likely to be noticed. Mothers consciously refrain from rewarding older children with hugs and kisses because physical demonstrations of approval are no longer seen as appropriate for youngsters past the ages of five or six. Similarly, Gusii mothers are much more likely to resort to caning a child under six years old, but to abandon caning for other punishments such as withholding food for an older child. As Tarong children grow older, parents exchange physical forms of punishment for ridicule and sharp comments. Older children are also less susceptible to threats about retribution from supernatural creatures, so parents begin to rely more on realistic warnings that a bad child may be kidnapped by the nonhumans or hurt by some large animal. Rewards and extravagant praise also become less frequent. Rather, a child can now expect occasional, carefully targeted complements. Banoi mothers use placation and indulgence as the major strategy for achieving compliance in a prelinguistic baby. By contrast, threats become the principle way of socializing young children who have begun to understand language. Threats of physical punishment are also leveled at young children, but it is only when the child is somewhat older that hitting becomes a genuine technique of socialization.

Children's Responses to Punishment

Typically, a child will accept whatever punishment is doled out by an adult without attempting to retaliate. For instance, Jamaican children never strike their parents. On the one occasion that a little girl was seen to hit her mother as a reflexive response to a flogging, the child was horror-struck by her own action, and made sure to avoid her mother for a number of days afterward. The mother was amused by the incident but her daughter never knew it. Children may also sometimes actively respond to punishment or to the threat of punishment. Truk children sometimes decide to teach their parents a lesson by running away after receiving a punishment that they felt was unfair. The child will hide out for a while, frightening the parents. When the youngster is finally found, all is forgiven. Jamaican children soon discover that they can avoid a flogging if their parents are unable to hold them physically, and youngsters, therefore, run away and hide if they can when a flogging is imminent. This gives the parent's temper a chance to cool. Jamaican youngsters are punished for accidental misbehavior such as breaking an object, and it is also common for a child to try to hide the accident to avoid being punished.

Different Treatment for Different Children

While some socialization strategies may be habitually used by adults in a given culture, parents also recognize that each child is different and responds differently to some specific child training strategy. Tairan mothers note that one technique works for one child while another works better for another child. As these women say: "You cannot scold this one because she is so sensitive. The boy you cannot scold because he would get so angry he would not be able to understand the wrong he did." Similarly, a Mixtecan mother may be forced to repeat a command a number of times before a child finally obeys. A woman may eventually resort to punishing a disobedient child, but discipline for noncompliance is by no means inevitable. Girls eventually comply, while a boy, by contrast, may avoid carrying out his mother's orders at all.

Barry, Herbert, III, Lili Josephson, Edith Lauer, and Catherine Marshall. (1977) "Agents and Techniques for Child Training: Cross-Cultural Codes 6." *Ethnology* 16: 191–230.

Beaglehole, Ernest, and Pearl Beaglehole. (1941) *Pangai: Village in Tonga.*

Benedict, Ruth. (1946) *The Chrysanthemum and the Sword.*

Brandt, Vincent. (1971) *A Korean Village.*

Cohen, Yehudi A. (1966) *A Study of Interpersonal Relations in a Jamaican Community.*

Geertz, Hildred. (1961) *The Javanese Family: A Study of Kinship and Socialization.*

Gladwin, Thomas, and Seymour Sarason. (1953) *Truk: Man in Paradise.*

Goldschmidt, Walter. (1976) *The Culture and Behavior of the Sebei.*

Hara, Hiroko Sue. (1967) *Hare Indians and Their World.*

Harner, Michael J. (1973) *The Jivaro: People of the Sacred Waterfalls.*

Hilger, M. Inez. (1951) *Chippewa Child Life and Its Cultural Background.*

———. (1952) *Arapaho Child Life and Its Cultural Background.*

Hitchcock, John T., and Leigh Minturn.(1966) *The Rajputs of Khalapur, India.*

Hogbin, Ian. (1964) *A Guadalcanal Society: The Kaoka Speakers.*

Lefley, Harriet Phillips. (1973) *Effects of an Indian Culture Program and Familial Correlates of Self-Concept among Miccosukee and Seminole Children.* Unpublished dissertation, University of Miami: Coral Gables, Florida.

LeVine, Robert A., and Barbara B. LeVine. (1966) *Nyansongo: A Gusii Community in Kenya.*

Maretzki, Thomas W., and Hatsumi Maretzki. (1966) *Taira: An Okinawan Village.*

Norbeck, Edward. (1954) *Takashima: A Japanese Fishing Village.*

Nydegger, William F., and Corinne Nydegger. (1966) *Tarong: An Ilocos Barrio in the Philippines.*

Piker, Steven.(1965) *An Examination of Character and Socialization in a Thai Peasant Community.*

Ray, Verne. (1933) *The Sanpoil and the Nespelem: Salishan Peoples of Northeastern Washington.*

Romney, A. Kimball, and Romaine Romney. (1966) *The Mixtecans of Juxtluahaca, Mexico.*

Wagley, Charles. (1949) "The Social and Religious Life of a Guatemalan Village." *American Anthropologist* 51: 3–150.

Wallace, Ernest, and E. Adamson Hoebel. (1952) *The Comanches: Lords of the South Plains.*

SOCIETIES

In a number of cultures around the world, young people, especially at or around puberty, are initiated into a society of some sort. Sometimes, individuals are then graduated into other societies as they grow older. Societies generally provide members with a sense of comraderie. They also mark life cycle transitions, confer certain privileges upon their membership, define roles, and often serve to enforce social norms.

At the age of 12, the average North American Arapaho boy became a member of a ceremonial society, or lodge. Males were then graduated through a series of seven more such societies, and membership in a particular society was confined to males within a particular age range. The first two societies were comprised of adolescent boys. In comparison with the remaining societies, they were not associated with any powers, secrets, or obligations because males of this age were not expected to appreciate the importance of the societies. Each society had its own songs and dances and conducted ceremonies, which lasted for four days. Some older man instructed members of a lodge in the ritual associated with it. Arapaho females could also belong to societies beginning at 15 years of age. There were six female lodges, with membership yoked to age. An old woman instructed members in the rituals of their society. Boys under 12 and girls under 15 could not belong to societies, but some young children did participate in the dances of the societies, and smaller boys were sometimes recruited to do errands for older males on behalf of a society.

After his first initiation and sometimes before puberty, a North American Hopi boy joined at least one secret society. Males generally joined the same societies to which their godfathers belonged. A girl also joined the secret societies of her ceremonial aunt. Entrance into the societies was marked by a kind of rebirth ritual. New members observed a set of taboos and rites, and each received a new name. Entrance into a secret society signaled a number of important changes in a young person's life. The interpersonal ties of girls and boys were now expanded, as were the responsibilities and also the opportunities to engage in creative activities. For a boy, membership in the *kiva* meant inclusion in the world of men. He now had a place in the ceremonial life of his village and became privy to the esoteric knowledge associated with the society. Boys again joined one of four secret societies at a second initiation at adolescence. Two of these societies were concerned with war, hunting, and death and two with fertility. Each society had its own home in the underworld where individuals were assumed to go when they died, so entrance into a particular society at this time in a person's life determined the destination of the individual after death.

Among the Hopi, societies also provided a way of enforcing discipline. Thus, the parents of a chronically ill-behaved boy would choose a godfather who belonged to the Kachina Society, where the initiation rituals included a severe whipping. These whippings were understood to serve as a powerful sanction against bad behavior. Girls could also become members of the Kachina Society, and they might be whipped, but the whippings were much less harsh and were, thus, less effective disciplinary devices.

The *Poro* is a secret society that exists in a number of African groups, including the Kpelle, Mende, and Temne. All males are eligible to belong to the society, but membership is contingent upon a man's undergoing a set of arduous physical ordeals. At or around puberty, candidates for membership are secluded for a period of time, traditionally three to four years but now considerably shorter, in a "bush school." Here, the initiate undergoes severe psychological indoctrination and is taught to take on a new Poro identity. The Poro society acts in part as a regulator of social behavior. Its power to persuade people to act in accordance with its dictates stems from the fear that the society instills. The Poro is associated with the spirits of the dead, who are very powerful as conduits to the supernatural. The Poro is also believed to own medicines that can cause disaster in the world if the rules of the Poro are disobeyed. Because these characteristics of the Poro are shrouded in secrecy, they become potent influences on people's behavior.

Ember, Carol R., and Melvin Ember. (1988) *Anthropology.* 5th ed.

Hilger, M. Inez. (1952) *Arapaho Child Life and Its Cultural Background.*

Thompson, Laura, and Alice Joseph. (1947) *The Hopi Way.*

SUPERNATURAL INFLUENCES

In many cultures around the world, supernatural beings are thought to influence the welfare of infants and youngsters, and adults take measures to protect their children from harm brought about by the supernatural. Sometimes, precautions begin to be taken even before a baby is born. Thus, for example, in Indonesia, Javanese parents worry about the influences of evil spirits upon a fetus, especially one who is under seven months old and, therefore, not fully formed. As a result, a pregnant woman stays near home in the daytime and shuts the doors and windows and refuses to go out in the evening when the spirits are at large, particularly if this is her first baby. If a spirit succeeds in entering a fetus, the woman might have a miscarriage. If the baby survives the pregnancy, it may exhibit odd behaviors and can die from convulsions.

Sometimes, the focus is upon newborns. The Toba of Bolivia believe that at the birth itself and also for some days afterward, a mother and her baby are susceptible to adverse supernatural forces who arrive in the form of invisible snakes and try to get into the house and enter the new mother, causing her and the baby to die if they succeed. They therefore take a number of precautions in an effort to ward off danger. The new mother is covered with clothing as a protection against evil spirits, and the father chants with a rattle all night outside the house, as the woman is particularly vulnerable at this time.

In some cultures, supernatural influences remain a threat throughout babyhood. In North America, Comanche babies wore charms to protect them from evil influences and to insure good health. Crow feathers were also attached to an infant's cradleboard to protect it from evil spirits, and a stuffed bat might also sit on a cradle to watch over a baby. In former times, if a newborn Japanese Takashima baby needed to be taken out of doors, then two dots of ink were placed on its forehead. This was intended to trick any devils or monsters who might otherwise hurt the baby into mistaking it for a dog. A Guatemalan Chimalteco baby's head remains covered for the first few months of life to protect it from the evil eye. Any stranger can have the evil eye even without knowing it and can, therefore, hurt a baby simply by looking at it. A man who is hot and therefore sweating is particularly dangerous because "his blood is stirred and his eyes are strong."

North African Teda babies are susceptible to a number of supernatural influences against which they must be protected. While she is nursing, a mother wears a silver forehead ornament with a white cowrie shell as a protection against the evil eye. And when a baby is eight or nine months old, it begins to wear around its neck a strip of leather with a white stone attached to it to guard against magicians and also the evil eye. Mothers, fathers, siblings, and neighbors all shower a Liberian Kpelle baby with attention, but no one praises an infant for fear of causing some envious person to use witchcraft on the newborn child. In North America, Hopi babies are never left alone for fear that evil spirits may cause them harm. As soon as a New Mexican Zuni baby was born, a perfect ear of corn was placed nearby to ward off witches. Later, turquoise and flint were put in the baby's cradle as protection against witchcraft, and the first time that an infant went out after dark, it was rubbed all over with charcoal so that it would be invisible to witches. Some parents did not like it if anyone other than a relative looked at their baby. The result of this pervasive anxiety about witches was that Zuni children grew up to be fearful of the dark and afraid as well to be left alone.

Some cultures assume that supernatural forces continue to threaten children throughout their early lives. In Okinawa, the Taira believe that children are influenced by both good and evil supernatural forces, and parents take measures to protect a child from evil spirits. For instance, ancestral spirits are assumed to affect the health and fate of an infant, and a baby who is chronically ill may be adopted by a foster family so that the influence of the ancestors of the biological household upon the baby may be diminished. The baby lives with its biological parents, but visits the adoptive family and worships their ancestors. The South American Yanomamö believe that children are especially susceptible to supernatural dangers because their souls are not yet firmly planted in their bodies and can still enter and leave a child more or less at will. Typically, a soul will break out of the body when a child cries, and a mother will try to quiet a baby as soon as it starts to scream so that the soul will be prevented from escaping. It is possible to retrieve the soul by sweeping the floor around the area where it most probably exited the child's body. Shamans regularly send evil spirits to the villages of their enemies, and a spirit will attack and eat the souls of children, making them ill and perhaps killing them.

In some societies, children themselves are assumed to have supernatural powers, and adults take measures to strengthen these abilities if they are desirable or to control them if they are not. In Ecuador, a newborn Jivaro baby is given mild hallucinogens to promote its supernatural powers. Older children who are disrespectful toward

their fathers are forced to take stronger hallucinogens. A girl is given mild hallucinogens between the ages of two and eight so that she will
acquire soul power and become a successful
worker and reproducer of children. Similarly, a
boy is given hallucinogens in order to help him
to see a vision, thus allowing him to develop such
valued qualities as honesty, industry, and intelligence. In Japan, if an Ainu child lies or steals
on a regular basis, or if the youngster is lazy, a
rite is performed in the hope of exorcising the
offending spirit that is responsible for the undesirable behavior. Sometimes, magic is practiced on children to promote some desirable
trait or to discourage an undesirable one. In
the Northwest Amazon, Cubeo boys are
treated with growth magic beginning when they
are around six years old and continuing through
adolescence.

See also ILLNESS

Chagnon, Napoleon A. (1983) *Yanomamö: The Fierce People.* 3rd ed.

Erchak, Gerald M. (1977) *Full Respect: Kpelle Children in Adaptation.*

Geertz, Hildred. (1961) *The Javanese Family: A Study of Kinship and Socialization.*

Goldman, Irving. (1963) *The Cubeo: Indians of the Northwest Amazon.*

Harner, Michael J. (1973) *The Jivaro: People of the Sacred Waterfalls.*

Karsten, Rafael. (1923) *The Toba Indians of the Bolivian Gran Chaco.*

Kronenberg, Andreas. (1981) *The Teda of Tibesti.*

Leighton, Dorothea, and John Adair. (1966) *People of the Middle Place: A Study of the Zuni Indians.*

Maretzki, Thomas W., and Hatsumi Maretzki. (1966) *Taira: An Okinawan Village.*

Munroe, Robert L., and Ruth H. Munroe. (1975) *Cross-Cultural Human Development.*

Norbeck, Edward. (1954) *Takashima: A Japanese Fishing Community.*

Thompson, Laura, and Alice Joseph. (1947) *The Hopi Way.*

Wagley, Charles. (1949) "The Social and Religious Life of a Guatemalan Village." *American Anthropologist* 51: 3–150.

Wallace, Ernest, and E. Adamson Hoebel. (1952) *The Comanches: Lords of the South Plains.*

SUPPLEMENTARY FOOD

While all human infants depend upon milk, and usually breast milk, for a good part of their nutrition, babies in a majority of societies also begin to eat supplementary foods early on in life. An infant begins to eat foods other than milk and water before 30 days of age in 39 percent of 80 cultures around the world. In Kenya, Gusii infants were traditionally given gruel made from grain beginning at birth or soon thereafter. The mother would pour the food into the baby's mouth and hold its nose, forcing it to swallow. Eventually, infants learned to drink the gruel from a bowl. Infants are introduced to supple-mentary food for the mother's convenience so that the baby will have something to eat when she is away from home and cannot nurse. When mothers are at home, however, they prefer to nurse rather than feeding gruel to the baby. Infants whose mothers have died or have no milk subsist on a mixture of gruel and cow's milk. But under normal circumstances, a child is not given cow's milk or adult foods until it is weaned, which may be anywhere between 11 and 30 months of age. Similarly, in Micronesia, Truk babies begin to eat solid food early on, and all infants include adult foods in their diet by 8 months of age. Very young babies are already given coconut water and sugarcane juice. The mother premasticates the sugarcane to produce juice, which is then transferred to the infant's mouth, but babies drink coconut juice on their own, spilling a good deal of it but managing to get some into their stomachs. If a baby does not like some adult food, the mother will make a substitution of some other food that is available. In Liberia, Kpelle babies are nursed on demand. A mother also begins force-feeding, or "stuffing," an infant beginning in the first week of life. The baby's nose is held, and rice water is poured down its throat. Crying and choking, the infant is forced to swallow. A 9-month-old baby begins to eat soft rice mush or prechewed rice, and a 12-month-old begins to eat most of the solid foods enjoyed by the rest of the household, including greens-and-hot-pepper relish.

Babies begin to eat supplementary food at between 1 and 6 months of age in 26 percent of 80 societies. In the Philippines, Tarong babies begin to eat supplementary food by about 4 months of age, and a baby may be seen chomping on a drumstick or eating cookies, fruit, bits of fish, rice, or anything else that it is able to chew, although parents say that infants should only be given foods that are easily digested. Children who are a year old are given rice at each meal and are offered anything else that the rest of the family is having. A child who is 18 months old depends upon breast milk for only a small part of its diet, and a 3-year-old is eating adult food, although children of this age may also have snacks between meals. Similarly, in India, Rajput infants may begin to eat supplementary food by 6 months of age. One-year-olds regularly eat solid foods such as bread, rice, and bits of candy, but infants younger than this survive mainly on breast milk, supplemented with cow's milk if the mother's supply of milk is inadequate. By the time infants are weaned, at an average of 3 years of age, they are eating the normal spicy adult diet. In Japan, Takashima babies begin to eat rice gruel and tangerine juice when they are 5 or 6 months of age. Soon, other soft foods are added to the infant's diet, and youngsters have been eating solid food for a long while by the time they are weaned at 2 years of age.

Another 21 percent of the 80 cultures are supplementing the baby's diet when it is between 7 and 12 months old, with two-thirds of these infants receiving solid food and the remaining third eating liquid or premasticated food. Guadalcanal Kaoka babies begin to be fed premasticated yams and bananas when they are around 6 or 7 months of age. A parent holds the baby in his or her lap and pushes the food into the baby's mouth with a finger. Soon the baby also begins to eat soft coconut flesh and steamed and crushed vegetables. An 18-month-old toddler also eats mashed yams, and the baby's diet is gradually expanded further. Neither fish nor pork is considered digestible, and youngsters under 4 years of age are not allowed to eat them. Only 14 percent of the 80 societies wait until after a baby's first birthday before introducing supplementary food into the infant's diet.

Women begin supplementary feeding for a variety of reasons. Often, mothers think that the addition of other foods is good for a baby's health. Among the Javanese of Indonesia, mothers do not believe that nursing provides sufficient nutrition for a baby. Therefore, they begin to feed infants mashed banana and rice paste two or three times a day beginning a few days after birth. Many infants refuse the food and they are not forced to eat it until after the first birthday. In many cultures, supplementary foods are introduced into a baby's diet so that the mother does not need to cart her baby along with her wherever she goes. Among the Banoi of Thailand, a nursing infant begins to eat rice and banana mush beginning anywhere from a few weeks to 10 months of age. Mothers say that the supplementary food is good for the baby's health, but the addition of other foods to the baby's diet also frees the mother up by allowing other people to feed the baby on occasion. Sometimes, mothers will supplement breast milk with milk from domesticated animals. Among the Sebei of Uganda, nursing infants are fed cow's as well as breast milk from the start so that they will grow strong. A mother will dip her fingers into the cow's milk and then allow a very young infant to suck it off. In the case of older babies, the milk is poured into the mouth. This causes the baby to gag, but some of the milk is ingested in the process. Sometimes, infants are also fed gruel by this method, although a mother will not usually give gruel to a baby until it can drink from a bowl. When there is not enough milk, the mother will soak plantains or potatoes in a vegetable broth and then feed the softened food to the baby. A mother may also resort to supplementary feeding if she is not producing enough milk to satisfy her baby's appetite. Among the Bolivian Jivaro, a baby begins to be left home for hours at a time when its mother returns to her garden to work. If a child nurse is attending the baby, she may try to feed it some chewed up boiled manioc if it cries from hunger. A mother who is not providing enough milk for her infant may supplement the baby's diet with chewed up manioc or beer. A baby whose teeth have begun to come in will also be given steamed hearts of palm and tidbits of chewed meat.

Sometimes, a baby's first supplementary feeding is preceded by some special ceremony or event. Among the Tairans of the Philippines, children undergo a procedure to protect them from digestive problems before they are allowed to eat solid food. A special grass is burned onto the skin around the navel when the baby is about 6 months old, leaving three rows of three small dots. The infant is then introduced first to rice water and eventually to tiny pieces of sweet potato and mashed fish. By the second birthday, a youngster is eating fish, vegetables, and potatoes. A child will, however, continue to nurse until the mother becomes pregnant again.

See also Eating; Nursing

Barry, Herbert, III, and Leonora Paxson. (1971) "Infancy and Childhood: Cross-Cultural Codes 2." *Ethnology* 10: 466–508.

Erchak, Gerald M. (1977) *Full Respect: Kpelle Children in Adaptation.*

Geertz, Hildred. (1961) *The Javanese Family: A Study of Kinship and Socialization.*

Gladwin, Thomas, and Seymour Sarason. (1953) *Truk: Man in Paradise.*

Goldschmidt, Walter. (1976) *The Culture and Behavior of the Sebei.*

Harner, Michael J. (1973) *The Jivaro: People of the Sacred Waterfalls.*

Hitchcock, John T., and Leigh Minturn. (1966) *The Rajputs of Khalapur, India.*

Hogbin, Ian. (1964) *A Guadalcanal Society: The Kaoka Speakers.*

LeVine, Robert A., and Barbara B. LeVine. (1966) *Nyansongo: A Gusii Community in Kenya.*

Maretzki, Thomas W., and Hatsumi Maretzki. (1966) *Taira: An Okinawan Village.*

Norbeck, Edward. (1954) *Takashima: A Japanese Fishing Community.*

Nydegger, William F., and Corinne Nydegger. (1966) *Tarong: An Ilocos Barrio in the Philippines.*

Piker, Steven. (1965) *An Examination of Character and Socialization in a Thai Peasant Community.*

Thompson, Laura, and Alice Joseph. (1947) *The Hopi Way.*

Swaddling

Swaddling refers to the custom of tightly wrapping a baby with a long swatch of material. Sometimes, the infant is swaddled from head to toe, arms pinned down

Navajo mothers with their children. The infant on the left has been tightly swaddled.

against its sides. Swaddling has been practiced in many East European as well as American Indian societies. The practice of swaddling is most often found in cooler climates and may serve in part as a solution to the problem of keeping the infant warm.

Swaddling can be more or less extreme. A Greek baby was traditionally wrapped so thoroughly that it resembled a stiff bundle. Sometimes, each leg would be wrapped separately and then the two would be wrapped together. The infant's arms would then be pinned to its sides, after which the baby was again wrapped from neck to foot. In many American Indian tribes, babies were swaddled prior to being placed in cradleboards. The Mixtecans of Mexico have adopted a less extreme form of swaddling. Here, babies wear cotton shirts, and their diapers are tied on with a separate strip of material. The infant is then wrapped in a blanket that is tucked under the armpits, restricting the infant to some extent. The baby remains swaddled in this manner, more or less continually, until it is about ten months of age. Mixtecan infants are typically subdued and do not move around much. Similarly, in Indonesia, a Javanese baby is bathed and massaged twice a day by the midwife for the first month of its life. The infant's arms are then placed at its sides and soft cloths are wound about its body, keeping it rigid. The baby's feet remain free and the swaddling is not tied, so infants can loosen the cloths by kicking. The swaddling will also be removed if a baby cries, and a mother whose infant is active and does not like to be bound will not use swaddling. Babies remain in swaddling for a few hours each day and are not wrapped at night.

In some cultures, adults say that swaddling is necessary to insure a baby's safety. In old Russia, the baby's entire body was wrapped, with only the feet peeking out of the swaddling. The wrapping was tight, so that the baby was "like a log of wood for the fireplace." Adults said that an infant who was not swaddled would tear off its own ears and break its legs. In Poland, swaddling was also practiced for the sake of the infant. In this case, the baby was viewed as too fragile to survive without the support that swaddling offered. Swaddling prevented the baby from breaking in two, and was understood to be one measure in a longer process of "hardening" the infant.

Swaddling retards motor performance while the baby remains wrapped. But babies quickly catch up with other infants once swaddling is discontinued. In North America, Hopi and Navaho babies, in spite of the fact that their legs were tightly wrapped, could flex their limbs like other, unwrapped babies, when the swaddling was removed for baths or changing. Similarly, although its hands were restrained for most of the day and night, a baby from either culture would make the same use of its hands as do other infants. Thus, swaddled babies used their hands, and even their feet, to carry objects to their mouths for sucking, and fingers were stuck into the mouth when the swaddling was removed temporarily. Similarly, Hopi and Navajo babies sat, crawled, and walked in the same order as other infants.

See also INFANTS, CARRYING DEVICES FOR

Benedict, Ruth. (1949) "Child Rearing in Certain European Countries." *American Journal of Orthopsychiatry* 19: 342–350.

Geertz, Hildred. (1961) *The Javanese Family: A Study of Kinship and Socialization.*

Romney, A. Kimball, and Romaine Romney. (1966) *The Mixtecans of Juxtlahuaca, Mexico.*

Whiting, John W. M. (1981) "Environmental Constraints on Infant Care Practices." In *Handbook of Cross-Cultural Human Development,* edited by Ruth H. Munroe, Robert L. Munroe, and Beatrice B. Whiting, 155–179.

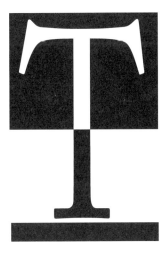

The temper tantrum is among the more dramatic kinds of behavior that young children are likely to display. Children who are throwing tantrums appear to be out of control and also seem to be in danger of harming themselves. Youngsters exhibiting a fit of temper may throw themselves about, strike other people, beat their own bodies, scream, and cry. Indeed, a tantrum is upsetting not only for the child who is throwing it but also for anyone who is witnessing the display. As disagreeable as a tantrum may be for both the actor and the observer, fits of temper on the part of young children are very common across cultures. Further, across societies, they occur in very predictable contexts.

A common trigger for the display of tantrums is the withdrawal of attention by the mother. In Micronesia, this is certainly a precipitating cause of fits of temper among Palauan youngsters. Thus, when they are about five years old, Palauan children suddenly discover that their mothers are no longer willing to indulge them in the way that they have come to expect. Young-sters of this age are no longer picked up and held, fed, cuddled, or amused on demand. Children respond to the withdrawal of indulgence with tantrums, throwing themselves on the ground and beating the earth with their fists while screaming, sobbing, and writhing. The display may initially have the intended effect. The mother gives in. But soon enough, children are required to resign themselves to the fact that they can no longer expect to be catered to by their mothers. Among the Alor of Indonesia, children between two and five years of age regularly throw temper tantrums. These fits are so pervasive and so long in duration that an outsider is immediately struck by them. Children commonly throw tantrums when their mothers leave for the fields in the morning. A youngster may first try to follow the mother and then resort to a fit of temper when she gets too far ahead to be pursued. Children who are having a tantrum may throw themselves to the ground, roll around, and hit their heads on the earth. The response of adults to tantrums is variable. A mother may ignore her child or threaten the youngster with the bogeyman. Sometimes, a woman may promise not to go to the fields and then sneak off when the child isn't looking. On occasion, women will hit children who are throwing tantrums. A strikingly similar drama is regularly played out among the Brazilian Mehinaku Indians. Here, a child whose mother attempts to go to the river on her own will shout, cry, and clutch at her legs in an attempt to prevent her from leaving.

Across cultures, temper tantrums are especially common among young children who suddenly discover that a new sibling has appeared on the scene. This is a special case of the withdrawal of attention that a child has come to take for granted. When a new baby is born into a household among the Takashima of Japan, the older child frequently throws temper tantrums, trying to push the new infant off the mother's lap. Women think of this as natural behavior on the part of the sibling. Older children may be given over to the care of a grandmother or older sister when a new baby arrives, in which case they adjust quickly, and demonstrations of jealousy more or less disappear.

Weaning is also a frequent trigger for tantrums. Among the Mehinaku Indians, a child of three is already eating the same food as adults. Nevertheless, youngsters resist being weaned, and fits of temper are the inevitable accompaniment of the weaning process. Most mothers give in and allow their youngsters to nurse when they cannot tolerate the screaming any longer. The Mehinaku child's anger at being weaned is exacerbated by the fact that the weaning of a child is usually associated with the birth of a new sibling. The older child, then, is responding to a variety of frustrations that happen to occur at more or less the same time. This is also a common state of affairs to which children across cultures have to resign themselves and to which they characteristically respond by throwing tantrums.

Children may also throw temper tantrums when they want something that is being withheld. Among the Banoi of Thailand, children soon come to expect that they will get their own way, and youngsters, especially those who have not yet been weaned, will throw tantrums, repeatedly hitting the mother if she does not meet the child's demands quickly enough. Children as old as seven years of age may also on occasion adopt the same strategy, but the mother will rarely give in to the demands of the older child the way she does to a younger one. Parents do not attempt to check aggression directed toward them by a child, and a mother will often go out of her way to distract and placate a little one who is being aggressive toward her. Jamaican children also have frequent emotional outbursts when they are hungry and want more food. Parents do not typically give in to these rages because they do not want their children to get used to having their stomachs full in case there is a shortage of food. Adults also ignore childish ti-

rades because they believe that children are prone to cry for no good reason. Therefore, there is no point in trying to calm a crying youngster. Infants are capable of working themselves up into such a rage that they become rigid and almost impossible to pick up. An older child who has a temper tantrum is punished.

Most Japanese boys between three and six years of age throw tantrums, and these fits of anger are so common that adults view them as a normal part of having a son. The youngster will scream and strike his mother, messing up her ornate hairdo in the bargain. Tantrums are frequently a boy's response to the teasing that is regularly employed as a socialization strategy among Japanese parents.

We may think of tantrums as a uniquely human display of emotion. But fits of temper also occur among the young of other species, and their occurrence elsewhere in the animal kingdom may help in an interpretation of their meaning in the human case. Infant and juvenile chimpanzees regularly throw temper tantrums that are striking in their similarities to the tantrums of human children. The young chimpanzee leaps into the air or throws itself onto the ground, perhaps beating at the earth with its hands and screaming loudly all the while. Chimpanzee tantrums occur when a young animal cannot immediately locate its mother or when it is being weaned. Often, the juvenile will stop in the middle of a display and secretly glance at its mother to determine what kind of affect the tantrum is having on her. Langur and baboon infants also throw tantrums, and such displays have also been observed in nonprimate species. For instance, pelican babies obtain food from their parents by begging. Sometimes, however, the young pelican will put on a more dramatic show, running toward the adult, throwing itself to the ground, beating its wings, and swinging its head back and forth. The infant pelican might disrupt the display long enough to peck at other nearby infants, thus driving them away. Sometimes, the baby might also shake and bite its own wings with its beak. Tantrums exhibited by other animals are similar to those displayed by human children not only in form but also in function. Thus, young chimpanzees, pelicans, baboons, and langurs, just like young human beings, seem to resort to fits of temper when they are being deprived of something that they want or when they wish to extract more of some commodity from an adult, and especially from a parent. Because we see the same kind of behavior implemented across species, and in the same contexts, the suspicion arises that we are witnessing a widespread, evolutionarily grounded strategy that promotes the survival of the actor. But how can this kind of violent behavior, and especially violent behavior that threatens to do harm to the actor him- or herself, be a way of promoting the youngster's survival? It is precisely the implied menace of tantrums to the actor that may make them effective. Parents are strongly motivated to see to it that their offspring are not harmed. Thus, tantrums begin to look like a form of blackmail. The youngster seems to be warning the parent: "If you don't give me what I want, I will hurt myself." The threat often works. Among the Wogeo of New Guinea, adults will do what they can to indulge whatever whim has caused a youngster to become angry. Sometimes, they try to distract the child with food. One little girl threw herself on the ground screaming when she discovered that her mother planned to leave her behind to visit the garden, and she kicked and bit anyone who tried to lift her up. The child's father fetched his wife back, and she remained at home all day nursing her daughter. There is no implication here that pelicans or chimpanzees, or even that young human beings, are consciously aware that tantrums will have this kind of effect on their parents. Rather, the claim is that the young of many species are biologically predisposed to throw tantrums as a way of trying to influence the behavior of their parents just because fits of temper in their children

do often frighten parents into acquiescing to the demands of their youngsters. The fact that juveniles in our own and other species seem to monitor the effects of these tantrums on observers makes temper tantrums look more like "strategies" that youngsters are actively using to manipulate the behavior of others and less like pure emotional responses to frustration.

Barnett, H. G. (1960) *Being a Palauan.*

Benedict, Ruth. (1946) *The Chrysanthemum and the Sword.*

Cohen, Yehudi A. (1966) *A Study of Interpersonal Relations in a Jamaican Community.*

Gregor, Thomas. (1985) *Anxious Pleasures: The Sexual Lives of an Amazonian People.*

Hogbin, H. Ian. (1943) "A New Guinea Infancy: From Conception to Weaning in Wogeo." *Oceania* 13: 285–309.

Munroe, Robert L., and Ruth H. Munroe. (1975) *Cross-Cultural Human Development.*

Norbeck, Edward. (1954) *Takashima: A Japanese Fishing Community.*

Piker, Steven. (1965) *An Examination of Character and Socialization in a Thai Peasant Community.*

Schaller, George B. (1964) "Breeding Behavior of the White Pelican at Yellowstone Lake, Wyoming." *Condor* 66: 3–23.

Trivers, Robert L. (1985) *Social Evolution.*

van Lawick-Goodall, Jane. (1968) "The Behavior of Free-Living Chimpanzees in the Gombe Stream Reserve." *Animal Behavior Monographs* 1: 161–311.

TOILET TRAINING

In all human societies, children are sooner or later required to learn the conventions of their culture in matters of elimination. This includes rules regarding where and when to eliminate as well as customs relating to hygiene. In most societies for which there is information, serious toilet training begins somewhere between one and three years of age. Toilet training of a child younger than a year of age is very unusual. It is equally unusual to find a child over three years old who is not more or less toilet trained.

Across cultures, toilet training routines differ in the degree to which they are easy to enforce. In part, this has to do with the age at which training begins. Older children are more easily trained both because they have greater physical control and because they can understand what it is that adults are asking of them and can go to the proper place for elimination on their own steam. Youngsters also sooner or later reach an age at which they want to imitate the actions of older children and adults. Thus, they are motivated to eliminate in the manner of grown-ups. As a result, while parents in Western cultures may hear about the traumas associated with toilet training, adults in some societies do not view toilet training as a problem. Among the Gusii of Kenya, toilet training does not begin until a child has been weaned, which does not take place until the youngster can walk tolerably well. This means that children will not begin training until they are around 26 months of age. Until training begins, when a baby urinates or defecates while being held, the mother will simply clean up the mess without showing any irritation. Once a mother decides that it is time for toilet training to begin, she will take the child to a spot near the house a number of times and show the youngster how to defecate there. Or she may simply tell the child to do what the older children do. A child who should now know the proper procedure will be caned for defecating in the house. At first, only daytime infractions are punished, but soon children are also expected to wake someone up to accompany them outside if they need to defecate at night. A child who defecates inside the house after training will also

be forced to clean up the feces. Adults are not as concerned about urination, and children tend to learn proper urination habits during defecation and modesty training. Toilet training takes anywhere from a week to a year. Quick results seem to be the result of severe punishment for mistakes. When training is prolonged, mothers seem not to be disturbed by indoor accidents on the part of their children. In Ecuador, Jivaro adults take no notice when a baby urinates or defecates in the house. Older children are told to go outside to relieve themselves, but a youngster who fails to do so is not scolded. Parents only begin to reprimand and sometimes spank recalcitrant children when they are five or so years of age. A Guatemalan Chimalteco mother does not tell her children to eliminate in private, and indeed, youngsters may initially urinate or defecate in the yard while talking to a parent. Soon, however, they learn to eliminate in privacy because they see that this is how the older children do it.

Where children wear little or no clothing, training is often relaxed, no doubt because accidents do not mean frequent cleaning and changing of garments. In Micronesia, Truk babies, who wear neither clothes nor diapers, regularly urinate and defecate in the house, and little attempt is made to stop them. A mother will take a baby outside in the morning and also when it is beginning to defecate, but otherwise the caretaker just cleans up after the infant. Youngsters who have begun to walk will be sent outside the house to eliminate, but children of this age are not reprimanded for accidents. Among the Mixtecans of Mexico, toilet training means learning to defecate or urinate at the corner of the patio. Young children do not wear pants, and adults do not worry very much about their toilet habits. When a child has begun to walk, the mother takes him or her outside and shows the youngster the proper spot for eliminating. A child who is being trained will first urinate right outside the door of the house, but will eventually head for the patio corner. Some mothers scold their children for mistakes, but others just allow their youngsters to train themselves. Children are typically trained by three years of age.

The toilet training regime typical of a society also depends in part upon the attitudes of the child's caretakers toward being soiled when the youngster urinates or defecates. Among the Tarong of the Philippines, babies are carried about or held for most of the day. As a result, they inevitably urinate on the people who are holding them. A mother whose baby wets her will simply shift the baby to a dry portion of her dress, but she will not rebuke the infant in any way. More of an effort is made to prevent a baby from defecating on another person, and anyone who is holding a baby will place a cloth under its buttocks. The cloth is then replaced when it is soiled. When an infant is able to sit with support, it is put on the porch at the first signs that it is about to defecate. A six-month-old baby is placed over the waste puddle in the corner of the porch when it has to urinate or defecate. More serious toilet training begins when youngsters are old enough to tell someone that they need to eliminate and to understand instructions about where to do so. A child who urinates in the wrong place is mildly scolded. Defecation in an inappropriate spot is treated less lightly, and a child who makes this kind of mistake may be slapped. Again, because children are not encumbered by elaborate clothing, training is easy, and parents do not face any resistance on the part of children who are being trained. A youngster has learned to defecate in the outhouse by the age of two and to urinate in the outhouse or in the corner of the porch by three.

Where accidents do not do permanent damage to furniture, rugs, or other expensive possessions, caretakers can also afford to be indulgent. Among the Indian Rajputs, babies wear only a short shirt during the day. When in their cots, they are placed on a sheet, which acts as a diaper. If a baby begins to urinate while being held, it is held away from the caretaker's body.

Courtyards, where Rajput infants spend most of their time, have mud floors, so the wet area is absorbed quickly. An infant sleeps with its mother, who holds the infant away from the bed if it urinates at night. If a caretaker can predict that an infant is about to move its bowels, she will hold the baby over the courtyard drain. A baby that soils itself is cleaned up immediately because the Rajputs believe that anyone who has ingested feces as a child will have the evil eye. Once Rajput children can walk, adults will take them to the courtyard drain, cattle compound, or street to urinate or defecate. Youngsters are able to witness adults eliminating in the appropriate places since adults urinate in public, and most are trained by the time they are two years old.

Sometimes, toilet training is very prolonged, with the result that a relatively old child is still not reliably trained. Among the Banoi of Thailand, infants urinate and defecate at will until they are around 12 or 18 months old. The mother simply cleans up the mess and washes the baby off. Toward the middle of the infant's second year, the mother may try to place the baby on a small pot when she thinks that the baby is about to eliminate. Sometimes, youngsters of this age will signal that they need to eliminate. The mother's efforts to anticipate when a child is about to eliminate, as well as the youngster's own attempts to communicate his intentions, become more frequent once the child can get around efficiently, at around two or three years of age. But until they are three years old, children are still regularly soiling themselves, and mothers take it for granted that they will do so. The mother of a three-year-old will more consistently remind her child to go over to the pot or to a hole in the floor when the child needs to eliminate. And by the time they are four or five, the now-constant reminders from adults as well as the example set by older children result in a youngster who is more or less trained. But it is not until children are seven or eight years old, when they have begun to go to school, that they display fully adult toilet habits, which include eliminating in the proper place and maintaining privacy in the process.

While children are typically not toilet trained until they are at least two years old, training is early in some cultures. In Uganda, a Sebei mother begins to take an infant outside to defecate once it is six months old. If the infant continues to have accidents after training has begun, the mother will put the feces on the baby's head. Nighttime mistakes are not punished until the child is able to go outside without help. Youngsters who are assumed to know better, however, are beaten if they soil themselves during the night. A Japanese Takashima mother will begin toilet training when the baby is six months old, unless it is winter and, therefore, too cold. The mother holds the infant over a receptacle in the yard a number of times a day for a few weeks, and babies begin to appreciate the point of this exercise. Most children are trained by the time they are two years old. Children aren't punished for mistakes, but a youngster who is old enough to be able to communicate the need to eliminate but forgets to do so may be scolded. And among the Hare of Canada, mothers begin toilet training as soon as they can, typically by six months of age and sometimes at two months. The mother holds the infant over a lard can or chamber pot acquired for the purpose. Most children have completed training by two years of age. When children of this age defecate in their pants, the mother will make them smell their clothing while ridiculing them.

Bedwetting is a problem for at least some children in a number of cultures. Banoi youngsters who reliably eliminate in the proper place during the day may still bedwet at night, and this is expected by their parents. Such mistakes are treated in the same way as other failures on the part of the child. Bedwetting is frequent among North American Zuni children long after they have learned proper toilet habits during the daytime, and some children continue to wet their beds until they are eleven or twelve years old. Canadian Hare parents avoid letting children drink much water in the nighttime to prevent bedwetting. Some mothers wake their children once during the night and hold them over the training pot. Jamaican children are expected to be toilet trained by five years of age. They continue to bedwet until late childhood, but are not punished because it is unreasonable to hold sleeping people responsible for their actions. Hopi children are not expected to control themselves at night until they are two years old. Some children, however, continue to wet their beds until they are six or seven. A girl who persists in bedwetting is expected to wash the soiled linen, while a boy is carried on the back of his maternal uncle at daybreak, accompanied by other boys, to a Water Clan house, where he is solemnly sung over and splashed with water. Tarong children who wet their beds are lightly scolded. Most youngsters have outgrown the habit by the time they are four years old. Tairan children do not usually have bedwetting problems, and youngsters who do wet their beds are embarrassed as well as concerned to be displaying such infantile behavior.

Benedict, Ruth. (1946) *The Chrysanthemum and the Sword.*

Cohen, Yehudi A. (1966) *A Study of Interpersonal Relations in a Jamaican Community.*

Gladwin, Thomas, and Seymour Sarason. (1953) *Truk: Man in Paradise.*

Goldschmidt, Walter. (1976) *The Culture and Behavior of the Sebei.*

Hara, Hiroko Sue. (1967) *Hare Indians and Their World.*

Harner, Michael J. (1973) *The Jivaro: People of the Sacred Waterfalls.*

Hitchcock, John T., and Leigh Minturn. (1966) *The Rajputs of Khalapur, India.*

Leighton, Dorothea, and John Adair. (1966) *People of the Middle Place: A Study of the Zuni Indians.*

LeVine, Robert A., and Barbara B. LeVine. (1966) *Nyansongo: A Gusii Community in Kenya.*

Maretzki, Thomas W., and Hatsumi Maretzki. (1966) *Taira: An Okinawan Village.*

Norbeck, Edward. (1954) *Takashima: A Japanese Fishing Community.*

Nydegger, William F., and Corinne Nydegger. (1966) *Tarong: An Ilocos Barrio in the Philippines.*

Piker, Steven. (1965) *An Examination of Character and Socialization in a Thai Peasant Community.*

Romney, A. Kimball, and Romaine Romney. (1966) *The Mixtecans of Juxtlahuaca, Mexico.*

Thompson, Laura, and Alice Joseph. (1947) *The Hopi Way.*

Wagley, Charles. (1949) "The Social and Religious Life of a Guatemalan Village." *American Anthropologist* 51: 3–150.

Whiting, John W. M., and Irvin L. Child. (1953) *Child Training and Personality.*

WALKING

Walking is actively encouraged in some cultures. Among the Guatemalan Chimalteco, children begin to walk at between 18 months and two years of age. Older brothers and sisters actively attempt to teach a little sibling to walk by taking the baby by the hands and helping it to toddle about. Once a youngster is able to walk on its own, a mother is very happy because she no longer has to pay as much attention to the toddler. Similarly, in Canada, an older Hare boy or girl will hold the hand of a baby to encourage it to walk. Infants begin to do so at about 15 months of age. Jamaicans encourage their children to walk early. For instance, a mother will hold food out and then beckon her infant to toddle over to fetch it. Adults say that they like children to walk as soon as possible because then they are able to do small chores. Jamaican infants generally begin to walk at one year of age. The Gusii of Kenya encourage their infants to stand and to walk, usually by holding the baby's hands and by guiding the infant as it toddles about. Or a child nurse may hoist an infant onto its feet and, saying "Ta, ta," prompt the baby to walk toward her. The goal here is not to accelerate motor development and parents are not especially proud that their infant has begun to walk early. Rather, adults are anxious to reduce the infant's fear of walking. But if there is a new baby on the way, a mother will direct the child nurse to teach an infant to walk early, as parents believe that a child should be able to walk and to be independent of its nurse before its "follower" comes along.

WALKING Every child with a normal genetic endowment and normal opportunity sooner or later begins to walk on his or her own. Children in Western societies start to walk at around one year of age, although there is actually considerable variation in the age at which perfectly normal children will take their first steps. In some cultures, adults are interested in encouraging their youngsters to walk as soon as possible, while in other societies early walking is discouraged. Beliefs also differ regarding what it takes to get a child to walk. Adults in some cultures assume that children will begin to walk on their own without any kind of intervention. As a result, they adopt a laissez-faire policy, allowing babies to learn to walk by themselves. In other societies, people assume that children need explicit training in order to learn to walk, and babies are provided with various aids designed to transform them into toddlers. In fact, practice of certain sorts may affect when and how a child walks. But children with no physical impediments inevitably learn to walk with or without the help of adults.

Adults in a number of societies provide special equipment of some sort to help a child to walk. Among the Jivaro of Ecuador, fathers build a railing around the open sides of the mother's bed so that infants who are learning to walk will have something to hold onto for support. In the Northwest Amazon, Cubeo infants are encouraged to walk, and a father will make a sling that passes between a baby's legs to make it easier for the youngster to sit, stand, and walk.

347

Sometimes, adults think that the ability to walk depends upon special training, sufficient strength, and the like. In these societies, adults make overt efforts to control the progress of the child. The Zhung !kwasi of the Kalahari Desert believe that a child needs training in order to succeed at sitting, standing, and walking, and parents pile sand around their babies to help them to sit upright. The Javanese of Indonesia do not allow infants to move on their own until there is evidence that their muscles are sufficiently developed. Babies are swaddled or else carried about for the first few months of life and are not supposed to be put on the ground at all until the seventh-month ritual. Infants, therefore, do not crawl. Parents may dangle a baby from their laps but only allow infants to be on their own when it is clear they are actually able to stand, squat, and toddle about by themselves.

Some cultures discourage early walking, sometimes because a mobile toddler is an inconvenience to have around and sometimes because walking children can more easily place themselves in the path of danger. Among the Taira villagers of Okinawa, a baby continues to be carried on the back of a caretaker for the first two or three years of life even though the baby is able to crawl by six months and to walk soon after. Adult baby tenders do not encourage crawling on the part of a baby because they are too preoccupied with their chores to be supervising a mobile infant. And child nurses prefer playing to keeping a crawling infant out of trouble. The reluctance to allow babies to crawl stems in part from the particular characteristics of Taira houses and in part from the kinds of tools that are used around the house by mothers. Floors are raised above the ground, making it easy for a crawler to fall over the side of the house. And women, who use sharp knives to weave bamboo baskets, work more efficiently if they do not have to worry that an unfettered baby will appropriate the knife as a toy. Babies do not mind being carried about and in fact seem to prefer being on the back of a caretaker to crawling about.

In some cultures, adults celebrate a child's first successful attempts at walking. In North America, the Chippewa celebrated when a baby first took a number of steps in succession. The parents gave the feast if the child first walked at home, and if it walked at a neighbor's house, then that is who would throw the feast. Other young children who lived nearby might be invited, or sometimes everyone in the neighborhood attended. The child's first real attempt at walking was similarly celebrated by the North American Arapaho in the past. Even when this custom fell into disuse, people were pleased when a toddler first walked because this meant that the youngster was growing normally. Whoever witnessed the child's first steps remembered it and would repeat to the youngster over the years: "I was the one who saw you take your first walk."

All normal children learn to walk with or without special aid or encouragement, and even when they are initially prevented from practicing walking. Thus, for example, babies who spend most of their time in cradleboards for the first months of life walk at the same time as infants who are allowed to move about freely. On the other hand, institutionalized infants who are deprived of sensory and social stimulation as well as opportunities to move about are slower to progress in all sorts of ways, and this includes walking. This suggests that extreme kinds of detours away from normal childhood experiences can get in the way of the normal acquisition of motor skills. Practice may also affect walking in subtle ways, allowing a child to become a more graceful walker than the youngster who has had less opportunity to practice walking skills.

See also PHYSICAL DEVELOPMENT

Cohen, Yehudi A. (1966) *A Study of Interpersonal Relations in a Jamaican Community.*

Geertz, Hildred. (1961) *The Javanese Family: A Study of Kinship and Socialization.*

Goldman, Irving. (1963) *The Cubeo: Indians of the Northwest Amazon.*

Hara, Hiroko Sue. (1967) *Hare Indians and Their World.*

Harner, Michael J. (1973) *The Jivaro: People of the Sacred Waterfalls.*

Hilger, M. Inez. (1951) *Chippewa Child Life and Its Cultural Background.*

———. (1952) *Arapaho Child Life and Its Cultural Background.*

LeVine, Robert A., and Barbara B. LeVine. (1966) *Nyansongo: A Gusii Community in Kenya.*

Maretzki, Thomas W., and Hatsumi Maretzki. (1966) *Taira: An Okinawan Village.*

Pinker, Steven. (1994) *The Language Instinct: How the Mind Creates Language.*

Super, Charles M. (1981) "Behavioral Development in Infancy." In *Handbook of Cross-Cultural Human Development,* edited by Ruth H. Munroe, Robert L. Munroe, and Beatrice B. Whiting, 181–270.

Wagley, Charles. (1949) "The Social and Religious Life of a Guatemalan Village." *American Anthropologist* 51: 3–150.

WEANING

In industrialized societies, a new mother may find herself faced with the decision of whether to breast-feed her baby or to use a bottle. For women in traditional societies and before natural milk substitutes were made available to them, however, the choice did not arise. Babies were breast-fed. But these mothers had another decision to make, and this had to do with when to wean a baby. By American standards, they opt to wean later rather than sooner. Thus, of 159 societies across the world, 83 percent wean when a youngster is two years old or older, 15 percent wean babies from one to two years of age, and a mere 2 percent wean infants at one year or less, the norm for American mothers. In some cultures, infants are still occasionally nursing at considerably older than two years of age. Thus, of 168 cultures, 21 percent include some youngsters who are still nursing from time to time at three years of age or older. For example, the North American Arapaho mother typically weaned a child at four years of age. But youngsters might still nurse occasionally at eight years, and people clearly remembered children of ten, eleven, and twelve who would interrupt their activities to nurse.

Reasons for Weaning

In many cultures, a woman will wean one child when she is pregnant with another. Among the Mixtecans of Mexico, infants are usually weaned at one to two years of age. Women generally nurse a baby for the first five or six months of a current pregnancy. Some mothers say that breast milk becomes sour and causes an infant to be ill beyond this point. Other women simply find it too taxing to nurse while they are pregnant. Among the Taira of Okinawa, a baby continues to nurse until the mother finds that she is pregnant, usually about two years after her last pregnancy. Ideas about how long to wait before weaning one child can affect a woman's attitudes about how long to wait before having another baby. The Gusii of Kenya do not like to wean youngsters until they can walk reasonably well and take care of themselves without constant surveillance. A woman, therefore, tries to prevent a new pregnancy until the current infant has attained a degree of independence. The Gusii believe that milk from a pregnant woman causes diarrhea in a nursing infant. Additionally, mothers fear that a nursing baby will consume all of the milk intended for the new infant. Women also claim that a pregnant woman's milk supply disappears when she is expecting a new baby. Mothers also feel that an infant who is already used to supplementary food and can get along on its own should begin to be prepared to have a new baby take its place. Thus, a mother will usually begin to wean a nursing baby early on in a new pregnancy. On an average, children are weaned at around 20 months of age, the earliest age of weaning being about 11 months and the latest around 30 months. Variations in the time of weaning have to do with whether the mother has become pregnant again.

While a new pregnancy is perhaps the most common reason for weaning a child, a mother may also decide to wean for other reasons. In the Philippines, the majority of Tarong babies are also weaned because the mother is pregnant. Most women wean infants between the fifth month of a new pregnancy and the birth of the new baby. A minority of infants stop nursing because the mother is ill, because nursing is interfering with her work, or because she is taking a trip and leaving the baby at home. Tarong infants are weaned anywhere between one and four years of age, and most mothers think that the best age for weaning is two or two-and-one-half years. To wean a baby before two years of age is considered unreasonable and weaning after the age of four is viewed as somewhat ridiculous. In India, Rajput women wean youngsters for one of three reasons. The mother may be ill, her milk supply may no longer be adequate, or a new baby may be on the way. Again, the most frequent reason is the pregnancy of the mother. Among the Jivaro of Ecuador, women do not wean an older child when a new baby is born, with the result that a youngster of six or seven may still be nursing. In Thailand, Banoi children are weaned at from two to five years of age, with youngest children often being weaned the latest. The timing of weaning is influenced by the demands of the mother's workload, by new pregnancies, and by a desire on the part of the mother

to be free from an ever-demanding and chronically dependent child. Sometimes, a woman will decide to wean a baby whose teeth have begun to grow in. In Micronesia, most Truk babies are weaned by two years of age, and some by a little over one year. A mother becomes motivated to begin weaning when her baby starts teething. As a result, an infant who is late to develop teeth may continue to nurse until the mother becomes pregnant again. Similarly, the Canadian Hare say that mothers wean babies "when their jaws become stronger and they start to hurt the mother." Sometimes, a woman will wean a baby because of pressure from her neighbors. If a Hare child has not been weaned by two-and-one-half years of age, the other women will talk about the mother of the youngster in an accusing manner.

When a new pregnancy is the inducement for weaning a nursing infant, the youngest child in a family will often end up being weaned at a later age than the older brothers and sisters. The average age of weaning for Rajput children is three years, usually because the mother is pregnant. But women who do not become pregnant again will usually allow youngsters to nurse as long as they wish, and a child may still be nursing on occasion at six years of age or older. Among the Chimalteco of Guatemala, a woman will allow a child to nurse until she becomes pregnant again, and sometimes the older child will continue to nurse until the new baby is a month or two old. Generally, infants are born every two years, but if a woman fails to have another baby, her youngest child will not be weaned so soon, and some youngsters are still nursing at five or six years of age. Frequently, children who are three or four years old will suck on or play with the mother's breast, and older children will nurse even though the mother is no longer producing milk.

Methods of Weaning

Across cultures, women employ a variety of strategies intended to persuade a child to abandon nursing. Gusii mothers depend upon a number of methods for weaning their children. Thus, some women smear their breasts with unpleasant substances such as pepper, goat dung, or sour juice. Some mothers will slap a child who still wishes to nurse and some will burn the child's arm with a caustic juice. A number of women try to wean their children by stuffing them with excessive quantities of solid food, hoping that the youngster will then "forget the breast." Sometimes, a woman will simply attempt to ignore the crying and pestering of her child. Many mothers will also wear a dress when they go to bed so that their youngsters, who are still sleeping with them, cannot get to the breast any longer during the night. Other women will continue to sleep naked, but with their backs to their babies. A mother who has special difficulty being stern with her child may send the youngster to live with a grandmother for a while. Weaning among the Gusii can take from a week to six months, but most typically goes on for a month or two.

Many Mixtecan women rub bitter herbs or dirt on their nipples to prevent their infants from nursing. Some women send the child to stay with a relative for a few days. A weaned baby who cries is often given coffee to drink, or milk if the family can afford it. In the daytime, scraps of food are also offered to babies as a substitute for nursing.

When a Tarong mother decides that it is time to wean her baby, she will usually make herself scarce for a day. Some female relative who is a favorite of the baby will then take the infant home and feed it a variety of treats such as fish, eggs, and candy. When the mother returns home and the baby wishes to nurse again, the mother tells the infant that it is no longer good to nurse. She then shows the baby her breast, which she smears with ginger, pepper, manure, or something similar. Or a woman might tell the child that her breast is hurt and that sucking would be bad for it. Most mothers send their infants

off to sleep with another adult in the same house or in another household during the weaning process. Sometimes, the child will continue to sleep in the house of the "one who is weaning him," especially if weaning occurs at the same time that a new baby is being born. An infant who cries during the night will be offered some tempting treat. Crying children, especially if they are older, may also be threatened with some bad consequence if they do not stop fussing. Thus, a recalcitrant child may be told that the nonhumans will come and take its heart, or that *Wawak,* the bogeyman who kills and eats bad children, will come. Because there is a woman who dresses up as *Wawak* and parades around the neighborhood once or twice a year, youngsters take these threats very seriously.

A Taira mother who has decided to wean a child may send the youngster off to sleep with some other relative. Or she may take an overnight trip to the city and leave the child behind. If the child still wishes to nurse, a mother may take a large patch of black paper ordinarily used to treat aches and bruises and paste it on her breast. She then tells the youngster that her breast hurts , and she will pretend to be hurt if the child tries to nurse. The black paper is often effective in persuading a child to avoid nursing. Some mothers prefer to place red pepper or bitter medicine on their breasts. A child who then tries to nurse will experience a burning sensation the mouth.

Among the Sebei of Uganda, mothers use a variety of strategies to wean their children. Most women smear red pepper on their breasts, but one mother used tobacco juice, and two women pinched a baby's cheeks when it tried to nurse. If a woman is dealing with an older child, she may try to talk the youngster out of nursing. One child was told that her new sibling would be taking her place at the mother's breast, and that she would have to stop nursing because there was not enough room for two children. Some women will comfort a child who is upset during weaning, but others just tell the child: "I don't want you anymore."

A North American Chippewa mother who was weaning a youngster would give the child a rind of bacon to suck, and babies might also be fed fish broth or well-boiled wild rice. Among the Truk of Micronesia, a mother may sometimes give her baby sugarcane or some other object to suck.

Sometimes, children will just lose interest in nursing. This occasionally happened among the North American Arapaho, especially in an older child. One woman remembered that her son weaned himself when he was four years old. He was so interested in playing that he no longer wished to be "bothered by nursing." Similarly, a seven-year-old girl who was still nursing occasionally just stopped asking to nurse after a visit to her grandmother's. A Sebei mother will wean a baby when she becomes pregnant again, especially if her breasts begin to hurt, because she attributes the pain to the nursing. In this case, the infant may stop nursing at four or five months of age. But youngest children may be allowed to nurse until they stop on their own or until other children make them ashamed by their continual teasing. In this case, a child may continue to nurse for four or five years. Sebei mothers prefer if possible to let a child nurse as long as it wants because weaning as a result of teasing by peers is easier than other methods of weaning.

Abruptness of Weaning

Societies differ regarding the abruptness with which a child is weaned. Once a Tarong mother decides to wean her baby, almost nothing can persuade her to relent, and weaning is finished in two or three days. Children are not prepared for weaning. One day, the baby is just told that it can no longer nurse, and from then on, the mother's breast is no longer available. By contrast, a Taira mother who has decided to wean her baby shows a good deal of indecisiveness for the first month of the weaning process. When the youngster wants to nurse, the mother will initially refuse, but if the child persists in demanding to be nursed, the woman will, in all likelihood, relent. A child who thus succeeds in wearing the mother down, however, is not treated in the nurturant and indulgent manner to which the younger baby is accustomed. Rather, onlookers will make fun of a child who is being weaned but still wants to nurse. In Thailand, a Banoi woman may show some ambivalence as she begins the weaning process, especially if she is weaning an older child because she is pregnant. She may begin weaning with a good deal of resolve only to give in and allow the fussing youngster to nurse. Mothers show this kind of indulgence because they know that the new baby will not be arriving for a number of months. As her pregnancy advances, a woman will show more determination and weaning will be successful. Weaning is abrupt in 23 percent of 159 societies and more gradual in the remaining 77 percent.

Distress at Weaning

In some Western cultures, some women resist nursing their babies in part because they have heard that weaning causes a considerable amount of distress in a baby who is used to being breast-fed. And children in some cultures are clearly very upset at being weaned. Indeed, among the Gusii, the translation of the word for weaning is "stamp on" or "step on," reflecting the expectation that the weaning process is a difficult one for a mother and child. And in fact, most Gusii mothers say that weaning was troublesome and that their children cried and were cranky. The typical way of comforting a child who is being weaned and is showing signs of distress is to give it solid food. Mothers also avoid or punish a child who persists in wanting to nurse. If Gusii weaning practices are harsh, this is because Gusii women believe that weaning will go more quickly and smoothly if the mother is severe with the child. Taira children show considerable distress while they are being weaned. They whine and throw tantrums and make it difficult for any caretaker to please them. Child nurses, who are frustrated by their suddenly difficult charges, become impatient with them.

In some cultures, weaning seems to be less taxing on a child. Most Rajput mothers report that they had no trouble weaning their children. A few women said that their youngsters were troublesome for three or four days. The most distressed Rajput child remained upset for twenty days. Weaned children do not typically try to nurse again once a new sibling is born. Truk mothers say that their youngsters do not show much distress at being weaned. A woman who has decided to wean her baby begins to feed it adult food more regularly and to pick up the infant to discourage it from crying. Usually, however, the mother also actively prevents the baby from trying to nurse by rubbing her breasts with wild pepper or the sticky sap of black breadfruit, and youngsters stop trying to nurse after only one or two attempts.

Sometimes, a child's perception of the weaning process is different from that of the mother. Among the Tarong, the abrupt weaning method causes a considerable amount of distress and crying on the part of children for a number of days, and youngsters remain sullen, unhappy, and fussy for some weeks or months later. A sunny, good-humored child may change to a whiny, miserable one who throws regular temper tantrums as a result of weaning. Mothers, however, do not think of weaning as being an especially difficult process unless the child's response is extremely and consistently negative.

Some children have an easier time with weaning than others, and this seems to be more a matter of the child's temperament than it is of age, sex, or the mother's method of weaning. Birth order does make a difference, so that eldest children are more likely to find weaning difficult than are later-born siblings. This is in part because the youngster is used to being the only child and is now being replaced by a new baby. It is also because this is the mother's first experience at weaning so that she is not as skilled as is the woman who has been through the weaning process before.

There is some indication that a child's response to weaning is partly related to the age at which weaning occurs. Thus, weaning appears to be least upsetting to relatively young and relatively old children, with youngsters of about two years of age having the hardest time. Thus, the overwhelming tendency of mothers to wait until a child is older than two years before beginning weaning may in part reflect this tendency for older children to adapt to weaning more easily. We see the lack of concern about weaning in older children reflected in the fact that, if mothers wait long enough, children eventually just lose interest in nursing and wean themselves.

Other Changes along with Weaning
Often, weaning means that there will also be other changes in a child's life. For New Guinea Kwoma children, weaning also means that the mother will no longer respond to their requests. Whereas the mother would formerly take the youngster into her lap, or scratch or pat the youngster at his or her request, the same demands are now ignored, and indeed the mother may punish a persistent child. In North America, a Navajo child who had been weaned was no longer allowed to sleep with the mother. Instead, weaned children slept under a single blanket with other siblings of roughly their own age. Mothers were less tolerant of crying in youngsters who had been weaned, and children who were no longer nursing might be jerked aside roughly if they got in the mother's way. For many Mixtecan babies, weaning is difficult, in part because a crying infant is no longer comforted by its mother. A baby who has not yet been weaned always evokes a nurturant response, including the offer to nurse, on the part of its mother when

it cries. But a weaned infant can no longer expect its mother to behave nurturantly whenever it is upset. Instead, an older child may be asked to take care of a youngster who is being weaned, so that weaning also means a gradual decrease in the amount of time that a child spends with the mother and the amount of maternal care that the youngster receives. Further, a baby who has stopped nursing is no longer carried in its mother's rebozo, so weaning also means giving up the physical contact to which the infant is accustomed.

Sometimes, the life of a weaned child remains more or less unchanged except for the fact that the youngster is no longer nursing. For a Banoi child, weaning means a sudden lack of availability of the mother's breast. But otherwise, the child's life and relationship with the mother remains much the same. Thus, the mother is just as affectionate and gives just as much attention to her youngster after weaning as she did before. She spoon-feeds the weaned child while holding the youngster in her lap and plays and talks soothingly to the child much as she always has done. Nevertheless, Banoi children do tend to show frustration at being weaned.

Health Problems with Weaning

Nursing is known to promote the health of children because the mother's milk carries antibodies that help youngsters to fight disease. Thus, weaning can mean that the child now has an increased susceptibility to illness. Indeed, Mixtecan mothers say that weaning is dangerous to the well-being of their children, and in fact a Mixtecan youngster is more likely to become sick during the months following weaning than while nursing. The increased resistance to illness that nursing promotes may also in part explain why mothers around the world prefer to wean late rather than early.

Nursing also provides a child with a dependable supply of protein. And indeed, the age at which mothers typically wean their youngsters

is related to the availability of other sources of protein in the diet of the culture. Thus, where sources of protein are scarce, weaning tends to be late. In these societies, a long postpartum sex taboo is also frequently instituted. This maximizes the chances that a woman will not become pregnant again too soon and will, therefore, be able to continue nursing for an extended period of time. It is interesting that polygyny is commonly legal in these societies. This means that a man will have sanctioned sexual access to another wife when one spouse is off limits because she is nursing, making it less likely that the nursing youngster will be unseated too soon by a new baby.

Barry, Herbert, III, and Leonora M. Paxson. (1971) "Infancy and Early Childhood: Cross-Cultural Codes 2." *Ethnology* 10: 466–508.

Gladwin, Thomas, and Seymour Sarason. (1953) *Truk: Man in Paradise.*

Goldschmidt, Walter. (1976) *The Culture and Behavior of the Sebei.*

Hara, Hiroko Sue. (1967) *Hare Indians and Their World.*

Harner, Michael J. (1973) *The Jivaro: People of the Sacred Waterfalls.*

Hilger, M. Inez. (1951) *Chippewa Child Life and Its Cultural Background.*

———. (1952) *Arapaho Child Life and Its Cultural Background.*

Hitchcock, John T., and Leigh Minturn. (1966) *The Rajputs of Khalapur, India.*

Leighton, Dorothea, and Clyde Kluckhohn. (1948) *Children of the People.*

LeVine, Robert A., and Barbara B. LeVine. (1966) *Nyansongo: A Gusii Community in Kenya.*

Maretzki, Thomas W., and Hatsumi Maretzki. (1966) *Taira: An Okinawan Village.*

Norbeck, Edward. (1954) *Takashima: A Japanese Fishing Community.*

Nydegger, William F., and Corinne Nydegger. (1966) *Tarong: An Illocos Barrio in the Philippines.*

Piker, Steven. (1965) *An Examination of Character and Socialization in a Thai Peasant Community.*

Romney, A. Kimball, and Romaine Romney. (1966) *The Mixtecans of Juxtlahuaca, Mexico.*

Wagley, Charles. (1949) "The Social and Religious Life of a Guatemalan Village." *American Anthropologist* 51: 3–150.

Whiting, John W. M. (1941) *Becoming a Kwoma.*

Whiting, John W. M. (1964) "Effects of Climate on Certain Cultural Practices." In *Explorations in Cultural Anthropology,* edited by Ward E. Goodenough, 511–544.

BIBLIOGRAPHY

Ackerman, Sandra. (1992) *Discovering the Brain.*

Ainsworth, Mary D. (1967) *Infancy in Uganda: Infant Care and the Growth of Love.*

Alford, Richard D. (1988) *Naming and Identity: A Cross-Cultural Study of Personal Naming Practices.*

Ammar, Hammed. (1954) *Growing Up in an Egyptian Village.*

Arensberg, Conrad. (1950) *The Irish Countryman.*

Ayres, Barbara. (1967) "Pregnancy Magic: A Study of Food Taboos and Sex Avoidance." In *Cross-Cultural Approaches: Readings in Comparative Research,* edited by Clellan S. Ford, 111–125.

Barnett, H. G. (1960) *Being a Palauan.*

Barry, Herbert, III, and John M. Roberts. (1972) "Infant Socialization and Games of Chance." *Ethnology* 11: 296–308.

Barry, Herbert, III, and Leonora M. Paxson. (1971) "Infancy and Early Childhood: Cross-Cultural Codes 2." *Ethnology* 10: 466–508.

Barry, Herbert, III, Irvin L. Child, and Margaret K. Bacon. (1959) "Relation of Child Training to Subsistence Economy." *American Anthropologist* 61: 51–63.

———. (1967) "Relation of Child Training to Subsistence Economy." In *Cross-Cultural Approaches: Readings in Comparative Research,* edited by Clelland S. Ford, 246–258.

Barry, Herbert, III, Lili Josephson, Edith Lauer, and Catherine Marshall. (1976) "Traits Inculcated in Childhood: Cross-Cultural Codes 5." *Ethnology* 15: 83–114.

———. (1977) "Agents and Techniques for Child Training: Cross-Cultural Codes 6." *Ethnology* 16: 191–230.

Barry, Herbert, III, Margaret K. Bacon, and Irvin L. Child. (1957) "A Cross-Cultural Survey of Some Sex Differences in Socialization." *Journal of Abnormal and Social Psychology* 55: 327–332.

Batchelor, John. (1895) *The Ainu of Japan.*

Beaglehole, Ernest, and Pearl Beaglehole. (1941) *Pangai: Village in Tonga.*

Beals, Alan R. (1962) *Gopalpur: A South Indian Village.*

Beattie, John. (1960) *Bunyoro: An African Kingdom.*

Benedict, Ruth. (1946) *The Chrysanthemum and the Sword.*

———. (1949) "Child Rearing in Certain European Countries." *American Journal of Orthopsychiatry* 19: 342–350.

———. (1955) "Continuities and Discontinuities in Cultural Conditioning." In *Childhood in Contemporary Cultures,* edited by Margaret Mead and Martha Wolfenstein, 21–30.

Bennett, Wendell, and Robert Zingg. (1935) *The Tarahumara: An Indian Tribe of Northern Mexico.*

Berk, Laura E. (1989) *Child Development.*

Blackwood, Beatrice M. (1935) *Both Sides of Buka Passage.*

Blos, Peter. (1962) *On Adolescence.*

Blount, Ben G. (1981) "The Development of Language in Children." In *Handbook of Cross-Cultural Human Development,* edited by Ruth H. Munroe, Robert L. Munroe, and Beatrice B. Whiting, 379–402.

Bowlby, John. (1969) *Attachment and Loss. Volume 1: Attachment.*

Bradburn, N. M. (1963) "n Achievement and Father Dominance in Turkey." *The Journal of Abnormal and Social Psychology* 67: 464–468.

Brandt, Vincent. (1971) *A Korean Village.*

Broude, Gwen J. (1975) *A Cross-Cultural Study of Some Sexual Beliefs and Practices.* Unpublished dissertation, Harvard University.

———. (1988) "Rethinking the Couvade: Cross-Cultural Evidence." *American Anthropologist* 90: 902–911.

———. (1990) "Protest Masculinity: A Further Look at the Causes and the Concept." *Ethos* 18: 103–122.

Broude, Gwen J., and Sarah J. Greene. (1983) "Cross-Cultural Codes on Husband-Wife Relationships." *Ethnology* 22: 263–280.

Brown, Roger. (1973) *A First Language: The Early Stages.*

Burton, Roger V., and John W. M. Whiting. (1963) "The Absent Father and Cross-Sex Identity." In *Studies in Adolescence,* edited by Robert E. Grinder, 89–106.

Carstairs, Morris. (1958) *The Twice-Born.*

Chagnon, Napoleon A. (1968) *Yanomamö: The Fierce People.*

———. (1983) *Yanomamö: The Fierce People,* 3d ed.

Childs, Gladwyn. (1949) *Umbundu Kinship and Character.*

Cohen, Yehudi A. (1964) *The Transition from Childhood to Adolescence: Cross-Cultural Studies of Initiation Ceremonies, Legal Systems, and Incest Taboos.*

Cohen, Yehudi. (1966) *A Study of Interpersonal Relations in a Jamaican Community.*

Colinder, Bjorn. (1949) *The Lapps.*

Czaplicka, M. A. (1914) *Aboriginal Siberia: A Study in Social Anthropology.*

Dawson, Warren W. (1929) *The Custom of the Couvade.*

Dentan, Robert. (1978) "Notes on Childhood in a Nonviolent Context: The Semai Case." In *Learning and Non-Aggression,* edited by Ashley Montagu, 94–143.

Dentan, Robert L. (1968) *The Semai: A Non-violent People of Malaya.*

Dorsey, George Amos, and James R. Murie. (1940) *Notes on Skidi Pawnee Society.*

Dorsey, J. Owen. (1884) *Omaha Society.* Third Annual Report of the Bureau of American Ethnology, 1881–1882.

Draper, Patricia. (1975) "Cultural Pressure on Sex Differences." *American Ethnologist* 2: 602–616.

DuBois, Cora. (1944) *The People of Alor.*

Edgerton, Robert B. (1971) *The Individual in Cultural Adaptation: A Study of Four East African Peoples.*

Edwards, Carolyn Pope. (1980) "Development of Moral Judgment and Reasoning." In *Handbook of Cross-Cultural Human Development,* edited by Ruth H. Munroe, Robert L. Munroe, and Beatrice B. Whiting, 501–528.

Elwin, Verrier. (1939) *The Baiga.*

———. (1947) *The Muria and Their Ghotul.*

Ember, Carol R. (1973) "Feminine Task Assignment and the Social Behavior of Boys." *Ethos* 1: 424–439.

———. (1981) "A Cross-Cultural Perspective on Sex Differences." In *Handbook of Cross-Cultural Human Development,* edited by Ruth H. Munroe, Robert L. Munroe, and Beatrice B. Whiting, 531–580.

Ember, Carol R., and Melvin Ember. (1988) *Anthropology*, 5th ed.

Erchak, Gerald M. (1977) *Full Respect: Kpelle Children in Adaptation.*

Erikson, Erik. (1950) *Childhood and Society.*

Fei, Hsiao-Tung. (1939) *Peasant Life in China.*

Fischer, W. F. (1963) "Sharing in Preschool Children as a Function of Amount and Type of Reinforcement." *Genetic Psychology Monographs* 68: 215–245.

Flannery, Regina. (1953) *The Gros Ventre of Montana*, part 1.

Foner, Nancy. (1984) *Ages in Conflict.*

Frayser, Suzanne. (1985) *Varieties of Sexual Experience.*

Freedman, Daniel G. (1974) *Human Infancy: An Evolutionary Perspective.*

Freud, Anna. (1948) *The Ego and the Mechanisms of Defense.*

Gabrenya, W. K., B. Latane, and Y. E. Yang. (1983) "Social Loafing in Cross-Cultural Perspective: Chinese on Taiwan." *Journal of Cross-Cultural Psychology* 14: 368–384.

Gabrenya, W. K., Y. E. Wang, and B. Latane. (1985) "Social Loafing on an Optimizing Task: Cross-Cultural Differences among Chinese and Americans." *Journal of Cross-Cultural Psychology* 16: 223–242.

Gayton, Anna. (1948) *Yokuts and Western Mono Ethnography.*

Gazzaniga, Michael. (1992) *Nature's Mind: The Biological Roots of Thinking, Emotions, Sexuality, Language, and Intelligence.*

Geertz, Hildred. (1961) *The Javanese Family: A Study of Kinship and Socialization.*

Gladwin, Thomas, and Seymour Sarason. (1953) *Truk: Man in Paradise.*

Goethals, George W. (1967) "Adolescence: Variations on a Theme." Paper presented at Boston University, April.

Goldman, Irving. (1963) *The Cubeo: Indians of the Northwest Amazon.*

Goldschmidt, Walter. (1975) "Absent Eyes and Idle Hands: Socialization for Low Affect among the Sebei." *Ethos* 3: 157–163.

———. (1976) *The Culture and Behavior of the Sebei.*

Gomes, Edwin H. (1911) *Seventeen Years among the Sea Dyaks of Borneo.*

Goodenough, Ward. (1951) "Property, Kin and Community on Truk." Yale University Publications in Anthropology 46.

Gorer, Geoffrey. (1938) *Himalayan Village: An Account of the Lepchas of Sikkim.*

Gregor, Thomas. (1985) *Anxious Pleasures: The Sexual Lives of an Amazonian People.*

Gusinde, Martin. (1937) *The Yahgan: The Life and Thought of the Water Nomads of Cape Horn.*

Hallpike, C. R. (1972) *The Konso of Ethiopia.*

Hara, Hiroko Sue. (1967) *Hare Indians and Their World.*

Harner, Michael J. (1973) *The Jivaro: People of the Sacred Waterfalls.*

Harper, Lawrence. (1989) *The Nurture of Human Behavior.*

Hart, C. W. M., and Arnold Pilling. (1960) *The Tiwi of North Australia.*

Henderson, Ronald W., and John R. Bergan. (1976) *The Cultural Context of Childhood.*

Herskovitz, Melville. (1937) *Life in a Haitian Valley.*

———. (1938) *Dahomey: An Ancient West African Kingdom*, v. 1.

Hilger, M. Inez. (1951) *Chippewa Child Life and Its Cultural Background.*

———. (1952) *Arapaho Child Life and Its Cultural Background.*

———. (1971) *Together with the Ainu.*

Hitchcock, John T., and Leigh Minturn. (1966) *The Rajputs of Khalapur, India.*

Hogbin, H. Ian. (1943) "A New Guinea Infancy: From Conception to Weaning in Wogeo." *Oceania* 13: 285–309.

Hogbin, Ian. (1964) *A Guadalcanal Society: The Kaoka Speakers.*

Honigmann, John J. (1949) *Culture and Ethos of Kaska Society.*

Howitt, A. W. (1904) *The Native Tribes of South-Eastern Australia.*

Jones, William. (1939) *Ethnography of the Fox Indians.*

Junod, Henri A. (1927) *The Life of a South African Tribe,* v. 1.

Kagan, Jerome. (1976) "Emergent Themes in Human Development." *American Scientist* 64: 186–196.

———. (1984) *The Nature of the Child.*

———. (1989) *Unstable Ideas: Temperament, Cognition, and Self.*

Kagan, Jerome, and Robert E. Klein. (1973) "Cross-Cultural Perspectives on Early Development." *American Psychologist* 28: 947–961.

Karsten, Rafael. (1923) *The Toba Indians of the Bolivian Gran Chaco.*

———. (1935) *The Headhunters of the Western Amazons.*

Kenyatta, Jomo. (1961) *Facing Mount Kenya.*

Kluckhohn, Clyde, and Dorothea Leighton. (1958) *The Navaho.*

Konner, Melvin J. (1981) "Evolution of Human Behavior Development." In *Handbook of Cross-Cultural Human Development,* edited by Ruth H. Munroe, Robert L. Munroe, and Beatrice B. Whiting, 3–51.

Konner, Melvin. (1982) *The Tangled Wing: Biological Constraints on the Human Spirit.*

Kronenberg, Andreas. (1981) *The Teda of Tibesti.*

Kuper, Hilda. (1963) *The Swazi: A South African Kingdom.*

Lambert, William W. (1971) "Cross-Cultural Backgrounds to Personality Development and the Socialization of Aggression: Findings from the Six Cultures Study." In *Comparative Perspectives on Social Psychology,* edited by W. W. Lambert and R. Weisbrod, 49–61.

Landauer, Thomas K., and John W. M. Whiting. (1981) "Correlates and Consequences of Stress in Infancy." In *Handbook of Cross-Cultural Human Development,* edited by Ruth H. Munroe, Robert L. Munroe, and Beatrice B. Whiting, 355–387.

Lane, R. B. (1965) "The Melanesians of South Pentecost." In *Gods, Ghosts, and Men in Melanesia,* edited by P. Lawrence and M. J. Meggitt, 250–279.

Lee, Richard B. (1979) *The !Kung San: Men, Women, and Work in a Foraging Community.*

Lee, Richard B., and Irven DeVore. (1976) *Kalahari Hunter-Gatherers: Studies of the !Kung San and Their Neighbors.*

Lefley, Harriet Phillips. (1973) *Effects of an Indian Culture Program and Familial Correlates of Self-Concept among Miccosukee and Seminole Children.* Unpublished dissertation, University of Miami, Coral Gables, Florida.

Leighton, Dorothea, and John Adair. (1966) *People of the Middle Place: A Study of the Zuni Indians.*

Leighton, Dorothea, and Clyde Kluckhohn. (1948) *Children of the People.*

LeVine, Robert A. (1973) "Patterns of Personality in Africa." *Ethos* 1: 123–152.

LeVine, Robert A., and Barbara B. LeVine (1966) *Nyansongo: A Gusii Community in Kenya.*

Levinson, David, and Martin J. Malone. (1980) *Toward Explaining Human Culture.*

Lewis, Oscar. (1951) *Life in a Mexican Village: Tepoztlán Revisited.*

Loeb, Edwin Meyer. (1926) *Pomo Folkways.*

Madsen, Millard C. (1971) "Developmental and Cross-Cultural Differences in the Cooperative and Competitive Behavior of Young Children." *Journal of Cross-Cultural Psychology* 2: 365–371.

Malinowski, Bronislaw. (1929) *The Sexual Life of Savages.*

Maretzki, Thomas W., and Hatsumi Maretzki. (1966) *Taira: An Okinawan Village.*

Marshall, Donald S. (1950) *Cuna Folk.* Unpublished manuscript, Harvard University.

Marshall, Lorna. (1959) "Marriage among the !Kung Bushmen." *Africa* 29: 335–364.

Maybury-Lewis, David. (1967) *Akwe-Shavante Society.*

Mead, Margaret. (1928) *Coming of Age in Samoa.*

———. (1931) *Growing Up in New Guinea.*

Messenger, John C. (1971) "Sex and Repression in an Irish Folk Community." In *Human Sexual Behavior,* edited by Donald S. Marshall and Robert C. Suggs, 3–37.

Minturn, Leigh, and John T. Hitchcock. (1966) *The Rajputs of Khalapur, India.*

Minturn, Leigh, and William W. Lambert. (1964) *Mothers of Six Cultures: Antecedents of Child Rearing.*

Munroe, Robert L., and Ruth H. Munroe. (1975) *Cross-Cultural Human Development.*

———. (1971) "Household Density and Infant Care in an East African Society." *Social Psychology* 83: 3–13.

Murdock, George P. (1936) *Our Primitive Contemporaries.*

Murphy, Yolanda, and Robert F. Murphy. (1985) *Women of the Forest.*

Nerlove, Sara Beth, and Ann Stanton Snipper. (1981) "Cognitive Consequences of Cultural Opportunity." In *Handbook of Cross-Cultural Human Development,* edited by Ruth H. Munroe, Robert L. Munroe, and Beatrice B. Whiting, 423–474.

Niblack, Albert F. (1890) *The Coast Indians of Southern Alaska and Northern British Columbia.* Annual Reports of the Board of Regents, Smithsonian Institute.

Norbeck, Edward. (1954) *Takashima: A Japanese Fishing Community.*

Nydegger, William F., and Corinne Nydegger. (1966) *Tarong: An Ilocos Barrio in the Philippines.*

Oliver, Douglas. (1955) *A Solomon Island Society.*

Opler, Morris. (1941) *An Apache Life-Way.*

———. (1942) "Adolescence Rite of the Jicarilla." *El Palacio* 49, 25–38.

Osgood, C. (1958) *Ingalik Social Culture.*

Palfrey House. (n.d.) "Cross-Cultural Ratings." Unpublished codes, Harvard University, Cambridge.

Parry, N. E. (1932) *The Lakhers.*

Piker, Steven. (1965) *An Examination of Character and Socialization in a Thai Peasant Community.*

Pinker, Steven. (1994) *The Language Instinct: How the Mind Creates Language.*

Pospisil, Leopold. (1958) *The Kapauku Papuans and Their Law.*

Powdermaker, Hortense. (1933) *Life in Lesu: A Study of Melanesian Society in New Ireland.*

Price-Williams, Douglas. (1981) "Concrete and Formal Operations." In *Handbook of Cross-Cultural Human Development,* edited by Ruth H. Munroe, Robert L. Munroe, and Beatrice B. Whiting, 403–422.

Raswan, Carl R. (1947) *Black Tents of Arabia.*

Ray, Verne. (1933) *The Sanpoil and the Nespelem: Salishan Peoples of Northeastern Washington.*

Richards, Audrey. (1940) *Bemba Marriage and Present Economic Conditions.* Rhodes-Livingstone Papers 4.

Robarchek, Clayton. (1979) "Learning To Fear: A Case Study of Emotional Conditioning." *American Ethnologist* 6: 555–567.

Roberts, John M., and Brian Sutton-Smith. (1962) "Child Training and Game Involvement." *Ethnology* 1: 166–185.

Roberts, John M., and Herbert Barry, III. (1976) "Inculcated Traits and Games Type Combinations: A Cross-Cultural View." In *The Humanistic and Mental Health Aspects of Sports, Exercise and Recreation,* edited by T. T. Craig, 5–11.

Rogoff, Barbara. (1990) *Apprenticeship in Thinking: Cognitive Development in Social Context.*

Rohner, Ronald P. (1975) *They Love Me, They Love Me Not: A Worldwide Study of the Effects of Parental Acceptance and Rejection.*

Romalis, Shelly. (1981) "An Overview." In *Childbirth: Alternatives to Medical Control,* edited by Shelly Romalis, 3–32.

Romney, A. Kimball, and Romaine Romney. (1966) *The Mixtecans of Juxtlahuaca, Mexico.*

Roscoe, John. (1911) *The Baganda: An Account of Their Native Customs and Beliefs.*

Rosen, B. C. (1962) "Socialization and Achievement Motivation in Brazil." *American Sociological Review* 27: 612–624.

Rosen, B. C., and R. D'Andrade. (1959) "The Psychological Origins of Achievement Motivation." *Sociometry* 22: 185–218.

Rosenblatt, Paul C., and Elizabeth L. Skoogberg. (1974) "Birth Order in Cross-Cultural Perspective." *Developmental Psychology* 10: 49–54.

Salo, Matt, and Sheila Salo. (1977) *The Kalderas in Eastern Canada.*

Schaller, George B. (1964) "Breeding Behavior of the White Pelican at Yellowstone Lake, Wyoming." *Condor* 66: 3–23.

Schlegel, Alice, and Herbert Barry, III. (1986) "The Cultural Consequences of Female Contribution to Subsistence." *American Anthropologist* 88: 142–150.

Segall, Marshall H., Pierre R. Dasen, and Ype H. Poortinga. (1990) *Behavior in Global Perspective: An Introduction to Cross-Cultural Psychology.*

Segall, Marshall H., Pierre R. Dasen, John W. Berry, and Ype H. Poortinga. (1990) *Human Behavior in Global Perspective.*

Shatz, Carla J. (1992) "The Developing Brain." *Scientific American* 267: 60–67.

Shirokogoroff, S. M. (1924) *The Social Organization of the Manchus.*

Shweder, Richard A., Manamohan Mahapatra, and Joan G. Miller. (1990) "Culture and Moral Development." In *Culture and Psychology: Essays on Comparative Human Development,* edited by James W. Stigler, Richard A. Shweder, and Gilbert Herdt, 130–204.

Simmons, Leo W. (1945) *The Role of the Aged in Primitive Society.*

Skinner, E. P. (1964) *The Mossi of the Upper Volta.*

Slobin, Dan I. (1990) "The Development from Child Speaker to Native Speaker." In *Cultural Psychology: Essays on Comparative Human Development,* edited by James W. Stigler, Richard A. Schweder, and Gilbert Herdt, 233–256.

Stephens, William N. (1962) *The Oedipal Complex: Cross-Cultural Evidence.*

———. (1963) *The Family in Cross-Cultural Perspective.*

Super, Charles M. (1981) "Behavioral Development in Infancy." In *Handbook of Cross-Cultural Human Development,* edited by Ruth H. Munroe, Robert L. Munroe, and Beatrice B. Whiting, 181–270.

Sutton-Smith, Brian, and John M. Roberts. (1981) "Play, Toys, Games, and Sports." In *Handbook of Cross-Cultural Psychology, v.*

4: Developmental Psychology, edited by H. C. Triandis and A. Heron, 425–471.

Symons, Donald. (1992) "On the Use and Misuse of Darwinism in the Study of Human Behavior." In *The Adapted Mind: Evolutionary Psychology and the Generation of Culture,* edited by Jerome H. Barkow, Leda Cosmides, and John Tooby, 137–162.

Textor, Robert B. (1967) *A Cross-Cultural Summary.*

Thompson, Laura. (1940) *Fijian Frontier.*

Thompson, Laura, and Alice Joseph. (1947) *The Hopi Way.*

Trivers, Robert L. (1985) *Social Evolution.*

Turnbull, Colin M. (1965) *Wayward Servants: The Two Worlds of the African Pygmies.*

Uchendu, Victor C. (1965) *The Igbo of Southeast Nigeria.*

Underhill, Ruth. (1936) *The Autobiography of a Papago Woman.*

———. (1939) *Social Organization of the Papago Indians.*

Urbanowicz, Charles F. (1973) "Tongan Adoption before the Constitution of 1875." *Ethnohistory* 20: 109–123.

van Gennep, Arnold. (1960) *The Rites of Passage.*

van Lawick-Goodall, Jane. (1968) "The Behavior of Free-Living Chimpanzees in the Gombe Stream Reserve." *Animal Behavior Monographs* 1: 161–311.

Waddington, C. H. (1962) *New Patterns in Genetics and Development.*

Wagley, Charles. (1949) "The Social and Religious Life of a Guatemalan Village," *American Anthropologist* 51: 3–150.

Wallace, Ernest, and E. Adamson Hoebel. (1952) *The Comanches: Lords of the South Plains.*

Warner, W. Lloyd. (1937) *A Black Civilization: A Social Study of an Australian Tribe.*

White, Robert W. (1959) "Motivation Reconsidered: The Concept of Competence." *Psychological Review* 66: 297–333.

Whiting, Beatrice B. (1971) "Folk Wisdom and Child Rearing." Paper presented at meetings of the American Association for the Advancement of Science, December.

———. (1972) "Work and the Family: Cross-Cultural Perspectives." Paper prepared for Women: Resources for a Changing World: An International Conference. Radcliffe Institute, Radcliffe College, April.

———. (1978) "The Dependency Hang-Up and Experiments in Alternative Life Styles." In *Major Social Issues: A Multidisciplinary View,* edited by S. Cutler and M. Winger, 217–226.

Whiting, Beatrice B., and Carolyn Pope Edwards. (1963) "A Cross-Cultural Analysis of Sex Differences in the Behavior of Children Aged Three through Eleven." *Journal of Social Psychology* 91: 171–188.

———. (1988) *Children of Different Worlds: The Formation of Social Behavior.*

Whiting, Beatrice B., and John W. M. Whiting. (1975) *Children of Six Cultures: A Psycho-Cultural Analysis.*

Whiting, John W. M. (1941) *Becoming a Kwoma.*

———. (1959) "Cultural and Sociological Influences on Development." In *Growth and Development of the Child in His Setting,* 5–9.

———. (1964) "Effects of Climate on Certain Cultural Practices." In *Explorations in Cultural Anthropology,* edited by Ward E. Goodenough, 511–544.

———. (1971) "Causes and Consequences of the Amount of Body Contact between Mother and Infant." Paper presented at the meetings of the American Anthropological Association, New York.

———. (1981) "Environmental Constraints on Infant Care Practices." In *Handbook of Cross-Cultural Human Development,* edited by Ruth H. Munroe, Robert L. Munroe, and Beatrice B. Whiting, 155–179.

Whiting, John W. M., and Irvin L. Child. (1953) *Child Training and Personality.*

Whiting, John W. M., Eleanor Chasdi, Helen Antonovsky, and Barbara Ayres. (1966) "The Learning of Values." In *The People of Rimrock: A Study of Values in Five Cultures,* edited by Evon Z. Vogt and Ethel M. Albert, 83–125.

Williamson, Laila. (1978) "Infanticide: An Anthropological Analysis." In Infanticide and the Value of Life, edited by Marvin Kohl, 61–75.

Wilson, Godfrey. (1936) "An Introduction to Nyakyusa Society." *Bantu Studies* 10: 253–292.

Woodburn, J. *The Social Organization of the Hadza of North Tanzania.* Unpublished dissertation, Cambridge University.

Yang, Martin C. (1945) *A Chinese Village: Taitou, Shantung Province.*

Zelazo, N. A., P. R. Zelazo, and S. Kolb. (1972) "Walking in the Newborn." *Science* 176: 314–315.

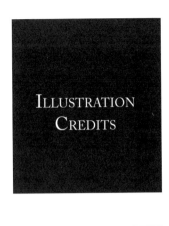

ILLUSTRATION
CREDITS

SUBJECT INDEX

CULTURE GROUP INDEX

Note: See the Subject Index on page 367 for general subject headings.